LEADERSHIP

FOR HEALTH PROFESSIONALS

Theory, Skills, and Applications

Gerald (Jerry) R. Ledlow, PhD, MHA, FACHE

Professor and Chair, Department of Healthcare Policy,
   Economics and Management
School of Community and Rural Health
UTHEALTH Northeast
University of Texas Health Science Center
Tyler, Texas

James H. Stephens, DHA, MHA, FACHE

Associate Professor and Distinguished Fellow in
   Healthcare Leadership
Department of Health Policy and Management
Jiann-Ping Hsu College of Public Health
Georgia Southern University
Statesboro, Georgia

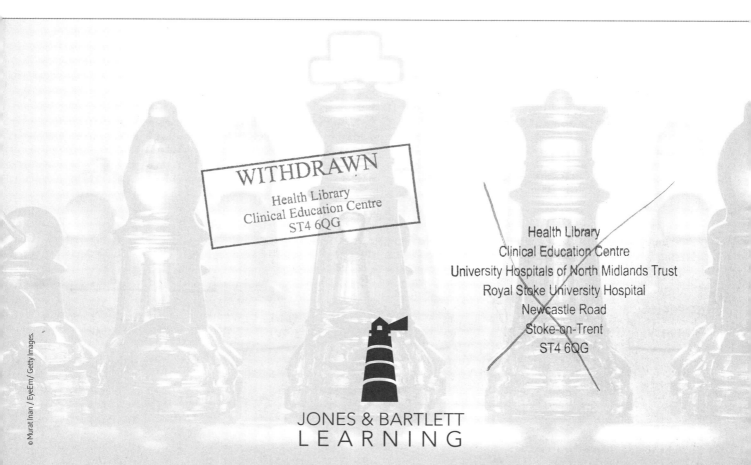

JONES & BARTLETT
LEARNING

World Headquarters
Jones & Bartlett Learning
5 Wall Street
Burlington, MA 01803
978-443-5000
info@jblearning.com
www.jblearning.com

Jones & Bartlett Learning books and products are available through most bookstores and online booksellers. To contact Jones & Bartlett Learning directly, call 800-832-0034, fax 978-443-8000, or visit our website, www.jblearning.com.

Substantial discounts on bulk quantities of Jones & Bartlett Learning publications are available to corporations, professional associations, and other qualified organizations. For details and specific discount information, contact the special sales department at Jones & Bartlett Learning via the above contact information or send an email to specialsales@jblearning.com.

13245-8

Production Credits

VP, Executive Publisher: David D. Cella
Publisher: Cathy L. Esperti
Editorial Assistant: Carter McAlister
Director of Production: Jenny L. Corriveau
Production Editor: Lori Mortimer
Production Services Manager: Colleen Lamy
Associate Marketing Manager: Alianna Ortu
VP, Manufacturing and Inventory Control: Therese Connell

Composition: Cenveo® Publisher Services
Cover Design: Kristin E. Parker
Director of Rights & Media: Joanna Gallant
Rights & Media Specialist: Jamey O'Quinn
Media Development Editor: Troy Liston
Cover Image: © Murat Inan / EyeEm/ Getty Images
Printing and Binding: Edwards Brothers Malloy
Cover Printing: Edwards Brothers Malloy

Library of Congress Cataloging-in-Publication Data

Names: Ledlow, Gerald R., author. | Stephens, James H., author.
Title: Leadership for health professionals : theory, skills, and applications
   / Gerald (Jerry) R. Ledlow, PhD, MHA, FACHE, Professor and Chair,
   Department of Healthcare Policy, Economics and Management, School of
   Community and Rural Health, UTHEALTH Northeast, University of Texas Health
   Science Center, 11937 U.S. Highway 271, Tyler, Texas 75708, James H.
   Stephens, DHA, MHA, FACHE, Associate Professor and Distinguished Fellow in
   Healthcare Leadership, Department of Health Policy and Management,
   Jiann-Ping Hsu College of Public Health, Georgia Southern University, 501
   Forest Dr., Building 303, Statesboro, GA 30460.
Description: Third edition. | Burlington, MA : Jones & Bartlett Learning,
   [2018] | Includes bibliographical references and index.
Identifiers: LCCN 2016052531 | ISBN 9781284109412
Subjects: LCSH: Health services administration. | Leadership.
Classification: LCC RA971 .L365 2018 | DDC 362.1068—dc23
LC record available at https://lccn.loc.gov/2016052531

6048

In Memorium

M. NICHOLAS COPPOLA, PHD

M. Nicholas Coppola, PhD, served his country as a U.S. Army Officer in the Army Medical Department as a Medical Service Corps Officer. He also served as program director for the U.S. Army-Baylor University Masters of Health Administration and the Texas Tech University Health Sciences Center Clinical Practice Management Masters programs. Dr. Coppola was well published and contributed greatly as my coauthor on the first two editions of *Leadership for Health Professionals: Theory, Skills and Applications* published by Jones & Bartlett Learning. He was also a long-time friend and father to three children. Dr. Coppola passed away on June 30, 2015. You will be missed and remembered, my friend.

Dr. Jerry Ledlow

Courtesy of Dr. M. Nicholas Coppola.

© Murat Inan / EyeEm / Getty Images.

CONTENTS

NEW TO THE THIRD EDITION

In addition to updating each chapter with relevant examples of executive leadership, this *Third Edition* addresses important issues regarding healthcare competencies, as researched by the nation's leading professional organizations and associations in healthcare leadership and administration. All chapters also include additional emphasis on an "application to practice" framework based on evidentiary leadership outcomes. Material on leading partnerships, health information systems, supply chains, inter-professional teams, and successful governance of managerial finance and outsourcing are also introduced. Scholars and students alike will also enjoy reading contemporary material relating to new statutory and regulatory issues that health executives must navigate. Finally, new material regarding healthcare reform, value-based purchasing, leadership competency models for today's leaders, the 4Ps of Health Analytics, inter-professional teams, leadership transparency, and ethical responsibilities of leadership are presented.

CHAPTER 1

Chapter 1 includes minor updates and additional references.

CHAPTER 2

The discussion of leadership personality assessments in Chapter 2 has been revised, emphasizing application to practice. The following topics have also been added to this chapter:

- Social competence
- Leadership locus of control
- Planned behavior
- New material in the Jungian Assessments and Emotional Intelligence sections
- Minor updates and additional references

CHAPTER 3

This is an all new chapter on leadership challenges of today. It includes a macro-system health system model and corresponding leadership competency model. The previous edition's Chapter 3 on the anatomy and physiology of theory and models is included as Appendix B.

CHAPTER 4

This chapter has received high praise as an authoritative chronology of leadership. Minor additions and references have been added to the chapter.

CHAPTER 5

Chapter 5 introduces additional new material on leadership competencies and personal responsibilities in the health professions. Competency assessment tools discussed include those offered by the American College of Healthcare Executives, the Healthcare Leadership Alliance, the National Center for Healthcare Leadership, and the Association of University Programs in Health Administration. Tools for maintaining personal competence are addressed through forming relationships, networks, and alliances. Self-determination, reliance, and power are explored along with minor reference additions and updates.

CHAPTER 6

To build on material in Chapter 5, Chapter 6 has been updated to foster an application to practice framework in executive leadership development. The chapter continues to addresses the following with minor reference updates:

- Strategic (calculated, premeditated, and deliberate) leadership
- Situational assessment

- Environment scanning
- Competency attainment through continuing health education

CHAPTER 7

Chapter 7 includes new citations to keep the chapter relevant and up to date.

CHAPTER 8

Chapter 8 has added a model (PAARP) and discussion on Inter-professional Teams in Health Organizations. The Omnibus Leadership Model discussion has been moved to Appendix C in this edition. Additionally, new references were added.

CHAPTER 9

Chapter 9 features the CAAVE (Competitive, Avoiding, Adaptive, Vested, and Empathetic) Model as a way of exploring leading systems, transactional leadership, and leadership through the application of strategic positioning. Leading partnerships, shared services, and leveraging outsourcing success are all explored through an evidentiary and outcomes-based approach that is both practical and easy for the early careerist to understand. New references have been added to update the chapter.

CHAPTER 10

In this chapter the importance of statutory and regulatory compliance issues surrounding executive decision making are addressed through historical precedents and law. Cases associated with the False Claims Act, the Federal Medicare/Medicaid Anti-Kickback Statute, Stark Law, Health Insurance Portability and Accountability Act (HIPAA), and the Emergency Medical Treatment and Active Labor Act are new examples. Leadership decision making relating to end-of-life decisions, abortion, spiritual preferences, and euthanasia are addressed in a manner that fosters critical thinking in early careerists. Additional references have been added to the chapter.

CHAPTERS 11 AND 12

Criteria from the Baldrige National Quality Award was added to Chapter 11 in the previous edition to help support a leader's need to measure outcomes in the health profession. New citations have been added to keep the chapters relevant and up-to-date. In Chapter 12, material pertaining to chief executive officers was updated and expanded.

CHAPTER 13

A minor update of references was completed for this chapter.

CHAPTER 14

Roughly 80% of the material presented in Chapter 14 was new to the *Second Edition*. The chapter now focuses on integrated delivery and financial systems that are wedded to ancillary areas of information systems, supply chains, operations management responsibilities, and materials/logistics management. Additional references and expansion of supply chain/material management were added to the *Third Edition*.

CHAPTER 15

In the previous edition, new material on managing disruptive patient care providers was introduced in order to recognize the unique political and sensitivity issues that surround this population of employees. This chapter provides a framework suggested by The Joint Commission to assist in developing policy for documentation and action. An update of references was completed for this edition.

CHAPTER 16

Chapter 16 is new to the *Third Edition*. This chapter was added as a mid-edition release in late 2014. It covers a leader's framework for using data, information, and knowledge, considering the dynamic changes to the health industry. The 4Ps of Health Analytics is the base model for this chapter.

CHAPTER 17

Although largely unchanged from the previous editions, Chapter 17 (which was Chapter 16 in earlier editions) includes material on a recommended mentoring philosophy for early careerists. An update of references was completed for this edition.

FOREWORD

Courtesy of General David Rubenstein.

The success of any enterprise derives from executive leaders, who entrust senior leaders, who entrust junior leaders, who, in turn, trust and empower the people who are doing the work. This truism applies to organizations of all forms and fashions.

Leading in healthcare organizations is no different, but nonetheless, it is unique. Leaders in health care deal with closely held guilds and tribes, each one based on profession-specific legal, educational, and aspirational philosophies. They stand apart while having to work together. One would think that working together would be intuitive, given the common denominator that members of these guilds and tribes share—keeping the patient before them healthy or returning them to health and supporting those providing that effort. In reality however, that teamwork and single focus require intense work, the work of leaders.

During a 35-year Army career I lived, learned, and led in a leadership environment. The military performs magnificently well at developing, testing, and advancing leaders. Interestingly, however, the Army's definition of a leader would apply perfectly well in any civilian organization: "An Army leader is anyone who by virtue of assumed role or assigned responsibility inspires and influences people to accomplish organizational goals. Army leaders motivate people both inside and outside the chain of command to pursue actions, focus thinking, and shape decisions for the greater good of the organization."[1]

The intersection of these two leadership aspects, the focus on teamwork and the need to have that person who inspires and influences the team, generates the question of how to best develop leaders. As most leaders eventually do, I have developed my own mantra that guides my leadership actions and efforts. The mantra is a simplistic 14 words long: take care of people, take care of equipment, pay attention to detail, have fun. The problem with a mantra born of experience, though, is that the thought is based on years of personal education, training, trial and error, mistakes, successes, and lessons learned. How does the developing leader best look behind the veil and discover the foundation upon which the mantra is based?

That is a question Dr. Jerry Ledlow and Dr. James Stephens tackle head on in their in-depth work. The professional and popular literature is replete with thousands upon thousands of leadership titles that compete for our attention. What makes this edition of *Leadership for Health Professionals* the title you want to read? This text addresses the needs of health leaders at various career stages: those in training, young leaders in the field, and more seasoned leaders who bear the scars of experience. The authors, contributors, and reviewers have fine-tuned their successful previous edition with skill and attention to detail. The reader's path travels through a rich field of empirical research, philosophical narrative, and use-today tools.

This edition will serve to meet the immediate needs of the student and also serve as a long-term reference. *Leadership for Health Professionals* is also well suited for the experienced leader who is selflessly performing within the profession and organization as a mentor and coach.

David Rubenstein, FACHE
Major General, United States Army, Retired
Clinical Associate Professor, Texas State University
Past Chairman, American College of
Healthcare Executives

REFERENCE

1. Department of the Army. *Army Leadership* (Army Doctrine Publication 6-22). 2012, 1.

A NOTE FROM THE AUTHORS

As the authors of this book, we want to thank you for purchasing and using this textbook for professional development, instruction, and education. We believe that the title of this book says it all: *Leadership for Health Professionals: Theory, Skills, and Applications*. Up to this point, there has not been a development-focused textbook, specific to health organizations and health professionals, that combines the classical knowledge of leadership theory in the literature with the time-honored best practices and outcomes associated with the skills and applications practiced by industry leaders. This is the third edition aimed at providing leadership-focused learning for health leaders. Until the publication of this book, students, educators, and professionals were placed in the position of having to buy two (or more) texts or supplement their readings with multiple journal articles to achieve the compilation of knowledge presented in these pages.

This textbook captures our collective hope of enabling and encouraging ever-improving leadership practice, continuous leadership development, and ultimately a more effective, efficient, and efficacious health industry. From our own practical experience, academic study, and facilitation of leadership instruction over the past 28 years, we fervently posit that great leadership practice is one of a few critical factors necessary to ensure quality healthcare delivery, good health status in our communities, and high levels of productivity in our society. As part of our ongoing effort to improve leadership practice, we developed this book and the associated materials for your use as a learning system.

The foundation of this health leadership learning system is informed by the following definition: **Leadership** is the *dynamic* and *active* creation and maintenance of an organizational *culture* and *strategic systems* that focus the collective energy of both *leading people and managing resources* toward *meeting the needs of the external environment* utilizing the most efficient, effective, and, most importantly, efficacious methods possible by moral means. As a system, the text is based on the hierarchical learning stages of Bloom's Taxonomy of the Cognitive Domain. It takes advantage of our experiences in facilitating leadership instruction to graduate students from all walks of life and with varying levels of practical health experience for more than a decade. Put simply, the material, concepts, theories, models, applications, and skills integrated within this system greatly facilitate learning. A graduate student, reviewing this work from a student's perspective, wrote the following:

> As a student, I have learned that the material taught in a course is often not as valuable as the way in which it is taught. The authors have succeeded in integrating the content of leadership practice with learning how to lead in their text, *Leadership for Health Professionals: Theory, Skills, and Applications.* Students will be eager, as was I, to learn the methods employed within this rich text. The health industry is a dynamic and engaging environment where the only constant is change. This text allows the student to become engaged in the material and extrapolate the roles, obligations, and responsibilities of leaders and managers. Drs. Ledlow and [Stephens] have spent years instructing health leaders and have simplified the exercise of learning into a concise, easy-to-follow format that can be straightforwardly adapted into today's ever-changing leadership environment. The reiteration of material sets a foundation, expands upon the context, and then places the information into a health context. This repetition makes it easy to learn and maximize what a student gains from a course. This text illustrates how to address continuity and stabilization in an environment ripe with change and uncertainty.

From a content perspective, themes of leadership principles, applications, and constructs such as organizational culture, cultural competency, ethical frameworks and moral practice, scientific methodology, leader competencies, external and internal assessment and evaluation, communication, planning, decision making, employee enhancement, and knowledge management are woven through the entire text and the supplemental materials. These themes are presented in multiple contexts throughout the book and echoed in multiple chapters. To wit, the most important constructs and concepts are presented in an early chapter, further expanded and explored in a middle chapter, and then used in context in a later chapter. The reiteration of key leader systems, actions, and behaviors provides additional opportunities for learning within a leadership course. Many times, students have not been exposed much to the material presented in a leadership course, so multiple interactions with critical content material are both efficacious and pedagogically sound. In practice, students learn more with construct and content reiteration in a time-limited semester or term.

Collectively, the authors of this book have more than 68 years of professional leadership experience that spans the continuum of health care from ambulatory clinics, to large multisite and multidisciplinary health entities, to academia. In this text, we combine our practitioner knowledge and experience and our academic experience to elucidate the competencies and learning outcomes required for graduate programs. In combining both practitioner knowledge and industry best practices in graduate education, it is our desire that you will find the studying, learning, and/or instructing of health leadership more effective, efficient, and efficacious and will enjoy a competitive advantage in your own career. It is our expectation that through studying this text, your leadership will bring about a better health organization, community, industry, and society through your application of the theories, skills, and concepts presented in this textbook.

In closing, we believe strongly that learning is a life-long process that requires continuous exposure to, thinking about, and reflection on new information that can be turned into knowledge that is "actionable" in your leadership practice. Although this book went through a rigorous peer review process, we actively encourage feedback on its content from students, educators, and professional executives in the field. If any part of this book requires additions or contains omissions, please contact us. We also encourage active contribution to this text for future editions. Should you or your colleagues desire to share for consideration any cases, models, exercises, or written text for inclusion in future editions, please do not hesitate to contact us with your ideas and suggestions. Thank you to all who have provided feedback to make this third edition more efficient, effective, and efficacious. As in the previous edition we welcome your feedback, and your contributions may be included in future versions of this text.

Thank you for allowing us to take part in your leadership development and practice!

PREFACE: THE PURPOSE OF THIS LEADERSHIP TEXT

The purpose of this text is to provide you with a foundation not only for the study of leadership practice and theory, but also for the broader concept of leading people and health organizations across multiple and interconnected disciplines. A second goal is to bridge theory and the abstract concepts of leadership with the practical or concrete operational behaviors and action of leaders. This goal is integrated with the discussion of the popular evidence-based leadership of today. We meet these goals by utilizing a four-tier strategy that walks students, early careerists, and practicing health leaders through the foundations of leadership, leadership principles and practices, the complexity of leadership in health care and finally into the world of leading people and managing resources into the future.

Although the discipline of leadership, with its myriad related topics, theories, and models, is rather large and extensive in the literature and knowledge base, the authors' perspective focuses on the most pertinent leadership content, theories, models, principles, and strategies that produce results in the health industry. The authors have put many of these theories and models into practice during the course of successful practitioner careers. Of course, the health industry differs in many ways from other services and products industries: Many times efficacy is more important than efficiency, patient outcomes are more important than profits/margin, the "rational man" theory of economics is set aside when certain injuries or illnesses invade our families such that chaos or irrational economic decisions prevail, and society holds the health industry to an extremely high standard of perfection. Moreover, health organizations are extremely complex, run continuously, and are highly regulated and scrutinized. These realities create a distinctive leadership niche—that of the health leader. This text is intended specifically for the person filling that role.

This text combines both the scholarship of the academy of leadership and the practicalities involved in leading people and managing resources in the real world. With more than 50 years of combined experience leading people in complex organizations, the authors hope to impart that experience to the next generation of health leaders in a way that is both meaningful and useful to scholars and practicing health professionals.

People are led and resources are managed! This text has multiple objectives. It was created to provide you with an understanding of leadership principles; an ability to apply leadership principles through actions, behaviors, and processes in a dynamic world; a capacity to synthesize leadership theories and models to create a personalized leadership model; and the ability to evaluate leadership theories, models, principles, and ideas in a sound manner. Most important, the intent of this text is to develop an increasingly competent and confident cadre of leaders for the health industry so that complex health systems, population health status, and a multidisciplinary health workforce can be improved, enhanced, and strengthened to successfully overcome the significant challenges that society faces now and in the future. Six key trends in the health industry, identified in 2009, clearly highlight the need for quality, competent, and enthusiastic leadership:

1. Quality and performance reporting will shift from value-add to essential.
2. Asset rightsizing will provide new levers to fund strategic growth.
3. Departmental autonomy will fade as technology enables an enterprise view.
4. Care architecture will drive smarter facility design.
5. Effective leaders will be part policymaker, part entrepreneur.
6. Managing clinical staff will require new thinking and methods.[1]

To achieve success in the health industry, an organization must demonstrate focused and intelligent effort. Leaders are the catalysts for organizational, group, and individual greatness. This text seeks to make you a better leader who can lead a group or organization to accomplish great achievements; the ultimate goal is for you to have a fulfilling health career. The authors applaud your enthusiasm to become a better leader! Wolf offers simple yet pertinent insight into the application of leadership:

- Leaders lead by example; they do not ask people to do something they would not do themselves.
- Leaders perform consistent rounding (walking the floors and engaging employees in their own work environments) and also maintain an open door policy, making the administrative offices a welcoming place to all staff.
- Employee input is sought and encouraged, both individually and through employee groups, and is supported by a non-punitive environment.[2]

This text serves as your road map to start your leadership journey, a multidisciplinary journey. In essence, this text is a catalyst to begin or continue your leadership development.

REFERENCES

1. Vachon, M. (2009). Six trends for your next strategy session agenda. *GE Healthcare Performance Solutions* [booklet], p. 2.
2. Wolf, J. A. (2008). Health care, heal thyself! An exploration of what drives (and sustains) high performance in organizations today. *Performance Improvement, 47*(5), 38–45. doi:10.1002/pfi.210, p. 39.

IN THIS TEXT

This text is intended to build foundational leadership knowledge and bridge the gap between theory and practice to enhance the skills and abilities of the reader and student of leadership in health organizations. The authors use "Focused Content Cycling" where concepts/topics are presented to form a foundation and then expanded upon in the following chapters and again later in the text, used in one or more contexts or situations to maximize awareness, learning, and the potential to bridge theory to practice for the reader. These goals are accomplished in the book's four parts, each of which consists of four chapters, with Part 4 containing five chapters. In addition there are three appendices: Appendix A contains insights from health leaders; Appendix B is Chapter 3 from the first and second editions titled, "The Anatomy and Physiology of a Theory," and it should be read prior to reading Chapter 4 of the textbook; and Appendix C is a portion of Chapter 8 from the first and second editions titled, "The Omnibus Leadership Model." A summary of the four parts provides a good overview of the content of this textbook.

PART 1: LEADERSHIP FOUNDATIONS

Part 1 is divided into four chapters. Chapter 1 defines leadership from historical, cultural, and contemporary perspectives. Chapter 2 assesses individual leadership styles and allows the student to relate his or her style to the various leadership theories and case studies presented in the text. Chapter 3 describes the challenges of today requiring health leadership. Chapter 4 provides a classical and historical review of leadership theories as they have evolved over the last several hundred years, especially since the 1930s.

PART 2: LEADERSHIP IN PRACTICE

Part 2 focuses on leadership in action and the knowledge, skills, and abilities required of a health leader. Chapter 5 outlines the personal responsibilities leaders have to maintain relevancy in skills, tools, abilities, and education. Chapter 6 focuses on applying those skills, tools, abilities, and education to communication, planning, decision making, managing knowledge, and training. Chapter 7 provides the health leader with a road map to success in personal leadership development by using the leader "crawl–walk–run" methodology. Chapter 8 looks at some new methods in practice that help guide and hone leader skills; emphasis is placed on "leading people and managing resources" in the health organization.

PART 3: LEADERSHIP IN HEALTH ORGANIZATIONS

The third major module in this textbook focuses specifically on the complexity of health organizations. Chapter 9 begins by exploring the complex world of health and describing how leaders can identify and manage horizontal, vertical, institutional, and resource-dependent environments. It is followed by Chapter 10, which offers a sound review of ethics and morality in health and discusses a leader's responsibility to manage and maintain an ethical framework that fosters a moral environment. Chapter 11 is a unique chapter on measuring and defining outcomes of health leadership initiatives that apply the model building techniques discussed in Chapter 2. Part 3 concludes with Chapter 12's special analysis of the unique and interdisciplinary roles of health leaders, focusing specifically on physicians, nurses, administrators, and department heads.

PART 4: LEADING PEOPLE AND MANAGING RESOURCES INTO THE FUTURE

Part 4 contains five (5) chapters. Chapter 13 offers suggestions for leaders in the next decade, with a specific emphasis on globalization and an understanding that many discussions in this book focus on Western philosophies of leadership; other worldviews of leadership are presented. Next, Chapter 14 impresses on the reader that healthcare systems such as the supply chain and financial areas such as revenue management must be understood, improved, and integrated into other systems for a coherent whole in the effort to lead people and manage resources in an efficient, effective, and efficacious manner. Chapter 15 outlines the responsibilities of leaders in the management of nonperforming employees. Tips, strategies, and best practices are introduced throughout this part of the textbook. Chapter 16 explores the 4Ps of Health Analytics and incorporates models from HIMSS along with the 4Ps model. The textbook closes with Chapter 17's discussion of mentoring and succession planning.

To illustrate concepts detailed throughout the book, Appendix A, describing the experiences of seven healthcare leaders, has been included.

MINI-CASES

In addition to the cases listed in the Leadership Mini-Cases table, there are 35 mini-cases that go with various chapters in the textbook. The mini-cases can be found on the publisher website.

LEADERSHIP MINI-CASES

Case	Title of Case	Textbook Chapter Link (Parts 1 and 2)	Textbook Chapter Link (Parts 3 and 4)
Stephens Case 1	Replacing the Radiology Contract	Chapters 5 and 6	Chapters 10 and 15
Bradshaw Case 1	Implementing an Information System: Electronic Health Record	Chapter 6	Chapter 12
Bradshaw Case 2	Ineffective Subordinate Leader	Chapters 2 and 5	Chapters 15 and 17
Bradshaw Case 3	Values and Vision Conflicts	Chapters 5 and 6	Chapter 10
Sack Case 1	Physician Leadership Development	Chapter 7	Chapter 12
Sack Case 2	Cultural Change	Chapter 4	Chapters 9 and 13
Smith Case 1	Evidenced-Based Leadership: A Formula for Success?	Chapters 4 and 8	Chapters 11 and 13
Smith Case 2	Ownership and Accountability Culture	Chapter 5	Chapters 9 and 13
Riley Case 1	Pharmaceutical Inconsistencies	Chapter 5	Chapters 11 and 14
Detty and Meadows Case 1	Improving Data Management Processes	Chapter 6	Chapter 14

© Murat Inan / EyeEm / Getty Images.

ACKNOWLEDGMENTS

As in any major project, when writing a book teamwork, collaboration, compromise, and dedication are required for a successful outcome. Our Triune God, first and foremost, has nurtured, loved, and cared for me and my family to enable all that I am, with all my flaws paid for by Christ. My beautiful wife, Silke, and my wonderful daughters, Sarah, Rebecca, and Miriam, supported and encouraged my work for this textbook: Thank you, and I love you all very much. Dr. James Stephens, my partner in this third edition, provided a value-added collegial environment while working intelligently and diligently on the many aspects of this textbook and supporting materials: Thank you for your collaborative spirit and dedication. Lastly, I greatly appreciate and empathize with the myriad health leaders—those now on the stage and those waiting in the wings—who provide the organizational nourishment, direction, and moral fiber for the health industry on a daily basis. I am greatly encouraged by those health leaders who "lead people and manage resources" in our dynamic world.

Gerald (Jerry) R. Ledlow, PhD, MHA, FACHE

xxiv ACKNOWLEDGMENTS

I would like to acknowledge Dr. Ledlow for asking me to join him as coauthor on the third edition of *Leadership for Health Professionals*. It has been a very interesting and informative process. Dr. Ledlow and I have worked together on many academic projects in our careers, and I know we will have new ventures in the future. I would also like to thank Dr. Dave Schott for his assistance. Dave has been one of my doctoral students, and I was chair of his dissertation committee. Also, I want to express my appreciation to Ms. Jennifer Dewey, who is my graduate assistant in the Master of Healthcare Administrative Program, as well as an MHA student herself, for her involvement with this edition. Finally, I wish to thank my wife, Mary Linda, for a wonderful marriage and for her support of my careers both in academics and as CEO of large healthcare systems, for being a wonderful mother to Robert, Craig and Eric, and a grandmother to Emily and Julian. I love her very much.

James H. Stephens, DHA, MHA, FACHE

AUTHOR BIOGRAPHIES

GERALD (JERRY) R. LEDLOW, PHD, MHA, FACHE

Dr. Gerald (Jerry) R. Ledlow, as a board-certified healthcare executive and fellow in the American College of Healthcare Executives, has led team members and managed resources in health organizations for more than 30 years, including 15 years as a practitioner and more than 14 years as an academically based teacher–scholar. He has successfully held a variety of positions: (1) executive-level positions in corporate and military health systems in the areas of clinical operations, managed care, supply chain and logistics, information systems, and facility management; (2) management positions in health services, medical materials, and the supply chain; and (3) various academic leadership positions as the director of doctoral programs at two universities, director of academic affairs, director of student services, and director of the center for survey research and health information, as well as holding tenured faculty positions at three doctoral research universities. Dr. Ledlow earned his PhD in organizational leadership from the University of Oklahoma, a master of health administration degree from Baylor University, and a bachelor of arts degree in economics from the Virginia Military Institute. He has held tenured graduate faculty positions at Central Michigan University and at Georgia Southern University. Currently, Dr. Ledlow is a tenured Professor and Chair of the Department of Healthcare Policy, Economics and Management in the School of Community and Rural Health at the University of Texas Health Science Center Northeast in Tyler, Texas.

Dr. Ledlow has taught 25 different graduate-level courses, including teaching doctoral- and master's-level students in the topic of health leadership. "Dr. Jerry" (as his students call him) has made presentations on health-related topics and health leadership models and applications across the globe; he has presented to myriad audiences internationally, nationally, and locally. He has published in many venues (e.g., journals, book chapters) and has been author, contributing author, editor, and reviewer for several books.

Dr. Ledlow is married to his beautiful wife, Silke, and has three fantastic daughters, Sarah, Rebecca, and Miriam. He is a regional editor for the *Journal of Global Business and Technology*, is on several publication review teams, and participates as a member of various task forces and committees internationally, nationally, and at the state level. Years ago, Dr. Jerry was a National Registry–certified emergency management technician as a volunteer and was deployed to combat zones as a commissioned officer in the U.S. Army Medical Service Corps.

He received the Federal Sector Managed Care Executive of the Year Award in 1998 and the American College of Healthcare Executives' Regent's Award in 1997 and in 2003. His interests are health industry oriented and focus on the areas of leadership, management, decision sciences, supply chain and logistics, community preparedness for terrorism and disasters, socioeconomic constructs of health and community health status, and any project that has the potential to improve the health of communities through moral, effective, efficient, and efficacious health leadership and management practices.

JAMES H. STEPHENS, DHA, MHA, FACHE

Courtesy of Dr. James Stephens.

Dr. James Stephens earned a doctorate of health administration degree at the Central Michigan University School of Health Sciences, a master of health administration degree at the Indiana University School of Medicine, and a bachelor of science in business administration at the Indiana University School of Business. He is a fellow in the American College of Healthcare Executives (ACHE) and is board certified.

Dr. Stephens has held senior executive positions in large medical centers and health systems for 25 years, with 18 years at the president and CEO level. Before joining the Georgia Southern University faculty, he held faculty/staff positions at University of Kentucky, Ohio University, University of Indianapolis, and Butler University.

Dr. Stephens has served on many healthcare and civic organizational governing boards, including the Kentucky and Indiana Hospital Associations, Chamber of Commerce, United Way, Boy Scouts, and the International Rotary Club.

He has been awarded Excellence in Teaching at Georgia Southern University, Excellence in Service Award at Ohio University, Sagamore of the Wabash (highest award from the Governor of Indiana), Kentucky Colonel (highest award from the Governor of Kentucky), Indiana Governor's Award for Volunteerism, Indiana University Alumni Association President's Award, Lincoln Trail Red Cross Award, and Equal Opportunity Award of Merit by the Urban League. He is also a Paul Harris Fellow in International Rotary. He and his wife have been recognized as Special Donations by International Rotary for their contribution to the Polio-Plus Program.

Dr. Stephens' interests include healthcare systems, disparity issues in urban/rural communities, CEO leadership development and succession planning, healthcare governance, strategic planning, and new healthcare delivery models.

Currently, Dr. Stephens is an associate professor and distinguished fellow in healthcare leadership and the director for the master of healthcare administration program within the Jiann-Ping Hsu College of Public Health at Georgia Southern University. He teaches doctoral- and master's-level courses, including healthcare finance, healthcare economics, leadership and strategic planning, and communication in healthcare organizations.

Dr. Stephens has published many articles, book chapters, and case studies, in addition to delivering national and international academic presentations.

CONTRIBUTORS

Donald M. Bradshaw, MD, MPH, FAAFP, FACHE, FACPE
Senior Vice President, Defense Health Operations Manager, Health Solutions Business Unit
Science Applications International Corporation (SAIC)
Falls Church, Virginia

Jameson Tyler Croft, MHA
Surgical Services Senior Materials Coordinator
Southeast Georgia Health System
Brunswick, Georgia

Paul E. Detty, MD, MHA
Six Sigma Green Belt
Midwest Medical Center
Lancaster, Ohio

Karl Manrodt, PhD
Professor and Chair, College of Business Administration
Georgia College and State University
Milledgeville, Georgia

William Mase
Assistant Professor, Department of Health Policy and
    Management
Jiann-Ping Hsu College of Public Health
Georgia Southern University
Statesboro, Georgia

Phil Meadows, MBA
Senior Data Analyst, Six Sigma Black Belt
Midwest Medical Center
Lancaster, Ohio

Crystal A. Riley, PharmD, RPh, MSHCA, CPHQ
Associate Director, Federal Relations
The Joint Commission
Washington, D.C.

David Schott, DPH, MBA, MPH
Assistant Administrator of Strategy and Business Analytics
South Georgia Medical Center
Valdosta, Georgia

Michael Sack
President and CEO
Hallmark Health
Melrose, Massachusetts

Susan Reisinger Smith, DHA, MSN, RN
Vice President, Clinical Practice, Research, and Education
Gentiva Home Health
Macon, Georgia

LEADERSHIP FOUNDATIONS

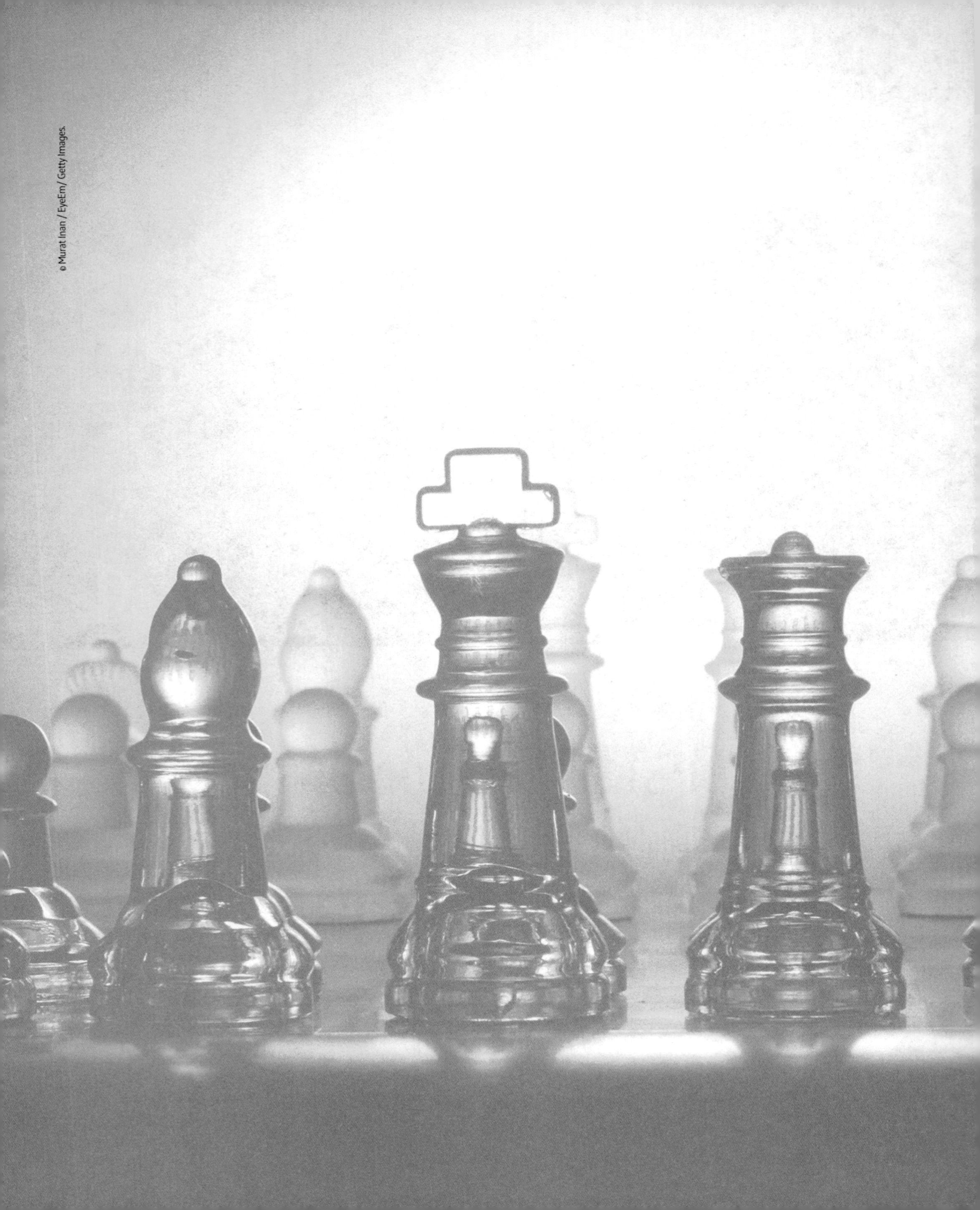

LEADERSHIP THOUGHT

The leader is a stimulus, but he is also a response.
Edward C. Lindeman, *Social Discovery*

Health professionals, health organizations, and communities served critically need leadership from competent and well-trained administrators and clinicians. Being in a position of leadership is the most important job of any health professional anywhere along the continuum of care. Holding a position of leadership in the health professions may mean making life or death decisions regarding patient care. Here, physicians are recognized for their ability to heal, nurses for their prowess in maintaining patient care, and administrators and ancillary staff for their ability to manage the daily operations of support for continued access and delivery of care. In other situations, leaders in supervisory roles may control the lives of countless others in employment entities regarding issues of merit raises, personnel layoffs, promotion opportunities, and the creation of positive and enriching job environments. In extreme conditions, leaders in high executive positions are responsible for the survival of their entire organization. This may involve providing a continuum of care to thousands of covered lives, as well as the continued employment of hundreds of fellow working healthcare professionals. Indeed, leaders are the individuals who make the healthcare history others read and write about.

As a result, leaders in health organizations are essential. Leadership is as important today as at any time in history, if not more so. Leadership has been important to human endeavor for thousands of years. Debates about leadership and the ways in which leaders came into power have been prevalent for centuries. Some leaders are born with instinctive leadership skills, charisma, and insights into human motivation. Even so, all great leaders must devote time, energy, and study to various aspects of leadership to master the discipline, while developing superior competencies in situational assessment, motivation, communication, and understanding dynamic group behavior. Whatever the case, health professionals should consider the discipline of leadership as one of the more important aspects of personal and professional education. Leadership in the health industry is required to navigate and successfully solve problems of cost, quality, and access to care across the continuum of care in our society. People are led; resources are managed—knowing the difference makes all the difference.

LEARNING OBJECTIVES

1. Outline why the study of leadership is important to professionals in the health industry and what the challenges in the industry requiring quality leadership are.

2. Explain and give examples of leadership as compared with management, and state why health organizations need both leaders and managers.

3. Relate and discuss the application of a prescriptive leadership model compared to a descriptive leadership model.

4. Distinguish the phases of leadership thought from ancient to modern times, and identify unique characteristics associated with each of these phases.

5. Relate the phases of leadership thought to modern leadership practices and research.

6. Evaluate the health industry's need for leadership today and into the next decade.

INTRODUCTION

People are led and resources are managed. Knowing this critical and sometimes subtle difference is the beginning of leadership wisdom. Leadership wisdom is an essential component to being successful in a fast-paced, ever-changing, and highly complex health environment.[1] Today, *evidence-based leadership* is a common term, as are *evidence-based management* and *evidence-based medicine*. *Evidence-based* means that the practice of leadership, management, and medicine is informed by empirical evidence from the structure, process, and especially, the outcomes of practice. This text provides foundations, principles, and strategies for leadership that are also informed by quantitative and qualitative evidence. Performance initiatives such as value-based purchasing, pay for performance, and accountability requirements, coupled with electronic medical records

"meaningful use" criteria, and community assessment and integration, all require strong leadership.

This chapter presents some of the basic definitions and distinctions of leadership. Specific emphasis is placed on defining the importance of leadership study in the healthcare environment and its appropriate place in the field of both academics and professional practice. Leadership is differentiated from management; although there are certainly differences between these two skills, health organizations need leaders and managers who are consistently focused on the direction of the enterprise. Emphasis is placed on both descriptive (tells about leadership) and prescriptive (gives direction and guidance) notions of leadership. In summary, this chapter provides an overview of the complex and exciting topic of leadership.

Within the realms of graduate education, business practice, and organizational analysis, there is no topic more important than the study of leadership. The contemporary study of leadership is a centuries-old, enormously complex discipline; however, fewer topics inspire more interest and have more stakeholder consequences than leadership in any organization in any industry. In the highly complex health industry, the role of leadership is further pronounced, and adept leadership is clearly necessary for success. Furthermore, no great leaders of our time have become successful and prosperous without first understanding the principles of leadership.

As scholars, future practitioners, and current practitioners, we need to perform at least two roles—that is, to wear two hats. One of these hats is that of the practitioner, who is directly in touch with the delivery of human services in health systems and leadership change for process improvement. In this role, you work closely with individuals and families, as well as other groups, organizations, and communities as a helping professional; from this perspective, you are positioned to observe the issues and emerging trends that are the greatest challenges for those people you serve in living healthy and fulfilling lives. The other hat you wear is that of scholar. In other words, early careerists must be capable of becoming a critical consumer of leadership research by personal study. Leaders must be aware of both the practices and habits of successful leaders, as well as the recognized traits and skills that are commensurate with leadership success as documented in the literature over the years.[2,3] For example, as a working health executive, suppose you encounter an issue with outside stakeholders with which you are unfamiliar. It is to your benefit to turn to the archived literature and search out articles and research that can help you gain deeper understanding of the problem facing you. Because of your training in leadership gained from this text, as well as from your mentors and educators, you can approach this literature with a basic understanding of the foundations of leadership and select the most appropriate course of action based on both your burgeoning experience and the successful practices documented in the literature of best practices.

Leadership is holistic. This means that leadership requires leading laterally or collaboratively and not just from the upper echelons in a top-down approach. Leadership entails leading the people, the structure, and the processes of the organization. In addition to the many definitions of this concept, there is an abundance of literature on leadership in general, leadership principles, and topics related to leadership. As a topic, leadership is of immense interest to international militaries, governments, businesses, and health organizations. Leadership and attributed outcomes in schools are commonly taught but likewise encompass varying approaches and lines of thought.[4]

WHY STUDY LEADERSHIP?

Simply stated, leadership is complex. To become a leader, an individual must possess a strong didactic educational background, be focused on taking care of people and resources simultaneously, and be confident in his or her own abilities. Furthermore, a successful leader must have extraordinary critical thinking skills, be a life-long learner, and be willing to (graciously) accept information that may be counterintuitive to his or her sensibilities or current understanding. Additionally, leadership requires—but is not limited to—having the ability to profoundly understand both the big picture and the minutiae, the possibilities and the potential roadblocks, and to do so coupled with the ability to motivate sustainable enthusiasm and focus among key stakeholders, staff, and the community. Finally, leadership may ultimately be about having foresight, hindsight, and vision; the personal presence to garner trust; and the art of knowing not just how to delegate but also how to elicit others' desire to always do their best—including knowing when to seek help and not feeling badly about doing so. At the end of the day, leadership is about having that special "something" that makes others feel they are contributing in a meaningful way to the greater good. This is why we study leadership.

Leaders of any organization encounter issues and decision-making challenges in everyday life. Some decisions are easily solved, whereas others may call for a critical analysis of the situation, a split-second judgment, an assessment made by one individual, or decisions made by a group. Whatever the circumstances, the decisions that are made will have consequences for human resources and the organization. It is, therefore, necessary for individuals to be trained in leadership and to become well equipped to make the right decisions at the right time.[5]

The concept and discussion of leadership is ancient; the discipline of leadership study can be consistently traced back to Machiavelli in 1530, but the first documentation of leadership dates back to 2300 BCE. However, leadership theory and research is a relatively modern discipline. Indeed, the first relevant theories were not proposed until the mid-1800s. From approximately 1840 to 1880, "great man" theorists Carlyle, Galton, and James studied great men from history who exhibited certain traits and suggested that those traits led to successful leadership.[6] This theory was later abandoned for more valid and reliable theories of leadership based on best practices and sound discovery. For nearly 125 years some of the greatest minds have attempted to catalogue and archive best practices in leadership for the benefit of the next generation of leaders and the current chief executives in the field. Although this area is a relatively modern topic of study, numerous qualitative and quantitative experiments continue to generate new journal articles each year. Clearly, the study of leadership is complex and ongoing, and the current and newer theories of leadership vary with its definitions as defined by the authors.[7] The authors of this text welcome you to the world of the study of leadership research and practice and encourage you to join the many generations who came before, in search of continuing education and new tools for your leadership toolkit.

Leadership is one of the few academic disciplines that is difficult for early careerists to embrace without both didactic training and real-world experience. Although some leaders may possess natural predispositions that allow them to become successful in small circles in colloquial events, successful leadership practitioners will agree that as their ever-increasing circles of influence grow, it becomes necessary to develop and hone natural predispositions while simultaneously cultivating the skills necessary to bring them to the next level of leadership. Leadership skills and traits that enable a person to become successful within one circle with one group of individuals with particular skill sets and academic disciplines may not allow the same person to become successful in the increasingly more complex concentric circles.[8–10] All leaders along the continuum of care must engage in lifelong learning to be successful.

Many early careerists find that the transition from being a follower and an employee to becoming one who leads others and takes responsibility can be difficult. Mistakes must be made and experience accumulated at lower supervisory levels to gain a perspective on which kind of leader each individual can become. However, without knowing the best practices of leaders, the strategies leaders employ for success, and the natural predispositions emulated by leaders, it will be difficult for early careerists to become successful.[11] Also, the health environment is continually changing. For example, recent literature suggests the need for new models of nurse leadership to deal with dynamic change and to serve as the bridge between clinical and administrative practice in health organizations.[12]

Those early in their career will become engaged with many facets of leadership over their tenure in the industry. For example, you may have a natural predisposition toward introversion or extroversion. Although these traits may already be well known to you, formally diagnosing them provides a road map to developing those skills lacking in persons who are determined to be leaders; it also can identify current strengths to build upon. If an early careerist is already leaning toward extroversion, he or she may already be comfortable in delivering clear goals and sharing vision statements with future groups of employees. For those on the other side of the spectrum, developmental opportunities are suggested, such as joining professional organizations and speaking groups where it may be possible to practice developing extrovert tendencies.

Leadership is a "universal phenomenon."[13,14] As long as people are part of the equation of health systems as workforce members and patients, leadership will be a critical component of successful organizations. "Since the effectiveness of the leader has frequently determined the survival or demise of a group, organization, or an entire nation, it has been of concern to some of the foremost thinkers in history, like Plato, Machiavelli, and von Clausewitz. If leadership were easy to understand, we would have had all the answers long before now."[15] Today, leadership far too often focuses more on coping strategies than on leading strategies. As scholars and experienced leadership practitioners in the health industry, the authors believe that leadership needs to be dramatically improved to enhance today's systems and deal with the challenges our society faces. It is not acceptable to merely perpetuate the status quo. The complexity and pace of change in the health industry further emphasize the need for leadership competence. For more than three decades, leadership in the health industry has been a concern. The need for leadership remains salient, and the dynamic elements of the industry are increasing. Consider the Patient Protection and Affordable Care Act, the ICD-9 transition to ICD-10, the explosion of social media, the growth of electronic medical records and meaningful use criteria amid the constant expansion of technology, the increase in community needs integration into healthcare delivery planning and implementation, the necessity for preparedness planning for disasters, the squeeze of reimbursement with value-based purchasing, the initiation of Lean Methodology into health industry culture, and the need for leaders and managers to understand and improve the healthcare supply chain for competitive advantage and cost avoidance. These realities are significant and tangible to health organizations, and there are plenty of other important items that could be mentioned. All point to the necessity for competent leadership throughout health organizations—from the top to the bottom, from administrators to physicians to nurses to technicians, to revenue and supply chain managers. Coping is not leading. Leading people and managing resources in an efficient, effective, efficacious manner with moral means are key. Creating your personal leadership plan will be important for you to contribute to industry-wide success and to your own success. Learning from the past and bringing that knowledge to the present day is a salient method for establishing and mastering leadership competence.

The coping strategy nature of leadership has been a concern for at least the past two decades, if not longer. In 1989, Warren Bennis talked about this issue in *Why Leaders Can't Lead: The Unconscious Conspiracy Continues*, in which he discussed the restrictions leaders place on themselves. More recently, Jo Manion, in 1998's *From Management to Leadership: Interpersonal Skills for Success in Health Care*, discussed the critical decline of skills and the overall lack of leadership in the healthcare industry. Hints of self-protection and self-promotion have begun to taint the noble profession of health leadership. It seems there is a significant lack of morality, knowledge, skills, and abilities at the individual leader level.

In the past decade, nurse managers have learned that they must rely on more "leadership" capabilities than on "nurse" capabilities to be successful.[16] In 2000, Ian Morrison posited several leadership challenges for different sectors of the health industry. He called on political organizations to create consensus, reduce party indifference, and reform Medicare. In the realm of managed care, he noted the need for innovation, a sustainable business strategy, and the establishment of a positive public image. In his estimation, the pharmaceutical and medical technology industries need to take care of rising costs while keeping their primary focus on developing new drugs and devices. As for hospitals and health systems, he called on them to reconcile the differences between improving general health and delivering sick care. Morrison then turned his attention to individual players within the healthcare field. Physicians must advocate for physician leadership, move beyond nostalgic views of the medical profession in years past, and take a more active role in developing organizational models. He then targeted leaders and their support teams:

> Public health leaders and workers must: (1) decide to participate in the mainstream of medical care . . . ; (2) decide how to incorporate the ideas of public health into the mainstream political agenda without sounding too much like socialism for the average American (socialism and fiscally irresponsible social justice ideology will not "play well" in mainstream America); and (3) [recognize that] the public health community can be incredibly self-righteous about having a monopoly on compassion for the poor. . . .[17,18]

To tackle these challenges, leadership is required. Those who wish to lead must be competent; competence starts with knowing what you know and what you do not know. There are four states of knowing:

- Unconscious incompetence, where "we do not know that we do not know"
- Conscious incompetence, where "we know that we do not know"

- Conscious competence, where "we know how to perform a skill but must consciously think about it"
- Unconscious competence, where performance of a skill is second nature[19]

Moving from one state of knowing to another takes considerable effort. Becoming a "conscious leader" takes study, effort, trial, error, and evaluation. Clearly, the most successful health leaders are not lucky but rather are competent at leading people to do important and tremendous tasks and achieve great success. Successful leaders have discipline, persistence, and humility while continuously working to improve their capabilities.

Studying, learning, and applying leadership knowledge, skills, and abilities are crucial to being a successful leader in the health industry. Regardless of where and at what level you lead—as a laboratory chief, physical therapy director, clinical office administrator, or health system chief executive officer—leadership knowledge, skills, and abilities are important to you, your organization, and the communities you serve. The health industry in the United States is destined for renewal; leadership will be essential to the health industry throughout this period of change.[20]

Regardless of cultural identity, all leaders of health organizations lead people and manage resources. Their work involves focusing the collective energy of leading people and managing resources toward meeting the needs of the external environment in the most efficient, effective, and—most importantly—efficacious approach possible (that is, focusing on the mission of the organization). It is important for leaders to understand that the individuals who make up the health workforce are people with vastly different education, training, and experience. These same individuals also have vastly different roles within the organization—and no leader can ever hope to understand the complexity of all aspects of jobs within the system. As a result, the good leader's job is to successfully motivate individuals within the organization toward goal-directed behavior that supports the leader's vision and organization's mission. As Presidential Medal of Freedom recipient Eric Hoffer has suggested, "The leader has to be practical and a realist yet must talk the language of the visionary and the idealist."[21]

The last important job of leaders is the management of nonhuman resources in the system. The role of a healthcare administrator, healthcare executive, public health leader, or healthcare manager is to merge the complexity of leading people and the complexity of managing resources into a culture that serves communities by maintaining and improving the health of individuals in those communities. This is done by influencing the people and distributing the resources under their stewardship to serve those individuals who come to health organizations for assistance, by building strong and effective relationships with their communities, and, especially, by building working relationships with the public health infrastructure in their communities.

INTRODUCTION TO LEADERSHIP IN ACADEMICS AND PRACTICE

Leadership has never been defined based on any one experience, theory, or historical study; rather, leadership is the product of several cumulative factors from several different cultural disciplines. The education and development of a leader require a broad perspective that emphasizes leadership as both a process and a set of scientific/technical and artistic/relational skills and abilities in need of development.[22,23]

History is replete with stories and examples of fearless, selfless leaders—people who have risked their lives and fought on against seemingly insurmountable odds or who have been able to motivate those around them to go beyond what they believed they were capable of accomplishing. For example, anthropology, archeology, social anthropology, political science, psychology, business, communication, and numerous other disciplines have all contributed to the foundations of leadership theory and practice. Leadership has been observed and documented for centuries: "leaders as prophets, priests, chiefs and kings served as symbols, representatives, and models for their people in the Old and New Testaments, in the Upanishads, in the Greek and Latin classics, and in the Icelandic sagas."[24] Initiated by necessity, leadership in practice was observed and documented by scholars of the era, and the connection between leadership practice and academic understanding of leadership began. Four thousand three hundred years ago, in the *Instruction of Ptahhotep* (2300 BCE), three qualities were attributed to the pharaoh's leadership.[25] In many ways, the documentation, study, synthesis, and evaluation of leadership have been a key basis of humans' historical record.

Most modern studies and research have been U.S. or "Western" based, although recently some effort has been devoted to international applications of leadership. This has not always been the case: In ancient times, "the subject of leadership was not limited to the classics of Western literature. It was of as much interest to Asoka and Confucius as to Plato and Aristotle."[26,27] However, much of our current literature on leadership is greatly influenced by Western culture and the documentation of history through the exploits of Western leaders, such as during the time of the Roman Empire. Remnants of the Roman Empire attest to the power of leadership in society, as illustrated in **Figures 1-1**, **1-2**, and **1-3**.

FIGURE 1-1 Ancient ruins of the Roman empire: Early "leadership" documentation can be attributed to ancient Egyptian, Greek, Roman, Chinese, and Persian societies.

Courtesy of Dr. Gerald Ledlow.

FIGURE 1-2 The ruins of the ancient Roman senate.
Courtesy of Dr. Gerald Ledlow.

Until the 1930s–1940s, emphasis on leadership focused on trait theories and the "great man" theory. Trait theory assumes that individuals possess certain traits or attributes that serve as the catalyst to leadership and securing leadership roles. Behavioral theory gained acceptance in the 1940s; this research phase focused on which styles or behaviors leaders used and how those styles contributed to subordinate satisfaction, performance, and quality. It was

FIGURE 1-3 Signs of leadership power and influence in ancient Rome.
Courtesy of Dr. Gerald Ledlow.

behavioral research that first acknowledged that leadership and leading could be a learned skill. Very recently (considering the more than 4,300 years of leadership information and knowledge), situational leadership has gained favor. This line of research suggests that successful leaders must assess the situation and then choose the appropriate leadership style to make the greatest positive impact on subordinate effort; it assumes that leaders have a full "toolbox" of capabilities. **Table 1–1** describes the three phases. All phases of leadership research build on each other and are interwoven into various models of leadership.

Is there "truth" in all three phases of research? What can you take away from each phase of study and information? Hundreds of leadership theories have been proposed, although only a dozen or so really show promise.

Despite 4,300 years of leadership practice, observation, and scholarly synthesis and evaluation, what we know about leadership continues to elude mastery. When examining the major leadership theories commonly accepted by practitioners and theorists, the similarities of the theories may be intuitive for many leaders, *but the lessons often have not been learned.* "For example, the following components are shared across theories: (1) vision, (2) inspiration, (3) role modeling, (4) intellectual stimulation, (5) meaning-making, (6) appeals to higher order needs, (7) empowerment, (8) setting of high expectations, and (9) fostering collective identity … models basically share similar beliefs about the role of vision in providing direction and meaning."[28,29]

THINKING ABOUT LEADERSHIP

Leadership is both an art and a science (**Table 1–2**).[30] Fundamentally, the leadership art encompasses relationships, interpersonal skills, timing and tempo, power, and intuition. The science of leadership embodies technical

Table 1-2 Leadership as a Science Compared to an Art

Science	Art
Technical skills orientation: forecasting, budgeting.	Relationship oriented: networking, interpersonal relationships.
Decisions are based more on analysis.	Decisions are based more on perceptions of people.
Developing systems is important to organizations.	Developing relationships and networks is important to organizations.
Expert systems.	Experts as people.
Cost control and evaluation of value are important.	Image and customer relationships are important.

Ledlow, G., & Cwiek, M. (2005). The process of leading: Assessment and comparison of leadership team style, operating climate and expectation of the external environment. *Proceedings of Global Business and Technology Association.* Lisbon, Portugal: Global Business and Technology Association.

acumen, skills, and principles along with expertise in the business of health.

From this very broad thought process, six important foundations must be in place for true leadership success, even as the individual strives to better balance the science and the art of leadership. First, communication knowledge, skills, and abilities need to be in place. This means that the individual leader knows how, what, and when to communicate to important constituencies, and how to become known as authentic and genuine. A keen sense of communication means that the leader understands, interprets, and utilizes nonverbal and symbolic communication as well as verbal means. Second, consistency of behavior and temperament is highly prized, both by subordinates and by those to whom the leader is accountable. Third, emotional intelligence is a valued foundation for the leader, because it connotes the ability to monitor self and social settings, and then to govern behavior accordingly. Effective leadership is not a mystery, although neither is leadership an exact science. Studies suggest that an individual's leadership style has an important impact on the working atmosphere of the company. The ability of the leader to establish a relationship with the organization may be defined by the leader's self-awareness of his or her emotional intelligence. Fourth, the effective leader understands the powerful relationship between trust and understanding; increased trust leads to greater understanding, and increased understanding in turn leads to greater trust. Fifth, a leader must be adaptive. Numerous studies have demonstrated that one leadership style

Table 1-1 Leadership Theory and Model Categorization Through Time

Great Man and Trait Phase (Circa 450 BCE–1940s)	Behavioral Phase (1940s–1960s)	Situational Phase (1970s–Present)
Attempted to determine which specific traits make a person an effective leader	Attempted to determine which particular behaviors/styles leaders utilize to cause others to follow them	Attempts to explain effective leadership within the context of the larger work situation

is not enough for effective leadership. Leaders should be able to be flexible and adapt to varying situations, because the environment is continually changing and leaders must respond to that change.

A leader's ability to adapt to numerous situations is profoundly evident with regard to leading people and managing resources within systems that support patient care practice and improve and maintain good quality community health status. These systems, such as large core business components, clinical and patient care, supply chain, revenue management, and financial and human resources, as well as subsystems, such as preparedness and contingency operations, community assessment, and others, must have leadership and integration to work seamlessly together to fulfill the mission of the health organization. The complexity required for leading these systems is a true adaptive challenge for leaders.

Finally, the role of integrity cannot be overstated. In many ways, the previous five foundations are part of what is considered integrity in leadership. That is, a leader with integrity communicates in a fair and balanced manner; is consistent in living a life of integrity, on and off the job; and is trustworthy and understood, because the leader values trusting and understanding others. Integrity in leadership, however, includes many more elements. Leadership integrity means sometimes standing alone to act in a moral fashion. It means doing the right thing for the organization while not forgetting the rights and sensibilities of individuals. It means putting the interests of others before and above one's own. Integrity, coupled with competence, forms the necessary foundation for a successful health leader.

Many leadership theories and models contain elements of both the science and artistry of leadership, either directly or by implication. Consider the model asserted by Chambers of the six agencies of leadership: (1) communication, (2) participation, (3) preparation, (4) identification of options, (5) closure (move beyond past conflicts, negativity, and inequity), and (6) celebration.[31] Of these six agencies, some are artistic, some are scientific, and others could work both ways. The science is embodied in processes and tasks associated with evaluating, planning, decision making, and training. The artistry of leadership is embodied in processes and tasks associated with relationship building, communicating, persuading, coaching, and evaluating or establishing context. The scientist-leader and the artist-leader both envision, create and develop, and implement. The key is to produce the best possible results through solid leadership—to do that which must be done to balance science and art. Where the scientist and the artist converge is in the creation, implementation, refinement, and maintenance of communication systems, strategic planning, decision-making systems, employee enhancement mechanisms, organizational learning, and knowledge management.

Although leaders are gifted in different ways, with different personalities and varying skill sets, all leaders can grow, become more skillful, and become more competent so that they can achieve greater effectiveness. The common factors shared by those who succeed in becoming great leaders in the health industry are the desire to learn more about themselves, the motivation to learn and practice new skill sets, and the need to become more tomorrow than what they are today. This is not the easiest path, but it is the path that optimizes the likelihood of leadership effectiveness and success.

DEFINING LEADERSHIP

Numerous studies have demonstrated that leaders, and more specifically, the characteristics, styles, and traits that leaders exhibit, influence organizational performance and success. Thus definitions of leadership and development of definitions and applications for leadership in the health environment are very important. Different perceptions and paradigms exist across the literature. *Perception* is how people see something within a context; *paradigm* is how they understand something in a context. Perceptions and paradigms may be "right" or "wrong."[32] The five characteristics of paradigms, according to Harris and Nelson, are

- Paradigms mitigate uncertainty.
- Uncertainty leads to unpredictability, so individuals are driven to find a paradigm to make sense of the situation.
- Past successes lead individuals to use the same paradigm, thereby causing them to neglect situation-based or other solutions.
- Paradigms are imitated when homogeneous groups lead paradigm solutions.
- As long as they are logically optimal, paradigms continue to be used even though they may be flawed.[33]

Different perceptions and paradigms create different definitions of leadership. The complexity of leading and the complexity of the industry or organization where leadership occurs increase that ambiguity.

The definition of leadership found in a typical dictionary—in this case, *Webster's Dictionary*—is somewhat tautological. The first two entries in *Webster's* state that "leadership is the position of office of the leader" and "leadership is the capacity or ability to lead." Further review of the term *leader* is similarly tautological, with definitions stating a leader is "one who leads." Perhaps scholarly researchers of leadership theory do not know how or where to apply leadership theory within the environment. After a thorough review of the literature over a 50-year period, Yukl has suggested that there are as many definitions of leadership as there are researchers attempting to study it.[34] Additionally, new definitions associated with leadership continue to be introduced into the literature every year.

When the famed Native American and cavalry fighter Geronimo was asked what made him a good leader, he replied, "The ability to ride a strong horse." Although this statement may seem somewhat humorous and superfluous to us in modern times, the ability to ride a strong horse was certainly a cultural competency in Geronimo's day. Without the personal courage and fortitude to ride bareback on a stallion (an activity deemed dangerous by even the most skilled Olympic equestrian medalists), Geronimo may not have become the great leader he was among nineteenth-century Native Americans.

Another familiar cultural icon is the famed World War II leader, General Douglas MacArthur. MacArthur's definition of leadership had nothing to do with health care (or peace). He was reputed to have said that a leader's only mission was to win wars.[35] In contrast, the Nobel Peace Prize leader Mahatma Gandhi suggested that leadership was all about getting along with other people. Somewhere in the middle of the dove in Gandhi and the hawk in MacArthur stood our nation's first African American Secretary of State, General Colin Powell (**Figure 1-4**). Powell has provided numerous quotes describing leadership; however, he has suggested that overall, leadership is about problem solving.

Management guru Peter Drucker suggested that leadership was not about being liked but about obtaining results. Finally, President Dwight Eisenhower stated, "Leadership is the art of getting someone else to do something you want done because he wants to do it."[36] The lack of a clear, parsimonious, accepted, and applied model of leadership is a fundamental weakness within the literature. Additionally, few leadership studies actually define leadership before researching variables associated with it.

Within the refereed literature, leadership is said to be as much an art as a science. Leadership is also a cultural phenomenon, allowing for different traits and characteristics to emerge as successful parables across society. Lastly, leadership is a dynamic and evolving paradigm that takes on different literal and figurative definitions over the centuries. With so many available and partisan positions on leadership, it is easy to understand why there continues to be vehement debate on defining, testing, framing, and understanding this concept.

FIGURE 1-4 Secretary of State Colin Powell and Dr. Nick Coppola (coauthor on the first two editions of this text; passed away June 2015) at a leadership conference in Washington, D.C.
Courtesy of Dr. Gerald Ledlow.

Conservative leadership empiricists suggest the understanding of leadership is founded in traditional research methods and may be discerned through the development of testable hypotheses and the operationalization of demonstrable unit variables that are derived from latent constructs. Liberal leadership enthusiasts advocate acceptance of leadership as an art; however, like beauty itself, its definition may lie in the eye of the beholder. One person's leader may be another's despot. Additionally, framing leadership is not culture-free; one's understanding of this concept lives in a sea of bias (or differing perceptions and paradigms). Techniques and activities developed in one society may need to be adapted to be effective in another. U.S. society recognizes leadership regardless of age or gender, whereas Asian and Middle Eastern societies place heavy emphasis on gender and age as precursors to recognition of a leader.

Akin to cultural awareness is the perspective of time. For more than two millennia, many leaders were selected to fill their positions based on their associations with feudal guilds, religious associations, or tribal rituals. In early Greek and Roman societies, leaders were often recognized and rose through the ranks into important senate and military positions through associations with other men of power. Finally, leadership recognition was often a matter of genetics and bloodlines, similar to the situation found in European and Asian monarchies.

With such a broad base and so many potential starting points for leadership, is it possible that the terms *leader* and *leadership* may have been misunderstood and leadership constructs misapplied? Early geographic, anthropological, and scientific literature is often flawed and full of assumptions and opinions often presumed to be fact until something better comes along. A whimsical example is the flat earth theory, which was largely abandoned after the invention of the telescope and the circumnavigation of the globe by early mariners. Other flawed scientific research is less amusing and has produced harmful consequences.

Organizational literature is likewise peppered with misnomers and reevaluated ideas.[37] Older theories, such as Fredric Taylor's scientific management, management by objectives (MBO), and even participatory management, are rarely used and applied as theoretical frameworks within modern literature. These earlier theories suggested micromanagement, a high degree of structure, or consensus making were cornerstones to management success. Contemporary literature suggests that treating employees like objects, restricting their freedom, and allowing too much creativity are counterproductive to organizational goals. Managers must possess some of the skills of the leader to be successful in the practice of management, but management is separate from the leadership discipline itself;

that is, leadership is just one of the many assets a successful manager must possess. Care must be taken in distinguishing between the two concepts. The main aim of a manager is simply to maximize the output of the organization through administrative implementation.

Some authors have suggested that the terms *leader* and *leadership* are culturally confounded with alternative and nonequivalent positions. For example, these terms are culturally confounded with the terms associated with *manager*, *supervisor*, *public figure*, and several other nonleadership or nonleader designations. This misapplication has had an adverse impact on health policy and planning, because the wrong caliber of individual is made responsible for areas of responsibility over and above his or her level of competence. The simple truth is that people are led and resources are managed.

A basic definition of leadership, as identified by Peters and Waterman, might suggest that leadership is "the process of influencing others to accomplish the mission by providing purpose, direction, and motivation."[38] These authors may have defined this term best when they suggested the following:

> It is patient, usually boring coalition building. It is purposeful seeding of cabal that ... will result in the appropriate ferment in the organization. It is shifting the attention of the institution through the language of management systems. It is altering agendas [for] new priorities. It is being visible [both in good and not so good times]. It's listening carefully, frequently speaking with encouragement, and reinforcing words with believable action. It's being tough when necessary.

Numerous definitions and variants of definitions can be found in the literature. A few definitions of leadership (emphasis added) are provided here:

- In 1961, Tannenbaum, Weschler, and Massarik defined leadership as *interpersonal influence*, exercised in a situation, and *directed* through the *communication* process, toward the attainment of a specified goal or goals.[39]
- In 1974, Stogdill stated that leadership is the initiation and maintenance of *structure* in expectation and *interaction*.[40]
- In 1982, in their bestselling book *In Search of Excellence*, Peters and Waterman defined leadership as guiding an organization toward success.[41]
- In 1984, Rauch and Behling suggested that leadership is the process of *influencing* the activities of an organized group toward *goal* achievement.[42]
- In 1990, Jacobs and Jacques stated that leadership is a process of giving purpose (meaningful direction) to

collective effort, and causing *willing effort* to be expended to achieve purpose.[43]

- In 1994, Yukl noted that most definitions of leadership reflect the assumption that it involves a "social influence process whereby intentional influence is exerted by one person over other people to structure the activities and relationships in a group or organization."[44]

- In 1999, it was suggested that "the unique and important function of leadership, contrasted with management or administration; is the conceptualization, creation and management of *organizational culture*."[45]

- In 2000, Blanchard, Hersey, and Johnson suggested that leadership is the ability to foster and succeed in obtaining good outcomes and noted that leadership is the result of training, not just the consequence of an accident or good fortune.[46]

- In 1990, Covey stated that leaders catalyze commitment to and vigorous pursuit of a clear and compelling vision while at the same time inspiring and leading the group to achieve high performance standards.[47]

- In 2005, Gupta suggested that leadership is a discipline, and that the ability to effectively discipline an organization's structure and habits consistently is a positive technique.[48]

- In 2008, Ling and colleagues suggested that leadership requires an individual's ability to motivate and instill pride in followers so that followers operate beyond self-interest and do what is necessary for the good of the organization.[49]

- In 2009, Ledlow and Coppola defined leadership as the ability to assess, develop, maintain, and change the organizational culture and strategic systems to optimally meet the needs and expectations of the external environment.[50]

Schein's well-established paradigm of leadership is an excellent example of implied scientific and artistic elementalism; that is, the unique and important function of leadership, contrasted with management or administration, is defined as the conceptualization, creation, and management of *organizational culture*.[51] *Culture* is a learned system of knowledge, behavior, attitudes, beliefs, values, and norms that is shared by a group of people.

> Leaders go beyond a narrow focus on power and control in periods of organizational change. They create commitment and energy among stakeholders to make the change work. They create a sense of direction, then nurture and support others who can make the new organization a success.[52–54]

Other important elements of leadership (including leadership teams) include the cultural impact of leadership. An important consideration in this realm is the cultural impact of communication on leadership effectiveness. The need to be skillful with regard to cultural differences illustrates not just the global challenges of leadership but also the richness of different styles of leadership, individually and as a leadership team. The areas of greatest interest include individualism versus collectivism, time perception, and high versus low communication contexts.

For health leaders in particular, and for leaders in general, for that matter, the definition of leadership used in this text comes from integrating ideas, study, and research from many scholars and practitioners that came before: *Leadership* is the *dynamic* and *active* creation and maintenance of an organizational *culture* and *strategic systems* that focus the collective energy of both *leading people and managing resources* toward *meeting the needs of the external environment* utilizing the most efficient, effective, and efficacious methods possible by moral means.

There is, however, a distinction between what is considered management and what is considered leadership. A manager tends to be more reactive and stays more closely coupled to organizational policies, standards, guidelines, and established processes. A health leader tends to be more proactive and more involved in developing the organizational culture and strategic systems (such as the supply chain, human resources, revenue management, and financial and clinical operational systems of the core organizational functions) necessary to maximize the efficiency, effectiveness, and efficacy of the organization within the external environment.

Leadership is one of the most widely debated and broadly defined organizational theories within the realm of organizational behavior. Strong partisan opinions abound, such that leaders are differentiated by disciplines or positions. The study of leadership has occupied tens of thousands of pages and decades of debate within the refereed literature, with little agreement on discussion and few results to show for these efforts.[55] A review of searchable databases at the Library of Congress in Washington, D.C., performed by employing a series of partially overlapping searches using the terms *leader*, *leadership*, *manager*, *executive*, *supervisor*, and *director*, covering printed material from 1945 to 1995, suggested the common media (comprising television, radio, and newspapers) has popularized the term *leadership* above the other terms.

The discussions of leadership and leaders have transcended traditional boundaries in recent decades, with these terms being used synonymously and extended to describe behavior and phenomena in management, supervisory positions, coaching, education, role models, celebrities, political representatives, inspirational personnel, sports figures, and subject matter experts, among others. Despite well-respected literature that distinctly separates leadership from other identifiers, the term *leadership* continues to be used to describe a plethora of activities in society.[56]

Because of this misapplication, the terms *leader* and *leadership* have dominated the fashionable connotations associated with nonequivalent positions, resulting in a popularly accepted hierarchy. Being a leader is perceived as better than being just a manager, supervisor, or subject matter expert. Being designated a leader rather than a manager (or something else) results in an artificial perception of status, which translates into a "feel good" perception for the individual.

Perhaps this evolution is, in part, associated with the increasing competition for the best employees and other cultural changes that have occurred within society in the past century. A review of want ads in *The Washington Post* finds few vacancies for "secretaries" but identifies several requests for "administrative assistants." Janitorial positions are advertised as "custodial engineers." The American College of Healthcare Executives contains a directory of search firms that suggests few hospitals are hiring "medical doctors." Instead, the current spin appears to be searching for "physician-leaders."

As a result of these ever-broader applications, the term *leadership* has become ubiquitous within the literature and society. Consequently, leadership constructs are no longer viewed as distinct and mutually exclusive. A review of the literature, in fact, suggests there is no single construct unique to leadership theory. Researchers of leadership theory are often forced to borrow from the plethora of micro-organizational theories in the discipline to explain phenomena associated with leadership theory.

What is your definition of leadership? What is your definition of management? Are your definitions of these two terms different?

DEFINING MANAGEMENT

There is a definite difference between leaders and managers. For example, one researcher has suggested that managers think incrementally, whereas leaders think radically. Moreover, Predpall states that "Managers do things right, while leaders do the right things."[57] Another distinction is that leaders do not manage daily operations, but rather they create vision and motivation; in contrast, managers implement objectives and programs.[58]

Several authors have suggested that leaders must have good managerial skills to organize and delegate tasks;

however, not all managers have the ability to direct complex health organizations and guide vision and strategy.[59] As Maxwell has suggested, an individual is either a follower or a leader: There is no in between—you are either a reactor or an imitator, not both.[60]

As a final distinction, leaders must let vision, strategies, goals, and values become the guideposts for their actions and behaviors rather than attempting to merely control others. This is starkly different from the managerial function, which almost by definition has an inherent obligation to know the daily duties and productivity of the people under the manager's supervisory control.[61]

As a reading of the body of leadership literature quickly reveals, many researchers over the decades have blurred the lines between leadership and management.[62] Today, much of this fuzziness still exists. Within this gray area, you should decide for yourself what makes an excellent manager and what defines an excellent leader. Leadership and management are compared in **Table 1-3**.

A further distinction can be seen in the values associated with team building and relationship nurturing. For example, managers may be involved with evaluating outcomes of employees, whereas leaders are responsible for selecting the original talent in the organization. Another example might suggest that managers oversee the daily accountability to a fiscal budget, whereas leaders direct the strategy that dictates where elements of resources will be allocated. Finally, managers may act as facilitators between employees and the upper leadership team, whereas the leadership team itself instills and builds trust through maintaining a healthy, surviving, and prosperous organization where the job security, benefits, and livelihoods of employees are maintained.[63]

In the simplest terms, management is the process of getting activities completed efficiently and effectively with and through other people.[64,65] Management functions and sets of knowledge, skills, and abilities have been researched for several decades. The most widely accepted approach for classifying managerial skills is in terms of a categorization system (called a *taxonomy*). Those skills are defined as follows:

- *Technical skills*: Knowledge about methods, processes, procedures, and techniques for conducting specialized activity; the ability to use those tools and equipment relevant to the activity
- *Interpersonal skills*: Knowledge about human behavior and interpersonal processes; the ability to understand the feelings, attitudes, and motives of others; the ability to communicate effectively; the ability to establish effective relationships
- *Conceptual skills*: General analytical ability; logical thinking; proficiency in concept formation and conceptualization of complex and ambiguous

Table 1-3   Comparison of Leadership and Management

Leadership	Management
Longer time horizon	Shorter time horizon
Vision, then mission oriented	Mission oriented
Organizational validity (Are we doing the right things?): environmental scanning and intuition	Organizational reliability (Are we doing things correctly and consistently?): compliance with rules and policies, and rule development
Does the organization have the correct components (people, resources, expertise) to meet future as well as current needs?	How can current components work best now?
Developing and refining organizational culture to meet external environment needs	Maintaining organizational climate to ensure performance
Timing and tempo of initiatives and projects	Scheduling of initiatives and projects

Ledlow, G., & Cwiek, M. (2005). The process of leading: Assessment and comparison of leadership team style, operating climate and expectation of the external environment. *Proceedings of the Global Business and Technology Association.* Lisbon, Portugal: Global Business and Technology Association.

relationships; creativity in idea generation and problem solving; the ability to analyze events and perceive trends, anticipate changes, and recognize opportunities and potential problems (inductive and deductive reasoning)

- *Administrative skills*: The ability to perform a particular type of managerial function or behavior (planning, organizing, delegating, negotiating, coaching, conducting meetings)[66–68]

Indeed, leadership and management research, literature, and practice have intermingled to a high degree. A leader can be a manager, and a manager can be a leader. Many times, depending on your job role and responsibilities, you have to be both leader and manager. Typically, the higher a person moves up the career ladder, the more extensively leadership thinking, behaviors, and actions are used. Successful organizations have both effective leaders and effective managers. The key to success is the consistency and focus on the organization's mission across the leadership and management team. Both leaders and managers are on the same health organizational team, focused on similar outcomes, but performing their responsibilities differently to ensure successful results.

In summary, the difference between management and leadership is based on experience and potential. For example, managers are usually employees who have experience in the field and discipline within the area of work and production with which the organization is associated. They are generally individuals who have worked their way up through the ranks of a company from "mailroom"-type

activities to a position where their knowledge of policies, practices, and procedures creates a stable environment of institutionalism such that daily operations are consistent and operations of daily reoccurring work remain relatively constant. Managers will know each layer of work under them and, in many cases, be able to perform the duties of their subordinates. In stark contrast is the leader, who may be a new arrival to the organization, yet whose careful risk taking, vision, wisdom, and ideas are capable of breaking down barriers and propelling the organization toward new levels of productivity and performance.[69]

ORGANIZATIONS NEED LEADERS AND MANAGERS

Leaders are essential to organization achievement and success. Managers are essential to organization achievement and success. Both leaders and managers must work in concert to develop an effective system with which to administer an organization. Henry Mintzberg, a prominent management researcher, scholar, and author, describes management in terms of roles.[70] As you read through the descriptions of these managerial roles, consider the leader and manager comparison presented earlier in this chapter, and determine whether a leader or a manager, or both, would perform the roles defined by Mintzberg.

In Mintzberg's work, chief executive officers were observed. During this process, managerial work was categorized as encompassing 10 roles: three that involved mainly *interpersonal contact* (figurehead, leader, and liaison);

three that involved *information processing* (monitor, disseminator, and spokesperson); and four that related to *decision making* (entrepreneur, disturbance handler, resource allocator, and negotiator). Managerial roles can be independent of situations that rely on traits and behavioral theories, although this line of research has proved more valid with the situational approach—where managers move from role to role depending on the situation. The Mintzberg roles for managers are as follows:

- *Figurehead*: Based on formal authority; symbolic duties of a legal and social nature.
- *Leader*: Responsible for making the organization function as an integrated whole in pursuit of the mission/goals of the organization.
- *Liaison*: Behavior intended to establish and maintain a web of relationships internal and external to the organization.
- *Monitor*: Continually seeking information from a variety of sources (situational analysis, environmental "scanning").
- *Disseminator*: Special access to information not available to subordinates; passing on of information to subordinates and, in some degree, to peers and superiors.
- *Spokesperson*: Obligation to transmit information and express value statements to people outside of the organization.
- *Entrepreneur*: Initiator and designer of controlled change; exploiting change to improve the current situation or position for future risk.
- *Disturbance handler*: Dealing with sudden crises that cannot be ignored (conflict, for example). Typically, the manager gives this role priority over others.
- *Resource allocator*: Authority to allocate scarce resources (power).
- *Negotiator*: Negotiations requiring substantial commitment of resources are facilitated by the manager having the authority to make commitments.[71]

Leaders and managers have different perspectives on the health organization and their personal roles within that organization. Both need to be on the same page to meet the organization's mission and vision. Again, an administrator or executive can be both a leader and a manager depending on the situation, job position, and immediate role required at the time. As long as the health industry remains dynamic, both leaders and managers are essential to the organization's success and survival; coordination and consistency of their efforts are keys to determine how well the strategic leadership/management system performs over time.

LEADERS AND SYSTEMS: INDIVIDUAL, GROUP, ORGANIZATION, AND INDUSTRY SUCCESS

Leadership requires a predetermined vision of an individual, group, organization, and industry as a whole. The complexity of the leader's actions and behaviors increases as one moves from individual to group, to organization, and so on. As complexity increases, the need for a predetermined vision, consistency, development of a strategic leadership and management system, and development of an improved culture intensifies as well. Leaders use strategic systems to direct the organization, but people are still led and resources are managed. In health organizations, a number of systems are integrated (or should be integrated) to provide tools for leaders to lead, including strategic human resource management systems, strategic supply chain systems, financial and revenue management systems, information and decision support systems, a strategic planning system, and a strategic network of internal and external stakeholders.

A significant system used by leaders is that of the leadership and management team. The members of this team, when aligned with the mission and vision of the organization, are the developers of organizational culture; strategic decision makers; directional, competitive, and adaptive strategists; and prime movers in the organization. The more knowledge, skills, abilities, and propensities the leadership team brings to the collective table, the better able the organization is to be successful in dynamic or changing times.

Leadership at the health industry level is difficult because of the industry's enormous size, unaligned motivations, differing incentives, scarcity of resources, and, especially, lack of a unifying and widely accepted (consensus of all stakeholders) common vision. However, there is a desperate need for a unified leadership effort at the industry level. Maybe you are the leader who will fill that gap.

DESCRIPTIVE AND PRESCRIPTIVE THEORIES

Leadership theories and models can be descriptive, prescriptive, or both descriptive and prescriptive. Descriptive theories and models illustrate, define, and capture leadership phenomena but do not recommend or prescribe specific actions, behaviors, or processes to employ. Prescriptive theories and models provide recommendations to the leader-practitioner with regard to actions, behaviors, or processes to use to be a successful leader. Some leadership theories and models both describe and prescribe.

THE STUDY OF LEADERSHIP: WHAT'S IN IT FOR ME?

All disciplines across the spectrum of education discuss leadership in one form or another. Whether they are chemists or musicians, successful individuals must know how to motivate people toward goal-directed behavior. The study of leadership provides the tools needed to accomplish this outcome and make you successful in your own endeavors in achieving success.

Being a leader is a special privilege. To have power, influence, and control over the lives of employees is a special responsibility. Of course, with that responsibility come special rewards, similar to those associated with being a parent. It is a special privilege to guide, nurture, and coach a group of employees toward an organizational objective and then share in the pride of accomplishing that objective. It is a joy to celebrate the success of those whom you lead. It is rewarding to mentor and develop the next generation of leaders and managers under your guidance as they look to you to provide them with the examples, tools, skills, insights, and judgments needed to be successful. And similar to the joy of parenthood, when your employees move on to assume positions of responsibility of their own and later call to say "thank you" for helping them to become successful, you can share in that special pride and reward that all leaders experience when they have successfully passed the reins of responsibility to one of their protégées.[72,73]

Leadership continues to be a concern in the forefront in healthcare delivery organization senior management discussions, professional literature, and academic literature. Recent leadership literature is plentiful in health leadership domains. The following provides the evidence.

- Leaders must have the ability to motivate as well as inspire; they also need to be willing to change leadership strategies and behaviors in order to remain effective.[74] "Leaders often integrate values into sustainable development," and sustainable development is important to balance the needs for today's society as well as the needs of the future.[75]
- Communication style and personality are traits that leaders rely on every day, and these are connected in overall leadership qualities. The authors suggest that communication styles, specifically expressive

and precise communication styles, add value over personality traits in leadership outcomes.[76]
- The demand for healthcare, accountability, quality of care, and patient satisfaction relate back to leadership training and professionalism within the healthcare industry. In many countries, a comprehensive development of strategic management and effective leadership skills must be learned to facilitate growth and achievement within the organization.[77]
- Although the Mayo Clinic forefathers followed the servant leadership model, it is important to inspire and motivate Mayo colleagues to fulfill the positive patient experience. The Mayo Clinic's physicians currently utilize transformational leadership to motivate and inspire the faculty and staff at Mayo in addition to using servant leadership; leadership development is essential to provide the best quality services to Mayo's patients.[78]
- "Effective leadership is critical for optimizing cost, access, and quality in healthcare."[79] Tailored programs in leadership should be focused on medical professionals to develop specific competencies within their roles. Overall leadership development should include collaboration, adaptation, initiative, a vision to promote quality healthcare, and active leadership experience.[80]
- Leadership is "a combination of position, responsibilities, attitude, skills, and behaviors that allows someone to bring out the best in others and the best in their organization, in a sustainable manner."[81]

What's in it for you? To be the best leader and have the best career in serving others that you can achieve. As you study leadership, you should focus on several goals. You may add your own goals to the following list:

- Define, describe, and categorize leadership knowledge, skills, and abilities.
- Understand leadership principles that contribute to successful groups and organizations.
- Apply leadership principles in thought, in writing, and then in practice.
- Analyze, compare, and deconstruct the various leadership theories, models, and skills.
- Combine elements from personal study to develop, refine, and defend a personal model of leadership that you can use in practice.
- Compare and contrast several leadership theories, models, and skills, and summarize the expected outcomes of the various leadership elements.
- Mentor, coach, and guide others in the health professions to be better leaders.

SUMMARY

This chapter focused on the basic definitions and distinctions of leadership. Specific emphasis was placed on defining the importance of leadership study in the healthcare environment and its appropriate place in the field of both academics and professional practice. Leadership was differentiated from management, and a distinction between managers and leaders was presented. Final emphasis was placed on descriptive (tells about leadership) and prescriptive (gives direction and guidance) theories and models before the basic goals of leadership study were presented. The importance of leadership today was presented to compel health professionals, established in the profession as well as new to the profession, to strive to achieve leadership competence to successfully lead people and manage resources throughout the dynamic health industry.

DISCUSSION QUESTIONS

1. Why is the study of leadership important to early careerists in the health industry? What are the challenges in the industry that require quality leadership?
2. Can you explain and give examples of leadership as compared with management? Why might health organizations need both leaders and managers?
3. Compare the application of a prescriptive leadership model to the application of a descriptive leadership model. What is the difference?
4. What distinguishes the phases of leadership thought from ancient to modern times, and what are the differences of each of the phases?
5. Can you relate the phases of leadership thought to modern leadership practices and research and provide examples?
6. What is your evaluation of the health industry's need for leadership today and into the next decade? Which specific leadership knowledge, skills, and abilities are particularly important today?

EXERCISES

1. What is leadership, and why is leadership vital to successful health organizations? Write a paragraph that supports your definition and another paragraph explaining why health organizations need leadership.
2. Distinguish between leadership and management. How are leadership and management similar? How are they different? Answer this question in three to four paragraphs.
3. Construct a list of leadership principles based on the actions and behaviors of a leader (preferably a health leader) you observe or have observed. Why are those principles successful or not successful in leading the organization? In two to three paragraphs, list and relate observed principles to outcomes.
4. Upon considering the trait, behavior, and situational leadership phases of research, which phase seems most relevant today in the health industry? Are there underlying constructs from each phase that can work together to form a coherent leadership model that explains leadership and can predict organizational outcomes? Break down each phase and relate the underlying constructs to leadership in health organizations today, paying particular attention to organizational outcomes.
5. Which attributes do you (or would you) look for in a manager? Which attributes do you look for in a leader? In your answers to these questions, is there a theoretical link in your response? (Can you reference this chapter, another reading, or a lecture that forms a connection to your responses?) Compile a list of manager attributes and a list of leader attributes. Categorize each manager and leader attribute as a "trait," a "behavior," or a "situational" attribute, and summarize the major themes of your lists in one to two paragraphs.
6. Critique one of the following articles, or an article provided by your instructor, in four to five paragraphs. Relate the critiqued article to the content in this chapter in two to three paragraphs.
   a. Boehnke, K., DiStefano, A. C., DiStefano, J. J., & Bontis, N. (1997). Leadership for extraordinary performance. *Business Quarterly*, *61*(4), 56–63.
   b. Gerstner, C. R., & Day, D. V. (1997). Meta-analytic review of leader–member exchange theory: Correlates and construct issues. *Journal of Applied Psychology*, *82*(6), 827–844.

c. Jelinek, M., & Litterer, J. A. (1995). Toward entrepreneurial organizations: Meeting ambiguity with engagement. *Entrepreneurship: Theory and Practice, 19*(3), 137–169.

d. Mintzberg, H. (1996). Musings on management. *Harvard Business Review, 74*(4), 61–67.

e. Calhoun, J. G., Dollett, L., Sinioris, M. E., Wainio, J. A., Butler, P. W., Griffith, J. R., & Warden, G. L. (2008). Development of an interprofessional competency model for healthcare leadership. *Journal of Healthcare Management, 53*(6), 375–389.

REFERENCES

1. Adams, A. (2007). Developing leadership wisdom. *International Journal of Leadership in Public Services, 3*(2), 39–50; Howard, J., Shaw, E. K., Felsen, C. B., & Crabtree, B. F. (2012). Physicians as inclusive leaders: Insights from a participatory quality improvement intervention. *Quality Management in Health Care, 21*(3), 135–145.

2. Pounder, J. (2008). Transformational leadership: Practicing what we teach in the management classroom. *Journal of Education for Business, 84*(1), 2–6.

3. Marques, J. F. (2006). Awakened leadership. *Performance Improvement, 45*(7), 35–38.

4. Evers, C., & Katyal, K. (2007). Paradoxes of leadership: Contingencies and critical learning. *South African Journal of Education, 27*(3), 377–390.

5. Rowold, J., & Rohmann, A. (2008). Relationships between leadership styles and followers' emotional experience and effectiveness in the voluntary sector. *Nonprofit and Voluntary Sector Quarterly, 38*(2), 270–286.

6. Ledlow, G. R., & Coppola, M. N. (2009). Leadership theory and influence. In J. A. Johnson (Ed.), *Health organizations: Theory, behavior, and development* (pp. 167–191). Sudbury, MA: Jones & Bartlett.

7. Turnock, B. (2004). *Healthcare leadership: What it is and how it works.* Sudbury, MA: Jones & Bartlett.

8. Dreachslin, J. L. (2007). The role of leadership in creating a diversity-sensitive organization. *Journal of Healthcare Management, 52*(3), 151–155.

9. Matkin, G. S., & Barbuto, J. E. (2012). Demographic similarity/difference, intercultural sensitivity, and leader–member exchange: A multilevel analysis. *Journal of Leadership and Organizational Studies, 19*, 294–302.

10. Cook, M. J., & Leathard, H. L. (2004). Learning for clinical leadership. *Journal of Nursing Management, 12*, 436–444.

11. Dreachslin, J. L. (2007). Diversity management and cultural competence: Research practice and the business case. *Journal of Healthcare Management, 52*(2), 79–86.

12. Hurley, J., & Linsley, P. (2007). Leadership challenges to move nurses toward collaborative individualism within a neo-corporate bureaucratic environment. *Journal of Nursing Management, 15*(7), 749–755.

13. Bass, B. M. (1990). *Bass & Stogdill's handbook of leadership.* New York: Free Press, p. 4.

14. Yunlu, D. G., & Murphy, D. D. (2012). R&D intensity and economic recession: Investigating the moderating role of CEO characteristics. *Journal of Leadership and Organizational Studies, 19*, 284–293.

15. Fiedler, F. E. (1996). Research on leadership selection and training: One view of the future. *Administrative Science Quarterly, 41*(2), 242.

16. Surakka, T. (2008). The nurse manager's work in the hospital environment during the 1990s and 2000s: Responsibility, accountability and expertise in nursing leadership. *Journal of Nursing Management, 16*(5), 525–534.

17. Morrison, I. (2000). *Health care in the new millennium.* San Francisco, CA: Jossey-Bass, p. 30.

18. Morrison, note 17, pp. 16–38.

19. Beebe, S. A., & Masterson, J. T. (1997). *Communicating in small groups: Principles and practices* (5th ed.). New York: Addison-Wesley Educational.

20. Morrison, note 17.

21. Hoffer, E. (2002). *Encyclopædia Britannica 2003 Ultimate Reference Suite CD-ROM.* Encyclopædia Britannica, Inc. Chicago, IL: Encyclopædia Britannica.

22. Kolenda, C. (2001). *Leadership: The warrior's art.* Carlisle, PA: Army War College Press.

23. Andrews, D. R., Richard, D. C. S., Robinson, P., Celano, P., & Hallaron, J. (2012). The influence of staff nurse perception of leadership style on satisfaction with leadership: A cross-sectional survey of pediatric nurses. *International Journal of Nursing Studies, 49*(10), 1103–1111.

24. Bass, note 13, p. 3.

25. Lichtheim, M. (1973). *Ancient Egyptian literature. Vol. 1: The old and middle kingdoms.* Los Angeles, CA: University of California Press.

26. Bass, note 13, p. 3.
27. Ramthun, A. J., & Matkin, G. S. (2012). Multicultural shared leadership: A conceptual model of shared leadership in culturally diverse teams. *Journal of Leadership and Organizational Studies*, *19*, 303–314.
28. Conger, J. A. (1999). Charismatic and transformational leadership in organizations: An insider's perspective on these developing streams of research. *Leadership Quarterly*, *10*(2), 156–157.
29. Fryers, M., Young, L., & Rowland, P. (2012). Creating and sustaining a collaborative model of care. *Healthcare Management Forum*, *25*(1), 20–25. Retrieved from http://www.sciencedirect.com/science/article/pii/S1048984316000059.
30. Lynn, L. E. Jr. (1994). Public management research: The triumph of art over science. *Journal of Policy Analysis and Management*, *13*(2), 231–287.
31. Chambers, H. E. (1999). The agencies of leadership. *Executive Excellence*, *16*(8), 12.
32. Harris, T. E., & Nelson, M. D. (2008). *Applied organizational communication: Theory and practice in a global environment* (3rd ed.). New York: Lawrence Erlbaum Associates, Chapter 2.
33. Harris & Nelson, note 32.
34. Yukl, G. (1994). Leadership in organizations (3rd ed.). Englewood Cliffs, NJ: Prentice Hall, p. 3.
35. Puryear, E. (1971). *Nineteen stars: A study in military character and leadership*. Novato, CA: Presidio Press.
36. Zaleznick, A. (2004). Managers and leaders: Are they different? *Harvard Business Review*, *82*(1), 74–81.
37. BrainyQuote. (n.d.). Leadership quotes. Retrieved from http://www.brainyquote.com/quotes/keywords/leadership.html.
38. Peters, T. J., & Waterman, R. H. (1982). *In search of excellence*. New York: Harper and Row.
39. Yukl, note 34.
40. Yukl, note 34.
41. Peters & Waterman, note 37.
42. Yukl, note 34.
43. Yukl, note 34.
44. Yukl, note 34.
45. Schein, E. H. (1999). *The corporate culture survival guide: Sense and nonsense about culture change*. San Francisco, CA: Jossey-Bass.
46. Blanchard, K., Hersey, P., & Johnson, D. E. (2000). *Management of organizational behavior: Leading human resources* (8th ed.). Upper Saddle River, NJ: Prentice Hall.
47. Covey, S. (1990). *Principle-centered leadership*. Provo, UT: Institute for Principle-Centered Leadership.
48. Gupta, A. (2005). Leadership in a fast-paced world: An interview with Ken Blanchard. *American Journal of Business*, *20*(1), 7–11.
49. Ling, Y., Simsek, Z., Lubatkin, M. H., & Veiga, J., (2008). The impact of transformational CEOs on the performance of small- to medium-sized firms: Does organizational context matter? *Journal of Applied Psychology*, *93*(4), 923–934.
50. Ledlow & Coppola, note 6.
51. Schein, note 45.
52. Kent, T., Johnson, J. A., & Graber, D. A. (1996). Leadership in the formation of new health care environments. *Health Care Supervisor*, *15*(2), 28–29.
53. Adair, J. (2010). *Effective leadership masterclass: Secrets of success from the world's greatest leaders*. London: Pan.
54. Maccoby, M. (2000). Understanding the difference between management and leadership. *Research Technology Management*, *43*(1), 57–59. Retrieved from http://www.maccoby.com/Articles/UtDBMaL.shtml.
55. Zaleznik, A. (1992, March/April). Managers and leaders: Are they different? *Harvard Business Review*, *70*(2), 126–135.
56. Ledlow & Coppola, note 6.
57. Predpall, D. F. (1994, May/June). Developing quality improvement processes in consulting engineering firms. *Journal of Management in Engineering*, 30–31.
58. Maxwell, J. C. (1993). *Developing the leader within you*. Nashville, TN: Nelson.
59. Leonard, G. (2011). Principles of execution: Insights from Steve Jobs on visionary leadership. *Strategic Portfolio Execution and Governance: Real People, Real Insights*. Retrieved from http://www.-principlesofexecution.com/principles-of-execution/2011/09/insights-from-steve-jobs-on-visionary-leadership.html.
60. Maxwell, J. C. (2002). *Leadership 101: What every leader needs to know*. Nashville, TN: Nelson.
61. Predpall, note 57.
62. Borkowski, N., Deckard, G., Weber, M., Padron, L. A., & Luongo, S. (2011). Leadership development initiatives underlie individual and system performance in a US public healthcare delivery system. *Leadership in Health Services*, *24*(4), 268–280.
63. Maccoby, M. (2000). Understanding the difference between management and leadership. *Research Technology Management*, *43*(1), 57–59.
64. Sharma, S. (1995). Development of management thought. Retrieved from http://choo.fis.utoronto.ca/FIS/Courses/LIS1230/LIS1230sharma/history4.htm.
65. George, B. (2010). Authentic leaders. *Leadership Excellence*, *27*(10), 16.

66. Katz, R. L. (1955, Jan/Feb). Skills of an effective administrator. *Harvard Business Review*, *33*(1), 33–42.

67. Mann, F. C. (1965). Toward an understanding of the leadership role in formal organizations. In R. Dubin, G. C. Homans, F. C. Mann, & D. C. Miller (Eds.), *Leadership and productivity* (pp. 68–103). San Francisco, CA: Chandler.

68. Stewart, K., Wyatt, R., & Conway, J. (2012). Unprofessional behaviour and patient safety. *International Journal of Clinical Leadership*, *17*(2), 93–101.

69. University of Edinburgh School of Engineering. (2009). Welcome to the ME96 leadership pages. Retrieved from http://www.see.ed.ac.uk/~gerard/MENG/ME96.

70. Mintzberg, H. (1973). *The nature of managerial work*. New York: Harper and Row.

71. Prather, J. (2009). *Soldiering on*. Waco, TX: Baylor Line.

72. Prather, note 71.

73. Rubenstein, H. (2005). The evolution of leadership in the workplace. *Journal of Business Perspective*, *9*(2), 41–49.

74. Akins, R., Bright, B., Brunson, T., & Worthman, W. (2013). Effective leadership for sustainable development. *Journal of Organizational Learning and Leadership*, *11*(1), 29–36. Retrieved from http://web.b.ebscohost.com.ezproxy.ttuhsc.edu/ehost/detail/detail?vid=6&sid=a9052a2a-dcb1-4dd5-9f79-af4ffdcce30f%40sessionmgr113&hid=112&bdata=JnNpdGU9ZWhvc3QtbGl2ZQ%3d%3d#db=bth&AN=91539352.

75. Akins et al., note 74, p. 29.

76. Bakker-Pieper, A., & de Vries, R. E. (2013, January 10). The incremental validity of communication styles over personality traits for leader outcomes. *Human Performance*, *26*(1), 1–19. doi:10.1080/08959285.2012.736900

77. Kumar, S., Adhish, V. S., & Deoki, N. (2014, February 4). Introduction to strategic management and leadership for health professionals. *Indian Journal of Community Medicine*. *39*(1), 13–16. Retrieved from http://www.ijcm.org.in/text.asp?2014/39/1/13/126345.

78. Peters, D. E., Casale, S. A., Halyard, M. Y., Frey, K. A., Bunkers, B. E., & Caubet, S. L. (2014, May). The evolution of leadership: A perspective from the Mayo Clinic. *Physician Executive*, *40*(3), 24–30. Retrieved from http://web.b.ebscohost.com.ezproxy.ttuhsc.edu/ehost/detail/detail?sid=d710c2c1-1431-48ab-8ddd-0&hid=114&bdata=JnNpdGU9ZWhvc3QtbGl2ZQ%3d%3d#db=bth&AN=96107054.

79. Stoller, J. K. (2013). Commentary: Recommendations and remaining questions for health care leadership training programs. *Academic Medicine*, *88*(1), 12–15. doi:10.1097/ACM.0b013e318276bff1

80. Stoller, note 79, p. 12.

81. Vender, R. J. (2014, July 22). Leadership: An overview. *The American Journal of Gastroenterology*, 1–6. doi:10.1038/ajg.2014.199

DETERMINING YOUR OWN LEADERSHIP STYLE

Personally I am always ready to learn, although I do not always like being taught.

Sir Winston Churchill

This chapter introduces the influence of personality and physiology on leadership dynamics. Students are introduced to various leadership and personality assessment tests. After completing the assessment tests, students are asked to write a summary essay integrating findings of their own leader and personality outcomes. This summary and the tests that precede it assist students in identifying a penchant for certain leadership styles. The assessments will assist students in understanding and relating to theories, models, and evolutionary trends in the literature.

LEARNING OBJECTIVES

1. Name and describe at least four assessments related to leadership.

2. Explain your personality type, leadership style, principles, and foundational skills as informed by leadership and leadership-related assessment instruments.

3. Produce results of at least four leadership-related assessments, and prepare and apply those results to your leadership persona.

4. Identify and distinguish your leadership style, principles, and foundational skills (both strengths and weaknesses) based on the results obtained from leadership-related assessment instruments.

5. Based on self-assessments of your personality type, leadership style, principles, and foundational skills, devise a plan to improve your weaknesses while leveraging or enhancing your strengths.

6. Critique and interpret your unique leadership persona, and relate your leadership persona with examples from your life experiences.

INTRODUCTION

Developing and utilizing a personal leadership model or plan that is efficient, effective, and efficacious starts with understanding your unique propensities of leadership. How your personality integrates with a leadership model and identifying strengths and improvement domains begin with these analyses and self-reflective exercises. It is well worth the time and effort to "know thyself." Understanding your personality is essential for effective leadership.[1] Without an understanding of self, there cannot be a clear understanding of how others perceive you as a leader. As a result, the first step in improving your ability to lead people in health organizations is to understand yourself.[2] To take that first step, gaining an understanding of your personality type, leadership style, and associated leadership skills is paramount. What you know, who you know, and, perhaps most importantly, what you know about yourself all matter![3,4] This chapter starts the journey to understanding yourself. As part of this effort, you can work to become a better leader by adding knowledge, skills, and abilities to your leadership "toolbox" by identifying your strengths, weaknesses, and propensities. This is a lifelong endeavor. Just as you have a dominant personality type (the personality you naturally have), so too do you have a dominant leadership style, a dominant conflict management style, and so forth. Even so, you can learn, practice, and master other styles, which then become part of your repertoire to lead people and manage

resources. Understanding your strengths, weaknesses, and propensities is important to enable you to construct your leadership plan and model to propel your career. This is because even without your understanding them, your strengths, weaknesses, and propensities will shape your career.[5] Through understanding, you can propel your career in the direction best suited to your leadership style.

Although there are several personality and diagnostic leadership assessments available on the Internet today, we have selected four that provide a strong foundation of self-awareness. These assessment tests can give you insights into the building blocks of personality most commonly identified by peers, subordinate employees, and supervisors. Additionally, the selected tests are similar to those an employer may use as part of the hiring process for a new employee. Furthermore, any candidate applying for a new position should be ready for the face-to-face and/or telephone interview. During this conversational part of the interview, a candidate should be prepared to share personal traits and professional self-assessments with the potential employer. These may include issues regarding conflict management, decision making, problem solving, and creativity. Having a prior foundation of personal self-assessment and test outcomes will better prepare the candidate for not only personal self-awareness but also for how those self-assessments can be leveraged for success to a prospective employer and his or her organization.[6,7] Personality testing is used in the workplace to predict work-related behaviors; there is also a connection between personality traits and emerging leaders.[8] Leadership styles can be related to particular leadership models such as transformational, transactional, and structure, relation, and change models. Eight personal work traits are important in leadership behavior: social ability, emotional intelligence, cooperation, perfectionism, endurance, creativity, self-confidence, and positive attitude.[9]

To begin your journey to understanding yourself, this chapter introduces a variety of assessment-related topics: the Jungian model (based on the research of Carl Jung, a notable Swiss psychiatrist and influential scholar for his work in personalities in the late nineteenth and early twentieth centuries), which many know as the Myers–Briggs personality indicator; introvertedness and extrovertedness (type A/B personality indicators); creative and empirical thinkers (left- and right-brain thinkers); and the propensity to lead and learn through visual, auditory, reading, or kinesthetic (VARK) constructs. Prior to completing the leadership-related assessments, you will complete the enneagram diagnostic to discern whether your personal motivational objectives mirror those of traditional leaders.

The assessments focus on the test taker's propensity and affiliation in relationship to traditional leadership or traditional managerial roles. Other assessments provide diagnostics that evaluate risk taking, charisma, vision, and empirical leadership characteristics. This chapter also discusses the constant battle a leader experiences between his or her natural predispositions and the precepts taught in leadership training and their mechanical execution. Although we do not present these tests as a panacea for leadership diagnosis, we do suggest that certain ability–job fit characteristics may become clearer after completing these self-assessments.

KNOW THYSELF: WHAT KIND OF LEADER ARE YOU?

Newt Gingrich, the former Republican Speaker of the U.S. House of Representatives, once said of former Democratic President Bill Clinton that he did not like to talk with Clinton for too long a period of time, because after a while he began to agree with him.[10] Although former White House Press Secretary George Stephanopoulos may have made this comment jovially in his book *All Too Human*, the statement was fundamentally accurate in more ways than one. President Clinton was widely admired for his natural charisma, political savvy, and social skills that inspired followership and easy friendship. The same might not be true of his spouse, former Secretary of State Hillary Clinton,[11] who has grown and matured in political

creditability through nearly two decades of on-the-job leader training coupled with personal and professional self-development. What one leader possesses intrinsically and naturally, the other honed through application of best practices and understanding of leadership styles, principles, and skills. In other words, some leaders have natural abilities, whereas others must work to learn those abilities.

All leaders, regardless of their natural abilities, experience, education, and training, must be aware of their own personal areas for improvement so that they can grow and become more successful. As a result, we ask you to consider the following questions:

- What kind of leader are you?
- What are your strengths and weaknesses?
- Are you aware of how those strengths and weaknesses support or fail to support your leadership style?

TRAITS OF LEADERS

There is an ongoing debate, within both the literature and professional practice, over whether leaders are born or made. This argument centers on the premise that those qualities that make leaders successful cannot be taught. Such qualities might include ambition, motivation, and a strong work ethic.

There is a general agreement in the literature that these qualities are inherent within individuals who emerge as leaders in the organizational workplace. Certainly, many great leaders of our time have possessed these qualities. However, qualities—or *traits*—of motivation, ambition, and work ethic are difficult to measure by themselves. Most often, proxy outcomes are assigned to these qualities as justification for their presence. Such proxy variables might include education (if the individual is motivated, he or she might pursue higher education for an advanced degree), number of hours worked, or number of jobs held at one time—all of which might lead outside agents to conclude that the individual possesses a strong work ethic. Although motivation and ambition are certainly good qualities for leaders to possess, they are not by themselves precursors to successful leader outcomes.

Take, for example, the Ponzi scheme created by former tycoon Bernard Madoff.[12] Well known as an extremely ambitious and motivated individual, Madoff became the architect of one of the greatest financial scams in U.S. history.[13] Clearly, ambition and motivation by themselves are not traits of leadership.

Another example might be Adolf Hitler. Using basic leadership theories of followership and transformation, Hitler might effectively be designated a leader through the example of his successful rebuilding of Germany after

World War I. Nevertheless, to refer to Hitler as a leader—after considering the totality of his "work"—is insulting to the profession of leadership. No, Hitler does not occupy a position in the highly regarded field of leaders. He was, at best, a despot and a dictator.[14] Leaders must be moral actors.

New leader models have emerged in the field of leadership that screen out dictators and despots from the honored study of those individuals who have earned the designation of *leader*.

PERSONALITY PROFILING IN ACTION

From 2004 through 2007, the program director of Baylor University's joint master's degree in health administration (MHA) and business administration (MBA) program conducted a series of personality assessments on members of the entering graduate class.[15,16] One of the personality self-assessments was the VARK test.[17] This self-completed survey provides users with a profile of their unique learning preferences. The scores profile an individual as having a predisposition for learning through visual, auditory, reading/writing, or kinesthetic (i.e., doing) constructs or modalities.

In the past, it was suggested that those individuals who score low in the auditory predisposition on the VARK test may have difficulty in the graduate and postgraduate settings, because oral lectures are the preferred method of delivering information in the traditional classroom. To test this hypothesis, 165 graduate students in Baylor's MHA/MBA program (approximately 41 in each class) were followed through 4 years of classroom dynamics. **Table 2-1** profiles the outcomes for these graduate students.

Table 2-1 suggests some common traits are associated with graduate students selected to attend a traditional full-time university. Although discrepancies are common, and reasonable variance is assumed between scores within the bounded rationality of standard personality diagnosis, in 2006, only two students identified themselves as having a preferred learning modality associated with listening to lectures (auditory). In the other years, the number of auditory learners was consistent and steady over time,

which suggests this learning style preference might be a shared trait among graduate classes in traditional academia. Furthermore, the percentage of students who preferred the reading/writing and visual styles stayed relatively consistent over the years.

The data recorded in 2005 were unique insofar as the class had no stabilizers for auditory learning. As a result, the class as a whole often became frustrated and irascible when faced with the prospect of long lectures. The feedback received on end-of-course evaluations for professors who refused to change or modify their teaching methods from lecture to case study was extremely poor ($n = 2.8$ on a 5-point scale). As the program director, Dr. Nick Coppola continually made recommendations to the faculty to modify teaching styles for the benefit of the class. Those faculty members who modified their teaching practices for the second term received significantly higher end-of-course evaluations ($n = 3.8$ on a 5-point scale). Those faculty members who did not modify their teaching practice continued to receive poor feedback for their entire teaching year with those students. Knowing how the students learned was helpful to the professors, and it made them better educators. Health leaders can apply the same information to their leadership styles and adapt their message delivery to their subordinates' propensities.

This small example demonstrates two points. First, personality profiling does provide insights into leading people that can result in positive outcomes. Second, those professors who were savvy and aware of how their teaching practice (i.e., their leadership style) was affecting the students were able to adapt and modify situations to create win–win opportunities for both themselves and the students.

THE IMPORTANCE OF UNDERSTANDING PERSONALITIES IN THE WORKFORCE

The average worker will change jobs seven to nine times over the course of his or her career. The decision to depart a current place of employment may be based on advancement opportunities or dissatisfaction with the current work

Table 2-1 VARK Learning Outcomes at Baylor University's MHA/MBA Program ($n = 164$)							
VARK Test 2004		**VARK Test 2005**		**VARK Test 2006**		**VARK Test 2007**	
Aural	9	Aural	2	Aural	9	Aural	9
Kinesthetic (doing)	8	Kinesthetic (doing)	22	Kinesthetic (doing)	12	Kinesthetic (doing)	10
Read/write	8	Read/write	10	Read/write	8	Read/write	8
Visual	18	Visual	9	Visual	11	Visual	12

environment. Whatever the specific reason given, the pursuit of new leadership opportunities is often driven by the seeker's interest in matching his or her educational and work history against published criteria about a new job. However, matching only past experience and educational accomplishments will not produce a positive outcome when seeking to match skills with available openings.[18]

Personality dynamics influence success in the workplace in many ways. Performance, personal satisfaction, and outcomes are all enhanced when the employee and the work environment are in alignment—that is, when there is synchronization with personality. Synchronization is a process that includes many dimensions of an individual's abilities, such as education and experience, ability to learn, mental "hard-wiring," personality archetypes, leadership dynamics, and physical abilities.[19] Understanding the personalities of subordinates, peers, and superiors in the health organization is important for health leaders. This understanding informs the health leader of the expectations of others and provides insights into motivation, competitiveness, team building, coalition building, and interpersonal relationships and communication.

LEADERSHIP AND PERSONALITY SELF-ASSESSMENT

The following section identifies some of the more popular personality and leadership self-assessments available on the Internet. These sites provide free leadership and personality self-assessments that are highly commensurate with many of the private and for-profit assessments that can be purchased. In fact, for many large for-profit organizations, personality screening is a necessary precursor to being offered a position in the company. Many large-scale organizations have found that a basic interview and reference checking are just small parts of a larger interview process. Personality assessment via computerized testing is becoming more common, as organizations have realized that nearly all references provided by candidates result in positive narratives. Additionally, a favorable half-day interview may not provide the organization with a complete picture of the individual's predisposition for participatory, autocratic, and authoritarian leadership styles or level of mastery of critical leadership skills such as communication.

Many organizations are weary of the litigation potential when an individual is hired, only to be terminated for failing to get along with coworkers or adapt to existing workplace dynamics. As a result, personality self-assessment has become a piece of the overall picture of the job candidate developed by organizations prior to making a final offer of employment. As such, it is incumbent on early careerists to

not only become aware of their own personality archetype but also to gain some experience with personality assessment prior to any real-world screening process so that nervousness and second guessing do not occur during the actual corporate screening process.

Upon completing each of these personality diagnostics, the test taker is supplied with a free assessment of his or her scores by the hosting website. Although there are often no right or wrong answers, and all tests are subject to issues of reliability and validity, many of these assessments, if taken consistently over the period of weeks or months, will provide similar responses over time.

Drs. Ledlow and Stephens suggest that in the university course setting, four to six self-assessments should be completed, based on the learning outcomes of the course. Upon completing these assessments, you should write a two- to three-page integrated self-assessment based on the diagnostic outcomes. This essay should list professional strengths for the career field that the test taker is about to enter, as well as areas of potential professional development where weaknesses are identified. One last note: Everyone—leader and follower alike—has weaknesses and areas of career and professional performance that can be improved.

The following section is exciting and fun but can also be scary and anxiety provoking. The goal is to "know thyself" as a health leader and to learn to identify and leverage your strengths while shoring up your weaknesses to create more potential for great leadership—your great leadership—in the health industry. The assessments can be found at the reference attached to each section's heading.

LEADERSHIP AND PERSONALITY ASSESSMENTS

EMOTIONAL INTELLIGENCE[20]

Emotional intelligence (EI) is the subset of social intelligence that involves the ability to monitor one's own and others' feelings and emotions, to discriminate among them, and to use this information to guide one's thinking and actions. "This big idea is that success in work and life depends on more than just the basic cognitive abilities typically measured by IQ tests and related measures; it also depends on a number of personal qualities that involve the perception, understanding, and regulation of emotion."[21] Two pieces of EI are energy and maturity. Energy is the liveliness and stamina with which people approach their work. Maturity is described as people's refinement, social graces, tact, capacity to grow and change, and ability to interpret signals from others. Both of these elements contribute to EI. It is important to be aware of your inner emotional self so that you can conduct yourself in the best manner when managing others.[22]

EI is one of the more difficult concepts for individuals to understand, improve, and master. It is based on a variety of nonintellectual factors that can influence behavior. Some leaders are unaware of how their EI affects their superiors and subordinates. In fact, many individuals will reassign negative outcomes and behaviors to those around them and be completely unaware of their personal effect on others' actions.[23,24]

EI is a relatively new concept in leadership, having only been studied since the early 1980s.[25] Many definitions of EI can be found in the literature. Notably, the Institute for Health and Human Potential defines EI as the ability or capacity to perceive, assess, and manage the emotions of oneself and of others. EI might also be thought of as having "street smarts." Street smarts are those characteristics most often possessed by highly charismatic leaders that allow them to exercise savvy and poise in controlling relationships among outside agents and stakeholders. Executives possessing this ability have a better understanding of how to manage the complex relationships in teams and foster positive relationships with rivals while attaining control and collegiality among organization members. Fostering EI in organizations and teams is an essential factor in successful organizations and should not be overlooked.[26]

The four salient constructs of the emotional intelligence model are (1) self-awareness, (2) self-management, (3) social awareness, and (4) social skills.[27] These constructs are slanted toward the relational or "art" aspect of leadership. At the same time, these constructs can and should merge to form a secondary level of "intelligence" that is ever present and that monitors the technical and relationship orientations of the leader. Conscious engagement and mastery leads to subconscious implementation; this is the internal gyroscope that many successful leaders learn to depend on. "Those who use the emotional intelligence framework to guide their thoughts and actions may find it easier to create trust in relationships, harness energy under pressure, and sharpen their ability to make sound decisions—in other words, they increase their potential for success in the workplace."[28] The dynamic culture leader connects the four EI constructs with this "internal gyroscope" to analyze him- or herself and the organization and to merge the appropriate levels of science and art in creating an organizational culture that can withstand ever-changing environmental challenges.[29]

SOCIAL COMPETENCE AND LOCUS OF CONTROL

The other important skill area to develop is social competence, which includes such attributes as social awareness, collaboration, empathy, and teamwork. Dye suggests that in order for EI to flourish, an early careerist needs to take an integrated approach to self-awareness, which includes drawing simultaneously from both social and personal outcomes and experiences.[30] The key, then, is to cultivate and sustain a high level of both personal and social competence and then to develop strategies for identifying and responding appropriately to behavioral patterns in the environment. This is done through personal self-perspective by simply monitoring reactions and emotions in the environment and leveraging personal behavior and visceral instincts accordingly. These efforts can also be gauged by interpreting the reactions of those around you. For example, each workplace develops a certain tone and tenor based on the personnel who work there. Some may respond in unexpected ways consistent with certain styles and behaviors of management. The socially competent leader will know how to adjust his or her level of autocratic, intimate, participative, and interpersonal communication with others in a manner that predicts and fosters workplace behavior over time. This reflects what is called *locus of control*.

Persons with a high locus of control are able to process, receive, and transmit information absent of emotional content. For example, an individual who worked very hard on a business case analysis that was not approved by his or her boss during a large staff meeting should refrain from an emotional outburst in front of other staff members. Likewise, leaders with a high locus of control would refrain from displaying a threatening demeanor when asked to support positions of contention in an organization where subordinate employees have a differing opinion.

Within the health professions, having a high locus of control can be important when discussing such volatile issues as end-of-life care and right-to-life issues. Leaders in the health profession must possess the sensitivity to recognize certain intangible elements in bio- and clinical ethics that are both ineffable and important to the success of a nonpartisan leadership.

Although seemingly suggesting "common-sense" workplace activities, leaders who fail to maintain a high locus of control and control their instinctive emotions eventually can become workplace hazards to themselves and the employees they supervise.

HEMISPHERE DOMINANCE[31]

The hemisphere dominance personality assessment indicates the brain hemisphere (right or left) that dominates in the test taker. Most professionals are aware there is a dominant side of the brain; however, these same professionals are often unaware of the influence this hardwiring has on the day-to-day activities of professional performance. For example, "right-brained" individuals tend to be more creative. Professionals with dominant right brains may be best suited for creating new product and service lines, developing long-range strategic plans, and forecasting threats on the environmental horizon. In contrast, "left-brained" individuals are more detail oriented, methodical, and calculating. They prefer implementing strategic plans to developing them. Although it is difficult to change one's predisposition for creativeness versus detail orientation, creative thinkers can make specific adjustments in their daily business of work to become more organized, whereas more concrete thinkers can exercise creative elements of their brain by engaging in more creative arts such as writing, music, or painting.

JUNGIAN ASSESSMENTS[32]

Scholars have suggested that all individuals are born with a personality archetype. Over the years, family, society, and the environment all exert influences on this archetype. Working professionals should be aware of their natural predispositions (as measured by Jungian assessments) so that certain characteristics can be leveraged or weaknesses avoided. The most popular assessment of this kind is the Myers–Briggs Type Indicator (MBTI), which has been a reliable source of documenting personality since World War II. The MBTI focuses on four dimensions of personality: extraversion or introversion, sensing or intuition, thinking or feeling, and judging or perceiving;[33–36] "[T]he four opposing dimensions are extroversion-introversion, sensation-intuition, thinking-feeling, and judgment-perception."[37] (Two preferences are identified in each dimension.) The MBTI results indicate the test taker's preferred style and remain fairly stable throughout a person's career.

Extroverts prefer the company and collaboration of teams, whereas *introverts* prefer comfort zones that involve the interaction of just a few people. Extroverts tend to be "charged" by other people and interaction with others, whereas introverts tend to be "charged" by quiet reflection and isolated activities. Extroverts can be alone and function very well, just as introverts can be with other people for long periods and function very well. Extroverts tend to be more assertive, whereas introverts have refined listening skills.

Sensing individuals seek empirical affirmation from the environment—that is, reassurance that history plays a critical role in today's decision and will impact tomorrow. *Intuitive* personality types prefer more latent cues from the environment for decision making and, at the extreme, ignore the past.

Thinking individuals tend to be very strong at execution, whereas the strength of *feeling* individuals resides with interaction. Logic and cause-and-effect reasoning are valued by the thinking profile, whereas emotion and the impact of decisions on the organization are important to the feeling-oriented individual.

Judging people carefully weigh all of the options and alternatives. They tend to be more structured in their approaches to implementation. In contrast, *perceiving* individuals find confidence in their own heuristics (rules of thumb with which to make decisions) and prior knowledge for decision making. Perceiving individuals tend to be more spontaneous.

TYPE A AND B PERSONALITY INDICATORS[38]

In the 1940s and 1950s, when personality archetypes and behavior theories were emerging as seminal fields of study to add to the trait theory literature, it was posited that people were hardwired to fit into one of three neat, clear-cut predispositions for the purposes of personality classification—namely, Type A, Type B, and Type A/B individuals.[39]

Type A individuals are competitive, inquisitive, and easily bored with routine; they have a "short fuse," often feel impatient, and may be aggressive. These individuals may also have a difficult time relaxing, staying focused on details, and maintaining stability in any one place for long periods of time. Type B people are the direct opposite: They can relax easily, tend to maintain focus on activities and projects, see stability as comforting, and can be perceived as more social and easygoing.[40] Type A/B individuals may present characteristics of both personality traits and present characteristics in either dimension depending on environment, circumstance, and mood. Type A/B personalities are said to be balanced personalities and can find comfort in a variety of situations.

Although there is no direct evidence that any of the personal predispositions aids in leadership development and success, a growing body of work suggests that Type A individuals have higher burnout and mortality rates.[41]

There is general agreement in the literature that individuals are predisposed to present behaviors in either the Type A or B modality. Even so, it may be possible for individuals to switch over and mimic personality characteristics and behaviors of the other dynamic based on their education, work stimulus, and coping skills.

Knowing which archetype best defines an individual creates leverage in the workplace. Successful Type B individuals will know when to "turn on" and become excited and committed to projects and ventures. This posture can be mimicked until the work is completed. Likewise, Type A individuals can present a high locus of control and know when to mitigate their own emotions and instincts to perform more cooperatively in group work and interdisciplinary team dynamics.

THE VARK TEST[42]

As mentioned earlier in this chapter, a VARK assessment provides insight into an individual's predisposition toward a particular learning style. Most people have a dominant learning style, a secondary style, a tertiary style, and a least preferred style. Some individuals may also have high abilities in more than one style. Although the VARK test may seem somewhat oriented to university education, all organizations have a set of continuing education and professional development competencies that must be achieved for an individual to advance or maintain employment in the workplace. By knowing which specific modality fosters a higher learning outcome for him- or herself, an individual can maximize use of his or her discretionary time to focus on those events that promote the greatest transfer of information. Such examples of different professional development activities might include on-site conferences, webinars, distance learning, traditional education, and personal self-development through reading, listening to audiobooks, or working on computer-based problems or games.

Although learning styles change over time, prudent early careerists will conduct a personal self-assessment of their own preferred learning modality. It is important for young leaders to know that potential organizations may or may not appreciate individual learning styles. For example, if an individual is an auditory learner in an organization that emphasizes verbal communication, the probability for successful synchronization between that individual and the organization should be enhanced. Conversely, an auditory learner in an environment where mass reading of policy and procedure statements is necessary may not fare as well. Thus health leaders should be aware of their preferred methods of learning—that is, whether they emphasize visual, aural, reading, or kinesthetic traits. Other assessments use the terms *visual verbal* (reading), *visual nonverbal* ("visual" referring to pictures, figures, and graphs), *auditory* (aural), and *learning by doing* (kinesthetic) to describe the learning style preferences. Collectively, these characteristics are referred to as VARK.[43,44] *Visual learners* prefer graphs, pictures, and flowcharts to help them understand complex phenomena. These learners feel most comfortable surrounded by blueprints and matrixes but may be distracted by debates and decision discussions.

Aural learners are stimulated by conversation and debate. These learners may often be more interested in the discussion of decision making than decision making itself. They "think out loud" and may often use other employees as sounding boards for new ideas.

Reading and writing (R/W) learning preference is a common characteristic among healthcare executives. These individuals prefer cross-referencing written material, writing summaries, and emailing thoughts. They do well with complex tasks and multitasking.

Kinesthetic learners require practical exercises, a hands-on approach, or meticulous simulation to learn efficiently. These learners prefer learning through experience to alternative preparatory methods. However, they are rapid processors of information in an on-the-job environment. Kinesthetic learners are also more comfortable with ambiguity.

THE NEW ENNEAGRAM TEST[45]

Enneagrams are said to be natural encodings in the neural tissue of the brain that provide a physical predisposition to behave in a certain way based on environmental stimulus. Similar to left- and right-brain dominance, the way in which each brain forms relationships within itself to process information is unique.[46] As a result, it is incumbent on health leaders to be aware of these visceral tendencies to see if there is any opportunity for professional development or self-awareness.

Enneagrams identify the test taker's natural inclination toward behavior. The results can be classified into nine primary constructs or types: Reformer, Helper, Motivator, Romantic, Thinker, Skeptic, Adventurer, Leader, and Peacemaker.[47–51]

The *Reformer* is the perfectionist and obedient child who must do everything right. Individuals with this tendency prefer that others get along with them and prefer to dictate terms in groups and interdisciplinary teams. This behavior stands in contrast to that of the *Helper*, who will seek to engage in supportive relationships with others to gain favor and acceptance.

The *Motivator* is the high achiever who seeks to pull those around him or her toward success. The Motivator may not try to conform those around him or her to his or her own standards of excellence; rather, the Motivator will pull those in his or her inner circle toward goals and objectives.

The *Romantic* strives for warm and collegial connections with those in the workplace. Words of approbation are very important to the Romantic, because individuals with this tendency do not thrive in a critical atmosphere. The Romantic may work well in small groups of known colleagues but may have difficulty in new environments.

The *Thinker* sees the world as "overstimulating" and confusing and will need privacy to contemplate actions in the environment. Type B personalities are most often Thinkers. Thinkers will often be plainspoken and direct, and they sometimes communicate without tact. However, they are often detail oriented and factually accurate. They leave little room for discrepancy or speculation. When a Thinker finally speaks, there often is little room for alternative positions and opinions.

The *Skeptic* is eager to investigate life and propositions. Skeptics, sometimes called "Challengers," have a great lust for life and a keen intellectual curiosity. They are most often Type A archetypes, challenge institutionalism, and may demonstrate creative and right-brain thinking. At the same time, they have a need for social integration and can be tactful and wary of irritating relationships.

The *Adventurer* wants excitement, pleasure, and fun. Individuals in this category see work as a game; however, they can have difficulty organizing activities and projects themselves. They prefer stimulating conversation to the labor of work, and they prefer to be the center of attention without taking responsibility. The Adventurer is an odd mix of a charismatic personality coupled with a degree of avoidance behavior. He or she may be the "idea person" in the organization who wants someone else to produce the concepts that he or she has suggested. A difficult archetype to pin down, the Adventurer may succeed best when surrounded by talented subordinate personnel.

The *Leader* archetype is not always presented in some assessments, because researchers believe that the leadership construct is a composite of several modalities coupled with environmental opportunities. However, in many enneagram tests, the Leader may not be the individual who inspires followership or who occupies a director role in project management; rather, the Leader in this case may be called the "Asserter." Asserters have strong personalities and are direct, self-reliant, and seemingly unfettered by the opinions of those around them. At the same time, the Leader can be supportive of those close to him or her.

Peacemakers do not want to be part of the spotlight, nor do they think of themselves as important or special to the group dynamic. They tend to avoid prominent leadership roles and prefer to "hide in plain sight" by neither confronting antagonists nor supporting commonly agreed-upon direction. Far from being lazy, the Peacemaker can provide a neutral sense of direction between competing priorities and introduce new ones if carefully coddled and treated well within the group dynamic.

DYNAMIC CULTURE LEADERSHIP ALIGNMENT ASSESSMENT[52]

Individual assessment is important, as is a leadership team evaluation. An accurate assessment can yield many positive results, including the ability of the team to better align itself to bring real diversity of style, skills, experience, and abilities into the health organization. In this model, cultural and individual diversity are valued because they enable the organization to better respond to dynamic organizational and external environments. A diverse leadership team brings robustness to solving organizational problems, as long as focus and adherence to team goals are maintained.

An assessment that looks at leadership as a team—across organizational levels, operating environments, and external environment needs—is especially valuable.[53] This assessment intends to evaluate the leadership styles and propensities of the leadership group of an organization, the organization's operating style, and the perceived external environment expectations of the organization. It can also be used as an individual assessment for leadership, management, technical (science) and art (relationships) propensities, communication, planning, decision alignment, employee enhancement, and knowledge management constructs.

Figures 2-1 and **2-2** illustrate the use of such an assessment tool for a leadership team of a hospital. Two continua are defined: leadership–management and science–art. The leadership–management continuum provides a method to quantify a person's propensity for leadership behaviors/functions or management behaviors/functions. The science–art continuum assesses leaders in terms of their preferences for technical skills and abilities (science), such as forecasting, analysis, budgeting, decision making, and related capabilities, by comparing them to relational skills and abilities (art), such as interpersonal relationships, team building, and related capabilities.

The reliability of the assessment tool and model is moderately strong in Figures 2-1 and 2-2, which illustrate the results with a sample size of 85 leaders from four different hospitals, two different university colleges, and a U.S. Army Medical Department Regional Command

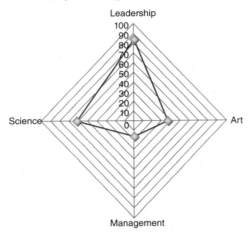

FIGURE 2-1 Dynamic culture leadership assessment: Community hospital leadership team style.

Ledlow, G., & Cwiek, M. (2005). The process of leading: Assessment and comparison of leadership team style, operating climate and expectation of the external environment. *Proceedings of Global Business and Technology Association.* Lisbon, Portugal: Global Business and Technology Association.

(Department of Defense). Graduate students (a total of 58) have taken this assessment as well. Thus the total number taking this assessment for purposes of internal reliability is $n = 143$. Although this is not a very large number, early results with this tool appear promising. The preliminary internal reliability and internal consistency measures are near or above reasonable levels; for example, Cronbach's coefficient alpha measures were between 0.68 and 0.89 (where 0.7 is reasonable for the social sciences and 0.77 is strong or good) for the constructs of the model.

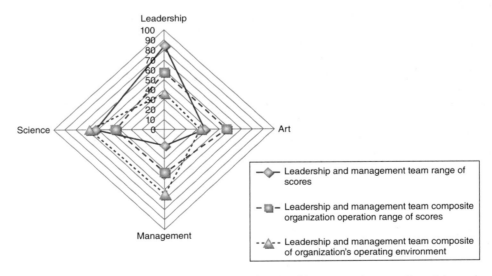

FIGURE 2-2 Dynamic culture leadership assessment: Comparison of leadership team style, operating style, and external environment requirements for a community hospital.

Ledlow, G., & Cwiek, M. (2005). The process of leading: Assessment and comparison of leadership team style, operating climate and expectation of the external environment. *Proceedings of Global Business and Technology Association.* Lisbon, Portugal: Global Business and Technology Association.

STUDER GROUP[54]

The Studer Group is a leadership and organizational consulting firm with a large hospital clientele. The Leader as Coach assessment is a quick evaluation of the test taker's coaching propensity. The test instrument groups the assessment outcomes into one of three categories: high, middle, or low coaching capability.

OTHER LEADERSHIP ASSESSMENTS

Many other leadership and leadership-related assessments are available on the Web; however, health leaders must be able to separate research-based assessments from those that are not empirically based. Does the assessment discuss or reveal internal consistency or reliability measures such as Cronbach's coefficient alpha (where 0.7 is reasonable, 0.77 is good, 0.8 to 0.89 is very good, and 0.9 and higher is excellent) or other measures of the assessment's credibility? Does the assessment have ecological validity or does it make sense or justify the real world?

Another way to look at the value of an assessment tool is in terms of its usefulness. An assessment's usefulness is in question if decisions, increased knowledge, or increased self-awareness cannot be achieved through use of the assessment. Of course, some assessments are wonderful as "ice breakers" to get subordinates, peers, superiors, and multilevel groups to talk about themselves and learn about others with whom they work in the health organization. Some assessments are great ways to encourage people to open up at meetings where they do not know one another very well, for early stages of team building, and other group activities where people must "gel" to accomplish a task or a set of tasks.

Can you distinguish research-based assessments and useful assessments from fun or icebreaker assessments? The following assessments are presented for your review.

Leadership Diagnostics[55]

This assessment is more speculative in nature. It evaluates a leader's potential to be a "twenty-first-century leader" based on several constructs such as team building.

Anthony J. Mayo[56]

This assessment determines whether the test taker is one of three leadership types: the entrepreneur, the manager, or the charismatic. Based on a book about brilliant leaders, it compares the test taker to successful contemporary leaders from several industries.

Dale Kurow[57]

This assessment evaluates leadership skills from a direct superior-to-subordinate basis. Also, individual leadership questions support the evaluation for this dichotomous assessment.

Price Group[58]

Are you more of a leader or a manager? This assessment tries to answer this question based on a series of skills- and actions-based questions.

THE RELATIONSHIP BETWEEN PERSONALITY ARCHETYPE AND LEADERSHIP

The research is in agreement that personality archetypes do affect leadership style, success, and outcomes in the workplace.[59–61] Although difficult to manage without a high degree of self-awareness, the first step in any leadership development process is to recognize potential weaknesses or areas for improvement. Some of this understanding will come with experience. Other professional development areas will present themselves with personal self-recognition. This chapter has provided some tools for the latter kind of diagnosis.

By the time many students get to college, they have already established certain predispositions toward one or more of the personality archetypes presented in this text. Simple predispositions may be perceived as habits at first, such as reading alone or studying to music. These habits, or preferred predispositions, may provide clues to early discovery of mental hardwiring. Social networking and competing in sports and intramurals may suggest a tendency toward Type A behavior, whereas preferring the company of small groups of intimate friends and social clubs may suggest a predisposition for Type B behaviors.

If an individual aspires to become a CEO of a large and munificent healthcare organization and is predisposed to Type B personality traits, he or she must either reconsider entering a career field where high external presence is mandatory or gradually exercise those areas of his or her personality that may be lying dormant but are open to cultivation. Remember, leadership styles, knowledge, skills, and abilities can be learned as well as enhanced. Malcolm Gladwell, in his book *Outliers: The Story of Success*, suggests that 10,000 hours of practice, experience, trial and error, and self-discovery are required to become a master or an expert in anything, with rare exception to this standard.[62] Gladwell also states that the average graduate student has an intelligence quotient (IQ) of 115 or higher[63]; this point suggests that you are intellectually poised to learn and master health leadership whether you are innately gifted or just willing to learn.

STRATEGIES TO MAXIMIZE YOUR NATURE-VERSUS-NURTURE LEADERSHIP STATE OF BEING

Numerous strategies are available to early careerists to help them cultivate dormant personality capabilities. For example, joining professional organizations is critical for success, because they provide opportunities for exercising leadership skills in closed and friendly environments that may not have direct visibility in the workplace. For instance, if an individual is predisposed to be a Skeptic, volunteering to support a continuing health education event with a local professional organization can provide the opportunity to be a Follower without the pressure of being scrutinized in terms of professional outcomes that may end up in a performance appraisal in the workplace. The classroom setting is uniquely suited for trial and error; mistakes are used to learn and improve rather than having negative career implications. Take advantage of the classroom environment to practice leadership by volunteering for group leader roles, community service project leadership, and similar opportunities. Find ways to lead people in a useful endeavor and to manage resources in useful endeavors; build up your experience to achieve the 10,000 hours of practice!

Within the workplace, early careerists can seek out professional mentors who are not in their direct supervisory chain to provide both education and candid professional development advice from a nonperformance-appraisal perspective. Although joining a professional organization may provide an opportunity for mentorship, many large organizations now have formal mentor programs where mentees can be paired up with volunteer mentors in a structured environment.

Self-development and self-directed learning may be the easiest method for individuals to gain a perspective on how to develop and cultivate dormant leader traits. Many professional development books include self-diagnostic scales that provide tools and strategies to augment leader skills.

Finally, the value of self-awareness and acceptance cannot be underscored enough in this chapter. Although none of the assessments in this chapter is by itself a 100% valid and reliable predictor of personality traits and leadership skills, each should be considered one part in your personal puzzle. The synthesis of these assessments should form an initial picture of your current situation—a situation you can improve and develop into becoming a great health leader. To ignore these assessments because you are not pleased with the outcome is essentially tantamount to ignoring your own potential.

USING WHAT YOU LEARN ABOUT YOURSELF

What do you do once you learn about your personality, your strengths, and your weaknesses? The important reality is this: You can learn, adapt, improve, and change to be a better leader. Several theories and models, presented in this text, can help you develop a plan to become a better leader; in essence, that is what this text is about. It is about assisting you to be a better leader. For example, goal-setting theory is a great framework to use to set goals for yourself, and your motivation will spur you on to achieve your goals. Another theory, the theory of planned behavior (TPB), is a framework to assist you in improving, once you know yourself.

TPB was proposed by Icek Ajzen in 1985 in his article "From Intentions to Actions: A Theory of Planned Behavior." According to the theory, human action is guided by three kinds of considerations: beliefs about the likely outcomes of the behavior and the evaluations of these outcomes (behavioral beliefs), beliefs about the normative expectations of others and motivation to comply with these expectations (normative beliefs), and beliefs about the presence of factors that may facilitate or impede performance of the behavior and the perceived power of these factors (control beliefs).[64] The theory was developed from the theory of reasoned action, which was proposed by Martin Fishbein together with Icek Ajzen in 1975. This theory was grounded in models dealing with attitudes such as learning theories, expectancy-value theories, consistency theories, and attribution theory.[65] The addition of the construct of perception of behavioral control differentiates the theory of reasoned action from TPB. Ajzen's three considerations are crucial in improvement (including self-improvement, as is the context in this chapter), leading projects, and directing programs when changing people's behavior.[66]

In order to apply TPB to your leadership improvement project, the key constructs or concepts are salient. The theory of planned behavior helps to clarify how to change the behavior of people. TPB predicts deliberate behavior, because behavior can be deliberative and planned as opposed to purely spontaneous.[67] As shown in **Figure 2-3**, TPB posits that individual behavior is driven by behavioral

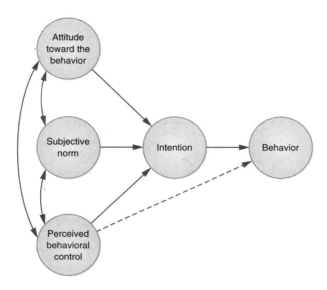

FIGURE 2-3 Theory of planned behavior.

Reprinted from *Organizational Behavior and Human Decision Processes*, 50, Ajzen, I. (1991). The theory of planned behavior, Pages 179-211, Copyright 1991, with permission from Elsevier.

intentions, where behavioral intentions are a function of an individual's attitude toward the behavior, the subjective norms surrounding the performance of the behavior, and the individual's perception of the ease with which the behavior can be performed (behavioral control). Attitude toward the behavior is the individual's positive or negative feelings about performing a behavior. The subjective norm is an individual's perception of whether people important to the individual think the behavior should be performed. Behavioral control is defined as one's perception of the difficulty of performing a behavior.[68] Goal-setting theory can reinforce TPB by setting goals to obtain a specific behavior within an organization, whether it be a health behavior, human actions, or adopting a new technology, or a way of improving yourself and your leadership competence, styles, or behaviors. Basically, once you determine what to improve, you determine how to improve, surround yourself with those leaders who can reinforce your improvement plan, and implement your improvement plan. That is, in essence, the theory of planned behavior.

In applying the theory of planned behavior, identify your attitudes, the subjective norms (of your colleagues that influence you), and your perceived behavioral control, and then devise an improvement plan. Once you have a plan and goals, work toward achieving your goals. Knowing yourself is the first step.

SUMMARY

This chapter provided a small sample of minimal diagnostic self-examinations that provide usable information for professional development in a course setting. Although the authors do not recommend taking all of these assessments, when completed under the supervision of your course director, these evaluations will support the learning outcomes of your program.

Following successful completion of several of these assessments, you should conduct an analysis and look for trends and patterns that may reveal areas of personality dominance or personality void. You may then write a paper integrating your personal findings into one composite essay. The final essay should include a personal plan to hone existing traits while also cultivating knowledge, skills, and abilities that may present themselves for development later. Ideally, the course director, executive in residence, or professional community leader will sit down with each student and provide a mentoring session aimed at leadership and career success.

Strong personalities with high levels of education dominate the health environment. As a person progresses up the corporate ladder, he or she will encounter new and different personality types at all levels. Leaders will most likely have to develop different personality skill sets to foster and cultivate relationships in the various environments in which they work. Traits associated with all types of leadership roles include integrity, honesty, the development of goals, and motivational skills.[69] Knowing oneself will provide an edge for success and a platform for improvement and mastery of leadership. Lastly, the theory of planned behavior provides a framework to think about, plan, and then improve your leadership behaviors, competencies, and ultimately, your organization's performance.

DISCUSSION QUESTIONS

1. Describe four leadership, leadership-related, or personality assessments that were most informative for you. Did other students select the same assessments? Why or why not?
2. Distinguish the various typologies (categories) used in personality assessments and personality archetype assessments, and explain the differences associated with the various types.
3. Relate two or more assessments from this chapter to your personal situation: Were the assessment results complementary or contradictory? Why do you think these results occurred?
4. From the assessments (two or more), identify the health leader most appealing to you (a real leader or a fictitious one whom you create). Using the assessments' constructs and typologies, why is that health leader appealing?
5. Compile and categorize your assessment results, summarize the results, and tell the group your plan for leadership mastery.
6. Appraise the empirical strength of the various assessment instruments, critique two or more assessments, and justify your critique.

EXERCISES

1. In two pages or less, name and describe at least four assessments related to leadership you used.
2. In a three-page essay, explain your leadership style, principles, and foundational skills as related to leadership assessment instruments, using at least four assessments.
3. Produce results of at least four leadership-related assessments, apply those results to your leadership persona, and attach the results to your three-page essay from Exercise 2.
4. In a two-page document attached to your essay and results document, identify and distinguish your leadership style, principles, and foundational skills strengths and weaknesses based on your leadership-related assessments' results.
5. Based on self-assessments of your personality style, leadership style, principles, and foundational skills, devise a plan to improve your weaknesses while leveraging or enhancing your strengths. Add this work to your essay, results, and strengths and weaknesses document.
6. In a two- to three-page document, critique and interpret your unique leadership persona, and relate your leadership persona to examples from your life experiences. Attach this work to your previous work. Return to and read this document once a month until you have achieved your goals for improving your leadership capabilities.

REFERENCES

1. Johnson, P. (2012). *Unstoppable leadership: Changing your relationships, thinking and influence.* New York: Global Next Publications.
2. Didato, S. V. (2012). *Who are you? Test your personality (know yourself).* Boston: Black Dog and Leventhal.
3. Mitra, B. (2012). Personality development and soft skills. London: Oxford University Press.
4. Ledlow, G., & Cwiek, M. (2005, July). The process of leading: Assessment and comparison of leadership team style, operating climate and expectation of the external environment. *Proceedings of the Global Business and Technology Association.* Lisbon, Portugal: Global Business and Technology Association.
5. Clark, K. D., & Waldron, T. (2016). Predictors of leadership behavior in early career white-collar professionals: The roles of personal characteristics and career context. *Journal of Leadership & Organizational Studies,* 23(1): 27–38, first published on May 26, 2015.

6. Tuber, S. B. (2012). *Understanding personality through projective testing*. Plymouth, UK: Jason Aronson.

7. Coppola, M. N., & Kerr, B. (2012). Your post-military career: Getting the job you want! *American Academy of Medical Administrators (AAMA) Annual Conference*, Boston.

8. Bergman, D., Lornudd, C., Sjoberg, L., & Von Thiele Schwartz, U. (2014). Leader personality and 360-degree assessments of leader behavior. *Scandinavian Journal of Psychology*, *55*(4), 389–397. doi: 10.1111/sjop.12130

9. Bergman et al., note 6a, p. 391.

10. Stephanopoulos, G. (1999). *All too human: A political education*. Boston: Little, Brown.

11. Kellerman, B. (2008). Leadership lessons from Hillary Clinton's election results. Harvard Business Review Blog Network. Retrieved from http://conversationstarter.hbsp.com/2008/02/leadership_lessons_from_hillar.html.

12. Healy, J. (2009, June 29). Madoff is sentenced to 150 years for Ponzi scheme. *New York Times*. Retrieved from http://www.nytimes.com/2009/06/30/business/30madoff.html?_r=1&hp.

13. Lambiet, J. (2008, Dec. 12). Bernie Madoff's arrest sent tremors into Palm Beach. *Palm Beach Daily*. Retrieved from http://www.palmbeachdailynews.com/news/content/news/2008/12/12/ponzi1212.html/

14. Coppola, M. N. (2004). A propositional perspective of leadership: Is the wrong head on the model? *Journal of International Research in Business Disciplines*, *11*, 620–625.

15. Coppola, M. N. (2008). *Observations and outcomes of graduate students based on VARK profiling* [white paper]. San Antonio, TX: Fort Sam Houston.

16. Coppola, M. N., Kerr, B. J., Ledlow, J. R., & Fulton, L. V. (2010, Nov. 10). Using the VARK learning test to optimize delivery of health administration course content and competency fulfillment. Association of University Programs in Health Administration Annual Conference [webinar].

17. Fleming, N. D., & Mills, C. (1992). Not another inventory, rather a catalyst for reflection, to improve the academy. *Academy of Management Journal*, *11*, 137.

18. Coppola, M. N., & Carini, G. (2006). Ability job-fit self-assessment. *Healthcare Executive*, *21*(2), 60–63.

19. Coppola & Carini, note 15.

20. Queendom. (n.d.). Emotional intelligence test. Retrieved from http://www.queendom.com/tests/access_page/index.htm?idRegTest=1121.

21. Ybarra, O., Kross, E., & Sanchez-Burks, J. (2014). The "big idea" that is yet to be: Toward a more motivated, contextual, and dynamic model of emotional intelligence. *Academy of Management Perspectives*, *28*(2), 93–107, p. 93. Doi:10.5465/Amp.2012.0106

22. Dye, C. F. (2010). *Leadership in healthcare, essential values and skills* (2nd ed.). Chicago, IL: Health Administration Press.

23. Kluemper, D. H. (2008). Trait emotional intelligence: The impact of core self-evaluations and social desirability. *Personality and Individual Differences*, *44*(6), 1402–1412.

24. Smith, L., Ciarrochi, J., & Heaven, P. C. L. (2008). The stability and change of trait emotional intelligence, conflict communication patterns, and relationship satisfaction: A one-year longitudinal study. *Personality and Individual Differences*, *45*, 738–743.

25. Gardner, H. (1983). *Frames of mind*. New York: Basic Books.

26. Cherniss, C., & Adler, M. (2000). *Promoting emotional intelligence in organizations*. Washington, D.C.: American Society for Training and Development.

27. Lanser, E. G. (2000). Why you should care about your emotional intelligence: Strategies for honing important emotional competencies. *Healthcare Executive*, *15*(6), 7–9.

28. Lanser, note 23, p. 9.

29. Ledlow & Cwiek, note 4.

30. Dye, note 18.

31. Mind Media. (n.d.). Left brain right brain test. Retrieved from http://www.mindmedia.com/brainworks/profiler.

32. HumanMetrics. (n.d.). Jung typology test. Retrieved from http://www.humanmetrics.com/cgi-win/JTypes2.asp.

33. McCrae, R. R., & Costa, P. T. (1989). Reinterpreting the Myers–Briggs Type Indicator from the perspective of the five-factor model of personality. *Journal of Personality*, *57*, 17–40.

34. Boyle, G. J. (1995). Myers–Briggs Type Indicator (MBTI): Some psychometric limitations. *Australian Psychologist*, *30*, 71–74.

35. The Myers & Briggs Foundation. (2012). Retrieved from http://www.myersbriggs.org.

36. Harvey, R. J. (1996). Reliability and validity. In A. L. Hammer (Ed.), *MBTI applications* (pp. 5–29). Palo Alto, CA: Consulting Psychologists Press.

37. Fretwell, C. E., Lewis, C. C., & Hannay, M. (2013). Myers–Briggs Type Indicator, A/B personality types, and locus of control: Where do they intersect? *American Journal of Management*, *13*(3), 57–66, p. 58. Retrieved from http://t.www.na-businesspress.com/AJM/FretwellCE_Web13_3_.pdf.

38. Goolkasian, P. (n.d.). Personality type A/B. Retrieved from http://www.psych.uncc.edu/pagoolka/TypeAB.html.

39. Jenkins, C. D., Zyzanski, S. J., & Roseman, R. H. (1971). Progress towards validation of a computer-scored test for the Type A coronary-prone behaviour pattern. *Psychosomatic Medicine, 33*, 193–202.

40. Kuiper, N. A., & Martin, R. A. (1989). Type A behavior: A social cognition motivational perspective. In G. H. Bower (Ed.), *The psychology of learning and motivation: Advances in research and theory* (Vol. 24, pp. 311–341). New York: Academic Press.

41. Friedman, M., & Rosenman, R. H. (1974). *Type A behavior and your heart.* New York: Knopf.

42. VARK. (n.d.). The VARK questionnaire. Retrieved from http://www.vark-learn.com/english/page.asp?p=questionnaire.

43. Fleming, N. D. (2001). *Teaching and learning styles: VARK strategies.* Honolulu, HI: Honolulu Community College.

44. Leite, W. L., Svinicki, M., & Shi, Y. (2010). Attempted validation of the scores of the VARK: Learning styles inventory with multitrait–multimethod confirmatory factor analysis models. *Educational and Psychological Measurement, 70*, 323–339.

45. 9types.com. (n.d.). The new enneagram test. Retrieved from http://www.9types.com/newtest/homepage.actual.html.

46. Riso, D. R., & Hudson, R. (1996). *Personality types: Using the enneagram for self-discovery.* Boston, MA: Houghton Mifflin.

47. Palmer, H. (1995). *The pocket enneagram: Understanding the 9 types of people.* San Francisco, CA: Harper Press.

48. Putnoi, J. (2000). *Senses wide open.* Berkeley, CA: Ulysses Press.

49. 9types.com. (n.d.). The nine types. Retrieved from http://www.9types.com/index.php.

50. Eclectic energies. (n.d.). Introduction to the enneagram. Retrieved from http://www.eclecticenergies.com/enneagram/introduction.php.

51. Smith, J. A., & Casteel, M. (2011). *How the enneagram works: A quick reference guide.* Lilburn, GA: Wells-Smith Partners.

52. Ledlow, G. R., & Coppola, M. N. (2011). *Leadership for health professionals.* Burlington, MA: Jones & Bartlett Learning.

53. Conger, J., & Toegel, G. (2002). A story of missed opportunities: Qualitative methods for leadership research and practice. In K. W. Parry & J. R. Meindl (Eds.), *Grounding leadership theory and research: Issues, perspectives, and methods* (pp. 175–197). Greenwich, CT: Information Age.

54. StuderGroup. (n.d.). Tools. Retrieved from http://www.studergroup.com/tools_andknowledge/tools/index.dot.

55. Center for Coaching and Mentoring. (n.d.). Are you ready to manage in the 21st century? Retrieved from http://www.coachingandmentoring.com/Quiz/21stmanager.html.

56. Mayo, A. J. (2005). Which type of leader are you? Retrieved from http://www.fastcompany.com/articles/2005/08/quiz.html.

57. Kurow, D. (n.d.). Leadership quiz. Retrieved from http://dalekurow.com/kurow/services/leadership-quiz.

58. The Price Group. (n.d.). True leader quiz. Retrieved from http://www.pricegroupleadership.com/tl_quiz.shtml.

59. Judge, T. A., & Bono, J. E. (2000). Five-factor model of personality and transformational leadership. *Journal of Applied Psychology, 85*, 751–765.

60. Chemers, M. M., Watson, C. B., & May, S. T. (2000). Dispositional affect and leadership effectiveness: A comparison of self-esteem, optimism, and efficacy. *Personality and Social Psychology Bulletin, 26*, 267–277.

61. Rychlak, J. F. (1963). Personality correlates of leadership among first level managers. *Psychological Reports, 12*, 43–52.

62. Gladwell, M. (2008). *Outliers: The story of success.* New York: Little, Brown.

63. Gladwell, note 57.

64. Ajzen, I. (1991). The theory of planned behavior. *Organizational Behavior and Human Decision Processes, 50*, 179–211.

65. Ajzen, I. (2009). Theory of planned behavior. Retrieved from http://www.valuebasedmanagement.net/methods_ajzen_theory_planned_behaviour.html.

66. Armitage, C. J., & Connor, M. (2001). Efficacy of the theory of planned behavior: A meta-analytic review. *British Journal of Social Psychology, 40*, 471–479.

67. Ajzen, note 60.

68. Furneaux, B. (2005). Theories used in IS research. Retrieved from http://www.istheory.yorku.ca/theoryofplannedbehavior.htm. Content removed due to copyright restrictions.

69. Nicol, E. D., Mohanna, K., & Cowpe, J. (2014). Perspectives on clinical leadership: A qualitative study exploring the views of senior healthcare leaders in the UK. *Journal of the Royal Society of Medicine, 107*(7), 277–286. Retrieved from http://www-ncbi-nlm-nih-gov.ezproxy.ttuhsc.edu/pubmed/25013095.

TODAY'S HEALTH LEADERSHIP CHALLENGES

*Many of us see surprise events and talk about the crisis ahead. Really good leaders see these challenges
as opportunities to shepherd people and organizations toward a successful future.*
Major General (Ret.) David Rubenstein

Change is inevitable. Industry and organizational change are necessary for organizations and professions to remain relevant and serve the external environment well. The health industry is no different when it comes to change except for one key aspect—the speed and volume of change in the health industry have been defined as "white water change"—that is, changes that come fast and with great volume. The health industry has gone through vast changes and continues to change at a staggering pace, since the passing of the Social Security Amendments (Titles 18 and 19) that instituted Medicare and Medicaid in the mid-1960s. Today's health organizations are trying to successfully navigate the Patient Protection and Affordable Care Act (ACA), value-based purchasing, community health needs assessment, transition from ICD-9 to ICD-10 coding systems, electronic health records, meaningful use criteria, and the like. In order for organizations to successfully navigate change while continually improving health outcomes within the communities they serve, leadership at multiple levels of the industry and within the organization is critical. Leaders must become efficient, effective, and efficacious in leading people and managing resources. Competencies for today's health leader must be continually honed, improved, and mastered to propel health organizations to greater and greater levels of value.

LEARNING OBJECTIVES

1. Outline why the dynamic forces within the industry are important to professionals in the health industry, and identify challenges that require quality leadership intervention strategies.

2. Explain and give an example of one aspect of change in the industry today, and link the leadership competencies that are necessary for successfully navigating the organizational changes required to deal with this change.

3. Relate, discuss, and explain the importance of the application of a leadership competency model to contemporary health industry change.

4. Distinguish the different aspects or domains of change in the health industry and how those domains impact leadership capability, and explain how the synergy of those changes impacts leadership capability and organizational success.

5. Relate the health reform efforts of the past decade to leadership needs at the health organization level.

6. Evaluate the health industry's needs for leadership today and into the next decade.

INTRODUCTION

There are a multitude of challenges facing the health organization leader today. This chapter will serve as an introduction for the concepts that we will revisit throughout our discussions of leadership for health professionals. Two contributing authors, Drs. William Mase and Dave Schott, collaborated with Drs. Ledlow and Stephens on this chapter; Drs. Mase and Schott are professionally trained in public health policy. Because the health industry is integrating public health and healthcare delivery (along with shared financial and service risk) it is prudent to attend to the aspects of integration between these two vital segments of the industry. This chapter intends to provide a foreshadowing of what health leaders need to understand, be aware of, and strategically and operationally plan for in order to successfully lead people and manage resources amid this dynamic turbulence. To support the introduction of the complex challenges facing today's health leaders, we have developed a visual representation of the current situation; this visual representation structures the discussion. The discussion is focused on health leadership over the next decade.

Figure 3-1 illustrates the flow of information and the interconnected nature of the health leadership competencies and how policy affects and is affected by the various domains of healthcare leadership. The second half of the chapter presents major contemporary leadership development and competency domains. These domains are presented as they relate to the various challenges discussed in the first half of the chapter.

POLITICAL INFLUENCE

Political influence is the ability of those wielding the political power to shape and control the political behavior of others and to lead and guide the behavior of others in a desired direction. Political behavior can include many different activities, all of which are concerned with public policy.[1] Because the ultimate purpose of obtaining political influence is to shape and control public policy, the policies of an organization or nation will change over time depending on the views and influence of those with political power. The primary tools by which government officials shape and control public policy are legislation and statutes.

LEGISLATION AND STATUTES

Legislation is a law that has been enacted by a governing body. A statute is the formal written enactment of a legislative authority at any level—city, state, or country.[2] Legislation and statutes related to health are of great concern to healthcare executives because they govern nearly every aspect of health care, from reimbursement for procedures to facility maintenance. Health policy includes the decisions, plans, and actions that are undertaken to achieve a specific healthcare goal within society. When

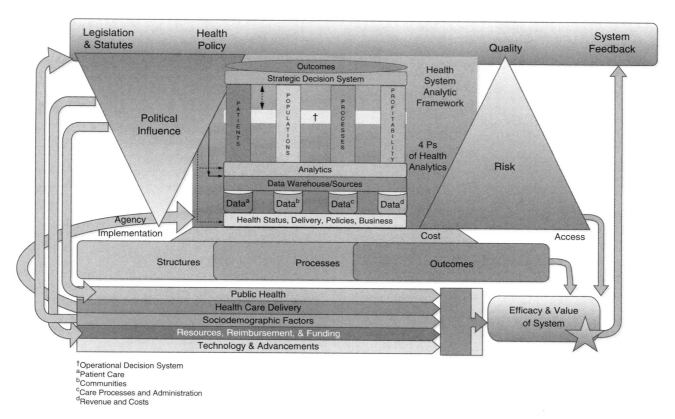

FIGURE 3-1 Today's health leadership challenges.

constructed successfully, health policy can achieve multiple aims. First, it can define a vision for the future, which in turn, helps to establish targets and reference points for the short and mid-term. Second, it can outline priorities and the expected roles for different groups and individuals.[3]

Once enacted, health policies are implemented by government agencies. When agencies implement policy, they do so through creation of regulations. Laws do not always include all of the details needed to explain how an individual or business must act to follow the law. Therefore, Congress authorizes certain government agencies to create regulations.[4] These regulations set specific requirements regarding what is legal and what is not. For the healthcare industry, many of the governing regulations are interpreted, "translated into practice," and put in place and enforced by the Centers for Medicare and Medicaid Services (CMS).

The risks associated with the creation or implementation of new policy can be large. To help describe these risks, as well as quantify the benefits from policy programs, it is common to use models or theoretical frameworks to describe the process. When enacting policy that affects the U.S. health system, there are three main areas that should be impacted by the policy decision: cost, quality, and access. Theoretically,

these three areas are opposed to one other. This oppositional relationship is described as the "Iron Triangle" of health care.

THE IRON TRIANGLE OF HEALTH CARE

The first mention of the Iron Triangle model was in a 1994 book by physician William Kissick. The model describes the relationship between cost, quality, and access to care. In its purest form, the model states that if two of the components move in a positive direction, the third must move in a negative direction. For example, when cost and quality increase, access must decrease. Kissick postulated this model after reflecting on the major issues within the U.S. healthcare system.

Costs include any costs associated with providing health care. Total cost includes what is charged to patients, either directly or as an insurance deductible. Quality is typically measured in patient outcomes. Quality care leads to improved health status for the individual receiving the care. Access to care is the ease of obtaining care for a patient.

Factors that can negatively affect access include the number of physicians accepting patients, healthcare facilities, and availability of equipment.

The Iron Triangle model has been criticized as not being a rigid relationship but instead just a general guideline.[5] However, there are still very few instances that "break" the iron triangle relationship. The conditions that "break" the relationship described by Kissick are:

- Increasing efficiency
- Decreasing regulation
- Improving technology

These situations are the exception rather than the norm. The Iron Triangle model has been used to describe the cost increases that occurred after the passage of the ACA in 2010.[6]

THE DONABEDIAN MODEL

Postulated by Avedis Donabedian, a physician at the University of Michigan in 1966, the model provides a framework for examining health services and evaluating the quality of care. The purpose of the Donabedian model is to modify structures and processes in a healthcare delivery network to improve outcomes. According to Donabedian, *structures* include all factors that can change the context of care delivery.[7] *Processes* include every action that takes place to provide care. Typically this is thought to include all of the clinical steps, such as diagnosis, treatment, patient education, and preventive activities. Processes are further subdivided into technical and interpersonal processes. Outcomes include the impact of providing health care to individuals and the communities in which they live. This includes changes to health status, behavior changes, and knowledge changes.

The goal of any leadership initiative is positive outcomes for the organization. Drawing conclusions regarding program outcomes may require large sample sizes or long time periods to account for random variation. In an effort to ensure that outcomes and project goals are met, modern programs are data driven. Since 1986, the Joint Commission has worked to create an evaluation system based on continuous data collection and periodic feedback on specific performance measures.[8] Over time, performance measures and standard scores have been developed and are published for the public on affiliated websites, such as the Centers for Medicare and Medicaid Services Hospital Compare website located at (https://www.medicare.gov/hospitalcompare/search.html). Value is a main focus of the efforts in these areas. What is valuable to the community that you serve?

DISRUPTIVE INNOVATION

Disruptive innovation is a hot topic in health care today. At the American College of Healthcare Executives (ACHE) congress in 2016, disruptive innovation took center stage in a discussion regarding the federal goal to tie 20% of Medicare payments to value and quality through alternative payment models by the end of the year. This CMS goal is disruptive to the industry because it is the first time that explicit goals for alternative payment models have been set for Medicare. There are a few leading health systems well ahead of other organizations in this effort. Those leading systems have a three-part goal:

1. Improve the patient experience of care.
2. Improve the health of populations.
3. Reduce the cost per capita of health care.[9]

You may notice that these three goals are in direct conflict with the Iron Triangle relationship we just discussed. How are these health systems able to achieve these goals? Can change occur through disruptive innovation?

The healthcare industry moves at a rapid pace, and one of the more recent examples of disruptive innovation is robotic and laparoscopic surgery. Prior to laparoscopic techniques a cholecystectomy required a large incision in the abdomen. Laparoscopic techniques allowed for the large incision to be replaced by four much smaller incisions. The net effect was an increased level of safety in the procedure, faster OR turnover, and a decreased length of stay with better patient outcomes. Robotic surgery has further expanded on these benefits.[10]

The demand for these disruptive innovations is created by manufacturers, providers, and patients. However, if the learning curve associated with disruptive innovation is not managed, unintended consequences of rapid acceptance may lead to patient harm. When adapting disruptive innovations, it is important to consider all factors, including potential harm, benefit, and learning curve management. It has been suggested that one of the best ways to cope with rapid change and disruptive innovations is using the "manage, steer, and create" model. Under this model, healthcare leaders are encouraged to manage the present, steer to the next horizon, and create the future.[11] The health leader of the present, and surely into the future, will also see a myriad of data-driven and "big data-" driven tools, programs, and solutions that will either stand alone for utilization of the health organization or will embed or interface with existing clinical and enterprise resource planning information systems; these will be organic to the health organization's information system or exist in an open-architecture or cloud environment. These disruptive innovation software systems will require leadership to evaluate their value and usefulness based on the health organization's strategic and operational plans, mission, values, and goals.

PUBLIC HEALTH

The American public health system is charged with providing assessment, policy development, and assurance functions. These three assigned functions are further subdivided into the 10 essential services, which include: (1) monitoring health; (2) diagnosing and investigating; (3) informing, educating, and empowering; (4) mobilizing community partners; (5) developing policies; (6) enforcing laws; (7) linking to provide care; (8) assuring a competent workforce; (9) evaluating systems; and (10) conducting research (**Figure 3-2**).

Public health powers operate at the national level, state level, and local level. Through the effective division of powers the public health system can carry out the 10 essential services by addressing public health–related concerns

at the local level. The primary functions of promoting and protecting the health of people and the communities in which they live is achieved through the effective coordination of all system-mandated activities. Public health is best defined as the collection of publicly available healthcare-related services that seek to address population-level health. These population-level pro-health services can be seen as complementary to the healthcare delivery systems that function to treat illness at the individual level. While a physician treats individuals with an illness, public health professionals seek to prevent people from getting sick or injured in the first place.[13] Typically, this is done through changing behavior patterns and promoting wellness. Notable activities of public health include vaccine development, health education, tracking of disease and environmental issues, and developing policy. Public health organizations are typically divided into five core areas: biostatistics, epidemiology, community health, environmental health, and health policy and management.

Biostatistics is the use of analytical tools to examine data relating to living organisms. The most visible use of biostatistics in health care is the development and analysis of clinical trials for pharmaceuticals. Epidemiology is the

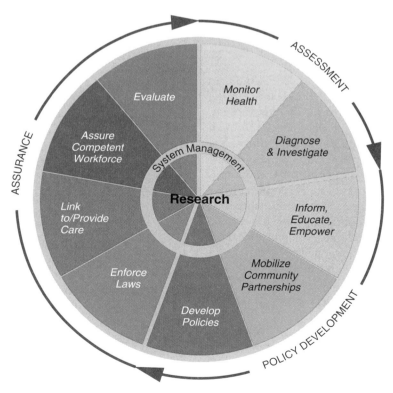

FIGURE 3-2 CDC training cycle.[12]

http://www.cdc.gov/healthliteracy/training/page1299.html.

branch of public health that deals with the incidence, distribution, and control of disease or other health-related factors. Community health is best known for health education and promotion resulting from the study and improvement of health characteristics in geographical areas. Environmental health includes monitoring and improving the environment outside as well as within facilities. Finally, health policy and management specializes in recommending and implementing policy as well as managing the programs that result from policy implementations.

The primary goal of the public health system is to improve the health status within communities through controlling activities or environmental variables that could lead to adverse health outcomes. Of course the efforts of public health are not able to prevent all morbidity, so the ability to deliver tertiary care is still necessary. A physician or other licensed medical professional usually provides hands-on healthcare delivery either in a stand-alone facility, such as a nonaffiliated physician's office, or through a healthcare organization.

HEALTHCARE DELIVERY

The healthcare delivery system in the United States is arguably the most complex system for delivering care in the world. This complexity results from the fragmented nature of services provided, the large number of organizations providing care, and the existence of both private and public insurance as well as self-pay.

Outside of the United States, most developed countries have a single-payer system that is controlled by the government or an agency controlled by the government. These national health plans are typically financed through taxes imposed on the population. These systems are often much less complex because there is either a single (government) payer or government with a self-pay option.

Whether in the United States or elsewhere, healthcare organizations are under increasing pressure to deliver increased efficiency and greater value and to simultaneously increase the quality of care. These policy and public opinion mandates are concurrent with the increasing complexity and needs of patients, which is forcing delivery of care model reform.[14]

RESOURCES, REIMBURSEMENT, AND FUNDING

In 2010, U.S. healthcare spending cost about $2.6 trillion. For decades the rate of healthcare spending in the United States has grown faster than the growth rate of the economy as a whole.

Per capita spending on health care in the United States is the highest in the world; however, the health outcomes of the citizens are not the best in the world. For example, the United States ranks comparatively low on measures such as infant mortality, life expectancy at birth, and healthy life expectancy. In 2011, the United States spent $8,508 on health care per person and received an overall ranking of 11. The United Kingdom, which ranks 1, spent $3,406 per person.[15] It was thought that the enactment of the ACA would lead to lower costs; however, this has yet to occur. In fact, costs continue to rise post ACA—although at a rate of about half that of previous years. Sources are conflicted about the cause of the declining rate, but evidence points to the aftereffects of the 2011 recession in the United States.[16]

REIMBURSEMENT

In the United States, when healthcare organizations provide care to insured patients, the healthcare organizations are reimbursed after the fact by insurance companies. Because private insurance reimbursement rates are determined through direct negotiations with the health system and the process can differ among insurers, we will focus on Medicare reimbursement to illustrate the process.

Hospitals are reimbursed for inpatient Medicare services provided through the Inpatient Prospective Payment System (IPPS). The payment comes in the form of a per discharge or per case basis for Medicare beneficiaries with inpatient stays. The claim filed by the hospital needs to include all outpatient diagnostic services as well as any admission-related outpatient services provided prior to admission to the healthcare organization. When patients are discharged they are assigned diagnosis related groups (DRGs), a classification system that groups similar clinical conditions and procedures provided during the patient's hospital stay. When assigning the DRG to the Medicare beneficiary, the hospital uses the principal diagnosis and up to 24 secondary diagnoses, which can be used to list comorbidities or complications. Based on these diagnosis codes and other factors, such as gender, age, and discharge disposition, the DRG is assigned.[17] Medicare reviews cases submitted for reimbursement and pays or rejects claims based on published criteria found on the CMS website. Rejected claims can be appealed by healthcare organizations in a series of formal appeals.

In addition, bundled pricing, such as that now required with total joint care (such as joint replacement) bundled pricing for Medicare (federal agency responsible is CMS), will change the reimbursement landscape.[18] Bundled pricing will facilitate the establishment of narrow networks of providers—a few providers in a given geographical area who are most efficient and have quality patient outcomes—to be utilized for services by Medicare health insurance plans. Higher cost providers—those that have not reduced supply chain, labor, and other costs to perform procedures—will be left out of the network. This is important because the commercial market–that is, health plans that are not Medicare or Medicaid and are usually established with employee benefits–tends to follow the federal programs of Medicare and Medicaid for pricing and reimbursement. Understanding the "value proposition" in health care is increasingly part of the business of health care and healthcare services.

FUNDING

Health care in the United States is generally funded from three sources, self-pay, private insurance, and government insurance.

Individuals typically use self-pay methods for care not covered by other sources. Credit cards or other generic means of borrowing are sometimes used for this purpose, but there are two options available for individuals to save in advance for self-pay, flexible spending accounts (FSAs) and health savings accounts (HSAs).[19]

FSAs are typically offered by employers. They allow employees to have a certain amount of money deducted from their paychecks and deposited into the FSA. The money in an FSA can be used to pay for out-of-pocket healthcare expenses. As an incentive to employees the money deposited into the FSA is not subject to federal income tax. However, the money in the FSA is usually forfeited at the end of the year, so careful planning is required on the part of the employee.[20]

HSAs are also used to pay out-of-pocket expenses. Unlike an FSA, HSAs earn interest and the unused balance is not forfeited at the end of the year. Typically, people who have health insurance plans that limit their reimbursements enough to be classified as high deductible are eligible for an HSA.[21]

Currently, about 17% of healthcare costs across the United States are funded out-of-pocket. As you may expect, charges for individuals are typically higher than for insurance companies, because insurance companies are able to negotiate rates based on volume. This can lead to individuals who pay out-of-pocket receiving extremely large bills for health services. In fact, many personal bankruptcies are related to medical expenses. To avoid this the ACA requires almost everyone to have some form of health insurance.[22]

Private insurance is purchased from insurance companies, which must be accredited in each state were they sell their product. Most private insurance is purchased by businesses as a benefit for employees; premiums are typically shared by the business and the employee. Because the cost of employer-provided health insurance is not considered taxable income, it is essentially government-subsidized. Individuals may purchase private insurance on their own, but these applications are typically evaluated closely to identify risks to the insurance company.[23]

In 2010, the private insurance market in the United States was fundamentally changed by the passage of the ACA. The purpose of the ACA is to increase availability, affordability, and use of health insurance in the United States. One of the primary methods by which the ACA seeks to accomplish this is through the expansion of the private insurance market, creating incentives for employers to provide insurance and penalties for individuals who choose not to purchase insurance. For the purposes of risk pooling and reducing program overhead, the ACA created insurance marketplaces within each state. These insurance marketplaces impose minimum standards for the insurance plans sold within them, and there are separate marketplaces for individuals and small businesses.[24]

Government insurance programs include Medicare and Medicaid as well as programs for active military and Native Americans. The Medicare program is designed to provide health insurance to the elderly, disabled, and individuals requiring dialysis. Medicaid covers individuals living below a certain level of income and those with certain disabilities. Approximately 30% of the population is covered by government insurance or government-provided care. The ACA increased federal funding for state Medicaid programs in the short term and expanded eligibility criteria. However, states are not penalized for not complying with the new criteria, so the total number of individuals who will enroll in the program is uncertain.[25]

SOCIODEMOGRAPHIC FACTORS

Sociodemographic factors are things such as age, race, ethnicity, languages, as well as income and education.[26] There is a growing body of research suggesting that these factors affect health outcomes, in addition to influencing how people are viewed by others and how people view the world. For the health leader sociodemographic factors come down to two questions: Do you know who your high-risk patients and high utilizers are? Do you know precisely where they live?

According to Dr. David Nash, in a presentation at the 2015 ACHE Congress on Healthcare Leadership, the number one health predictor in 2015 is your ZIP code. This stems from the observation that large disparities in health can be found among pockets of population that live short distances from each other. A commonly cited example is the Washington, D.C., area. Babies born in Montgomery, Arlington, or Fairfax counties can expect to live 6 to 7 years longer than babies born in Washington, D.C. These counties are one ZIP code apart—just a few stops on the subway. Observations like this can be used to predict the percentage of patients who share that risk factor and determine strategies to improve care coordination and delivery.[27]

Basic electronic health record (EHR) systems, however, are not equipped for this kind of data analysis; more advanced systems using predictive analytics are needed. In order to elevate a health system from basic EHR usage to predictive analytics there are numerous paths and options with regard to software. In order to facilitate decision making by the healthcare organization, a model such as the 4Ps of Health Analytics can be used to structure the discussion and formulate a plan of action.

THE 4 PS OF HEALTH ANALYTICS

To effectively guide and direct their organizations, health leaders need information. Starting with raw data gathered from various operational, governmental, and other systems, how do health leaders create an organizational culture based on knowledge utilization? How do health leaders take data, place them in context, integrate information from multiple domains, take action based on the information, promote organizational learning from those actions, and improve strategies and operations of the healthcare organization? With the changes in the healthcare industry that require closer connections to the community's health care, organizations serve those communities with more assumption of risk for the health status of those communities. What model can health leaders use to achieve a knowledge-based organization? Complicated ideas are often shown as a model. A *model* is a simplified substitute for an event or situation that is being studied or predicted. Models can be used in multiple ways. The most common is to describe a situation or prescribe a course of action. A *descriptive* model describes *how a system should function* according to the model. A *prescriptive* model shows *how to make a system function* according to the model. The most useful type of model is a combination of the two concepts, a model that

is both prescriptive and descriptive. Models of this type describe how something works and show how to make it work as described.

Due to the complex nature of the health industry there are many models regarding the operation of health organizations. This is true of health analytics—health information for analysis and decision making—because it is an exciting, rapidly evolving field, even by health industry standards. The implication of change is relevant—the health industry is a dynamic industry. Recent changes from healthcare reform, policy changes, and the need to demonstrate value in health services delivery have created an environment where new models of health analytics, health information utilization, and health technology are required.

The 4 Ps of Health Analytics describes the interconnections between the four major categories of data found in health organizations: patients, populations, processes, and profitability (called "net margin" for not-for-profit [NFP] organizations). Traditionally, these four types of information have been used separately. When data are not easily accessed or integrated with other data from complementary domains, they are referred to as being in an *information silo*. As computer systems evolved, it became possible to store data in an electronic database which, when properly implemented, allows for information that, previously in a silo, can be used with other data sources. Another term for these electronic databases is *data warehouse* or *enterprise data warehouse*. A data warehouse is a system that creates a central repository of data and makes that data available for reporting and data analysis.

Patient data are data pertaining directly to the demographic information, history, diagnostics, treatment, care plans, and outcomes of care of the patient; these data are contained in the electronic medical record (EMR) system. *Population data* refer to the communities where health organizations are located. The data in this category are related to improving community health status and to the health and well-being of the community as a whole. *Process data* include information on the way business is conducted within the healthcare organization; these data (or elements of the data) can be found in enterprise resource planning (ERP) systems and organizational documents. *Profitability data* ("net margin" for NFP health organizations) include data on the ability of a health organization to generate income, such as cost of services, amount billed, and expected reimbursement along with expenses; these data can be found in ERP systems and organizational documents. The goal for a healthcare organization is this: How can data be turned into actionable operations that maximize efficiency, effectiveness, and efficacy?

TECHNOLOGY AND ADVANCEMENTS

Improvements in technology have created the era of "big data," a term used to describe the exponential growth and availability of data.[28]

The growth of big data has provided researchers and business professionals with access to unprecedented amounts of data. Combined with the ever-increasing power of computers, the newly available big data can be used to examine the effectiveness of existing processes and improvement efforts.

In health care, the mandated use of EMR is fueling big data throughout the industry. When coupled with a business intelligence or enterprise resource planning system, nearly all of the clinical, as well as business processes, will generate data that can be used to track process effectiveness.

EFFICACY AND VALUE OF THE SYSTEM

The efficacy and value of the health system can be traced back to the improvement in health status for the communities that it serves. Because the ultimate goal of healthcare organizations is to improve the health status of the communities they serve, all metrics used to track efficacy and value should support this outcome.

The trend in the U.S. health industry is for leaders to become more efficient, effective, and efficacious in leading people and managing resources, while simultaneously achieving high performance and quality outcomes within their organization. To keep up with this trend, measurement and assessment have become necessary competencies for leaders. However, before any leader can become skilled in these areas, he or she must understand the differences between the constructs of efficiency, effectiveness, efficacy, performance, and quality. Today's leader must also identify how the operationalization of salient variables for these constructs can assist in leading highly successful organizations.[29]

Terms such as *efficiency* and *effectiveness* are called constructs. Constructs are those things that lack identification through one of the five senses. As a result, to maximize opportunities for achieving highly effective, efficient, efficacious, performing, and quality organizations, it is incumbent on the health leader to recognize the differences between these constructs (as they are generally understood in the healthcare arena) and be able to use common indicators (e.g., variables)

that are also understood by internal and external stakeholders. Failing to use appropriate terminology (e.g., constructs and variables) that is universally understood and applied consistently within and outside the organization may result in conflicting messages. For this reason, it is incumbent upon the leader to "stay on message," adhere to industry standards in terms of the definition and use of commonly accepted and widely employed health terminology, and measure these variables consistently.

Efficacy and value of the health system are determined through the aggregate data collected from the five major areas we just discussed: public health; healthcare delivery; sociodemographic factors; resources, reimbursement, and funding; and technology and advancements.

The efficacy and value of the health system will also be redefined by population demographics. As the millennial generation takes over a larger percentage of the workforce, the cultural changes that they have brought to other areas will also occur in the workplace. Examples of these changes include pervasive usage of mobile technology, the Internet, and innovative services such as ride-sharing mobile applications. As the first generation that has had access to personal computers for their entire lives, millennials have a different perspective on these technologies; technology is not the "new" way to get things done but the "easiest" way to get things done. This complete embracing of technology has been disastrous for industries that have failed to adapt (think of newspapers and record companies); it has been a great boost to industries that embrace change.[30]

According to some sources, millennials are one of the unhealthiest generations. This is leading to an increased utilization of health services by millennials at an earlier age.[31] While this is not necessarily good for the health of their generation, it could prove good for health care—an industry that typically adopts business process innovations more slowly than other sectors. As millennials interact with the health system they could potentially drive systematic changes to the healthcare industry.

SYSTEM FEEDBACK

System feedback in the healthcare delivery system is the end result of the efficacy and value provided by the system. Based on the magnitude and nature of the feedback, existing policies are either supported or modified. In some cases, feedback with regard to the efficacy and value of the system indicates the need for new policy, to create a shift in the trajectory of the system.

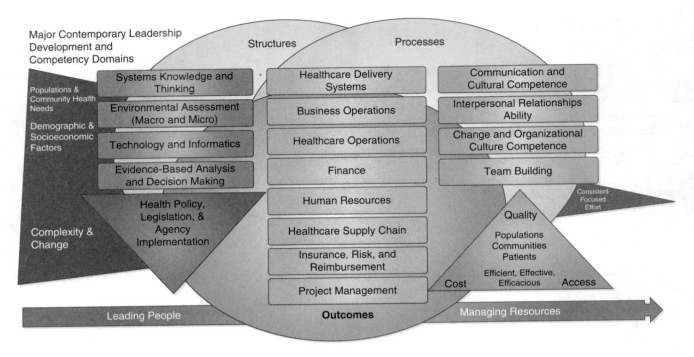

FIGURE 3-3 Major contemporary leadership development and competency domains.

STRUCTURES, PROCESS, AND OUTCOMES

The assertion that today's challenges require healthcare leadership is supported by several development and competency domains developed by Drs. Ledlow and Stephens (**Figure 3-3**).

The structures, processes, and outcomes of the Donabedian model encompass the majority of competency domains required of today's health leaders. As discussed in the first half of the chapter, the Donabedian model was designed as a tool to improve the outcomes of health services by modifying the structures and processes that create those outcomes. Outside of these competency domains we find the population health needs, including demographic and socioeconomic factors that increase the complexity and change facing the organization. In order to manage these external influences, a constant focused effort must exist within the processes of the organization. This relationship is represented by the red triangle behind the Donabedian model. William Kissick's Iron Triangle can be found at the juncture of outcomes and processes. Based on its position within the competency

domain map we can see that quality is directly influenced by the processes of the organization, with cost as an outcome; both of these modify the access to care in the community. The yellow constructs above the Iron Triangle are process changes, or leadership competencies that improve healthcare quality. Opposite the Iron Triangle, the triad of health policy, legislation, and agency implementation is represented.

COMPLEXITY AND CHANGE

Healthcare executives must be able to lead and manage change within their organizations. The ACA, new payment models, and a changing market are driving healthcare executives to launch new strategies within their organizations. But how can healthcare executives ensure that they are truly leading change? The key is to understand the difference between managing change and leading change. It has been suggested that ineffective leadership in times of change has caused much of the fatigue and frustration in the healthcare industry.[32] According to a recent ACHE seminar, this is because burnout of clinicians and staff of their organizations is associated with leaders making changes without considering the greater context or how their decision relates to the vision of the organization.[33]

POPULATION AND COMMUNITY HEALTH NEEDS

Population health is a growing topic in health care, which, if you think about it, is long overdue. With the move to value-based care, healthcare organizations have an increasing focus on population health and the needs of the community, because it is the measure by which they will be evaluated for reimbursement of service provision. Healthcare services that are high in value for the patient result in improved health status for the individual. On a community scale, this results in decreased morbidity and mortality rates, improving the health status of the community. In 2015, the number one factor to predict health status was not blood pressure, age, or cholesterol level; it was your ZIP code.[34] In many population centers, the average health status of residents can vary widely, even among relatively close areas. As classic example of this is Washington, D.C.

Figure 3-4 illustrates different life expectancies at birth in the metropolitan Washington, D.C., area.[35] These differences in life expectancy are reflected in the health status of those communities and driven by demographic and socioeconomic factors.

Examples of these demographic and socioeconomic factors include, race, age, education level, and proximity to environmental hazards. These factors will affect the payer and case mix index at healthcare facilities within the community. Advanced analytics are being used in some parts of the country by healthcare organizations to map out the community in terms of health status. Utilizing analytic tools such as community mapping will help to identify trends so that the healthcare organization is able to manage health-related trends within the communities they serve.

Even utilizing advanced techniques, consistent focused effort will be required for health systems to improve the health of their communities while managing expenses and covering their costs.

SYSTEMS KNOWLEDGE AND THINKING

Systems knowledge and thinking is a way of investigating and communicating complex issues. The core of systems thinking is seeking to understand how things are connected to each other in the total system.[36] In health care,

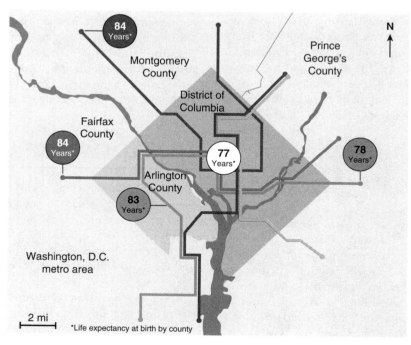

FIGURE 3-4 Your ZIP code may be more important to your health than your genetic code.

Reproduced from Robert Wood Johnson Foundation.

there are many interconnected systems and processes that contribute to providing care for patients. It may be hard to realize how simple actions such as proper facility maintenance or proper receiving of items via three-way matching can contribute to patient care, but everyone who works in health care must be aware of the interconnected nature of the various systems within a healthcare organization.

In order to determine the possible effects of an action, healthcare leaders can perform an environmental scan. Environmental scanning is a process of systematically surveying and interpreting relevant data to determine opportunities and threats.[37] All healthcare leaders must be able to assess the overall situation currently facing their organization, and this requires an assessment of both internal and external environments. A situational assessment must be an objective and honest look at the multiplicity of factors that could affect the health organization's success in achieving its vision, mission, strategies, and goals. One tool commonly used for the internal assessment is SWOT analysis, which investigates internal strengths and weaknesses and external opportunities and threats.[38]

Situational assessment and continuous environmental scanning are crucial if organizations hope to survive in the dynamic health industry. It is the responsibility of a leader and a leadership team to remain current about and relevant to situational and environmental change that can or will affect the organization. Forces that contribute to the health industry's rapid and dynamic environment are varied but cumulative; as a consequence, they have a additive impact on the industry. "Technology, demography, economics, and politics drive change, not only as individual factors but interacting to make the rate of change faster."[39] With regard to technological changes and the evolution of informatics, models such as the earlier mentioned 4 Ps can be used to guide the adoption process.

Healthcare delivery systems are made up of several subsystems that affect each other and are affected by the environment. It is for these reasons that systems knowledge and environmental scanning are essential tools for healthcare leaders, as discussed. Business operations are activities that support provision of care to patients but may not be directly related. Examples of business operations include supply chain, finance, and human resources. Healthcare operations, also called clinical operations, include activities directly related to providing patient care. Healthcare operations are typically led by physicians or advanced practice nurses. Examples include emergency room care, radiographic services, and surgical services.

FINANCE

Under the control of the Chief Financial Officer, the finance department is responsible for the financial accounting of an organization and assisting in making strategic decisions. The exact activities overseen by the finance department will vary among organizations, but it will always include day-to-day transactional accounting and related activities.[40] With the financial accounting covered, other activities such as securing external funding or providing financial reporting for strategic planning can take place. In the typical healthcare organization, some business functions such as supply chain management report up through finance.

HUMAN RESOURCES

Human resources (HR) within the healthcare organization is seen as potential source for innovation in the transition to value-based care. According to a survey by the American Society for Healthcare Human Resources Association (ASHHRA), HR can play a key role in managing healthcare reform goals through screening, shadowing programs, and continuing education.[41] The survey was referring to the role HR departments play in organizational culture. If individuals are hired who are not the right fit for the organization, replacing them is often extremely costly to the organization. To insure that hired individuals are a right fit for the organization, some health systems are using behavioral assessments, pre-hiring shadowing, and keeping communication channels open between HR and other departments within the facility.

HEALTHCARE SUPPLY CHAIN

The supply chain integrates with the healthcare provider to diagnose, treat, and care for a patient; if you remove either the supply chain or the provider of care from the equation, health care is significantly less effective, less efficient, and less efficacious. Patient safety, cost of care, quality of care, and access to care are intimately connected to the healthcare supply chain.

Supply chain management is the purposeful direction of the flow of goods. This includes the transport and storage of raw materials, work in progress, and finished goods from the point of production to the point of usage. A supply chain is an interconnected network of people and organizations that are involved in the production of products and services.

If they produce a product, every organization has some sort of a supply chain. Here, we will focus on the supply chain and logistics of healthcare organizations; the material presented also generally applies to other types of businesses. Supply chain management is an important area of growth for healthcare organizations for several reasons; the most obvious is the cost associated with mismanagement of the supply chain. It is estimated that in the United States supply chain costs in health care are typically around 40 to 45% of the operating cost of the organization,[42] and the associated costs are likely to continue to increase. Other estimates suggest that the healthcare supply chain is attributed to 30 to 35% of the annual operating costs of healthcare organizations; with a low of 30% or high of 45%, healthcare organizations must effectively manage their supply chain. Recent estimates suggest that there may be as much as $20 billion in efficiencies that could be gained by improving healthcare supply chain operations and management across the health industry.[43]

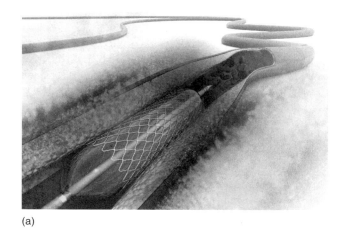

(a)

As healthcare treatments increase in complexity, the associated costs tend to increase. An example of this is stents used in percutaneous coronary intervention (PCI), a procedure used to treat narrowing of the coronary arteries in patients with coronary heart disease. The first stent was implanted during a PCI procedure in the mid-1980s.[44] Because of the success of the procedure, the use of stents became more commonplace. After a few years, certain complications began to appear. These complications were attributed to the material used to make the stents. Eventually, in 2001, a new stent was introduced to improve the outcomes of PCI procedures. The new stents are drug eluting, which means that they are coated in and secrete medication that reduces the risk of complications that were associated with the older type of stent. The increased level of safety associated with drug-eluting stents (DES) comes at a price. PCI procedures done with DES cost about $2500 more per procedure than they would have if basic, older version, stents were used.[45] However, the improvement in quality of care, now accepted as a standard of care (the level and type of care expected in the industry that produces higher quality outcomes), is required to perform this procedure in the healthcare organization. **(Figure 3-5)**

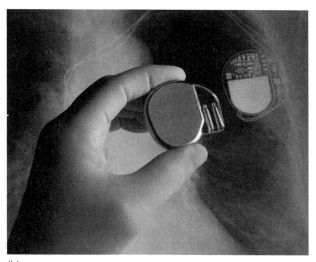

(b)

As the cost of medical supplies and devices continues to increase, the total expense associated with the supply chain increases as well. Currently, supply chain management is second only to labor in terms of expense for the average health system. If the cost of supply chain management continues to increase at the current rate, it is estimated that costs associated with the supply chain could exceed those associated with labor by 2022.[46] Technological advances are

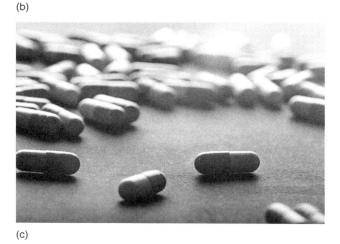

(c)

FIGURE 3-5 Technologies supported by the supply chain. a) Stent; b) Pacemaker; c) Pharmaceuticals.

a) © hywards/Shutterstock; b) © Science Photo Library/Getty Images; c) © Oleksii Fedorenko/Shutterstock.

enabling organizations to more efficiently and consistently manage supply chain operations, billing practices, and compliance while providing flexibility for different processes within the system of care. "In all industries, not just health care, three out of four chief executive officers consider their supply chains to be essential to gaining a competitive advantage within their markets."[47] According to Vance Moore, CEO of ROi (the supply chain entity within the Sisters of Mercy Health System based in St. Louis, Missouri), in a 2008 presentation in Chicago, the trend in the cost of the healthcare supply chain continues to grow where, if the trend continues, supply chain could equal labor cost for annual operating expenses for hospitals and health systems between the years 2020 and 2025.[48] Clearly, maximizing efficiency of the healthcare supply chain is an increasing concern amid increasing costs but with increasing quality.

Increased cost is partly due to a concept called *total cost economics*. Total cost economics, sometimes called *total cost of ownership*, is the complete cost of an item or procedure, including direct and indirect costs. An example of direct cost is the list price of the item. However, there are usually additional "hidden" costs associated, which are called *indirect costs*. An example of an indirect cost is additional training for physicians or specialized storage needs for new medical devices or supply items.

Healthcare organizations have to remain diligent when it comes to managing their supply chain, especially through times of rapid technological advancement. The consequences of supply chain disruptions in healthcare organizations can prove deadly for patients. Due to the consequences associated with running out of items necessary for patient care, all hospitals seek to maintain a reserve level of essential items in stock. However, there is room to streamline the supply chain in almost all facilities. A streamlined supply chain can create a competitive advantage for an organization through the elimination of unnecessary purchasing and storage of items. A *competitive advantage* is an attribute or process that outperforms competitors in a specific area. An example of a business that maintains a competitive advantage due to its supply chain is WalMart. Can the healthcare supply chain provide competitive advantage for healthcare organizations? Can the healthcare supply chain increase value to the delivery of care? The answer to both questions is "Yes." However, the healthcare industry needs to focus on improving its supply chain.

Healthcare organizations, individually and as an industry, are behind other industries when considering supply chain structure, coordination, management, and value. Other industry leaders understand a simple reality, and this simple reality is important to think about and understand when working to improve the supply chain. That reality is: Funds, information, and products are closely linked together. It is imperative for health care, using a team approach, to make improvements to supply chain operations, management, and information systems that drive their care delivery processes by providing the "technology of care" to providers of care. In the healthcare supply chain, these statements are generally true:

- Supplies are traditionally the second largest expense category for providers.
- Providers are getting supplies today.
- Providers are paying for every part of the supply chain.
- Providers control a very small portion of the cost of products used in their facilities.
- Providers have very little control or impact on the quality of supply service.
- Providers believe that the supply chain is a necessary evil and that it does not play a significant role in the quality of patient care.[49]

An excerpt from a healthcare supply chain book written for senior healthcare executives follows; the situational assessment today reveals similar findings.

Today's healthcare supply chain characteristics:

- *Multiple systems, multiple processes that lack cohesiveness and uniformity*—Many health systems, if not stand-alone facilities, use different materials, management information systems, and processes across facilities and departments.
- *High distributor fees*—Most healthcare organizations spend hundreds of thousands of dollars, if not millions each year on outside parties for supply (medical/surgical and pharmaceutical) distribution.
- *Service quality failures and service frequency did not match need*—Distributors commonly fill between 80% to 90% of the order. This causes a tremendous number of product shortages for clinicians each day. At times, distributors overfill orders causing excessive stock on shelves and higher costs for the overage and cost of storing the items. As for frequency, many healthcare organizations receive supplies based on distributors' schedules not based on clinical needs.
- *Wholesalers lead pharmacy processes*—The medications obtained, primarily from outside distributors/wholesalers, control the systems and processes for medication sourcing, ordering, receiving, and distribution.
- *Inconsistent management processes*—Many healthcare organizations manage the supply chain operation in different ways within the same facility. In some

cases, each department seems to be a unique entity with regard to supply chain operations.

- *Limited usable data*—In many healthcare organizations, identical products are named differently depending on facility and/or department. This reality limits the ability to aggregate data for decision making, volume purchasing, and bulk ordering, thus impacting the bottom line.
- *Many intermediaries*—The majority of distributors service many customers and stock what sells for *them* best, not necessarily what is needed or wanted. This means that most healthcare organizations get supplies, or are sourced, from many different distribution facilities to meet their needs or are directed to use what the distributor stocks in that particular service region.[50]

Opportunities clearly exist in the healthcare supply chain for improvement, higher value, better patient care, and enhanced integration of information for quality decision making. This chapter intends to assist in that industry effort.

PROJECT MANAGEMENT

Traditionally, physicians have been individual thinkers and actors. Successful methods and technologies from other sectors have been slow to be adopted. This is, perhaps, because medical school and graduate medical education has been traditionally focused on the individual.[51] As the focus on quality continues to increase in health care, it is becoming clear that lessons learned in other industries must be adopted by healthcare organizations.[52] Some key lessons that can be learned from project management include the importance of collaboration and sharing vision, proper execution of a plan, the role of technology, and being mindful of costs.[53] These key project management lessons focus around open and honest communication with team members while driving results toward the mission and vision of the organization.

Managing risk is another important aspect of project management, especially in health care. With the proliferation of patient-centered medical homes, accountable care models, episode of care payments, and global payment, healthcare organizations face increasing levels of competition and decreasing levels of payment.[54] For years, the U.S. healthcare system has been working to combat issues of increasing costs and disparities in the quality of care provided. This situation prompted the government to create and pass the ACA in 2010.

One of the changes brought by the ACA was the accountable care organization (ACO). An ACO is a re-envisioned payment and care delivery system that is designed to help address the issues of cost and health disparities in health care. ACOs do this by being a provider-led organization that is responsible for the overall cost and quality of care provided. ACOs are incentivized based on treatment cost savings achieved while meeting quality of care standards.[55]

One side effect of the regulatory pressures brought about by the ACA is healthcare organization consolidation. New payment systems, as well as requirements to use new technologies, have given many small healthcare organizations a choice: join forces with another organization or close the doors. Recent studies have shown that as healthcare organizations consolidate, health insurance companies increase their premiums. This holds true for insurance plans on and off the ACA–created health insurance marketplaces.[56]

When planning and managing projects within the healthcare organization, these external forces and cost drivers must be accounted for if the healthcare organization is to adapt to market conditions and successfully complete its planned projects.

GOAL-SETTING THEORY

Goal-Setting Theory was developed by Edwin Locke in 1968. According to the theory, goals are the aim of an action or behavior. Setting a specific outcome, or goal setting, can be done for any verifiable or measurable outcome. In short, goals are the aim of an action or behavior. Between 1968 and 1980, studies showed that specific, well-defined goals led to a greater improvement in performance than an easy goal or a goal that was vague. This performance is further enhanced through feedback mechanisms and availability of required resources to perform the tasks required.

According to Locke, there are seven steps to optimize goal setting:

1. Specify objectives or tasks to be done.
2. Specify how performance will be measured.
3. Specify the standard to be reached.
4. Specify the time frame involved.
5. Prioritize goals.
6. Rate goals for difficulty and importance.
7. Determine the coordination requirements.[57]

When working through the process, it is important for leaders to ensure that new goals do not conflict with other organization goals. Some other risks associated with using this theory are creating an environment where excessive risk is acceptable, adding unwanted stress, or eroding employee confidence.

Since the theory was originally published, goal-setting theory has been applied in various industries and management situations, most notably in the logging industry. As a result of the work done since the 1968 publication of the theory, Locke began to explore the relationship between goal-setting theory and expectancy theory in the early 1990s. Expectancy theory says that low goals may be easier to obtain but that they do not provide as much satisfaction as more difficult goals.[58]

COMMUNICATION AND CULTURAL COMPETENCE

Health leaders need to have exceptional communication skills. They must learn techniques for clarifying what someone else is saying and for being clear in their own communication. Mintzberg's study on managerial work revealed that managers' activity was characterized by "brevity, variety, and fragmentation"; managers were continually seeking information, preferring oral communications to written reports.[59,60] This finding applies to leaders as well. The preference for oral communication may be difficult for health leaders to enact but nonetheless is important. As an example of personal preference for oral communication, it has been noted that within the first 7 months of President Barack Obama's administration, he had more White House press conferences than George W. Bush did in his 8 years as president.[61] Although verbal communication may be time consuming, given the of employees and the public for such communication, it is a very valuable tool that is essential to achieve success and increase understanding across diverse constituent groups.

Simply put, communication is the process of *acting on information*.[62] Communication contributes tremendously to the culture and climate of the healthcare organization. A response—feedback—is an essential aspect of the communication process. Obstacles to communication, called noise, either in the channel or in the mind of the receiver, may contribute to an inaccurate understanding of the intended message. Communication is the main catalyst behind the motivation efforts and strategies utilized by leaders.[63] "Various management [leadership] practices, including goal setting, reinforcement, feedback, and evaluation, require communication."[64] There are three goals of communication:

- Assuring understanding
- Achieving intended results
- Acting ethically and morally

Communication is a process of active transaction (transactive), which means messages are sent and received simultaneously. Everything you do or do not do, say or do not say, communicates something. You cannot not communicate.

As globalization increases, healthcare leaders need to be culturally aware, understand, and lead people from diverse backgrounds, diverse educational portfolios, and diverse outlooks. In today's global economy, it is commonplace for subordinates, peers, and superiors to be from different geographic, national, and cultural backgrounds. Likewise, patients, customers, and their families are more diverse. This trend requires a culturally competent and adaptive perspective for both the health leader and the health organizational culture the leader maintains. It adds complexity to the health leader's landscape from both internal and external environmental perspectives. In turn, this complexity lends credence to demands for a dynamic culture leadership mentality and process to create a robust organizational culture amid an environment of change, the speed of which is increasing.

Globalization causes concern when discussing differing perceptions across cultures:

- Individualist (self-oriented) and collectivist (team-oriented) cultures will have significantly different perceptions of work and performance.
- Power distance (higher power means more physical space): High-power cultures tend to be authoritarian, whereas power is more equally distributed in low-power cultures.
- Uncertainty avoidance (risk taking and plan implementation without all information and organizational coupling) is thick with rules and guidelines.
- Gender equality: Assertive, material, and competitive cultures tend to be masculine, whereas collaborative, harmonious, and nurturing cultures take on a feminine persona.
- High-context communication cultures transfer meaning with more emphasis on the situation, whereas low-context communication cultures emphasize the sender's responsibility to transfer meaning more than the situation.[65]

Situational leadership applications fit nicely in the paradigm of a culturally competent leader, considering the complexity of globalization. Leadership expectations differ depending on the culture, society, nation, or ethnic group to which leaders belong (and reside and practice). It is difficult to find much in the literature on leadership outside the Western perspective, for example. The Western perspective in the literature is predominantly based on research conducted in the United States, the United Kingdom, Australia, or Europe. "To date [as of 2004] more than 90% of the organizational behavior [including leadership] literature reflects U.S.-based research and theory."[66]

INTERPERSONAL RELATIONSHIP ABILITY

The Purpose-Assemble & Charter-Align-Resource—Perform, or PAARP, model (**Figure 3-6**), when followed throughout the lifecycle of a team, can result in improved morale of team members, improved outcomes, and greater value to the organization. Throughout the team lifecycle, identifying purpose and continual communication are keys. Proposed by Stephens, Ledlow, and Schott, the PAARP model postulates that the actions of interprofessional teams occur in five distinct phases that repeat as necessary depending on the type of team.

According to PAARP, the actions of leadership give purpose to a group. There are several theories that can assist the leader in providing this purpose: the great groups approach, goal-setting theory, and the theory of planned behavior. Great groups are a common subject when it comes to planning teams, but so many of the associated principles are quickly glanced over for the sake of expediency. It is important to remember that not only does a leader create a great group; it is the group that makes the leader great. For the group to succeed, the right people need to be in the right jobs. With the right people in place, the great group is focused on results and achieving their goal.[67] Team members must align, resource, and perform tasks as laid out by leadership through the defined purpose and assembly of the group. Once tasks are complete, the standing group is repurposed for its next task or, for single-purpose groups, adjourned.

CHANGE AND ORGANIZATIONAL CULTURE COMPETENCE

There is a growing trend to incorporate organizational culture into leadership theories and models. This is a rather new emphasis but a critically important one. Leaders build culture in everything they do—from role modeling, to assigning responsibilities, to communicating with others—including how they communicate and what they do not do or do not say. Models with an organizational culture emphasis require leaders to determine, develop, and maintain an organizational culture that can best meet the expectations, if not thrive, in the external environment. This perspective envisions a more important and dramatic role for organizational culture as a construct—a leadership role—compared to that assigned under the situational leadership philosophy. *Leaders must now create culture!* The Dynamic Culture Leadership model enables leaders to create the culture of excellence that is required in healthcare organizations.

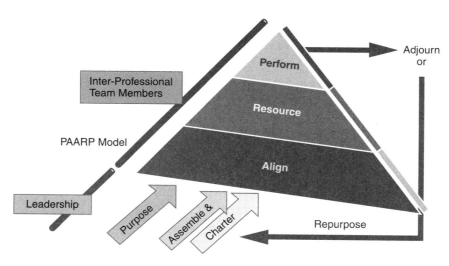

FIGURE 3-6 The PAARP model.

THE DYNAMIC CULTURE LEADERSHIP MODEL[68]

Due to the increasingly dynamic nature of the healthcare environment, superb leadership is required at all levels of the healthcare organization. This reality is the catalyst for the development of the dynamic culture leadership (DCL) model. Leadership in this model is recognized at three levels as the critical ingredient in the recipe for overall success: at the personal level, at the team level, and at the organizational level. The challenge is to focus the knowledge, skills, and abilities of organizational leaders appropriately and to empower the total organization to complete its mission, reach its vision, and compete successfully in an environment that constantly changes.

TEAM BUILDING

Surprisingly, many healthcare organizational leaders are unfamiliar with the process of team building. This may be due to the fact that they moved into organizations with relatively large and stable groups of employees who are comfortable in their positions. It may also be because the leader has become a prominent figure in his or her field of study through excellence in the execution of skills (as might be the case with a surgeon, for example). This level of leader acknowledgment is different for a middle-level health leader and especially for a CEO of a large healthcare organization who maintains responsibility for many elements of the enterprise. Without the experience of leading increasingly larger groups, the leader may not be fully aware of the life cycle and evolution associated with standing, ad hoc, and process action teams.

SUMMARY

There are a multitude of challenges facing the health organization leader today. This chapter served as an introduction for concepts that will be revisited in more detail. Because the healthcare industry is integrating public health and healthcare delivery, along with shared financial and service risk, it is prudent to attend to the aspects of integration between these two vital segments of the industry. This chapter provided a small yet vital foreshadowing of what health leaders need to understand, be aware of, and strategically and operationally plan for in order to successfully lead people and manage resources amid dynamic and turbulent times. Leadership competence is crucial across multiple and complex domains. Understanding the competency domains needed for successful leadership in today's health industry sets the stage for mastery of necessary knowledge, skills, and abilities to lead. Healthcare organizations need competent leaders as much today as at any time in the industry's history.

DISCUSSION QUESTIONS

1. Outline why the dynamic forces in the industry are important to professionals in the health industry, and identify challenges requiring quality leadership intervention strategies.
2. Explain and give an example of one aspect of change in the industry today, and link leadership competencies necessary for successfully navigating the organizational changes required for dealing with the change.
3. Relate, discuss, and explain the importance of the application of a leadership competency model to contemporary health industry change.
4. Distinguish the different aspects or domains of change in the health industry and how those domains impact leadership capability. Explain how the synergy of those changes might impact leadership capability and organizational success.
5. Relate the health reform efforts of the past decade to leadership needs at the health organization level.
6. Evaluate the health industry's need for leadership today and into the next decade.

EXERCISES

1. Outline at least four dynamic forces in the health industry, and explain why they are important to health professionals. For one of the forces, identify challenges requiring quality leadership intervention strategies.
2. Explain and give a specific example of one aspect of change in the industry today. Link leadership competencies from the competency model in this chapter that might be necessary for successfully navigating

the organizational change required to deal with the change.

3. Relate, discuss, and explain the importance of the application of a leadership competency model to contemporary health industry change. Evaluate your own ability in each competency domain from the model.

4. Distinguish the different aspects or domains of change in the health industry and how those

domains impact leadership capability. Explain how the synergy of those changes might impact leadership capability and organizational success.

5. Relate the health reform efforts of the past decade to leadership needs at the health organization level in a one-to two-page narrative essay.

6. Evaluate the health industry's need for leadership today and into the next decade based on issues set forth in this chapter.

REFERENCES

1. Way, A. L. (2005). Political power, influence, PS201H-1C. Retrieved from http://www.proconservative.net/CUNAPolSci201PartOneC.shtml.
2. Animal Protection of New Mexico. (2009). How to understand the differences between statutes, regulations, ordinances and common law. Retrieved from http://www.apnm.org/publications/animal_law/how_to/understand.php.
3. World Health Organization. (2004). WHO | Health policy. Retrieved from http://www.who.int/topics/health_policy/en/.
4. U.S. Environmental Protection Agency. (2013). The basics of the regulatory process | laws and regulations. Retrieved from http://www2.epa.gov/laws-regulations/basics-regulatory-process.
5. Lui, Davis MD. (2012). The iron triangle of health care is not law, but an observation. Retrieved from http://www.kevinmd.com/blog/2012/10/iron-triangle-health-care-law-observation.html.
6. (2013). Why healthcare costs are about to explode. *Forbes*. Retrieved from http://www.forbes.com/sites/realspin/2013/06/30/why-healthcare-costs-are-about-to-explode/.
7. Donabedian, A. (1988). JAMA Network | JAMA | The quality of care: How can it be . . . . Retrieved from http://jama.jamanetwork.com/article.aspx?articleid=374139.
8. Nadzam, D. M., Turpin, R., Hanold, L. S., & White, R. E. (1993). Data-driven performance improvement in health care: The Joint Commission's Indicator Measurement System (IMSystem). *The Joint Commission Journal on Quality Improvement*, 19(11): 492–500. PMID: 8313012
9. King, A. K., & Sax, C. H. (2016). Integrating disruptive innovation while leading your core mission. [Presentation]. American College of Healthcare Executives Annual Congress. March 16, 2016.
10. King & Sax, note 9.
11. King & Sax, note 9.
12. Centers for Disease Control and Prevention. (n.d.). Health literacy for public health professionals: Core functions of public health: Assurance. Retrieved from http://www.cdc.gov/healthliteracy/training/page1299.html.
13. American Public Health Association. (2014). What is public health? Retrieved from https://www.apha.org/what-is-public-health.
14. Harvard Business School. (2009). Managing health care delivery. Retrieved from http://www.exed.hbs.edu/programs/mhcd.
15. (2014). US health system ranks last among eleven countries on . . . . Retrieved from http://www.commonwealthfund.org/publications/press-releases/2014/jun/us-health-system-ranks-last.
16. FactCheck. (2014). ACA impact on per capita cost of health care. Retrieved from http://www.factcheck.org/2014/02/aca-impact-on-per-capita-cost-of-health-care/.
17. Centers for Medicare and Medicaid Services (CMS). (2012). Acute care hospital inpatient prospective payment system. Retrieved from https://www.cms.gov/Outreach-and-Education/Medicare-Learning-Network-MLN/MLNProducts/downloads/AcutePaymtSysfctsht.pdf.
18. Comprehensive care for joint replacement payment model for acute care hospitals furnishing lower extremity joint replacement services, final ruling. Retrieved from http://federalregister.gov/a/2015-29438.
19. Trivedi, A. (2015). Overview of health care financing. Retrieved from http://www.merckmanuals.com/professional/special-subjects/financial-issues-in-health-care/overview-of-health-care-financing.
20. Trivedi, note 19.
21. Trivedi, note 19.

22. Trivedi, note 19.
23. Trivedi, note 19.
24. Trivedi, note 19.
25. Trivedi, note 19.
26. (2014). Sociodemographic factors affect health outcomes. Retrieved from http://essentialhospitals.org/institute/sociodemographic-factors-and-socioeconomic-status-ses-affect-health-outcomes/.
27. (2015). Using technology to map out a population health strategy. Retrieved from http://www.stjosephhospital.com/Population-Health-Stategy.
28. (2014). What is big data? SAS. Retrieved from http://www.sas.com/en_us/insights/big-data/what-is-big-data.html.
29. Aday, L. A. (1998). Introduction to health service research and policy analysis. In L. A. Aday, C. E. Begley, D. R. Lairson, & R. Balkrishnan (Eds.), *Evaluating the healthcare system: Effectiveness, efficiency, and equity* (pp. 45–172). Ann Arbor, MI: Health Administration Press.
30. (2015). Millennials cleaning up another Boomer mess. *Forbes.* Retrieved from http://www.forbes.com/sites/davechase/2015/11/03/millennials-cleaning-up-another-boomer-mess-this-time-healthcare/.
31. Millennials, note 30.
32. Hegwer, L. (2015, November 1). Leading change from the c-suite: 3 leaders share their strategies. *Healthcare Executive*, 11–18.
33. Hegwer, note 32.
34. Buell, J. (2015, September 1). Using technology to map out a population health strategy. *Healthcare Executive*, 11–18.
35. Buell, note 34.
36. Peters, D. (2014). The application of systems thinking in health. Retrieved from http://www.health-policy-systems.com/content/12/1/51.
37. (2012). Strategic planning: What are the basics of environmental . . . . Retrieved from http://www.shrm.org/templatestools/hrqa/pages/cms_021670.aspx.
38. Van der Werff, T. J. (2009). Strategic planning for fun and profit. Retrieved from http://www.globalfuture.com/planning9.htm.
39. Griffith, J. R. (1999). *The well-managed healthcare organization* (4th ed.). Chicago: Health Administration Press, p. 1.
40. (2011). Roles and responsibilities of a finance department. Retrieved from http://www.jasmith.com/roles-and-responsibilities-of-a-finance-department/.
41. (2014). Innovating human resources. *Healthcare Finance News.* Retrieved from http://www.healthcarefinancenews.com/news/innovating-human-resources.
42. Pennic, J. (2014). 5 ways supply chain can reduce rising healthcare costs. Retrieved from http://hitconsultant.net/2013/05/13/5-ways-supply-chain-can-reduce-rising-healthcare-costs/.
43. Ledlow, G., Corry, A., & Cwiek, M. (2007). Optimize *your healthcare supply chain performance: A strategic approach.* Chicago: Health Administration Press, pp. 2–5.
44. Newsome, L. (2010). History of coronary stents. Retrieved from http://www.apsf.org/newsletters/html/2007/winter/12_protocol.htm.
45. Ryan, J. (2006). Are drug-eluting stents cost-effective? *Circulation.* Retrieved from http://circ.ahajournals.org/content/114/16/1736.full.
46. Pennic, note 42.
47. Ledlow et al., note 43, p. 2.
48. Moore, V. (2008). Clinical supply chain. [Presentation]. American College of Healthcare Executives National Congress. Chicago, Illinois.
49. McCurry, M., & Moore, V. (2005, October 20–21). Resource optimization and innovation. Sisters of Mercy Supply Chain Summit 2005. Branson, MO.
50. Ledlow et al., note 43, pp. 2–4.
51. (2013). 5 lessons healthcare can learn from project management. Retrieved from http://www.medicalpracticeinsider.com/blog/business/5-lessons-healthcare-can-learn-project-management.
52. (2015). Need for project management [pdf P(1)] Docs-Library.com. Retrieved from http://www.docs-library.com/pdf/1/need-for-project-management.html.
53. (2013). 5 lessons healthcare can learn from project management. [Blog]. Retrieved from http://www.medicalpracticeinsider.com/blog/business/5-lessons-healthcare-can-learn-project-management.
54. (2015). Delivery and payment models—private sector initiatives. Retrieved from https://www.ahip.org/Map/AlternativeDeliveryPaymentModels/.
55. (2012). Embracing Accountable Care: 10 Key Steps — America's . . . . Retrieved from https://www.ahip.org/Marketplace/White-Papers-and-Case-Studies/Embracing-Accountable-Care-10-key-Steps.aspx.
56. (2015). Impact of hospital consolidation on health insurance . . . . Retrieved from https://www.ahip.org/Epub/Impact-of-Hospital-Consolidation/.
57. Locke, E. A. (1986). *Generalizing from laboratory to field settings.* Lexington, MA: Lexington Books.
58. Mento, A. J., Locke, E. A., & Klein, H. J. (1992). Relationship of goal level to valence and

instrumentality. *Journal of Applied Psychology*, 77(4), 395–405.

59. Mintzberg, H. (1989). *Mintzberg on management: Inside our strange world of organizations*. New York: Free Press.

60. Mintzberg, H. (1973). *The nature of managerial work*. New York: Harper & Row.

61. CBS Evening News. (2009). Obama going prime time to help ailing health initiative. Retrieved from http://www.cbsnews.com/blogs/2009/07/22/politics/politicalhotsheet/entry5179382.shtml.

62. Beebe, S. A., & Masterson, J. T. (1997). *Communicating in small groups: Principles and practices* (5th ed.). New York: Addison-Wesley Educational Publishers, p. 3.

63. Cusella, L. P. (1987). Feedback, motivation, and performance. In F. M. Jablin, L. L. Putnam, K. H. Roberts, & L. W. Porter (Eds.), *Handbook of organizational communication* (pp. 624–679). Newbury Park, CA: Sage.

64. Harris, T. E. (1993). *Applied organizational communication: Perspectives, principles and pragmatics*. Hillsdale, NJ: Lawrence Erlbaum Associates, p. 454.

65. Harris, T. E., & Nelson, M. D. (2008). *Applied organizational communication: Theory and practice in a global environment* (3rd ed.). New York: Lawrence Erlbaum Associates, Chapter 2.

66. House, R. J. (2004). Preface. In R. J. House, P. J. Hanges, M. Javidan, P. W. Dorfman, & V. Gupta (Eds.), *Culture, leadership and organizations: The GLOBE Study of 62 societies* (p. xxv). Thousand Oaks, CA: Sage.

67. CBS News. (2013). The 10 rules of great groups. Retrieved from http://www.cbsnews.com/news/the-10-rules-of-great-groups/.

68. Ledlow, G., Coppola, N., & Cwiek, M. (2008). Leadership and transformation. In J. A. Johnson (Ed.), *Organizational theory, behavior, and development* (pp. 193–212). Sudbury, MA: Jones & Bartlett.

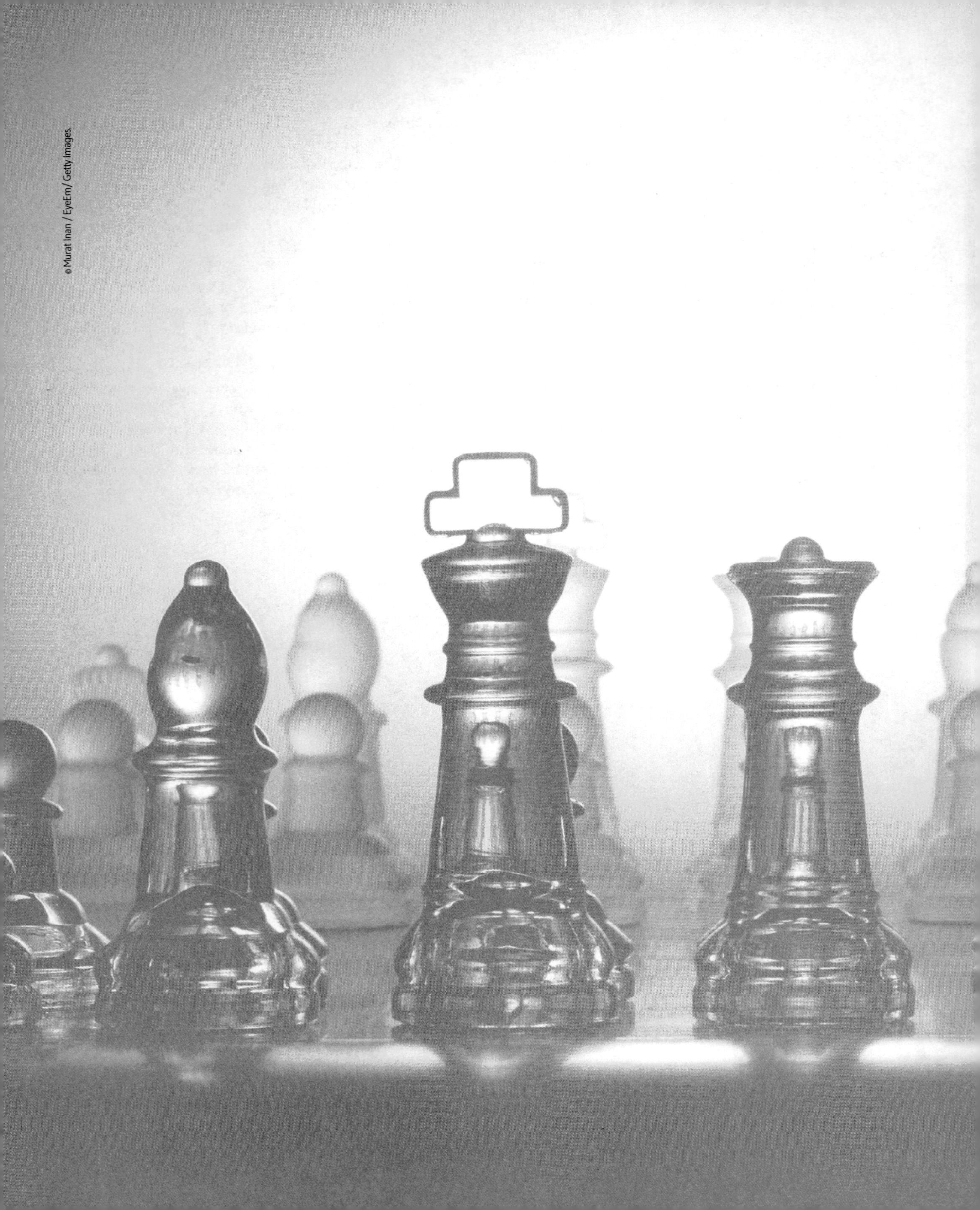

CHRONOLOGY OF LEADERSHIP STUDY AND PRACTICE

One's feelings waste themselves in use of words; they ought all to be distilled into actions and into actions which bring results.

Florence Nightingale

This chapter provides a historical summary and overview of leadership theory as it has evolved over the ages. Major theories and models are presented. Early documents (2300 BCE) outlining leadership principles and definitions (400 BCE) are addressed, with the discussion then proceeding through the contemporary and accepted models of the twentieth and twenty-first centuries. This chapter presents the theories and models in the original light that the creating authors intended. Strengths and weaknesses of each theory, as well as applications and strategies for use, are integrated into each theoretical overview.

LEARNING OBJECTIVES

1. Describe the progression of leadership thought as portrayed in theories and models from the "great man" and trait phase, to the behavioral phase, to the situational or contingency phase.

2. Distinguish constructs of a trait theory or model, a behavioral theory or model, and a situational or contingency theory or model of leadership, and interpret those constructs' value in the present day.

3. Apply a behavioral theory or model and a situational or contingency theory or model of leadership, and demonstrate the application in an example based on a definition of leadership.

4. Compare and contrast, through the use of illustrative diagrams, two or more behavioral or situational/contingency theories or models of leadership.

5. From the progression of leadership thought, design, create, and explain a personal leadership model applicable to leading health organizations today.

6. Appraise and relate constructs and variables from the progression of leadership thought to your personal leadership model for leading health organizations today.

INTRODUCTION

The study of historical leadership is important for both students and early careerists for several reasons. First, as with the study of any historical theory grounded in the literature, it is important to know where the study of the discipline began so that leaders do not repeat mistakes of the past or spend effort on advocating philosophies no longer considered relevant in the study of leadership. Second, early careerists will recognize opportunities and best practices discovered by predecessors that, if applied properly, can aid them in developing competencies in their own leadership practice. Third, leadership theories and models have built upon one another over time; contemporary leadership theories, models, and practices have a lineage stretching back for decades—if not centuries—that have paved the way and informed modern leadership thought. Learning from the past is important to improve the future, and it is crucial for individual leader development.

These are the most salient reasons to study the history of leadership thought. In reality, hours-long discussions could be sustained pondering many other reasons to explore the history of the discipline. You can learn from the past and build upon the work and thinking of others to develop your leadership plan and model for your career in the health industry. For practical purposes, better known theories and models are presented in this chapter; a thorough discussion of leadership theories and models could easily run to thousands of pages.

Which theories and models and which constructs and variables form the basis for your leadership model? Read this chapter critically not only to learn about leadership theories and models but also to form the basis of your leadership plan/model. This is not "just history" but a focused exploration of leadership history through theory and models, so you can learn from history and use it to your advantage. How will your career look if you are a better leader than anyone else? How will it look if you are one of a hundred or a thousand others with similar leadership capabilities? Build your leadership plan to lead people and manage resources.

The progression of leadership thought is a constructivist approach over time; that is, early theories and models form the foundations or stepping stones for the next theories or models proposed. As you read about the theories and models, list the constructs and variables associated with each theory or model under the various phases of leadership thought, and begin to identify which constructs and approaches are salient to health leadership in today's environment. As you study the progression of leadership thought and research, think about which theories and models are descriptive, prescriptive, or both. Ultimately, you should begin to identify leadership constructs and approaches that resonate with your own philosophy, thereby enabling you to build a preliminary personal leadership model that you can use in your career.

There are three distinct phases of leadership thought: (1) "great man" and trait theories and models, (2) behavioral theories and models, and (3) situational or contingency theories and models (**Table 4-1**). A fourth phase may now be in an early stage of development; this potential phase incorporates organizational culture into situational leadership practice.

Some theories and models from earlier phases did overlap somewhat with part of another phase of leadership thought. Nevertheless, in general, the theories and models presented in this chapter can be classified into a specific phase based on the constructs and variables they incorporate rather than the chronological time period in which they emerged. When leaders' traits—for example, height or eye color—are utilized to distinguish them or measure success or select another leader, traits are the overriding factor of the theory or model. Likewise, when an individual "great" leader, such as Alexander the Great or George Washington, is identified and characterized for the purposes of measuring success, identifying another leader, or role modeling, the basis of the theory or model is considered a "great man" phase approach. Upon reflection, great man and trait theories and models are very similar and, therefore, tend to be grouped together. Behavioral theories are behavior or action based. In other words, successful leaders perform some action or behavior or a set of actions or behaviors, such as showing concern for people by rounding (i.e., walking around the workplace talking with subordinates purposefully). Situational (or contingency) theories and models incorporate the context

or situation or environment into the leadership approach to identify avenues for success that can be attributed to the leader. Situational leadership requires leaders to be flexible, and to build and develop the competencies, knowledge, skills, and abilities (especially situational assessment) needed to adapt styles and practices to the current situation. The "toolbox" of leadership—that is, the capability to use several styles, practices, or "tools"—is most important in situational leadership theories and models.

GREAT MAN AND TRAIT LEADERSHIP PHASE

Great man and trait theories and models concentrated on individual leaders who were considered "great." The characteristics or traits of those leaders were identified as reasons for their success. Other models focused simply on traits without identifying a great man. "Great women" were also identified, such as Joan of Arc, but to a lesser degree because of social norms and cultures that prevailed prior to the 1900s. Many "great leaders"—both women and men—could serve as the focus of a great man theory or model. The cultural norm through the early twentieth century was encapsulated by Dowd in 1936, who argued that there is no such thing as leadership by the masses. According to his view, the individuals in every society possess different degrees of intelligence, energy, and moral force, and in whatever direction the masses may be influenced to go, they are always led by the superior few.[1] Beginning in the time of Moses, great leaders have shaped civilization.[2]

Although pure trait theory has fallen into obsolescence, traits of leadership are still very important to the subject of leadership.[3] Based more heavily on description, these theories and models propose emulation of what great leaders do and which traits they possess; prescription is indirect and "universal," in that situational context and behavior adaption are not incorporated into this genre of leadership thought. Some of the more accepted (for their time) theories and models of this phase are presented here.

XENOPHON: AN EARLY LEADER THEORY (400 BCE)

As early as 400 BCE, Xenophon (**Figure 4-1**) first defined leadership and its impact on organizations; later, Bennis stated the converse notion—namely, that the most important (and underlying) issue is lack of leadership.[4] Today, leaders in a variety of organizations must understand the role and importance of effective leadership, leadership development, and succession planning in achieving organizational success.

Table 4-1 Progression of Leadership Thought by Phase		
"Great Man" and Trait Phase (Circa 450 BCE–1940s)	**Behavioral Phase (1940s–1960s)**	**Situational or Contingency Phase (1970s–Present)**
Attempted to determine which specific traits make a person an effective leader. Great leaders are the focus of trait identification.	Attempted to determine which particular behaviors and styles leaders use to cause others to follow them. Which behaviors and styles were successful was a focus of the theories.	Attempts to explain effective leadership within the context of the larger work situation and environment where the leader adapts styles, strategies, and applications to best fit the situation or by selecting a leader who best fits the situation based on the leader's style and strategies.

FIGURE 4-1 Xenophon.
Photo courtesy of MyOliveTrees [www.myolivetrees.com].

FIGURE 4-2 Niccolo Machiavelli.
Photo courtesy of Santiago Soto Borreiros.

Unfortunately, leadership and leadership development do not confine themselves to a single checklist, comprehensive model, or flowchart. Xenophon wrote *Anabasis*, which served as a guide to Alexander the Great during his conquests. Restated in modern terms, Xenophon's key idea was that leaders guide their people (their army) to success by demonstrating courage and modeling "leadership." A key characteristic of a leader, from Xenophon's perspective, was horsemanship; being a great horseman was critical to role modeling leadership. In the warfare of the time, horses were essential, and mastery of horsemanship was a valuable leader attribute.

Xenophon's writings included *On the Cavalry Commander*,[5] which described the successful military leader. The strength of this body of work was its focus on military leadership and its value as a unique source of wisdom for future leaders such as Alexander the Great. The weaknesses were its focus on characteristics and skills indirectly linked to subordinates' performance or motivation.

Machiavelli: Narcissist Theory (1530)

Although leadership has been discussed from the earliest times, one of the first formal documents written about leadership and organizational structure was Niccolo Machiavelli's *The Prince* (1527). Machiavelli (**Figure 4-2**) suggested that the qualities of a good leader were to be malevolent and feared. The major theme of Machiavelli's work was "the end justifies the means." Although behavioral discussions are presented in Machiavelli's

work, the overtones of trait and great man approaches are clear throughout his book. At the same time, the lack of consideration of consequences and the inherent immorality of his strategies should be apparent. The strengths of this work are its pragmatic approach, which served as fodder for political science thought; its weaknesses are the cynical nature of the discussions. Also, the focus on leaders' use of fear as a motivational tool is clearly suspect.

From approximately 1840 to 1880, great man theorists Carlyle, Galton, and James studied great men from history who exhibited certain behaviors and possessed certain characteristics. They documented successful outcomes of these "great" leaders, such as prosperity, political standing, or affluence. Based on the study of these characteristics, the theorists suggested that to be a good leader, a person would have to emulate the characteristics of these men. Such characteristics often centered on an individual's race and gender. Not surprisingly, many of the great men identified in the early chronicles were Anglican, male, and Caucasian (such as George Washington, depicted in **Figure 4-3**). In the past, some authors advocating this theory combined great man and trait theories into a common field of study; others did not.

Carlyle, Galton, and James's Great Man Theory (1840–1880)

In the early study of great man theories, an inordinate amount of weight was placed on certain immutable variables such as gender, race, height, and oration. Mutable variables, such as social class, education, and religion, also

FIGURE 4-3 George Washington: A great man theory icon.
© Victorian Traditions/Shutterstock.

factored heavily into the early great man theories. As the study of historical figures evolved, scholars began to examine commonalities among great historical figures and developed a finite list of traits associated with leadership. The primary focus on traits eventually evolved into a distinct discipline called *trait theory*. This niche concept suggested that leaders are defined by various characteristics, such as intelligence, extraversion, experience, education, confidence, and initiative. In early trait-based theories, possession of these traits was said to distinguish a leader from a follower.[6]

LEWIN, LIPPITT, AND WHITE'S TRAIT THEORY (1938–1939)

The emphasis on traits was solidified as an acceptable practice in 1938 and 1939 when Lewin, Lippitt, and White's research emerged as the benchmark studies of their time.[7,8] These scholars studied the leadership styles of two groups of 10- and 11-year-olds in mask-making clubs. During the experiment, they noted that the two groups demonstrated two distinct leadership behavior types: authoritarian or democratic. The study led to the subsequent examination of the effects of these leadership styles on production, group tension, cooperation, and feelings of "we'ness" versus "I'ness." Lewin, Lippitt, and White's early work has become some of the more often-cited and highly quoted leadership and social psychology studies of the modern era. This work aided in the migration to the behavioral phase. Accordingly, much of the modern research in leadership theory traces its roots back to these early studies. Unfortunately, the failure of Lewin, Lippitt, and White's theory to identify any single trait or behavior, or set of traits or behaviors, that could systematically explain leadership success across various situations promoted a paradigm shift in leadership study, such that researchers began to analyze the effects of situations on leader behavior.

STOGDILL'S LEADER TRAITS AND SKILLS

Stogdill performed reviews of trait theory research well after the great man and trait phase of leadership had ended. From his analysis of that literature, he compiled a list of traits and skills of the successful leader. "However, Stogdill makes it clear that recognition of the relevance of leader traits is not a return to the original trait approach."[9] **Table 4–2** lists the traits and skills Stogdill found consistently in the trait literature.

BEHAVIORAL LEADERSHIP PHASE

The behavioral phase of leadership study and thought emerged in the middle of the twentieth century when theorists realized that the traits and great man arguments were unable to totally explain the phenomenon of leadership. In particular, the question of which actions and behaviors facilitated leadership success lay at the heart of leadership research of this period. An important assumption

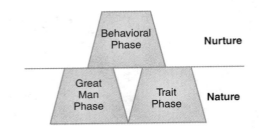

FIGURE 4-4 Leadership thought progression.

of this behavioral phase was the notion that leadership could be learned or nurtured.

Bandura's social learning theory[10] emphasizes the importance of observing and modeling the behaviors, attitudes, and emotional reactions of others. People can learn through observation. According to Bandura, most human behavior is learned observationally through modeling: from observing others, one forms an idea of how new behaviors are performed, and on later occasions this coded information serves as a guide for action. Social learning theory explains human behavior in terms of continuous reciprocal interaction among cognitive, behavioral, and environmental influences. Social learning theory advocates that individuals imitate or copy modeled behavior from observing others, the environment, and the mass media. Earlier theories and models accepted the idea that leadership was inherited, genetic, and based on nature. Although it seems less dramatic now, this shift in thought from only nature being at work to a combination of nature and nurture being recognized as part of leadership marked a huge step in research and leadership practice (**Figure 4–4**). Leadership could be learned! More prescription is assumed in these theories and models compared to the earlier phase of leadership. Even so, the behavioral phase was built upon the great man and trait phase of leadership thought.

MCGREGOR'S THEORY X AND THEORY Y (1950)

At the sunset of the trait phase and the dawning of the behavioral phase of leadership research, the concept of Theory X and Theory Y emerged. In the 1950s, McGregor hypothesized that leaders generally hold one of two contrasting sets of assumptions about people. He additionally suggested that these two dichotomous sets of assumptions would influence leadership behavior. For example, if managers/leaders assumed that their followers were lazy, indifferent, and uncooperative, then they would be treated accordingly (Theory X). Conversely, if they

Table 4-2 Stogdill's Leader Traits and Skills	
Traits	**Skills**
Adaptable to situations	Clever (intelligence)
Alert to social environment	Conceptually skilled (abstract to operational)
Ambitious and achievement oriented	Creative
Assertive	Diplomatic and tactful
Cooperative	Fluent in speaking
Decisive	Knowledgeable about group tasks
Dependable	Organized
Dominant	Persuasive
Energetic	Socially skilled
Persistent	
Self-confident	
Tolerant of stress	
Willing to assume responsibility	

Data from Yukl, G. (1994). *Leadership in organizations* (3rd ed.). Englewood Cliffs, NJ: Prentice Hall, p. 256.

viewed their subordinates as energetic, bright, and friendly, they would treat them quite differently (Theory Y). These leadership attitudes toward followers would soon condition the leader to behave in a certain manner. In essence, this theory exemplifies a self-fulfilling prophecy.

Those leaders who hold Theory X assumptions would be autocratic and very directive, and those who hold Theory Y would be democratic and consensus-building oriented. A Theory X leader would view a subordinate who was late as irresponsible and would require stricter control over his or her behavior, whereas a Theory Y leader might speculate that this same subordinate found his or her job boring and might need additional opportunities to stimulate the person and improve performance (and behavior). The real contribution of McGregor's work was the suggestion that a manager/leader influenced a leadership situation by these two dichotomous assumptions about people.

- *Theory X*: People are lazy, extrinsically motivated, incapable of self-discipline, and want security and no responsibility in their jobs.
- *Theory Y*: People do not inherently dislike work, are intrinsically motivated, exert self-control, and seek responsibility.

Theory Y leaders assess themselves (internal modifiers) in areas such as preferred leadership style, motives and limitations, and past experiences. They also assess external modifiers, such as characteristics of the task, time constraints, organizational norms, structure and climate, past history with group, economic and legal limits, and degree of stability of the organization. Once the assessment is complete, the Theory Y leader chooses a leadership style (which may include an autocratic style depending on the situation). A Theory X leader has one leadership style—autocratic—and has a limited view of the world; that is, he or she does not consider internal and external modifiers. There is also a hint of situational or contingency leadership research in McGregor's theory. The weakness of this model is its dichotomous nature.

STOGDILL AND COONS'S OHIO LEADERSHIP STUDIES (1950)

In 1947, under the direction of Stogdill, the Ohio State Leadership Studies[11] were conducted. The goal of these studies was to determine whether a relationship exists between effective leader behavior and subordinates' satisfaction and performance. Two dimensions of leader behavior that emerged from these studies were consideration and initiating structure. The consideration focused on psychological closeness between the leader and followers, whereas the initiating structure dealt with concern for actively directing subordinates toward job completion or goal attainment.

Surprisingly, some people who rated highly on both constructs of consideration and initiating structure were not always the most effective leaders. Further research along these lines indicated that both of these dimensions were needed for effective leadership. It was found to be more important for a leader to strike a balance in terms of what is appropriate for the situation than to consistently display high consideration and high structure at all times (**Table 4-3**).

The following summaries delineate the conclusions of how effective leader behavior relates to follower satisfaction and performance:[12]

Consideration

1. Employee satisfaction with a leader depends on the degree of consideration displayed by the leader.
2. Leader consideration affects employee satisfaction more when jobs are unpleasant and stressful than when they are pleasant and have low stress.

Table 4-3 Initiating Structure and Consideration

Manager's Consideration		Manager's Initiating Structure	
		High	Low
	High	High performance	Low performance
		Low grievance rate	Low grievance rate
		Low turnover	Low turnover
	Low	High performance	Low performance
		High grievance rate	High grievance rate
		High turnover	High turnover

Data from Gordon, J. (1991). *A diagnostic approach to organizational behavior* (3rd ed.). Englewood Cliffs, NJ: Prentice Hall.

3. A leader who rates high on consideration can exercise more initiating structure without a decline in employee satisfaction.
4. Consideration given in response to good performance will increase the likelihood of future good performance.

Initiating Structure

1. Initiating structure by a leader that adds to role clarity will increase employee satisfaction.
2. Initiating structure by a leader will decrease employee satisfaction when structure is already adequate.
3. Initiating structure by a leader will increase performance when a task is unclear.
4. Initiating structure by a leader will not affect performance when a task is clear.

The major drawback to the Ohio State Studies was the limited consideration given to situational differences that may influence leader effectiveness. From this point, you can see the development of research (future studies) leaning toward situational leadership.

UNIVERSITY OF MICHIGAN LEADERSHIP STUDIES (1950)

Conducted around the same time as the Ohio State Studies, the University of Michigan leadership studies sought answers to many of the same research questions as their Ohio State counterparts. Not surprisingly, the Michigan study results were similar to those conducted at Ohio State, thus supporting some convergent validity assumptions. Like the Ohio State Studies, the Michigan studies suggested that leaders could be grouped into one of two classifications: employee oriented or production oriented. The research suggested that highly productive supervisors spent more time planning departmental work and supervising their employees. The same supervisors spent less time working alongside and performing the same tasks as subordinates. The successful supervisors accorded their subordinates more freedom in specific task performance and tended to be employee oriented. In contrast, the employee-focused leader spent his or her time forging relationships and maintaining harmony in the work environment. Such a leader was less interested in written policies and formalized delegation of responsibilities.[13] In the end, leaders with both an employee orientation and a production orientation were the most successful.

KATZ'S SKILLS THEORY (1955)

In 1955, Robert Katz proposed three categories of skills leaders should have: technical skills, human skills, and conceptual skills. Technical skills relate to knowledge and capabilities the leader needs to be competent and proficient in certain activities. Human skills are nearly self-evident: They are the skills leaders need to relate to and to interact with other people. Such skills would include excellent communication skills, the ability to work with groups and teams, and the social skills to get each member of the team to perform at his or her maximum potential. Conceptual skills are a bit more difficult to define: They are the many skills that allow the leader to understand what needs to be done, how it should be done, and when to do it. Leaders need to be able to conceptualize ideas to be able to see the "big picture."

Katz identified the level of importance that each of these three areas has for each level of management. The most important skills for top-level management are human and conceptual; the most important skills for mid-level management are human; and the most important skills for supervisory management are technical and human. Mid-level managers also need a fair degree of technical and conceptual skills, whereas technical skills are not as important for top-level leadership and conceptual skills are not as important for supervisory management.[14,15] A summary of the skills follows:

- *Technical skills*: Knowledge about approaches, methods, processes, procedures, and techniques for conducting specialized work, and the ability to use those tools and equipment relevant to the activity
- *Interpersonal skills*: Knowledge about human behavior and interpersonal relationships; the ability to understand the feelings, attitudes, and motivations of others; the ability to communicate and deal with conflict effectively; and the ability to build effective relationships
- *Conceptual skills*: Analytical ability, logical thinking, proficiency in concept development and the capability to make sense of complex and ambiguous relationships, creativity in idea generation and problem solving, and the ability to analyze events and perceive trends, anticipate changes, and recognize opportunities and problems (inductive and deductive reasoning)
- *Administrative skills* (added as a fourth category by later researchers): the ability to perform particular types of managerial functions or behaviors (e.g., hiring, planning, organizing, budgeting, delegating, negotiating, coaching, mentoring, and conducting meetings)

ARGYRIS'S PERSONALITY AND ORGANIZATION THEORY (1957)

In 1957, Argyris published a seminal work called *Personality and Organization*. It was one of the first publications to relate organizational learning and success with a leader's ability to achieve synchronization between his or her vision and goals with the subordinate's or employee's perception or tolerance of the vision and goals. To demonstrate this theory, Argyris posited two sets of organizational values he called "theories in use" and "theories in action."

Theories in use suggest that, given a basic scenario dealing with organizational norms, cultures, or values in a stable environment, an individual's outcome can be forecasted and predicted. The theory suggests there is an implicit acknowledgment of what we should do as leaders and managers; that is, the person's predicted answers are conducive to the behavior and effort expected in the organization.

Theories in action are those activities that occur in the organization that are dissimilar from the predicted theories in use. For example, if organizational norms and behaviors call for a multicultural workforce and the personnel hired reflect only one gender or race, there could be a disconnect between organizational goals and organizational outcomes. In this case, the two may not be in synchrony.[16–18]

This early leader theory on managing and leader organizations acknowledges that organizations are part and parcel of the humans who work in them. Sufficient training, branding, and communication of institutional norms, values, and objectives are the leader's responsibilities.

Training and culture shifts can increase the effectiveness of a leader's ability to ensure that the actions and thoughts executed come from the same (desired) agenda.[19] For example, multicultural sensitivity training can provide an opportunity for personnel in organizations to become more tolerant of different races and demographic characteristics. Extreme methods of applying this theory may include organizational reengineering, where personnel in the organization who are incapable of unlearning irrelevant predispositions and do not support the organization are moved to different parts of the organization or "right-sized" out of a job.

BLAKE AND MOUTON'S MANAGERIAL GRID (1964)

In 1964, Blake and Mouton offered what was then a very unique approach to leadership. Their managerial grid is a behavioral leadership model based on four constructs: concern for production, concern for people, motivation, and leadership style. Motivation can be negative (motivate by fear) or positive (motivate through desire and encouragement). Motivation is rarely shown (perhaps due to the difficulty in determining motivation type and amount).

Essentially, Blake and Mouton identified five different managerial styles based on the priority the individual leader assigns to product versus people: Country Club, Team Leader, Impoverished, Produce or Perish, and Middle of the Road. The first two styles place far more importance on people than on product, the second two emphasize product, and the last one rides the fence, emphasizing neither product/production nor the person or people/subordinates. **Figure 4-5** depicts the managerial grid.

In the Mouton–Blake managerial grid, the least effective leadership style is the Impoverished style, because such a person does not really care about either product or people. The most effective is Team Leader, because such an individual places a high priority on both the product and the people and will look for win–win solutions that will satisfy the needs of all. This leader is not naive; he or she does realize that in some situations it is not possible to reach a solution that will satisfy everyone. Another key facet of the Mouton–Blake managerial grid is that each leadership approach is understood to be important and useful given certain circumstances and in certain situations. There are clear connections between Blake and Mouton's work

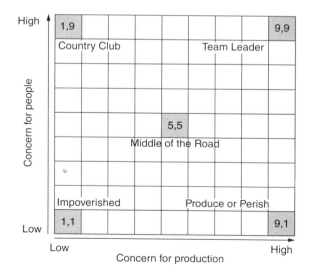

FIGURE 4-5 Blake and Mouton's managerial grid.

Data from Blake, R., & Moulton, J. (1964). *The managerial grid: The key to leadership excellence.* Houston: Gulf Publishing Company.

on the managerial grid and Hersey and Blanchard's 1977 situational leadership model. Although the managerial grid is taught in most graduate management and leadership programs, there is no research validating its efficacy.[20,21]

SITUATIONAL OR CONTINGENCY LEADERSHIP PHASE

We turn now to more recent research in leadership theory. Situational leadership theories and models—also called contingency models, because the leader model should change contingent (based) on the situation at hand—are more applicable to health organizations today because the healthcare environment is dynamic and stakeholder relationships are multifaceted and complex. Contingency or situational theories and models assert that no single way of leading works well in all situations. Instead, leaders need the ability to change styles and select those skills that best deal with the organizational situation at hand. Effective leaders diagnose the situation, identify an appropriate leadership style, and then determine whether its implementation is possible. At least four dimensions must be evaluated when assessing situational or contingent leadership research:

- *Subordinate*: Expertise, experience, resources, motivation, task load, and knowledge of the job
- *Supervisor/leader/manager*: Values, attitudes, level of influence, and level of authority
- *Task characteristics*: Complexity, time, risk, autonomy, ambiguity, uncertainty, and workload
- *Organizational culture*: Coupling, communication environment, ambiguity and uncertainty tolerance, balance of work, social and personal life, planning emphasis, decision-making alignment, employee enhancement, and level of knowledge management and learning orientation

The other significant element in situational leadership is the emergence of organizational culture within the situational context. Simply stated, culture is a group's unique view of the world. Every organization—whether a family or a health system conglomerate—has an overriding organizational culture and various sets of subcultures. Leaders must attend to cultural issues to be successful.

Some researchers have suggested that leadership strategies in any setting have strong underlying similarities but must change as the setting changes over time. Even if the health organization remains essentially the same, change in the environment, such as the recent changes in healthcare delivery, may require leaders

to change their strategy/style to be effective. Culture comes into the discussion of leadership as an influence on leadership style selection; organizational culture has grown in importance over the past decade in that leaders can actually develop culture—not merely assess and adapt to it. This realization may be leading into another phase of leadership thought; this idea is discussed briefly in the next section of this chapter.

To provide a simple example of situational leadership in action, suppose that subordinates have the expertise and competence needed to perform an organizational task. In such a case, an employee-oriented leadership style will be more effective than a task-oriented leadership style. In contrast, if leader and follower both have the same attitudes, then followers may be more willing to accept a task- or production-oriented leadership style.

This phase of leadership—the phase currently in vogue—immerses behaviors into the context of the leadership situation and environment. Situational assessment skills are critical to this body of knowledge on leadership. Thus leaders can be "made" through nature, can be nurtured, and now must consider situational factors and adapt to those situations to be successful. Leaders must also adapt! This phase has more potential for prescription and not just description of theories and models. As illustrated in **Figure 4-6**, leadership models are a progression, wherein later approaches build on the knowledge of the past. A number of different models of leadership fit under the general category of contingency. Given that this phase constitutes the most widely accepted set of theories and models today, several approaches falling under this rubric are highlighted in this section.

EXCHANGE THEORY

Exchange theory focuses on a vertical dyad linkage approach that comprises the connection between the leader and those being led. This approach emphasizes the interaction of the leader with the subordinate group. The leader exchanges

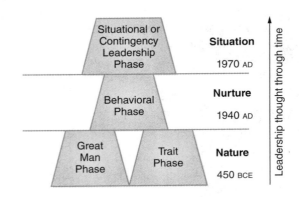

FIGURE 4-6 Leadership thought progression revisited.

resources, such as increased rewards, increased job latitude, influence on decision making, and open communication, for members' commitment to higher involvement in organizational functioning. This line of research embraces social exchange theory, which suggests that leaders must offer something in exchange (e.g., bonus, increased status) for improved or additional performance by subordinates. It is the precursor of modern transactional leadership theory.

According to exchange theory, the leader categorizes followers into two groups: (1) the cadre or in-group and (2) the hired hands or out-group. With the in-group, the leader allows greater latitude, which in turn yields higher performance ratings, lower propensity to quit, greater supervisory relationships, and greater job satisfaction. The out-group receives less latitude and, therefore, demonstrates poorer performance outcomes.

This approach has been criticized because it relies on narrow information and situations, does not study the organizational outcomes associated with this exchange relationship, and utilizes exchanges in diverse and inconsistent ways.[22] The important point is that social exchange is a viable way of regarding leadership and is directly linked to transactional leadership theory.

Fiedler's Contingency Model (1946)

In the mid-1960s, Fiedler introduced a contingency model of leadership.[23] In this model, Fiedler proposed that the performance of any group depends on the leader's style in terms of motivation and relationship to the subordinates and the favorability of the situation. De Jonge[24] explains that Fiedler was the first to discuss this approach, and it is Fiedler's approach that has been researched most often. Fiedler identified three variables related to the context: group atmosphere, task structure, and leader's power position. For this researcher, the performance of any group depended on two other factors, which became known as "leadership style" and "situational favorableness"; these two factors determine how effective the leader will be.[25] The term *leadership style* is a leader's manner of behaving and acting in a work environment, is strongly dependent upon his or her personality, and is relatively stable.

Fiedler identified three situational factors that are present in any situation: (1) leader–member relations; (2) task structure; and (3) position power of the leader. A leader using a task-oriented style (notice the progression from the Ohio State and University of Michigan studies) will most likely be successful when subordinates have enough of the following attributes:

- *Leader–member relations*: The amount the group trusts and respects the leader and is willing to follow his or her directions

- *Task structure*: The amount in which the task is clearly specified and defined or structured
- *Position power*: The leader's amount of official power— that is, the ability to influence others due to the leader's position in the organization (also known as "legitimate power" in French and Raven's power taxonomy)

The antithetic leader style is indicated when a lack of enough leader–member relations, task structure, and position power would suggest the leader use a relationship-oriented style. Fiedler's theory defines leadership effectiveness in terms of work group performance. Group performance is contingent upon the situational constructs and match between (1) a person's leadership style and (2) the "favorableness" of the leadership situation where the following relationship holds:

Group performance = Leadership style + Situational favorableness

According to Yukl, to determine a person's leadership style, Fiedler developed a measure called the least preferred coworker (LPC) scale.[26] This instrument describes the one person with whom the leader worked least well among all the workers he or she has supervised. Such an evaluation classifies people into three types:

- Those who are relationship oriented—who see good interpersonal relationships as a requirement for task accomplishment and find satisfaction from these close relations
- Those who are task oriented—who focus on task completion and worry about interpersonal relationships afterward
- The middle-LPC people—who are flexible and not overly constrained with either relationship or task completion

Situational favorableness refers to the extent a particular situation enables a leader to influence a group of subordinates. Three factors are used to measure this aspect of the model:

- *Leader–member relations*: The quality of the relationship between the leader and followers (the most important construct because it directly contributes to the influence the leader will have over subordinates)
- *Task structure*: Step-by-step clarity of a task (the higher the degree of task structure, the more influence the leader will have)
- *Position power*: The ability for the leader to reward and punish subordinates by hiring, firing, and promoting them

Several important issues exist regarding Fiedler's model of leadership. First, evidence suggests that other situational variables, such as training and experience, contribute to leader effectiveness. Second, there is some doubt regarding whether the LPC scale is a true measure of leadership style; critics contend its interpretation is speculative and inadequately supported.[27] Some researchers argue that the reliability of the measurement of leadership style using the LPC is low and the range and appropriateness of the three situational components are narrow.

ERIKSON'S PSYCHOANALYTIC THEORY (1964)

Psychoanalytic theory was a derivative of the early Freudian studies of personality and development. The factors that were originally thought by Freud to affect only an individual's relationship with the environment and close family members have now been extended to consider their influence on teams and organizations. Psychoanalytic theory has become an interesting tool, which has been used over the past 50 years to study the various influences on followership, leadership, and group and organizational dynamics in both large organizations and smaller groups built on interpersonal relationships.[28–30]

In 1964, Erikson posited psychoanalytic theory as a study of attachment and childhood development.[31] Over time, however, psychoanalytic theory became recognized as an opportunity to research "intrigue" in the leadership literature. For example, Erikson's initial theory posited that a variety of unconscious factors stimulate and motivate behavior. For some individuals, followership may be stimulated by a need of a subordinate to replace a father figure with a person of authority in the workplace. Consequently, a father's mentoring and emotional attachment for children within the family dynamic may extend to the need to display those tendencies by subordinates in the workplace. All this occurs through an unconscious need to follow or lead others.[32]

In many cases, a charismatic leader may be viewed as a father figure by followers in the organization.[33,34] The charismatic leader may display those qualities that are desired or sought after by subordinates in the workplace who are seeking to have as their guide a leader who will exhibit patriarchal behaviors. In a pure tribal sense, a natural pecking order (informal chain of command) is established that may (or may not) establish legitimate lines of authority in the workplace.

Although natural predispositions to follow and obey may present themselves in the workplace, the same might be said of the opposite tendencies—in other words, the inclination to rebel and disobey.[35] Predispositions in the environment toward certain traits may evoke (unconsciously or otherwise) certain outcomes, leading to negative results.[36,37] For example, if a new leader in an organization has a more rigid philosophy of leadership that emphasizes adherence to an 8 AM to 5 PM workday, as opposed to the more flexible self-directed and autonomous philosophy espoused by that leader's predecessor, the employees may present as "organizational disrupters" and noncompliant. In this case, the employees may not be rebelling against the new leader as much as demonstrating their predisposed feeling to rebel against the rigid schedule and the perception of authoritative leadership. The resistance may derive from the employee's unconscious being, related to a sense of negative control and helplessness directorship experienced in adolescence.

A leader's awareness of his or her predisposition to lead or follow is crucial in any self-diagnosis and application. Those who are predisposed to be followers may be uncomfortable in filling the leader role and may perform better with fewer leaders over them to provide praise and structure. Similarly, those predisposed to lead and mentor others in a personal and predisposed manner may be uncomfortable in environments characterized by stricter organizational norms and reporting mechanisms.

HOUSE'S PATH–GOAL THEORY (1971)

Path–goal theory, which was developed by Robert House in 1971, suggests that a leader can affect subordinates' performance, satisfaction, and motivation by (1) offering rewards for achieving performance goals, (2) clarifying paths toward these goals, and (3) removing obstacles to performance.[38] This theory adds the elements of clarity (step-by-step instructions, for example) and explicit effort by the leader to remove barriers blocking goal achievement for the subordinate to the leadership discussion. The ability and effects of the leader's efforts are influenced and moderated by the subordinate's personality (e.g., the subordinate's locus of control [as described by Rotter, either internalizer or externalizer], self-perceived ability, and self-efficacy) and characteristics of the environment (e.g., the amount of task structure, organizational coupling, and team orientation).

Victor Vroom was very active in developing theories that fall within this realm, including expectancy theory (a motivational approach). Vroom's 1964 theory is significantly connected to House's path–goal theory of leadership and the situational leadership theory introduced by Hersey and Blanchard. The constructs of leadership styles in the path–goal theory have similarity to those found in

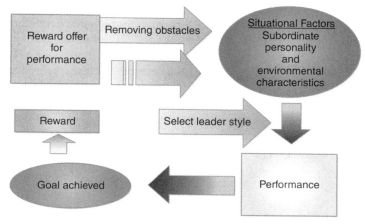

Leadership Styles
Directive: leader gives specific guidance to subordinates.
Supportive: leader is friendly and shows concern for subordinates.
Participative: leader consults with and considers recommendations by subordinates.
Achievement oriented: leader sets high goals and expects subordinates to achieve them.

FIGURE 4-7 Path–goal theory.

situational leadership theory. The path–goal theory began with just two options for a leader's behavior: supportive or directive. This model was then subsequently expanded to incorporate McClelland's achievement orientation and participation. According to House, the leader can influence employee performance by "offering rewards for achieving performance goals; clarifying paths towards goals, removing obstacles to performance."[39]

Path–goal theory now encompasses four leadership behavior options: directive, supportive, achievement oriented, and participative (**Figure 4–7**). Each approach has its time and place. When a task is not structured, when it is complex, or when employees lack the skills to adequately perform the task, the leader needs to use the directive approach. When the task is boring and routine, the leader needs to be supportive. When a task is unstructured but could be challenging for the worker, the leader might be more achievement oriented, offering encouragement to build employee confidence. When the task is totally unstructured, the leader might be more effective by using a participative approach.

VROOM, YETTON, AND JAGO'S NORMATIVE DECISION-MAKING MODEL (1973)

Vroom, Yetton, and Jago's normative decision-making model was intended to help leaders make more effective decisions while at the same time garnering support for those decisions

from their subordinates. These researchers identified five styles of decision making, ranging from very autocratic to consultative. Because it incorporates the idea that leaders make decisions differently based on different situations, their model falls under the very broad umbrella of contingency models. Vroom, Yetton, and Jago suggested that four major categories of decision-making styles exist, with two subcategories appearing under three of the major categories:[40]

Autocratic Type 1: The leader uses information that is easily available and makes the decision alone.
Autocratic Type 2: The leader collects information from followers, makes the decision alone, and then informs others.
Consultative Type 1: The leaders share the problem individually with those persons whom he or she considers to be relevant, asks for ideas and suggestions, and then makes the decision.
Consultative Type 2: The leader shares problems with relevant others as a group, asks for ideas and suggestions, and then makes the decision alone.
Group-Based Type 1: The leader brings one other person into the decision-making process for the purposes of sharing information and making the decision.
Group-Based Type 2: The group makes the decision with the leader, with consensus being the priority.[41,42]
Delegative: The leader gives the responsibility and authority to make the decision to someone else.

The strengths of this model include (1) its incorporation of the reality that decisions are made in situational context, (2) the broad range of decision-making styles, and (3) its inclusion of leader and group dynamics in the decision-making process. Weaknesses include (1) the lack of understanding of decision load, technology, and leader and subordinate attention and (2) the lack of acknowledgment of irrational decision making.

GRAEN'S LEADER–MEMBER EXCHANGE AND VERTICAL DYAD LINKAGE THEORIES (1975)

The leader–member exchange theory (LMX) was proposed in 1975 by Graen and Cashman. This model suggests that leaders accomplish work through various personal relationships with different members of the subordinate group. Leaders give tasks that are more positive to members whom they feel support them. LMX suggests behavior is not consistent across subordinates. As a result, leaders classify subordinates into two groups: an in-group and an out-group (similar to the classifications used in Fiedler's contingency theory). Subsequently, the leader adapts his or her behavior to account for individual subordinate needs for direction, contact, and supervision. This creates a unique relationship with every different member of the group, called a "dyad." Graen and Cashman later coined the term *vertical dyad linkage* (VDL) to describe the situation in which leader–group interactions, judgments, and opinions are formed by the leader and the members of each dyad. With this theoretical model of leader behavior, the emphasis is on the interaction of the leader with the supervised group. For example, the leader exchanges resources, such as increased job latitude, influence on decision making, and open communication, for members' commitment to higher involvement in organizational functioning.

This line of research embraces the social exchange theory, which suggests that leaders must offer an exchange (e.g., bonus, increased status) if they hope to obtain improved or additional performance by subordinates. The LMX approach has been criticized because it does not study the organizational outcomes associated with the exchange relationship and because it links exchanges in diverse and inconsistent ways. Nevertheless, the obvious reality is that many leaders do treat employees differently based on personal relationships, suggesting that LMX theory merits additional attention.

LMX theory emphasizes the "two-way relationship between supervisors and subordinates [and] aims to maximize organization success by establishing positive interactions between the two."[43] Research has shown that there is a significant relationship between an employee's performance and commitment and the quality of the relationship between leader and follower. LMX is said to increase employee commitment and loyalty to the company, and the research consistently concludes that "committed employees are associated with better organizational performance, have a lower turnover rate, and have lower absenteeism."[44]

Graen and colleagues originally called this relationship a vertical dyad linkage, only later referring to it as the leader–member exchange theory. Miner also points out that Graen and colleagues' theory has commonalities with Vroom's normative decision-making model.[45] Graen and colleagues are basically saying that the relationship between manager and subordinate must be positive and of high quality. The quality of this linkage will have a direct impact on performance and job satisfaction.

Two types of dyadic relationships are of great importance in LMX, which Graen referred to as "relationships with informal assistants and ordinary members ... leadership and supervisory relationships and in-group and out-group relationships or high- and low-quality relationships."[46] Each is a dyad. The most important dyadic relationship remains that between the manager and the subordinate. As leaders form higher quality relationships with employees, those employees begin to feel as though they are part of the in-group. However, the in-group will always have more responsibilities and more influence in decision making as well as greater job satisfaction compared to the out-group. A low-quality relationship between the leader and an employee leads to a feeling of being in the out-group.[47] Leaders use a more participative approach with in-group employees and a more directive style with out-group employees.

HERSEY AND BLANCHARD'S SITUATIONAL LEADERSHIP THEORY (1977)

In the late 1970s, Hersey and Blanchard discussed situational leadership.[48] They initially called their model the life-cycle theory of leadership but later renamed it *situational leadership theory* (SLT). Initially, Hersey and Blanchard identified four possible styles of leadership: telling, selling, participating, and delegating. Notice how similar these styles are to those identified by other theorists. Although SLT also falls under the broad umbrella of contingency theory, it is different from the other theories found within this realm.[49]

In Hersey and Blanchard's model, the leader must determine what these researchers refer to as the "maturity of the follower." This determination dictates the degree of supervision that employees need. Employees with low maturity are those with low motivation or those with few or no skills in the task activities. Telling or directing is the leadership style most appropriate with such workers. Low to moderately mature employees need a combination of telling and personal attention. Moderate to highly mature employees require attention as well as sharing in decision making, and highly mature employees need freedom to make their own decisions.[50] This is really a very sensible approach: The less motivated and/or less skilled employees require more direction (more telling). As employees become more mature, more motivated, and more highly skilled, they need little or no direction or even encouragement.

From 1969 through 1977, Hersey and Blanchard developed SLT,[51] which they formally defined as a leadership style driven by the situation at hand. This model specifies the readiness of followers, defined as the ability and willingness to accomplish a specific task, as the major contingency that influences appropriate leadership style. SLT is based on the relationships among three components:

- Directive behavior (task behavior) the leader provides followers
- The amount of supportive behavior (relational behavior) a leader provides[52]
- The development level (maturity) of the follower, which is derived from the amount of competence and commitment demonstrated while performing a specific task

In the last component, *competence* is the degree of knowledge or skills gained from education, training, or experience needed to do the task, and *commitment* is defined as the combination of confidence and motivation displayed by the follower in reference to doing the task. A follower can be competent but not committed to doing a task; consequently, he or she may need support to regain the devotion to accomplish the task.

SLT also suggests that the individual leadership style demonstrated should match the maturity of the subordinates who are being led.[53] Thus, according to this theory, there is no one best style of leadership. Instead, people in leadership and management positions become more effective when they select a leadership style that is appropriate to the development level of the individual or group they want to influence. Maturity is assessed in relation to a specific task and the psychological maturity and job experience of the follower. The leader may then exercise various levels of delegating, participating, selling, and telling to coax employees to complete their assigned tasks and achieve the desired goals. Application of the correct leadership style based on the developmental level of the follower or group is the key ingredient in the SLT model; however, sometimes situational variables may affect the leadership style—for example, time constraints, supervisory demands, and job demands. Each style varies the leadership approach based on the aforementioned situational factors. The most recently described leadership approaches include additional dimensions of leadership, such as whether the leader utilizes a transactional or transformational style.

As summarized in **Figure 4-8**, SLT posits that leaders must use different styles depending on the situation: telling and directing (S1); selling and coaching (S2); participating and supporting (S3), or delegating (S4). Subordinate competence and commitment moderate the leader's style.

Although contingency and normative decision-making approaches are types of situational theories, Hersey and Blanchard's approach is more centric, because it depends on the number of tasks and people that the leader adopts in reference to the level of subordinates' commitment and competence. In Figure 4-8, notice how subordinate development level D1 relates to S1 (directing) leader behavior, D2 relates to S2 (coaching) leader behavior, and so on. The greater the subordinates' level of commitment and competence, the less the leader has to provide task-based and relation-based leadership. SLT holds that successful

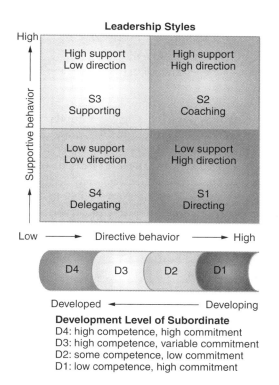

FIGURE 4-8 Situational leadership.

leadership is achieved by selecting the correct leadership style based on the readiness of the followers.

In critiquing the SLT, some researchers have questioned its conceptual clarity, validity, robustness, and utility, as well as the instruments used to measure leadership style. Of course, others have supported the utility of the model.

HOUSE'S CHARISMATIC LEADERSHIP MODEL (1977)

Based on the earlier suggestion of Max Weber, who posited the dimension of charismatic leadership that he called *charismatic domination* in the early 1920s, House revisited the construct of charisma. Building on the earlier theories, he proposed a theory in 1977 specifically called charismatic leadership.[54] Recent studies have extended this theoretical base to examine the degree of an employee's or subordinate's identification with a team or work group as a function of charismatic leadership.[55]

Charismatic leadership inspires followership through intangibles in personality that cannot be measured directly in an individual. Making the dynamic even more complex, charisma may be identified in a leader by subordinates but cannot be directly operationalized as any one set of traits or skill sets. Similar to the adage "Beauty is in the eye of the beholder," charisma is in the eye of the beholder; however, levels of acceptance and acknowledgment cannot be uniformly communicated by the members of the organization. Charisma, like the definition of any construct itself, cannot be measured directly by any tangible property in a universal way.

Charismatic leaders inspire trust, faith, and confidence in nonmechanical ways. They have a natural predisposition to be self-assured and comfortable in their own skin. They rarely second-guess themselves and are generally extroverts. Charismatic leaders are always "turned on" in one dimension or another—that is, they may be the individual at a social gathering everyone wants to talk to, or they may be the voice of direction and order in an otherwise panicked and disordered atmosphere.

It is very difficult for those without natural charisma to mimic those who possess this natural ability on a long-term basis. Environmental change and culture shifts will make the mechanical charismatic leader unable to function for long periods of time in work or social situations; fatigue and apathy will set in. Being charismatic cannot be acted.

For those leaders with natural charismatic qualities, opportunities exist to leverage these inherent capabilities in the organization. Consider a leader with a natural predisposition to inspire and befriend who can combine this ability with learned executive skills and competencies

in organizational dynamics; this blending can lead to success for the adept leader. For example, a CEO negotiating policy change in a legal market may know little about the financial structure of the merger's initial public offering valuation; however, the CEO may excel in maintaining a positive dialogue with stakeholders that will maintain calm during the times of unfamiliarity that allow the change to occur.[56–58]

Despite the many positives associated with charismatic leadership, there are also disadvantages for use of this leadership style. Charismatic leaders may be prone to avoiding professional discourse and could be challenged on ideas. They may surround themselves with "yes men" during long stints of leadership that result in organizational institutionalism and stagnation. In the worst-case scenario, charismatic leaders may be prone to narcissism and feel superior to people who are not within their immediate circle of influence.[59,60]

BURNS'S TRANSFORMATIONAL LEADERSHIP MODEL (1978)

Two of the more recent theories of leadership that are frequently discussed are transactional and transformational leadership theories. Transactional leadership was first described by Max Weber in 1947 and was revisited in 1981 by Benjamin Bass, who hypothesized that transactional leaders believe workers are motivated by rewards. That is similar to McGregor's Theory X description of one type of subordinate. The transformational leadership model is a situation-influenced theory that suggests the situation influences the leader to adapt a style most fitting to the specific circumstances at hand. This style may be transactional or transformational, or some combination of the two. In practice, a combination of these approaches is the most practical leadership strategy to undertake in health organizations. The knowledge, skills, and abilities of a health leader to use transformational and transactional leadership are critical for success in today's environment.

The descriptors applied to transactional leadership are "working to achieve specific goals, rewarding employees, [responding] to employees and [their] self-interests."[61] Because a trade—an exchange of work and effort for rewards—occurs, transactional leadership is perceived as an economic model of leadership.[62] A potential negative outcome with this model is that employees may not be motivated to accomplish certain tasks if there is no reward attached to performance and positive outcomes.

Around 1978, James MacGregor Burns first distinguished between transactional and transformational leadership styles. Burns based his theories on other sources, such as Maslow's hierarchy of needs and Kohlberg's theories of moral development.[63] Burns believed the transactional leader lived in keeping with certain values, such as fairness, responsibility, and integrity. Transformational leadership is sometimes viewed as the polar opposite of transactional leadership, though in reality that perception is inaccurate. Transformational leaders are charismatic; they have vision, empathy, self-assurance, commitment, and the ability to assure others of their own competence; and they are willing to take risks.[64,65] "Transformational leadership refers to the process of building commitment to the organization's objectives and empowering followers to accomplish these objectives."[66]

Bass describes Burns's expectation of transactional leadership as follows:

> Transactional leadership involves values ... relevant to the exchange process such as honesty, fairness, responsibility, and reciprocity ... bureaucratic organizations enforce the use of legitimate power and respect for rules and tradition rather than influence based on inspiration. For Burns, leadership is a process, not a set of discrete acts. Burns (1978) described leadership as "a stream of evolving interrelationships in which leaders are continuously evoking motivational responses from followers and modifying their behavior as they meet responsiveness or resistance, in a ceaseless process of flow and counter-flow."

Bass summarized Burns's take on transformational leadership thusly:

> At the macro-level of analysis, transformational leadership involves shaping, expressing, and mediating conflict among groups of people in addition to motivating individuals.[67]

Building on Burns's work, Bernard Bass argued that rather than the two leadership styles being polar opposites, there was a linear progression from transactional to transformational leadership. Bass also believed that transformational leadership should be measured in terms of how it affects employees, such as how much they trust and respect the leader. According to Bass, transformational leadership must be grounded in moral foundations that include inspirational motivation, individualized consideration, intellectual stimulation, and idealized influence. These concepts position the transformational leader in a place similar to that identified in servant–leader models, such as the model proposed by Greenleaf.[68]

From this discourse, Bass (1985) proposed a theory of transformational leadership that is measured in terms of the leader's influence on subordinates or followers. Subordinates or followers "connect" to the transformational leader through trust, admiration, a sense of loyalty, and respect for the leader.

Transformational leaders, in turn, create an environment that propels subordinates and followers to greater performance and greater deeds[69] than previously expected, in three ways: (1) by making followers aware of the importance of their performance and task outcomes; (2) by replacing their own self-interest with the good of the group, team, and organization; and (3) by energizing and motivating followers' higher order needs.[70] In more recent research, transformational leadership has been identified as the most important predictor of individual success and active involvement in healthcare delivery teams (multidisciplinary teams).[71] In addition, based on modern investigations of transformational leadership as it influences follower-group behavior in China, leaders assume that both a group and an individual can receive knowledge and information in the same manner; however, that is not the case. Providing knowledge to others is a voluntary act, and the leader must have strong communication and motivational skills to pass this information on to a group or individual.[72]

An individual's behavior toward a leader includes respect, personal feelings, and possibly individual differences with the leader. It is important for a leader to develop a relationship with the individual that relates to the development of sharing knowledge and information. A group must be looked upon as a team—not as a competition among group members. A group must function together in cooperation, affiliation, and equality in receiving knowledge and information.[73]

In summary, transformational leadership focuses on four constructs. Bass's original theory included three behaviors of transformational leaders; the fourth was added later:

- *Charisma*: The leader influences followers by arousing strong emotions and identification with the leader.
- *Intellectual stimulation*: The leader increases follower awareness of problems and influences followers to view problems from a new perspective.
- *Individualized consideration*: The leader provides support, encouragement, and developmental experiences for followers.
- *Inspirational motivation*: The leader communicates an appealing vision using symbols to focus subordinate effort and to model appropriate behavior (role modeling; Bandura's social learning theory).[75,75]

In support of this theory, Fairholm, in an assessment of empowering leadership techniques that closely resemble transformational leadership, suggests that leaders fulfill the following responsibilities:

- Utilize goal setting.
- Delegate to followers.
- Encourage participation.
- Encourage self-reliance.

Table 4-4 Transformational Leadership Variables: Possible Predictors

Construct	Charisma	Inspiration	Motivation	Intellectual Stimulation	Individualized Consideration
Variables	Ascendancy	Confidence	Ascendancy	Ascendancy	Ascendancy
	Sociability	Personal adjustment	Sociability	Internal locus of control	Sociability
	Less thinking than feeling	Pragmatism	Sensing		Extroversion
	Internal locus of control	Nurturance	Internal locus of control		Feeling
	Self-acceptance	Femininity			Self-acceptance
		Less aggression			

Data from Bass, B. (1998). *Transformational leadership: Industrial, military, and educational impact.* Mahwah, NJ: Lawrence Erlbaum Associates.

- Challenge followers.
- Focus on followers.
- Specify followers' roles.[76]

Transformational leadership can be measured by an instrument called the Multifactor Leadership Questionnaire (MLQ). Using this tool, global attributes, specific traits, and combinations of assessments have been applied to validate forecasts of retrospective and concurrent transformational leadership through measurement.[77] Several different approaches have been used to confirm the reliability and validity of MLQ assessments. According to Bass, promising predictors (variables categorized by construct) include those listed in **Table 4-4**.

Under situational or contingency theory, transformational leadership and transactional leadership are viewed as encompassing a range of viable styles from which a leader can select depending on the situation. Like Burns, Bass considers transactional leadership to entail an exchange of rewards for compliance. Transactional behaviors include the following:

- *Contingent reward*: Clarification of work required to obtain rewards
- *Active management by exception*: Monitoring subordinates and corrective action to ensure the work is effectively accomplished
- *Passive management by exception*: Using contingent punishments and other corrective action in response to obvious deviations from acceptable performance standards[78,79]

Bass regards theories such as leader–member exchange theory and path–goal theory as descriptions of transactional leadership. He views transformational and transactional leadership as distinct but not mutually exclusive processes; the same leader may use both types of leadership at different times in different situations.[80]

The strengths of transformational leadership are its pragmatic approach, intuitiveness, flexibility, attention to individual and groups of subordinates, and motivation orientation. Its weaknesses hinge on validation and testing: Much of the research in this area has been descriptive and qualitative; few quantitative data exist. Qualitative research focuses on theory building, using such methods as biographies, observation activities, informal interviews, and the like. In contrast, quantitative research is a theory testing methodology that tries to prove causality: This action causes that specific outcome to happen. This approach is normally associated with statistical applications such as the general linear model (*t*-tests, analysis of variance [ANOVA], analysis of covariance [ANCOVA], regression) or relationships (such as correlations).

In the qualitative research that has been done on transformational leadership, this model shows real promise. For example, Bennis and Nanus conducted a multiyear study of transformational, dynamic, innovative leaders that included 65 top-level corporate leaders and 30 leaders of public-sector organizations. They collected data through unstructured interviews (3–4 hours each) and supplemented interviews with observation. Several themes were associated with successful transformational leaders:

- *Ability to meet external expectations to develop an effective vision* that is right for the times, right for the organization, and right for the people who are in the organization
- *Ability to develop a clear and appealing vision* to focus collective organizational energy toward a consistent set of strategies, goals, and objectives

- *Ability to inspire* others by leveraging the basic human need to feel and be important and valuable
- *Ability to facilitate decision making, take initiative, and delegate decision making* to extend authority and discretion to all levels appropriately (empowerment)
- *Ability to develop commitment and trust across all stakeholders* by communicating vision and embedding it in the culture of the organization
- *Ability to develop systems of internal and external environmental scanning, monitoring, analysis, and forecasting*
- *Ability to be a great facilitator of organizational learning and developer of knowledge management systems*, using experimentation to encourage innovation and to test new products, services, and procedures[81]

In the healthcare arena, transformational leadership is a critical health leader style associated with success. "Transformational leaders motivate others to do more than they originally intended and often even more than they thought possible."[82]

In summary, transformational leaders tend to have the following characteristics:

- Idealized
  - Followers seek to identify with and emulate their leader.
  - The leader puts the needs of others over his or her own needs.
  - The leader uses power only when needed.
- Inspiring
  - Produce commitment to goals.
  - Arouse team spirit.
- Intellectually stimulating
  - Expands the use of the followers' abilities.
  - Encourages creativity.
  - Tries new approaches to problems.
  - Followers' ideas are not criticized.
- Individually considerate
  - Supporting, mentoring, and coaching.
  - New learning opportunities are created in a supportive environment.
  - "Management by walking around."
  - Delegation of tasks.[83]

Transactional leaders tend to have the following characteristics:

- Contingently rewarding
  - Followers rewarded for satisfactory completion of assignments
- Active in managing by exception
  - Monitors standards, mistakes, and errors
  - Takes corrective action

- Nontransactional passive leaders
  - Laissez–faire attitude
  - Avoidance or absence of leadership[84]

Transformational leaders may choose to use a transactional leadership style based on the situation; it is not a "this or that" decision. In reality, *successful health leaders use both transformational and transactional leadership styles*, many times simultaneously. However, the laissez-faire and avoidance or absent style is not recommended to be used often. It is important to remember "the performance of the organization is the ultimate measure of a leader."[85]

BENNIS'S COMPETENCY-BASED LEADERSHIP (1985–1993)

Building on earlier work by Burns, Bennis proposed his competency-based model of leadership.[86,87] The competency-based model has been widely embraced by professional organizations and executives alike. This model suggests that the skills and tools necessary to lead organizations must be learned—whether through incremental on-the-job training (OJT), formal education, or years of professional development. Bennis interviewed some 90 executives from various sectors and identified four areas of competency:

- Creating attention through vision
- Creating meaning through communication
- Becoming a person of trust
- Self-development

The competency-based model suggests strongly that leaders are made and not simply born (the antithesis of the great man leadership theory). That is, in any complex and dynamic organization, there are certain educational requirements that require years of exposure and specific training to achieve parity with peers in similar positions. Becoming a chief of a department of surgery is one example—one cannot successfully hold such a position without years of medical education and a successful practice of medicine.

THE BOUNDARYLESS LEADER (1994)

In 1994, Ronald Ashkenas proposed a model of multifaceted/ nonlinear leadership that was achieved by creating an organization that was "boundaryless." In this philosophy, the informal structures in the organization are as important as the formal ones. Additionally, lines of responsibility are overlapping and not mutually exclusive. The idea was that leaders needed to influence and leverage performance by driving change at the employee level and that letting anyone in the organization have the ability to take ownership for that change was important. In Ashkenas's article "Beyond the Fads: How Leaders Drive Change with Results," he laid out the steps that he believed a leader should take to structure successful leadership change within an organization. The theory suggests that if employers want improved performance from their employees they need to challenge them to create and adhere to short-term goals, develop quick fixes to problems themselves as they arise, and take ownership and responsibility for actions during and after processes. The theory also suggests that innovation and metrics, not opinion and preference, drive change. The theory relies heavily on maintaining best practices, as well as reflecting and expanding on current policy, practices, and procedures when necessary. Finally, this theory is niche and professionally focused; that is, the theory suggests that horizontal organizations may be best able to perform in this environment.[88,89]

KOUZES AND POSNER'S LEADERSHIP FRAMEWORK (1995)

In 1995, Kouzes and Posner[90] developed a twist on earlier leadership frameworks; they suggested that leadership is successful only if a shared vision can be communicated to followers that changes their values, thereby resulting in goal-directed behavior and positive work-related outcomes.[91] To achieve this vision, the leader must be aware of the intangibles that exist in the ideals that motivate those employees around them. According to Covey (as cited by Kouzes & Posner, 1995):[92]

> Leaders "ignite" subordinates' passions and serve as a compass by which to guide followers. They define leadership as "the art of mobilizing others to want to struggle for shared aspirations." The emphasis lies in the follower's desire to contribute and the leader's ability to motivate others to action. Leaders respond to customers, create vision, energize employees, and thrive in fast-paced "chaotic" environments. Leadership is about articulating visions, embodying values, and creating the environment within which things can be accomplished.

To achieve this positive outcome, Kouzes and Posner developed five constructs of action: Challenging the Process, Inspiring a Shared Vision, Enabling Others to Act, Modeling the Way, and Encouraging the Heart.[93]

Challenging the Process

Leaders must be capable of not only creating a vision but also for helping others to understand why certain workplace architectures or policies must be unlearned and new

structures developed in their place; those new structures are created from learning or doing new things. As a metaphor, the adage "better the devil you know than the devil you don't" is valid here. Many people, once they are trained and become comfortable with one process for accomplishing missions, must be convinced that an alternative process can result in better outcomes or future benefit to (preferably) the organization and/or the individual. In this respect, the leader is more effective when not just implementing new ideas and programs, but also identifying the weaknesses and lack of legitimacy of current programs and policies. Articulating these necessary changes to subordinates is paramount.

Inspiring a Shared Vision

Once processes are challenged and problems with these processes are successfully communicated, there must be an effort to communicate the vision to followers in a manner that results in the desired behavior changes. This goal is difficult to accomplish and may be threatened by barriers of age, subcultures, incentives, and education. For example, communicating a vision to transform Medicare may be difficult to translate to persons younger than age 30, who are a half a lifetime away from collecting benefits themselves. Similarly, complex issues involving deficits and fiscal responsibility can be difficult to communicate even to those with advanced degrees. As an example, an effective political talking point might be that "Homeowners could see their taxes increase by $64 per year if we cannot expand our tax revenue by creating new jobs," as opposed to stating, "We need to create 400 new jobs so that the county can increase its annual tax revenues by $3,064,000."[94] Inspiring a shared vision requires personal and frequent communication with an appealing aspiration that connects to subordinates in a personal way.

Enabling Others to Act

Words without resources will not yield any return on investment. If calling community members to volunteer for action is requested by leaders, then infrastructure must be in place to ensure that those volunteers are able to produce some form of usable output. The dominant political parties in the United States, for example, are aware of this reality, and this explains why both the Democratic and Republican parties place preaddressed and unsigned letters to various congressional and senatorial leaders on their websites. These letters may lobby in favor of a certain position or request a certain vote be made in an upcoming hearing. Through such tactics, the leaders of each party may challenge the process and provide a vision and then follow up by providing a concrete opportunity for the person's voice to be heard.

Modeling the Way

In a daily example of leadership, the leader demonstrates a "Do as I do" philosophy. Sometimes seen as a trait of leadership theory on its own, modeling can be an effective methodology of living by example the values that others then seek to emulate; this social learning theory–based model was originally developed by Albert Bandura. For example, during President Jimmy Carter's administration, the United States experienced an energy crisis; in a television address to the nation, Carter urged viewers to conserve energy by turning down their thermostats and keeping their houses cooler during winter months. Carter led the country in this modeling effort by ordering White House thermostats set to 65 degrees Fahrenheit.[95] Although the effort had little effect on the energy crisis of the day, the President's effort to model conservation through behavior remains one of his most widely cited White House exploits.

Encouraging the Heart

In this final construct of leadership strategy, Kouzes and Posner suggest that no followership will occur without an emotional connection from leader to follower that is derived from simple leader encouragement. This construct was so highly regarded when it was proposed in 1995 that the

authors eventually introduced it as a leadership theory of its own in 1999.[96] In this relatively simple leadership theory, the authors suggested that becoming a leader who is recognized as someone who cares about and understands people results in engenderment and loyalty that cannot be duplicated with other artificial means. The authors of this book prefer to think of this concept as an updated version of the *Pygmalion effect*.

Pygmalion, a character in Greek mythology, sculpted a statue of such beauty in ivory that he eventually fell in love with his own creation. He named the statue Galatea and later prayed to the gods that she be brought to life, which eventually happened. This Greek myth later became generalized in the sciences as the Pygmalion effect. This model has been suggested as a means through which leaders can believe in and encourage their employees over a constant period of time with the hopes that they will "come to life" and emulate the expectations leaders have for them. Unfortunately, the model has a notable weakness, known as the "halo effect"; that is, if a leader has a preconceived notion that, for example, women are lower achievers than men, then the leader may interpret outcomes incorrectly as well. Although some constructs of this model remain the subject of debate, leaders can never go wrong with appropriate, simple praise and acknowledgment of employee accomplishments and efforts!

See the box for a story that highlights the tenets of Kouzes and Posner's leadership model by viewing this framework in the light of ongoing efforts to enact healthcare reform.

CHALLENGING THE PROCESS: EVENTS THAT CHANGED HISTORY

During the latter part of the 1980s and prior to the 1990 U.S. election cycles, less than 10% of the U.S. public ranked health care among the nation's most important problems in any public survey conducted at that time. By 1992, however, when the presidential debates took place between candidates Bill Clinton and George H. W. Bush, Americans ranked health care as the second biggest problem facing the nation, just behind the economy. What happened in those 2 years to dramatically increase the importance of health care to the American public? Roberts (1994) explains that emphasizing this issue started out as a risky political move by a democratic senatorial candidate in 1990, and it was capitalized on by then-Governor Bill Clinton during the 1992 presidential election.

In 1990, senatorial candidate Harris Wofford of Pennsylvania became the first candidate in U.S. history to become elected to political office based solely on a platform of reforming health care. For decades, the U.S. healthcare system had been considered too difficult to fix or too challenging for the common worker to understand. As a result, politicians and candidates for office steered away from this issue. Indeed, this may have remained the case in the 1992 presidential election as well—at least until Wofford was able to capitalize on the misunderstandings and frustration associated with the healthcare system by the citizens of Pennsylvania and win the election.

In preparing for the 1992 Democratic presidential nomination, Bill Clinton changed his platform priorities from crime and the U.S. deficit to healthcare reform. If the strategy had been successful for a senator from Pennsylvania, his election team reasoned, then Clinton might potentially use this avenue to propel him to the presidency.

(continues)

(continued)

The attack on the mismanagement of health care in the United States came largely as a surprise to presidential incumbent George H. W. Bush. Only 2 years earlier (in 1990), Bush had received the largest popular support of any sitting president since Theodore Roosevelt for actions he had taken during the Gulf War. Bush, who was widely viewed as a master of foreign policy but had a notable history of underestimating political crises at home, seemed almost bored with the topic of health care during one 1992 presidential debate. Throughout the discussion, Bush could be seen on camera checking his watch, waiting for the debate to end.

According to most healthcare historians, it was during this period that the U.S. public embraced health care as a national issue because of what later became known as the "Wofford factor." Before 1990 and 1992, healthcare debates may have been witnessed only in graduate classrooms and hospital faculty meetings. From a retrospective point of view, Clinton's and Wofford's campaigns served as the crucible for a debate that continues to shape the political landscape today.

Data from: Roberts, M. J. (1994). *Your money or your life: The health care crisis explained.* New York: Main Street Books; Dreyfuss, R. (1993). America's healthcare crisis: A case of media malpractice. Retrieved July 22, 2009, from http://www.fair.org/index.php?page=1532.

BUCKINGHAM AND CLIFTON'S MANAGERIAL AND STRATEGIC LEADERSHIP (2001)

Buckingham and Clifton[97] suggest that leadership is a process of focusing on follower strengths rather than trying to eliminate weaknesses. Understanding the "hard-wiring" people possess, through nature and nurture, is a tool to accomplish this goal.[98]

It is imperative for leaders to conduct a self-assessment to really understand themselves, their organizational direction, and the strengths and weaknesses of their subordinates prior to trying to change the behavior of others. After all, leaders cannot develop the strengths of anyone in the workplace if they do not know how to find, name, and develop their own talents. Thus, according to this philosophy, the best strategy is to identify the individual's total strengths and, based on that understanding, to capitalize on these existing strengths. At the same time, it is also important to improve those areas in which the individual is weak.

In 2003, Wise noted that this model was particularly helpful in the nursing profession.[99] One of the "strengths" found to be of particular interest in nurses was empowerment. Nurses, who are often caught between several stakeholders (patient, provider, administrator, counselor, advocate, and supply chain/logistician), have a greater need to be empowered by their leaders than many other patient care and stakeholder authorities. Responding to this fact of life, leaders who recognize this need in nurses for empowerment can nurture, support, and grow this intrinsic need while learning to give up some power to improve the care process in the organization.

ULRICH, ZENGER, AND SMALLWOOD'S (1999) AND NOHRIA, JOYCE, AND ROBERTSON'S RESULTS-BASED LEADERSHIP

Results–based leadership[100] may have its roots in the path–goal theory methodology proposed by House; however, in this modern-millennium twist, results are tied to desired outcomes, which may themselves be tied to competencies. Competencies act as goals for leaders to achieve in strategy and training; likewise, employees are wedded to those competencies through achieved attributes such as education, training, and certifications. For example, if a hospital executive desires to improve patient outcomes in his or her facility by lowering morbidity and mortality rates, the end results might be achieved through hiring and directing personnel who are knowledgeable in achieving those outcomes by learning the competencies associated with those results. Several articles have been written linking such quality outcomes to leadership, as well as linking competencies to training rather than to demographic variables or other influences.[101–103]

Nohria, Joyce, and Robertson[104] also suggest that the key to achieving excellence for leaders is to focus on the organizational strategy. They insist that if a strategy is communicated clearly (and competency-based communication is the key to achieving that feat), then customers, employees, and shareholders will receive this communication in a uniform way that results in similar and desired outcomes.

THE ARMY LEADERSHIP MODEL (2007) AND MINISTRY L-MODEL (1995)

Closing out this review of the evolution of seminal leadership theories, two lesser known models of leadership are presented here; these models, the Army leadership model[105] and the Ministry L-model,[106] are rarely cited or quoted in academic texts and scholarly journals.

Academic and scholarly journals tend to disregard military and religious models of leadership, as part of a "good intentions" bias that is meant to avoid offending those who may be less tolerant of military or religious affiliations. This view may be shortsighted, however. More than 1 million people currently serve on active duty in the U.S. military, and there are an additional 8 million retired military people and their families in the United States. Many have been exposed to the fundamentals of the Army leadership model. As a result, this model is ripe for scholarly review.

A similar argument can be made for the Ministry L-model proposed by Rick Warren. Warren's seminal thesis on spiritual leadership has inspired millions. His presence as a national leadership and spiritual leader was so highly regarded by President Barack Obama that Warren was chosen as the person to deliver his invocation during the 2008 presidential inauguration.[107] Tens of millions of people are members of religious organizations and institutions in the United States.

The Army leadership model makes a distinction from previously described models in that it incorporates a definition of leadership into its conceptual model. In this model, leadership is defined as "influencing people by providing purpose, direction, and motivation while operating to accomplish the mission and improving the organization." Defined constructs are character, knowledge, and application—more commonly summarized as be–know–do.

Be–know–do emphasizes the philosophy that one must lead by example. Leading by example means that a leader will do what he or she says and says what he or she will do. Such a model implies that a high value is placed on morality and posits that a leader is the organization's role model. Concomitantly, the leader must be both the legitimate leader of the organization and the individual most highly versed in the technical and strategic skills of the organization.

Variables derived from the be–know–do philosophy include values, attributes, skills, and actions. The Army leadership model differs somewhat from traditional applications, however. A key premise in this model is the notion that leadership is a process that requires experience. Additional, didactic education and training are a must. It is not uncommon for officers in the military to return to school for periods of weeks, months, or years between major rotational assignments (i.e., those that occur every 3 to 4 years). Upon an officer's retirement from active duty after 20 years, it may be conceivable that the individual spent 5 years (or more) of his or her 20-year career in classrooms and training centers. In this regard, the Army leadership model is dissimilar to previous theories in which education and experience are seen as falling outside of the model's discussion. **Figure 4-9** shows a conceptual view of this model.

Finally, the ministry model of leadership, sometimes referred to as the L-model, suggests a *leadership by behavior* construct (role modeling). In this regard, values and institutional beliefs act as guidelines for daily life. These values can be summed up in one simple expression: Follow

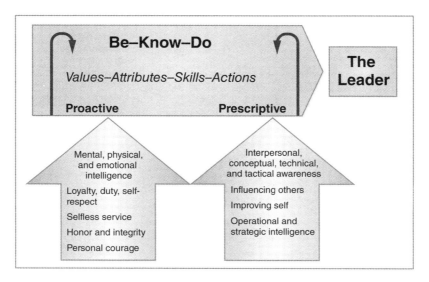

FIGURE 4-9 U.S. Army conceptual leadership model.
Data from Department of the Army. (2007). *Field manual M-22-100: Army leadership.*

the golden rule of "Do unto others as you would have others do unto you."

Seminal constructs in the ministry model are discipleship, servanthood, gifting, traits, skills, organizational management, and transformational leadership. The ministry model also suggests an overriding higher order principle as the cornerstone of moral living. Although rarely used outside religious practices and spiritual family units, the religious model of leadership has been the most distinctly applied and followed model by citizens in the United States for the latter part of the twentieth century and into the twenty-first century.[108]

The Army leadership model and Ministry L-model are two examples of lesser known leadership models. However, these models may enjoy a higher level of practical application and individual internalization than many other academically derived leadership models.

LEADERSHIP AS MANAGING ORGANIZATIONAL CULTURE

There is a growing trend to incorporate organizational culture into leadership theories and models. This is a rather new emphasis, but a critically important one. Leaders build culture in everything they do—from role modeling, to assigning responsibilities, to communicating with others, including how they communicate and what they do not do or do not say. Models with an organizational culture emphasis require leaders to determine, develop, and maintain an organizational culture that can best meet the expectations of, if not thrive in, the external environment.

This perspective envisions a more important and dramatic role for organizational culture as a construct—a leadership role—compared to that assigned under the situational leadership philosophy. *Leaders must now create culture!*

Take into consideration the changing governmental, societal, and economic situations with regard to health systems and hospitals (especially not-for-profit hospitals), where community needs assessments and emergency/disaster preparedness assessments must be conducted and findings integrated into the services and planning of the health systems and hospitals. This is not only an operational change but also a cultural change that leaders must integrate efficiently, effectively, and efficaciously into the fabric of the organizations they lead.

The next leadership phase may very well be the *culture creation contingency leadership* (CCCL) phase, which combines situational or contingency leadership with organizational culture creation, refinement, and enhancement (**Figure 4-10**). In this phase of leadership thought, leaders are proactive (culture developers, creators, modifiers) rather than reactive (culture is considered to determine a leadership style or actions), as is assumed in the situational leadership phase; this is the greatest difference between the two lines of thought. Even so, the CCCL phase builds on the past. Notably, Edgar Schein's work on organizational culture, and specifically on mechanisms of organizational culture, lies at the heart of this discussion. Developing models such as the dynamic culture leadership model, which incorporates transformational, transactional, and team leadership into an organizational culture development process, would be considered a synthesis of leadership and organizational culture concepts.

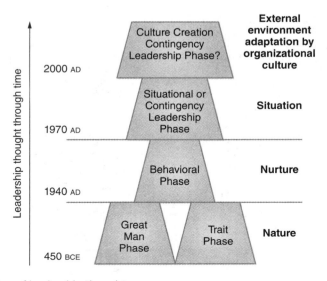

FIGURE 4-10 A possible progression of leadership thought.

SUMMARY

This chapter provided a historical summary and overview of leadership theory as it has evolved over the ages. The theories and models of leadership have evolved dramatically over the centuries, with later theories and models building on their predecessors. For example, early documents (dating back to 2300 BCE) of leadership principles and definitions (such as Xenophon's definition of leadership from 400 BCE) served as key resources for later philosophers who developed the contemporary and accepted models of the twentieth and twenty-first centuries. This chapter presented the theories and models in the original light that their creators intended. Strengths and weaknesses of each theory, as well as applications and strategies for use, were explored within each theoretical overview.

In simple terms, the progression of leadership thought builds from a "nature" perspective to weave the idea of "nurture" (learning and experience) into the discussion, then incorporates situational adaption, and finally adds organizational culture development into the formula for leader success. A healthcare leader focused on success will understand and hone leadership capabilities from nature, build capabilities through nurture (learning, study, and experience), adapt styles and practices to dynamic situations, and develop or create organizational culture based on external expectations to be successful. This effort of building leadership capabilities and practicing leadership must be performed in a moral and efficacious manner. The continued growth and development of leadership theories depend on researchers to understand how leaders influence outcomes, organizations, and followers.[109] Continued development is needed to grow and build upon existing leadership (knowledge) models and to develop new ones (models) to understand the changing role of leader as well as follower.[110]

A synopsis of leadership dichotomies is a great "reality check" for understanding and applying knowledge from the historical perspective of leadership models and theories. A few examples of this practical understanding follow.

A good leader must be:

- Confident but not cocky [overconfident at the detriment of the team or mission]
- Courageous but not foolhardy
- Attentive to details but not obsessed by them
- A leader and a follower
- Humble not passive
- Calm but not robotic
- Strong but have endurance[111]

From the discussion and overview of historical leadership models and theories, what can we garner from this journey in the past? In essence, leadership success could be formulized across all leadership thought phases (see **Table 4–5**).

Leader success = Individual (Nature + Nurture) × Situational adaptation × Organizational culture × Personal + Subordinate accountability

Table 4-5 Summary of Leadership Theories and Models

Theory	Goal	Antecedent Framework	Constructs	Variables	Relationship	Utility for Greater Understanding in Practice
Carlyle, Galton, and James's "great man" theory (1840–1880)	Identify immutable traits of past leaders so future leaders can be identified	Most likely Machiavelli	Physical characteristics	Immutable physical characteristics	Procession of characteristics is leadership.	Evolved into trait theory over time
Lewin, Lippitt, and White's trait theory (1938–1939)	Identify mutable traits of past leaders so that future leaders can be identified	Great man theory	Intelligence, physical stature, extraversion	Outcomes of intelligence, extraversion, physical stature	Those with "leadership" traits should be good leaders.	Incorporated into broader leadership models such as behavioral and situational theories

(continues)

Table 4-5 Summary of Leadership Theories and Models   (continued)

Theory	Goal	Antecedent Framework	Constructs	Variables	Relationship	Utility for Greater Understanding in Practice
McGregor's Theory X and Theory Y (1950)	Identify lazy and self-motivating personnel	Early trait theories	Laziness and motivation	Various	Laziness equals failure and motivation equals success.	Suggests motivated leaders can achieve more than lazy leaders
Stogdill and Coons's Ohio Leadership Studies (1950)	Identify individual dimensions of behavior	Early trait theories	Initiating structure and consideration	Work-related variables and satisfaction	Leaders who set high standards while respecting employees achieve high outcomes.	Organizational management design
Michigan Leadership Studies (1950)	Identify leader objectives associated with performance effectiveness	Early trait theories	Employee oriented and production oriented	Satisfaction and goal attainment	Focus is on employee task performance.	Task organization and employee workload
Katz's skills theory (1955)	Identify individual dimensions of behavior	Early trait theories	Technical, conceptual, and human abilities	Various traits and outcomes	Must have all three to be successful	Production outcomes
Argyris's personality and organization theory (1957)	Organizational learning	Fledgling humanistic theories	Organizations, learning, and employee mental maps	Governing, action, and consequences	Institutional norms and cultures	Measurement of organizational outcomes affected by the leader
Blake and Mouton's managerial grid (1964)	Focus on attitudes	Early trait theories, motivation, and management research in practice	Concern for results and concerns for people	Satisfaction, outcomes, and productivity	Those with high ratings for both people and results are most effective.	Team building and consensus making
Erikson's psychoanalytic theory (1964)	Psychoanalysis theory	Early studies of Freud (1913) and Fromm (1941)	Father figure role, mentoring, and love	Pleasing and fear proposition: My subordinates are my children; they must respect me.	Intersubjective object, relational context	Early behavior studies on loyalty and engendering
Fiedler's contingency model (1964)	Identify variables affecting group performance	Motivation and management	Situation favorableness/ preferred coworker scale	Task and relationship orientation	The more favorable the relationship (or perceived relationship) between the leader and the follower, the higher the degree of task orientation.	Psychology, management teams

						Utility for Greater Understanding
Theory	**Goal**	**Antecedent Framework**	**Constructs**	**Variables**	**Relationship**	**in Practice**
House's path–goal model (1971)	Predict leadership effectiveness based on communication of leader intent; expectancy motivation theory	Earlier works in expectancy, motivation, and leader intent; Vroom's expectancy theory	Perception of work, self-development, and path to goals; Communications: directive, supportive, participative, and achievement oriented	Rewards, goals, accomplishments, personal characteristics, environment	Leader behavior will be motivational to the extent it assists subordinates to accomplish assigned goals.	Management communication
Vroom–Yetton–Jago's normative decision-making model (1973)	No one decision-making model is appropriate.	Earlier work in decision making	Quality or rationality of the decision, the acceptance, or the commitment on the part of subordinates to execute the decision effectively, and the amount of time required to make the decision	Various	Better decision making is achieved through balancing construct dimensions.	Decision making
Graen's leader–member exchange and vertical dyad linkage (1975)	Tasks are accomplished based on personal relationships.	Katz and Kahn's (1966) work on motivation, equity, and organizational citizenship behavior	Vertical dyad linkage	In-group and out-group	Satisfaction will be higher with the in-group, leading those individuals toward goal attainment.	Motivation, satisfaction, delegation
Hersey and Blanchard's situational leadership model (1977)	Four leader choices: tell, sell, participate, or delegate	Graen's leader–member exchange theory, vertical dyad linkage, and other antecedent theories	Directive behavior, supportive behavior, development level	Structure variables of time, supervisory demands, and job demands	Optimizing the leadership based on the environmental constraints maximizes outcomes.	Delegation and decision making
House's charismatic leadership model (1977)	Influence and followership	Max Weber, early theories on charisma	Dominance, influence, confidence, and values	Success, culture, and change	Followership is achieved through some divine personality trait that cannot be measured.	Various organizational and individual trait outcomes

(continues)

Table 4-5 Summary of Leadership Theories and Models   (continued)

Theory	Goal	Antecedent Framework	Constructs	Variables	Relationship	Utility for Greater Understanding in Practice
Burns's transformational leadership model (1978)	Leaders and followers raise each other to higher levels of motivation.	Max Weber's charismatic leadership theory	Charisma, intellectual stimulation, environment	Rewards	Followers of a transformational leader feel: trust, admiration, loyalty, and respect	Motivation and satisfaction
Bennis's competency-based leadership (1985–1993)	Learned skills specific to the organizational dynamic can make leaders successful.	Transformational leadership, communication; social learning theory (Bandura)	Creating attention by vision, creating meaning by being a person of trust, self-development	Education, skills, and training	Education and experience lead to success.	Professional development
Kouzes and Posner's leadership framework (1995)	Eliminate institutionalism through inspired change	Burns's transformational leadership, theory of planned behavior, social learning theory (Bandura)	Challenging the Process, Inspiring a Shared Vision, Enabling Others to Act, Modeling the Way, Encouraging the Heart	Organizational outcomes	Eliminating institutionalism and inspiring change result in different outcomes.	Culture change
Warren's ministry L-model (1995)	Leadership by behavior	Spiritual teachings	Discipleship, servanthood, gifting, traits, skills, organizational management, transformational leadership	Outcomes	Modeling behavior results in the reflection of that behavior by others.	Applying the omnibus leadership model
Buckingham and Clifton's managerial and strategic leadership model (2001)	Leverage personality	Trait theories	Personality and enneagrams	Verbal and nonverbal communication characteristics	Weaknesses are hard to change; focus on developing strengths.	Personality assessment to drive organizational outcomes
Ulrich, Zenger, and Smallwood's results-based leadership (1999); Nohria, Joyce, and Roberson's results-based leadership (2003)	Achieve desired results	House's path–goal theory, goal-setting theory, social learning theory	Performance	Outcomes	Outcomes are tied to goals.	Organizational strategy
Army leadership model (2007)	Leading by example	Earlier trait and transformational leader theories	Be–know–do	Organizational outcomes	The leader is both the legitimate authority and the organizational expert.	Determining educational/ training factors that influence organization and team outcomes

DISCUSSION QUESTIONS

1. Describe the progression of leadership thought as portrayed in theories and models from the great man and trait phase, to the behavioral phase, to the situational or contingency phase.
2. Distinguish constructs of a trait theory or model, a behavioral theory or model, and a situational or contingency theory or model of leadership, and interpret those constructs' value in the present day. Does the culture creation contingency leadership phase emerge as a new phase based on your interpretation? Why or why not?
3. Apply a behavioral theory or model of leadership and a situational or contingency theory of model of leadership; demonstrate these applications using examples based on a definition of leadership you produce. Were you drawn more to descriptive or prescriptive theories and models?
4. Compare and contrast, with illustrating diagrams, two or more behavioral or situational/contingency theories or models of leadership.
5. Referring to the progression of leadership thought, design, create, and explain a personal leadership model applicable to leading health organizations today.
6. Appraise and relate constructs and variables from the progression of leadership thought to your personal leadership model applicable to leading health organizations today.

EXERCISES

1. In one paragraph each, describe a trait, behavioral, and situational/contingency theory or model of leadership.
2. Distinguish situational leadership theory from transactional leadership and from transformational leadership. What is similar and what is different for each theory of leadership?
3. Prepare a personal definition of leadership, and construct a personal application-based model of leadership geared toward healthcare organizations today from the theories and models of the situational or contingency phase of leadership, categorizing the descriptive and prescriptive elements. Your paper should be two to three pages long.
4. Analyze the strengths and weaknesses of your personal application-based leadership model from Exercise 3. In a one- to two-page paper, modify your personal application-based leadership model to overcome the weaknesses you identify.
5. In a three- to four-page paper, summarize at least four of the following articles from the literature on transformational and transactional leadership models:
   a. Avolio, B., Bass, B., & Jung, D. (1999). Re-examining the components of transformational and transactional leadership using the Multifactor Leadership Questionnaire. *Journal of Occupational and Organizational Psychology, 72,* 441–462.
   b. Bass, B. (1999). Ethics, character, and authentic transformational leadership behavior. *Leadership Quarterly, 10*(2), 181–217.
   c. Conger, J. A. (1999). Charismatic and transformational leadership in organizations: An insider's perspective on these developing streams of research. *Leadership Quarterly, 10*(2), 145–179.
   d. Yukl, G. (1999). An evaluation of conceptual weaknesses in transformational and charismatic leadership theories. *Leadership Quarterly, 10*(2), 285–305.
   e. Barling, J., Weber, T., & Kelloway, E. K. (1996). Effects of transformational leadership training on attitudinal and financial outcomes: A field experiment. *Journal of Applied Psychology, 81*(6), 827–832.
6. Interpret, critique, defend, and support a position based on your appraisal of the situational leadership theory by reading the following scholarly debate literature:

   Additional sources for the situational leadership theory (use if needed):
   Hersey, P., & Blanchard H. (1993). *Management of organizational behavior: Utilizing human resources* (6th ed.). Englewood Cliffs, NJ: Prentice Hall, Chapters 8–17.

   Scholarly debate regarding the situational leadership theory:
   Graeff, C. L. (1983). The situational leadership theory: A critical view. *Academy of Management Review, 8,* 285–291.
   Hersey, P. (1985). A letter to the author of "Don't be misled by LEAD." *Journal of Applied Behavioral Science, 21,* 152–153.
   Lueder, D. C. (1985). A rejoinder to Dr. Hersey. *Journal of Applied Behavioral Science, 21,* 154.

Lueder, D. C. (1985). Don't be misled by LEAD. *Journal of Applied Behavioral Science, 21,* 143–151.

Vecchio, R. P. (1987). Situational leadership theory: An examination of a prescriptive theory. *Journal of Applied Psychology, 72,* 444–451.

REFERENCES

1. Dowd, J. (1936). *Control in human societies.* New York: Appleton-Century.
2. Landis, E. A., Hill, D., & Harvey, M. R. (2014). A synthesis of leadership theories and styles. *Journal of Management Policy and Practice, 15*(2), 97–100. Retrieved from http://www.na-businesspress.com/JMPP/LandisEA_Web15_2_.pdf, p. 97.
3. Bass, B. (1990). *Bass & Stogdill's handbook of leadership: Theory, research and managerial applications* (3rd ed.). New York: Free Press, p. 38.
4. Nanus, B. (1992). *Visionary leadership.* San Francisco: Jossey-Bass.
5. Internet Classics Archive. (n.d.). Works by Xenophon. Retrieved from http://classics.mit.edu/Browse/browse-Xenophon.html.
6. Ledlow, J. R., & Coppola, M. N. (2009). Leadership theory and influence. In J. A. Johnson (Ed.), *Health organizations: Theory, behavior, and development* (pp. 167–191). Sudbury, MA: Jones & Bartlett.
7. Lewin, K., & Lippitt, R. (1938). An experimental approach to the study of autocracy and democracy: A preliminary note. *Sociometry, 1,* 292–300.
8. Lewin, K., Lippitt, R., & White, R. (1939). Patterns of aggressive behavior in experimentally created social climates. *Journal of Social Psychology, 10,* 271–301.
9. Yukl, G. (1994). *Leadership in organizations* (3rd ed.). Englewood Cliffs, NJ: Prentice Hall, p. 256.
10. Isom, M. D. (1998, November 30). The social learning theory. Retrieved from http://www.criminology.fsu.edu/crimtheory/bandura.htm.
11. Gordon, J. (1991). *A diagnostic approach to organizational behavior* (3rd ed.). Englewood Cliffs, NJ: Prentice Hall.
12. Filley, A. C. (1978). *The complete manager.* Champaign, IL: Research Press, pp. 57–60.
13. Ledlow & Coppola, note 6.
14. Mumford, M. D., Zaccaro, S. J., Connelly, M. S., & Marks, M. A. (2000). Leadership skills: Conclusions and future directions. *The Leadership Quarterly, 11*(1), 155–170.
15. Yukl, note 8, p. 256.
16. Argyris, C. (1957). *Personality and organization.* New York: HarperCollins.
17. Argyris, C. (1962). *Interpersonal competence and organizational effectiveness.* Homewood, IL: Dorsey Press.
18. Argyris, C. (1964). *Integrating the individual and the organization.* New York: Wiley.
19. Argyris, C. (1993). *Knowledge for action: A guide to overcoming barriers to organizational change.* San Francisco: Jossey-Bass.
20. Leadership Champions. (2008). Vroom–Yetton–Jago normative leadership decision model. Retrieved from http://leadershipchamps.wordpress.com/2008/11/06/vroom-yetton-jago-normative-leadership-decision-model/.
21. Boje, D. M. (2009). Traditional situation leadership theories. New Mexico State University. http://business.nmsu.edu/~dboje/388/2009_book/pdf/Chapter23TraditionalSituationLeadershipTheories.pdf.
22. Yukl, note 9.
23. Blair, G. M. (1997, February 7). Contingency models. Science and Engineering, University of Edinburgh. Retrieved from http://www.see.ed.ac.uk/~gerard/MENG/ME96/Documents/Styles/conti.html.
24. 12Manage. (n.d.). Contingency theory. Retrieved from http://www.12manage.com/methods_contingency_theory.html.
25. 12Manage, note 24.
26. Yukl, note 9.
27. Yukl, note 9.
28. Shapiro, R. L. (1991). Psychoanalytic theory of groups and organizations. *Journal of the American Psychoanalytic Association, 39,* 759–781.
29. Kernberg, O. F. (2004). *Contemporary controversies in psychoanalytic theory, technique, and their applications.* New Haven, CT: Yale University Press
30. Winer, J. A., Jobe, T., & Ferrono, C. (1984). Toward a psychoanalytic theory of the charismatic. *Annals of Psychoanalysis, 12,* 155–175.
31. Erikson, E. H. (1964). *Insight and responsibility.* New York: Norton.
32. Kernberg, note 29.
33. Winer et al., note 30.

34. Towler, A. (2005). Charismatic leadership development: Role of parental attachment style and parental psychological control. *Journal of Leadership and Organizational Studies, 11*(3), 247–258.

35. Rubinstein, B. B. (1975). On the clinical psychoanalytic theory and its role in the inference and confirmation of particular clinical hypotheses. *Psychoanalytic Contemporary Science, 4*(3), 57.

36. Ray, J. J. (1990). The old-fashioned personality. *Human Relations, 43*, 997–1015.

37. Ray, J. J. (1988). Why the F scale predicts racism: A critical review. *Political Psychology, 9*(4), 671–679.

38. 12Manage. (n.d.). Path–goal theory (house). Retrieved from http://www.12manage.com/-methods_path_goal_theory.html.

39. Clark, D.R. (2015). Path–goal leadership theory. Retrieved from http://nwlink.com/~donclark/leader/lead_path_goal.html.

40. Boje, note 21.

41. Boje, note 21.

42. Leadership Champions, note 20.

43. Truckenbrodt, Y. B. (2000, Summer). The relationship between leader–member exchange and commitment and organizational citizenship behavior. *Acquisition Review Quarterly, 233–244.* Retrieved from http://www.au.af.mil/au/awc/awcgate/dau/truck.pdf.

44. Truckenbrodt, note 43.

45. Miner, J. B. (2005). *Organizational behavior 1: Essential theories of motivation and leadership.* Armonk, NY: M. E. Sharpe.

46. Miner, note 45.

47. Boje, note 21.

48. Hersey, P., & Blanchard, K. (1974). *So you want to know your leadership style?* Englewood Cliffs, NJ: Prentice Hall.

49. Hersey, P., & Blanchard, K. (1993). *Management of organizational behavior* (6th ed.). Englewood Cliffs, NJ: Prentice Hall.

50. Bass, B. M. (1990). From transactional to transformational leadership: Learning to share the vision. *Organizational Dynamics, 18*(3), 19–30.

51. Hersey, P., & Blanchard, K. (1969). *Management of organizational behavior: Utilizing human resources.* Englewood Cliffs, NJ: Prentice Hall.

52. Jin, M., McDonald, B., & Park, J. (2016). Followership and job satisfaction in the public sector: The moderating role of perceived supervisor support and performance-oriented culture. *International Journal of Public Sector Management, 29*, 3.

53. Hersey & Blanchard, note 48.

54. House, R. J. (1977). A 1976 theory of charismatic leadership. In J. G. Hunt & L. L. Larson (Eds.), *Leadership: The cutting edge* (pp. 189–207). Carbondale, IL: Southern Illinois University Press.

55. Cicero, L., & Pierro, A. (2007). Charismatic leadership and organizational outcomes: The mediating role of employee's work group identification. *International Journal of Psychology, 42*(5), 297–306.

56. Towler, A. (2005). Charismatic leadership development: Role of parental attachment style and parental psychological control. *Journal of Leadership and Organizational Studies, 11*(3), 15–25.

57. Crandall, D. (2006). *Leadership lessons from West Point.* New York: John Wiley and Sons.

58. Waldman, D. A., & Yammarino, F. J. (1999). CEO charismatic leadership: Levels of management and levels of analysis effects. *Academy of Management Review, 24*, 266–285.

59. Crandall, note 57.

60. Waldman & Yammarino, note 58.

61. Bryant, S. E. (2003). The role of transformational and transactional leadership in creating, sharing and exploiting organizational knowledge. *Journal of Leadership and Organizational Studies, 9*(4), 32–45.

62. Bryant, note 61.

63. Burns, J. (1978). *Leadership.* New York: Harper & Row.

64. Gooty, J., Gavin, M., Johnson, P. D., Frazier, M. L., & Snow, D. B. (2009). In the eyes of the beholder: Transformational leadership, positive psychological capital, and performance. *Journal of Leadership and Organizational Studies, 15*(4), 353–367.

65. Bass, note 3.

66. Yukl, note 9, p. 350.

67. Yukl, note 9, p. 351.

68. 12Manage. (n.d.). Servant-leadership (Robert K. Greenleaf). Retrieved from http://www.12manage.com/methods_greenleaf_servant_leadership.html.

69. Bass, note 3.

70. Yukl, note 9.

71. Savic, B. S., & Pagon, M. (2008). Individual involvement in health care organizations: Differences between professional groups, leaders, and employees. *Stress and Health: Journal of the International Society for the Investigation of Stress, 24*(1), 71–84; Moreno, V., Hickman, M., & Cavazotte, F. (2012). Effects of leader intelligence, personality, and emotional intelligence on transformational leadership and managerial performance. *Leadership Quarterly, 23*(3), 987–991.

72. Li, G., Shang, Y., Liu, H., & Xi, Y. (2014, August). Differentiated transformational leadership and knowledge sharing: A cross-level investigation. *European Management Journal*, *32*(4), 554–563.

73. Li et al., note 72.

74. Yukl, note 9; Anderson, M. H., & Sun, P. Y. T. (2012). Civic capacity: Building on transformational leadership to explain successful integrative public leadership. *Leadership Quarterly*, *23*(3), 309–323.

75. Bass, note 3.

76. Fairholm, G. (2003). *The techniques of inner leadership: Making inner leadership work*. Westport, CT: Praeger.

77. Bass, B. (1998). *Transformational leadership: Industrial, military, and educational impact*. Mahwah, NJ: Lawrence Erlbaum Associates.

78. Yukl, note 9.

79. Bass, note 3.

80. Yukl, note 9, p. 352.

81. Bennis, W. G., & Nanus, B. (1985). *Leaders: The strategies for taking charge*. New York: Harper and Row.

82. Avolio, B. J., & Bass, B. M. (2002). *Developing potential across a full range of leadership: Cases on transactional and transformational leadership*. Mahwah, NJ: Lawrence Erlbaum Associates, p. 1.

83. Avolio & Bass, note 28.

84. Avolio & Bass, note 82.

85. Avolio & Bass, note 82, p. 19.

86. Bennis & Nanus, note 77.

87. Bennis, W. (1989). *On becoming a leader*. Wilmington, MA: Perseus.

88. Ashkenas, R. N. (2005). Beyond the fads: How leaders drive change with results. In *Human resource planning*. Retrieved from http://www.questia.com/read/1G1-16482369/beyond-the-fads-how-leaders-drive-change-with-results.

89. Malsbury, M. (2010). Leadership models: Then and now. *American Chronicle*. Retrieved from http://www.americanchronicle.com/articles/view/162416.

90. Kouzes, J. M., & Posner, B. Z. (2007). *The leadership challenge* (4th ed.). New York: John Wiley and Sons.

91. Boulais, N. A. (2002). Leadership in children's literature: Qualitative analysis from a study based on the Kouzes and Posner leadership framework. *Journal of Leadership Studies*, *5*, 54–63.

92. Covey, S. R. (2004). *The 8th habit: From effectiveness to greatness*. New York: Free Press.

93. Kouzes, J. M., & Posner, B. Z. (2003). *The leadership challenge* (3rd ed.). San Francisco: Jossey-Bass.

94. Lubbock County Democratic Talking Points. (July 2009). Lubbock, TX.

95. Koncius, J. (2009, June 6). Former Chief Usher of White House offers rare glimpse of first families. *Washington Post*. Retrieved from http://domesticblog.com/2009/07/06/former-chief-usher-of-white-house-offers-rare-glimpse-of-first-families/.

96. Kouzes, J. M., & Posner, B. Z. (1999). *Encouraging the heart: A leader's guide to rewarding and recognizing others*. San Francisco, CA: Jossey-Bass.

97. Buckingham, M., & Clifton, D. O. (2001). *Now, discover your strengths*. New York: Free Press.

98. Coppola, M. N., & Carini, G. (2006). Ability job-fit self-assessment. *Healthcare Executive*, *2*, 60–63.

99. Wise, P. S. (2003). *Leading and managing in nursing*. St. Louis, MO: Elsevier Health Sciences.

100. Ulrich, D., Zenger, J. H., Zenger, J., & Smallwood, W. M. (1999). *Results-based leadership*. Boston: Harvard Business School Press.

101. Harrison, J. P., & Coppola, M. N. (2007). Is the quality of hospital care a function of leadership? *Health Care Manager*, *26*(3), 1–10.

102. Harrison, J., & Coppola, M. N. (2008). Is the quality of hospital care a function of leadership? [Poster presentation]. Annual Research Meeting sponsored by the Academy of Health, Washington, D.C., June 8, 2008.

103. Coppola, M. N., Lafrance, K. G., & Carretta, H. J. (2002). The female infantryman: Testing the possibility. *Journal of Military Review*, *6*, 55–60.

104. Nohria, N., Joyce, W., & Roberson, B. (2003). What really works. *Harvard Business Review*, *79*(11), 85–96.

105. Department of the Army. (2007, January 1). *Field manual M-22-100: Army leadership*. Washington, D.C.: Author.

106. Warren, R. (1995). *The purpose driven church*. Grand Rapids, MI: Zondervan.

107. Grossman, C. L. (2008, December 22). Rick Warren and Barack Obama's inaugural address. *USA Today*. Retrieved from http://content.usatoday.com/communities/religion/post/2008/12/60306978/1.

108. Warren, note 106.

109. Dinh, J. E., Lord, R. G., Gardner, W. L., Meuser, J. D., Liden, R. C., & Hu, J. (2014). Leadership

theory and research in the new millennium: Current theoretical trends and changing perspectives. *Leadership Quarterly*, *25*(1), 36–62. doi:10.1016/j.leaqua.2013.11.005

110. Landis, E. A., Hill, D., & Harvey, M. R. (2014). A synthesis of leadership theories and styles. *Journal of Management Policy and Practice*, *15*(2), 97–100. Retrieved from http://www.na-businesspress.com/JMPP/LandisEA_Web15_2_.pdf.

111. Willink, J., & Babin, L. (2015). *Extreme ownership: How U.S. Navy SEALS lead and win*. New York: St. Martin's Press, pp. 277–278.

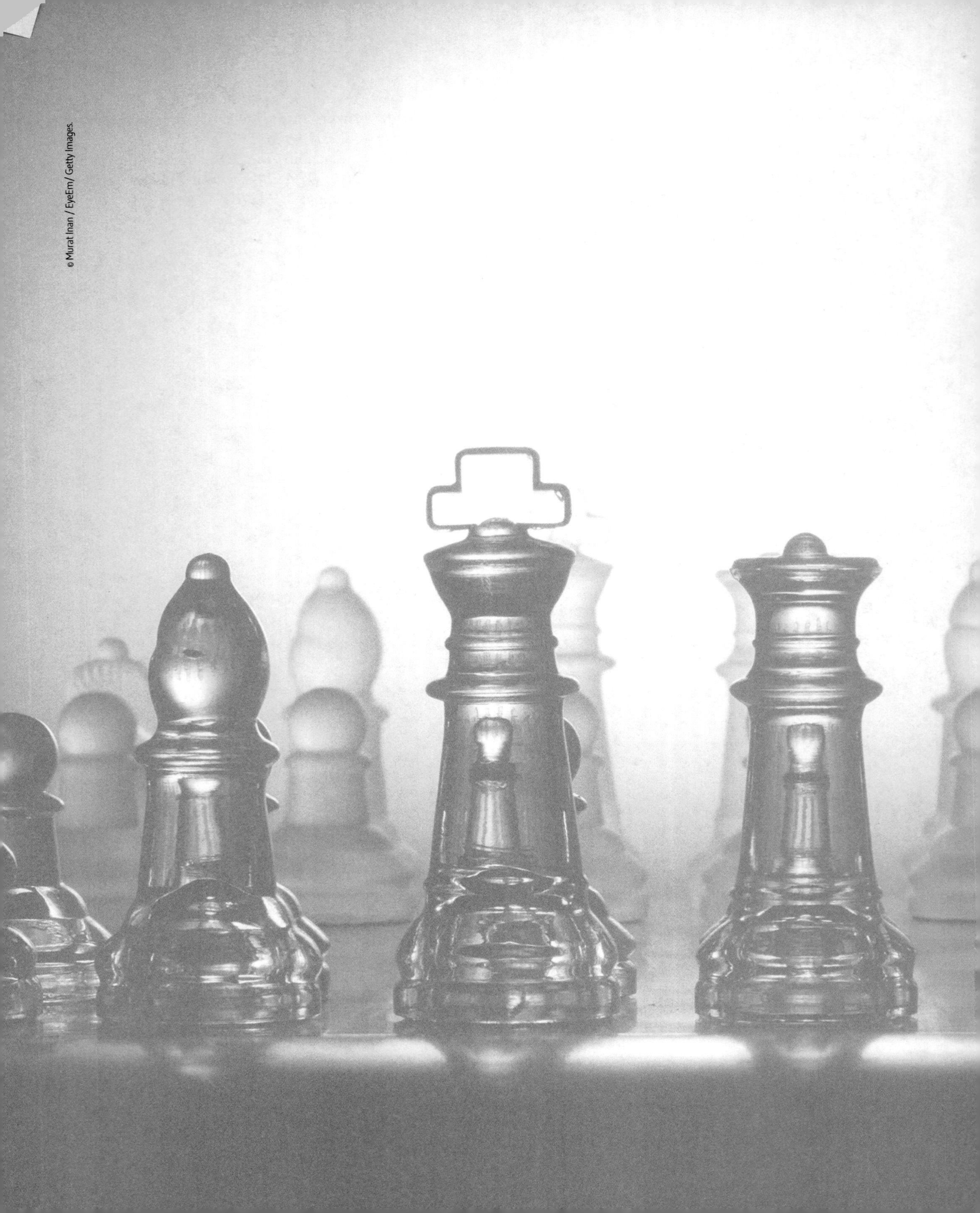

PART 2

LEADERSHIP IN PRACTICE

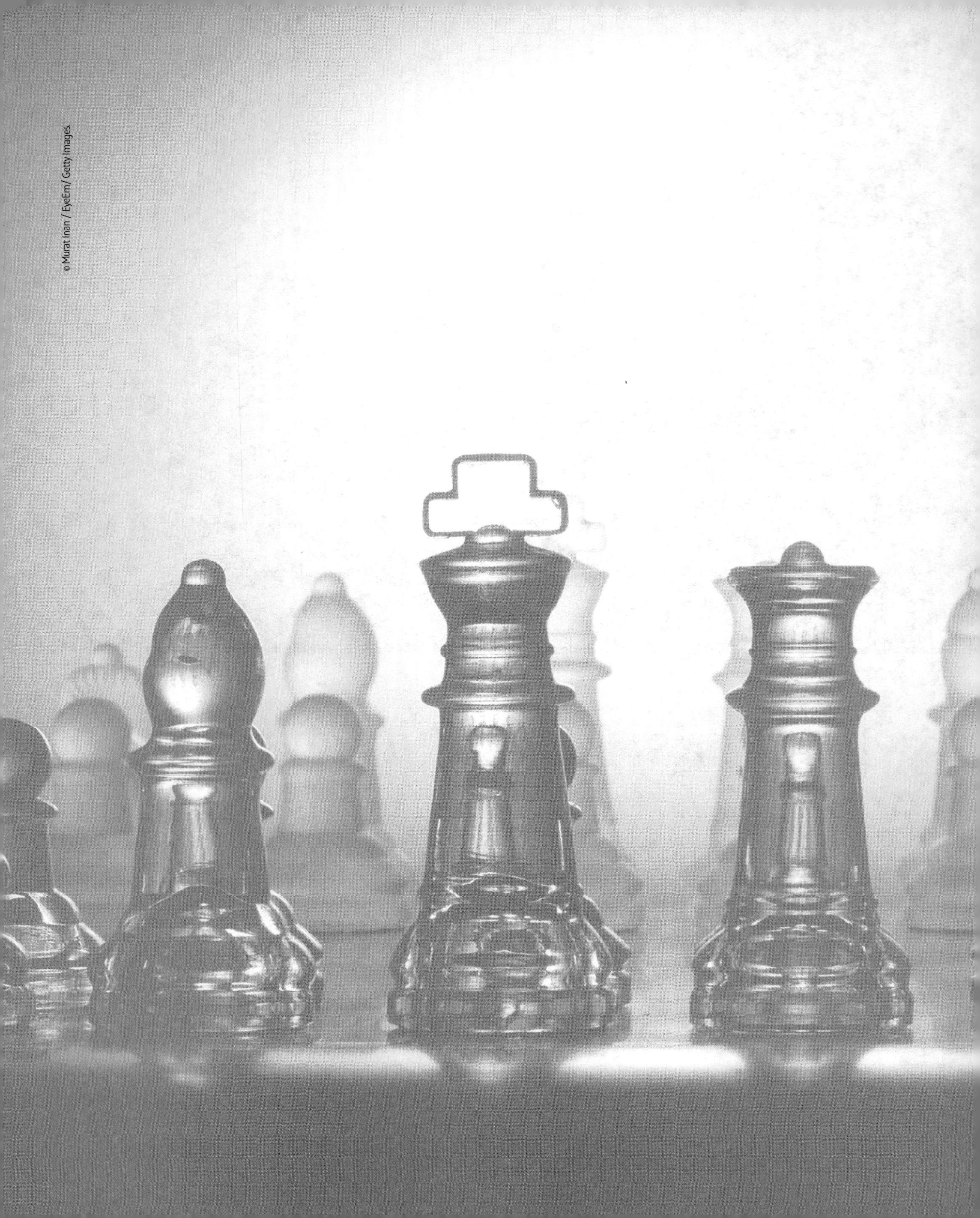

© Murat Inan / EyeEm/ Getty Images.

CHAPTER

5

Leadership Competence I: Professional Competencies and Personal Skills and Responsibilities

Men are conquered only by love and kindness, by quiet, discreet example,
which does not humiliate them and does not constrain them to give it. They dislike to be
attacked by a man who has no other desire but to overcome them.
Giosuè Borsi, *A Soldier's Confidences with God*

This chapter presents the personal competencies a leader must develop, build, and maintain to be successful. It also discusses leadership knowledge, skills, and abilities and the ability–job fit a leader has with his or her organizational environment. Emphasis is placed on the understanding that health leaders work in a highly complex environment with a very educated and interdisciplinary workforce. Based on the complexity and diversity of the health industry workforce, competence in leading people begins with understanding the elements of motivation, influence, and power combined with the ability to communicate to those diverse audiences. Leadership success is often based on the leader's capabilities in terms of motivation, influence, power, interpersonal relationships, communication, and inspiring teams. The chapter begins with a summary of leadership competencies from experts in the industry.

LEARNING OBJECTIVES

1. Describe the complexity of the healthcare industry in terms of workforce, environment, and societal expectations, and explain how a health leader's mastery of competencies, influence processes, motivation, interpersonal relationships, and communication capabilities is necessary to successfully navigate that complexity.

2. Explain how the complexity of the health workforce may lead to communication failure and conflict, and summarize the use of quality communication and conflict management skills to successfully motivate subordinates, build interdisciplinary teams, and lead a health organization based on commitment rather than compliance or resistance.

3. Predict the outcomes of continuous use of the avoiding and competing strategies in a health organization compared with the compromising, accommodating, and problem-solving strategies; predict the outcomes of face-to-face communication compared with use of the memoranda communication channel and media to disseminate ambiguous and urgent messages.

4. Analyze the health leader competencies in terms of the knowledge, skills, and abilities discussed in this chapter, differentiating the competencies described here with those not discussed, and provide support for your assessment.

5. By combining several theories and models, design an influence, power, and motivation leadership model for use in health organizations focused on subordinate commitment; modify this model for use with an interdisciplinary health team or group, and explain why this modification is necessary.

6. Evaluate competencies (knowledge, skills, and abilities) found in leadership practice concerning situational assessment, interpersonal relationships, influence processes, motivation, and communication necessary to successfully lead healthcare organizations, and demonstrate support for your evaluation.

COMPETENCIES IN THE HEALTH PROFESSION

A profession, such as health leadership, administration, and management, is defined by standards of practice. In this dynamic industry, individuals in the profession are expected to be competent in various aspects of the position—in this case health leadership. Thus "competencies" are constructs or factors a professional in the health industry should be able to know, understand, apply, assess, integrate with the situational aspects of the industry, and evaluate. As noted by Dr. Mary Stefl, a forerunner in academic education and a leading author in competency development in health care, "health executives in all professional settings must navigate a landscape influenced by complex social and political forces, including shrinking reimbursements, persistent shortages of health professionals, endless requirements to use performance and safety indicators, and prevailing calls for transparency."[1] Furthermore, she notes that leaders and managers are expected to continually do more with less. Developing competencies that are specific to the role an individual plays in the health setting aids healthcare

organizations in communicating to executives the skills necessary for leading in these changing times. Baldrige National Quality Award criteria also hold leadership competencies and the application of sound, moral, and effective leadership in high regard.

Today's healthcare executives and leaders must have management talent sophisticated enough to match the increased complexity of the healthcare environment.[2] In practical terms, as highlighted by Antonakis and House within the Instrumental Leadership model, leadership is about *getting things done*.[3] Competencies in health care are important because they set professional standards by adding to the value of health education. Competencies are skills, knowledge, and attitudes that allow a health professional to perform to standards set within the profession. Establishing and implementing these competencies are based on education, training, and professional development.

The health administration profession began to explore the concept of competency–based education to produce qualified healthcare executives in the 1990s. Early careerists in the health professions were taught that competencies in the health profession were composed of four key points that would assist graduates in achieving competence in executive positions: technical skills, such as finance and human resources; a perceptive view of the industrial aspects in health care, such as clinical process and various healthcare institutions; the explanation of analytic and conceptual concepts; and the interpretation of and acknowledgment of emotional intelligence.[4,5]

Calhoun, Vincent, Calhoun, and Brandsen also have been leaders in the health education process for developing competencies. They have suggested that "during the last decade there has been a growing interest in adopting a competency-based system in various areas of education, training, and professional development."[6] As a result, they list a number of competency initiatives that include calls for the following:

1. Both curricular content and process review in health administration and related training programs
2. Rethinking and reform of current educational practices
3. Evidence-based, outcomes-focused education in health management; and policy education

They also suggest that competencies in healthcare administration optimize organizational effectiveness by better equipping students with more than just the textbook information needed to succeed in the industry. However, they have suggested that in spite of governmental mandates and accrediting body specifications for improvement of education, the debate about the use of competency models, the competencies themselves, and competency-based education (CBE) still continues in a number of postsecondary educational settings—both within and outside the professions.[8,9]

Competencies can also be described as a characteristic of a person that results in effective performance on the job. As a result, professionals are better prepared for excellence in the working world of the health professions. Competencies can also be thought of in terms of actual performance. A person can have the education and training to be a hospital administrator, but actually performing the job is another matter altogether. Mastery of specific competencies related to healthcare administration is the true measure of performance in the workplace.

In health care, competencies are used to define discipline and specialty standards as well as expectations.[10] The competency validation process should begin in the academic setting. Setting formal standards as a profession will give health professionals clear direction on what they should be doing to be a successful leader within their organization. However, it is important to note that both the academic world and healthcare organizations need to be on the same page in terms of accepted competencies and expectations.

The need for competencies has been an issue throughout the healthcare industry for decades. During the twentieth and twenty-first centuries there has been a growing interest in competency-based systems in various areas of education, training, and professional development. As a result, a number of competency initiatives have been undertaken across the health professions, including administration and medicine. Organizations that are able to hire leaders with competencies in healthcare management benefit from the ability of a leader to more quickly tackle the specifics of his or her job, retain staff who thrive under leadership that has the skills of collaboration and team building, and maintain a ready pool of exemplary employees who are competent to move up and through an organization, strengthening its quality of service as well as operations.

The reason that competency is important in healthcare administration is that health care continues to change, and this requires a highly skilled workforce that readily adapts for lifelong learning. A prerequisite for ensuring this is the identification and specification of skill sets or competencies that accommodate those transformation processes. Additionally, leaders should recognize the development of competencies as a continual process that results in continual improvement.

The focus on individual leadership competencies in health care is a continuation, and product, of earlier work by dozens of healthcare icons, including Abraham Flexner, Dr. Ernest A. Codman, Avedis Donabedian, and John R. Griffith (to name only a small handful).

ABRAHAM FLEXNER

Abraham Flexner is credited with shepherding in the scientific age of medicine. In 1910 he wrote *Medical Education in the United States and Canada*. This seminal piece of healthcare literature was used at that time as the basis to close more than 60 of the 155 operating medical schools in the United States that were still basing medical education on anachronistic practices. Flexner found that some medical schools were still awarding medical degrees based on apprenticeships and teaching students with woefully outdated and irrelevant curricula, and that none of the medical schools based their education on any one particular standard. As a result, Flexner recommended that all physicians needed formal didactic education, that this education be conducted in a university setting by skilled medical educators, that it conform to a recognized curriculum, and that standards and practices (early terms for competencies) be developed that would allow for uniform learning outcomes regardless of where the medical student earned a degree. Flexner's report also recommended that physician education be based on both a scientific foundation and empirical knowledge. Using this methodology, it may be suggested that medical students of the era were the first of their generation to be taught to think critically; that is, to transcend the gaps between knowledge and abilities in the development of new skills.[11,12]

ERNEST A. CODMAN

In 1917 Dr. Ernest A. Codman wrote *A Study in Hospital Efficiency as Demonstrated by the Case Report of the First Five Years of a Private Hospital*. Codman practiced medicine in the early 1900s during the start of the industrial revolution, and the U.S. healthcare system's burgeoning interest in standardization (another early precursor term for competence). Today, Codman is credited with developing the "end results" methodology, which was a precursor to outcomes assessment. Codman's end results methodology involved studying the delivery of patient care practices that resulted in more favorable outcomes (such as lower morbidity and mortality). However, unlike his contemporary Abraham Flexner, Codman's efforts to improve patient outcomes in the Boston hospital in which he practiced were not met with approbation from peers. In fact, Codman was eventually asked to resign his medical position from the Massachusetts Medical Society for advocating policies and practices that none of his colleagues thought prudent or necessary. However, there was a growing trend within U.S. health care to meet the quality demands of a rapidly growing and more discerning patient base. As a result, the American College of Surgeons (an early precursor to the American Medical Association) eventually adopted Codman's end result methodology as an early quality process to deliver better care. Today, we refer to this collective process of a population of providers all evaluating and treating patients in a similar way that results in the most favorable outcomes as *standards of practice*.[13,14]

AVEDIS DONABEDIAN

Avedis Donabedian's work in health care is most commonly associated with the construct of quality. Donabedian published three volumes on healthcare quality and divided quality assessment into three focal areas: structure, process, and outcome. Since the 1960s there have been numerous efforts at measuring and improving quality by assessing the clinical process by way of the Healthcare Effectiveness Data and Information Set (HEDIS) measure and the Institute for Healthcare Improvement's (IHI's) 100,000 Lives Campaign, which was promoted to spur healthcare organizations to systematically use evidence-based guidelines for specific medical issues. Other quality improvement efforts have led to the employment of the Hospital Consumer Assessment of Healthcare Providers and Systems (HCAHPS) survey, which is a general healthcare satisfaction survey of care, and the Hospital-Based Inpatient Psychiatric Services (HBIPS), which is a set of core psychiatric measurements developed in concert with the Joint Commission, the National Association of Psychiatric Health Systems (NAPHS), the National Association of State Mental Health Program Directors (NASMHPD), and the NASMHPD Research Institute.[15,16] Although the aforementioned may seem like an alphabet soup of professional organizations and jargon, the key for early careerists is to recognize that these professional organizational metrics do, in fact, flow from the current knowledge, best practices, standards, and outcomes assessment within the field. As such, these professional organizations provide the "variables, measures, and operationalization" through which competencies are evaluated.

JOHN R. GRIFFITH

John R. Griffith has been an educator and scholar in the health professions for over 50 years. He is a past chair of the Association of University Programs in Health Administration (AUPHA) and has previously served as a commissioner for the Accrediting Commission on Education in Health Services Administration (now called the Commission on Accreditation Healthcare Management Education [CAHME]). His textbook, *The Well-Managed Health Care Organization*, is necessary reading for candidates who want to take the Board of Governors exam in order to become Board Certified in Healthcare Management through the American College of Healthcare Executives (ACHE). Finally, the material developed by the Griffith Leadership Center is strongly considered by a variety of professional organizations, university programs, and other entities as practical guidance from research and as advisory/best practices for the profession.[17]

COMPETENCY ASSESSMENT TOOLS

AMERICAN COLLEGE OF HEALTHCARE EXECUTIVES

The American College of Healthcare Executives (ACHE) has developed a competencies assessment tool that healthcare executives can use in assessing their expertise in critical areas of healthcare management. The competencies are derived from the Healthcare Leadership Alliance (HLA), and the self-assessment is designed to help identify areas of strengths and weaknesses to develop a personal development plan. The competencies in this self-assessment tool comprise a subset relevant to management and leadership tasks typically performed by affiliates of ACHE, regardless of work setting or years of experience. ACHE suggests its competency self-assessment can be a powerful tool in facilitating feedback about gaps in skills necessary for optimizing performance.[18]

HEALTHCARE LEADERSHIP ALLIANCE

The Healthcare Leadership Alliance (HLA)—a consortium of six major professional membership organizations—used research from and experience with its individual credentialing processes to posit five competency domains common among all practicing healthcare managers. The organizations of the HLA are ACHE, American College of Physician Executives (ACPE), American Organization of Nurse Executives (AONE), Healthcare Financial Management Association (HFMA), Healthcare Information and Management Systems Society (HIMSS), Medical Group Management Association (MGMA), and its educational affiliate, the American College of Medical Practice Executives (ACMPE). The necessary competencies they have developed are:

1. Communication and relationship management
2. Professionalism
3. Leadership
4. Knowledge of the healthcare system
5. Business skills and knowledge

NATIONAL CENTER FOR HEALTHCARE LEADERSHIP

The Robert Wood Johnson Foundation created the Health Research and Development Institute, which revolved around creating a foundation for qualified leadership within U.S. health systems. To align initiatives with current shortcomings in the healthcare administration field, a group of 200 professionals gathered in 2001 at the National Summit on the Future of Education and Practice in Health Management and Policy.

This group also identified specific facets of the overall healthcare administration problems. Deficiencies in expenditures, cost, quality, and patient satisfaction; difficulty attracting young professionals and leaders; lack of clear collegiate accreditation in healthcare administration; insufficient practical experience; lack of support for young managers; failure to provide opportunities for advancement

for women and minorities in management positions; and a shortage of individuals being prepared for senior management positions of healthcare systems were the main focuses on improvement in education and training that came out of this summit.

In response to this, the Robert Wood Johnson Foundation funded two grants, one of which established the National Center for Healthcare Leadership (NCHL). This center was seen as

> ... [a] formal structure to carry out the mission of encouraging stronger managerial leadership in the healthcare field. This group encourages broad participation throughout various career stages, establishes baseline data for the industry, identifies core competencies for superior performance, identifies best means for career preparedness, and strengthens values and diversity levels within the talent pool for executive management throughout the country. The NCHL succeeded in developing a protocol for evaluating organizational culture, aligning human resource systems with the organization's competency model, creating the most widely used health leadership competency model (the Lifelong Leadership Inventory [LLI]), and other projects to develop graduate students in health management education programs.[19]

The LLI can assist leaders in self-assessing their stage of professional competence.[20,21]

ASSOCIATION OF UNIVERSITY PROGRAMS IN HEALTH ADMINISTRATION

AUPHA lists five core competencies of healthcare professionals: communication and relationship management, leadership, professionalism, knowledge of health care, and business skills. These are defined as follows:

1. *Communication and relationship management*: A healthcare executive should be able to communicate clearly and respectfully with patients, customers, industry leaders, partners, department heads, and hospital workers. He or she should be able to create meaningful relations with peers and promote constructive interaction between individuals and groups in all situations.
2. *Leadership*: For obvious reasons, a healthcare leader needs to have the ability to create a shared vision for and inspire his or her entire team. He or she must also be able to create and implement a strong organizational plan for his or her hospital or institution.
3. *Professionalism*: A hospital executive must maintain the utmost professional, ethical, and moral conduct

at all times, thereby setting a high standard of excellence for his or her team members.

4. *Knowledge of health care*: A good healthcare executive is on top of healthcare system policies, the latest innovations in healthcare technology, and the ever-changing political landscape of the industry.

5. *Business skills*: Business skills are needed to run a hospital like a business. Healthcare leaders need to have a good grasp of business principles, systems thinking, and business management in order to reach the higher levels of healthcare employment.

THE COMPLEX AND DYNAMIC HEALTH ENVIRONMENT

The health industry exists in a highly dynamic environment. If the environment were static (i.e., not changing), the workforce homogeneous and consistent, and the technology of health simple, the need for and the value of leaders would be much lower. In effect, the dynamic and complex environment of health necessitates competent and motivated leaders. Because the environment, workforce, technology, and systems are complex and dynamic, highly effective leadership in the health realm is essential. In addition, societal expectations for health organizations and health professionals are very high; in truth, the expectation for these organizations and professionals is to be error free, or flawless. How long would a pharmacy director keep his or her job if 5%, or even 3%, of that section's work was erroneous? How successful would a physical therapy director or branch chief of the clinic be if new therapies and technologies were adopted 5 or 10 years after a competitor had adopted them? Would the director of the supply chain for a hospital be successful if that person did not keep up with the latest medical and surgical items needed by the hospital to meet the professional or national standard of care? Of course, the responses in these scenarios would not be favorable; in fact, failure in these areas would be career minimizing for these hypothetical individuals. Clearly, the dynamic environment of the health industry requires competent leaders throughout the organization, from chief executive officer to section or branch director.

In today's health industry, the needs for professionalization and competence are especially important. Competence means recognizing and having the ability to utilize the capabilities associated with leadership. It requires mastery of the special skills and learning from experiences that are required to become a "professional." Many organizations in the United States focus on increasing the competence of professionals of health organizations. Many of these organizations or associations are populated by executives in the profession who are committing their time and resources for the causes that are important to them. Without this kind of interdisciplinary exchange, increasing competence levels of the industry, one leader at a time, might not be achievable.

THE COMPLEX AND HIGHLY EDUCATED WORLD OF THE HEALTH WORKFORCE

The health workforce is a complex assortment of individuals characterized by different backgrounds, educational experiences, certifications, specialties, and work locations. Reviewing the workforce reports from the federal Health Resources and Services Administration, Bureau of Health Professions,[22] provides some appreciation of the diversity and heterogeneity of the health workforce. As a whole, the health workforce accounts for nearly 12% of the total U.S. workforce.[23]

Leaders in the health sector must be able to foster a culture that is conducive to change and growth as well as develop the full potential of their staff members and volunteers. Understanding culture is a big part of this effort. Put simply, a major component of culture is the human element. Culture includes the sum total of knowledge, beliefs, art, morals, laws, customs, and shared patterns of behaviors, interactions, cognitive constructs, and affective understanding that is acquired by a particular society through socialization.[24] These shared patterns distinguish the members of one group from the members of another group. Studies have found that the values that vary from one culture to another significantly influence the constitutional effectiveness of the organization. Each of these groups has its own specialized training, norms, beliefs, and values, which may differ from those espoused by other groups.

In stable times, such individual dynamics may be masked and subgroups submissive; in contrast, in turbulent times, these internal groups may seek some degree of autonomy. Moreover, the training, education, and experience of health administrators, doctors, nurses, allied health professionals, and other paraprofessionals may result in the presentation of certain cultural concepts that are unique and may be expressed in different ways, such as aggressive needs for autonomy or increased advocacy for patient care versus financial survivability of the healthcare organization.[25]

Mechanisms that reinforce norms and behaviors arise when the leader focuses attention on specific, high-priority goals and objectives. These characteristics are taught by the leaders and, in turn, adopted by the staff and the supporters of the organization. In a reciprocal relationship, the culture influences leadership as much as leadership influences culture. The adroit leader in a health organization has a direct impact on the culture, which can affect how decisions are made with respect to fundraising, volunteers, and placement within the organization.[26]

For a leader in today's complex world, the important issues are threefold: (1) the leader's ability to focus a diverse group of individuals toward the mission, vision, and tasks of the organization; (2) the leader's ability to determine which individuals, with their unique sets of knowledge, skills, and abilities, should be employed, and where and how they should be utilized to the greatest value of the organization; and (3) the leader's use of the skills of communication and motivation, as well as culture development and maintenance to create systems and processes that are effective, efficient, and efficacious so that the organization can be successful within the environment in which it performs its mission. These leadership challenges are salient for leaders throughout the industry regardless of their level in a specific organization. As leaders progress upward in responsibility and accountability in a health organization, the complexity widens and deepens. Those are rather large leadership tasks!

The myriad of specialties in the health workforce underlines the advancement and specialization of the application of knowledge, skills, abilities, and technologies of the industry. Multidisciplinary teams, whether in clinical, administrative, or allied health, are becoming more prevalent in the delivery of care, administration of health organizations, and improvement in health status of communities. Understanding the different knowledge, skills, abilities, and perspectives each health professional brings to an issue, opportunity, or challenge that the organization faces is important for leaders. Effective handling of this need is essential so that the proper mix of professionals can be formed into a team, proper resources can be provided, and appropriate expectations can be set for the multidisciplinary team. Learning about each discipline and knowing which capability each type of health professional can competently perform will allow the leader to make the most efficient use of the most valuable resource—people.

Table 5-1 presents a simple summary of a current snapshot of the health workforce.

These various specialties and disciplines all have different education, licensure, credentialing, and licensure maintenance requirements. Therefore, different professional associations and societies, as well as credentialing and accreditation associations, have been developed to provide a set of standards for each distinct profession. These associations and societies also provide valuable connections and updates concerning the macro- and micro-environmental forces that are changing the health industry.

A recent collaboration of five professional associations, the Healthcare Leadership Alliance (HLA), has created five domains that encompass a total of 300 competencies for the health leader and manager. An extract of competencies, focusing on leadership and management from Domain 2: Leadership, is provided in **Table 5-2**. Although this table focuses on the leadership domain, leaders should possess the competencies identified in each domain.

The professional associations involved in the collaboration to create this list of competencies are essential to leaders and managers in the health industry. The associations' mission or charter (i.e., their reason to exist, their purpose), taken as a whole, is to keep their membership—the leaders, managers, and stakeholders of the health industry—current on changing environmental forces. One of the many ways they perform this mission is to maintain close relationships with the legislative, judicial, and political entities of U.S. society.

Health industry leaders should seek membership in these associations and certification as appropriate to their career track and personal career goals. This is a sincere and strong recommendation. **Table 5-3** lists some of these associations and provides contact information for the National Center for Healthcare Leadership and the Association of University Programs in Health Administration.

Health leaders should become members and earn the appropriate certification from a professional association of the health industry. The associations and societies listed in Table 5-3 are the best known in the industry for leadership careers. For example, the NCHL provides essential services and information for the health leader. AUPHA and CAHME provide instructors of health industry leadership and management students with the standards and specialty certification for their programs. In addition, specialty associations exist to serve women, Asian, and African American health leaders and managers. Of note, recognized universities may be regionally accredited as institutions of higher learning, whereas specific colleges and specific programs are specialty accredited, such as with health administration regarding CAHME. Other specialty accrediting bodies for health industry leadership and management programs include the Council on Education for Public Health (CEPH)[36] and the Association to Advance Collegiate Schools of Business (AACSB).[37]

Many leaders come from clinical or technical programs, backgrounds, and practical experiences. These leaders include, but are not limited to, physicians, physical therapists, pharmacists, occupational therapists, audiologists and speech pathologists, optometrists, and nurses. For would-be health leaders, maintaining membership

Table 5-1 Health Workforce Specialty Categories and Disciplines	
Category	**Specialties**
Medicine	• Physicians of medicine (MD) and physicians of allopathic medicine (DO) • Many specialties, such as neurology, pathology, radiology, psychiatry, and surgery (e.g., thoracic, cardiac, orthopedic) • Many specialties, such as pediatrics, family medicine, obstetrics and gynecology, internal medicine, ophthalmology, and cardiology
Nursing	• Registered nurses (RN) • Advance practice nurses (NP or APN) • Licensed practical and vocational nurses (LPN)
Dentistry	• Dentists of surgery (DDS) and dentists of medical dentistry (DMD) • Dental hygienists • Dental assistants
Nonphysician clinicians	• Physician assistants (PA) and podiatrists (DPM) • Chiropractors • Optometrists and opticians
Pharmacy	• Doctors of pharmacy (PharmD) • Pharmacists • Pharmacy technicians and aides
Mental health	• Psychologists • Social workers • Counselors
Allied health	• Physical therapy, occupational therapy, speech-language pathology and audiology, and respiratory therapy • Various technicians and technologists (laboratory, emergency medical, radiology), paramedics, medical and clinical technologists, and nuclear medicine technologists • Medical records and health information technologists and technicians, dieticians and nutritionists, home health aides and nursing aides, orderlies and attendants
Health administration	• Health system and hospital administration, nursing home/long-term care administration, home health administration, health insurance, and integrated system administration • Medical practice administration, clinical practice administration, and technical area administration • Public health administration as a whole and/or, for example, in environmental health science, epidemiology, community and social behavior, health policy, maternal women and children, and biostatistics

and certification for your clinical or technical specialty is important, but securing membership in one of the professional leadership and management health associations, the one that provides the best fit for you, is also important for your personal growth, professional development, and upward career mobility. Not only are your leadership knowledge, skills, and abilities important, and not only is the environmental scanning support important, but the broader network of similar leaders that you will develop can also assist you and your organization greatly throughout your career.

Industry segment associations are valuable assets not just to the health industry as a whole, but also to your organization. These associations include the American Hospital Association, American Medical Association,

American Dental Association, and American Nurses Association, among many others. Maintaining connections and good relationships with these organizations will assist your organization in environmental scanning and situational assessment activities as well.

As a health leader, you are responsible for maintaining your competence and your subordinate team's competence, and for striving for and achieving organizational success. Leaders should regularly seek out continuing education, much of which is provided by the health professional associations, not just for themselves, but also for their subordinates. Most certifications you earn as a health leader, or as a clinician or technician for that matter, require regular continuing education credits or units. The next section expands on the topic of learning and competence.

Table 5-2 Leadership Domain 2: Healthcare Leadership Alliance (HLA) Competency Directory

Domain	Knowledge/Skill	Competency	Skill Area	Key Words	Core/Specialty	ACHE	ACMPE	AONE	HFMA	HIMSS
						— Core and Specialty Competencies Relevant to the Professional Organization (X indicates relevancy)				
Domain 2: Leadership	Knowledge of	Leadership styles/techniques		Methods, models	Core	X	X	X	X	X
Domain 2: Leadership	Knowledge of	Personal journey disciplines		Methods, models	Specialty			X		
Domain 2: Leadership	Skill	Gain physician buy-in to accept risk and support new business ventures	Facilitate	Decision making	Core	X	X	X	X	X
Domain 2: Leadership	Skill	Adhere to legal and regulatory standards	Be accountable	Regulation	Core	X	X	X	X	X
Domain 2: Leadership	Skill	Advocate and participate in healthcare policy initiatives (e.g., uninsured crisis, medical malpractice, access to health care, patient safety)	Advocate	External factors	Core	X	X	X	X	X
Domain 2: Leadership	Skill	Anticipate and plan strategies for overcoming obstacles	Think strategically	Problem solving	Core	X	X	X	X	X
Domain 2: Leadership Core	Skill	Anticipate the need for resources to carry out initiatives	Think strategically	Needs	Core	X	X	X	X	X
Domain 2: Leadership	Skill	Assess the organization including corporate values and culture, business processes, and the impact of systems on operations	Analyze	Organization	Core	X	X	X	X	X
Domain 2: Leadership	Skill	Champion solutions and encourage decision making	Promote	Decision making	Core	X	X	X	X	X
Domain 2: Leadership	Skill	Create an organizational climate that encourages teamwork	Develop	Culture	Core	X	X	X	X	X
Domain 2: Leadership	Skill	Create an organizational climate that facilitates individual motivation	Develop	Culture	Core	X	X	X	X	X
Domain 2: Leadership	Skill	Develop external relationships	Develop	External relations	Core	X	X	X	X	X
Domain 2: Leadership	Skill	Encourage a high level of commitment to the purpose and values of the organization	Promote	Vision, goals	Core	X	X	X	X	X

(continues)

Table 5-2 Leadership Domain 2: Healthcare Leadership Alliance (HLA) Competency Directory (continued)

Domain	Knowledge/Skill	Competency	Skill Area	Key Words	Core/Specialty	Core and Specialty Competencies Relevant to the Professional Organization (X indicates relevancy)				
						ACHE	ACMPE	AONE	HFMA	HIMSS
Domain 2: Leadership	Skill	Establish a compelling organizational vision and goals	Develop	Vision, goals	Core	X	X	X	X	X
Domain 2: Leadership	Skill	Establish an organizational culture that values and supports diversity	Develop	Culture	Core	X	X	X	X	X
Domain 2: Leadership	Skill	Explore opportunities for the growth and development of the organization on a continuous basis	Develop	Organization	Core	X	X	X	X	X
Domain 2: Leadership	Skill	Foster an environment of mutual trust	Develop	Culture	Core	X	X	X	X	X
Domain 2: Leadership	Skill	Hold self and others accountable for organizational goal attainment	Be accountable	Vision, goals	Core	X	X	X	X	X
Domain 2: Leadership	Skill	Incorporate and apply management techniques and theories into leadership activities	Integrate	Methods, models	Core	X	X	X	X	X
Domain 2: Leadership	Skill	Plan for leadership succession	Develop	Staff	Core	X	X	X	X	X
Domain 2: Leadership	Skill	Promote and manage change	Manage	Decision making	Core	X	X	X	X	X
Domain 2: Leadership	Skill	Promote continuous organizational learning/improvement	Develop	Organization	Core	X	X		X	X
Domain 2: Leadership	Skill	Represent physician interests in negotiating and managing relationships with hospitals, insurance companies, and others (e.g., fair market value of services, on-call coverage of specialists)	Advocate	Physicians	Core	X	X	X	X	X
Domain 2: Leadership	Skill	Support and mentor high-potential talent within the organization	Develop	Staff	Core	X	X	X	X	X

Key: ACHE: American College of Healthcare Executives; ACMPE: American College of Medical Practice Executives; AONE: American Organization of Nurse Executives; HFMA: Healthcare Financial Management Association; HIMSS: Healthcare Information and Management Systems Society; HLA: health leader attributes.

Table 5-3 Professional Associations for Health Leaders and Managers

Health Professional Association and Web Address	Mission
American College of Healthcare Executives (ACHE) www.ache.org	ACHE is an international professional society of more than 40,000 health executives who lead hospitals, healthcare systems, and other healthcare organizations. ACHE is known for its prestigious FACHE credential, signifying board certification in healthcare management, and its educational programs, including the annual Congress on Healthcare Leadership, which draws more than 4,500 participants each year. ACHE's established network of more than 80 chapters provides access to networking, education, and career development at the local level.[27]
Medical Group Management Association (MGMA) www.mgma.com	The mission of MGMA is to continually improve the performance of medical group practice professionals and the organizations they represent. MGMA serves 22,500 members who lead and manage 13,600 organizations in which almost 280,000 physicians practice. Its diverse membership comprises administrators, chief executive officers, physicians in management, board members, office managers, and many other management professionals. They work in medical practices and ambulatory care organizations of all sizes and types, including integrated systems and hospital and medical school–affiliated practices. Three related organizations and their boards of directors and committees help MGMA fulfill its commitment to members. • *American College of Medical Practice Executives (ACMPE)*: The standard-setting and certification organization for group practice professionals • *MGMA Center for Research*: The research and development companion to MGMA that conducts quantitative and qualitative research to advance the art and science of medical group management • *MGMA Services Inc.*: A wholly owned, for-profit subsidiary of MGMA that was established to further the provision of high-quality medical management services and assist medical group practices in delivering efficient and effective health care[28]
American Organization of Nurse Executives (AONE) www.aone.org	AONE is the national organization of nurses who design, facilitate, and manage care. With more than 6,500 members, AONE is the voice of nursing leadership in health care. Since 1967, this organization has provided leadership, professional development, advocacy, and research to advance nursing practice and patient care, promote nursing leadership excellence, and shape public policy for health care. AONE's 48 affiliated state and metropolitan chapters and its alliances with state hospital associations give the organization's initiatives both regional and local presences. AONE is a subsidiary of the American Hospital Association.[29]

Healthcare Financial Management Association (HFMA) www.hfma.org	HFMA is the United States' leading membership organization for healthcare financial management executives and leaders. Its more than 39,000 members—ranging from CFOs to controllers to accountants—consider HFMA a respected thought leader on top trends and issues facing the healthcare industry. HFMA members can be found in all areas of the healthcare system, including hospitals, managed care organizations, physician practices, accounting firms, and insurance companies. At the chapter, regional, and national levels, HFMA helps healthcare finance professionals meet the challenges of the modern healthcare environment in the following ways:
	• Providing education, analysis, and guidance
	  ◦ Building and supporting coalitions with other healthcare associations to ensure accurate representation of the healthcare finance profession
	  ◦ Educating a broad spectrum of key industry decision makers on the intricacies and realities of maintaining fiscally healthy healthcare organizations
	  ◦ Working with a broad cross-section of stakeholders to improve the healthcare industry by identifying and bridging gaps in knowledge, best practices, and standards
	Vision: To be the indispensable resource for healthcare finance
	Purpose Statement: To define, realize, and advance the financial management of health care by helping members and others improve the business performance of organizations operating in or serving the healthcare field[30]

(continues)

Table 5-3 Professional Associations for Health Leaders and Managers (continued)

Health Professional Association and Web Address	Mission
Healthcare Information and Management Systems Society (HIMSS) www.himss.org	HIMSS is the healthcare industry's membership organization exclusively focused on providing global leadership for the optimal use of healthcare information technology (IT) and management systems for the betterment of health care. Founded in 1961, and with offices in Chicago; Washington, D.C.; Brussels; Singapore; and other locations across the globe, HIMSS represents nearly 50,000 individual members and more than 570 corporate members who collectively represent organizations employing millions of people. HIMSS frames and leads healthcare public policy and industry practices through its advocacy, educational, and professional development initiatives designed to promote information and management systems' contributions to ensuring quality patient care. **Vision**: Advancing the best use of information and management systems for the betterment of health care **Mission**: To lead change in the healthcare information and management systems field through knowledge sharing, advocacy, collaboration, innovation, and community affiliations[31]
National Center for Healthcare Leadership (NCHL) www.nchl.org	NCHL is a not-for-profit organization that works to assure that high-quality, relevant, and accountable leadership is available to meet the challenges of delivering quality patient health care in the twenty-first century. Its goal is to improve health system performance and the health status of the entire country through effective healthcare management leadership.[32]
Association of University Programs in Health Administration (AUPHA) www.aupha.org Commission on Accreditation of Healthcare Management Education (CAHME) www.cahme.org	AUPHA is a global network of colleges, universities, faculty, individuals, and organizations dedicated to the improvement of healthcare delivery through excellence in health administration education. Its membership includes the premier baccalaureate and master's degree programs in health administration education in the United States and Canada. The association's faculty and individual members represent more than 230 colleges, universities, and healthcare organizations. When asked what they value most highly about AUPHA membership, these members cite the opportunity to meet and network with colleagues who share similar interests, learning about the issues facing the field, and witnessing the latest products and services for the healthcare industry.[33] **Vision**: Improve health by promoting excellence and innovation in healthcare management education. **Mission**: AUPHA fosters excellence and innovation in healthcare management education, research, and practice by providing opportunities for member programs to learn from one another, by influencing practice, and by promoting the value of healthcare management education.[34] **Program Certification and Accreditation**: Programs seeking full membership in AUPHA must have achieved proven excellence as indicated by undergraduate certification or graduate accreditation. Certification and accreditation are processes of external peer review through which programs are examined to determine quality of the curriculum, infrastructure, and outcomes. Certification of undergraduate programs is available through AUPHA. Accreditation of graduate programs is carried out by the CAHME.[35]

LEADERSHIP KNOWLEDGE, COMPREHENSION, SKILLS, AND ABILITIES

Knowledge focuses on recalling information with familiarity gained through education, experience, or association, whereas *comprehension* is the understanding of the meaning of the information, such as of a science, an art, or a technique, in order to interpret and translate that information into action. A *skill* is the effective and timely utilization of knowledge that is comprehended; it is the learned power of doing something competently through a developed aptitude. *Ability* is the physical, cognitive, or legal power to competently perform through natural aptitude or learned or acquired proficiency and competence. In essence, knowledge, comprehension, skills, and abilities are sequential, and the notions of competence and proficiency are critical to these definitions. Leaders grow in knowledge, comprehension, skills, and abilities through education, study, experience, mentoring, and observation. Most, if not all, of these capabilities are learned.

Leaders may find the taxonomies developed by Benjamin Bloom useful as they reflect on their own capabilities and as they evaluate and develop subordinates whom they lead. Bloom's theory is based on three types of learning, or three learning domains (categories):

- *Cognitive*: Mental skills (knowledge)
- *Affective*: Growth in feelings or emotional areas (attitude)
- *Psychomotor*: Manual or physical skills (skills)

Trainers often refer to these three domains as KSAs (knowledge, skills, and attitudes [abilities]). Thus this taxonomy of learning behaviors can be thought of as "the goals of the training process." That is, "after the training session, the learner should have acquired new skills, knowledge, and/or attitudes [and abilities]."[38] "Bloom's Taxonomy is a way to classify instructional activities or questions as they progress in difficulty. The lower levels require less in the way of thinking skills. As one moves down the hierarchy, the activities require higher-level thinking skills."[39]

Table 5–4 describes the cognitive domain within Bloom's Taxonomy.[40] The cognitive domain involves knowledge and the development of intellectual skills. This includes the recall or recognition of specific facts, procedural patterns, and concepts that develop intellectual abilities and skills. There are six major categories in Table 5-4, which move from the simplest behavior to the most complex. The categories can be thought of as degrees of difficulty; that is, the first one must be mastered before the next one can be tackled.

A revision of the cognitive domain in 2001 updated the terminology and uses active verbs.

1. *Remembering*: Retrieving, recognizing, and recalling relevant knowledge from long-term memory
2. *Understanding*: Constructing meaning from oral, written, and graphic messages through interpreting, exemplifying, classifying, summarizing, inferring, comparing, and explaining
3. *Applying*: Carrying out or using a procedure through executing or implementing
4. *Analyzing*: Breaking material into constituent parts, determining how the parts relate to one another and

Table 5-4 Bloom's Taxonomy of the Cognitive Domain (Original Version)	
Category and Examples	**Key Words and Actions**
Knowledge: Recall of data or information *Examples: Defines leadership; identifies items from a list*	Defines, describes, identifies, knows, labels, lists, matches, names, outlines, recalls, recognizes, reproduces, selects, states
Comprehension: Understands the meaning, translation, interpolation, and interpretation of instructions and problems; states problem in own words *Example: Explains the steps and sequence of willful choice decision making; translates information and equations into a spreadsheet*	Comprehends, converts, defends, distinguishes, estimates, explains, extends, generalizes, gives examples, infers, interprets, paraphrases, predicts, rewrites, summarizes, translates
Application: Uses a concept in a new situation or unprompted use of an abstraction; applies what was learned in the classroom to novel situations in the workplace *Examples: Uses quantitative methods to determine employee performance outliers; uses a policy to determine an employee's merit raise increase or bonus*	Applies, changes, computes, constructs, demonstrates, discovers, manipulates, modifies, operates, predicts, prepares, produces, relates, shows, solves, uses
Analysis: Separates material or concepts into component parts so that their organizational structure may be understood; distinguishes between facts and inferences *Examples: Determines sequential work process steps and transition points of a larger work system; gathers information and assessments to identify training needs in a department or unit*	Analyzes, breaks down, compares, contrasts, deconstructs, diagrams, differentiates, discriminates, distinguishes, identifies, illustrates, infers, outlines, relates, selects, separates
Synthesis: Builds a structure or pattern from diverse elements; puts parts together to form a whole while emphasizing a new meaning or structure *Examples: Composes an organizational policy, operations, or process manual; organizes, plans, and leads a process improvement project*	Categorizes, combines, compiles, composes, creates, designs, devises, explains, generates, modifies, organizes, plans, rearranges, reconstructs, relates, reorganizes, revises, rewrites, summarizes, tells, writes
Evaluation: Makes judgments about the value of ideas or materials *Examples: Selects the most effective, efficient, and efficacious solution to a health delivery problem; explains and justifies a project or annual budget*	Appraises, compares, concludes, contrasts, criticizes, critiques, defends, describes, discriminates, evaluates, explains, interprets, justifies, relates, summarizes, supports

Adapted from Bloom, B. S. (1956). *Taxonomy of educational objectives. Handbook I: The cognitive domain.* New York: David McKay. Retrieved from http://www.nwlink.com/~Donclark/hrd/bloom.html#cognitive.

to an overall structure or purpose through differentiating, organizing, and attributing

5. *Evaluating*: Making judgments based on criteria and standards through checking and critiquing

6. *Creating*: Putting elements together to form a coherent or functional whole; reorganizing elements into a new pattern or structure through generating, planning, or producing[41]

Next, we turn to the affective domain within Bloom's Taxonomy. This domain includes the manner in which we deal with things emotionally, such as feelings, values, appreciation, enthusiasms, motivations, and attitudes.

The five major categories are listed in **Table 5-5** from the simplest behavior to the most complex.

The psychomotor domain includes physical movement, coordination, and use of the motor-skill areas. Development of these skills requires practice, and achievement in this domain is measured in terms of speed, precision, distance, procedures, or techniques in execution. **Table 5-6** lists the seven major categories in the psychomotor domain in order from the simplest behavior to the most complex.

Understanding and utilizing these taxonomies will assist health leaders in evaluating their own progress in learning about leadership and applying leadership capabilities;

Table 5-5 Bloom's Taxonomy of the Affective Domain (Original Version)	
Category and Examples	**Key Words and Actions**
Receiving Phenomena: Awareness, willingness to hear, selective attention. *Examples: Listens to others with respect; listens for and remembers name of newly introduced person*	Asks, chooses, describes, erects, follows, gives, holds, identifies, locates, names, points to, selects, sits, replies, uses
Responding to Phenomena: Active participation in activities; learns from stimulus; attends and reacts to particular phenomenon; shows compliance in responding, willingness in responding, or satisfaction in responding (motivation) *Examples: Participates in discussions; gives presentations; questions new ideas, concepts, and models to understand them; knows rules and follows them*	Answers, aids, assists, complies, conforms, discusses, greets, helps, labels, performs, practices, presents, reads, recites, reports, selects, tells, writes
Valuing: The worth or value a person attaches to a particular object, phenomenon, or behavior; ranges from simple acceptance (compliance) to commitment; based on the internalization of a set of specified values; clues often expressed in overt behavior and are often identifiable *Examples: Demonstrates belief in the democratic process; is sensitive to individual and cultural differences; speaks up appropriately on matters one feels strongly about*	Completes, demonstrates, differentiates, explains, follows, forms, initiates, invites, joins, justifies, proposes, reads, reports, selects, shares, studies, works
Organization: Organizes values into priorities by contrasting different values; resolves conflicts between those values and creates new (or modified) value system; emphasis is on comparing, relating, and synthesizing values *Examples: Recognizes the need to balance freedom with responsible behavior; accepts responsibility for own behavior; explains role of systematic planning to solve problems; accepts professional ethical standards; balances abilities, interests, and beliefs as well as organization, family, and self*	Adheres, alters, arranges, combines, compares, completes, defends, explains, formulates, generalizes, identifies, integrates, modifies, orders, organizes, prepares, relates, synthesizes
Internalizing Values: Has a value system that controls one's behavior; behavior is pervasive, consistent, predictable, and characteristically that of a learner *Examples: Shows self-reliance when working alone; cooperates in group activities (teamwork); uses an objective approach to problem solving; displays professional commitment to an ethical framework and moral practice at all times; revises judgments and behaviors in light of new evidence; values people for what they are and how they behave, not on appearance*	Acts, discriminates, displays, influences, listens, modifies, performs, practices, proposes, qualifies, questions, revises, serves, solves, verifies

Adapted from Krathwohl, D. R., Bloom, B. S., & Masia, B. B. (1973). *Taxonomy of educational objectives, the classification of educational goals. Handbook II: Affective domain.* New York: David McKay. Retrieved May 12, 2009 from http://www.nwlink.com/~Donclark/hrd/bloom.html#affective.

Table 5-6　Bloom's Taxonomy of the Psychomotor Domain (Original Version)	
Category and Examples	**Key Words and Actions**
Perception: The ability to use sensory cues to guide motor activity; ability ranges from sensory stimulation to translation. *Examples: Detects nonverbal communication cues; estimates where a ball will land after it is thrown; adjusts height of forklift forks in relation to pallet*	Chooses, describes, detects, differentiates, distinguishes, identifies, isolates, relates, selects
Set: Readiness to act; includes mental, physical, and emotional sets; these three sets are dispositions that predetermine a person's response to different situations. *Examples: Knows and acts upon a sequence of steps in a care delivery process; recognizes one's abilities and limitations; shows desire to learn a new process (motivation)*	Begins, displays, explains, moves, proceeds, reacts, shows, states, volunteers
Guided Response: The early stages of learning a complex skill, which include imitation and trial and error; adequacy of performance is achieved by practice. *Examples: Solves a financial or mathematical equation as demonstrated; follows instructions to conduct an activity*	Copies, follows, reacts, reproduces, responds, traces
Mechanism: The intermediate stage of learning a complex skill; learned responses have become habitual and the movements can be performed with some confidence and proficiency. *Examples: Uses a personal computer and software program; drives a car*	Assembles, calibrates, constructs, dismantles, displays, fastens, fixes, grinds, heats, manipulates, measures, mends, mixes, organizes, sketches
Complex Overt Response: The skillful performance of motor acts that involve complex movement patterns. Proficiency is indicated by a quick, accurate, and highly coordinated performance, requiring a minimum amount of energy; performs without hesitation, an automatic response. *Note: Same as Mechanism but performed more quickly, better, and more accurately.* *Examples: Operates a computer and software program quickly and accurately; displays confidence while addressing a group*	Assembles, calibrates, constructs, dismantles, displays, fastens, fixes, grinds, heats, manipulates, measures, mends, mixes, organizes, sketches
Adaptation: Skills are well developed and the person can modify movement patterns to fit special situations and requirements. *Examples: Responds effectively and efficiently to unexpected situations and experiences; modifies instruction to meet the needs of the learners; uses a machine or medical instrument in a new way (not as intended) successfully*	Adapts, alters, changes, rearranges, reorganizes, revises, varies
Origination: Creates new movement patterns to fit a particular situation or specific problem. Learning outcomes emphasize creativity based on highly developed skills. *Examples: Constructs a new theory or model; develops a new and comprehensive training program*	Arranges, builds, combines, composes, constructs, creates, designs, initiates, makes, originates

Adapted from Simpson, E. J. (1972). *The classification of educational objectives in the psychomotor domain.* Washington, D.C.: Gryphon House. Retrieved from http://www.nwlink.com/~Donclark/hrd/bloom.html#psychomotor.

moreover, it will assist leaders in structuring the development of their subordinate team members. Motivating and inspiring to focus the collective energy of a diverse workforce toward the mission and vision of the health organization are paramount to leadership success. The next section provides an overview of motivation and inspiration theories, models, and applications.

MOTIVATION AND INSPIRATION

In the health leader's array of knowledge, skills, and abilities, motivation and inspiration rank high on the list. Carnevale states that "creating a climate that enhances motivation, with the commensurate increase in productivity, is a requirement."[42] Motivation is all about getting a person to start and persist on a task or project. Inspiration is the emotive feeling of value a person experiences while performing a worthy task or project.

Motivation and inspiration in the present day are rooted in the concepts of influence and, to some degree, power. Leaders use motivation and inspiration to influence subordinate actions. Traditionally, leadership thinking rested on the concepts of power and influence. However, the modern-day art of leadership requires a more subtle approach to the misconception of aggressive power and "arm-twisting" influence. The well-educated and complex health workforce will resist the use of errant influence and positional power. Rather, as a twist on motivation must derive from authority and power, Drenkard states that effective leaders do not necessarily have to possess the greatest amount of authority, but must be good communicators, encouragers, and motivators.[43]

Perhaps not surprisingly, many leaders, academics, and scholars disagree about the best use of power and influence. "There is more conceptual confusion about influence processes than about any other facet of leadership."[44] This section begins with a brief discussion of where influence "exists" for a person; this is followed by a discussion on group affiliation, and then influence as a concept is explored.

Subordinates in health organizations look to leaders, and especially senior executives, as champions and sources of inspiration. Inspirational motivation in health organizations can be achieved when the leader passionately believes in the vision and is able to motivate others through this passion. The leadership team plays an important role in ensuring the success of the organization. This team determines the direction of the organization, while also ensuring that the details behind each event are managed well. Leaders have the responsibility of being concerned about the task of the organization and the support of the organization's stakeholders. Successful health organizations have leaders who not only provide the overall vision for the organization, but also step in and play a pivotal role by motivating and recognizing the efforts of subordinates that contribute to success.[45]

Ethics and morality also play a key role in motivating others; collectively, they represent a crucial characteristic for a leader to possess. The success of the organization may rise and fall on the perception of the community regarding the morals of the organization. Subordinates and the community expect leaders to use their best judgment and to do what is right. Although leadership distinctions may depend on the execution of skills and abilities, such as charisma, the distinction of authentic leadership rests heavily on perceptions of morality.[46] To gain widespread support, the organization must demonstrate the sincerity of its mission and stay true to the values it supports as an organization.

LOCUS OF CONTROL

To understand where or how people are motivated and inspired, it is important to recognize each person's perspective on influence. Rotter used a personality scale that measured locus of control orientation as a means of assessing influence.[47] People with a strong internal locus of control orientation (a belief that they control their own destiny and success) believe that events in their lives are determined more by their own actions than by chance or uncontrollable forces. (Leaders and managers tend to be "internals.") In contrast, people with a strong external control orientation believe that events are determined mostly by chance or fate and that they can do little to improve their lives. Research by Miller and Toulouse associated effective management (leadership) with managers (leaders) with an internal locus of control orientation.[48,49] According to this research, some people are influenced inside themselves (internalizers) and some are influenced outside of themselves (externalizers). In reality, both an internalizer and an externalizer are present inside each person. As a health leader, it is important to understand the people you lead—specifically, to understand which subordinates are more internally oriented and which are more externally oriented.

GROUP AFFILIATION

Schutz's theory of affiliation suggests that individuals form groups in response to three kinds of needs:

- *Inclusion need*: The need to be included
- *Control need*: The need for status and power
- *Affection need*: The need to give and receive warmth and closeness

These needs are cyclical; groups pass through observable phases of inclusion, control, and affection.[50] When a leader balances a subordinate's need for inclusion with his or her needs for control and affection within a group environment, the seeds of a powerful organizational or group culture are planted. In a study published in the research literature in 2007, charismatic leadership attributes used by leaders positively contributed to social identification processes and to social identity applied to the workplace.[51] This suggests that leaders can positively influence group affiliation.

Ideally, the leader's subordinate group will be formed into a cohesive team. The health leader's understanding and active use of the insight provided by Schutz's theory could prove very valuable in developing a high-performing, effective, and efficacious team.

INFLUENCE

In the simplest terms, leader influence on one or more subordinates may have one of three possible outcomes:

- *Commitment*: The person internally agrees with a decision or request from the leader and makes a great effort to carry out the request or implement the decision effectively.
- *Compliance*: The person is willing to do what the leader asks but is apathetic rather than enthusiastic about it and will make only a minimal effort. The leader has influenced the person's behavior but not the person's attitudes.
- *Resistance*: The person is opposed to the proposal or request, rather than merely indifferent about it, and actively tries to avoid carrying it out.[52]

Clearly, commitment is what every leader desires from each team member or members. The reason motivation is linked with inspiration is that leaders should communicate how the task, project, or action is integrated with a subordinate's job activities and provide individualized consideration and concern for that subordinate.

SELF-DETERMINATION THEORY

Self-determination theory (SDT) is a motivation theory that focuses on human motivation, personality, and well-being.[53] This macro theory assists in investigating people's inherent growth and psychological needs and the conditions that promote self-motivation and personality integration.[54] SDT begins with the assumption that people are active organisms that have only three basic psychological needs: autonomy, competence, and relatedness.[55] Autonomy concerns the feeling of choice and having the ability to initiate one's own behavior, whereas relatedness is associated with respecting others and the sense of relying on others.[56] Competence is related to the ability of the individual to complete a challenging task and achieve a desired outcome.[57] When these needs are supported and satisfied within a social context, people experience more vitality and self-motivation, as well as enhanced well-being.[58]

To create an environment that is conducive to satisfying the three basic psychological needs—autonomy, relatedness, and competence—leadership must first develop an interpersonal environment and appropriate relationships with their subordinates. Leaders should allow subordinates to participate in the decision-making and planning processes. This will encourage autonomy and self-empowerment. To promote relatedness and competence, health leaders should equip employees with the fundamental information needed to complete challenging tasks; they should set obtainable goals and encourage staff to use problem solving to formulate solutions. This will give team members or employees the satisfaction of achieving a desired outcome and allow them to depend on each other to achieve a mutual goal.

To promote intrinsic motivation and intrinsic goals, team members or employees should be rewarded with positive praise, public praise, achievement certificates, and other rewards, not just increased pay or salary. Team members should be allowed to choose their own goals, as long as the goals are in alignment with the organization's goals. This will also promote autonomy. If the goals or tasks are interesting to the employee, intrinsic motivators are used, and the task is performed for the satisfaction of completing the task. To create an environment that promotes autonomy orientation, leaders should limit unnecessary rules, thus promoting workers' empowerment. This gives subordinates a sense of authority, by allowing them the ability to make decisions based on the values of their work environment. Employees then tend to be self-regulated and orient toward the values of the organization when deciding how to behave and perform. This macro theory is the applied expression of social exchange–based theories, discussed next.

MOTIVATION BASED IN SOCIAL EXCHANGE THEORY: EXCHANGE AND EXPECTANCY THEORIES

Social exchange theory requires that leaders give something in exchange (e.g., higher salary, bonus, increased status) for improved or additional performance by subordinates. Under this theory, relationships can be described in terms of their rewards, costs, profits, and losses. As long as rewards exceed costs (group membership is profitable), group membership is attractive. In social exchange theory, cohesiveness of group members becomes a salient issue.

Exchange theory, as developed by Graen, emphasizes the interaction of the leader with the subordinate or supervised group. The leader exchanges resources, such as increased job or task choices and latitude, influence on decision making, and open communication, for members' commitment to higher involvement in organizational functioning.[59] Under this theory, the leader categorizes followers into two groups: (1) the cadre or in-group and (2) the hired hands or out-group. With the in-group, the leader allows greater subordinate choices and decision making that contribute to higher performance, lower propensity to quit, greater supervisory relationships, and greater job satisfaction. The out-group receives less latitude and, therefore, has poorer performance outcomes. Social exchange theory and the application of Graen's exchange theory are both salient factors in leadership. With a basic understanding of exchange theory, Vroom's expectancy theory of motivation can be studied.

According to Vroom's expectancy theory,[60] motivation depends on a person's belief that effort will lead to performance, and performance will lead to rewards that are valued. If any of these three variables (expectancy, instrumentality, and valence) decreases in value, then motivation decreases. Likewise, as the variables increase in value, motivation increases. *Expectancy* is the subordinate's belief that effort will result in quality performance; it focuses on how the employee perceives the relationship between his or her effort and performance. *Instrumentality* is the belief in the reward for quality performance; it refers to the perceived relationship between performance and outcome. *Valence* is the level of self-satisfaction in the reward and in the quality performance. In other words, how valuable is the outcome? Does the person think if he or she tries hard, he or she can achieve the outcome, and does the person think he or she can really achieve the outcome?

Integrating well with expectancy theory in the realm of motivation and inspiration, Cleavenger and Munyon state that transformational leadership is most effective when the leader is able to emphasize the importance of the work being performed; the leader must give meaning to the employee's work.[61] There are five job characteristics, structured by the leader, that impact work outcomes within the genre of expectancy theory, motivation, and inspiration:

- *Autonomy*: The freedom an individual has in carrying out work
- *Skill variety*: The extent to which an individual must use different skills to perform his or her job
- *Task identity*: The extent to which an individual can complete a whole piece of work
- *Task significance*: The extent to which a job impacts others' lives
- *Feedback from the job*: The extent to which a job imparts information about the individual's performance[62]

Social exchange theories and models are closely integrated with goal setting, the subject of the next subsection.

GOAL-SETTING THEORY: A MOTIVATIONAL THEORY

Goal-setting theory,[63–65] which was originally developed by Edwin Locke, is an effective motivational and inspirational leadership approach. Goals are the aim of an action or behavior. They can be set for any verifiable or measurable outcome. "Goals provide order and structure, measure progress, give a sense of achievement, and provide closure."[66] Locke's basic assumption is that goals are immediate regulators of human action. An individual synthesizes direction, effort, and persistence to accomplish goals (**Figure 5-1**).

To maximize the effectiveness of goal setting, specific and challenging goals should be established to focus action

FIGURE 5-1 Locke's goal-setting theory constructs and application.

and effort over time to accomplish tasks. From 1968 to 1980, 90% of all studies conducted in this area showed that specific, well-defined, and challenging goals led to greater improvements in performance compared to vague and easy goals.[67] Individuals must commit to setting goals to produce results; the more difficult (challenging yet reasonable) the goal, the better the individual will perform.

Individuals need leadership support (feedback, reward mechanisms, and required resources [time, training, and material goods]) to maximize performance when applying goal setting. "Goal setting and regular communication increase the challenge of the job, make it clear to workers precisely what they are expected to do, and deliver a sense of pride and achievement."[68] Locke suggests seven steps to follow to apply and optimize goal setting:

1. Specify objectives or tasks to be done.
2. Specify how performance will be measured.
3. Specify the standard to be reached.
4. Specify the time frame involved.
5. Prioritize goals.
6. Rate goals as to difficulty and importance.
7. Determine the coordination requirements.[69]

Leaders must ensure that the goals they set do not conflict with one another or with organizational goals. For groups, every group member should have verifiable, specific goals, as well as an overall group goal to counter social loafing. Smaller groups (three to eight people) are more effective than larger ones in goal setting.[70] The use of management by objectives (MBO) is an approach for leaders to utilize goal setting,[71] whereby mutually acceptable goals can be developed with subordinates.[72] Locke's model, coupled with SMART goals, is an excellent model; SMART is an acronym for specific, measurable, attainable, relevant, and time-bound.[73]

Leaders should be cognizant of the drawbacks of goal setting, which include excessive risk taking and excessive competitiveness. Indeed, goal failure can reduce subordinate confidence and create unwanted stress. However, the benefits of goal setting outweigh the negative potential aspects of applying the theory. "Goal-setting theories provide specific explanations for why people are motivated. Difficult, specific, and mutually developed goals will assist individuals in being motivated. Although goal setting is extremely useful, many individuals are motivated more by climate [current atmosphere or "feeling" of the workplace; an easily changed phenomenon], culture, and affiliation."[74]

Goal setting integrates well with other motivational theories. Although goal setting is a principal component of many motivational and performance theories, research in this genre has largely focused on locus of control influences and expectancy theory relationships. For the health leader, the merging or synthesis of related theories provides a powerful repertoire for utilization in a multitude of situations. Some examples of results from the evaluation of merged theories are as follows:

- Considering the theory of locus of control, internalizers tend to have better performance than externalizers with regard to goal setting and applying goal setting.[75]
- In the merger of expectancy theory and goal-setting theory, goal setting is negatively related to valence (setting low-level goals does not satisfy individuals as well as setting high-level goals), and instrumentality is positively related to goal setting (difficult goals give the individual a greater sense of achievement, self-efficacy, and skill improvement than do easy goals).[76]

Clearly, motivation and influence are critical to leadership success. The understanding, application, and enhanced skill and ability a leader gains by using applied theories such as goal setting are invaluable.

POWER, INFLUENCE, AND THE BASIS OF POWER

Power is the capacity of a leader or agent to influence the values, beliefs, attitudes, and behaviors of another person, group, or organization. Using power to influence a change of behaviors is less difficult than changing attitudes; attitudes are less difficult to change than either beliefs or values. Power and influence can be characterized in several ways; the two methods presented here are the most universal.

Power can be discussed in terms of Kelman's social influence theory[77,78] and the process of social influence. Power and influence, serving as a catalyst, prompt three responses to varying degrees; that is, the subordinate or target of a leader's power- and influence-based request or requirement may demonstrate instrumental compliance, internalization, and/or identification.

- *Instrumental compliance* is defined as a subordinate's or target person's fulfillment of the leader's requested action for the purpose of obtaining a tangible reward or avoiding a punishment controlled by the agent. This is an example of transactional leadership in action from a foundation of the social exchange theory.
- *Internalization* is defined as a subordinate or target person's commitment to support and implement

requests (and actions required to fulfill the request) made by the leader because they are perceived to be intrinsically desirable and correct in relation to the target's values, beliefs, attitudes, self-image, and culture.[79] In this response, the request or proposal becomes integrated with the target person's underlying values and beliefs. It is an example of transformational leadership in action.

- *Identification* is defined as a subordinate's or target person's imitation of the leader's behavior and/or adoption of the same attitudes to please the leader. This is an example of social learning theory in action and is closely linked to role modeling.

Another method to consider in terms of the use of power and influence on subordinates, peers, stakeholders, and possibly superiors results in three possibilities: commitment, compliance, or resistance.

- *Commitment* occurs when the person, group members, or organizational members who are the focus of power and influence from the leader internally agree with a decision or request from the leader; they then implement an approach to fulfill the request or implement the decision effectively, efficiently, and efficaciously. Commitment implies attitude change in the subordinates.

- *Compliance* occurs when the person, group members, or organizational members are willing to do what the leader desires but in a mechanical or apathetic manner, applying only moderate to minimal effort. Compliance implies that the subordinate's behavior, but not his or her attitude, has changed due to the leader's influence.

- *Resistance* happens when organizational members are opposed to the leader's request and actively avoid carrying it out, perhaps even taking steps to block actions to fulfill the leader's request.

The most recognized basis of power and influence comes from French and Raven's Power Taxonomy. **Table 5-7** is presented in tandem with Kelman's model for purposes of synthesis and comparison.

Agenda power—the authority and control of agenda items—is similar to information power but can be recognized as a source of power as well: Consider the secretary's or assistant's control of meeting agenda items on behalf of the leader (superior). Moreover, health leaders have power from legitimate or formal power, also called position power: "Position power includes potential influence derived from legitimate authority, control over resources and rewards, control over punishments, control over information, and control over the organization of the work and the physical work environment."[80]

Table 5-7 French and Raven's Power Taxonomy and Kelman's Power and Influence Outcomes		
French and Raven's Power Taxonomy	Description	Kelman's Influence Processes
Reward	Person complies to obtain rewards controlled by the agent.	Instrumental compliance
Coercive	Person complies to avoid punishment by the agent.	Instrumental compliance
Legitimate (also called formal)	Person complies because the agent has the right to make the request; person is under the chain of authority.	Instrumental compliance, internalization, and identification
Expert	Person complies because the agent has special knowledge.	Internalization
Referent	Person complies because he or she admires or identifies with the agent and wants the agent's approval.	Identification
Information*	Control of information by agent is a source of power.	

*Added by Yukl.

Data from French, J. R. P., & Raven, B. H. (1959). The bases of social power. In D. Cartwright (Ed.), *Studies of social power* (pp. 150–167). Ann Arbor, MI: Institute for Social Research; Kelman, H. C. (1958). Compliance, identification and internalization: Three processes of attitude change. *Journal of Conflict Resolution, 2,* 51–56; Kelman, H. C. (1974). Further thoughts on the process of compliance, identification, and internalization. In J. T. Tedeschi (Ed.), *Perspectives on social power* (pp. 125–171). Chicago: Aldine; Yukl, G. (1994). *Leadership in organizations* (3rd ed.). Englewood Cliffs, NJ: Prentice Hall, p. 202.

Power is maintained, if not increased, by its wise use. The use of power is particularly important in organizational culture; who controls resources, who receives those resources, and how resources are used all contribute to the cultural disposition of the organization. Bolman and Deal, in their reframing organizational leadership model (specifically, under the "political" construct), overtly suggest that leaders must use power and resource distribution wisely. Again, consistent and predetermined leadership actions, when using power and distributing resources, are paramount to ensure leader success.

Power and influence, and the basis of power, change in all organizations. "Power is not static; it changes over time due to changing conditions and the actions of individuals and coalitions."[81] Subcultures in health organizations have also been shown to create and build resistance to power, influence, and change.[82] Controlling your emotions is "power's crucial foundation"[83] across all professional situations. Health leaders who control their emotional "self," are cognizant of their sources and level of power. They are also sensitive to subcultures in the organization and to sources and level of power in others, and they will best navigate amid coalitions and groups in moving the health organization forward in a positive direction. Of course, as in motivation, influence and power, competence, network building, interpersonal relationship building, and communication competencies are also vital to leadership. Next, concepts of leadership network building, interpersonal relationships, personal development, and communication are discussed.

FORMING RELATIONSHIPS, NETWORKS, AND ALLIANCES

Leaders are rarely successful in any organization without the assistance of positive relationships and networks. Knowledge and education can only help an individual achieve certain levels of success. The ability to build relationships and networks is critically important at early stages of leadership development. However, as the junior leader emerges from initial leader development jobs into more responsible and complex positions in dynamic organizations, his or her success is no longer a function of skills and tools as much as the ability to influence the behaviors of those outside the organization; outside stakeholders form the basis for networks and alliances in the organizational environment.[84,85] In support of this notion, Mintzberg found that leaders spend 44% of their time dealing with outside agents and stakeholders, and the rest of their time talking to internal (or other) elements associated with organizational survival.[86,87]

For health organizations, policies are official expressions and, at least, implied guidelines of expected behavior, decision making, and thinking within the organization. Because policies help organizations attain objectives, they must be consistent with the health organization's mission. However, when determining policies, health organizations must take into account the needs of the stakeholders who make up outside networks and alliances. These external stakeholders include the community, patients, providers, and insurers.

Stakeholders are constituents with a vested interest in the affairs and actions of health organizations. They include individuals, groups, and organizations affected by the health organization's decisions and actions. A well-thought-out and implemented philosophy about stakeholders is a prerequisite to a health organization's strategic planning effort, resource allocation and utilization, customer service strategies, and ability to cope with the external environment in general. Stakeholders can be classified into three groups:

- *Internal stakeholders* "operate entirely within the bounds of the organization and typically include management and professional and nonprofessional staff."[88]
- *Interface stakeholders* "function both internally and externally to the organization" and include medical staff, the governing body, and stockholders in the case of for-profit health organizations.
- *External stakeholders*, such as suppliers, patients, and third-party payers, including government entities and officials, interact with the organization, provide resources, or use services of the organization. The health organization needs this stakeholder group to survive. Other external stakeholders include competitors, special-interest groups, local communities, labor organizations, and regulatory and accrediting agencies.

Health organizations must assess stakeholders to determine which ones are most important, which ones pose potential threats, and which ones have the potential to cooperate with the health organization. Such an assessment suggests appropriate health organization behavior toward stakeholders, ranging from ignoring, to negotiating, to co-opting and cooperating. Asking a stakeholder group that the health organization has previously ignored to assist the organization with significant influence or resources would be futile. The assessment of stakeholders should also capture conflicting priorities, needs, demands, incentives, and political and financial pressures as related to the association with the health organization.

Balancing the demands of multiple stakeholders with different interests is a major challenge. Levey and Hill suggest that the need for health organization managers (leaders) to balance demands can pose "moral dilemmas arising from responsibilities to patients, governing boards, (professional) staff, and community."[89] Balancing these demands is necessary to maintain ethical values and social responsibility and to prevent inappropriate demands made by single-interest stakeholders from predominating.

The stakeholder philosophy should be consistent with continuous quality improvement. "For example, patients as consumers were passive stakeholders until this decade."[90] Patients are major stakeholders, as are third-party payers; both aggressively seek to influence the health organization. External stakeholders are a fact of life; responding to their legitimate interests while minimizing the effects of inappropriate demands is necessary.

Health organizations are dynamic, heterogeneous entities composed of numerous suborganizations and interdependent processes. These linkages, when changed, affect other internal departments as well as the external environment. Various types of health organizations are found in both the private (owned by private individuals or groups) and public (owned by government) sectors. Health organizations may be institutions, the most prominent of which are hospitals and nursing facilities, or they may be programs and agencies, such as public health departments and visiting nurse associations. All interact with, influence, and depend on their internal environments to provide the range of health services that, in turn, interact with, influence, and depend on the external environment that the organization serves.

In earlier eras, traditional approaches to leadership development were based on the notion that an individual's formal education prior to employment would provide enough learning to span an entire career. Today, however, restructuring efforts, coupled with continuous environmental and technological change, have contributed to rapid job obsolescence at all organizational levels; as a result, leaders need to rely more on outside relationships to ensure organizational success.[91] This emerging focus on managing alliances and networks mandates that leadership development efforts concentrate as much on networking across the entire organization with stakeholders as on the technical requirements of leadership.

Networks can be seen as living systems that adapt and change over time. As more individuals and groups join the network, they become dependent on one another for "group" survival and future growth.[92] If one area of a network is threatened, other partners in the alliance may be less likely to abandon "one of their own" and move off to recruit new replacements if there is a friendship in place. Although relationship and network building may be difficult for many early careerists to understand and embrace, the practical reality of working and operating in the health environment requires a formal and informal network to achieve results. This need usually becomes apparent during the first few months in a new position. The application of the knowledge, skills, and abilities presented here will assist you in dealing with these kinds of real-world situations as they arise in the workplace.

Health organizations establish supply chains; such a chain is both a network and an alliance between two or more organizations. In today's collaborative, customer-driven, networked economy, forming and sustaining strategic business relationships with customers, suppliers, and partners have become mission-critical imperatives. If done well, the creation of collaborative relationships will lead to greater success and profitability for the organizations involved. As with all other aspects of business, specific steps are followed in forming these relationships—namely, planning, preparing, interaction, and analysis and refinement. These relationships are complex and require investigation and consideration of what each party wants out of the relationship.[93]

FORMAL AND INFORMAL NETWORKS

The support of formal and informal networks—that is, groups of individuals connected in some way—is important for the leader to perform his or her duties. Formal professional networks include peers and superiors at the health organization as well as professional links to members of associations to which the leader belongs. Informal networks tend to be associated with friendship and longevity. Internal networks in the health organization assist leadership to accomplish goals and objectives as well as to move the organizational culture toward the desired state. External networks within the health professions and in the community are also important for career progression and health organization integration and acceptance in the communities served. The basis of building networks, whether internal or external, is interpersonal relationships.

Formal networks in the workplace tend to mirror an organizational wire diagram or organizational structure diagram. These relationships are generally supervisory in nature and carry with them an annual performance appraisal of some sort.

Health leaders in the higher positions can be great leaders, or, unfortunately, not-so-great leaders. If you encounter great leaders, learn from them. With not-so-great leaders, look to them to learn what not to do. Some leaders in the upper echelons of the hierarchy may not lead through charisma, motivation, and values-driven philosophies, but rather use coercion and legitimacy of position to manipulate their subordinates. Leaders of this sort do not care about or know the feelings of those under them. They focus only on organizational outcomes and lead through a bottom-line mentality. It may be difficult to work for such leaders; however, for those in job-lock situations with few options for employment elsewhere, the legitimate and coercive boss can dominate a formal network of subordinates for years, with his or her power unchecked.[94,95] What is important, when working under a not-so-good leader, is to be a great leader to those who follow you and are subordinate to you. You can be a great leader at whatever level position you hold.

Informal networks are relationships with others within or outside of the health organization that exist through mutual understanding. They are based on the strengths and values of each member of the informal group and the shared aspiration of members' success. Such may be the case with the local community hospital or health organization and the local entity itself. For example, the president of a local health organization cooperative or association benefits from the wide participation of local affiliated hospitals. The larger the network, the more legitimacy and creditability the cooperative or association may have among its peers in the community when it comes time to lobby local government for changes in policy or recognition of its members. In turn, the chief executive officers (CEOs) of the local hospitals and healthcare networks benefit from the opportunity to ally with a large assortment of peers and stakeholders in the local community and establish alliances to achieve various economies of scales on issues, resulting in better outcomes for both parties.[96,97]

From an individual perspective, the same lesson may be applied on a personal level within an organization. The locally elected union representative may have formal reporting relationships within the vertically integrated facility itself; however, if the internal union leader and the legitimately appointed CEO do not have a positive relationship, contract negotiations and employee complaints may result in less than cordial and collegial discussions. In the worst-case scenario, risk management issues may evolve into lawsuits and litigation rather than leading to open discussion, problem solving, arbitration, and mediation.[98,99]

From a more pragmatic perspective, the essential tasks of many leaders in nonprofit health organizations may include fundraising and lobbying of state and local officials for funding. Although a CEO may be able to justify needs and budget expenses to outside agents and stakeholders, many CEOs of these types of organizations find that it is their ability to influence and leverage personal relationships that results in the advantageous distribution of funds and the personal contributions of charitable donors.[100] Given this factor, organizational survival may depend as much on the CEO's informal professional network as on the development of strategic plans and leadership of internal subordinates.

INTERPERSONAL RELATIONSHIPS[101]

Building relationships while in a leadership role is not always easy. Nevertheless, you can build relationships in a professional manner while maintaining your position of power and authority. If honesty, inclusion, and sincerity (the building blocks of trust) are the basis of your quality communication, and if that communication is culturally competent, then you can maintain your role while building relationships. You can gauge the nature of each relationship based on disclosure levels; leaders must consciously draw the line when determining their personal level of disclosure. Disclosing too much or too soon or too often can reduce your position of power and authority; being personally "disclosure conservative" is a good initial approach when building new relationships.

For health leaders (or any other leaders, for that matter), interpersonal relationships are required, are beneficial, and enhance leadership capability and success. Certain elements or factors facilitate improved, positive, and mutually beneficial relationships. In 1989, Yukl proposed a taxonomy of managerial behaviors in which one of the four major domains of managerial life was "building relationships"; in this construct, managing conflict, team building, networking, supporting, developing, and mentoring were the actual behaviors and activities that leaders were recommended to engage in to strengthen relationships.[102] A health organization leader should establish, enhance, and grow relationships with a myriad of organizational stakeholders both internal and external to the organization. There is no better method to build relationships than going to visit people in their own environment or location; this kind of "management by walking around" is a powerful approach.

The next section provides an overview of four key factors that will enhance relationships. Each factor described has monumental importance, though many factors play a role in forging and maintaining solid relationships.

FACTORS TO STRENGTHEN RELATIONSHIPS

A *relationship* encompasses the feelings, roles, norms, status, and trust that both affect and reflect the quality of communication between members of a group.[103] Relational communication theorists assert that every message has both a *content* and a *relationship* dimension:

- Content contains specific information conveyed to someone.
- Relationship messages provide hints about whether the sender/receiver likes or dislikes the other person.

Communicating with someone in a manner that provides both content and positive relationship information is important. Language, tone, and nonverbal communication all work together to provide communicative meaning that is interpreted by another person. Consider the following points about nonverbal communication:[104,105]

- Nonverbal communication is more prevalent than verbal communication and consists of the following elements:
  - Eye contact
  - Facial expressions
  - Body posture
  - Movement
- People believe nonverbal communication more than verbal communication.
  - Sixty-five percent of meaning is derived from nonverbal communication.
- People communicate emotions primarily through nonverbal communication.
  - Ninety-five percent of emotions are communicated nonverbally.

Frequent communication that is timely, useful, accurate, and in reasonable quantity is needed to reinforce and validate the relationship. Thus one important factor in developing quality interpersonal relationships is *quality communication of sufficient and desired frequency*.

A second factor is *disclosure*, which was mentioned briefly earlier in this chapter. Disclosure relates to the type of information you and the other person in the relationship share with each other; disclosure is one factor that can help you "measure" or evaluate the depth and breadth of a relationship. The "deeper" the information disclosed, the closer the bond of the relationship. Also, the broader the topics of information and experience sharing (e.g., family, work, fishing together, or playing golf) between people, the closer the bond of the relationship. Disclosure or self-disclosure is strongly and positively correlated with trust; that is, more trust means more disclosure. Again, trust starts with quality communication.

Self-disclosure can be categorized and measured. In Powell's model,[106] level 5 illustrates a weak relationship bond, whereas level 1 shows a strong relationship bond:

- *Level 5*: Cliché communication
- *Level 4*: Facts and biographical information
- *Level 3*: Personal attitudes and ideas
- *Level 2*: Personal feelings
- *Level 1*: Peak communication (rare; usually with family or close friends)

Self-disclosure can be summarized as having the following characteristics:[107]

- A function of ongoing relationships
- Reciprocal
- Timed to what is happening in the relationship (contextual/situational/relational)
- Should be relevant to what is happening among people present
- Usually moves in small increments

A third factor in building strong interpersonal relationships is *trust* (mentioned briefly in relation to self-disclosure). Trust is built and earned over time through honest interaction (communication and experiences). It is an essential component of a quality, positive relationship. Honesty, inclusion, and sincerity are directly linked to building trust. *Honesty* means being truthful and open concerning important pieces of information that you share with another person. *Inclusion* entails including the other person in the relationship in activities and experiences that are important to the other person, to you, and to both of you. Inclusion is also about making sure the other person is part of the "group" in the organization. *Sincerity* is meaning what you say, meaning what you do, and not keeping a record or an account of the relationship (not keeping score). In support, intelligence and *trustworthiness* would rank as highly desirable at all levels of leadership by subordinates; interpersonal skills (e.g., cooperativeness, emotional stability) would be seen as more desirable in low-level leaders, while dominant traits (e.g., ambition, assertiveness) would be seen as more desirable in higher-level leaders.[108] Over time, if honesty, inclusion, and sincerity are the basis of your interactions with others, positive and quality relationships will begin to grow.

A fourth factor in forging successful relationships is *cultural competence*. This factor is based not only on ethnic or national dimensions, but also on socioeconomic factors. For instance, consider the cultural differences in surgeons as opposed to nurses as opposed to facility technicians or linen staff or consultants. Every stakeholder group and every individual has a varying culture of uniqueness. Understanding those cultural issues, or "walking a mile in someone else's shoes," is a factor important to building solid interpersonal relationships. Understanding and modifying your approach to relationship building and enhancement based on cultural differences will serve you well in leadership positions.

COMMUNICATION AND CULTURE

Health leaders need to have exceptional communication skills. They must learn the techniques for clarifying what someone else is saying and for being clear in their own communication. Mintzberg's study on managerial work revealed that managers' activity was characterized by "brevity, variety, and fragmentation"; managers were continually seeking information, preferring oral communications to written reports.[109,110] This finding applies to leaders as well. The preference for oral communication may be difficult for health leaders to enact, but nonetheless is important. As an example of personal preference for oral communication, it has been noted that within the first 7 months of President Barack Obama's administration, he had more White House press conferences than George W. Bush did in his 8 years in the same position.[111] Although verbal communication may be time consuming, given the needs of employees and the public for such communication, it is a very valuable tool that is essential to achieve success.

Simply put, communication is the process of *acting on information*.[112] Communication contributes tremendously to the culture and climate of the health organization. A response—feedback—is an essential aspect of the communication process. Obstacles to communication, called noise, either in the channel or in the mind of the receiver, may contribute to an inaccurate understanding of the intended message. Communication is the main catalyst behind the motivational efforts and strategies used by leaders.[113] "Various management [leadership] practices, including goal setting, reinforcement, feedback, and evaluation, require communication."[114] There are three goals of communication:

- Understanding
- Achieving the intended effect
- Being ethical (moral)

Communication is a process of active transaction (transactive), which means messages are sent and received simultaneously. Everything you do or do not do, say or do not say, communicates something. You cannot not communicate. Communication media, which encompass what and how to communicate, are discussed next.

MEDIA RICHNESS THEORY

Media richness theory[115–117] was originally developed by Daft and Lengel and later updated with the inclusion of computer-mediated communication[118] by D'Ambra

and Rice. It explains and predicts why certain types of technologies, called media channels or media, are effective (or not effective) in communication efforts. This theory is important to health leaders, because selecting the appropriate communication media channel, such as a face-to-face meeting, a telephone call, or an email, can predict the likelihood of successful communication to others, such as superiors, subordinates, and peers. Today, it is all too easy to send off an email. In many situations, however, email, as a media channel, is not a good choice if you wish to have your communication understood as you meant and, therefore, receivers of your message may not take the proper action you expect.

In media richness theory, various media are placed on a "richness" continuum based on the following factors (**Figure 5-2**):

- Potential for instant feedback
- Verbal and nonverbal cues that can be processed by senders and receivers
- Use of natural language versus stilted or formal language
- Level of focus on individual versus a group or mass of people

This theory indicates that ambiguous or potentially ambiguous messages should be sent with richer media to reduce the level of potential (or actual) misunderstanding. *Ambiguity*, also called *equivocality*, is based on the ability of the receiver, in this context, to ask questions. In other words, does the receiver know which questions to ask and how to get started?

Different from ambiguity is uncertainty, although these two constructs complement each other. Uncertainty resolution is "having the question answered" and having the appropriate information to proceed with an action, task, or project. "Uncertainty is a measure of the organization's ignorance of a value for a variable in the [information] space; equivocality is a measure of the organization's ignorance of whether a variable exists in the [information] space."[119] More information reduces uncertainty.[120] In the workplace, the more similar the work performed by subordinates (or the workforce in general) is, the more ambiguity exists, whereas the more dependent each segment of the work process or work flow is on other segments, the more uncertainty exists (**Figure 5-3**).

It is vital for leaders to reduce ambiguity and uncertainty to the greatest extent possible. The richer the media utilized, the greater the chance of leader communication success, the greater the chance of reducing ambiguity, and the greater the chance of reducing uncertainty. Unfortunately, richer media, such as face-to-face communication, cost more in

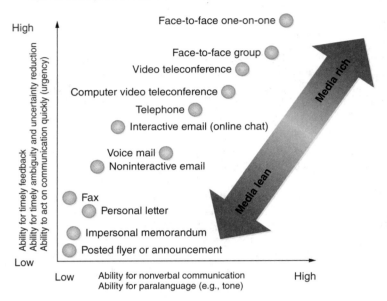

FIGURE 5-2 Media richness theory media channel continuum.

terms of resources (e.g., time, travel, meeting space) than do less rich media.

Health leaders will be more effective if they master the basics of media richness theory. Some important points to reflect on for leadership success are as follows:

- Select media channels to reduce ambiguity.
- Select media channels to reduce uncertainty.

- The more complex the issues, the more group members like face-to-face meetings.
- Computer-mediated communication (CMC) deals more with tasks but less with group relationships.
- CMC may increase polarization.
- CMC works best with linear, structured tasks.
- CMC increases individual "information processing" requirements.

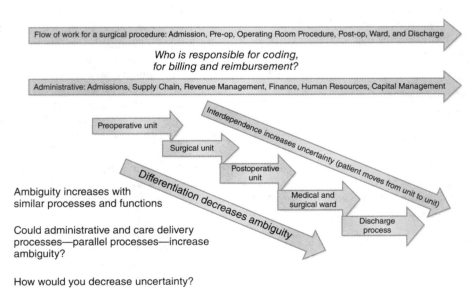

FIGURE 5-3 Ambiguity and uncertainty in health organization work process.

- People with technological skills gain more power in CMC group communication.
- More cliques and coalitions form with CMC than with face-to-face communication.

SYMBOLIC CONVERGENCE THEORY

Bormann developed symbolic convergence theory,[121] which explains how certain types of communication function to shape a group's identity and culture, and this, in turn, influences other dynamics such as norms, roles, and decision making. As part of this process, a group develops "fantasy" themes and stories. The key points are that groups develop a unique "group identity" (culture, personality) built on shared symbolic representations related to the group and that these cultures evolve through the adoption of fantasy themes or group stories. Stories provide insight into a group's culture, values, and identity.[122]

COMMUNICATION ENVIRONMENTS

Health organizations function best in communication environments that are open and honest, are free of fear and unnecessary anxiety, and support diverse teams of professionals. Gibb suggests that organizational communication environments promote either a defensive or a supportive communication climate. According to Beebe and Masterson, the following behaviors used by leaders (as well as by others, because subordinates tend to follow the leader's example) contribute to defensive or supportive communication environments:

- *Evaluative versus descriptive communication*: Evaluation is "you" language; description is "I" language. Descriptive language leads to more trust and greater group cohesiveness.
- *Problem orientation*: Such an orientation is more effective in reducing defensiveness (rather than attempting to control communication).
- *Strategic versus spontaneous communication*: Strategic communication (controlling) suggests manipulation, creating distrust, whereas spontaneous communication is inclusive.
- *Superiority versus equality in communication*: Supportive climates occur when participative and equity-based communication is used.
- *Certainty versus provisionalism*: Flexible, open, and genuine thinking fosters a more supportive climate than "knowing it all."[123]

The health organization's leader and leadership team—from the smallest unit leader all the way to the top of the hierarchy of the organization—set the example and develop the communication environment. The communication environment is a major foundational element of organizational culture. Which type of communication environment do you want to foster as a leader? Is one environment better at enabling more quality and productivity in the health organization than another environment?

Another communication environment model suggests that a culture may be either disconfirming or confirming based on communicative responses. In essence, a confirming communicative response causes people to value themselves more. A disconfirming communicative response causes people to value themselves less. Health leaders should work to be much more confirming than disconfirming, an effort that takes practice and work. Think about which responses are confirming and which responses are disconfirming.

Listening is yet another valuable leadership skill. Listening contributes to a supporting and confirming communication environment to build a culture of achievement. It encompasses the following aspects of communication:

- *Hearing*: Receiving the message as sent
- *Analyzing*: Discerning the speaker's purpose
- *Empathizing*: Seeing and understanding the speaker's viewpoint

"People seen as good leaders are also seen as good listeners."[124] A simple, yet effective listening model to practice and master has been summarized as follows: "(1) stop, (2) look, (3) listen, (4) ask questions, (5) paraphrase content, and (6) paraphrase feelings."[125]

Informal leadership within an organization is a reality. Miner states that organizational theory has overlooked the significant influence of informal groups and informal communication; 70% of organizational communication is informal, and those communications are up to 90% accurate.[126] Miner lists four characteristics of "informal leaders" that should be adopted by formal leaders; all of these characteristics influence the communication environment of the organization: (1) recognition of subgroups, (2) recognition of their difference from formal groups, (3) recognition of their influence and power, and (4) recognition of the esteem informal leaders command.[127]

Sometimes, despite the best efforts at communication, conflict may arise. A leader's wise use of conflict management knowledge, skills, and abilities is essential for effectiveness, efficiency, and efficacy in a health organization, as discussed next.

CONFLICT MANAGEMENT[128]

Conflict is both inevitable and necessary for a vibrant organization. Health leaders will surely meet with situations of conflict and, therefore, must master conflict management styles and techniques. Five frameworks form the basis of modern conflict management theory and application: psychodynamic theory, field theory, experimental gaming theory, human relations theory, and intergroup conflict theory.

Conflict that is channeled and managed effectively is a rational route to change, improvement, thought creation, and organizational longevity, if not outright survival. The existence of conflict means there are opportunities to find improved alternative solutions to the current state of affairs. Of course, conflict also can negatively affect the organization; even so, pessimism should not be the overriding default attitude assumed by leadership or management—or human existence for that matter. Leaders and managers can manage conflict and train others to apply skills and tools of conflict to achieve successful and improved outcomes in their professional lives. Leaders communicate meaning in everything they do. If messages are incongruent, goal conflicts and inconsistencies soon become part of the organizational culture.[129–131]

Hand-in-hand with conflict management are interpersonal relationships. Learning, as an organization, to constructively manage and succeed in conflict situations is a foundational construct of leadership and management.

Conflict occurs wherever interdependent people or groups (i.e., people or groups who depend on one another in some fashion for some need) have different goals[132] or aspirations of achievement amid an environment of scarce resources. Simply put, conflict arises when people, individually or in groups, must work together with other individuals or groups who have different goals, needs, or desires in an environment where a full complement of resources is not available to satisfy those goals, needs, or desires. We all live, work, and socialize with other people and share the limited resources available (rarely, if ever, are resources not limited), so conflict will happen and does happen to varying degrees of intensity. At one end of the spectrum, conflict can be a situation identified by two parties, such that those parties identify the problem and work together to solve it (problem-solving style). At the other end of the spectrum is violence (competing style) that inflicts bodily harm, such as in a war, which is the failure of conflict management.

Conflict is both an individual and a group phenomenon. Western society tends to teach children to "smooth over" conflict. For example, you may remember a parent saying, "Play nice" or "You have to learn to share." Fairness, morals, social norms, and mores, along with the application of any of the multiple distributive justice methods, contribute to conflict situations when one party believes that a less than equitable distribution of resources has occurred.

Quality conflict management should produce the following outcomes:

- A wise agreement if an agreement is possible
- An efficient solution
- A potentially innovative solution
- Movement toward positive change in the organization
- A better relationship between the conflicting parties (or at least should not damage the relationship)

Given these expectations, how can the health leader manage conflict? Basically, different situations require different styles; training organizational stakeholders on the effective use of conflict styles is also imperative. Conflict occurs because of differing preferences and nuances, over distribution of resources, and from differing values, difficult relationships, and differing perceptions. Primary tension (initial conflict over an issue or difference) is followed by secondary tension (conflict over the process for actually dealing with the issue of difference), and both require leadership intervention, conflict management, and conflict styles training for the conflicting parties. (The preference is to train all subordinates and staff.) "Groupthink," a negative group decision, occurs when there is no conflict (**Figure 5-4**).

Conflict Styles

Six basic conflict management styles have been identified.[133,134–138] Although each person has a dominant (primary) style and a secondary style that are relatively stable (like personality style), all six styles can be learned, applied, and mastered. Conflict styles are a learned skill set. The more you learn and practice, the more flexible you will be in conflict situations. Later in this chapter, a decision tree is shown that can help you select which conflict style to use based on the situation (by answering several yes or no questions). It is imperative to understand and be able to apply different conflict styles because situations differ from day to day.

The six styles presented here represent an amalgam of the work of multiple scholars created for the purpose of expanding your knowledge:

1. Accommodating
2. Avoiding
3. Collaborating
4. Competing
5. Compromising
6. Problem solving

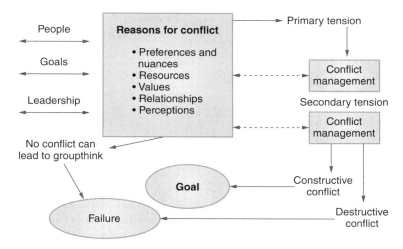

FIGURE 5-4 Conflict illustrated.

The best style to use in any case depends on the situation. It is important to note that during conflict situations, one party may select (knowingly or unknowingly) one style and the other party may select a different style. Only in problem solving do both parties knowingly choose that style and work together. The following summaries identify the situational context associated with each conflict management style.

Accommodating

- When you find you are wrong; to allow a better position to be heard, to learn, and to show your reasonableness
- When issues are more important to others than to you; to satisfy others and maintain cooperation
- To build social capital for later issues
- To minimize your losses when you are outmatched and losing the conflict
- When harmony and stability are especially important
- To allow subordinates to develop by learning from their mistakes

Avoiding

- When an issue is trivial or more important issues are pressing
- When you perceive no chance of satisfying your needs
- When the potential disruption outweighs the benefits of resolution

- To let people cool down and regain perspective
- When gathering information supersedes immediate decision making
- When others can resolve the conflict more effectively
- When issues seem a result of other issues

Collaborating

- To find an integrative solution when both sets of concerns are too important to be compromised
- When your objective is to learn
- To merge insights from people with different perspectives
- To gain commitment by incorporating concerns into a consensus
- To work through feelings that have harmed an interpersonal relationship

Competing

- When quick, decisive action is vital (e.g., emergency situations, such as a disaster or terrorism incident or accident)
- On important issues where unpopular actions need implementing (e.g., cost cutting, enforcing unpopular rules, discipline)
- On issues vital to company welfare and survival when you know you are right
- Against people who take advantage of noncompetitive behavior

Compromising

- When goals are important, but not worth the effort or potential disruption of competing
- When opponents with equal power are committed to mutually exclusive goals
- To achieve temporary settlements to complex issues
- To arrive at expedient solutions under time pressure
- As a backup when collaboration or competition is unsuccessful

Problem Solving

- May not always work (it takes two to make this style work)
- Requires the identification of a broader range of strategies
- Points for problem solving
  - Both parties have a vested interest in the outcome (the resolution).
  - Both parties believe a better solution can be achieved through problem-based collaboration.
  - Both parties recognize that the problem is caused by the relationship, not the people involved.
  - The focus is on solving the problem, not on accommodating differing views.
  - Both parties are flexible.
  - Both parties understand that all solutions have positive and negative aspects.
  - Both parties understand each other's issues.
  - The problem is looked at objectively, not personally.
  - Both parties are knowledgeable about conflict management.
  - Allowing everyone to "save face" is important.
- Successful outcomes are celebrated openly.

The various conflict management styles should be used contingently based on the situation that presents itself in conflict environments. The dynamic nature of healthcare organizations requires leaders to become competent in using each conflict style. Again, training organizational stakeholders is also critically important. To show the contingent nature of conflict styles, a merging of styles with a well-known leadership model is highlighted in **Figure 5-5**. From a leadership contingency perspective, it might be helpful to review the results of the Ohio State and Michigan University leadership studies, where conflict management styles can be arrayed as shown in the figure, similar to leadership styles.

Essential steps for leaders in conflict management follow. When you are in the early stages of conflict, you should take these steps:

- Stay calm and rational.
- Use facts (do your homework).
- Understand the resource implications and limitations surrounding the conflict.
- Listen to how you feel and know what you want or need.
- Try to imagine what the other(s) feel, want, and need.
- Use a process to select a strategy such as the decision tree method (discussed later).
- Rehearse your strategy.
- Be prepared to modify your approach if necessary.

When you are in the midst of conflict, keep these tenets in mind:

- Separate the people from the problem or conflict as much as possible.
- Focus on interests, not positions.
- Avoid always having a "bottom line."
- Think about the worst and best solutions and know what you can "live with."

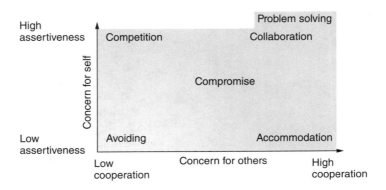

FIGURE 5-5 Conflict styles regarding concern for self and others.

This figure is an aggregation of multiple scholars' work[115–120] and a modification of the leadership studies at Ohio State and Michigan University accredited to Stogdill and Likert. For the leadership component, "Concern for task" was replaced by "Concern for others."

- Generate several possibilities before deciding what to do.
- Insist that the result (resolution) be based on some objective standard.

Negotiation is similar to conflict resolution. In fact, Fisher, Ury, and Patton's 1991 work, *Getting to Yes: Negotiating Agreement Without Giving In*, Second Edition, contains some especially salient points for conflict management. These recommendations reinforce guidelines presented earlier in this chapter and lean toward the problem-solving style of conflict:[139]

- Do not bargain over positions.
- Separate the people from the problem.
- Focus on interests, not positions.
- Invent options for mutual gain.
- Insist on using objective criteria to resolve the issue.
- Use your "best alternative to a negotiated agreement." (What is the worst-case scenario if nothing is resolved?)
- Get the other party to negotiate.

Next, we turn our attention to the process of selecting a conflict style based on the situation. With six styles to select from, it is important to study all of them and become familiar with the styles so that the selection method—a decision tree—becomes understandable. Remember that five styles are under your "control," whereas the sixth style, problem solving, requires that both parties consciously agree to select that style.

Conflict Style Selection

Selecting a conflict style depends on several factors, including the interpersonal relationship with others (that is, those in the conflict against you), resources available (such as time), resources not available, and importance of the issues at hand. In the decision tree model, these factors take the form of high/yes or low/no answers to the following questions:

1. Is (are) the issue (issues) important to you?
2. Is (are) the issue (issues) important to the other party?
3. Is the relationship with the other party important to you?
4. How much time is available and how much pressure/stress is there to come to resolution? (With this question, an answer of "high" means high pressure.)
5. How much do you trust the other party?

To obtain an overview of the decision tree process, examine **Figure 5-6**, noting the questions at the top of the graphic and the associated high/yes and low/no answers to each of these questions. Follow the path until you come to a conflict management style that is recommended given the conflict situation.

An example illustrating two points, use of the decision tree and cautionary notes associated with each style, is provided here. In this scenario, you are in a conflict situation with another employee at the hospital. You have prepared yourself by reviewing all of the points made previously in this chapter. Now you answer the questions based on the decision tree model (follow along on the decision tree in Figure 5-6):

1. Is the issue important to you? *You determine the answer is "low."*
2. Is the issue important to the other party? *You determine the answer is "high." (Why else would this person make such a big deal out of it?)*
3. Is the relationship with the other party important to you? *You determine the answer is "low." (Caution: How does this equate to using the avoiding style? Eventually, the avoiding style will cause the relationship with the other person or party to deteriorate.)*
4. How much time is available and how much pressure/stress is there to come to resolution? *You determine there is "high pressure" to come to resolution.*
5. How much do you trust the other party? *You determine you do not really trust the other person, so the answer is "low."*
6. Outcome: *The style recommended is the avoiding style.*

Conflict management is a critical and necessary skill that includes both technical (styles and decision tree) and relationship (communication and trust building) components. Conflict is a state of nature; hence the application of conflict styles requires good judgment on the leader's part.

OVERVIEW OF CULTURE

Culture is a learned system of knowledge, behavior, attitudes, beliefs, values, and norms that is shared by a group of people.[140,141] Culture is a difference that makes a difference.[142] Cultural differences have been classified (initially from the work of Hofstede) into the following categories (four categories are presented here, though several more are possible):

- Language
- Context (high versus low)
- Contact (high versus low)
- Time (monochronic versus polychronic)

Language is the structure, rules, and enunciation of symbols. Spanish, English, Mandarin Chinese, German, and Flemish are examples of languages.

High-context cultures place more emphasis on nonverbal communication; physical context is important in interpreting

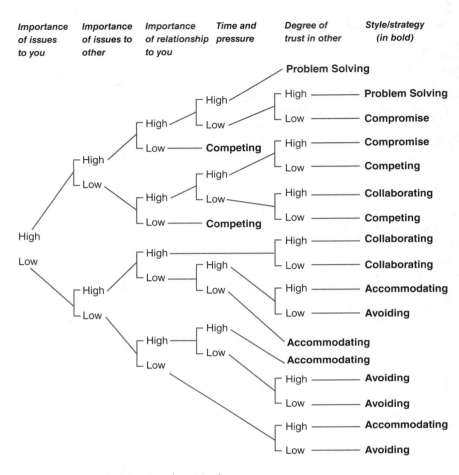

FIGURE 5-6 Conflict management style decision tree (modified).

Data from Folger, J. P., Poole, M. S., & Stutman, R. K. (1997). *Working through conflict: Strategies for relationships, groups, and organizations* (3rd ed.). New York: Addison-Wesley Educational Publishers, p. 201.

the message, and the stress is on the receiver of a message to understand the intended meaning (**Figure 5-7**). Low-context cultures place more emphasis on verbal expression; the sender is responsible for relaying meaning to the receiver verbally. Sometimes, people from a high-context culture will find people from a low-context culture less credible or trustworthy. Someone from a low-context culture may be more likely to make explicit requests for information ("Talk to me," "Do you know what I mean?"). In contrast, a person from a high-context culture expects communication to be more indirect and relies on more implicit cues.[143] People from high-context cultures may consider a low-context person overbearing, dominant, and talkative.

Contact preferences among cultures also differ. People from some cultures are more comfortable being touched or being in close proximity to others (high contact), whereas some people want more personal space, typically have less eye contact, and are uncomfortable with being touched by others (low contact). Contact, as a variable, is similar to the notion of personal and social space. Some people want larger areas of space, whereas others are comfortable with less space.

Monochronic and polychronic cultures differ with perceptions and use of time. Monochronic cultures are precise; time is to be used and manipulated. Polychronic cultures are not as precise on time; time is what it is, events flow in their intended pattern as they happen. It is not unusual to have a monochronic culture person arrive at a scheduled meeting 5 minutes early, only to be irritated and upset by the time a polychronic culture person arrives 30 minutes past the scheduled time. Although organizational rules such as adherence to schedules (organizational coupling) are important, some understanding of time perception differences can reduce potential anger when people from differing cultural perspectives understand the perceptions of the others. Thus, strategies to bridge cultural differences, specifically for communicative purposes, are important, as discussed next.

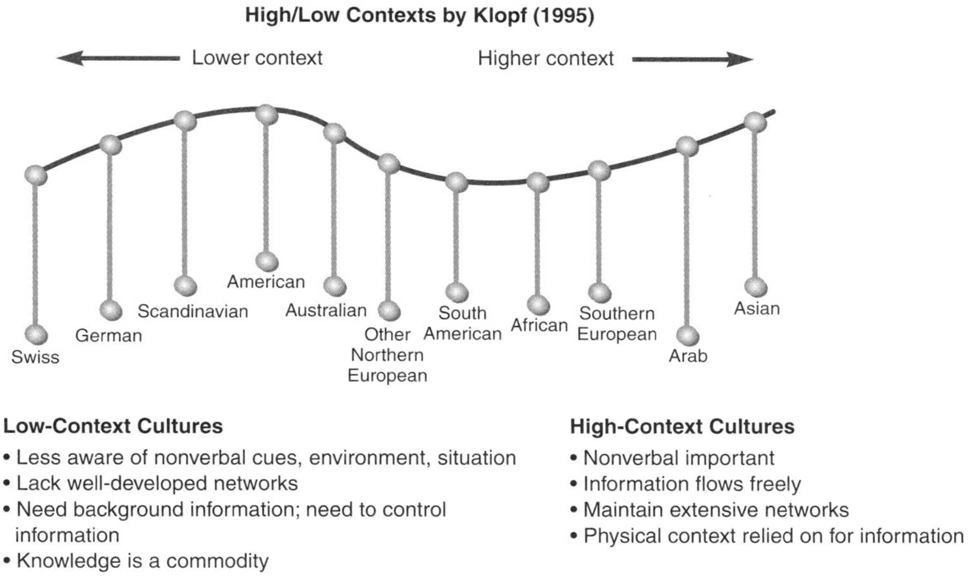

High/Low Contexts by Klopf (1995)

◄———— Lower context   Higher context ————►

American

Scandinavian   Australian   South
German   American   African   Southern
Swiss   Other Northern   European   Asian
                   European   Arab

Low-Context Cultures
• Less aware of nonverbal cues, environment, situation
• Lack well-developed networks
• Need background information; need to control information
• Knowledge is a commodity

High-Context Cultures
• Nonverbal important
• Information flows freely
• Maintain extensive networks
• Physical context relied on for information

FIGURE 5-7 High- versus low-context cultures continuum.

Data from Beebe, S. A., & Masterson, J. T. (1997). *Communicating in small groups: Principles and practices* (5th ed.). New York: Addison-Wesley Educational Publishers, pp. 152–158.

BRIDGING CULTURAL DIFFERENCES IN COMMUNICATION

Individuals hold cultural assumptions when engaged in work within the health organization; this is particularly apparent when involved in group problem solving and decision making. "All communication, problem-solving, decision making, etc. ... is filtered through the cultural perspective group members hold."[144] Beebe and Masterson recommend the following strategies to bridge cultural differences:

• *Develop mindfulness*: Be consciously aware of cultural differences; your assumptions and other people's assumptions may be (and probably are) different.
• *Be flexible*: You may have to adapt and change according to the perceptions and assumptions others hold.
• *Tolerate uncertainty and ambiguity*: Be patient and tolerant.
• *Resist stereotyping others and making negative judgments about others*: Do not be ethnocentric; ethnocentrism leads to defensive (not open or confirmatory or supportive) communication environments.
• *Ask questions*: Develop common ground rules and ask for additional meaning (paraphrase and ask about feelings).
• *Be other oriented*: Be empathetic and sensitive to others where the key is to bridge cultural differences.[145]

Just as there are global cultural differences, so there may be unit or discipline or location differences within the same industry and organization. The next section discusses this phenomenon.

COORDINATED MANAGEMENT OF MEANING

At the organizational or unit level, individuals and groups embody their own cultural identity; this is certainly true in health organizations. Coordinated management of meaning (CMM) is an interactional theory that focuses on how individuals organize, manage, and coordinate their meanings and actions with one another. This theory was developed by Pearce in 1976 and updated by Pearce and Cronen in 1980. "The theory proposes that the interpretation of a conversation or message will be shaped by the context or nature of the relationship between the interactants as well as the self-concept and culture of each individual."[146] Consider the cultural differences of operating room nurses and technicians and surgeons relative to physical therapists and therapy aides relative to pharmacists and pharmacy technicians while you review the constructs of this theory.

At the highest and deepest level, *cultural patterns* provide a person's unique view of the world and how he or she fits into that world through his or her various roles, behaviors, and beliefs; this level is very stable and difficult to change. The next construct level is *life scripts*, which expands on cultural patterns by "holding" a person's self-identity, self-efficacy, and expectations of rewards and punishments based on that identity; this level is stable and nearly as difficult to change compared with the cultural patterns construct. The following quote sheds light on constructs in the model that are more likely (although not easy) to modify, subject to influence and change.

> *Contracts* define and specify expectations of the particular relationship based on the kinds of episodes that occur within the relationship. *Episodes* define the kind of activity that occurs between individuals based on the kinds of and sequencing of messages being exchanged. *Speech acts* identify the intent of the speaker and content is the decoding of the substance of the message. *Raw sensory data* concern the audio and visual signals that reach the brain.[147]

This logical relationship between levels produces constitutive rules for determining meaning. Constitutive rules stipulate how meanings at one level determine meanings at another level. Regulative rules specify what is appropriate

given the nature of the relationship, the episode, and what the other person has said. Thus the CCM theory may be connected to Rokeach's values–beliefs–attitudes model in the following way: (1) values link to cultural patterns and life scripts; (2) beliefs link to life scripts and contracts; and (3) attitudes link to contracts, episodes, and speech acts.

The CMM theory brings into focus practical elements of Shutz's theory of affiliation, communication environments and culture, media richness theory, and interpersonal relationships. It also has strong links to Bolman and Deal's reframing organizational leadership model. Health leaders who understand motivation and influence and apply culturally sensitive communication approaches can effectively use motivation-based theories and models, such as goal setting, to focus a multidisciplinary team of health professionals on the mission and vision of the organization in an effective, efficient, and efficacious manner. **Figures 5–8** and **5–9** graphically illustrate the CMM model and the hierarchy of how meaning impacts people from low (raw data) to high (cultural patterns within the model's continuum).

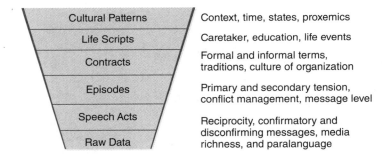

FIGURE 5-8 Coordinated management of meaning: hierarchy.

Data from Folger, J. P., Poole, M. S., & Stutman, R. K. (1997). *Working through conflict: Strategies for relationships, groups, and organizations* (3rd ed.). New York: Addison-Wesley Educational Publishers, p. 58.

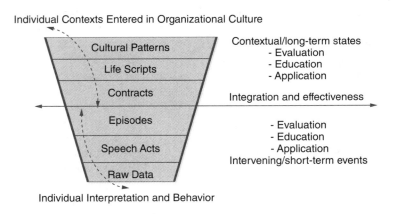

FIGURE 5-9 Coordinated management of meaning: impact.

Data from Beebe, S. A., & Masterson, J. T. (1997). *Communicating in small groups: Principles and practices* (5th ed.). New York: Addison-Wesley Educational Publishers.

SUMMARY

A leader has personal responsibility to maintain—if not advance—relevancy in his or her environment. To ensure that he or she does so, leadership competencies and the ability–job fit between a leader and his or her organizational environment are key considerations. Health leaders work in a highly complex environment with a highly educated and interdisciplinary workforce. Leadership success is often based on the leader's capabilities related to motivation, influence, interpersonal relationships, communication, situational assessment, and inspiring teams.

Networks and alliances are key ways to expand the leader's sphere of influence. Health leaders must take into account the various factors that play roles in interpersonal relationship building, communication as an environment for leadership effectiveness, communication culture, and conflict management.

For the beginning careerist, using the applications, ideas, and principles presented in this chapter both for your leadership model and for practice will serve you well. Additionally, seeking out a mentor who clearly has earned the respect of others by establishing many quality relationships will benefit you for many years; learn from your mentor in the areas of motivation and inspiration, forming networks and alliances, developing interpersonal relationships, and managing conflict.

DISCUSSION QUESTIONS

1. How would you describe the complexity of the health industry in terms of workforce, environment, and societal expectations? How would a health leader's mastery of competencies, including interpersonal relationship building, influence processes, motivation, power, and communication capabilities, enable the leader to successfully navigate this complexity?

2. Explain how the complexity of the health workforce may lead to communication failure and conflict. Summarize ways to use quality communication and conflict management skills to successfully motivate subordinates, build interdisciplinary teams, and lead a health organization based on commitment rather than compliance or resistance.

3. Can you predict the outcomes of continuous use of the avoiding and competing strategies compared to the compromising, accommodating, and problem-solving strategies in a health organization? What might be the outcome of using face-to-face meetings compared to that when using memoranda communication channel/media for ambiguous and urgent messages?

4. How would you analyze the health leader competencies in terms of the knowledge, skills, and abilities discussed in this chapter, differentiating the competencies presented here with those not discussed? Support your assessment.

5. How would you design, by combining several theories and models, an influence, power, and motivation leadership model for use in health organizations focused on subordinate commitment? Could you modify this model for use with an interdisciplinary health team or group? Explain why this modification was utilized.

6. Evaluate competencies (knowledge, skills, and abilities) found in leadership practice concerning building interpersonal relationships, influence processes, motivation, power, and communication that are necessary to successfully lead health organizations. Support your evaluation. How would you use those capabilities?

EXERCISES

1. Define the complexity of the health industry in terms of the workforce and label possible up-to-date and continuous information sources for the health workforce that are affecting the health industry. Use a cost–quality–access model to determine the cumulative impact of several changes on the health industry.

2. In a three-page (or less) paper, distinguish potentially differing motivational factors for each major health workforce group and predict which applications of building interpersonal relationships, influence, and motivation theories or models would work best for each group.

3. In a two- to three-page paper, construct models of communication for a health organization that could be used by a leader for individuals, groups/teams, and the entire organization. As part of your discussion, demonstrate which elements of your models are similar and dissimilar.

4. Select two theories or models of influence, power, and/or motivation. In a two-page paper, identify the constructs and leadership behaviors/actions, and analyze the effectiveness of the theories or models in a health organization setting for achieving commitment, achieving compliance, and achieving resistance. Relate components of quality leader communication to this analysis and illustrate whether they would result in changes to your outcomes.

5. In a two-page paper, explain how goal-setting theory, expectancy theory, and locus of control work together; also, relate how a health leader can utilize the synthesis of these theories to have a productive workforce at the individual subordinate and team or group level.

6. In a two- to three-page paper, evaluate and justify the combined competencies of your professional association's health leaders, considering the complexity of the health industry.

REFERENCES

1. Stefl, M. E. (2008). Common competencies for all healthcare managers: The healthcare leadership alliance model. *Journal of Healthcare Management*, *53*(6), 360–374.

2. Stefl, note 1.

3. Antonakis, John & House, Robert J. (2004). On instrumental leadership: Beyond transactions and transformations. Paper presented at the UNL Gallup Leadership Institute Summit, Omaha.

4. Robbins, J. C., Bradley, H. E., Spicer, M., & Mecklenburg, A. B. (2001). Developing leadership in healthcare administration: A competency assessment. *Journal of Healthcare Management*, *46*(3), 188.

5. Calhoun, J. G., Vincent, E. T., Calhoun, G. L., & Brandsen, L. E. (2008). Why competencies in graduate health management and policy education? *Journal of Health Administration Education*, *25*(1), 17–35.

6. Calhoun et al., note 5.

7. Calhoun et al., note 5.

8. Boyatzis, R. E. (1996). Competencies for HR professionals: An interview with Richard E. Boyatzis. *Human Resource Management*, *35*, 119–131.

9. Calhoun, J., Dollett, L., Sinioris, M., Wainio, J., Butler, P., … , Warden, G. (2008). Development of an interprofessional competency model for healthcare leadership. *Journal of Healthcare Management*, *53*(6), 375–391. Retrieved from CINAHL with full text database.

10. Anthony, M. (2002). What are your core competencies? [book review]. *Journal of Research Administration*, *33*(2), 89–91. Retrieved from ABI/INFORM Global (Document ID: 544971301).

11. Berliner, H. (1975). A larger perspective on the Flexner report. *International Journal of Health Services*, *5*, 573–592.

12. Flexner, A. (1910). *Medical education in the United States and Canada*. Boston: Merrymount Press.

13. Codman, E. A. (1917/1996). *A study in hospital efficiency: As demonstrated by the case report of the first five years of a private hospital*. Oakbrook Terrace, IL: Joint Commission on Accreditation of Healthcare Organizations.

14. Corwin, E. (1946). *The American hospital*. New York: The Commonwealth Fund.

15. Donabedian, A. (1966). Evaluating the quality of medical care. *Milbank Memorial Fund Quarterly*, *44*, 166–206.

16. Liptzin, B. (2009). Quality improvement, pay for performance, and "outcomes measurement": What makes sense? *Psychiatric Services*, *60*, 108–111.

17. University of Michigan School of Public Health. (n.d.). John R. Griffith, MBA, FACHE. Retrieved from http://www.sph.umich.edu/iscr/faculty/profile .cfm?uniqname=jrg.

18. American College of Healthcare Executives. (2011). ACHE healthcare executive competencies assessment tool. Retrieved from http://www.ache.org /pdf/nonsecure/careers/competencies_booklet.pdf.

19. Robert Wood Johnson Foundation. (2006). New national center for healthcare leadership creates source for better management education and training. Retrieved from http://www.rwjf.org/reports /grr/049126.htm.

20. National Center for Healthcare Leadership. (2012). Lifelong leadership inventory. Introduction to lifelong leadership inventory. Retrieved from http://nchl .org/Documents/Ctrl_Hyperlink/doccopy5759 _uid3162012419032.pdf.

21. Stefl, M. E., & Bontempo, C. A. (2008). Common competencies for all healthcare managers: The

healthcare leadership alliance model/practitioner application. *Journal of Healthcare Management*, *53*(6), 360–373; discussion, 374. Retrieved from http://search.proquest.com/docview/206729682?accountid=27965.

22. Health Resources and Services Administration, Bureau of Health Professions. (2013). Bureau of Health Professions Work Force. Retrieved from http://bhpr.hrsa.gov/healthworkforce/allreports.html.

23. New York Center for Health Workforce Studies. (2006, Oct.). The United States health workforce profile. Health Resources and Services Administration grant report. Retrieved from http://bhpr.hrsa.gov/healthworkforce/reports/.

24. Hatch, M. J. (1993). The dynamics of organizational culture. *Academy of Management Review*, *18*, 657–693.

25. Schneider, B. (1990). *Organizational climate and culture*. San Francisco, CA: Jossey-Bass.

26. Hatch, note 24, pp. 657–693.

27. American College of Healthcare Executives. (n.d.). About ACHE. Retrieved from http://www.ache.org/aboutache.cfm.

28. Medical Group Management Association. (n.d.). About MGMA-ACMPE. Retrieved from http://www.mgma.com/about/.

29. American Organization of Nurse Executives. (n.d.). About AONE. Retrieved from http://www.aone.org/membership/about/welcome.shtml.

30. Healthcare Financial Management Association. (n.d.). About HFMA. Retrieved from http://www.hfma.org/Content.aspx?id=38.

31. Healthcare Information and Management Systems Society. (n.d.). About HIMSS. Retrieved from http://www.himss.org/about.

32. National Center for Healthcare Leadership. (n.d.). About NCHL. Retrieved from http://www.nchl.org/ns/about/aboutnchl.asp.

33. Association of University Programs in Health Administration. (n.d.). About AUPHA. Retrieved from http://www.aupha.org/i4a/pages/index.cfm?pageid=3275.

34. Association of University Programs in Health Administration. (n.d.). Vision & mission. Retrieved from http://www.aupha.org/i4a/pages/Index.cfm?pageID=3285.

35. Association of University Programs in Health Administration. (n.d.). Program certification & accreditation. Retrieved from http://www.aupha.org/i4a/pages/index.cfm?pageid=3518.

36. Council on Education for Public Health. (n.d.). Home page. Retrieved from http://ceph.org/.

37. Association to Advance Collegiate Schools of Business. (n.d.). Home page. Retrieved from http://www.aacsb.edu.

38. Clark, D. (2010). Bloom's taxonomy of learning domains. Retrieved from http://www.nwlink.com/~Donclark/hrd/bloom.html.

39. Bloom, B. S., Engelhart, M. D., Furst, E. J., Hill, W. H., & Krathwohl, D. R. (1956). *Taxonomy of educational objectives: The classification of educational goals; Handbook 1: Cognitive domain*. New York: Longman.

40. Clark, D. (2010). Bloom's taxonomy of learning domains. Retrieved from http://www.nwlink.com/~Donclark/hrd/bloom.html#cognitive.

41. Anderson, L. W., & Krathwohl, D. R. (Eds.). (2001). *A taxonomy for learning, teaching and assessing: A revision of Bloom's taxonomy of educational objectives, complete edition*. New York: Longman, pp. 67–68.

42. Carnevale, A. P. (1991). *America and the new economy*. Washington, D.C.: Department of Labor.

43. Drenkard, K. (2013). Transformational leadership. *The Journal of Nursing Administration*, *43*(2), 57–58.

44. Yukl, G. (1994). *Leadership in organizations* (3rd ed.). Englewood Cliffs, NJ: Prentice Hall, p. 193.

45. Sorcher, M., & Brant, J. (2002, February). Are you picking the right leaders? *Harvard Business Review*, p. 78.

46. Cooper, T. L. (1998). *The responsible administrator: An approach to ethics for the administrative role*. San Francisco: Jossey-Bass.

47. Rotter, J. B. (1966). Generalized expectancies for internal versus external control of reinforcement. *Psychological Monographs*, *80*, 609.

48. Miller, D., & Toulouse, J. (1986). Chief executive personality and corporate strategy and structure in small firms. *Management Science*, *32*, 1389–1409.

49. Miller, D., Ketsde Vries, M., & Toulouse, J. (1982). Locus of control and its relationship to strategy, environment, and structure. *Academy of Management Journal*, *25*, 237–253.

50. Beebe, S. A., & Masterson, J. T. (1997). *Communicating in small groups: Principles and practices* (5th ed.). New York: Addison-Wesley Educational Publishers.

51. Cicero, L., & Pierro, A. (2007). Charismatic leadership and organizational outcomes: The mediating role of employees' work-group identification. *International Journal of Psychology*, *42*(5), 297–306.

52. Yukl, note 44.

53. University of Rochester. (n.d.). Self-determination theory: An approach to human motivation

and personality. Retrieved from http://www.psych .rochester.edu/SDT/theory.php#References.

54. Ryan, R. M., & Deci, E. L. (2000). Self-determination theory and the facilitation of intrinsic motivation, social development, and well-being. *American Psychologist*, 55(1), 68–78.

55. O'Shaughnessy, M. S. (2009). Individual behavior and motivation. In J. A. Johnson (Ed.), *Health organizations: Theory, behavior, and development* (pp. 90–93). Sudbury, MA: Jones & Bartlett.

56. O'Shaughnessy, note 55.

57. O'Shaughnessy, note 55.

58. Ryan & Deci, note 54.

59. Graen, C. (1976). Role making processes within complex organizations. In M. D. Dunnette (Ed.), *Handbook of industrial and organizational psychology* (pp. 1201–1246). Chicago: Rand McNally.

60. Vroom, V. H. (1964). *Work and motivation.* New York: McGraw-Hill.

61. Cleavenger, D., & Munyon, T. P. (2013). It's how you frame it: Transformational leadership and the meaning of work. *Business Horizons*, 56, 351–360.

62. Cleavenger & Munyon, note 61.

63. Locke, E. A. (1968, May). Toward a theory of task motivation and incentives. *Organizational Behavior and Human Performance*, 157–189.

64. Locke, E. A., Shaw, K. N., Saari, L. M., & Latham, G. P. (1981). Goal setting and task performance: 1969–1980. *Psychological Bulletin*, 90(1), 125–152.

65. Locke, E. A., & Latham, G. P. (1984). *Goal setting: A motivational technique that works!* Englewood Cliffs, NJ: Prentice Hall.

66. Quick, T. L. (1985). *The manager's motivation desk book.* New York: Wiley, p. 124.

67. Locke & Latham, note 65.

68. Rosenbaum, B. L. (1982). *How to motivate today's workers.* New York: Wiley, p. 103.

69. Locke & Latham, note 65.

70. Locke, E. A., & Chesney, A. A. (1991). Relationships among goal difficulty, business strategies, and performance on a complex management simulation task. *Academy of Management Journal*, 34(2), 400–424.

71. Latham, G. P., & Baldes, J. J. (1975). The practical significance of Locke's theory of goal setting. *Journal of Applied Psychology*, 60, 122–138.

72. Baron, R. A. (1983). *Behavior in organizations: Understanding and managing the human side of work.* Boston: Allyn & Bacon.

73. Value Based Management.net. (2007, May 23). Motivation and management: Vroom's expectancy theory. Retrieved from http://www .valuebasedmanagement.net/methods_vroom_ expectancy_theory.html.

74. Harris, T. E. (1993). *Applied organizational communication: Perspectives, principles and pragmatics.* Hillsdale, NJ: Lawrence Erlbaum Associates, p. 454.

75. Locke et al., note 64.

76. Mento, A. J., Locke, E. A., & Klein, H. J. (1992). Relationship of goal level to valence and instrumentality. *Journal of Applied Psychology*, 77(4), 395–405.

77. Kelman, H. C. (1958). Compliance, identification and internalization: Three processes of attitude change. *Journal of Conflict Resolution*, 2, 51–56.

78. Kelman, H. C. (1974). Further thoughts on the process of compliance, identification, and internalization. In J. T. Tedeschi (Ed.), *Perspectives on social power* (pp. 125–171). Chicago, IL: Aldine.

79. Ifinedo, Princely (2016). Applying uses and gratifications theory and social influence processes to understand students' pervasive adoption of social networking sites: Perspectives from the Americas. *International Journal of Information Management*, 36(2), 192–206. Retrieved from http://www.sciencedirect .com/science/article/pii/S0268401215001085.

80. Yukl, G. (1994). *Leadership in organizations* (3rd ed.). Englewood Cliffs, NJ: Prentice Hall, p. 197.

81. Yukl, note 80, p. 209.

82. Jermier, J. M., Slocum, J. W. Jr., Fry, L. W., & Gaines, J. (1991). Organizational subcultures in a soft bureaucracy: Resistance behind the myth and façade of an official culture. *Organization Science*, 2(2), 170–194.

83. Greene, R. (1998). *The 48 laws of power.* New York: Penguin, p. xix.

84. Coppola, M. N., Erckenbrack, D., & Ledlow, G. R. (2009). Stakeholder dynamics. In J. A. Johnson (Ed.), *Health organizations: Theory, behavior, and development* (pp. 255–278). Sudbury, MA: Jones & Bartlett.

85. Vicere, A. A., & Fulmer, R. M. (1997). *Leadership development by design.* Boston: Harvard Business School Press.

86. Mintzberg, H. (1989). *Mintzberg on management: Inside our strange world of organizations.* New York: Free Press.

87. Mintzberg, H. (1973). *The nature of managerial work.* New York: Harper & Row.

88. Fottler, M. D., Blair, J. D., Whitehead, C. J., Laus, M. D., & Savage, G. T. (1989). Assessing key stakeholders: Who matters to hospitals and why? *Hospital and Health Services Administration*, 34, 527.

89. Levey, S., & Hill, J. (1986). Between survival and social responsibility: In search of an ethical balance. *Journal of Health Administration Education, 4,* 227.

90. Blair, J. D., & Whitehead, C. J. (1988). Too many on the seesaw: Stakeholder diagnosis and management for hospitals. *Hospital and Health Services Administration, 33,* 154.

91. Lawrence, J. (1999). Exceed your goals. *Hospital and Health Networks, 73*(10), 5–10.

92. Davis, S., & Meyer, C. (1999). *Blur: The speed of change in the connected economy.* New York: Warner.

93. Shuman, J., & Twombly, J. (2003, April). The link between entrepreneurial thinking and alliance management. *The Rhythm of Business.* Retrieved from http://www.rhythmofbusiness.com/articles/2003 /4/25/the-link-between-entrepreneurial-thinking -and-alliance-manag.html.

94. Harmaakorpi, V., & Niukkanen, H. (2007). Leadership in different kinds of regional development networks. *Baltic Journal of Management, 2*(1), 80–96.

95. Graen, G. B., & Graen, J. A. (2006). *Sharing network leadership.* Charlotte, NC: IAP Press.

96. Levinson, H. (2003). Management by whose objectives? *Harvard Business Review, 81*(1), 107–116. Retrieved from http://ezproxy.library.capella.edu /login?url=http://search.ebscohost.com/login.aspx?d irec=true&db=bth&AN=8796896&site=ehost-live.

97. Harmaakorpi & Niukkanen, note 94.

98. Lippitt, M. (2007). *Fix the disconnect between strategy and execution.* Retrieved from http://proquest.umi. com.library.capella.edu/pqdweb?did=1327907261 &sid=3&Fmt=3&clientId=62763&RQT=309&VN ame=PQD.

99. Harmaakorpi & Niukkanen, note 94.

100. Grace, K. S. (2006). *Over goal! What you must know to excel at fundraising today.* Medfield, MA: Emerson & Church.

101. Ledlow, G. R. (2009). Conflict and interpersonal relations. In J. A. Johnson (Ed.), *Health organizations: Theory, behavior, and development* (pp. 158–163). Sudbury, MA: Jones & Bartlett.

102. Yukl, note 44.

103. Beebe & Masterson, note 50, p. 71.

104. O'Hair, D., Friedrich, G. W., Wiemann, J. M., & Wiemann, M. O. (1997). *Competent communication* (2nd ed.). New York: St. Martin's Press.

105. Beebe & Masterson, note 50.

106. Beebe & Masterson, note 50.

107. Beebe & Masterson, note 50.

108. Nichols, A. L., & Cottrell, C. A. (2014). What do people desire in their leaders? The role of leadership

109. level on trait desirability. *The Leadership Quarterly, 25,* 711–729.

109. Mintzberg, note 86.

110. Mintzberg, note 87.

111. CBS Evening News. (2009). Obama going prime time to help ailing health initiative. Retrieved from http://www.cbsnews.com/blogs/2009/07/22 /politics/politicalhotsheet/entry5179382.shtml.

112. Beebe & Masterson, note 50, p. 3.

113. Cusella, L. P. (1987). Feedback, motivation, and performance. In F. M. Jablin, L. L. Putnam, K. H. Roberts, & L. W. Porter (Eds.), *Handbook of organizational communication* (pp. 624–679). Newbury Park, CA: Sage.

114. Harris, note 74, p. 454.

115. Daft, R. L., Lengel, R. H., & Trevino, L. K. (1987). Message equivocality, media selection, and manager performance: Implications for information systems. *MIS Quarterly, 11*(3), 355–366.

116. Daft, R. L., & Lengel, R. H. (1986). Organizational information requirements, media richness, and structural design. *Management Science, 22*(5), 554–571.

117. Daft, R. L., & Wiginton, J. (1979). Language and organization. *Academy of Management Review, 4*(2), 179–191.

118. D'Ambra, J., & Rice, R. E. (1994). Multimethod approaches for the study of computer-mediated communication, equivocality, and media selection. *IEEE Transactions on Professional Communication, 37*(4), 231–339.

119. Daft & Lengel, note 116, p. 557.

120. Daft et al., note 115.

121. Beebe & Masterson, note 50.

122. Beebe & Masterson, note 50.

123. Beebe & Masterson, note 50.

124. Ledlow, note 101.

125. Ledlow, G. R., Bradshaw, D. M., & Shockley, C. (2000). Primary care access improvement: An empowerment–interaction model. *Military Medicine, 165*(2), 390–395.

126. Ledlow, G., Cwiek, M., & Johnson, J. (2002). Dynamic culture leadership: Effective leader as both scientist and artist. In N. Delener & C. Chao (Eds.), *Global Business and Technology Association International Conference: Beyond boundaries: Challenges of leadership, innovation, integration and technology* (pp. 694–740). New York: Global Business and Technology Association.

127. Schein, E. H. (1999). *The corporate culture survival guide: Sense and nonsense about culture change.* San Francisco: Jossey-Bass.

128. Folger, J. P., Poole, M. S., & Stutman, R. K. (1997). *Working through conflict: Strategies for relationships, groups, and organizations* (3rd ed.). New York: Longman.

129. Burton, J. (1990). *Conflict: Resolution and prevention.* New York: St. Martin's Press.

130. Beebe & Masterson, note 50, p. 116.

131. Beebe & Masterson, note 50, pp. 116–117.

132. Miner, R. C. (2013). Informal Leaders. *Journal of Leadership, Accountability and Ethics, 10*(4), 57–61.

133. Miner, note 132

134. Cahn, D. (Ed.). (1990). *Intimates in conflict: A communication perspective.* Hillsdale, NJ: Lawrence Erlbaum Associates.

135. Canary, D. J., Cupach, W. R., & Messman, S. J. (1995). *Relationship conflict.* New York: Sage.

136. Cupach, W. R., & Canary, D. J. (1997). *Competence in interpersonal conflict.* New York: McGraw-Hill.

137. Folger et al., note 128.

138. Hocker, J. L., & Wilmot, W. W. (1995). *Interpersonal conflict* (4th ed.). Madison, WI: WCB Brown & Benchmark.

139. Fisher, R., Ury, W., & Patton, B. (1991). *Getting to yes: Negotiating agreement without giving in* (2nd ed.). New York: Penguin.

140. Schein, note 127.

141. Beebe & Masterson, note 50, p. 153.

142. Beebe & Masterson, note 50, p. 153.

143. Beebe & Masterson, note 50, pp. 155–156.

144. Beebe & Masterson, note 50, p. 199.

145. Beebe & Masterson, note 50.

146. Folger et al., note 128, p. 57.

147. Folger et al., note 128, p. 58.

LEADERSHIP COMPETENCE II: APPLICATION OF SKILLS, TOOLS, AND ABILITIES

Thinking always ahead, thinking always of trying to do more, brings a state of mind in which nothing seems impossible.

Henry Ford

This chapter presents additional knowledge and empirically based skills and abilities (a leadership toolbox full of "tools") required for a health leader's success in organizational practice. The leader's application of these skills, tools, and abilities is valid for small groups as well as all members of an organization. Strategies for leaders in effecting planning and situational assessment, decision making, and training that result in positive outcomes are addressed; these strategies, in turn, result in practical leadership actions and applications based in "active" leadership. Leadership is the active, conscious, focused, and consistent application of organizational theories and models of how health organizations operate; thus, the application of organizational theory and behavioral models is leadership.

LEARNING OBJECTIVES

1. Describe planning, decision making, and training in health organizations, and provide examples of each.

2. Summarize the planning process and the decision-making process within the context of leadership.

3. Apply and relate at least two different decision-making models to a leadership situation.

4. Differentiate the levels or components of the planning process and distinguish each level or component from the others.

5. Plan and design a quality improvement program based on a system of rational decision making for a health organization.

6. Compare and contrast willful choice to garbage can models of decision making, training leaders to training staff, and cultural competence to ethics and morality.

PLANNING

Planning is an essential leadership skill. It requires knowledge about planning and the ability to structure and develop a system of planning. Planning is an essential and critical component to successful leadership; effective planning and consistent leadership practice are vital to linking the clinical and administrative domains.[1] Health leaders plan at all levels of an organization. Specifically, they plan the operational actions necessary within their area of responsibility to implement the senior leadership team's strategic or operational plans. Health leaders who can understand, apply, and evaluate planning will have advantages over those who haphazardly plan or fail to plan.

Starting from the highest level of health organization strategic and operational plans, leaders at subordinate levels should (and many say must) develop strategies and operational practices that achieve the goals and objectives of the high-level plans at their subordinate level of the organization. Each level of the organization should (again, many say must) have goals and measureable objectives with time lines and accountable owners that contribute to the mission and to achieving the vision of the health organization. Wise leaders at all levels of the organization should (must) acquire the strategic and operational plans of the organization and seek counsel with their supervisory leader on how best to contribute to the organization's mission or vision at their level of leadership. Wise leaders also hold themselves accountable to fulfill goals and objectives at their level and report results regularly (monthly, quarterly, etc.) to those they lead as well as those they report to in the leadership hierarchy.

For some scholars, such as Yukl, planning is a step in decision making.[2] For others, planning is a cultural imperative and a method for leaders to guide the organization to its most effective, efficient, and efficacious outcomes.[3,4] Planning occurs formally, informally, strategically (how the organization can best serve its purpose in the external environment), and operationally (how the internal capabilities and resources of an organization can be used effectively, efficiently, and efficaciously to achieve the strategies and goals of the organization as documented in the strategic plan).

A set of basic definitions will assist in understanding the differences in the term *planning*:

- *Planning* is a process that uses macro- and micro-environmental factors and internal information to engage stakeholders to create a framework, template, and outline for section, branch, or organizational success. Planning can be strategic, operational, or a combination of both.

- *Strategic planning* is concerned with finding the best future for the organization and determining how the organization will evolve to realize that future. It is a stream of organizational decisions focused in a specific direction based on organizational values, strategies, and goals. The focus is on external considerations and how the organization can best serve the expectations, demands, and needs of external markets.

- *Operational planning* is about finding the best methods, processes, and systems to accomplish the mission/purpose, strategies, goals, and objectives of the organization in the most effective, efficient, and efficacious way possible. The focus in operational planning concerns internal resources, systems, processes, methods, and considerations.

Planning is vital to the survival of the organization. Indeed, creating a plan is an investment in improving the organization. Improvement is realized through internal change and evolution. Developing and focusing the organization to best meet the needs and demands of its customers and others (stakeholders) that affect the organization lie at the heart of planning. Because the environment, technology, information, people, financing, and governmental policies and laws are constantly changing, the organization itself must evolve to survive, succeed, and prosper. Planning is a journey—but this journey must have a destination, and this destination must be planned. In other words, it is a planned journey forward in time. In that light, planning includes both a process (developing and achieving goals and objectives) and an outcome (the plan itself).

Planning is a process. This process involves moving an organization along a predetermined path based on its values. Similar to the decisions involved in planning a real-world trip (e.g., which road to take, which stops to make, and who will drive), the organizational planning process entails deciding which goals are important to the organization and which objectives must be met to reach those goals.

Planning has an outcome. This outcome paves the way to a better future state based on organizational values and the external environment. Improving effectiveness, efficiency, efficacy, customer satisfaction, employee satisfaction, financial performance, and many other possible elements are a part of moving the organization to reach a better future state.

The desired future state constitutes the vision of the organization; the vision is what the combined staff of the organization strive to achieve. If you know where you are going, planning the trip and getting commitment from your staff are much easier. Also, organizational resources (including your energy and time) can be devoted to reaching set goals and having a positive outcome (turning the vision of your organization into a reality).

In this light, the process comprises a journey that must be planned knowing that different ways of doing things, different stops, and different issues will be encountered along the way. The vision represents the final destination. The destination must be determined and the journey must be planned. As a health leader, you are critical in

determining the vision (outcome/destination) and the process (journey/goals and objectives) that will ensure the organization reaches its intended vision.

For all health organizations, mergers, departmental restructuring, implementation of new technologies, and market changes may indicate a need for the organization to develop a strategic plan to support its overall plan. Strategic planning can be described as an organizational planning process that analyzes the current situation of an organization and forecasts how the organization will change or evolve over a specified period of time. The health leader is an integral part of a successful strategic plan. Strategic planning on the part of an organization and its leaders requires both thought and action, however. In health organizations, strategic thought includes the "ideas, reasons, and processes for changing the future state of your organization."[5] Within the component of strategic thought exist the vision, intent, and planning affecting the path that the organization takes in moving toward its future.

If the strategic plan is a road map, then the organizational vision is the final destination, describing where the organization is going. The vision depicts a perfect situation in which the future destination can be obtained. The health leader must energize his or her followers to buy in to the vision so that the organization can begin its strategic journey on the correct path. The strategic vision must be tested and retested to ensure that it has won buy-in from all stakeholders (external and internal).

A vision may require many drafts and revisions to ensure that the needs of all stakeholders are met. In the dynamic world of the health industry, leaders need to recognize that the strategic vision should be tangible. To be tangible, the vision should be stated in the form of concrete ideals rather than using generalizations, should identify a direct relationship between the organization's values and culture and the future direction of the organization, and should communicate a unique future to stakeholders.[6]

Once an organizational vision is developed, intent must be established. Intent describes how the organization will be affected if change does not occur. Organizational leaders must outline how these impacts or crises could potentially influence the viability of the organization. Examples of crises might include market changes, advances that cause older technology to become obsolete, personnel shortages, and decreased reimbursement from payers. From the journey perspective, having the wrong intent is analogous to driving in the wrong direction without a road map.

Once the vision and intent have been established, the strategic plan needs to be developed. From the road map perspective, this means that the quickest, most efficient route must be drawn to the final destination (i.e., the vision). One can assume that a good plan will lead to an effective outcome—namely, achieving the vision.

Strategic thought is followed by the component of tactical action, which includes commitment, execution, and accountability. In the health industry, tactical action encompasses the feelings, practices, and metrics for changing the future state of the organization.[7] If strategic thought is the plan for the journey to reach the final destination, then tactical action is the journey itself, including the mechanism for getting there. Tactical action requires commitment within the organization, execution of the plan, and accountability for this effort within organizational leadership.

Commitment, like the strategic vision, requires buy-in by the organization and its internal and external stakeholders. It involves a relationship between organizational leaders and followers; in contrast, each party has a clear understanding of the strategic vision and his or her role in reaching this vision. Without commitment on all levels, it is impossible to achieve the strategic vision effectively and efficiently. From a leadership perspective, a leader can foster commitment within his or her team by serving as a model and demonstrating a strong commitment to the plan and vision. A leader cannot expect to achieve buy-in from followers if he or she has not fully committed to the vision.

During the execution phase of the strategic plan, each team member performs his or her assigned duty. Without a strong, unified commitment, execution of the plan will be a dismal failure. It is the leader's responsibility to enhance motivation and maintain commitment within the team, particularly when team members encounter obstacles. The health leader must be supportive of his or her team members, supporting them by providing them with the needed skills, equipment, and materials to effectively carry out their roles in the plan. In many ways, the health leader's effort in this phase echoes the precepts of House's path–goal theory.

Leaders and followers require consistent feedback about performance during execution of the plan. To ensure that they receive this information, measures must be put in place to gauge successes (or lack thereof) during this time. Successes should be acknowledged between leaders and followers. After all, employees want to know that the plan is working correctly. Lack of success should be analyzed and modified to determine inconsistencies within the execution of the plan.

THE LEADER'S ROLE IN PLANNING

Most people look for leaders who have a vision and who can direct them in the path of the mission. There can be many leaders within a single organization, and each leader will have a vision for his or her tasks or responsibilities. The morale of the organization can sometimes depend on the attitudes espoused by visionaries of the organization. Staff members of an organization look to the visionaries to lead by example. In planning, leadership should come from within the organization; the effort should be exciting, with followers are excited to follow. Health leaders provide the structure, process, macro direction, shared outcome for all stakeholders, motivation, accountability, influence, obstacle removal, resources, and persistence in the overall effort of *directing, staffing, organizing, controlling,* and *rewarding.*

Planning is the fundamental function of leadership from which all other outcomes are derived. The first step in planning is establishing the organizational situational assessment; then, the vision, mission, strategies, goals, objectives, and action steps are developed. Without this structure and signposts as first steps, the organization cannot move forward.

The vision provides the motivational guidance for the organization, and typically it is defined and promoted by senior leadership. It explains *how* the organization intends to achieve its goals, whereas the mission defines *why* the organization pursues the goals it does. Both vision and mission are "directional strategies."

The mission statement is the organization's reason for being. It provides guidance in decision making as well, ensuring that the organization stays on the track that its leaders have predetermined. From the mission statement, strategies to achieve the mission and, ultimately, the vision are devised. Goals are broad statements of direction that come from strategies. This multilevel approach focuses and narrows effort for each section within the health organization. Objectives, in pursuit of achieving goals, are very specific.

Goals further refine the strategies focused on in the mission. They are expected to be general, observable, challenging, and untimed.[8] Goals are general in nature; in contrast, objectives are highly specific. Notably, different perspectives often switch goals with objectives and objectives with goals. Whatever framework you select for your organization, try to be consistent. It is not important if goals are at a higher level than objectives, or vice versa; what matters is the process of planning—a planning and execution culture should grow and mature in your health organization. Erven promotes objective development within the "SMART" framework; to be SMART, objectives must be "specific, measurable, attainable, rewarding, and timed."[9]

The phase in which action steps or tactics are established and implemented follows all of the preceding activity. Action steps or tactics represent a fifth level of planning; they provide the most specific approach for describing the *who*, *what*, *when*, *where*, and *how* elements of the activities needed to accomplish an objective.

Planning can be described as an ongoing process of thinking and implementing at multiple levels. At each level, health leaders engage in directing, staffing, organizing, and controlling. Along the way, such leaders must remember that "what gets measured gets done"; thus all planning objectives and action steps must be measurable, assigned to an accountable and responsible person, and set within a time period. Periodic progress reviews, either monthly or quarterly, are essential to see the movement toward success.

In addition to this effort of *directing*, *staffing*, *organization*, and *controlling*, *rewarding* is important. These five elements are crucial as leaders embrace the foundations and functions of planning. Health leaders must publicly praise success and reward those who have achieved predetermined action steps, objectives, and goals.

As U.S. General and President Dwight Eisenhower once said, the plan is important but the process of planning is even more important. The team building, achievement, and success orientation that a culture of planning and implementation brings to an organization is invaluable in ensuring its success over both the short and long term. Situational assessment and environmental scanning are vital elements to establish and maintain a culture of successful planning in a health organization.

SITUATIONAL ASSESSMENT AND ENVIRONMENTAL SCANNING

All health leaders must be able to assess the situation currently facing their organization, which requires an assessment of both internal and external environments. A situational assessment must be an objective and honest look at the diverse factors that could affect the health organization's success in achieving its vision, mission, strategies, and goals. One tool commonly used for the internal assessment is SWOT analysis, which investigates internal strengths and weaknesses and external opportunities and threats.[10]

SWOT analysis offers insight into both the internal and external factors that might affect the organization's performance and success; however, every organization needs more information about the environment than just its potential opportunities and threats. Choo reports that it is important to obtain information about relationships, trends, and information in the external environment; health leaders need to know which influences are acting on the industry and even the economy.[11] A focused environmental scan concentrates

on specific information, such as how many consumers bought a particular product or service in the last year. External scanning, whether focused or general, is essential for planning and forecasting the organization's performance into the future.

Situational assessment and continuous environmental scanning are crucial if organizations hope to survive in the dynamic health industry. A leader's and leadership team's responsibility is to remain current about and relevant to situational and environmental change that can or will affect the organization. Forces that contribute to the health industry's rapid, dynamic environment are varied but cumulative; as a consequence, they have a cumulative impact on the industry. "Technology, demography, economics and politics drive change, not only as individual factors but interacting to make the rate of change faster."[12]

Another approach is to look at the dynamic environment as comprising macro-environmental forces and health micro-environmental forces. In an approach that has been validated over the last two decades, in 1992 Rakich, Longest, and Darr outlined a series of categories that leaders can scan (environmental scanning) to keep current and relevant in the industry:

1. Macro-environmental forces
   a. Legal [regulatory, executive orders, and case law] and ethical forces
   b. Political (including government policy) forces
   c. Cultural and sociological (including values [beliefs and attitudes]) forces
   d. Public expectations (including community, interest groups, and media)
   e. Economic forces
   f. Ecological forces

2. Healthcare environmental forces [also called micro-environmental forces]
   a. Planning and public policy (regulation, licensure, and accreditation) forces
   b. Competitive forces
   c. Healthcare financing (third-party payers, public and private, and financial risk)
   d. Technology (equipment, material, and supply entities) forces
   e. Health research and education
   f. Health status and health promotion (wellness and disease)
   g. [Integration with other health disciplines and organizations] Public health (sanitation, environmental protection, etc.) forces[13]

The Rand Corporation has suggested that the immense pressure exerted by cost-containment efforts and the rapid speed of change are major factors that can influence the health industry.[14] Multiple forces have cumulatively contributed to change in the health industry in recent decades. Compare the health organizations of the 1960s or 1970s to those of today: There is a vast difference between the two organizations. The speed of that change in a mere 40 to 50 years is astonishing, as are the gains in the ability of healthcare delivery systems to diagnose, treat, and rehabilitate patients who present with health needs.

For example, consider the life expectancy of people living in the 1960s compared to today. "Between 1961 and 1999, average life expectancy in the [United States] increased from 66.9 to 74.1 years for men and from 73.5 to 79.6 for women."[15] Projections for 2015 estimate life expectancy to be 76.4 years for males and 81.4 years for females, according to the U.S. Census Bureau.[16] Trends in aging are also tied to life expectancy, but have profound implications for health services.[17]

This dynamic whirlwind, often called *white water change*, frames a picture of the world that the health leader must navigate. Although there have been tremendous successes in this industry, health leaders must continue to recognize the dynamic nature of the industry and challenge their organizations, groups, teams, and individuals to become more efficient, effective, and efficacious, while functioning under significant cost-containment pressure. From a practical viewpoint, Kotter suggests eight steps to transform organizations in dynamic situations (italics added):

1. *Establish a sense of urgency* by examining market and competitive realities and identifying and discussing crises, potential crises, or major opportunities.
2. *Form a powerful guiding coalition* by assembling a group with enough power to lead the change intended [from any level of the organization] and encourage the group to work together as a team.
3. *Create a vision* to help direct the change effort and develop strategies for achieving that vision.
4. *Communicate the vision* by using every vehicle possible to communicate the new vision and strategies and by teaching new behaviors by the example of the guiding coalition [at lower levels of the organization, the leader translates the senior leadership's vision for his or her section, branch, or unit into understandable and actionable tasks for that level and situation].
5. *Empower others to act on the vision* by getting rid of obstacles to change, changing systems or structures that seriously undermine the vision, and encouraging risk taking and nontraditional ideas, activities, and actions.
6. *Plan for and create short-term wins* by planning for visible performance improvements, creating those

improvements, and recognizing and rewarding employees involved in the improvements.
7. *Consolidate improvements and produce still more change* by using increased credibility to change systems, structures, and policies that don't fit the vision; hiring, promoting, and developing employees who can implement the vision; and reinvigorating the process with new projects, themes, and change agents.
8. *Institutionalize new approaches* by articulating the connections between the new behaviors and corporate [organizational] success and developing the means to ensure leadership development and succession.[18]

Kotter's eight steps are a sequence of leader actions and are cybernetic; that is, a feedback loop goes from the last step back to the first step. Leaders of health organizations should consider the changes in the macro- and micro-environments by assessing them against the *cost*, *quality*, and *access* health assessment constructs for the community members whom they serve. This analysis, for the segment of the continuum of care (from self-care and health promotion and prevention to primary, secondary, and tertiary care to long-term care and hospice care) for which the leaders are responsible, should be integrated into the holistic aspect of health and the health infrastructure available (or needed) in the community. Leadership depends on a leader's ability to make quality and consistent decisions. The discussion here now turns to the complexity of decision making and how to develop an efficient, effective, and efficacious decision-making culture to dovetail into the organization's planning culture.

DECISION MAKING AND DECISION ALIGNMENT[19]

Decision making occurs in all organizations. Health organizations, for example, face many decisions each day. The decision-making process begins with identifying a question or problem—that is, an area needing improvement or an operational issue. Problems, issues, questions, and operational challenges come to leaders and managers from many different people, both within and outside the health organization. Acknowledging and accepting the inevitability of decision making under paradoxical circumstances are necessary to avoid inappropriate reactions, and doing so can open the door to alternative solutions.[20]

Leaders and managers usually are taught to use the rational decision-making model, which focuses on analytical (quantitative) methods; when necessary, they may couple this approach with group methods (qualitative) such as the normative group technique (brainstorming, alternative categorization, prioritizing alternatives, and selecting an alternative based on group consensus) to triangulate the final result (using both quantitative and qualitative methods) and identify an effective decision.

In reality, decision making is not as sterile and ordered as most have been taught. Both willful choice (rational) decision-making models and reality-based ("garbage can") models are used in organizations amid a myriad of tools and techniques. Thus there are three major domains of decision making:

- Willful choice or rational models
- Reality-based or garbage can models
- Combinations of willful choice and reality-based models

Likewise, three types of decision-making methods are used:

- *Quantitative methods*: Tools such as multiple attribute value, probability-based decision trees, analytical mathematical models, linear programming, and similar tools
- *Qualitative methods*: Tools such as focus groups, interviews (formal and informal), normative group techniques, and similar tools
- *Triangulation methods*: Combinations of quantitative and qualitative methods where, classically, qualitative methods are perceived as "theory building" and quantitative methods are described as "theory testing, validating, or confirming"

A review of bounded rationality, willful choice, and reality-based decision-making models is presented next. More time is spent on reality-based models because this decision-making method is the least well known but may be the most applicable to health organization leaders and managers.

BOUNDED RATIONALITY IN DECISION MAKING

Decision making must occur within the bounded rationality of the environmental context in which the problem must be solved. In modern times, with the advent and availability of the Internet, the bounded rationality of information available for decision making is immense and global. The bounded rationality for any problem spans the parameters in which the rational resources are available to the decision maker to accomplish positive outcomes. Organizational culture influences decision making as well. As noted in a study of military officers published in 2009, officers with

an embedded "forcefulness" and "decisiveness" culture in team leadership roles were more spontaneous and less rational in decision making than their equally ranked team members.[21] Clearly, then, bounded rationality is influenced by organizational culture.

Prior to the dawn of the Information Age and the widespread use of the Internet, information was considered to be a scarce resource that was difficult to find—a perception that has changed dramatically, to the point that we live in an age characterized by "information overload." Unfortunately, the vast amounts of information available do not always include all of the information necessary or completely accurate information with which to make the best decisions. Additionally, information may not be in a form that is immediately useable by those who need it. As a result, the most the health leader can hope to achieve is the best decision possible based on the information that is known. With any decision at hand, different levels of ambiguity and uncertainty will surround the issue. Decisions made easily and with little risk tend to have less ambiguity and uncertainty associated with them, whereas complex, difficult, and more risky decisions tend to have much more ambiguity and uncertainty embedded within them.

Complicating this feature of human decision making is the fact that, although much more information is available today, decision makers may not have access to all the proper information regardless of tools available to them. Furthermore, searching out that information may require far more time than decision makers have to arrive at a decision. Not all information or sources will be identifiable, but time will advance in any case. The decision maker will need to arrive at the best decision that can be made at the time. As a consequence, health leaders must often "satisfice" by seeking "a satisfactory reward rather than seeking the maximum reward."[22]

WILLFUL CHOICE DECISION-MAKING MODELS

Today's decision-making models and current understanding imply that decisions are made by rational, intentional, and willful choice. Choice is guided by four basic principles: (1) unambiguous (you know which questions to ask) knowledge of alternatives, (2) probability and knowledge of consequences, (3) a rational and consistent priority system for alternative ordering, and (4) heuristics or decision rules to choose an alternative.[23] These models assume that alternatives are selected based on the greatest utility (via cost-benefit analysis, for example) for the organization, given the environmental situation (e.g., as assessed via a SWOT analysis in strategic planning), and in line with the organization's objectives, goals, and mission. The decision-making models used in engineering, operations analysis and research, management science, and decision theory represent variations on the rational and willful choice model.[24]

The six-step model of decision making[25] applies the analytical willful choice model as follows:

1. Identify the problem.
2. Collect data.
3. List all possible solutions.
4. Test possible solutions.
5. Select the best course of action.
6. Implement the solution based on the decision made.

This practical model assumes that time and information are abundant, energy is available, and goal congruence of participants (everyone is focused on the same set of goals) has been achieved.

Criticism of Willful Choice Models

Well-known leadership and management concepts consider preplanning (short- and long-term) as the method to solve ambiguity (not knowing what to do) in business. As task complexity increases and time availability decreases, however, the challenge of planning and problem solving becomes increasingly difficult.[26] The rapid pace of operations and change in health care today makes traditionally based organizations less adaptive and flexible in complex environments.[27] Information and time are assumed to be abundant and relatively free resources in rational and willful choice models; moreover, organizational participants in the decision-making process are assumed to have similar (if not the same) goals.[28] Perhaps not surprisingly, these assumptions are the basis of criticisms of the willful choice model. Theories of agency (for conflict management) and economics (scarce resources—namely, time and information) have proposed to resolve contradictory issues associated with willful choice as an explanatory model. Both the theories of agency and economics depend on rational participants to validate the models.[29] The reality of the healthcare industry suggests that individual and group preferences change as underlying variables associated with the decision vary, environmental factors evolve, and other organizational decisions are made.[30,31] In addition, preferences of participants in the decision-making process often vary in illogical and emotionally dependent ways. Although accounted for in the willful choice models, time and information are not considered to be as valuable or scarce in these models as reality actually suggests they are.

Neoclassical economic theory suggests that the greatest good occurs when individuals are free to pursue self-serving interests.[32] This relationship further confounds the underlying assumptions of the willful choice decision-making models. It is unreasonable to assume that each participant in a decision-making process will have similar self-serving goals and similar joint organizational goals most of the time. These contradictions add further credence to the view that willful choice models should be used when the goals of participants are similar, time and information are available in sufficient quantities, and participants are well trained in the use of the model.

We do not mean to suggest that one should not use willful choice models, but rather that these models should be used in *appropriate* situations. This leaves the leader and manager in a tough situation: Which model should be used when the willful choice model conditions cannot be met? Other options include reality-based models. In the discussion that follows, the garbage can model is highlighted as an extension of rational decision-making models. It adds to the available methods of decision making for the leader and manager in health organizations.

REALITY-BASED DECISION-MAKING MODELS

Reality-based models, such as the garbage can model, are intended to extend the understanding of organizational decision making by emphasizing a temporal context (the situation at one point in time) and accepting chaos as reality. Rational (willful choice) decision-making models are a subset of reality-based models. In ambiguous (do not know what to ask or do) situations where time and information are limited or constrained and "perfect information" is impossible to acquire, where organization structure/hierarchy is loosely coupled, and where the organizational persona seems to embody organized anarchy (chaos), analytical decision-making models do not fit reality. The garbage can model, which was originally designed to reflect decision making in universities, has been cited to explain decision-making processes in various organizations and situations. This kind of model also has been introduced as a possible method for understanding processes such as how an organization learns.[33] For the past two decades, researchers have observed that willful choice models of decision making underestimate the chaotic nature and complexity characterizing actual decision-making situations; a large percentage of decisions are made by default—that is, when decision-making processes are followed without actually solving anything.[34]

Garbage Can Model Concepts

Organized anarchy, *chaos*, and *bedlam* are terms that describe organizational decision making. "Garbage can decisions can occur in any organization but are more likely to be found in 'organized anarchies,' where decisions are made under ambiguity and fluid involvement of participants."[35] Garbage can models represent attempts to find logic and order in the midst of decision-making chaos. In this model, garbage—defined as sets of problems, solutions, energy, and participants—is dumped into a can as it is produced (streams of "garbage" in time); when the can is full, a decision is made and removed from the scenario.[36]

> Numerous empirical observations of organizations have confirmed a relatively confusing picture of decision making. Many things seem to be happening at once, technologies are changing and poorly understood; alliances, preferences, and perceptions are changing; solutions, opportunities, ideas, people, and outcomes are mixed together in ways that make interpretation uncertain and leave connections unclear.[37]

In management arenas (and specifically in acquisition decisions), the decision-making load, speed required in decision making, uncertainty, and equivocality (i.e., ambiguity—not knowing which questions to ask or what to do) are commonly encountered factors that influence the decision-making process.[38] Thus the temporal nature of decision-making processes, if taken as "snapshots" in time, would show a sequential arrival of problems, solutions, and information in a complex mix of participants, environmental factors, and consequences of prior decisions as reality in the "organized chaos" of decision making in organizations. Recognizing that time is not static and multidimensionality is ever present, the garbage can model depicts the chaotic nature of decision making through the jumbled mixture of elements in the garbage can.

Concepts are grounded in the ambiguous and uncertain states of nature for the garbage can model. Originally, three states of nature contributed to the model. All three states are immersed in ambiguity and, to a lesser degree, in uncertainty: (1) The greater the ambiguity of technology, (2) the more diverse the preferences of participants (the fewer preferences that are known, the greater the level of uncertainty) and of the organization, and (3) the greater the level of participation (in more specific terms, attention of participants), the more prevalent the garbage can processes in organizational decision making.

Ambiguity is defined as ignorance. Not only does this definition imply lack of knowledge, but it also indicates a lack of understanding of which questions to ask, which information is available, and which kind of connectivity exists between problem and solution sets and the consequences of implementing solutions. Ambiguity of participation exists when participants in the decision-making process have competing time demands that battle for attention that would otherwise be necessary to solve a problem (make a decision). Because measurement of participation ambiguity depends on many extraneous variables in a sea of limitless situational factors, it is difficult to quantify. Yet, attention and energy variations among participants are considered a "given" phenomenon in decision-making processes.

Extending the original concepts in the three-factor model, Takahashi proposed three additional state-of-nature ambiguities to the model: (1) fluid participation, (2) divorce of solutions from discussion, and (3) job performance rather than subjective assessments.[39] Regarding individual preference, Pablo and Sitkin suggest that the more risk averse a decision maker is, the less tolerant of ambiguity he or she is.[40]

Loose coupling in organizations fosters adoption of the garbage can decision-making approach. Loose coupling, in this sense, is defined as a more informal, differentiated focus, such that members of the organization focus less on following the rules, yet structured connectivity of intraorganizational entities is still present. Loose coupling tends to allow a more flexible organization.[41] Organizations that are loosely coupled can more readily adapt to change and shifts in environmental factors.[42–44] The strength of the feedback loops present determines organizational coupling: Stronger feedback loops imply tighter coupling, whereas weaker loops suggest loose coupling.[45] Four criteria[46] are measured to determine the coupling status in organizations:

- *Formal rules*: The more closely the rules are followed, the more tightly coupled the organization. (In entrepreneurial organizations, formal rules are not as important.)
- *Agreement on rules*: The greater the employee congruence, the tighter the coupling. (Entrepreneurial firms agree on social norms rather than formal rules.)
- *Feedback*: The closer the feedback in time, the tighter the coupling.
- *Attention*: Empowered individuals allocate energy and time to prioritized projects in their area. (Participation, competence, and empowerment foster focused attention to areas of responsibility.)

In the garbage can model, the concept of loose coupling is required to understand decision making. As a thinking exercise, consider where a health leader should establish the level of coupling in a health organization; refer to **Figure 6-1** when contemplating this question.

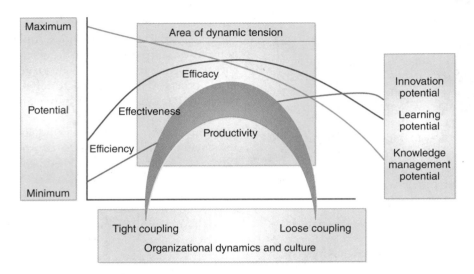

Innovation, learning and knowledge management and organizational coupling
Tension: efficiency, effectiveness, efficacy, productivity.
Where should health organizations focus? Consider mission, vision, strategies, goals, and external
(e.g., error-free delivery of care) and internal (capabilities) assessments.

FIGURE 6-1   The Ledlow and Johnson model (revised by Ledlow): Coupling and the tension of innovation, learning, and knowledge management.

Reproduced from Johnson, J., Ledlow, G., & Kerr, B. (2005). Organizational development, training and knowledge management. In B. Fried, J. Johnson, & M. Fottler (Eds.), *Human resources in healthcare: Managing for success* (2nd ed.). Chicago: Health Administration Press.

Temporal order replaces sequential order. Time is spatial in that a multitude of issues, problems, information flows, and sensing mechanisms can bombard decision makers in short or long time blocks. How problems and information to resolve the problems arrive in time has relatively equal priority with the evaluation of their importance. Arrival time and sequence in the current context both influence how much attention the decision maker pays to the situation:

> The process is thoroughly and generally sensitive to load. An increase in the number of problems, relative to the energy available to work on them, makes problems less likely to be solved, decision makers more likely to shift from one arena to another more frequently, and choices longer to make and less likely to resolve problems.[47]

Individuals in the decision-making process, directly and indirectly, are interconnected and influence the context of the decision at hand.

Obviously, attention demands influence decision making. Time and energy must be allocated to understand, evaluate, and formulate a problem; then to synthesize relevant information; next to evaluate options; and finally to

choose an alternative to counter or terminate the problem. Individuals focus on some things and do not attend to others in the same space of time. Corporate actions, outcomes, and responsiveness are the results of dynamic organizational processes, not heuristics of individual choice.[48] Time and energy combine to form "attention." Attention is a dynamic concept that is highly dependent on load (i.e., the number of decisions that need to be made).

Lending support to the garbage can concept, rational choice in organizational decision making can be skewed by rituals and symbolism. Symbolic rituals associated with decision-making processes, at times, may derail rational attempts to understand the process. Decision making is a process that reassures the organization that values, norms, and logic are upheld; in this light, decision making is a ritual.

Lastly, decision making as a process focuses on showing control and logic in a world of complexity and rapid change. Saying, "We made a decision" and "We own the process" implies control of human existence by logical choice. Whatever way the choice ritual makes one feel, decision making is not rational. For this reason, a depiction of organized chaos rationalized by imperfect participants among a myriad of complex and synergized variables is more appropriate, as shown in **Figure 6-2**.

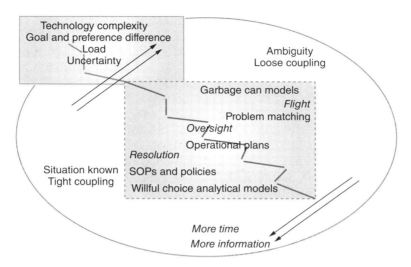

FIGURE 6-2 Conceptual garbage can decision-making model.

Decision possibilities in the garbage can run the gamut from willful choice models to garbage can–based models. Decisions by "flight," "resolution," and "oversight" are prominent categories in the latter model. *Flight* is defined as a decision maker's intentional movement (attention shift) to another area of concern (problem). *Resolution* comprises a decision that uses classical decision-making processes such as willful choice models.[49] *Oversight* is defined as decision makers activating a process or procedure before a problem becomes apparent, such as development of a standard operating procedure or use of an established and documented process. Much of the research shows that flight is a significant result of many decision-making processes; in essence, decisions were "overcome by events" or were not made, but rather were allowed to either resolve or escalate themselves. So, what does a leader or manager do to deal with the reality of decision making?

OPTIMIZATION OF DECISION MAKING

If a health organization has decision-making processes that resemble the garbage can environment, understanding the issues and proactively creating an environment that improves decision making can benefit the organization as a whole. Simulation results as part of garbage can studies revealed that decision making by resolution is not the most likely result of decision-making processes unless flight results are greatly constrained or decision load is light. Instead, flight and oversight[50] are more likely to occur— that is, either decisions are not made or predetermined and established processes (such as standard operating procedures) are used to a greater degree than might be noted with willful choice models. Given these findings,

why not reengineer organizations to foster decision making based on the goals of the organization, where clearly defined yet challenging goals are set and managers direct subordinates to focus, persist, and provide effort in achieving the goals,[51] comprehend technology, and logically apply rational decision-making processes? The answer is simple: Organizations do not exist to make decisions, but rather to serve the external environment. An organization structured to make decisions will not serve its customers well and eventually will be eliminated from the marketplace.

Imperfect decision making can be expected. In light of the ambiguous reality of information, preference, differences, incongruent goals, and sporadically occurring problems coupled with information bombardment of the temporally "exposed" decision maker, the garbage can model represents a reasonable extension of willful choice theories. Humans strive for processes of willful choice, yet, as the garbage can model proposes, fail to achieve rationality in decision making due to time, energy, attention, uncertainty, ambiguous information, and decision-making load issues. Leaders who can grasp the dynamics of the garbage can are better prepared to position their organizations to make good decisions amid organized chaos and competition.

Given this understanding, it seems clear that leaders and managers in health organizations should develop an organizationally sensitive *system of decision making* with the understanding that decision making is not always orderly. To do so, they should focus on the following tasks:

- Evaluating the situation and decisions that need to be made across the organization (or within your area of responsibility) and categorizing decisions by quantity, urgency, information needed to make the decision, and variance in decision outcomes

- Developing readily available information concerning core business functions
- Standardizing, documenting, and training team members on decisions that need to be made routinely, where the same or a similar decision outcome is required, and "pushing" those decisions to the lowest levels of the organization as possible but requiring feedback loops
- Determining decision-making load (quantity in a set time frame) and information available to make decisions for the existing decisions (those not standardized)
- Determining the importance of a decision to the organization by creating a system of risk determination, prioritization (urgency), and technological requirements for nonstandardized decisions
- Training team members on the decision-making system and processes

When a decision or decisions need to be made, a health organization leader should take the following steps:

1. Evaluate the priority and risk of the decision to be made, and determine whether this is a standardized decision or a decision that needs to be worked through.
2. Evaluate time available, resources available, participant attention, goals, and incentives.
3. Determine which decision-making method to use: oversight, based on established documented processes such as standard operating procedures; resolution, using a willful choice model; or pushing the decision to the appropriate level, individual, or group. It is also important to know when you do *not* need to make a decision (flight), based on the importance and risk level of the decision at hand.

To develop a reality-based decision-making system, the leader and manager must understand that decision making is not a sterile and orderly process in most cases. Importantly, organizational decision making *should be aligned* (decisions should be in accordance) with the organization's *mission* and *vision* statements and *strategic planning–based goals and objectives*.

TOOLS OF DECISION MAKING

Early careerists need to be aware of the various tools of decision making for future leadership study and practice. Study (e.g., taking a course) and practice of both quantitative and qualitative decision-making tools are highly recommended. This section highlights quantitative methods, qualitative methods, and triangulation, a combination of quantitative and qualitative methods. It is recommended that each tool mentioned here (and others not mentioned) be researched (perhaps on the Internet), discussed, practiced, and role played with others in the class, group, or organization. Facilitating the decision-making process in a group or organization is an essential skill of leaders and managers, and a working familiarity with decision-making tools is a prerequisite to mastering this skill.

Quantitative Methods

Quantitative methods include mathematical and computational analytical models to help leaders understand the decision-making situation (data turned into information, which is then turned into knowledge) and produce mathematical outcomes of solutions. Some models are rather simple; others are highly complex. Quantitative models assist in assigning a "number" to uncertainty. Models include multiple-attribute value and multiple-utility methods, linear programming, probability, and decision trees based on Bayes' theorem, and can be as complex as discrete and dynamic simulation. In general, simulation uses theoretical distributions and probabilities to "model" the real-world situation on the computer. From this computer model, response variables produce "outcomes" that can be evaluated.

Quantitative models take time and understanding of the important elements (also known as factors or variables) associated with the decision that needs to be made. In most health organizations, quantitative models are gaining momentum, though qualified (highly trained and well-practiced) analysts who understand health processes and can perform a range of quantitative analyses remain difficult to find and hire. Even with quantitative analyses in hand, many times leaders and managers skew decisions toward the qualitative side of decision making.

Six Sigma is a methodology that is growing in prominence in the health industry. Quantitative methods are critical to Six Sigma, which is a fact-based, data-driven philosophy of quality improvement that values defect prevention over detection. The Six Sigma technique drives customer satisfaction and bottom-line results by reducing variation and waste. It can be applied anywhere variation and waste exist, and every employee should be involved in its implementation. Six Sigma is used by many business organizations; health organizations are now using this philosophy as well to improve the work processes in their facilities.

Six Sigma is used to evaluate the capability of a process to perform defect free, where a *defect* is defined as anything that results in customer dissatisfaction.[52] The higher the Sigma level, the lower the number of defects. At the Six Sigma level, there are approximately 3.4 errors per 1 million opportunities, a virtually error-free rate.[53] Among early adopters of this approach are some of the most highly regarded health systems in the country—the Cleveland Clinic, the Mayo Clinic, and Johns Hopkins Medical Center, to name a few. These facilities consistently rank among the best hospitals in the world.[54]

Six Sigma is most successful when senior leadership makes a strong commitment to change and in institutions where patient satisfaction and error-free care are the driving forces. Health organization staff must be trained by professional Six Sigma trainers. The training includes a "lean" thinking that seeks to drive employees toward perfection. It comprises a set of tools of varying degrees of sophistication that can be helpful for a leader to improve the health organization.[55]

A complementary approach to Six Sigma is Lean Sigma. Lean Sigma focuses on fixing the broken systems and processes that hinder medical professionals from doing what they do best, empowering employees to make improvements, reducing time and costs, synchronizing processes, and improving quality and the patient experience.[56] This practice helps to create efficient processes and to decrease wasted time in a health facility. Lean Sigma provides the road map for fast and sustainable improvement while creating a work environment that strengthens and sustains the patient experience and increases the effectiveness of the health service and the provider of care.

Qualitative Methods

Qualitative methods include a variety of tools, ranging from personal intuition, discussions with team members, informal interviews, formal interviews, focus groups, nominal group techniques, and even voting. These methods are very useful in the decision-making process, because experience, intuition, and common sense can all be used by individuals as well as by groups.

Study and practice of qualitative methods are essential for leaders to facilitate decision making for themselves, groups, and organizations. The most notable leader decision-making tools of a qualitative nature are intuition, consensus, and coalition-based counsel.

Triangulation

The combination of quantitative and qualitative methods results in triangulation, a more thorough (albeit more time-consuming) method with which to make decisions. For example, a group may use nominal group techniques to develop a small set of possible solutions and then analyze each solution quantitatively. From there the leader can make a decision.

Training the group or organization to use triangulation is a good practice for resolving ("resolution" in reality-based models) decisions. Triangulation can also be used to develop standard operating procedures ("oversight" in reality-based models). Lastly, triangulation can be used to make improvements to processes within the organization. Kaizen theory (discussed later in this chapter) uses triangulation in the context of continuous quality improvement.

DECISION MAKING IN QUALITY IMPROVEMENT

Extending the discussion on decision making, quality improvement integrates well into the overall schema of decision systems. In essence, quality improvement is a distinct system characterized by seven phases: (1) decision making (identification of improvement areas), (2) situational assessment, (3) information gathering, (4) decision making (what to do with assessment and information to improve), (5) planning, (6) implementation, and (7) feedback. Quality improvement, as a system, is an organizational culture "flag" found in many excellent health organizations. The connection in this arena is simple: Where quality improvement systems exist, decision-making systems are embedded throughout the system of continuous quality improvement. Total quality management (TQM), Kaizen theory, and the Shewhart cycle are all quality improvement strategies; they are profiled in the remainder of this section.

Total Quality Management

The TQM principles were initially brought to Japan by W. Edwards Deming after World War II. Consequently, Japanese businesses have been practicing TQM for more than 50 years, with remarkable results: Japan was able to rebuild its war-torn economy and innovate, to the extent that it became one of the strongest economies in the world in the latter part of the twentieth century. Despite this proof that TQM can be used over the long term with successful results, many health leaders feel an urgency to adopt new management philosophies every few years.[57,58]

The key with TQM for any leader is to strive for documented and incremental decreases in variation and redundancy. This is a 14-step process:

1. Constantly strive to improve products and services.
2. Adopt a total quality philosophy.
3. Correct defects as they happen, rather than relying on inspection of end products.

4. Award business on factors other than price.
5. Continually improve the systems of production and service.
6. Institute training.
7. Drive out fear.
8. Break down barriers among staff areas.
9. Eliminate superficial slogans and goals.
10. Eliminate standard quotas.
11. Remove barriers to pride of workmanship.
12. Institute vigorous education and retraining.
13. Require that management take action to achieve the transformation.
14. Engage in proactive management.

The prudent health leader meets in collaboration with fellow leaders in the organization. Working through a facilitator, they write down each of Deming's tenets and outline those current organizational policies, practices, and procedures that have an impact on improving or impeding practices in the organization. When all of the information has been collected, the leader will be ready to establish new guidelines and break down barriers, as appropriate.

Kaizen Theory

Kaizen theory is another approach with ties to Deming's work but is a Japanese-originated philosophy that focuses on continuous improvement throughout a system. Because health leaders are ultimately responsible for all aspects of organizational dynamics within the health enterprise, this approach is noteworthy. Kaizen theory is as much of an organizational culture (how things are done here) as a system that can be taught.

Kaizen originated in Japan in 1950 when business management and government acknowledged that there were problems in the then-current confrontational management system, given the pending labor shortage in Japan. This theory considers the initial quality of a project as well as the incremental improvement of quality when planning for quality improvements. Researchers defined Kaizen theory as a strategy to include concepts, systems, and tools within the bigger picture of leadership. This approach involves people (subordinates) and organizational culture, all driven by the customer. Japanese business leaders then involve the workforce in the solution of the problem. A key idea behind this theory is the need to practice reactive problem solving to promote continuous adherence to quality standards.[59]

Kaizen focuses on continuous improvement (CI) in performance, cost, and quality. In fact, some sources use the terms *Kaizen* and *continuous improvement* interchangeably, reflecting the nature of the theory. Ellife described Kaizen, or continuous improvement, as a method that intensively focuses on improving every small detail of a process, recognizing that lots of small improvements, when executed continuously and embedded in the culture of an organization, can yield much more benefit than a few "big" programs.[60] The goal when implementing the concepts of this theory in an organization is to promote a culture of consistent standards and quality by addressing small problems or tasks. In other words, *Kaizen* signifies a series of small improvements that have been made in the status quo as a result of ongoing efforts.[61] Others suggest that CI can be generated and sustained through the promotion of a good improvement model and management support.[62]

A *Kaizen event* is a focused and structured improvement project, using a dedicated cross-functional team to improve a targeted work area, with specific goals and objectives, in an accelerated time frame. It is a complex organizational phenomenon, with the potential for altering both a technical system (i.e., work area performance) and a social system (i.e., participating employees and work area employees).[63] Kaizen events are usually short-term projects, sometimes lasting only 1 week.

The introduction of a Kaizen event in the health setting may be problematic, given that leaders could face multiple barriers to the proposed change from the start. For example, some have suggested that demarcations are traditionally more stringent in hospital settings; subordinates in different units in the health organization protect "their" territory. It is, therefore, necessary to have personnel from the different groups involved in patient care represented on a Kaizen team. The structure and composition of this team is crucial to the success of a health organization Kaizen event. Kaizen events typically use a semiautonomous team (a social system) to apply a specific set of technical problem-solving tools.[64]

In the healthcare arena, a Kaizen team should be composed of people from multiple disciplines to accurately address and manage events. Its members may, for example, consist of a physician, nurse, social worker, and physical therapist, depending on the event being addressed. Working as an interdisciplinary team ensures the sustainability of the improvements. Another positive side effect is that the group members can analyze one another's work processes to see how many steps each process actually includes and how much time is spent doing them. Kaizen covers many techniques and processes of CI; one that may be used in the health setting is the Shewhart cycle.[65]

Shewhart Cycle

The Shewhart cycle is also referred to as the Deming model and the plan–do–check–act (PDCA) cycle. This continuous quality improvement model consists of a logical sequence of these four repetitive steps for CI and learning.[66] The Shewhart cycle is a continuous feedback loop that seeks to identify and change process elements to reduce variation. The objective of this process is to plan to do something, do it, check for met requirements, and correct the process to achieve acceptable output performance. Performance improvement teams (PITs) are often developed in health organizations to address specific issues and work on problem solving by implementing the Shewhart cycle.

A PIT, which is a multidisciplinary group, may apply a model such as the Shewhart cycle to concentrate on quality improvement issues. Evidence-based data are used to analyze information within a PIT. Evidence-based practice in clinical performance, as well as administrative components, may help to reduce unnecessary tasks and procedures. The PIT can use the Shewhart cycle to tackle issues that affect the quality of care.

TRAINING

Training is a responsibility of leadership. Usually housed in the human resources department, it is the main vehicle for human resource development (HRD). Training functions as a key role of HRD by working to improve the organization's effectiveness, efficiency, and efficacy by providing employees with the learning needed to improve their current or future job performance based on the mission, vision, strategies, and goals of the organization.[67]

Training comprises a planned set of activities that proceeds through health organizational needs assessment, gap analysis (Do current employees lack certain capabilities?), training module development, trainer identification, logistics of training, the training itself, and training evaluation and refinement. Training in organizations should focus on the organizationally required knowledge, skills, and abilities (KSAs). Training of staff and subordinates is, of course, essential for the long-term success of the health organization. Usually employees who work at the highest levels (leadership) and the lowest levels (e.g., receptionists) receive the least amount of ongoing training in a health organization; this is a problem that needs to be rectified (considering that the lowest levels in a health organization usually welcome and often interact with patients). Leader training is often subsumed in the HRD training structure, when, in fact, it needs to be an ongoing effort that is just as prevalent as staff training.

Why should it be that some people develop into "take charge" types who organize everything around them, whereas others remain more laissez-faire in their approach to life? Maltby asks this basic question, noting that the

QUALITY LEADERS' BENCHMARKS

1775: Adam Smith, author of *The Wealth of Nations*, observed a pin factory in 1775 and concluded that the process of making a pin could be separated into 14 different steps and processes. After observing the process for a period of time, Smith defined the sentinel events of pin making and assigned these tasks to the personnel who showed expertise in each specific stage. The result: The factory went from producing hundreds of pins a week to thousands! However, Smith found that if certain elements of this fledgling assembly line suffered slowdowns, the entire output could be hindered or halted.

1920: Dr. Walter Shewhart of Bell Telephone developed one of the first true control charts. In a paradigm shift from management philosophies, instead of inspecting outcomes, Shewhart began inspecting the process. He developed some of the first process-control methodologies used in the United States. His primary data methods were statistics (outcomes), sampling (convenience), and control charts that could be supplied to management to measure events as they happened.

1950: Kaizen theory resulted in increase in productivity in Japan after World War II. Before World War II, Japanese products were seen as low quality and cheap; after the war, when Japanese factories and management philosophies were reestablished, Kaizen principles helped the country to establish dominance in the global marketplace. Eventually, the word *Japanese* became synonymous with the word *quality* in regard to factory-made items.

1950–present: W. Edwards Deming applied Shewhart's principles of quality control in his role as a consultant to several organizations while visiting Japan after World War II. From 1950 onward, he often visited Japan as lecturer and consultant (the Japanese honored him by naming the highest Japanese quality award after him). In spite of this popularity in Japan, Deming's principles were not adopted in the United States until the latter part of the 1980s. Today, the demonstration of TQM, Kaizen theory, and Shewhart principles are staples of many accreditation site visits for health leaders.

"question continues to dominate the study of leadership today. Volumes of research have been written."[68] Many definitions of leadership exist, and Maltby offers one taken from the writing of Jay Conger: This definition holds that leaders establish direction, gain commitment, and motivate members of the group.[69]

Developing some clarity about the "Born or made?" debate is essential to any discussion of leadership training. The current consensus is that the answer to this question is "both"; leaders are born *and* made. Most authors agree that although elements of leadership certainly can be taught to others, such training is far more effective among people with a predisposition to leadership. To be successful, training must be designed to (1) develop and refine certain of the teachable skills; (2) improve conceptual abilities; (3) tap individuals' personal needs, interests, and self-esteem; and (4) help leaders see and move beyond their interpersonal blocks.[70] Two of the more important health organization training efforts, for leaders and all subordinates, are cultural and moral competencies.

Cultural and Moral Competencies

Health leaders must work together as partners to increase general awareness and improve culturally diverse organizations. The U.S. Department of Health and Human Services defines *cultural competence* as behaviors, attitudes, and policies that come together on a continuum to work in an adverse cultural setting. The Robins Group defines it as a way of being that enables people and organizations to engage effectively in a variety of cross-cultural environments.[71] Because every organization is different, what constitutes appropriate cultural competence in one organization may be seen as being wholly inadequate in another organization. Thus cultural competence is "an approach that starts with the core values and cultural expectations of the specific organization."[72] It can also be defined as an understanding of the importance of social and cultural influences on patients' health beliefs and behaviors and a consideration of how these factors interact at multiple levels of the health delivery system (e.g., at the level of structural processes of care or clinical decision making). Clearly, it is important to devise interventions that take these issues into account to assure quality healthcare delivery to diverse patient populations.[73,74]

Cultural competence provides the knowledge, skills, and abilities that allow health leaders to increase their understanding and appreciation of cultural differences among groups of people. It focuses on behaviors, attitudes, and policies. This foundation facilitates exploration of different cultures, learning about cultural heritages, and appreciation of the effects of diversity on health care and the health industry. Culture and language have powerful effects in terms of how patients access and respond to all health services received from a health provider; leaders need to be aware of these issues.[75,76]

The Joint Commission suggests that all health leaders should be culturally competent. The U.S. government has presented a series of recommendations for national standards and outcomes-focused research to assure cultural competence in health care.[77,78] When cultural competency is lacking, patients and subordinates may mistrust both the leader and the health organization. For leaders, cultural competency is a learning process that will allow them to grow and expand their knowledge, sensitivity, and respect for those in the organization and for those whom the health organization serves. Cultural competency is expressed in the healthcare approaches used with patients of diverse ethnicities, races, national origins, and languages. Leaders need to be culturally competent to succeed.[79,80]

In a global community, the value of cultural competence is clear, particularly as ethnic, racial, and national diversity increase. These points of diversity further contribute to the mélange that is the organizational culture. Power can be used to block something from happening, or it can be used to ensure that something does happen. Power is essential if the organization hopes to accomplish anything: Some person or some group must have the power to make things work. "Power is the basis of the ability to get things done in organizations, and is therefore an essential element of organization and leadership."[81] Cultural competence, on the other hand, is a capability that adds to a leader's power.

All of these factors combine to form and influence leadership. Planning, decision making, and training can and do take place within organizations that serve and employ a variety of cultural types, but only cultural and moral competency can produce an organizational culture that encourages and allows employees to fully respond to leadership.

Ethics and Morality

Ethics can be defined as the theory of moral values.[82] There is a perception that all organizations are expected to work to the highest standards of integrity and ethics. Ethical standards and values are not created by laws or regulations, but rather by the board and trustees of an organization; they are then implemented by the leadership. Ethics is a framework for decision making and action, whereas morality is the level to which the ethical framework is applied. In many university programs, ethics is embedded in a health law or legal course. Ethics and morality are health leader responsibilities—a statement that holds true at all levels of the health organization. In simple terms, ethics relates to doing what is right; it is about using good and fair judgment; it is about responsible fiduciary use and distribution of resources. Ethical and moral behavior, personally and organizationally, is the leader's responsibility.

Health leaders must be ethical and moral agents of the organization. The success of the organization may rise and fall on the perception of the community regarding the morals of the organization. Staff members and the community expect the leaders to use their best judgment; leaders are held accountable for doing what is right. If a slip in morality occurs, unfavorable publicity might obscure all of the health organization's other positive efforts and smear the good name of the organizational "brand." Unfavorable publicity can have a dramatic effect on an initiative already in progress.[83] Although other leadership distinctions may depend on the execution of a skill set (such as planning) or a trait (such as charisma), the distinction of authentic leadership rests heavily on perceptions of morality. To gain support from both internal and external stakeholders, the health organization must display the sincerity of its mission and act consistently with its espoused values.

In nonprofit health organizations, losses due to fraudulent activities are particularly troublesome because they directly reduce the amount of resources available to address tax-exempt purposes.[84] Negative publicity for a health organization may also reduce contributions and lead to the loss of grants. Some organizations have publicly indicated their commitment to ethics, whereas others have done little to prevent ethical dilemmas from arising. It is important to read your health organization's ethical statements to see where it stands on these issues.

Over the years, various reports have appeared in the literature on the need for healthcare organizations to develop and implement organizational ethics programs. Health organizations should institute visible and effective leadership training programs in these areas. These programs should promote and inspire the ethical behavior of employees and executives alike. In 2009, Fine suggested that a moral discourse in the health leadership context is important; adding purpose and context to leadership model constructs should be based in ethical considerations and possibly adopting a feminist ethic of care perspective.[85]

In recent decades, several ethical scandals have adversely affected the health industry. Health leaders should be aware of these episodes and take steps to prevent them in their own organizations. Some of the more widely publicized scandals involved embezzlement by the president of the United Way of America,[86] improper use of funds by the head of the National Association for the Advancement of Colored People (NAACP),[87] and investment fraud by the head of the Foundation for New Era Philanthropy.[88] These examples show that ineffective leadership can have a huge impact on health organizations and the industry as a whole. The success of health organizations is sometimes rated by the quality of their charitable and beneficent activities; when these activities are associated with immoral behavior, the negative effects can be devastating.

The leaders of the health organization must demonstrate that they can operate in a consistently ethical and moral manner. Consistent, ongoing, and frequent training in cultural and moral competencies is imperative; this training should begin with new employee orientation and continue throughout the tenure of the employee regardless of position or status.

CONTINUING HEALTH EDUCATION: COMPETENCY ATTAINMENT

As we close out this chapter, we offer a perspective of knowledge, skills, and abilities (KSAs) in regard to continuing health education (CHE). For the purpose of this summary, we suggest that *knowledge* is recalling information with familiarity gained through education, experience, or association, whereas *comprehension* is understanding the meaning of the information. A *skill* is the effective and timely utilization of knowledge, and finally, an *ability* is the physical, cognitive, or legal power to competently perform and achieve positive outcomes. Many of the competencies needed to start a career may be learned in degree programs; however, once an individual moves away from traditional education and enters into professional practice, most, if not all, of these capabilities are learned through CHE. As early careerists will see, whether you are aware or not, you are constantly being evaluated and assessed on a combination of your skills, knowledge, and abilities in any professional practice setting entered.

The health workforce consists of a complex assortment of individuals with different backgrounds, educational experiences, certifications, specialties, and work locations. Approximately 12% of the U.S. workforce works in the health professions.[89] As a result, health leaders must continue to understand the dynamic nature of the industry to lead very diverse members of the healthcare team, which will require them to challenge themselves and their organizations to become more competent under significant external pressures.

WHAT IS CONTINUING HEALTH EDUCATION?

Continuing health education (CHE) involves activities, learning events, or individual efforts that result in a combination of recognized (and/or credentialed) and unrecognized (uncredentialed) knowledge. Formal CHE includes those activities sponsored through professional organizations or organizations of higher education that award credit toward certification, licensure, or accreditation, or apply to annual requirements for practice. These include:

- Formalized continuing health and/or medical education (CHE/CME)

- Certificate, graduate, and doctoral education
- Recognized didactic instruction

Informal CHE includes those activities, events, and efforts in which individuals engage to maintain proficiency or fill personal gaps in knowledge in personal practice. These may include:

- Mentoring (or being a mentee)
- Heuristics (a "rule of thumb" or organizing rubric)
- Community volunteerism
- Professional organizations (networking)

Table 6-1 provides a snapshot of the advantages and disadvantages of each type of CHE. An adroit health professional should keep him- or herself abreast of several different and ongoing types of CHE in his or her career to maintain appropriate competency within the profession.

Table 6-1 Advantages and Disadvantages of Formal and Informal Continuing Health Education

	Type	Description	Advantages	Disadvantages
Formal continuing education	Continuing health and/or medical education (CHE/CME)	Those didactic activities that are generally sponsored by professional organizations	• Recognized • Easily transferable • Peer reviewed • Panel of experts • Relevant to today's environment	• High cost • Geography • Seasonal times and opportunities for attendance • Limited focus to the profession • Often requires meeting face-to-face
	Certificate, graduate, and doctoral education	Those activities that are sponsored or take place in institutions of higher learning or education *Examples:* Texas Tech University Health Sciences Center, Central Michigan University	• Results in a focused set of transferable competencies across the profession • Permanent and often without expiration • May be conducted via distance learning	• Skills become dated and may lack relevancy over time • Quality may vary between degree-granting institutions
	Recognized didactic instruction	Those activities that are sponsored by or take place in peer professional organizations or educational organizations *Examples:* ACHE, MGMA, AMA, ANA, trade schools, colleges, and universities	• Credits often transferable across professions • Permanent and often without expiration • Provides a different point of view • Often relevant and necessary to profession	• Skills may become dated and may lack relevancy over time • Quality may vary between degree-granting institutions • May take months to years to learn skill • Costs may be prohibitive

Table 6-1 Advantages and Disadvantages of Formal and Informal Continuing Health Education (continued)				
	Type	**Description**	**Advantages**	**Disadvantages**
Informal continuing education	Mentoring	The close and personal relationship established between a senior and a junior professional—often in similar career fields *Example:* The CEO mentoring a new hire or junior employee	• Little to no cost • Creates loyalty and decreases turnover • Reaffirms leadership principles • Transfer of knowledge and skills specific to organization	• Skills learned in one organization may not be specific to another • Can create perception of favoritism
	Heuristics	Knowledge gained through experimentation and practice *Example:* A mid-level executive volunteering to do his or her first CBA (cost-benefit analysis)	• Heuristic opportunities surround us daily • Personal challenge • Demonstration of leadership to peers, superiors, and subordinates • Provides valuable set of marketable skills	• Skills are difficult to quantify and measure • May not be valued across organizations

SUMMARY

This chapter identified knowledge and empirically based skills and abilities (a leadership toolbox full of "tools") required for a health leader's success in organizational practice. Strategies for leaders in effecting planning, decision making, and training that result in positive outcomes ideally result in practical leadership actions and applications based in "active" leadership.

Planning, decision making, and training are integrated processes that are embedded in health organizations. Leaders can consciously make these processes better, more efficient, effective, and efficacious while reducing organizational stress. Understanding the nature of planning and decision making and becoming competent as a decision maker, facilitator, analyst, or decision-making assistant (a person who helps the primary decision makers) are critical for success as a leader and a manager; they are also necessary for success as a team member who is not filling a leadership or management role. Developing a system of planning,

decision making, and training, within the organizational context, and becoming a competent user of these systems are vital to achieving and maintaining excellence in health organizations. Given the dynamic changes in the health industry—considering health reform and implementation of the Patient Protection and Affordable Care Act, value-based purchasing impacting reimbursement, transition to electronic health records and meaningful use criteria, and movement to the ICD-10 version procedure codes from the ICD-9 version—the leader's ability to scan the environment, assess the internal organizational situation, and provide a vision to move the organization forward successfully is vital. Planning and decision making are the bridge between the opportunities and threats within the industry and strengths and weaknesses within the organization and the successful navigation to achieve the vision of the organization. A leader and/or leadership team is the catalyst, the essence, for organization success.

DISCUSSION QUESTIONS

1. Discuss the importance and use of planning, decision making, and training in health organizations and provide examples of each. How can planning, decision making, and training aid in developing organizational culture in health organizations?
2. Explain the planning process within the context of leadership. Explain the decision-making processes

used by health organizations. Predict how successful leaders can be when they master these tools of leadership. What might happen if they do not master these tools?
3. Use examples to apply and relate at least two different decision-making models to a leadership situation in a health organization. How are the models

different? When should each model be used in health organizations?

4. Illustrate the levels or components of the planning process and distinguish each level or component from the others. How does this structure help in planning and in progress review?

5. Relate how a quality improvement program is based on a system of willful choice decision making in a health organization. Can a reality-based decision-making model work in quality improvement? Why or why not?

6. Compare and contrast willful choice to garbage can models of decision making, training leaders to training staff, and cultural competence to ethics and morality. Justify your positions.

EXERCISES

1. Define the overall concepts of planning, decision making, and training; give examples of each as part of your definitions.

2. Generalize how a successful health leader prepares for (a) planning in a health organization, (b) developing a decision-making system in a health organization, and (c) ensuring that all employees are culturally competent in a health organization. Complete this exercise in two pages or less.

3. Prepare a list of internal and external stakeholders for a health organization in preparation for strategic planning; categorize each group.

4. In a two-page paper, compare and contrast the willful choice and garbage can models of decision making within a health organization context.

5. Organize a planning effort in preparation for a Kaizen theory or Shewhart cycle quality improvement project within a unit (keep it small) of a health organization. Describe this plan in three pages or less.

6. In a two- to three-page paper, appraise the concept of "coupling" within the context of decision making and ethics/morality in a health organization.

REFERENCES

1. Granda-Cameron, C., Lynch, M. P., Mintzer, D., Counts, D., Pinto, S., & Crowley, M. (2007). Bringing an inpatient palliative care program to a teaching hospital: Lessons in leadership. *Oncology Nursing Forum*, *34*(4), 772–776.

2. Yukl, G. (1994). *Leadership in organizations* (3rd ed.). Englewood Cliffs, NJ: Prentice Hall.

3. Ledlow, G., & Cwiek, M. (2005). The process of leading: Assessment and comparison of leadership team style, operating climate and expectation of the external environment. In N. Delener (Ed.), *Global Business and Technology Association Proceeding*. Lisbon, Portugal: Global Business and Technology Association.

4. Ledlow, G., Cwiek, M., & Johnson, J. (2002). Dynamic culture leadership: Effective leader as both scientist and artist. In N. Delener & C. Chao (Eds.), *Global Business and Technology Association International Conference; Beyond boundaries: Challenges of leadership, innovation, integration and technology* (pp. 649–740). New York: Global Business and Technology Association.

5. Eicher, J. P. (2006). Making strategy happen. *Performance Improvement*, *45*(10), 31–48.

6. Eicher, note 5.

7. Eicher, note 5.

8. Higgins, J. (1994). *The management challenge* (2nd ed.). New York: Macmillan.

9. Meyer, P. J. (2003). What would you do if you knew you couldn't fail? Creating S.M.A.R.T. goals. In *Attitude is everything: If you want to succeed above and beyond*. Meyer Resource Group.

10. Van der Werff, T. J. (2009). Strategic planning for fun and profit. Retrieved from http://www.globalfuture.com/planning9.htm.

11. Choo, C. W. (2001, October). Environmental scanning as information seeking and organizational learning. *Information Research*, *7*(1), 23–40.

12. Griffith, J. R. (1999). *The well-managed healthcare organization* (4th ed.). Chicago: Health Administration Press, p. 1.

13. Rakich, J., Longest, B., & Darr, K. (1992). *Managing health services organizations*. Baltimore, MD: Health Professions Press, p. 17.

14. Brook, R. H. (1998). Changes in the healthcare system: Goals, forces, solutions. *PharmacoEconomics*, *1*, 45–48. Retrieved from http://www.rand.org/cgi-bin/health/showab.cgi?key=1998_77&year=1998.

15. Harvard School of Public Health. (2008). Life expectancy worsening or stagnating for large segment of the U.S. population. Retrieved from http://www.hsph.harvard.edu/news/press-releases/life-expectancy-worsening-or-stagnating-for-large-segment-of-the-us-population/.

16. Centers for Disease Control and Prevention. (2003). Public health and aging: Trends in aging—United States and worldwide. *Morbidity and Mortality Weekly Report*, *52*(6), 101–106. Retrieved from http://www.cdc.gov/mmwr/preview/mmwrhtml/mm5206a2.htm.

17. Centers for Disease Control and Prevention, note 16.

18. Kotter, J. P. (1998). Leading change: Why transformation efforts fail. In *Harvard Business Review on change* (pp. 4–17). Boston: Harvard Business School Press.

19. Ledlow, G., & Stephens, J. (2008). Decision making and communication. In J. A. Johnson (Ed.), *Organizational theory, behavior and development* (pp. 213–232). Sudbury, MA: Jones & Bartlett.

20. Lavine, M. (2014). Paradoxical leadership and the competing values framework. *Journal of Applied Behavioral Science*, *50*(2), 189–205.

21. Thunholm, P. (2009). Military leaders and followers: Do they have different decision styles? *Scandinavian Journal of Psychology*, *50*(4), 317–324.

22. Simon, H. A., Dantzig, G. B., Hogarth, R., Piott, C. R., Raifia, H., Schelling, T. C., et al. (1986). Decision making and problem solving. In *Research briefings 1986: Report of the Research Briefing Panel on Decision Making and Problem Solving*. Washington, D.C.: National Academy Press. Retrieved from http://www.dieoff.org/page163.htm.

23. March, J. G., & Weisinger-Baylon, R. (1986). *Ambiguity and command: Organizational perspectives on military decision making*. Marshfield, MA: Pitman.

24. March & Weisinger-Baylon, note 23.

25. Argenti, P. A. (Ed.). (1994). *The portable MBA desk reference: An essential business companion*. New York: John Wiley & Sons.

26. Jelinek, M., & Litterer, J. A. (1995). Toward entrepreneurial organizations: Meeting ambiguity with engagement. *Entrepreneurship: Theory and Practice*, *19*(3), 137–169.

27. Jelinek & Litterer, note 26.

28. March & Weisinger-Baylon, note 23.

29. Swanson, D. L. (1996). Neoclassical economic theory, executive control, and organizational outcomes. *Human Relations*, *49*(6), 735–757.

30. March & Weisinger-Baylon, note 23.

31. Swanson, D. L. (1995). Addressing a theoretical problem by reorienting the corporate social-performance model. *Academy of Management Review*, *20*(1), 43–65.

32. Swanson, note 29.

33. Tsang, E. W. K. (1997). Organizational learning and the learning organization: A dichotomy between descriptive and prescriptive research. *Human Relations*, *50*(1), 73–90.

34. March & Weisinger-Baylon, note 23.

35. March & Weisinger-Baylon, note 23, p. 36.

36. Takahashi, N. (1997). A single garbage can model and the degree of anarchy in Japanese firms. *Human Relations*, *50*(1), 91–109.

37. March & Weisinger-Baylon, note 23, p. 16.

38. Pablo, A. L., & Sitkin, S. B. (1996). Acquisition decision-making processes: The central role of risk. *Journal of Management*, *22*(5), 723–747.

39. Takahashi, note 36.

40. Pablo & Sitkin, note 38.

41. Bennis, W., Parikh, J., & Lessem, R. (1996). *Beyond leadership: Balancing economics, ethics, and ecology* (rev. ed.). Cambridge, MA: Blackwell.

42. Pablo & Sitkin, note 38.

43. Jelinek & Litterer, note 26.

44. March & Weisinger-Baylon, note 23.

45. Van de Ven, A. H., & Poole, M. S. (1995). Explaining development and change in organizations. *Academy of Management Review*, *20*(3), 510–541.

46. Jelinek & Litterer, note 26.

47. March & Weisinger-Baylon, note 23, p. 18.

48. Swanson, note 29.

49. Takahashi, note 36.

50. Takahashi, note 36.

51. Locke, E. A., & Latham, G. P. (1984). *Goal setting: A motivational technique that works!* Englewood Cliffs, NJ: Prentice Hall.

52. Black, K., & Revere, L. (2006). Six Sigma arises from the ashes of TQM with a twist. *International Journal of Health Care Quality Assurance*, *19*(3), 259–266. Retrieved from ABI/INFORM Global database. Document ID: 1073443771.

53. Morgan, S., & Cooper, C. (2004). Shoulder work intensity with Six Sigma. *Nursing Management*, *35*(3), 29–32. Retrieved from ABI/INFORM Global database. Document ID: 583229661.

54. Hirst, R., & Weimer, D. (2008). Management systems keep hospitals from meeting goals. *Managed Healthcare*

Executive, 18(5), 26–27. Retrieved from ABI/INFORM Global database. Document ID: 1500296291.

55. Baker, P. (2005, March). Get the right blend. *Works Management, 58*(3), 26–28. Retrieved from ABI/ INFORM Global database. Document ID: 816940421.

56. Hirst & Weimer, note 54.

57. Burns, J., & Sipkoff, M. (1998). *1999 hospital strategies in managed care.* New York: Faulkner and Gray.

58. Coppola, M. N. (1998). The hidden value of managing worker's compensation costs in the hospital setting. In J. Burns & M. Sipkoff (Eds.), *1999 Hospital strategies in managed care*(pp. 227–255). New York: Faulkner and Gray.

59. Singh, J., & Singh, H. (2009). Kaizen philosophy: A review of literature. *ICFAI Journal of Operations Management, 8*(2), 51–72.

60. Ellife, S. A. (2004, May 3). Cutting out the fat. *Journal of Commerce,* p. 22. Retrieved from ABI/INFORM Global database. Document ID: 626516031.

61. Singh & Singh, note 59.

62. Chen, C. I., & Wu, C. W. (2004). A new focus on overcoming the improvement failure. *Technovation, 24,* 585–591.

63. Farris, J. A., Van Aken, E. M., Doolen, T. L., & Worley, J. (2008). Learning from less successful Kaizen events: A case study. *Engineering Management Journal, 20*(3), 10–20. Retrieved from ABI/INFORM Global database. Document ID: 1582589011.

64. Wennecke, G. (2008, Aug.). Kaizen–LEAN in a week: How to implement improvements in healthcare settings within a week. *Medical Laboratory Observer, 40*(8), 28, 30–31. Retrieved from ProQuest Medical Library database. Document ID: 1555010561.

65. Wennecke, note 64.

66. Singh & Singh, note 59.

67. Blanchard, P. N., & Thacker, J. W. (1999). *Effective training systems, strategies, and practices.* Upper Saddle River, NJ: Prentice Hall.

68. Singh & Singh, note 59.

69. Maltby, D. E. (2009). Leaders: born or made? The state of leadership theory and training today. Biola University. Retrieved from http://www.biola.edu/academics/professional-studies/-leadership/resources/leadership/bornormade/.

70. Maltby, note 69.

71. U.S. Department of Health and Human Services, Office of Minority Health. (n.d.). What is cultural competency? Retrieved from http://minorityhealth.hhs.gov/templates/browse.aspx?lvl=2&lvlID=11.

72. Nori-Robins, K. J. (2009). The Robins Group organization development consultants. Retrieved from http://www.kikanzanurirobins.com/newsletter.htm?newsletter=.

73. Berry-Cabán, C. S., & Crespo, H. (2008). Cultural competency as a skill for health care providers. *Hispanic Health Care International, 6*(3), 115–121.

74. Jirwe, M., Gerrish, K., & Emani, A. (2006). The theoretical framework of cultural competence. *Journal of Multicultural Nursing and Health, 12,* 3.

75. Berry-Cabán & Crespo, note 73.

76. Jirwe et al., note 74.

77. Rudd, K. M., & Stack, N. M. (2006). Cultural competency for new practitioners. *American Journal of Health-System Pharmacy, 63,* 912–913.

78. Berry-Cabán & Crespo, note 73.

79. Markova, T., & Broome, B. (2007). Effective communication and delivery of culturally competent health care. *Urologic Nursing, 27,* 3.

80. Wolf, K. E., & Calmes, D. (2004). Cultural competence in the emergency department. *Top Emergency Medical, 26*(1), 9–13.

81. Van Maanen, J. (2003, October 3). Summary of the three lenses. Retrieved from http://www.core.org.cn/NR/rdonlyres/Sloan-School-of-Management/15-322Fall2003/0C7013D1-D849-43FA-995C-42C096FD1B82/0/ses4_three_lenses.pdf.

82. Midkiff, K. A. (2004). Catch the warning signs of fraud in NPOs. *Journal of Accountancy, 197*(1), 29.

83. Hankin, J. A., Seidner, A., & Zietlow, J. (1998). *Financial management for nonprofit organizations.* New York: John Wiley & Sons.

84. Midkiff, note 82.

85. Fine, M. G. (2009). Women leaders' discursive constructions of leadership. *Women's Studies in Communication, 32*(2), 180–202.

86. Murawski, J. (1995, July 13). Former United Way chief gets 7 years in jail: Sentence praised by charities. *Chronicle of Philanthropy,* 37–38.

87. Greene, E. (1995, May 4). The NAACP: What went wrong? *Chronicle of Philanthropy,* 27–29.

88. Stecklow, S. (1997, Sept. 23). New Era's Bennett gets 12 years in prison for defrauding charities. *Wall Street Journal,* 15.

89. U.S. Department of Health and Human Services, Health Resources and Services Administration. (n.d.). National Center for Health Workforce Analysis. Retrieved from http://bhpr.hrsa.gov/healthworkforce/index.html.

LEADERSHIP ASSESSMENT AND RESEARCH: INDIVIDUAL, TEAM, AND ORGANIZATION

Great ability develops and reveals itself increasingly with every new assignment.
Baltasar Gracian, *The Oracle*

This chapter looks at techniques and applications of leadership, ranging from leading small groups of individuals to leading interdisciplinary teams in small- and large-scale organizations. These elements represent ordinal stages for developing competent leadership capabilities, which in turn are built on the "crawl–walk–run" methodology of health leader development. Mature leaders recognize that different skills are required to lead small groups of individuals than are needed to lead large and complex organizations. Individuals and teams may respond better to verbal communication and direct interaction, whereas leaders of large and complex organizations must develop alternative approaches to communication, such as well-written and well-developed policy and mission statements, or the nurturing and developing of human resources proxies to carry the leader's vision down the hierarchy of the health organization. This chapter examines best practices in communication, leadership archetypes, and some delegation, participatory, and collaborative practices in a group or team context.

LEARNING OBJECTIVES

1. Describe the cycle of leadership, and identify knowledge, skills, and abilities at each stage of the cycle that contribute to understanding health leadership development.

2. Explain Tuckman's model of the group dynamic process, and summarize its importance to health leaders in group or team supervision.

3. Construct a 5-year leadership development plan based on an ultimate health leadership position goal.

4. Compare and contrast a great group or team with one in a groupthink situation and one that is ineffective; distinguish how a health leader performs in each of these group or team situations.

5. Devise a health leader's checklist for leading and managing a group or team focused on superior performance and outcomes.

6. Evaluate health leader development, and explain and relate leader development opportunities and events to the cycle of leadership and the knowledge, skills, and abilities necessary to master each stage of the cycle.

CYCLES OF LEADERSHIP DEVELOPMENT

This chapter offers a methodology for leader development and training based on the crawl–walk–run (CWR) approach. Becoming a great leader starts with forming a foundation of knowledge, skills, and abilities, and building on that foundation. That is the basis for the CWR approach presented in this chapter; this approach, as presented, "walks" along with career levels of leadership roles, reviewing entry-level to senior-level positions in health organizations and what leaders need to do and master to move to the next level of responsibility. When using this philosophy, leader development starts with a backward planning approach. For example, an early careerist looking to enter into the dynamic world of health may see him- or herself rising to the position of president or chief executive officer (CEO) of a large and integrated healthcare delivery system that spans several geographic areas, employs hundreds (perhaps thousands) of personnel, controls policy for hundreds of millions of dollars' worth of equipment and facilities, and is responsible for the competent and safe care of hundreds of thousands of ambulatory and inpatient visits each year. Although this coveted position may be a goal for many entry-level careerists, one has to ask: How did the person currently in that job get there?[1]

The CEO of such an organization did not get to this position overnight. He or she engaged in years (perhaps decades) of incremental training and education that prepared the individual to assume such a complicated position of responsibility. These antecedent, or earlier, leadership positions probably involved entry-level positions in the health industry as the administrator for a group practice or administrative department in a hospital, or a clinical leader in a clinical service. The person may then have become an assistant or associate administrator in the same facility, or a larger one, where junior executives implemented policy and programs under the supervision of the chief operations officer (COO). The individual may have sought out a CEO position at a small organization with limited inpatient services, with specific rural and/or community missions. This job may have offered the opportunity for movement and advancement into subsequently larger and more complex organizations spanning greater responsibility across human resources as well as financial, revenue, logistical/supply chain, strategic, and other resources. Thus a CEO at a small organization may have moved to a larger organization over time. At each stage in this process, the individual gained competencies in areas relating to human resources and financial, revenue, logistical/supply chain, and strategic areas, to name only a few. These development positions made it possible for the individual to be successful in the complex job that he or she now holds as the president/CEO of a large and complex system.

In looking at this hypothetical life cycle model, it is apparent that in each phase in the developmental process, the

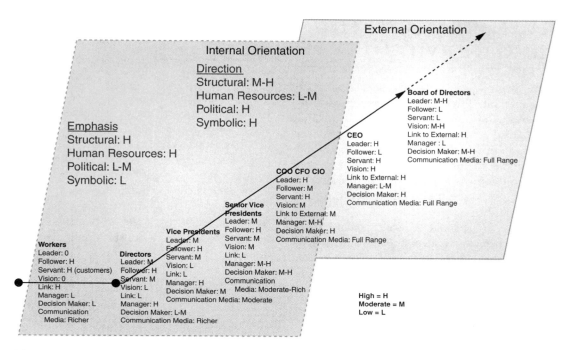

FIGURE 7-1 A hypothetical leadership–management–follower progression in a health organization. Bolman and Deal's constructs for reframing leadership and management in organizations are used as components of the model.

junior executive gained experience in managing ever larger budgets and leading ever greater numbers of people. The junior executive also transitioned from the responsibility of maintaining only personal equipment and property, or equipment of a colloquial nature, to being responsible for hundreds of individual pieces of property with a value exceeding hundreds of thousands, or even millions, of dollars. Additionally, nearly all entry-level positions offer at least a limited opportunity for strategic planning. In contrast, the senior healthcare executive makes his or her reputation on the ability to strategically plan for future events while balancing the simultaneous needs of dozens of tightly woven and interconnected echelons of competing priorities.

So again, we ask: *How does a person get to this level of leadership complexity?* In response, we offer the CWR methodology of leadership development. In **Figure 7-1**, progressive leadership levels are presented in a hypothetical health organization (e.g., under "Workers," "Vision" is assigned a value of 0 because most times the lowest levels of the organization do not develop vision—but should they be involved?). In the figure, Bolman and Deal's leadership orientation constructs, which include structural, human resources, political, and symbolic components, are shown as leader propensities of the positional level; in

reality, these constructs are situational and may be used at any level.

THE CRAWL–WALK–RUN METAPHOR

The CWR metaphor for leader development and training is based on how infants learn to move—from the crawling stage, to the walking stage, to the running stage in their motor ability. This theory also can be applied to their cognitive progress. The CWR premise is both a philosophical perspective and a practical approach to development in any venue. We do not learn to become experts in anything without gaining knowledge, skills, and abilities (KSAs) in a progressive manner.

As the adage says, "You can't run before you can walk." This statement makes obvious theoretical—if not ecological—sense. In education, in the practice called task analysis, each step in performing a task is analyzed to ensure that essential information or skills are not omitted in learning the whole task or process. Everything new that we learn is based on past knowledge and experience along with newly introduced KSAs. The process of advancement in health leadership is no different.

THE CRAWL: STRATEGIES FOR MANAGING INDIVIDUALS

The crawl stage begins with self-awareness. In human development, an infant slowly becomes aware of him- or herself and the surroundings. The infant also begins to understand that he or she can interact with the complex world around him or her. After several attempts and experiments, the infant becomes aware of simple cause-and-effect outcomes. The infant then wants to "go places." To get to where the infant wants to go, he or she crawls.

By completing a personal self-assessment, early careerists will have a road map to success that allows them to initiate their own journey toward leadership competence. The same premise holds true in learning and developing leadership skills. Entry-level management positions are characterized by contact with the unknown and unfamiliar. For example, early careerists are often unsure how to write effective memos and perform management analysis without being given all the variables and constraints to "crunch the numbers." They will likely be unsure of themselves in speaking up at meetings and interacting professionally with senior leaders and clients. They may be uncomfortable when chairing their first meeting, preparing an agenda in advance, scheduling a time, and so forth. There will be some anxiety at initiating ideas and, in the worst-case scenario, taking responsibility for the actions of those below them in the supervisory chain.

There is a specific reason why resumes of health executives boast similar phrases outlining how many people the executive supervised, the number of plants and facilities he or she was responsible for, and the size of the budgets managed. Prior to managing hundreds of people, the early careerist must learn to manage him- or herself and gain experience supervising and keeping track of others in an entry-level and supervisory role.

EXPLICIT LESSONS

From a mentoring standpoint, in the crawl stage, early careerists must be given very explicit lessons and directions to learn very basic knowledge, such as what a leader is, what leadership characteristics are, and what leaders do. For example, in the crawl stage in leadership development, the individual performs the tasks slowly and methodically. This analogy refers to the movement from the conscious incompetent to the conscious competent stage of learning. After experimentation, with greater experience, and recognizing the ability to fail without consequences, the young

executive gains confidence in standing up before groups, framing an opinion on basic courses of action, and being responsible for equipment.[2]

ROLE MODELING

In the crawl stage, there is a need for specific role modeling and/or instruction. Instructions must be explained in detail and their value communicated in the overall plan. After instruction or experience in observing actions, the young executive learns from role models and obtains the knowledge needed to duplicate steps in the process as he or she has been taught. During the crawl stage, the instructions should be relatively simple, so that the early careerist does not need a great deal of supervision to correctly perform the tasks as assigned.[3] Monitoring is still necessary, however, because not all early careerists learn things at the same rate and the progression can vary depending on who is being taught the basic skill set.

WHY ACTIONS ARE DONE

In the crawl stage, the early careerist must know why actions are being initiated, so that the decisions in dynamic organizations make sense. For example, an early careerist who is harshly judged because an email to a senior supervisor included spelling errors may not know that a marketing brochure mailed to thousands of stakeholders months earlier contained numerous spelling errors. The early careerist may not know that the chief executive placed special emphasis on spelling and grammar on all written documents developed within and outside the organization after the embarrassing event. As a result, what might have seemed to be an innocent email written hastily by an early careerist attempting to solve a complex task that was previously assigned may result in a perception of unprofessionalism individually and reflect poorly on his or her department as a whole. The early careerist must make it a point to read existing documents, ask questions, and consult with peers and mentors (sometimes peer mentors) who have been in the organization for a longer period of time. These "peer mentors" are probably aware of the unique professional landmines and informal barriers that exist in the organization. Subsequently, the mentor—either a peer or otherwise—can assist the early careerist in navigating the political waters.

EDUCATION

The crawl stage involves continuing education to augment previously learned classroom or didactic education.[4] In the crawl stage, the early careerist must grasp the many themes found in an "Introduction to Leadership" class or seminar. These include the topics mentioned earlier, but also encompass the student's definition of "leadership" and the difference between leadership and management. The crawl stage also includes becoming aware of the organizational field of health, the specifics of the health organization, and a burgeoning understanding of how one's own "mental hard-wiring" supports (or fails to support) events and opportunities in the environment. The crawl stage might not be defined so much by doing, as by learning.

Personality tests provide an opportunity for the early careerist—the future health leader—to develop an awareness of his or her strengths and weaknesses within the complex organizational environment. This will help the individual become aware of personal "blind spots" that might keep the early careerist from being successful. For example, a health organization that has a highly kinesthetic preference for learning (learning by doing things) may pose challenges to an early careerist who is fundamentally hard-wired to learn through reading. In the absence of this critical element of self-development, the early careerist will have to either enable him- or herself to learn differently or seek out employment with organizations that are not as action based. Such may be the case in health consulting and sales, where verbal communication and on-the-job training are considered more critical than formal or didactic education.

DEVELOPMENTAL TASKS

During the crawl stage of development, the prospective leader may not have the knowledge, skills, or abilities to lead a formal group in completing a complex task or process. Leadership is a very complex profession and requires extensive KSA development before the individual is prepared to lead a formal group in confusing and chaotic situations. It is possible during this stage for the mentor to assign developmental tasks to the early careerist to build these KSAs, such as writing white papers or participating in interdisciplinary process action teams. The crawl stage is also about followership and development of the understanding that to become a leader, one must be a good follower. Some characterize this as understanding the concept of loyalty and servant-leadership development.

The crawl stage is characterized by self-awareness as well as basic knowledge about leadership itself. It is a time to practice what has been learned and to demonstrate one's competencies through written and oral assignments. These beginning developmental lessons provide the foundation for later completion of more intricate and complex tasks in leadership functions.

SELF-IMPROVEMENT

It has been argued that leaders are born, not made. Current understanding suggests that leaders *can* be made or developed; of course, a combination of nature and nurture is at work. However, the patterns of behavior established through early leader development programs cannot be emphasized too strongly as influencing later outcomes. Organizations and industry leaders spend millions of dollars annually to support leadership development and mentoring programs geared toward successfully transitioning early careerists from the crawl stage to the walk stage of development. Moreover, certain activities in which the early careerist engages can specifically assist him or her in advancing up the leader ladder.

First, the crawling leader should be a volunteer. Volunteering to sit on committees, conduct extracurricular management analysis, and assist others who are involved in interdisciplinary team projects, and making it known to the organization that the individual is not limited by his or her own job description, sets a tone of success for the early leader.

Second, the early leader should join and support professional organizations. Joining professional organizations exposes the early careerist to broader pools of health professionals, albeit not in the same organization as the early careerist, who may offer career and mentoring advice. Professional organizations can also provide opportunities for professional advancement and acknowledgment, as well as continuing health, leadership, and management education.

Lastly, the early careerist should be a reader at the crawl stage. In the dynamic world of health, it can become immediately evident if one's relevancy is dated. For example, if an early careerist continues to refer to the Joint Commission as JCAHO, or cites the most recent version of the STARK laws as having been last updated at version II, this may signal to senior executives that the early careerist lacks creditability and relevancy. There are few items that can immediately affect (negatively, in particular) a recent graduate's creditability. Never rely on just one source of information for timely knowledge of health events and industry updates until you are confident and trust the source implicitly. Self-development and personal responsibility cannot be underscored enough in this regard. Early careerists should read fervently and stay attuned to the industry.

BENCHMARKING

From a mentorship perspective, senior leaders are seeking to develop potential leadership talent in others. Several identifying characteristics are referred to as *indicators* that an individual will make a good leader. First, managers will look at job performance of individuals and compare their performance with that of their peers. A good leader will go above and beyond the established requirements to accomplish a goal or complete a project. They will also do the job well, communicate well, treat people with respect, and be loyal to their supervisor and organization.

Potential leaders have strong interpersonal skills and have the ability to interact with individuals on a variety of levels. Empathy is considered to be an important leadership attribute by many people. Potential leaders develop trustful, reliable, and consistent relationships. They assist others to succeed. Potential leaders know the mission, vision, strategies, goals, and objectives of the health organization and can translate the larger plan into a series of smaller, more specific plans that can be used within their area of responsibility.

Potential leaders also demonstrate clear and concise written and verbal communication skills within the workplace. Strongly developed communication skills may indicate an individual's ability to address conflict. Individuals who are self-driven may be seen as having a strong work ethic and, therefore, may be identified as having leadership potential. Self-driven individuals may also have a tendency to be motivated when presented with a desirable task, demonstrating initiative and drive until the project reaches its completion.

Finally, individuals who have an ability to create an organizational vision and motivate others to buy into the vision have potential as future leaders. The ability to translate the health organization's "large" vision into a vision for the specific area of responsibility is a highly valued skill. The application of motivating action to accomplish the work needed to achieve the vision is even more important. Individuals who demonstrate such abilities have a complex understanding of the organizational vision and can be considered forward thinkers.

Once individuals with leadership potential are identified, the next step is to begin the process of developing these skills in the individual to prepare him or her for leadership opportunities of greater scope and scale. According to managers, strategies to promote early leadership development within individuals include exposure, increased responsibilities, special assignments, job rotation, and coaching. Individuals should have exposure to a number of factors, including interactions with senior executives, uncomfortable situations, customers, external resources, internal resources, different levels of the organization, and different degrees of risk. Exposure allows the early leader opportunities for trial-and-error learning and making mistakes in a nonthreatening environment. Assigning increased responsibilities to early leaders will allow for this kind of learning and leadership development. Other benefits of these interactions include opportunities to enhance tolerance to stressful situations, to improve communication within the team and organization, and to strengthen the leader's influence on his or her team.

Early leaders should also be given the opportunity to complete special assignments that will allow them to develop "transferable skills." Development of these skills will allow individuals to gain a better understanding and knowledge of the various roles within the organization. Rotating jobs will give the early leader the opportunity to learn about the skills and requirements needed to perform unfamiliar duties within the organization. A leader with a well-rounded knowledge of organizational culture will be able to meet the needs of the employees, their departments, and the organization as a whole.

Finally, early leaders need multiple opportunities to receive coaching and feedback regarding their performance. Opportunities for modeling and mentoring will allow the early leader a safety net as he or she begins to analyze his or her leadership performance.

Sometimes, early leaders may run into situations in which "derailment" may occur. Early leaders who begin to withdraw from communication or engagement; exhibit adverse effects from personal stressors, such as excessive familial or community obligations; fail to follow through on assignments and projects; and demonstrate immaturity and lack of self-control may be unprepared to handle the early leadership role. If intercepted early, derailment of the early leader can be avoided. Bolt and Hagemann offer strategies to prevent derailment of the early leader, including increasing communication and feedback, developing an action plan, providing more opportunities for coaching, and providing new opportunities or challenges.[5]

MEASURING THE SUCCESS OF THE CRAWL STAGE

The discussion of the crawl stage methodology presented here concludes by focusing on the measurement of crawl success by outside agents and stakeholders. This analysis is made through both empirical and evaluative thinking in regard to profession-driven standards and competencies. As a result, it is during the crawl stage that the early careerist begins to fully appreciate the profession that he or she is entering.

Empirical thinking is a skill-based approach that involves the memorization of lists, facts, and other entry-level competencies. Through this type of thinking, the early careerist demonstrates to superiors that he or she understands the technical nature of the organization. Possessing empirical thinking demonstrates to superiors and outside agents that the early careerist has spent time understanding the inputs, processes, and outputs of the organization. Additionally, it demonstrates a basic understanding of the organizational architecture. Empirical thinking may be analogous to the metaphor of an individual "learning the ropes." This phrase was developed by sailors in the British Navy centuries ago. The first task of any new sailor was to "learn the ropes" of the ship—that is, how the ropes were rigged to the masts, tethered to the sails, and connected to the moorings. Every sailor who boarded a ship for the first time learned the ropes so that he could contribute to the work of the ship. This same analogy can be applied to the business world.[6] Every profession has certain skills, traits, and entry-level competencies that must be memorized or performed in order to be acknowledged by senior leaders as meeting certain basic performance standards. Passage through this phase entails the movement from the unconscious incompetent or conscious incompetent to the conscious competent or unconscious competent stages of knowing. Execution of profession-driven empirical thinking demonstrates this competency.

The second standard that demonstrates a transition from the crawl stage to the walk stage of development is the execution of evaluative thinking. Evaluative thinking involves the ability to prioritize tasks within the health organization, to assign weighted values to projects based on organizational impact, and to screen the importance of new information filtering into the organization. Evaluative thinking allows the early careerist to make competent decisions on how to manage his or her day, perform tasks as assigned, and prioritize those tasks. A simple analogy may be a decision to spend time cleaning out one's email account versus planning for the weekly staff meeting where you are expected to provide input on a topic. Evaluative thinking allows early careerists to be competent not only in performing tasks, but also in performing them in the proper order to allow for maximum output.

Both evaluative and empirical thinking are based on organizational goals and organizational objectives and will differ from organization to organization. For example, the prowess gained in becoming a group practice manager of a multiple-physician cardiac practice will be different than the mastery demonstrated by a CEO in managing a larger healthcare system.

THE CRAWL TIME LINE

Assigning an organizational time line to the crawl stage is difficult because the time required to master the "crawl" is unique from individual to individual. Some crawl time may be spent in a degree program; in residencies, internships, or other practicum situations; and in the first professional positions in the health industry. Factors affecting advancement from the crawl stage to the walk stage include the size and complexity of the organization, the interdisciplinary nature of the job(s) to which the individual is assigned, the opportunity for outside professional development, and the desire and motivation of the employee to advance up the corporate ladder. These factors are variable and difficult to predict between organizations and individuals; however, the authors of this text, based on their more than 50 years of health and leadership experience, believe that it may take 5 to 10 years for a recently graduated student to advance prodigiously and effectively through the stages and tasks of the "crawl." This does not mean an early career health leader cannot perform entry-level tasks effectively; rather, it means that to advance to higher, more responsible positions within the industry, crawl-stage development is required.

THE WALK: STRATEGIES FOR MANAGING GROUPS AND TEAMS

In the walk stage, individuals learn more difficult and more complex information about leadership. The prospective leader is still in a safe environment and will most likely make mistakes, just as toddlers often fall down when they progress from crawling to walking. Training is more complex during the walk stage. Perhaps the leadership trainee begins learning about how to make changes in the organization, how to lead a project team, or how to deploy more comprehensive and complex communication skills. For example, the early careerist might learn how to lead successful and effective meetings. This skill incorporates excellent communication skills but also requires learning about facilitation of meetings. This is a skill every leader must have. For example, a meeting attendee who "takes over" or is talkative at inappropriate times should be seated at the corner of the meeting table or where the individual does not have easy face-to-face contact with other meeting attendees; this could reduce their inappropriate behaviors. This "knowledge" comes by learning from a mentor, in coursework, or from role modeling. Further capability elicited from this knowledge is then garnered from doing the task or using the knowledge appropriately.

In the walk stage, there is an increased emphasis on communicating evaluative and empirical information to groups or teams. As part of this phase, health leaders begin to understand the complexities and challenges of managing teams. A *team* is defined as an interdisciplinary group of individuals who are brought together to accomplish specific tasks or projects. The interdisciplinary nature of the team allows its members to accomplish what larger and unspecialized groups cannot perform as effectively. For example, a baseball team, where each player has demonstrated competency as a pitcher, catcher, infielder, or outfielder, is classified as a team.

A *group* is defined as two or more individuals who come from random disciplines with no apparent collective skills necessary to accomplish complex and specific tasks. A large group of competent baseball pitchers with 95-mph fastballs, for example, may lack the skills of an outfielder who can catch a fly ball and immediately throw the ball from left field to home plate. Whereas a group tends to be more random and may lack specific skill sets for tasks with great complexity, a team is more specialized.

In the walk stage, leaders begin to understand the complexities and challenges of managing teams. The Roman army discovered it was difficult for 1 person to manage more than 12 people simultaneously. This rule of thumb, or heuristic, has remained a metric for small-group leadership for more than two millennia. Developing leaders would be wise to not attempt to personally manage too many people simultaneously.

The walk stage becomes far more abstract, which inherently makes it more difficult and more comprehensive. The developing leader will need to access more resources during this stage of development. It is during the walk stage that developing leaders might be required to actually lead a group outside the training situation. Learning in the crawl stage about leading a group or team (from in-training leadership exercises in coursework, perhaps) can serve the leader well when leading a real group in a real situation. Role playing is one of the activities an instructor could adopt to support this type of learning. For instance, one company's motto in this regard is "Role before you roll," which means that company employees engage in role playing before attempting to bring a new product to market.[7,8]

Interdisciplinary leadership can be understood in terms of shared leadership. Shared leadership requires that all team members "carry responsibility for team process and outcomes, thereby accepting formal and informal leadership roles that shift according to the situation."[9] The leader managing the interdisciplinary team may step in and out as the primary leader, with other individuals taking over at times as primary leader—a "taking your turn" approach. A series of individuals may temporarily fill the role of primary leader when the situation requires the most appropriate

individual to be involved. Interdisciplinary leadership requires that individuals demonstrate competence and understanding of other disciplines to serve in the leader role in such a situation.

McCallin calls for a paradigm shift in which interdisciplinary leadership continues to be a form of "shared leadership" with a defined "practice leader." Under this approach, the practice leader accepts the role of managing the team, including the processes of development and coaching. The practice leader is also responsible for "coaching" other team members in the "art of shared leadership." This would include providing learning opportunities to find solutions to problems and achieve desirable outcomes.[10]

TEAM BUILDING

In the crawl stage, a person primarily manages him- or herself. By comparison, in the walk stage, the individual begins to lead larger numbers of people and manage greater quantities of resources. No leader can be successful without the ability to manage resources and lead small groups. As a result, one of the most critical tasks for young executives to master is the process of leading and building consensus in teams to produce positive outcomes for the health organization. Although the theoretical process of leading and building teams is often covered in organizational behavior texts, Ledlow and Coppola suggest that no health leader can be truly effective without first having dedicated him- or herself to the study of the theories, processes, and dynamics of team evolution. This knowledge may then be put in practice through experience.

Surprisingly, many health leaders are unfamiliar with the process of team building. This may be due to the fact that they moved into organizations with relatively large and stable groups of employees who were comfortable in their positions. It may also be because the leader has become a prominent figure in his or her field of study through excellence in the execution of skills, as might be the case with a surgeon, for example. This level of leader acknowledgment is different for a middle-level health leader and especially for a CEO of a large healthcare system who maintains responsibility for many elements of the enterprise. Without the experience of leading increasingly larger groups, the leader may not be fully aware of the life cycle and evolution associated with standing, ad hoc, and process action teams.

Given the importance of understanding this facet of team life, an overview of team-building strategies is provided here. The following analysis is based on the work by Coppola as published in *Healthcare Executive*.[11]

Tuckman's Model of the Group Dynamic Process

It is during the walk stage training that students will most likely learn about the stages of group development. The first lesson is that a group of individuals does not become a cohesive, productive group overnight without training or without time. The process of group formation occurs in conjunction with group learning.[12] A descriptive process provides insight or knowledge into this phenomenon. In 1965, Bruce Tuckman described a process of team development that developing leaders in the walk stage would be wise to understand.[13] This process includes five stages: forming, storming, norming, performing, and adjourning. As an addition to the Tuckman model, an initial stage is important in team development; that additional step is called the "informing" stage.[14] Understanding the steps in the team-building process will assist leaders in maximizing team output. Conversely, failing to understand life cycle issues in team development may result in team failure or decreased team productivity.

Leaders at the walk stage gain their first understanding of this process by managing interdisciplinary teams. During this phase, they come to recognize the importance of building and maintaining teams that produce positive outcomes within their organizations if they are to advance to higher levels of responsibility. However, the dynamics of organizing, maintaining, and guiding teams may be difficult and complex to manage. Teams go through stages of development and an organizational life cycle that may mirror the growth and development of the organization itself. Failing to understand organizational life cycle issues commonly encountered in team development may result in the leader's inability to manage more complex and interdisciplinary groups in later stages of personal growth and development.

Informing Stage

Prior to the development of any new team, or making additions to an existing structured team that rotates members in and out, there is an official notification of membership. This notification may be either verbal or written. In some cases, the individuals may be knowledgeable about the mission of the team and be familiar with other team members. During the informing stage, the prospective team member will form generalizations and opinions about the mission of the group. If not provided with enough structure, the individual may make judgments that prove counterproductive when the team initially meets and begins to work. Furthermore, if the candidate is knowledgeable about other team members, he or she may also form opinions and biases (good or bad) about other individuals in the group.

Informing Stage Strategy

Many leaders overlook this important stage of team development and pay little attention to its significance. Numerous threats to team productivity can be overcome in this initial stage through the formal presentation of vision and mission statements as well as clearly defined goals and objectives of the group, bounded in a specific time frame for performance and objective measurement. The face-to-face verbal communication of these strategic points by the leader to the group is critical (as suggested by media richness theory); it is a must, not just something that occurs "if the leader has time and opportunity."

Additional strategic considerations include the time frame for notifying individuals of their team membership and the latent period between notification and the first required meeting. Shorter periods of latency may affect an individual's motivation to be on the team if other important projects are competing for time and attention, not unlike constructs associated with the garbage can model of decision making. Longer periods of latency (90 days or more) may result in an individual moving out of the department or organization where the team assignment was made. A reasonable time for notification of team action is 15 to 30 days.

Other considerations should include a known desire of the individual to be on the team, the special skill set the member brings to the team, and outcomes obtained with similar projects. Finally, an implied task of leaders prior to appointing individuals to a group is a working knowledge of personality dynamics between members. Previous working relationships, both positive and negative, should be included as part of the decision-making process before informing anyone of team assignment.

Forming Stage

The forming stage might also be called the "discovery stage." Typical professionals and working adults may be overtly cordial during this stage and attempt to overcompensate by remaining passive and agreeable. Other commonly encountered dynamics include the initial group membership being dominated through individual conservatism and by those members with a high internal locus of control. If members have worked well together in the past, there will be an initial latent discovery period of testing between members, where mutual support and a reconfirmation of cooperation are established. For members who lack familiarity with one another, there is a desire to be overtly convivial and supportive. New ideas may be offered implicitly or posited as participatory questions, such as "What do you all think would happen if we did 'X'?" If no one has been formally appointed as the mentor or leader of the group, the team may wait for an informal leader to emerge who possesses the expert knowledge of small-group leadership or the information power necessary to accomplish the team mission.

At this stage, many members of the group may share the perception that there is only one best way to handle the problem or mission. In reality, more than half of the group members may have already made up their minds about what to do, but are reluctant in this genial stage to be perceived as overbearing and lacking participatory collegiality. Conflict is important at this stage to limit "groupthink." Groupthink is a phenomenon, first formally identified by Janus, in which a group may make a decision that is harmful, unwanted, or benign. Conflict that is constructive is important in group processes. Conflict management skills should be part of organizational members' training and specifically group or team training. Emphasis should be placed on the problem-solving style of conflict management.

Forming Stage Strategy

It is beneficial in the forming stage to have previously outlined team member roles. This groundwork will catalyze and expedite the protracted collegial followership that professionals often bring into the complexity of team and group dynamics. Establishing clear goals and objectives is important as well, because it aids in the variance and unbounded rationality of excessive "outside the box" decisions. Finally, establishing a time line for the team is important. Many teams will expand their stages of incremental development to fill the time allotted to complete the task. Providing a time to complete initial tasks and objectives may expedite the forming stage. During this stage, the leader has to balance group development (storming and forming) with urgency; this can be a difficult balancing act if significant time constraints are present.

Storming Stage

A team will arrive at the storming stage when a tipping point is achieved and the members of the team no longer feel an obligated sense of prioritizing collegiality over task accomplishment. In the storming stage, members may compete for leadership of the group, try to gain control over the group's creative development, and exhibit frustration with imperfect information or animosity toward others for failing to support their own ideas. In the storming stage, the proverbial "gloves are off" philosophy takes hold, and members become more interested in their own personal agendas and goals than in the team objectives.

In the storming stage, disrupters are typically present. Disrupters are people who have not been appointed as formal group mentors or who have not been recognized by the group as informal leaders. As a result, they may seek to exert control and dominance by exercising disruptive behavior. Outside of the leader role, the disrupter is the most common and most easily recognized role in any team dynamic situation.

Storming Stage Strategy

In this stage of group dynamics, many outside leaders and agents may want to intervene and provide management influence. Although seemingly productive, this path might be the worst one for a leader to follow. President Abraham Lincoln is credited with forming a "team of rivals" wherein competing personalities and strong partisan opinions were found to be necessary to achieve positive outcomes and maximize productivity. Intervening too quickly and discouraging professional discourse may result in a perception of group powerlessness and a perception that the team is merely a "rubber stamp" for the leader's vision. Frustration, professional discourse, and passionate competition between team members can be healthy and necessary to achieve higher goals. From a creative standpoint, when partisan personalities will not let go of their personal ideas and agendas, the only option is to develop a new collective idea that is truly accomplished through the input of all team members. Professional discourse is healthy and necessary; leaders should be wary of micromanaging the storming stage too soon.

Norming Stage

In the norming stage, individuals begin to relinquish their personal agendas. At this point, team roles have been clearly identified within the group and can be recognized by outside agents and stakeholders. Informal and formal leaders begin working together to accomplish tasks and achieve desired outcomes. Other participants in the group may assume one or more roles as followers, innovators, experts, or researchers, among other actor positions. In this stage, lingering disrupters may assume supportive roles or enter into passive positions by accepting delegation. Some individuals may exchange roles over the course of the team's tenure.

Norming Stage Strategy

Leaders may be initially bewildered by the task organization of the group and the agenda that the group is moving toward.

Leaders should be cognizant that the reason the group was formed was to complete a task or mission that could not be accomplished individually or through institutionalized practices and policies. They need to know that team members have gone through the informing, forming, storming, and norming phases and now possess a unique point of view of the problem under study. Leaders need to trust in the process and allow the team to accomplish its task(s). If one or more group members are not "norming" to the group, then the group leader or manager may need to remove them from the group or replace those members. However, replacing members at this stage will set back the group dynamic process and bring the group back to the earlier stages of team development. In essence, if the group leader assesses the situation and determines that certain group members will deter the group from performing the desired work, it is better to go with a smaller team or take more time to replace group members: This choice is the group leader's decision. The team or group is now ready to accomplish what it has been formed to do.

Performing Stage

In the performing stage, the team has developed new ideas and carefully thought out objectives. It would not have been possible for any one individual in the group working alone to develop these ideas and objectives. The adage, "None of us is as smart as all of us," is salient in this context. There is an increased recognition of superordinate goals and a realization that the organization's needs are superior to individualism. A sense of pride in team identity is recognized and a clear sense of "we-ness" over "I-ness" becomes visible. The "we-ness" culture of the group is developed and enhanced when a confirming communication climate is established by the group's leader or manager. This consideration is especially important in health organizations, and even more so with interdisciplinary teams.

In the performing stage, new responsibilities and new requests for information can be processed quickly. The team may be eager to demonstrate its ability to multitask and continue to be challenged. Products, ideas, and tasks are brought to fruition in this stage—there is visible output; there are tangible results.

Performing Stage Strategy

As the group's leader, first and foremost, you should say, "Thank you!" to team members. Recognize individuals in the group for their contributions. Make a point to understand the role each member played in the development of the new idea or product so that these talents and abilities can be used appropriately in the future.

In addition, take a step back and be supportive of the group's work. A potential threat to morale, future team building, and group productivity arises when a leader attempts to place his or her superfluous thumbprint on the product for the sole purpose of possession. Leaders need to know when to lead, but they also need to know when to support and trust in the collective wisdom of the team.

Adjourning Stage

In the adjourning stage, both internal and external stakeholders recognize the completion of the group's work. The reason for the team's formation has been accomplished and there is a recognition of the new (or updated) programs, polices, or procedures now in place. Members are ready to move on to their next positions of responsibility and assume new challenges.

Adjourning Stage Strategy

In this stage, document the process and save the output of member work. Incredibly, the good work of ad hoc teams (temporary teams or groups focused on a specific project), seasonal teams (e.g., Joint Commission preparation teams), and standing teams (organizational Six Sigma teams) is often lost in the process of personnel turnover and the dynamic turbidity and rapidity of the environment. More often than not, legacy files and best practices are discarded or reinvented with each new cycle of team formation. Given these possibilities, means of archiving best practices and lessons learned should be established. Now is the perfect time to build knowledge management and organizational learning systems. A team or group section, departmental, or even organizational (depending on the scope and scale of the work) presentation or briefing may be a good start to manage knowledge, diffuse knowledge to others, and provide a platform for organizational learning.

GOOD TO GREAT GROUPS AND TEAMS

Once a health leader has mastered the crawl stage and understands the process of team life cycle development and associated challenges in the walk stage, the leader can focus his or her attention on making good teams great. In health organizations, good group and team accomplishments are important. However, the dynamic and varied world of health also calls for great groups and teams, combined with great effort to achieve results that enhance everyone's professional life. The need for great groups is urgent, in order to solve the most pressing strategic and operational problems in the health industry and within health organizations.

The organizations of the future will increasingly depend on the creativity of their members to survive.[15]

Health leaders must understand the type of people who make for great groups. People in great groups have the following characteristics:[16]

- Intrinsically motivated, buoyed by the joy and challenge of problem solving
- Focused obsessively on fascinating projects
- Oblivious to "ordinary," bureaucratic, and trivial matters

These people love the discovery process and they have dazzling skills (such as [clinical], mathematical, statistical, [financial], or computer). They have the unique ability to identify problems and find creative, boundary busting solutions [with] hungry, urgent, quick minds; many have expansive interests with encyclopedic knowledge. They have the ability to see what others don't see in part because they have command of more data (and the ability to use it) in the first place.[17]

The key skill set for health leaders to develop is to gather, unite, and make an effective group of people, who individually are great, into a synergistic team capable of superior problem solving, persistent energy, and tremendous innovative capacity. Health organizations increasingly will require such teams if they are to compete in a competitive environment amid significant health challenges, where information is readily available and just-in-time learning is commonplace:

Great Groups tend to be less bureaucratic than ordinary ones. Terribly talented people often have little tolerance for less talented middle managers. Great Groups tend to be structured, not according to title, but according to role. The person [who] is best able to do some essential task does it.[18]

Every great group has a strong and visionary leader who has a talent for selecting or hiring people better than the leader; successful health leaders look for people of excellence who have the ability to work well with others. Health leaders, considering goal-setting theory, set challenging goals for the group or team: "Look how morale soars when intelligent people are asked to do a demanding but worthy task and given the freedom and tools to do it."[19] Successful health leaders have a vision and a plan to realize it, while being expert motivators. They make their group or team feel and know why their work is important; this kind of sharing improves problem solving and increases the pace of work.

Innovation through group performance is important to note as well. Traditional notions of individual-based leadership behaviors are no longer adequate to achieve innovation in healthcare organizations. A major contributing factor to limited innovation is that outdated leadership practices, such as leader centricity, linear thinking, and poor readiness for innovation, are being used in healthcare organizations. Through a qualitative case study analysis of innovation implementation, seven characteristics of innovation leadership, founded in team behaviors, were uncovered; the characteristics that were uncovered included boundary spanning, risk taking, visioning, leveraging opportunity, adaptation, coordination of information flow, and facilitation.[20] These characteristics describe how leaders throughout the system were able to influence and implement innovation successfully.

Bennis and Biederman suggest the following factors be considered as part of the team-building process:[21]

Killers of Groups

- Constraints and trivial structure/tasks
- Error-free environments
- Closed systems
- Military model of leadership (authoritative/strongly directive)

Enhancers

- Freedom and autonomy (failure is a learning event; errors are a natural part of learning)
- Risk taking
- Enabling and encouraging environment (confirming communication environment)
- "If you can dream it, you can do it" mentality

Take-Home Lessons

- *Greatness starts with superb people.* Recruit the best people possible. Recruit problem solvers who happen to be computer programmers, physicists, nurses, physicians, and so on.
- *Great groups and great leaders create one another.* Collaboration is critical; the standard command-and-control models of leadership/management do not work. Leaders of great groups must act decisively, but never arbitrarily.
- *Every great group has a strong leader.* A leader is an organizer of genius—a maestro who is a pragmatic dreamer and who has an original, yet attainable, vision. A good leader eliminates distractions and trivial matters (consider the path–goal model).
- *The leaders of great groups love talent and know where to find it.* They revel in the talent of others.
- *Great groups are full of talented people who can work together.* Sharing information and advancing the work are the only real social obligations.

- *Great groups think they are on a tremendously important mission.* These groups are filled with believers; doubters are dismissed. Their clear, collective purpose makes everything they do seem meaningful and valuable.
- *Great groups see themselves as winning underdogs.* They have to compete against challenges and against the odds.
- *Great groups are optimistic, not realistic.* They envision things that have not been done before.
- *In great groups, the right person has the right job.* The leader has achieved good ability–job fit and members are all competent of their peers' expectations.
- *The leaders of great groups give them what they need and free them from the rest.* Leaders stay focused on a path–goal approach to accomplishment.
- *Great groups share information effectively.* The leader ensures that a communication network exists and that everyone has full access to it.
- *Great groups ship.* They produce.
- *Great work is its own reward.* In Herzberg's two-factor theory, group members are intrinsically motivated by a transformational leader.

Bennis and Biederman used qualitative (as opposed to quantitative) research methods to come to these conclusions. Their work was mostly performed through histories, literature review, interviews, and possibly some observation (qualitative methods). Which model do they propose for leading great groups? Which conditions foster the creation of a great group? Which parts—or the whole of the model—will work (can be applied) in health situations? Enhancers of great groups can provide the answers to these questions.

Group Size and Composition

Another important factor in group and team dynamics is group size and composition. Shull, Delbecq, and Cummings determined that group size influences decision processes in several ways; for example, communication becomes difficult as the number of members increases and less time is available for each member to speak.[22] When the size of a group increases beyond eight members, the potential contribution from adding another member should be carefully weighed against the added difficulty of running an effective meeting and the project as a whole.

Janus's notion of "groupthink" (mentioned earlier in this chapter) is noteworthy when considering group issues. "Highly cohesive groups sometime foster a phenomenon called 'group think' (Janus, 1972); groupthink involves certain kinds of illusions and stereotypes that interfere with effective decision making."[23] Ensuring constructive conflict in the group or establishing and maintaining a "devil's advocate" role or contrarian role in the group can reduce the potential for groupthink.

OVERVIEW OF OTHER ESSENTIAL SKILLS IN THE WALK STAGE

Although learning how to manage and interact with teams is an essential skill that must be mastered by the developing leader, it is not the only skill set required. The developing leader must also gain experience with larger budgets, multidisciplinary task organization, and strategic planning. Several methodologies are available to help the developing leader to gain experience in these areas if there is not a direct opportunity in the workplace to do so.

Becoming involved in the local community can assist the developing leader in acquiring skill sets that are not immediately available in the workplace. Many local governments and communities have colloquial health boards and advisory committees that routinely seek volunteers. These organizations can assist the developing leader in obtaining experience in strategic planning and managing resources. Many of these boards have strategic plans that look forward into the future for 3 to 5 years and can be excellent places for a young health leader to practice skills related to strategic planning and forecasting, analysis, budgeting, and building interpersonal relationships and networks.

As with the crawl strategies, the developing leader in the walk stage can seek relevant opportunities in professional organizations. The opportunity to run for office or lead large committees may be available in the professional organization that will assist the developing health leader in working with teams across large distances (using teleconferencing technology) and provide him or her with an excellent opportunity to exercise leadership skills along an informal chain of influence.

Leading an event and becoming a host of a multidisciplinary health event are also good ways to expand the expression and development of the nascent leader. Hosting a local event and managing a committee of experts who provide continuing health education to a group of senior executives, for example, provide an opportunity for the developing leader to get noticed, to network within the community, and to become recognized as someone who can manage people in informal networks.

MASTERY OF WALK TASKS

In the walk stage, there is an implied understanding that material learned at the crawl stage has been mastered.

For example, the chief executive no longer gives detailed and explicit directions and instructions on how to complete tasks to the subordinate health leader; the subordinate health leader knows what to do to accomplish the assigned task. The young executive, at this stage, should have mastered basic skills in regard to participating fully on interdisciplinary teams; completing projects in a timely manner; producing thoughtful and correctly executed white papers, business case analyses, or other analyses; and taking on greater responsibility in terms of leading people and managing more materials, financial resources, and other logistical components of the health organization.

The young executive at this stage should begin to serve as a peer role model in the health organization rather than directly seeking mentorship for him- or herself. Although the CEO always has the responsibility to role model and mentor junior members of the organization,[24] young executives may begin to discover the benefits of being role models themselves during the walk stage.[25] At this point, the young executive has learned the complexities of the organization and is ready to assume some mentoring duties.[26] Thus the walk stage is characterized by the "powering down" or "pushing down" of the mission, vision, values, strategies, goals, and objectives of the CEO to the subordinate health leader, accompanied by the subordinate health leader's ability to translate higher-order organizational directives and competitive strategies into operational and tactical execution at the departmental, unit, and section levels. The subordinate health leader, by now, should be demonstrating leadership qualities and organizational values to more junior employees in the organization.

The young executive also relaxes from reacting to the environment. In the walk stage, he or she has mastered the basics of the organizational environment and become active in controlling events in a strategic and forecasted nature.[27–29] The leader in the walk stage also knows the difference between basic and complex competencies in the organization. A simple example can be found in the naive nature of how an organization measures productivity or executes a budget. A health leader at the entry level, and definitely at the middle level, after working in a health organization for a period of time should be responsible for explaining productivity measurement to more junior employees and administrative personnel, rather than seeking counsel from a more senior health leader concerning these issues.[30,31]

Measuring the Success of the Walk Stage

The young executive in the walk stage has sought out professional education and self-improvement in two

forms: didactic (continuing health education) and practical (on-the-job training). When these forms of development are combined, they provide for the ability to exercise competency in both empirical and evaluative thinking. These competencies were exercised in the crawl stage; however, when these two competencies are mastered and the skills of each executed in a combined and simultaneous fashion, one sees the emergence of critical thinking and the ability to apply that thinking to create positive outcomes in the health organization. Critical thinking is apparent when the young executive has demonstrated the capacity to merge both empirical thinking and evaluative thinking into seamless actions and decision making that result in favorable outcomes.[32,33]

Critical thinking is a skill that involves not only knowledge of content, but also concept formation and analysis. Furthermore, critical thinking encompasses the ability to reason and draw conclusions based on imperfect data, and the ability to recognize and avoid contradiction with imperfect information. Critical thinking is important in moral and ethical analysis, where gray areas exist and conflict and partisanship over processes and policy are evident. In extreme cases, the ability to think critically allows an individual to see both sides of controversial topics, such as euthanasia and right-to-life issues. In its simplest form, it allows an individual to balance enduring beliefs with behaviors. For example, it may be unwise to tell a subordinate employee that he has gained weight, even though it may be true. Excessive and unnecessary honesty—that is, honest discussions over issues that are not organizationally related or that may be personally hurtful to people's self-esteem—can be undesirable in leaders, and the adroit health leader knows how to balance the importance and consequence of individual action and deeds.[34] This facility directly relates to emotional intelligence.

There is a certain expectation that young executives will be able to anticipate organizational needs, take initiative in solving problems before they become too onerous, and find solutions to issues before they become apparent to others. This ability to anticipate is typically the product of multimodal training experiences that include volunteerism, personal self-improvement, affiliation with professional organizations, maintaining relevancy in the literature, and becoming a mentor to junior employees.[35]

The burgeoning mastery of critical thinking skills may be ineffable and difficult to notice in the workplace; however, the long-term effects of applied critical thinking on an individual's success in the organization are readily identified. The young executive who has mastered these skills is more likely to be promoted and advance within the

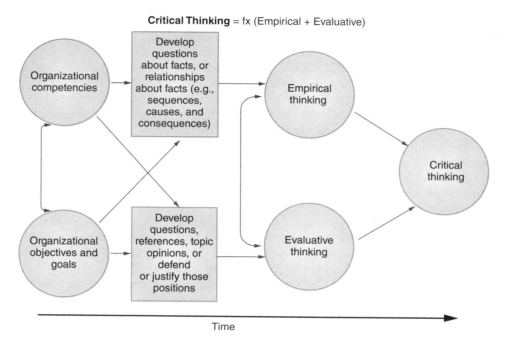

FIGURE 7-2 Conceptual model of critical thinking.

Reproduced from Coppola, M. N. (2004, March 8). Measuring critical thinking through analysis of moment structure (AMOS): A latent variable approach to evaluating effective outcomes. Whitepaper, Baylor University, Waco, TX.

organization than those individuals who are still educating themselves on empirical and evaluative competencies. Finally, when the young leader is seen advancing in the workplace through demonstrative stakeholder approval of senior leaders, the young leader has successfully graduated from the walk stage.

A conceptual model of critical thinking is depicted graphically in **Figure 7-2**. In this conceptual model, the ability to think critically is a function of combining empirical and evaluative thinking. These two constructs are, in turn, derived from the organizational mission, vision, strategies, goals, objectives, and competencies that represent the skill sets of the organization. In essence, they encompass the knowledge of the health organization, which (ideally) is archived and housed in the health organization's knowledge management system. As the model suggests, obtaining effectiveness in mastering organizational directive and competitive strategies, goals, objectives, and competencies results in a young leader successfully "learning the ropes" of the organization. Over a period of time, with appropriate experiences and opportunities, the young leader hones his or her empirical and evaluative thinking abilities. A tipping point finally occurs when these items are mastered and become an internalized part of the young executive's activities of

daily action and decision making. This is an example of unconscious competence: The health leader performs "leadership" as a natural part of who he or she is in the health organization.

THE WALK TIME LINE

Similar to the analysis provided in conjunction with the crawl time line, determining the necessary time to achieve critical thinking skills is difficult to judge. The walk time line will certainly involve graduate education, or similar continuing health education, resulting in the mastering of competencies associated with industry norms.[36] Mastery of competencies in the health environment might also be achieved through extensive and progressive on-the-job training. As with the crawl stage, advancement from the walk to the run stage will be based on unique factors in the environment that may include access to graduate and continuing health education, opportunities in the workplace to exercise skills, and the individual's motivation to challenge him- or herself by taking on new responsibilities in the health organization. These factors are also mutable and will vary from organization to organization and from individual to individual. As a guideline, it may take 7 to 15 years to master these advanced competencies.

THE RUN: STRATEGIES FOR LEADING ORGANIZATIONS

When aspiring health organization leaders have progressed successfully through the crawl and walk stages, it is time for them to run. In the run stage, the health leader has been screened and evaluated by outside stakeholders and deemed prepared to lead hundreds of people, manage millions of dollars, and direct strategic plans and policies that may affect the lives of tens of thousands of others; this stakeholder assessment is usually accomplished in the hiring of a senior health leader through screening and interview processes. Candidates who successfully survive these processes are placed in leadership positions, where they become accountable and responsible for the diverse, myriad responsibilities and challenges inherent in every health leadership position. They have the knowledge, they have gained the skills, they have practiced, and now it is time for them to become the leader. This is the most difficult part of the leadership development cycle, because the person who fills this position has a major responsibility—namely, he or she must get things done.[37] At this stage, the leader is ready to be effective as the head of departments or even as the head of the institution or organization. Leaders in this stage have the knowledge, skills, and experience required to lead gender-diverse, ethnically rich populations and motivate highly educated professionals who have received many different kinds of training; they also have the capabilities needed to integrate their health organizations with the communities they serve and to improve the health status of those populations through the organization's products and services.

In the run stage, the execution of complex skill sets allows the leader to lead and operate in the large-scale health organization. These complex skill sets include professional characteristics and qualities, the ability to manage change, the ability to manage crises, and the willingness to accept risk.[38] A final complex competency is the ability to think conceptually.

Professional characteristics of the leader in the run stage include demonstration of ethical behavior and actions, the moral courage to do the right thing, a strong preference for "we-ness" over "I-ness," organizational beneficence, and altruism. The senior leader of the health organization exercises the external presence necessary for the organization to be reflective of the leader's own personal characteristics. It is the leader whose honesty, values, and charisma become the mortar holding together the bricks from which the organization's personality is built.

Moreover, the senior-level executive must be able to manage change. Organizational change may stem from a variety of factors, including technological developments, market or environment changes, needs of the employees, economic changes, and social movements. The *green movement* is an example of environmental change, wherein conscientious consumers have begun making decisions about which goods and services to buy based on the organization's posture and efforts related to conservation. The health leader who does not look for opportunities in this movement to promote the organization's initiatives and values may face a loss of business as these consumers look for more eco-friendly organizations from which to purchase health products or services.

In managing change, the senior executive must be sensitive to fluctuations in the environment and be able to assess change, plan for change, and facilitate change. In this regard, it is important to remember that "to lead" is "to move the organization forward," and organizations move forward through change. Change becomes a catalyst for organizational improvement, and the senior leader is aware of this opportunity for improvement based on external or internal environmental pressures. Areas of change might, for example, include new staff, new services, new technology, redesigned tasks or jobs, or organizational culture change.

In managing change, the executive leader has the most important role when addressing crises to ensure that issues are addressed and handled effectively. It is no minor epiphany to say that many leaders earn their reputations on the ability to manage crisis. Hook explains that the principles for managing crisis situations may be classified into three groups: getting organized and oriented, developing a course of action, and implementing the plan.[39]

Another senior-level competency is the ability to accept personal risk and to engage in prudent organizational vulnerability. If the leader cannot do so, then leading an organization will not be possible. Risk taking often is the seminal and actionable element that distinguishes the fully mature and competent leader from less skilled persons who are still experimenting with factors in the run stage. An example of a leader engaging in personal leadership risk might be Barack Obama's bid for the U.S. presidency in 2008. The first-term senator from Illinois may have hindered his ability to become reelected to the Senate if running for President weakened his ability to legislate for the people of Chicago, or if he embarrassed himself professionally on the national stage. Of course, this run-from-behind personal risk was successful for Obama, and it serves as an excellent example of risk taking in leadership.

CONCEPTUAL THINKING

The ability to think conceptually might be considered the ultimate goal of a leader. In its simplest form, conceptual thinking is "outside the box" thinking. It is the ability to see what everyone else has not seen and to think and act in ways that others cannot think and are incapable of acting. Alternatively, conceptual thinking might be considered as the lack or absence of perceptual blindness. Perceptual blindness is a process of self-selected institutionalism where all future or current problems are addressed based on past practices and procedures. It also incorporates the concept of exercising personal bias and ignoring obvious factors in the environment that are contributing to the existing situation. In this regard, the theory of the hammer applies: When a person has a hammer as a tool, then all problems look like nails.

Conceptual thinking allows a leader to think strategically. Through strategic thinking, a leader is able to view tomorrow's world without the limits imposed by today's resources and other constraints. Strategic thinking involves anticipation of future events before they happen and the controlling of events on the horizon. The ability to think strategically, combined with the openness of the leader to explore different methods of practice and policy, allows the leader, and his or her organization, to adopt new technologies early and penetrate new markets ahead of competitors. In short, conceptual thinking provides an organizational advantage for both the leader and the organization within the health industry.

MEASURING THE SUCCESS OF THE RUN STAGE

Because the run stage is a continuous process of planning conceptually and thinking strategically, the measurement of the run stage can be framed in terms of the overall success of the organization as defined by market share or other organizational performance metrics. The latter metrics might include the return on investment on new projects and ventures, the rate of penetration into new markets, the development of new product lines, an increase in patient enrollment, satisfaction scores, and other similar measures.

In addition, the successful senior leader will attain a high level of approbation from the external stakeholders in the operational community. These stakeholders may be members of the governing board, outside advocacy groups, or unions. In its simplest form, success at the run stage is based on stakeholder satisfaction, organizational prosperity, and the creation of an organizational culture that is poised to thrive in a dynamic environment.

THE RUN TIME LINE

The time line for achieving success in the run stage may cover 10 to 20 years, or even take a lifetime to achieve.

For some individuals, success in this stage may never be fully realized. It is reasonable to suggest that some leaders may never be regarded as ready to lead large-scale health organizations, owing to a variety of mutable and immutable factors. Nevertheless, entry into this echelon of excellence should be a benchmark for all early careerists to achieve.

EFFECTIVENESS AND LEADERSHIP DEVELOPMENT

The overall effectiveness of any leader development or organizational life cycle can be measured and gauged only through stakeholder dynamics and health organizational performance. Effectiveness is defined as the ability to achieve approbation from outside stakeholders. In this respect, effectiveness is a qualitative term whose measurement is based on the individual preferences of those measuring the leader themselves. A review of the performance of the President of the United States provides a clear example of this dynamic in action. In approval polls, the President's overall satisfaction rate is based on an amalgam of priorities that are individually calculated by stakeholders and that result in a simple yes or no satisfaction rating. As suggested by the cliché, "Beauty is in the eye of the beholder," leader effectiveness is similarly based on the opinions and subjective judgments of stakeholders.

Stakeholders are constituents with a vested interest in the affairs and actions of the health leader and the health leader's organization. They include those individuals, groups, or organizations that are affected by the leader and that may seek to influence the leader. Stakeholders can be classified into three groups:

- *Internal stakeholders*: Operate entirely within the bounds of the organization and typically include management and professional and nonprofessional staff
- *Interface stakeholders*: Function both internally and externally to the organization and include medical staff, the governing body, and stockholders in the case of for-profit healthcare organizations
- *External stakeholders*: Those acting as suppliers, customers, patients, community members, and third-party payers, including government agencies, and those who provide resources, as well as other external stakeholders, including competitors, special-interest groups, local communities, labor organizations, and regulatory and accrediting agencies

The leader in any health organization needs these stakeholders to survive. However, the leader must also analyze all stakeholders in the environment to determine which are

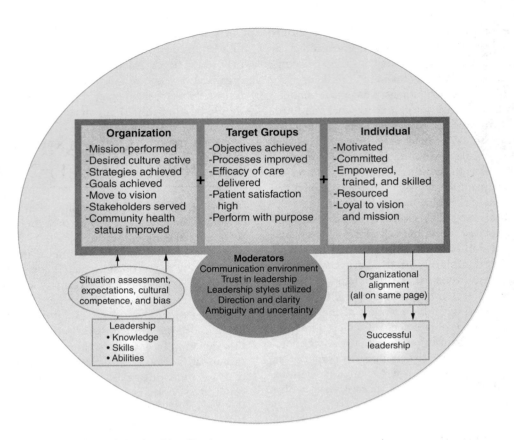

FIGURE 7-3 Macro constructs of health leadership effectiveness.

relevant, which groups could be potential threats, and which have the potential to cooperate. Balancing the demands of multiple stakeholders with different interests poses a major challenge for any leader. Achieving stakeholder approbation on a continual basis is a signature of the leader who has mastered empirical, evaluative, critical, and conceptual thinking skills.

When health leaders are fully competent at leading health organizations, large groups, large projects, and the like, the next salient issue becomes effectiveness. Simply put, how effective is the leader in the health organization?

Leading people and managing resources to accomplish the health organization's mission, strategies, goals, and objectives are major components. Creating a robust culture that is able to withstand and thrive in dynamic environments, developing future leaders, and moving the health organization in the appropriate direction to achieve its vision are other elements. **Figure 7-3**, which depicts major constructs of health leadership effectiveness, is provided for thought, reflection, and discussion; use it as a starting point for your own career planning.

SUMMARY

This chapter looked at techniques and applications of leadership in leading groups, ranging from small groups of individuals to interdisciplinary teams in small- and large-scale organizations. These elements are ordinal stages for developing competent leadership capabilities, which are in turn built on the crawl–walk–run methodology of health leader development. Mature leaders recognize

that different skills are required to lead small groups of individuals than are needed to guide large and complex organizations. Individuals and teams may respond better to verbal communication and direct interaction, whereas leaders of large and complex organizations must develop alternative approaches to communication, such as well-written and well-developed policy and mission statements, or nurturing and developing human resources proxies to spread the leader's vision down the hierarchy of the health organization. Groups, led well, can be the catalyst to innovation and achieving organizational goals and

vision. This chapter examined additional best practices in communication, leadership archetypes, delegation, and participatory and collaborative practices used in a group or team context.

DISCUSSION QUESTIONS

1. How would you describe the CWR cycle of leadership? Identify the knowledge, skills, and abilities at each stage of the cycle that contribute to understanding health leadership development. How do you "learn the ropes" in a health organization?
2. Explain Tuckman's model of the group dynamic process and summarize its importance for health leaders in group or team supervision. What is the most important stage and why?
3. Which elements would you include when constructing a 5-year leadership development plan based on an ultimate health leadership position goal? What is your goal, and how do you get there? Which empirical and evaluative competencies do you need to reach your goal?

4. Compare and contrast a great group or team, a team mired in a groupthink situation, and an ineffective group or team. Could you distinguish how a health leader performs in each of these group or team situations?
5. Which elements or components would be included in a health leader's checklist for leading and managing a group or team focused on superior performance and outcomes?
6. How would you evaluate health leader development as a concept? How would you relate leader development opportunities and events to the cycle of leadership and the knowledge, skills, and abilities necessary to achieve mastery in each stage of the cycle?

EXERCISES

1. In a one-page paper, describe the cycle of leadership and identify essential knowledge, skills, and abilities at each stage of the cycle that contribute to understanding health leadership development.
2. In a half- to one-page paper, explain Tuckman's model of the group dynamic process and summarize its importance to health leaders in group or team supervision.
3. Construct a 5-year leadership development plan for yourself. Then, in a one- to two-page paper, outline a development plan based on your ultimate health leadership position goal. How long will it take you to reach your ultimate goal?
4. In a one- to two-page paper, compare and contrast a great group or team, a team mired in a groupthink

situation, and an ineffective group or team. Also describe how a health leader performs in each of these group or team situations.
5. Devise a health leader's checklist for leading and managing a group or team focused on superior performance and outcomes; the checklist should be one half to one page in length.
6. In a two- to three-page paper, evaluate health leader development, and relate leader development opportunities and events to the cycle of leadership and the knowledge, skills, and abilities to achieve mastery at each stage of the cycle.

REFERENCES

1. Bolt, J. F., & Hagemann, B. (2009). Harvesting tomorrow's leaders. *T+D Magazine*, *63*(7), 52–57.
2. Kinney, M. (2008, July 17). What the Army taught me about teaching. Retrieved from http://www.insidehighered.com/views/2008/07/17/Kinney.
3. GlobalSecurity. (2005, April 27). Training. Retrieved from http://www.globalsecurity.org/military/library/policy/army/fm/7-21-13/chap5.htm.
4. Griffin, C. A., & Lockwood, C. A. (2009, May). Building active learning applications and opportunities into

a distance learning leadership course. Retrieved from http://gondor.bus.cba.nau.edu/Faculty/Intellectual/workingpapers/pdf/Lockwood_ActiveLearning.pdf.

5. Bolt & Hagemann, note 1.

6. Abramson, M. A. (2005). *Learning the ropes: Insights for political appointees.* New York: Rowman and Littlefield.

7. Lynn, D. (2004, May 20). Crawl, walk, run. Retrieved from http://startingit.blogspot.com/2004/05/crawl-walk-run.html.

8. Smith, M. K. (2005). Bruce W. Tuckman—Forming, storming, norming and performing in groups. Retrieved from http://www.infed.org/thinkers/tuckman.htm.

9. McCallin, A. (2003). Interdisciplinary team leadership: A revisionist approach for an old problem? *Journal of Nursing Management, 11,* 364–370.

10. McCallin, note 9.

11. Coppola, M. N. (2008). Managing teams in organizations. *Healthcare Executive, 23*(3), 70–74.

12. Raes, E., Kyndt, E., Decuyper, S., Van den Bossche, P., & Dochy, F. (2015). An exploratory study of group development and team learning. *Human Resource Development Quarterly, 26,* 5–30. doi:10.1002/hrdq.21201

13. Smith, note 8.

14. Coppola, note 11.

15. Bennis, W., & Biederman, P. W. (1997). *Organizing genius: The secret of creative collaboration.* New York: Addison-Wesley, p. 8.

16. Bennis & Biederman, note 15.

17. Bennis & Biederman, note 15, p. 17.

18. Bennis & Biederman, note 15, p. 104.

19. Bennis & Biederman, note 15, p. 9.

20. Bennis & Biederman, note 15.

21. Weberg, D., & Weberg, K. (2014). Seven behaviors to advance teamwork. *Nursing Administration Quarterly, 38*(3), 230–237. doi:10.1097/NAQ.0000000000000041

22. Yukl, G. (1994). *Leadership in organizations* (3rd ed.). Englewood Cliffs, NJ: Prentice Hall.

23. Shull, F. A., Delbecq, A. L., & Cummings, L. L. (1970). *Organizational decision making.* New York: McGraw-Hill.

24. Bagins, B. R., Coon, J. L., & Miller, J. S. (2000). Marginal mentoring: The effects of type of mentor, quality of relationship, and program design on work and career attitudes. *Academy of Management Journal, 43,* 1177–1194.

25. Hollister, R. (2001). The benefits of being a mentor. *Healthcare Executive, 16*(2), 49–50.

26. Seijts, G. H., & Latham, G. P. (2001). The effect of learning, outcome and proximal goals on a moderately complex task. *Journal of Organizational Behavior, 22,* 291–302.

27. Wallace Foundation. (2011). *The school principal as leader: Guiding schools to better teaching and learning.* New York: Author.

28. Thrall, T. H., & Hoppszallern, S. (2001). Leadership survey. *Hospitals and Health Networks, 75*(2), 33–39.

29. Seijts & Latham, note 26.

30. Huselid, M. A., Becker, B. E., & Beaty, W. (2005). *The workforce scorecard: Managing human capital to executive strategy.* Boston: Harvard Business Press.

31. Supon, V. (1998). Penetrating the barriers to teaching higher thinking. *Clearing House, 71*(5), 294–296.

32. Coppola, M. N. (2004, March 9). *Measuring critical thinking through analysis of moment structure (AMOS): A latent variable approach to evaluating effective outcomes* [Whitepaper]. Waco, TX: Baylor University.

33. Brookfield, S. D. (1991). Discussion. In Galbraith, M. W. (Ed.). (2004). *Adult learning methods: A guide for effective instruction* (pp. 187–204). Malabar, FL: Krieger.

34. Coppola, note 32.

35. Coppola, note 32.

36. Global Security, note 3.

37. Global Security, note 3.

38. Hook, J. R. (2008). Developing senior leaders: A theoretical framework and suggestions for applications. *International Journal of Organization Theory and Behavior, 11*(3), 411–436.

39. Alvesson, M., & Spicer, A. (2011). *Metaphors we lead by.* London: Sage.

LEADERSHIP MODELS IN PRACTICE

There are risks and costs to a program of action. But they are far less than the long-range risks and costs of comfortable inaction.
John F. Kennedy, May 12, 1961

This chapter presents practical models for both students of leadership and mature practitioners of the art and science of leadership to apply to their personal leadership practice. Two evolving models and one established model of leadership are described here; they should assist leaders in honing their personal leadership practice. These models are the *inter-professional team model, called the PAARP model,* the *dynamic culture leadership model,* and the *reframing organizations leadership and management model.* These models are prescriptive in that they provide a strategy for success and guidelines for practical implementation. Other differing, yet contemporary, leadership models are also presented from Lynn, Yukl, and Hargrove and Glidewell. An analysis and comparison of four of the models presented in this chapter is included as an example of model comparison and evaluation. Health leaders should consider the constructs of these models and think about how they might apply them in complex health organizational environments. The chapter concludes with a list of recommended leadership measurement tools with which to conduct leader evaluations.

LEARNING OBJECTIVES

1. Outline the constructs and processes of at least two contemporary leadership models presented in this chapter, and identify the prescriptive mechanisms of those models.

2. Distinguish at least two of the contemporary leadership models in this chapter from one other leadership theory or model from the situational leadership thought phase.

3. Apply the PAARP inter-professional team model from this chapter to a real or hypothesized health leadership situation or case, and explain the rationale for your decisions, actions, and behaviors.

4. Analyze and illustrate the contemporary leadership models' constructs that enable a health leader to develop, modify, or revise the organizational culture in a health enterprise.

5. Create a leadership model—either simple or complex—for your own use in health organizations, and relate your model to constructs found in models from this chapter and other constructs from other theories and models.

6. Compare and contrast two or more contemporary leadership models.

INTRODUCTION

The myriad of leadership and management models from the past century can be analyzed, assessed, and synthesized into modern, useful, and effective tools of health leadership and management practice. This chapter accomplishes this focused goal by introducing practical models, guides, and tools for leadership and management practice. First, the inter-professional team model, or PAARP, model (**Figure 8-1**) is presented as a method of planning, leading, and successfully creating a culture of inter-professional teamwork; health organizations must use team members from multiple disciplines, clinical and nonclinical, to achieve organizational results. Drawing from models and theories from previous chapters, the PAARP is a method that will serve health leaders well. Following the PAARP model, the dynamic culture leadership model (DCL) is presented to offer the health leader a prescriptive process of leading people and managing resources within a context of organizational culture development. Likewise, the reframing organizations model is offered as a method to positively and successfully apply leadership and management principles within a situational framework. The PAARP, DCL, and reframing organizations models can be mastered and used in a complementary fashion by health leaders. Additional models, with an analysis of those models, are also presented as modern and practical models for health leaders.

INTER-PROFESSIONAL TEAM MODEL: PAARP

The awareness of forces and factors of inter-professional teams assembling, chartering, aligning, resourcing, and performing is critical. In order to best understand these forces and factors we will first reexamine related theories and models from previous chapters, considering their constructs and tenets, which can enhance the inter-professional team and lead to greater, more focused and more efficient, effective, and efficacious performance. Considering Bloom's Taxonomy of the cognitive domain, the synthesis of models and theories is most appropriate in this aspect of health leadership, that is, facilitating inter-professional teams to improve the health organization and remedy issues that arise in a dynamic environment using the problem-solving capabilities of the inter-professional team. As the authors prepared for the third edition, a scholar and reviewer of this textbook recommended the inclusion of the concept of inter-professional team into this edition; this turned out to be a wonderful idea. From this suggestion, the following model emerged. The authors want to illustrate the "pieces" of the model and the sequence that is most salient for the PAARP model. The PAARP model development, with associated models and theories previously discussed, is first shown and later illustrated in a simple yet useful model.

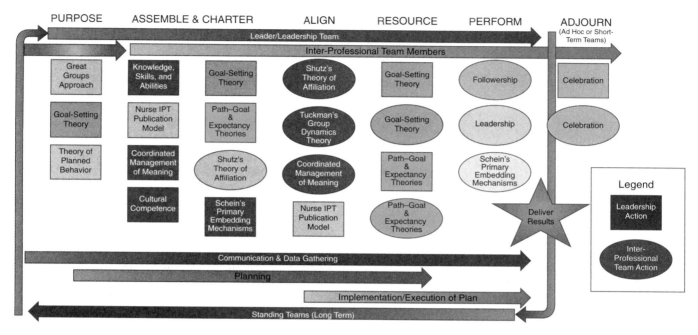

FIGURE 8-1 Inter-professional team model components.

The PAARP model, when followed throughout the life cycle of a team, can result in the improved morale of team members, improved outcomes, and greater value to the organization. Throughout the team life cycle, identifying purpose and continual communication are keys. The PAARP model proposed by Stephens, Ledlow, and Schott postulates that the actions of inter-professional teams occur in five distinct phases that repeat as necessary, depending on the type of team.

RESPONSIBILITIES OF LEADERSHIP WHEN FORMING A GROUP

Purpose

According to PAARP, it is the actions of leadership that give purpose to a group. There are several theories that can assist the leader in providing this purpose: the great groups approach, goal-setting theory, and the theory of planned behavior.

Great groups are a common subject when it comes to planning teams but so many of the associated principles are quickly glanced over for the sake of expediency. It is important to remember that not only does a leader create a great group but it is the group that makes the leader great. For the group to succeed the right people need to be in the right jobs. With the right people in place, the great group is focused on results and achieving their goal.[1]

A useful tool for determining goals that will motivate your inter-professional team is goal-setting theory.

Goal-setting theory plays a role throughout the PAARP process, beginning with the determination of purpose. When determining the purpose of your group, it is helpful to keep in mind Locke and Latham's five principles around goal setting:

1. Clarity
2. Challenge
3. Commitment
4. Feedback
5. Task complexity[2]

When setting goals they should be clear. One tool designed to aid in the creation of clear goals is the mnemonic SMART: specific, measurable, achievable, relevant, and timely. Goals should say who will accomplish them, how you will measure success, the goals should be achievable, the goals should also be aligned with the mission and vision, and goals should have a time period for completion.[3]

Goals should also be challenging and should strike a balance between performance and pressure. It is important to ensure that achieving challenging goals results in rewards for your team members. Another approach is to allow team members to set their own goals that contribute to the overall mission of the group. Allowing team members to set their own goals will increase their sense of commitment and empowerment.[4]

In addition to selecting the correct goals, leaders need to listen to feedback from their team members. This feedback will allow the leader to gauge the progress their team is making toward the goals. Based on the feedback, leaders have the opportunity to clarify the expectations of team members and adjust goals accordingly. When considering task complexity, care must be taken to ensure that work will not overwhelm the team, especially when assignments are complex. It is common for individuals who work in complex or demanding roles to push too hard and lose their work/life balance; this can ultimately result in reduced performance and eventual burnout.[5]

The theory of planned behavior[6] (TPB) (**Figure 8-2**) is also useful to the leader when thinking about the purpose of a group. TPB links the beliefs of an individual to his or her behavior and improves on the predictive ability of previous psychological theories.

Behavioral attitude encompasses the beliefs of the individual around the consequences of his or her behavior. Subjective norms are how the individual perceives the social pressures surrounding his or her behavior. Perceived behavioral control is an indication of the ease or difficulty of performing a particular action. According to TPB, these three elements form the intention of the individual with regard to performing or not performing a particular action. The intention of the individual, if strong enough, then results in the expression of the behavior. Leaders with a strong understanding of what influences the behaviors of their team members will be better able to assemble a team to achieve their goals.

Assemble and Charter

Assembling and providing the group charter are activities primarily related to leadership action. The leader must take into account the knowledge, skills, and abilities of their proposed team members. In addition to selecting team members who have the ability to perform the desired group activities, it is essential that the proposed group members have good interpersonal skills and are able to work together. This need is compounded in health care due to the high stakes of health care and the zero tolerance for error in clinical areas. One part of working together is cultural competence, which is being aware that individuals have different backgrounds, as described in TPB, which change their perceived behavioral controls and cause them to act differently in accordance with their culture and how they perceive the subjective norms of the organization.

Let us examine how this is related to the actions of inter-professional team members once the group is formed.

Assemble

As the group is assembled and given its charter by leadership, the members of the group begin to learn about each other and their role within the newly created team. For group members, there are three basic needs: the need for inclusion, the need for control, and the need for affection. The competing needs, to be included, to have power or status, and to give or receive warmth, are cyclical and groups will observably pass through each one of these phases.[7]

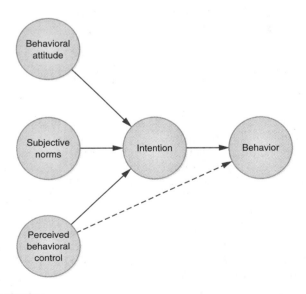

FIGURE 8-2 The theory of planned behavior.

Reprinted from Organizational Behavior and Human Decision Processes, 50, Ajzen, I. (1991). The theory of planned behavior, pages 179-211. Copyright 1991, with permission from Elsevier.

Align

The competing needs of the group members, as defined by Schultz, which are present in the Assemble phase, continue through the Align phase as group members find their place within the team. These needs are manifested through the forming, storming, norming, and performing phases as defined by Tuckman.

Forming occurs when the team first meets and learns its purpose. In the forming phase, group members tend to act somewhat independently of one other. Think back to your personal experiences joining groups for the first time. The generalized process is the same for teams at work, group projects at school, or recreational groups such as club sports.[8]

Storming begins shortly after the forming process and is when group members begin to form opinions about others in the group. These opinions are both positive and negative, ranging from admiration for a group member to distrust of the group leader. The storming phase lasts until any disagreements between the members are resolved. As you might imagine, sometimes groups never mature past the storming phase. Additionally, this is not a phase that can be skipped. Use of best practices by the leader during the Purpose and Assemble phases can, however, dramatically reduce the length of the storming process.[9]

Norming occurs as team members accept the goals of the team as their own and take responsibility for their part in achieving them. When the team reaches the norming phase, the members accept each other and learn to work together.

Performing, the final phase of group alignment per Tuckman, occurs when individuals are not only motivated, as in the norming phase, but knowledgeable and able to perform tasks and make decisions within their bounded reality with little to no supervision. Groups in this phase have mechanisms in place to handle conflict so that it can be resolved without reverting back to the storming phase.[10]

This type of conflict management is part of a larger system for how team members create and interpret meaning. These rules are an integral part of the makeup of the team, and as such, are constantly evolving with the team. This system of meaning is referred to as the coordinated management of meaning (CCM).[11] CCM has three basic domains: management, meaning, and coordination.

Management refers to the actual rules that govern the communication between individuals. Based on these rules, team members can coordinate and manage the meaning of what is communicated between group members. As might be expected, this management of meaning takes on different contexts depending on the relational position of the group members who are communicating. For example, when two peers communicate, messages may have a different meaning than when a team member and team leader communicate; this is because people organize meaning hierarchically.[12] CCM proposes that there are six levels to this hierarchy and that the higher levels of meaning may contradict or even override a lower level of meaning.

1. *Content*: The content of a message is the information transmitted during the communication, and it may not be enough on its own to draw meaning from the message. This ties into media richness theory (MRT), which ranks communication methods based on their "richness," or ability to transmit a message. The takeaway from the CCM content level and MRT is that transmitting a message via text may make the message less clear for the recipient than a "richer" communication method, such as face-to-face communication.[13]

2. *Speech*: The speech portion of the meaning domain of CCM is how the content is aggregated into phrases that convey additional meaning such as a promise, assertion, compliment, or threat.[14]

3. *Episodes*: Episodes are the entire situation of a communication between individuals. Episodes are also unique to each team member. They include the feelings toward the interaction by that team member and deeper meanings to phrases.[15]

4. *Relationships*: Relationships between group members weigh heavily on the interactions between individuals. This is perhaps the easiest-to-understand level of the hierarchy—consider how you would communicate differently with a parent, peer, child, or leader.

5. *Life scripts*: Life scripts are the combined effect of all episodes between participants.[16]

6. *Cultural patterns*: Cultural patterns are what is generally considered normal for a society when communicating.[17]

Clinical Inter-Professional Skills

Due to the additional complications of the healthcare environment, there are several other desirable competencies for inter-professional teams in health care.

- Patient centered
- Community oriented
- Sensitive to systems context across practice settings
- Applicable across health professions[18]

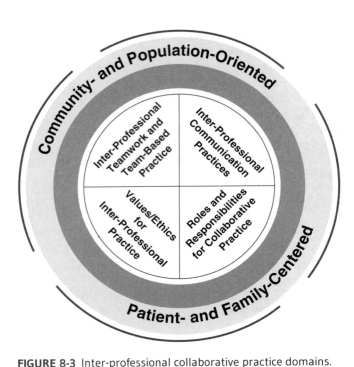

FIGURE 8-3 Inter-professional collaborative practice domains.

(2012). Core Competencies for Interprofessional Collaborative … Retrieved November 22, 2015, from http://www.aacn.nche.edu/education-resources/ipecreport.pdf.

Figure 8-3 illustrates the competencies identified by the American Association of Colleges of Nursing,[19] in association with other medical education bodies, as the four general competencies required to provide population-oriented and patient-centered care.[20]

Values for inter-professional practice and their related ethics are an important part of creating a professional identity that is interpersonal in nature. If the values and ethics are patient centered and population oriented, they will support the common good in health care while reflecting a shared commitment to creating a safer, more efficient, and more effective system of care.[21]

Roles and responsibilities, as well as an understanding of how professional roles and responsibilities complement each other, are essential for inter-professional relationships. Understanding these complementing roles is essential for an individual's own competency as well as collaborative practice.[22]

Inter-professional communication is a common area for health professions education but typically health professions students have little knowledge about or experience with inter-professional communication. In the move toward patient-centered care, communication competencies help prepare professionals for collaborative practice. Important aspects of inter-professional communication are the use of a common set of terms and defining acronyms before their use. Using undefined professional jargon creates a barrier to effective inter-professional care.[23]

Teams and teamwork behaviors apply in any setting where health professionals interact on behalf of shared goals for care with patients or communities. As such, it is critical for the inter-professional team member to be a good team player. Some behaviors involved with teamwork include cooperating with the patient-centered delivery of care and coordinating with other health professionals to increase the safety and effectiveness of care. As health care continues to evolve, the increasing levels of interdependence between teams embedded in health organizations will continue to increase.[24]

Resource

In Resourcing, the inter-professional team sets goals and expectations both for individual members and the team as a whole. The setting of goals was best described by Edwin Locke in his 1968 publication "Toward a Theory of Task Motivation and Incentives."[25] According to Locke this process can be summed up in seven steps:

1. Specifying objectives or tasks to be completed by the team
2. Determining how the performance will be measured
3. Specifying the standard to which the tasks or objectives must be completed
4. Specifying the time period in which the goal must be accomplished
5. Placing a priority on goals when more than one goal exists
6. Rating goals as to their difficulty and importance
7. Determining requirements for coordinating with team members[26]

It is worth noting that the difficulty of goals will also affect team performance. More difficult goals will be more satisfying to team members when they are attained, because they provide team members with a greater sense of self-efficacy, achievement, and skill improvement when compared to easier goals.[27]

Additionally, you must be aware of the role that leaders play in removing obstacles from the path of the group and allowing them to complete tasks on schedule. In support of this, path–goal theory describes four leadership styles that can be used, depending on the situation and team members involved: directive, supportive, participative, and achievement oriented.[28]

The directive approach requires the leader to inform team members what is expected of them. It is most effective when team members are unsure about a task or there is uncertainty within the environment. The supportive approach requires the leader to show concern for the team members while being approachable and friendly. This approach is most effective in situations where the assigned tasks are physically demanding. The participative approach has the leader consulting with his or her followers before making decisions. This approach is effective when the team members are highly experienced. An achievement-oriented approach requires a leader to set challenging goals for his or her team members and hold them accountable for performance at the highest level while showing confidence in their abilities. This approach works best in professional or competitive environments.[29]

Perform

The Perform phase focuses on followership, leadership, and embedding mechanisms.

Followership and leadership are reciprocal roles within the team. Robert Kelly described followership extensively and identified five general types of followers formed from a combination of two key underlying behavioral dimensions. The first dimension measures the extent to which an individual is an independent critical thinker, and the second is a measure of how active or passive an individual is with regard to group behavior.

1. *Sheep*: Sheep are team members who are very passive and require the leader to motivate them externally. Additionally, these team members lack commitment and require constant supervision from the leader.
2. *Yes-people*: These are team members who are committed to the goal of the team and do not question the actions of the leader. Team members who fall into this category will typically defend the leader against any criticism, even when that criticism proves to be valid.
3. *Pragmatics*: Pragmatics will tend to support the majority decision and tend to remain in the background of the group. They will never be the first to suggest a controversial or unique idea.
4. *Alienated*: Alienated individuals can usually be found questioning the actions of the leader and attempting to stall or bring down the efforts of the group through questioning the motivations of the leader. In addition to being critical of the leader, an alienated group member will commonly assume they can lead the group more effectively and view themselves as the true leader of the group.
5. *Star followers*: Star followers are independent, positive, and active. They evaluate the actions and decisions of the leader, and they will provide input and commentary, as they deem appropriate. Star followers are able to work independently and will generally succeed even when the group leader is not present.[30]

Primary embedding mechanisms come down to how a leader transmits culture. For example, what a leader holds up as important, his or her team will do the same. What the leader controls on a regular basis through emphasis will eventually become the focus of the team. The most important factor to remember here is that consistency of action on the part of the leader is essential to prevent the team from second-guessing the actions of the leader. According to Schein, leaders communicate their true feelings both explicitly and implicitly. If the leader is conflicted, his or her message will not be consistent, resulting in uncertainty and conflict within the organization. Health leaders must predetermine where and how to guide the team, and they must stay on task to meet goals.[31]

As seen in **Figure 8-4**, team members must align, resource, and perform tasks as laid out by leadership through the defined purpose and assembly of the group. Once tasks

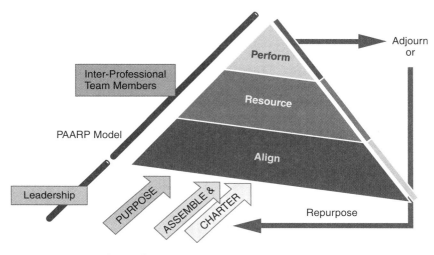

FIGURE 8-4 Inter-professional team model (PAARP).
Stephens, Ledlow, Schott

are complete, the standing group is repurposed for its next task or adjourned in the case of single-purpose groups.

THE DYNAMIC CULTURE LEADERSHIP MODEL[32]

Superb leadership is required at all levels of the health organization due to the increasingly dynamic nature of the health environment. This reality was the catalyst for the development of the dynamic culture leadership (DCL) model. Leadership in this model is recognized at three levels as the critical ingredient in the recipe for overall success: at the personal level, at the team level, and at the organizational level. The challenge is to focus the knowledge, skills, and abilities of organizational leaders appropriately and to empower the total organization to complete its mission, reach its vision, and compete successfully in an environment that constantly changes. This model is built on various theories and models from the leadership literature and related research. An overview of the DCL model is presented; this model is intended to fit within the situational and transformational leadership paradigm with an emphasis on organizational culture development. This model is appropriate for organizational, departmental, system, subsystem, or program leadership and should be used as a basis for developing a personal leadership plan or model.

The DCL model[33] provides both a descriptive and a high-level prescriptive process model of leadership. This model emphasizes a sense of balance that needs to be maintained to achieve a sustainable and continuing level of *optimized* leadership based on the changing macro and micro factors in the external environment. "Optimized leadership," like the concept "high quality," is not necessarily a norm to be achieved at all times. Rather, it is a worthy goal, an ideal state. No individual (and certainly no organization) can in all situations and at all times enjoy a steady state of higher-level leadership. Nevertheless, many individuals and organizations continuously optimize their ability to function at high leadership levels by consciously (and even unconsciously) cultivating the various elements of the model.

The basic assumptions of the DCL model are as follows:

- Due to the very dynamic nature of the environment (in this case, the health industry), it is critical for the leadership and management team to bring multiple knowledge, skills, abilities, perspectives, and backgrounds (DCL leadership alignment assessment) to the organization to enable it to successfully and proactively navigate the external environment and focus the internal people and resources on the mission, vision, strategies, goals, and objectives of the organization.
- Leadership is defined as the ability to assess, develop, maintain, and change the organizational culture to optimally meet the needs and expectations of the external environment through focusing the collective energy of the organization on the mission, vision, strategies, goals, and objectives of the organization.
- The leadership and management team should consciously determine the culture of the organization and guide and direct culture through communication improvement, organization-wide strategic planning, decision-making alignment, employee assessment and empowerment, and knowledge management and organizational learning (process constructs).
- Based on the predetermined organizational culture, mission, vision, and strategies, consistency of leadership and management are paramount.
- Situational and environmental assessment and scanning are key to adjusting organizational culture, mission, vision, and strategies.
- Transformational leadership and management (including transactional leadership approaches), where both the science and art of leadership and management are in concert with the external environment expectations, provide the best approach to lead people and manage resources in a dynamic world.

Optimized leadership is certainly attainable for any person and any organization, but it usually requires concentrated effort to overcome past habits, ideas, and tendencies. Ultimately, *individual* leaders make up the leadership team. The team, therefore, must be diverse in style and competencies while being anchored to a set of values and operating principles of the organization. The assessment instrument for individuals and teams for this model is based on a leadership–management continuum and an art–science continuum.

The characteristics of "leadership" as compared to "management," and "science" as compared to "art," are described in **Tables 8-1** and **8-2**. It is important to note that organizations need leaders, managers, scientists, and artists working together to achieve success over the long term. **Figure 8-5** illustrates the macro descriptive model, whereas **Figure 8-6** shows the prescription (or processes) associated with the model.

The differences in *leadership* versus *management* are shown in Table 8-1; the differences in *science* versus *art* are shown in Table 8-2. It is important to keep in mind that organizations need leadership as well as management mentality/capabilities, and science as well as art mentality/

Table 8-1 Explanation of the Leadership–Management Continuum in the Dynamic Culture Leadership Model

Leadership	Management
Longer time horizon	Shorter time horizon
Vision then mission oriented	Mission oriented
Organizational validity (Are we doing the right things?)—environmental scanning and intuition	Organizational reliability (Are we doing things correctly and consistently?)—compliance to rules and policies and rule development
Does the organization have the correct components (people, resources, expertise) to meet future as well as current needs?	How can current components work best now?
Developing and refining organizational culture to meet external environment's needs	Maintaining organizational climate to ensure performance
Timing and tempo of initiatives and projects	Scheduling of initiatives and projects

Reproduced from Ledlow, G., & Cwiek, M. (2005, July). *The process of leading: Assessment and comparison of leadership team style, operating climate and expectation of the external environment.* Proceedings of Global Business and Technology Association. Lisbon, Portugal.

Table 8-2 Explanation of the Science–Art Continuum in the Dynamic Culture Leadership Model

Science	Art
Technical skills orientation (e.g., forecasting, budgeting)	Relationship orientation (e.g., networking, interpersonal relationships)
Decisions based more on analysis	Decisions based more on perceptions of people
Developing systems (important to organizations)	Developing relationships and networks (important to organizations)
Expert systems	Experts as people
Cost control and evaluation of value are important	Image and customer relationships are important

Reproduced from Ledlow, G., & Cwiek, M. (2005, July). *The process of leading: Assessment and comparison of leadership team style, operating climate, and expectation of the external environment.* Proceedings of Global Business and Technology Association. Lisbon, Portugal.

capabilities, if they are to survive and thrive in their external environment.

The DCL model entails a leadership process, as shown in Figure 8-6, that emphasizes leadership team assessment, communication improvement, strategic planning, decision-making alignment, employee enhancement, and learning organization improvement. Leaders who regularly follow the sequence shown in Figure 8-6 have the best potential to deal with change in their environment while building a culture that will be effective even during times of change. Members of the leadership team must be ever thoughtful in maintaining their consistency relative to the organizational mission, vision, strategies, goals, and values, but also in terms of the model's constructs and process constructs. Examples of inconsistency might include instituting a defensive and disconfirming communication environment within a customer or patient service and care excellence (differentiation) strategy; using a subordinate decision-making tactic (i.e., pushing down decisions to the lowest level appropriate) without involving subordinates in strategic and operational planning; or maintaining a leadership team that is heavily skewed toward "leadership" and "art" whereas the external environment demands "management" and "science." Examples of consistency would be creating a culture based in a supportive and confirming communication environment; using a subordinate-involved planning process with decision making made at the lowest appropriate level; and initiating a customer service and patient care excellence strategy if the external environment expects such a strategy (today, excellent service and care are expected). The overriding theme is that leadership envisions, develops, and maintains an organizational culture that works amid a dynamic environment. A summary of model constructs and process constructs follows.

Briefly, the DCL model incorporates both "model" constructs and "process" constructs. In essence, model constructs are primarily the descriptive model. Model constructs include the following:

- *Science of leadership* includes all technical elements involved in leading and managing an organization, such as quantitative and qualitative analysis, decision-making assessments, finance and budgeting, job analysis and design, planning structures and processes, computer skills, and the like. Each process construct of the model has both science and art aspects; an integration of the two must be consistently used to ensure successful leadership of an organization.
- *Art of leadership* includes the elements involved in interpersonal relationships, network building and maintenance, intuition, coalition development, and the like.
- *Technical competence, relationship building, emotional intelligence, morality and trust building,* and *environmental*

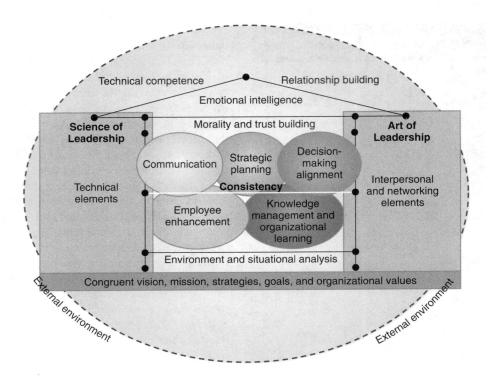

FIGURE 8-5 The dynamic culture leadership model.

Reproduced from Ledlow, G., & Cwiek, M. (2005, July). *The process of leading: Assessment and comparison of leadership team style, operating climate, and expectation of the external environment.* Proceedings of Global Business and Technology Association. Lisbon, Portugal.

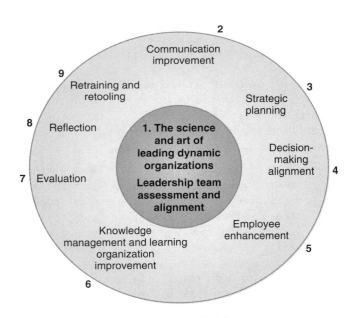

FIGURE 8-6 The leadership process (DCL) model.

Reproduced from Ledlow, G., & Cwiek, M. (2005, July). *The process of leading: Assessment and comparison of leadership team style, operating climate, and expectation of the external environment.* Proceedings of Global Business and Technology Association. Lisbon, Portugal.

and situational analyses are required at sufficient levels (and should be at high levels) across the leadership and management team to successfully lead people and manage the resources of the health organization.

- *Congruent vision, mission, strategies, goals*, and *organizational values* are essential so that a culture of consistency is developed throughout the organization. The leadership and management team must consciously assess the external environment (macro and micro factors) and predetermine these directional, competitive, adaptive, and cultural development strategies for the organization.

- *External environment* comprises all organizational stakeholders (anyone or any group that influences, serves, gets service, or is connected to the organization), the macro-environmental factors, the micro-environmental factors, and the synthesized set of expectations of the health organization.

Prescriptive elements of the model include assessing and aligning a robust leadership and management team that can utilize the knowledge, skills, abilities, and perspectives of all quadrants of the assessment instrument "diamond"; being consistent in developing and maintaining an appropriate culture; and the sequential and building utilization of the model's process constructs. Process constructs include the following elements:

- *Communication improvement* is the leadership and management team engagement in predetermined modeling, training, rewarding, and assimilating of the communication environment into the organization in the means that best contributes to an effective organizational culture. In health organizations, a confirming and supportive communication environment that is cognizant of media richness of communication channels and competent in conflict management should be the most effective, efficient, and efficacious.
- *Strategic planning* (includes operational planning) is the structured, inclusive process of planning to determine a mission, vision, strategies, goals, objectives, and action steps that are consistent with organizational values and that meet the external environment's expectations of the organization. Subordinate, internal, and external stakeholders should be included in the planning process, as appropriate to level and responsibilities. Continuous and "living" planning is a cultural imperative in dynamic environments.
- *Decision-making alignment* involves aligning decisions with the strategic and operational plan while understanding reality-based decision making (i.e., pushing down decisions appropriately and using policies and standard operating procedures for routine and consistent decisions).

- *Employee enhancement* is the assessment of employee knowledge, skills, abilities, experience, and trustworthiness and the practice of increasing or reducing responsibilities (such as making decisions) appropriate to the unit, group, and individual in line with the organizational culture as part of development and the strategic and operational plans.
- *Knowledge management and organizational learning* involve capturing what the organization knows and what it has learned so that improvements to effectiveness, efficiency, and efficacy can be achieved. Leadership, willingness, planning, and training are facilitators of organizational learning.[34]
- *Evaluating, reflecting, and retooling* is the leadership and management team's honest assessment of the DCL model cycle and ways to improve the cycle in the next repetition.

Using this process consistently not only improves the organization's ability to use these processes and produce an organizational culture that reflects the leadership's vision, but also enables the organization to maneuver in dynamic/changing situations.

Leadership team assessment and alignment are important. **Figure 8-7** illustrates the leadership team assessment (Step 1 in Figure 8-6) for 10 members of a hospital leadership team as it compares to the current operational environment and the expectations of the external environment. As shown in Figure 8-7, there is a tension between what the leadership team tends to be (more *leadership* oriented with a reasonable

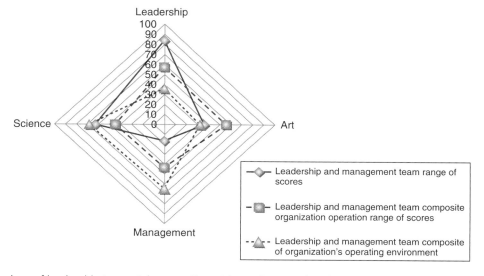

FIGURE 8-7 Comparison of leadership team style, operating style, and external environment requirements for a leadership team.

Reproduced from Ledlow, G., & Cwiek, M. (2005, July). *The process of leading: Assessment and comparison of leadership team style, operating climate, and expectation of the external environment.* Proceedings of Global Business and Technology Association. Lisbon, Portugal.

science and *art* balance) and the more *management* and *science* emphasis in leadership demanded by the external environment; the operating environment can be found between that tension. The external environment requirements, as perceived by the leadership team, are skewed toward *management* and *science* (the "analytical manager" quadrant). The perception of leadership would lead one to believe that the external environment requires greater cost control, accountability, and adherence to policies and rules, although relationships are still important, as is some leadership focus.

Assessing an organization's leadership team is essential. Aligning the team to bring diversity of style, skills, experience, and abilities is essential for organizations if they are to maintain a robust and resilient, and even opportunistic, personality. In this model and assessment, both cultural diversity and individual diversity are valued because they enable the organization to better respond to dynamic organizational and external environments. In contrast, diversity of focus and diversity of organizational goals are not advantageous; a diverse leadership team brings robustness to solving organizational problems as long as the focus on the vision, mission, and goals are similar across the leadership team. An assessment that looks at leadership as a team, across organizational levels, operating environments, and external environment needs, is far better than one that relies solely on individual leader assessments.[35]

Figure 8-7 shows the results of a leadership team style assessment, including operating style and external environment expectations. Note that a considerable disconnect exists between the leadership style and the external environment requirements. The organizational operating style is *balanced*, whereas the leadership style composite is *analytical leader* (skewed toward science and leadership) and the external environment is *analytical manager* (skewed toward science and management). This is hypothesized to represent a leadership coping strategy. Aligning additional leadership team members to bring in more management- and science-oriented members may be an appropriate strategy in this case. Alternatives to adding team members would be to "buy" or have consultation with people who might add management and science abilities to the organization. Such a strategy can cause a problem over the long term, however, in that institutional knowledge could be more easily lost with this approach. When leadership style by organizational level is compared, there is much more propensity for leadership than management, as one looks down the organizational hierarchy, than an organization may be able to tolerate over the long term. In essence, it is important to understand and know the leadership team's style and "personality" as it compares to its operating style (how business gets done), as well as the expectations of the external environment.

Leaders are gifted in different ways, with different personalities and varying skill sets. All leaders can grow and become more balanced and achieve greater effectiveness. Some common factors found in those who succeed in becoming dynamic culture leaders include the desire to learn more about themselves, the motivation to learn and practice new skill sets, and the need to grow and become more tomorrow than what they are today. This is not the easiest path to travel, but it is the path that optimizes the likelihood of leadership effectiveness and success.

The DCL model categorizes leaders and managers, and scientists and artists, based on the diamond configuration of the assessment tool. Overlaying this categorization scheme, on top of the assessment, are the following classifications: relationship leader, relationship manager, technical or analytic leader, technical or analytic manager, balanced leader, equalized leader-manager, and balanced manager (**Figure 8-8**). In which category would you put yourself? This same schema can be used in assessing the operating style of the organization (such as relationship-led operation or relationship-managed operation) and the external environment expectations (such as technical or analytically led environment or technical or analytically managed environment). The following discussion and figures illustrate a comparison between the leadership teams of two different hospitals.

COMPARISON: TWO COMMUNITY-BASED HOSPITALS

Two community hospital leadership teams were assessed using the DCL Leadership Alignment Assessment Tool.

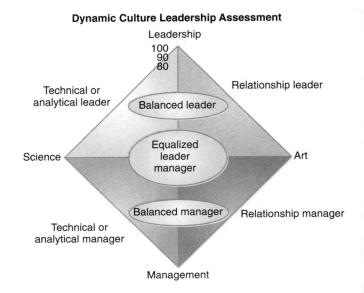

FIGURE 8-8 Categorization scheme for DCL model.

Table 8-3 Hospital Comparisons

	Hospital A	Hospital B
Type of facility	Short-term acute care	Short-term acute care
Type of control	Government, federal	Voluntary, nonprofit
Total staffed beds	76	88

The first hospital is a military community hospital in the Western United States and the other hospital is in the North Central/Midwest United States. The two hospitals, with similar services and case-mix indexes, are highlighted in **Table 8-3**.

When comparing the two hospitals, both Hospital A (federal) and Hospital B (nonprofit) are skewed strongly toward leadership and somewhat toward science. Hospital A is slightly higher in both areas than Hospital B. There is a moderate amount of diversity in the area of art and little in the area of management for both hospitals, with Hospital B having slightly higher scores. Both hospitals' leadership teams demonstrate the analytical leader, as compared to the relationship leader or relationship manager team composites. The perceived operating environment for both Hospital A and Hospital B is fairly balanced; however, Hospital B is now slightly skewed toward art and Hospital A toward science.

The external environment requirements, as perceived by Hospital A, are skewed toward management and science (the analytical manager quadrant); for Hospital B, they are slightly skewed toward leadership and science (analytical leader). For Hospital A, the perception is that the external environment requires greater cost control, accountability, and adherence to policies and rules, whereas in Hospital B, there is a balanced focus on vision and decision making based on analysis.

When leadership style by organizational level is compared, there is much more propensity for leadership than management as you go down the organizational hierarchy. However, and most interestingly, Level 3 and Level 4 are balanced with a slight skew for art and science for both Hospital A and Hospital B. At this level of the organization, both scientist and artist are needed to deal with dynamic environments. The DCL Leadership Alignment Assessment summaries and charts are shown in **Tables 8-4** through **8-7** and **Figures 8-9** through **8-18**.

Table 8-4 Hospital A DCL Scores

Organizational level (levels from CEO)	Levels 0–1	Level 2	Level 3	Level 4
Leadership	100	85	70	80
Art	50	25	50	40
Management	0	15	30	20
Science	50	75	50	60
Number in category	1	2	1	1

Table 8-5 Hospital B DCL Scores

Organizational level (levels from CEO)	Levels 0–1	Level 2	Level 3	Level 4
Leadership	100	80	74	80
Art	50	35	50	50
Management	0	20	26	20
Science	50	60	50	50
Number in category	1	2	5	2

Table 8-6 Hospital A DCL Mean Composite Scores

	Leadership and Management Team Range of Scores	Leadership and Management Team Composite Organization Operation Range of Scores	Leadership and Management Team Composite of Organization's Operating Environment
Leadership	84.00	56.92	36.00
Art	38.00	56.00	32.00
Management	16.00	43.08	64.00
Science	62.00	44.00	68.00

Table 8-7 Hospital B DCL Mean Composite Scores

	Leadership and Management Team Range of Scores	Leadership and Management Team Composite Organization Operation Range of Scores	Leadership and Management Team Composite of Organization's Operating Environment
Leadership	79.00	60.38	54.00
Art	48.00	44.00	44.00
Management	21.00	39.62	46.00
Science	52.00	56.00	56.00

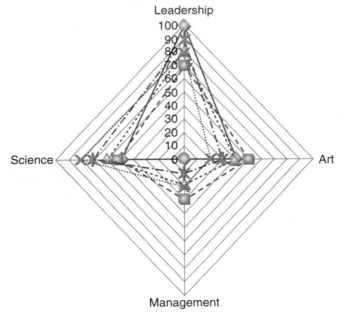

FIGURE 8-9 Hospital A DCL leadership team individual leader results.

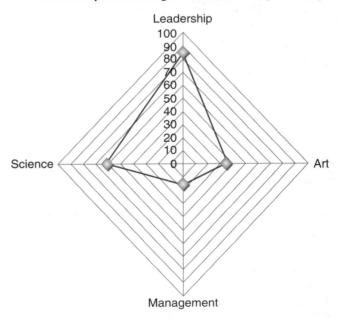

FIGURE 8-10 Hospital A DCL leadership team mean result composite.

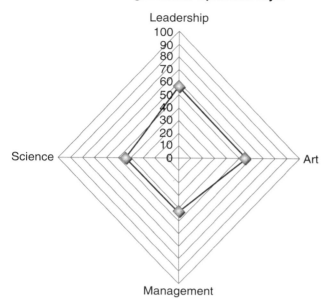

Leadership and Management Team's Composite of Actual Organization Operation Style

FIGURE 8-11 Hospital A DCL scores operating style mean composite.

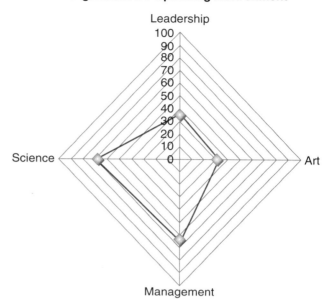

Leadership and Management Team's Composite of Organization's Operating Environment

FIGURE 8-12 Hospital A DCL scores external expectations style mean composite.

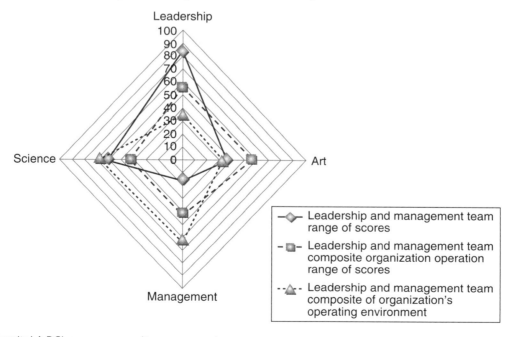

Comparison of Team Style, Actual Organization Operation Style, and Required Environment Style

FIGURE 8-13 Hospital A DCL mean composite scores overlay.

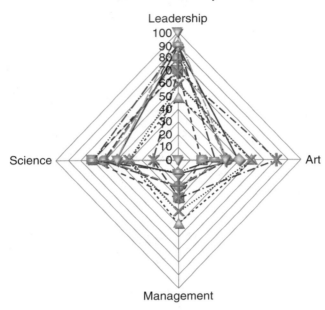

Leadership and Management Team Individual Scores as a Composite

FIGURE 8-14 Hospital B DCL leadership team individual leader results.

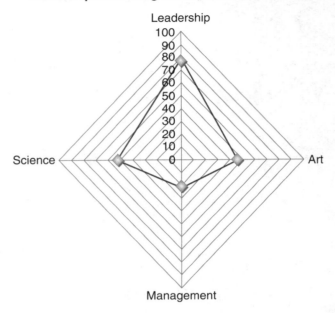

Leadership and Management Team Composite Style

FIGURE 8-15 Hospital B DCL leadership team mean result composite.

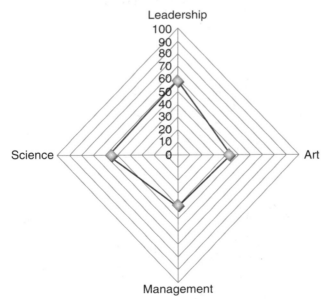

Leadership and Management Team's Composite of Actual Organization Operation Style

FIGURE 8-16 Hospital B DCL scores operating style mean composite.

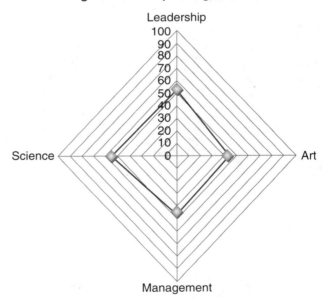

Leadership and Management Team's Composite of Organization's Operating Environment

FIGURE 8-17 Hospital B DCL scores external expectations style mean composite.

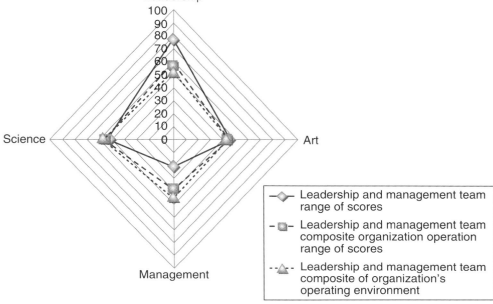

Comparison of Team Style, Actual Organization Operation Style, and Required Environment Style

Leadership and management team range of scores

Leadership and management team composite organization operation range of scores

Leadership and management team composite of organization's operating environment

FIGURE 8-18 Hospital B DCL mean composite scores overlay.

Which hospital leadership team is more "diverse"? Which hospital leadership team is more aligned with the operating climate and external environment expectations?

DCL AND ORGANIZATIONAL CULTURE

Organizations are more dynamic today than ever before. With the advent of the Information Age, the fluidity of professional and family life, and the competitive nature of the global marketplace, more of an entrepreneurial environment can be found in many of today's organizations:

> Entrepreneurial organizations reflect a different set of underlying assumptions principally because they shift the focus away from producing specific, predetermined behavior by means of direction and formal controls. Instead, they encourage coordination through the shared understanding that will enable individuals to choose effective actions themselves. Organization structure and control systems can no longer be depicted as tools that mechanically determine behaviors. We must shift our thinking away from the organization as an entity, to members' choice and understanding.[36]

Leaders in this environment cannot rest on the laurels of "cookie-cutter" methods, but must instead learn and become effective in developing teams of professionals within dynamic cultures. To see the reality of the dynamic nature of organizations today, one need simply consider the changes wrought by increased human diversity, information overload, the evolution of technology, the increasing sophistication of the consumer, and the introduction of e-commerce.

Leaders need to have a firm grasp of how they can develop an organizational culture that creates a thriving environment for their organization. In 1999, Edgar Schein defined "culture" as the basic assumptions and beliefs shared by members of a group or organization.[37] "A major function of culture is to help us understand the environment and determine how to respond to it, thereby reducing anxiety, uncertainty, and confusion."[38] The key question then becomes, how do leaders shape culture? Schein suggests that leaders have the greatest potential for embedding and reinforcing aspects of culture by using the following five primary mechanisms:[39]

- *Attention*: Leaders communicate their priorities, values, and concerns by their choice of things to ask about, measure, comment on, praise, and criticize.

- *Reaction to crisis*: This reaction increases the potential for learning about values and assumptions.
- *Role modeling*: Leaders set the example for others by their actions and behaviors.
- *Allocation of resources*: The distribution of resources to units within the organization.
- *Criteria for selection and dismissal*: Leaders can influence culture by recruiting people who have particular values, skills, and traits, and then promoting (or firing) them.

Schein also described five secondary mechanisms:[40]

- *Design of organizational structure*: A centralized structure indicates that only the leader can determine what is important; a decentralized structure reinforces individual initiative and sharing.
- *Design of systems and procedures*: Where emphasis is placed shows concern and reduces ambiguity.
- *Design of facilities*: For example, modern, clean, and eye appealing.
- *Stories, legends, and myths*: Stories to tell about great employees, leaders, or community figures that reinforce positive actions and behaviors.
- *Formal statements*: Creeds or mission and vision statements of the organization; many of these can be found framed and hanging on walls of the organization.

It is imperative that health organization leaders understand the various factors that influence culture. Culture is more stable and more difficult to change than climate, because climate usually does not remain stable over time. Whether employees are "happy" today (a climate indicator) is only of temporal importance. By comparison, culture indicators (e.g., processes, incentive systems, communication environment, understanding of goals and how they fit into the work to achieve success) are much more meaningful and important.

The DCL model is a set of constructs with the goal of unifying the various leadership theories that previously have received attention. Furthermore, the DCL model can be studied and employed immediately by leaders and organizational scholars intent on developing highly effective leadership. In their book *The Success Paradigm*,[41] Mike Friesen and James Johnson discuss the importance of leadership in the integration of quality and strategy to achieve organizational success. In this book, the leadership process is described as critical for success. The DCL model is presented as an application of theory to advance existing contingency leadership theories, coupled with a strategic process. It is, therefore, presented as a prescriptive model.

Today's complex, ever-changing organizations are experiencing a shortage in leadership effectiveness, not because of a lack of talent or goodwill, but because of the demanding balancing act required for success. This balance of scientist attributes and artist attributes defined in the DCL model provides the pathway for success. According to experts, leadership is the pivotal issue in organizational success. The DCL model is intended to become central to the understanding of leadership in organizations and the people who lead them.

The DCL model, in its current state of development, is being tested in both theoretical and practical ways. It currently provides a conceptual framework for the better understanding of complex organizations and serves as a model for advancing leader effectiveness. Furthermore, tools for leadership assessment and direct application are being refined to advance the practical utility of this model in all organizational settings. In summary, the DCL model includes the following recommendations:

- An assessment of the organization's leadership team and ultimately the development of a team should focus on building a team that is diverse in terms of the leadership, management, art, and science attributes, while simultaneously being rooted in the fundamental values, beliefs, and mission of the organization.
- An organization's leadership should focus on communication improvement, strategic planning, decision-making alignment, employee enhancement, and learning organization improvement in a regular, cyclical sequence.
- Leaders should become competent in the use of the process constructs (e.g., communication improvement, strategic planning) included in this model, so that predetermined and consistent alternative strategies and applications can be selected based on the situation.
- The sequence should be repeated based on the tempo of change in the environment: Rapid change creates a need to work through the sequence at a faster pace. It is estimated that in health care today, this sequence should be planned to take place every 3 to 4 years.

The DCL model, as a leadership team alignment, macro, and culture creation model, integrates well with the reframing leadership and management in organizations model, an episodic leader style selection, and the frame emphasis platform developed by Bolman and Deal. Both models possess descriptive and prescriptive elements that can be learned and embedded into the organization culture of health organizations.

BOLMAN AND DEAL'S REFRAMING LEADERSHIP AND MANAGEMENT IN ORGANIZATIONS MODEL[42]

Bolman and Deal suggest that leaders must be situational/contingency oriented. Critical variables assist leaders in choosing the emphasis and style they need to use to be successful. Four constructs are considered important in this model: structural, human resources, political, and symbolic. Each of these constructs is important in its own right, but some are more important than others at critical times. Recent research literature from late 2008 used Bolman and Deal's model to suggest several applications for this model in an academic healthcare organization.[43]

With Bolman and Deal's model, a leader must pay attention to the four organizational constructs, each of which has assumptions, attributes, and imperatives for the leader to consider. This section summarizes each of these dimensions. As we progress through this model, pay close attention to the application of the model.

The *structural* construct (called a "frame") deals with how organizations "structure" work processes, how they establish formal relationships, and how groups facilitate *coupling* (coupling is the level of adherence to organizational policies, rules, procedures, and social expectations). The structural frame assumptions are outlined here:

- Organizations exist to accomplish established goals.
- Organizational design/structural form can be designed to "fit" the situation.
- Organizations work best when governed by rationality and norms.
- Specialization permits more productivity and individual expertise.
- Coordination and control are essential to effectiveness.
- Problems originate from inappropriate structures and inadequate systems that can be resolved through restructuring and developing new systems (modern reengineering).

The *human resources* construct or frame embraces McGregor's Theory Y model. This dimension is critical to focus and synergize human energy in an organization. Human resources frame assumptions are as follows:

- Organizations exist to serve human needs (rather than the reverse).
- Organizations and people need each other.
- When the fit between the individual and the organization is poor, one or both will suffer: Individuals will be exploited or will seek to exploit the organization, or both.
- A good fit between individual and organization benefits both: Human beings find meaningful and satisfying work, and organizations get the human talent and energy that they need.[44]
- Moreover, the idea that people have needs is a central element in commonsense psychology.[45]

This model's essential theme regarding human resources management is best summed up in the following quotations:

The theories of Maslow, McGregor, and Argyris suggested that conflict between individual and organization would get worse as organizations became larger (with greater impersonality, longer chains of command, and more complex rules and control systems) and as society became better educated and more affluent (producing more people whose higher-level needs are salient).[46]

One solution to that problem [treating employees as children] is participation—giving workers more opportunity to influence decisions.[47]

The *political construct* or frame deals with resource allocation within an organization. The interesting aspect of this construct is that people create interesting webs of relationships to gain and reallocate resources. Political frame assumptions are based on power, conflict, and coalitions:

- "The propositions of the political frame do not attribute politics to individual selfishness, myopia, or incompetence. They assert that interdependence, difference, scarcity, and power relations will inevitably produce political forces, regardless of the players. It is naive and romantic to hope that politics can be eliminated in organizations. [Leaders and managers] can, however, learn to understand and manage political processes."[48]
- This frame suggests that organizational goals are set through negotiations among members of coalitions. A typical organization has a confusing set of multiple goals, many of which are in conflict with one another.
- "The political perspective suggests that the goals, structure, and policies of an organization emerge from an ongoing process of bargaining and negotiation among the major interest groups....the political view suggests that the exercise of power is a natural part of an ongoing contest."[49]

The *symbolic* construct or frame deals with meaning. This dimension gets at the heart of what organizational members feel about issues and events. Specifically, the meaning of the event is more important than the event. A *symbol* is something that stands for or means something else.

The symbolic frame seeks to interpret and illuminate the basic issues of meaning and faith that make symbols so powerful in every aspect of the human experience, including life in organizations. This frame presents a world that departs significantly from traditional canons of organizational theories: rationality, certainty, and linearity. It is based on the following unconventional assumptions:

- What is important is not the event but what it means;
- Events and meaning are loosely coupled;
- Most significant events and processes in organizations are ambiguous and uncertain;
- The greater the ambiguity and uncertainty, the harder rationality and logical approaches to analysis, problem solving, and decision making are to use;
- Faced with ambiguity and uncertainty, humans create symbols to decrease confusion, increase predictability, and provide direction; and
- Many organizational events and processes are more important for what they express than for what they produce: secular myths, rituals, ceremonies, and sagas that help people find meaning and order in experiences.

Symbolic phenomena are particularly visible in organizations with unclear goals and uncertain technologies; in such organizations, most things are ambiguous. Who has power? What is success? Why was a decision made? What are the goals? The answers are often veiled in a fog of uncertainty.[50]

Utilization of the symbolic frame focuses on three types of concepts:

- Concepts of meaning
  - Dilemmas and paradoxes are everywhere.
  - Organizations are full of questions that have no answers.
  - Organizations are full of problems that cannot be solved.
  - Organizations have many events that cannot be understood fully.
- Concepts of beliefs
- Concepts of faith

The leader uses the following tools within the symbolic frame:

- *Myths*: To reconcile differences and resolve dilemmas
  - Fairy tales
  - Stories
- *Metaphors*: To make confusion comprehensible
- *Scenarios and symbolic activities*: To provide direction amid uncertainty, to provide forums for socialization, to reduce anxiety and ambiguity, and to convey messages to external constituencies
  - Rituals
  - Ceremonies
- *Heroes, heroines, shamans, priests, and storytellers*: To provide guides to and interpretations of what life in organizations really means

Historically, all human cultures have used ritual and ceremony to create order, clarity, and predictability, particularly in dealing with issues or problems that are too complex, mysterious, or random to be controlled in any other way. We all create rituals to reduce uncertainty and anxiety.[51]

Important to the understanding of organizations and leading organizations, then, is culture. The four frames, when integrated, form a unique culture for each organization.

How do leaders effectively utilize Bolman and Deal's model? First we need to understand which actions leaders use in each frame. Let's look at each frame in an overview.

Structural Leadership

- Leaders do their homework.
- Leaders develop a new model of the relationship of structure, strategy, and environment for their organization.
- Leaders focus on implementation.
- Leaders continually experiment, evaluate, and adapt.

Though structural leadership has received less attention than it deserves, it can be a very powerful approach. Structural leaders lead through analysis and design rather than charisma and inspiration. Their success depends on developing the right blueprint for the relationship between their organization's structure and strategy, as well as on finding ways to get that blueprint accepted.[52]

Human Resources Leadership

- Leaders believe in people and communicate that belief.
- Leaders are visible and accessible.
- Leaders empower: they increase participation, provide support, share information, and move decision making as far down the organization as possible.

Human resource leadership has generated an enormous amount of attention. Until very recently, in fact, human resource concepts dominated the literature on managerial leadership. The human resource literature has focused particularly on interpersonal relationships between superiors and subordinates and on the value of openness, sensitivity, and participation. When they are successful, human resource leaders become catalysts and servant-leaders.[53]

Political Leadership

- Leaders clarify what they want and what they can get.
- Leaders assess the distribution of power and interests.
- Leaders build linkages to other stakeholders.
- Leaders persuade first, negotiate second, and use coercion only as a last resort.

Effective political leaders are advocates who are clear about their agenda and sensitive to political reality and who build the alliances that they need to move their organization forward.[54]

Symbolic Leadership

- Leaders interpret experience (transactional [exchange theory] versus transforming [inspire to reach higher needs and purposes]).
- Leaders are transforming leaders who are visionaries.
- Leaders use symbols to capture attention.
- Leaders frame experience (i.e., reduce the ambiguity and uncertainty through symbolism).
- Leaders discover and communicate a vision.
- Leaders tell stories.

Symbolic leaders are artists, poets, or prophets who use symbols and stories to communicate a vision that builds faith and loyalty among an organization's employees and other stakeholders.[55]

"Wise leaders understand their own strengths, work to expand them, and build teams that together can provide leadership in all four modes—structural, political, human resource, and symbolic."[56] In essence, a situational leader is what is advocated. "Leadership is always an interactive process between the leader and the led. Organizations need leaders who can provide a persuasive and durable sense of purpose and direction, rooted deeply in human values and the human spirit."[57]

The prescriptive aspect of the Bolman and Deal model is summarized in **Tables 8–8** and **8–9**. Upon reviewing the tables, you may notice that this model has significant connections to other theories, such as media richness theory.

Bolman and Deal propose that *pluralism* slows research by impeding communication, in that different disciplines and theories use different languages. Because they used interdisciplinary research on leadership to create their model, Bolman and Deal had to develop their own "language" and a common understanding for people to utilize the model. By doing so, these scholars reduced the "Tower of Babel" problem. When you apply, analyze, synthesize, and evaluate leadership theories and models in your own unique circumstances, it will be important to understand and create a common language (and be consistent).

Now we turn to three models that use different constructs but are inherently situational or contingency leadership models. After the summary of each model, an analysis of these models and the Bolman and Deal model is presented as an example.

Table 8-8 Bolman and Deal: Choosing a Frame

	Conditions for Salience
Structural	Clear goals and information; well-understood cause–effect relationships; strong technologies and information systems; low conflict; low ambiguity; low uncertainty; stable legitimate authority
Human resources	High or increasing employee leverage; low or declining employee morale and motivation; relatively abundant or increasing resources; low or moderate conflict and uncertainty; low or moderate diversity
Political	Scarce or declining resources; goal and value conflicts; high or increasing diversity; diffuse or unstable distribution of power
Symbolic	Unclear and ambiguous goals and information; poorly understood cause–effect relationships; weak technologies and information systems; culturally diverse

Adapted from Bolman, L. G., & Deal, T. E. (1991). *Reframing organizations: Artistry, choice, and leadership.* San Francisco: Jossey-Bass, p. 315.

Table 8-9 Bolman and Deal: Assessing Frame Selection

Question	Structural Frame	Human Resources Frame	Political Frame	Symbolic Frame
How important are commitment and motivation?	Unimportant	Important	?	Important
How important is the technical quality of the decision?	Important	?	Unimportant	Unimportant
How much ambiguity and uncertainty are present?	Low to moderate	Moderate	Moderate to high	High
How scarce are resources?	Moderately scarce	Moderately abundant to abundant	Scarce or increasingly scarce	Scarce to abundant
How much conflict and diversity are present?	Low to moderate	Moderate	Moderate to high	Moderate to high
Are we working in a top-down or bottom-up manner?	Top down	Top down	Bottom up	Top down or bottom up

Adapted from Bolman, L. G., & Deal, T. E. (1991). *Reframing organizations: Artistry, choice, and leadership.* San Francisco: Jossey-Bass, p. 326.

LYNN'S LEADERSHIP ART AND SCIENCE IN PUBLIC LEADERSHIP AND MANAGEMENT MODEL[58]

Lynn suggests that most situational leadership models are correct but are difficult to prove. As the number of practitioner-based models of situational leadership increases, Lynn strongly recommends that empirical research and evidence of effectiveness be employed to complement any practitioner model. An interdisciplinary balance of "art" and "science" is the best method for situational model development. "The use of conceptual frameworks delineating agency problems to study the incentive effects of goals is surely a better basis for advising practitioners than ideologically justified advocacy of performance measurement."[59] Agency theory and game theory provide a scientific "platform" from which to research, prove, and apply situational leadership theory. According to Lynn, having a way to think and conceptualize is more important to effective situational leadership than employing half-baked practitioner, "art-based" approaches.

Lynn's situational leadership perspective supports a long-term, individualized approach. Under this model, both practitioner-based and empirically supported concepts are integrated into a conceptual decision-making or thinking approach for leadership. The leader is more important than the organization in this decision-support–based framework. Skills paramount for leaders include evaluation, critical thinking, and synthesis of interdisciplinary ideas to develop an individual situational model of leadership.

In 1987, Lynn found that high-level public-sector officials (members of the Reagan administration) tried to change their organizations with varying success. Accordingly, Lynn noted that success depended on four factors:[60]

- Personality
- Skills and experience
- A design for change
- Favorability of the situation

YUKL'S MULTIPLE LINKAGE MODEL[61]

Based on a comprehensive leadership approach, the multiple linkage model was first introduced in 1971, with refinements to the model continuing to appear through the 1990s. This model, which was built on previous leadership models, embraces the contingency approach. The key issue is the interacting effects of leader behavior and situational variables on organizational performance.

Yukl advocates a more complex and comprehensive model than was offered by earlier contingency theories.

His model proposes that leaders, in the short term, evaluate and improve intervening variable situations for effectiveness. In the long term, leaders change the situation to better match their organizational strengths and achieve the mission. A transformational leader uses an entrepreneurial style and an articulate and clear vision to shift the situation toward a more favorable environment. Long-term situational variables include the following:

- A formal reward system (subordinate effort)
- Intrinsically motivating properties of the work itself (subordinate effort)
- Technology (performance)
- Geographical distribution (performance)
- Policies and procedures (performance)
- Informal practices that have evolved over time (performance)

Yukl's model suggests that leaders are in control (effective leaders, that is) of the situation more so than, or at least as much as, the organization's status quo or political environment. In this model, empirical evidence is more important than practitioner-based situational leadership schemes. The ability to evaluate short-term intervening variables, establish a long-term vision, and be the primary catalyst (director) driving long-term situational change—these characteristics are the essence of the effective situational leader. According to Yukl, evaluation, learning, interpersonal, and entrepreneurial skills (from empirical evidence) are the leader's most important skills.

HARGROVE AND GLIDEWELL'S IMPOSSIBLE LEADERSHIP MODEL[62]

Hargrove and Glidewell's model is based on "impossible jobs in leadership," such as the positions filled by elected officials, appointed officials, and persons working in the public goods and services arena. In this model, coping takes center stage rather than leading: "The commissioner must always be prepared, however, for a shift in focal concerns and be ready to respond by shifting resources to possible (sometimes impossible) professional mitigation of the problems stressed by the new concerns."[63] The prudent public administrator (commissioner) learns to evaluate coalitions—political, governmental, and public—and incorporate coalition concerns into an overall vision for the organization.

An entrepreneurial leader—one who is flexible, is dynamic, and stands with expert power—is able to direct the organization through political storms, and manages and maintains emotional and structural equilibrium, through choosing and using situational coping strategies. Hargrove and Glidewell suggest that an accommodation strategy works better than a consensus-creation strategy in this kind of scenario. Public "impossible jobs" have much ambiguity and uncertainty built into the situation: "'the moves' of commissioners must conform to rules that are constantly changing; in fact, the 'players' often disagree about what the rules are."[64] To deal with this level of uncertainty, the leader must develop a firm sense of intuition.

The more able a leader is at developing contingency plans, and the better he or she masters the ability to effectively and quickly implement contingency plans, the more effective the leader is perceived to be. The leader is tied to the situation he or she inherits in the public sector, especially in "impossible-type jobs"; evaluating coalition power, establishing expert power, choosing and using coping strategies, developing a relatively short-term vision based on accommodation, and celebrating marginal intermittent victories are the essence of such a person's situational leadership model. Hargrove and Glidewell's approach suggests that the organization is the catalyst, rather than the leader, with regard to situational variables and that the "art" of the leader as practitioner is more important than the empirical evidence of effective public leadership. An effective leader who tries to control situational variables may well be a leader who can change expectations of both the political machine and the public.

ANALYSIS AND COMPARISON OF FOUR MODELS

This analysis and comparison section is intended to help readers think critically about leadership models. Can you add insights to this analysis and comparison? The four leadership models analyzed and compared are Bolman and Deal's reframing organizational leadership model, Lynn's art and science of public management model, Yukl's multiple linkage model, and Hargrove and Glidewell's impossible leadership model. The four model citations follow:

- Bolman, L. G., & Deal, T. E. (1991). *Reframing organizations: Artistry, choice, and leadership.* San Francisco: Jossey-Bass.
- Hargrove, E. C., & Glidewell, J. C. (1990). *Impossible jobs in public management.* Lawrence, KS: University Press of Kansas.

- Lynn, L. E. Jr. (1994). Public management research: The triumph of art over science. Symposium on Public Management Scholarship. *Journal of Policy Analysis and Management, 13*(2), 231–287.
- Yukl, G. (1994). *Leadership in organizations* (3rd ed.). Englewood Cliffs, NJ: Prentice Hall.

Five critical concepts can be used to evaluate the perspectives of the four models: (1) the time horizon, (2) the foundation base of the model, (3) the focal point (leader or organization centered), (4) the system employed or suggested for the leader to use, and (5) the important skills that an effective leader must possess to use the respective model. **Table 8-10** presents the analysis and comparison of the models.

Regarding the time horizon, each model takes a slightly different approach. Yukl suggests that leaders use both a short-term strategy (affect intervening variables) and a long-term strategy (develop a vision and change situational variables). Bolman and Deal take a more immediate perspective overall. Because the reframing model is organization centered, short-term horizons and decision making are more important for the individual leader in this model. Hargrove and Glidewell suggest that, due to the ambiguous and dynamic nature of public jobs, a short-term horizon is most effective for leadership flexibility. Lynn, basing the model on integrating practitioner and empirical approaches, recommends that leaders develop individual synthesized situational models; thus development is a long-term endeavor, but individual approaches can be used in both the short- and long-term time horizons.

The four models also use differing perspectives of foundational grounding. Yukl recommends that an empirically grounded model (movement toward a solid theory) is the best approach. Lynn suggests that more empirically supported approaches are needed in the leadership literature. Bolman and Deal offer both empirical support and practitioner-based foundations for their model. Due to the lack of empirical evidence and the best practices (qualitative) nature of their work, Hargrove and Glidewell's model is grounded in practitioner-based evidence.

The focal point of each model can be derived from the disciplinary perspective of the model developer(s) and from the system employed or offered for the leader to utilize. Yukl comes from the behaviorist perspective, which suggests that leaders can individually provide the momentum and the environment for successful leadership. Yukl proposes that by employing behaviors that positively influence intervening variables in the short term and by articulating a clear vision to change situational variables into a more favorable position, leaders provide the focal emphasis of organizational life. Bolman and Deal, and Hargrove and Glidewell, coming from education and public administration disciplines, respectively, and collectively from organizational theory backgrounds, recommend "an organization influences leader" type of model. Evaluation of the situation, developing frames of analysis, and choosing an appropriate frame based on organizational reality are the essence of Bolman and Deal's model, whereas Hargrove and Glidewell suggest that the organizational realities determine the leader's choice of direction and coping strategies. Lynn focuses on the leader to develop a mixed (synthesized)

Table 8-10 Analysis and Comparison of Four Leadership Models

Situational Leadership Model	Time Horizon	Foundation	Focal Point	System Employed	Important Leader Skills
Yukl	Short and long term	Empirical evidence	Leader	Leader behavior in the short term, leader vision in the long term	Evaluation, learning, behavior effectiveness, and vision development
Bolman and Deal	More short than long term	More practitioner than empirical based	Organization	Decision–support system	Evaluation, decision making, application of "inert" knowledge
Hargrove and Glidewell	Short term	Practitioner based	Organization	Coping strategies	Evaluation, accommodation, coping scheme development
Lynn	More long than short term	More empirical than practitioner based	Leader	Individualized conceptual thinking and decision–support models	Evaluation, critical thinking, synthesis of interdisciplinary work

model, individualized to the leader, based on empirical evidence and relying on practitioner-based concepts, to construct a successful situational leadership approach.

All four models suggest that a leader's skill in evaluating the situation (situational analysis) is of paramount concern. Yukl, however, includes the importance of leader behavior development (short-term requirements) and vision development. Although all of the models incorporate an implied leader decision-making requirement, the Bolman and Deal model uses decision making in differing situations as a step in the leader's sequence of "frame" analysis. Hargrove and Glidewell mandate negotiation skill—specifically, accommodation—and the development of coping strategies as skills required for the successful leader. Lynn, requiring the leader to dive deeply into Bloom's educational learning taxonomy, requires the leader to synthesize leadership literature and material to develop an individualized situational model.

The four models come from different perspectives; the critical issues, as examined here, can be arranged in a series of continua. **Figure 8-19** offers an integrated look at the four models. Each of these situational leadership approaches is embedded in the developer(s)'s disciplinary perspective. Quite reasonably, each model requires the successful leader to master situation evaluation and learning skills. From there, each model depends on different critical concepts to provide the situational leader with a basis for action and decision making.

LEADERSHIP MEASUREMENT TOOLS

Much of the leadership research has been descriptive and qualitative; by comparison, fewer quantitative data are available. As a result, qualitative research has centered on a "theory building" methodology that uses such methods as biographies, observation activities, informal interviews, and the like. In contrast, quantitative research is a "theory testing" methodology that tries to prove causality—that is, one thing causes another thing to happen. This approach is normally associated with statistical applications such as the general linear model (t-tests, analysis of variance [ANOVA], analysis of covariance [ANCOVA], regression) or relationships (such as correlations). The theories highlighted in this text are but a small sample of the myriad leadership models that have been researched throughout the history of leadership. Truly, most leadership research has been conducted using surveys, observation, and factor analysis of experts. Rarely have leadership models that link leader styles, situational variables, and outcomes (performance) been evaluated. However, the models summarized in this text form the basis of much cutting-edge leadership thinking today and are most salient for health organization leadership.

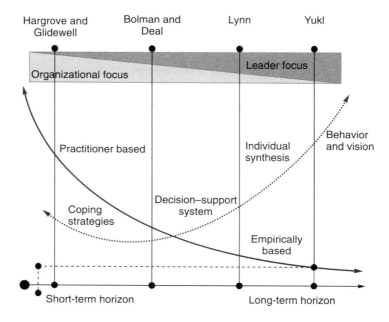

FIGURE 8-19 Four-model analysis and comparison: evaluation continua.

A review of the literature suggests that a plethora of descriptive tools are available to measure or evaluate a leader's style or success. Many of these tests use self-report scales. As a result, they introduce and maintain method bias. Despite this potential weakness, it is possible to control for bias by taking the test multiple times over a period of time. In this manner, a true response score might be found. **Table 8–11** profiles these various test tools (instruments), all of which have been used in the literature with varying degrees of utility. Although Table 8–11 is certainly not an all-inclusive list of leadership tools on the market, the goal here is to present a balanced approach to the tools on the market that are otherwise readily available and cost-efficient.

Table 8-11 Leadership Tests and Measurement Instruments

Test	Measures
Multifactor Leadership Questionnaire (MLQ)	MLQ is designed to measure various characteristics associated with transformational leadership. Three subscales pertaining to transformational leadership are included—charisma, individualized consideration, and intellectual stimulation.
Leadership Competency Inventory (LCI)	Developed for individual use, the LCI measures and identifies four competencies essential to effective leadership: information seeking, conceptual thinking, strategic orientation, and customer service orientation.
Leadership Skills Inventory (LSI)	Developed for individual use, the LSI evaluates and measures competency in terms of planning and organizational skills, oral and written communication skills, decision-making skills, financial management skills, problem-solving skills, ethics and tolerance, personal/professional balance skills, and total inventory score.
Leadership Practices Inventory (LPI), Individual Contributor	Developed for individual use, the LPI assesses five leadership practices: challenging the process, inspiring a shared vision, enabling others to act, modeling the way, and encouraging the heart.
Leadership Practices Inventory	The third edition of this instrument package approaches leadership as a measurable, learnable, and teachable set of behaviors. This 360-degree leadership assessment tool helps individuals and organizations measure their leadership competencies while guiding them through the process of applying leadership to real-life organizational challenges.
Leader Behavior Questionnaire	Developed for individual use, this instrument helps leaders to determine which changes or further skill developments are required for them to make full use of their capabilities for visionary leadership. The questionnaire is made up of 50 items measuring 10 key leadership scales: focus, respect for self and others, communication, bottom-line orientation, trust, length of vision span, risk, organizational leadership, empowerment, and cultural leadership.
Leader Behavior Analysis II, Revised	Developed for individual use, this self-scored questionnaire measures team leadership style flexibility, primary and secondary styles, effectiveness in matching leadership behaviors to the group situation, and tendencies to misuse or overuse various styles.
Leadership Team Alignment Assessment, Dynamic Culture Leadership (DCL)	The DCL instrument was developed to assess individual and group leadership versus management and science versus art "personalities" in comparison to organizational operating culture and external environment expectations. This assessment incorporates the DCL process: (1) communication improvement, (2) strategic and operational planning, (3) decision-making alignment, (4) employee enhancement, (5) knowledge management, and (6) repeat. A key premise is that a leadership team that is diverse (in leadership personalities), yet focused on organization goals, is better situated for internal and external changes and, therefore, for dynamic culture leadership.
Bolman and Deal's Reframing Organizations	This tool was developed for assessment of leadership ability in structural, human resources, political, and symbolic constructs called frames; it determines the leader's dominant, secondary, tertiary, and least apt frames.

SUMMARY

This chapter presented practical models for both students of leadership and mature practitioners of the art and science of leadership. Two evolving models and one established model of leadership were described at length: the inter-professional team model, or PAARP; the dynamic culture leadership model; and the reframing organizations leadership model created by Bolman and Deal. These models can assist young leaders in honing their personal leadership practice; they are intended to invoke thought, reflection, and discussion. They are also prescriptive in that they provide a strategy for success and a model for practical implementation. Other differing, yet contemporary, situational leadership models were also presented from Lynn (leadership art and science in public leadership and management model), Yukl (multiple linkage model), and Hargrove and Glidewell (impossible leadership model). A variety of leadership measurement tools are also available with which to conduct personal and organizational evaluations.

DISCUSSION QUESTIONS

1. Discuss the constructs and processes of at least two contemporary leadership models presented in this chapter and name the prescriptive mechanisms of those models.
2. Interpret the differences of at least two of the contemporary leadership models in this chapter from one other leadership theory or model from the situational leadership thought phase. Why did you select those models?
3. Explain how you would apply at least one contemporary leadership model from this chapter to a real or hypothesized health leadership situation or case; explain the rationale for your decisions, actions, and behaviors.
4. Identify and discuss the contemporary leadership models' constructs that enable a health leader to develop, modify, or revise organizational culture in a health enterprise.
5. How would you create a leadership model—either simple or complex—for your own use in health organizations? Relate your model to constructs found in models from this chapter and other constructs from theories and models you have learned about elsewhere.
6. Select two models from this chapter. Compare and contrast those contemporary leadership models. Is one better for leadership use in health organizations?

EXERCISES

1. In a two-page paper, outline the constructs and processes of at least two contemporary leadership models presented in this chapter, and state the prescriptive mechanisms of those models.
2. In a three-page paper, identify the differences between at least two of the contemporary leadership models in this chapter from one other leadership theory or model from the situational leadership thought phase.
3. Apply at least one contemporary leadership model from this chapter to a real or hypothesized health leadership situation or case; explain the rationale for your decisions, actions, and behaviors in three pages or less. Complete at least one leadership assessment from this chapter and report the results in one page or less.
4. In a two-page paper, analyze and illustrate the contemporary leadership models' constructs that enable a health leader to develop, modify, or revise organizational culture in a health enterprise.
5. In a paper that is 10 pages or less, create a leadership model—either simple or complex—for your own use in health organizations and relate your model to constructs found in models from this chapter and other constructs from theories and models.
6. In a three-page paper, compare and contrast two or more contemporary leadership models. An example can be found within this chapter, but do not use those specific models in your own work.

REFERENCES

1. CBS News. (2013). The 10 Rules of Great Groups. Retrieved from http://www.cbsnews.com/news/the-10-rules-of-great-groups/.
2. MindTools. (2007). Locke's goal-setting theory: Setting meaningful and challenging goals. Retrieved from https://www.mindtools.com/pages/article/newHTE_87.htm.
3. MindTools, note 2.
4. MindTools, note 2.
5. MindTools, note 2.
6. (2011). The theory of planned behavior, operationalized. Retrieved from http://publichealthnerds.blogspot.com/2011/06/theory-of-planned-behavior.html.
7. Beebe, S. A., & Masterson, J. T. (1997). *Communicating in small groups: Principles and practices* (5th ed.). New York: Addison-Wesley Educational Publishers.
8. Coppola, M. N. (2008, May/June). Managing teams in organizations. *Healthcare Executive, 23*(3), 70–74.
9. Coppola, note 8.
10. Coppola, note 8.
11. Folger, J. P., Poole, M. S., & Stutman, R. K. (1997). *Working through conflict: Strategies for relationships, groups, and organizations* (3rd ed.). New York: Longman.
12. West, R., & Turner, L. H. *Introducing communication theory analysis and application* (3rd ed.). McGraw-Hill Higher Education, p. 111.
13. Folger et al., note 11.
14. West & Turner, note 12, p. 111.
15. West & Turner, note 12, p. 111.
16. Folger et al., note 11.
17. Folger et al., note 11.
18. Interprofessional Education Collaborative Expert Panel (IECEP). (2011). Core competencies for interprofessional collaborative practice: Report of an expert panel. Washington, D.C.: Interprofessional Education Collaborative. Retrieved from http://www.aacn.nche.edu/education-resources/ipecreport.pdf.
19. IECEP, note 18.
20. IECEP, note 18.
21. IECEP, note 18.
22. IECEP, note 18.
23. IECEP, note 18.
24. IECEP, note 18.
25. Locke, E. A. (1968). Toward a theory of task motivation and incentives. *Organizational Behavior and Human Performance, 5*, 157–189.
26. Locke, E. A., & Latham, G. P. (1984). *Goal setting, a motivational technique that works!* Englewood Cliffs, NJ: Prentice-Hall, Inc.
27. Mento, A. J., Locke, E. A., & Klein, H. J. (1992, August). Relationship of goal level to valence and instrumentality. *Journal of Applied Psychology, 77*(4), 395–405.
28. Woolard, D. (2009). *Path–goal theory of leadership.* Campbell University, Buies Creek, NC.
29. (2013). Path–Goal Theory of Leadership. Retrieved from http://www.nwlink.com/~donclark/leader/lead_path_goal.html.
30. Kelley, R. E. (1988). In praise of followers. *Harvard Business Review, 66*, 142–148.
31. Schein, E. H. (1999). *The corporate culture survival guide: Sense and nonsense about culture change.* San Francisco, CA: Jossey-Bass.
32. Ledlow, G., Cwiek, M., & Johnson, J. (2002). Dynamic culture leadership: Effective leader as both scientist and artist. Global Business and Technology Association (GBATA) International Conference; Beyond Boundaries: Challenges of Leadership, Innovation, Integration and Technology; N. Delener & C-N. Chao (Eds.), pp. 694–740. First reported in the GBATA publication and provided again herein with permission by New Visions Network, LLC.
33. Ledlow et al., note 32.
34. Busch, M., & Hostetter, C. (2009). Examining organizational learning for application in human service organizations. *Administration in Social Work, 33*(3), 297–318.
35. Conger, J., & Toegel, G. (2002). A story of missed opportunities: Qualitative methods for leadership research and practice. In K. W. Parry & J. R. Meindl (Eds.), *Grounding leadership theory and research: Issues, perspectives, and methods* (pp. 175–197). Greenwich, CT: Information Age Publishing.
36. Jelinek, M., & Litterer, J. A. (1995). Toward entrepreneurial organizations: Meeting ambiguity with engagement. *Entrepreneurship: Theory and Practice, 19*(3), 137–169.
37. Schein, E. H. (1999). *The corporate culture survival guide: Sense and nonsense about culture change.* San Francisco, California: Jossey-Bass.
38. Yukl, G. (1994). *Leadership in organizations* (3rd ed.). Englewood Cliffs, NJ: Prentice Hall, p. 355.
39. Schein, note 37.
40. Schein, note 37.

41. Friesen, M., & Johnson, J. (1995). *The success paradigm*. London: Quorum.

42. Bolman, L. G., & Deal, T. E. (1991). *Reframing organizations: Artistry, choice, and leadership*. San Francisco, CA: Jossey-Bass.

43. Sasnett, B., & Clay, M. (2008). Leadership styles in interdisciplinary health science education. *Journal of Interprofessional Care, 22*(6), 630–638.

44. Bolman & Deal, note 42, p. 121.

45. Bolman & Deal, note 42, pp. 121–122.

46. Bolman & Deal, note 42, pp. 152–153.

47. Bolman & Deal, note 42, p. 154.

48. Bolman & Deal, note 42, pp. 189–190.

49. Bolman & Deal, note 42, pp. 203–204.

50. Bolman & Deal, note 42, pp. 244–245.

51. Bolman & Deal, note 42, p. 261.

52. Bolman & Deal, note 42, p. 434.

53. Bolman & Deal, note 42, p. 435.

54. Bolman & Deal, note 42, p. 445.

55. Bolman & Deal, note 42, p. 445.

56. Bolman & Deal, note 42, p. 445.

57. Bolman & Deal, note 42, pp. 448–449.

58. Lynn, L. E. Jr. (1994). Public management research: The triumph of art over science. *Symposium on Public Management Scholarship, Journal of Policy Analysis and Management, 13*(2), 231–287.

59. Lynn, note 58, p. 249.

60. Lynn, L. E. Jr. (1987). *Managing public policy*. Boston: Little, Brown.

61. Yukl, note 38.

62. Hargrove, E. C., & Glidewell, J. C. (1990). *Impossible jobs in public management*. Lawrence, KS: University Press of Kansas.

63. Hargrove & Glidewell, note 62, p. 34.

64. Hargrove & Glidewell, note 62, p. 39.

© Murat Inan / EyeEm / Getty Images.

LEADERSHIP IN HEALTH ORGANIZATIONS

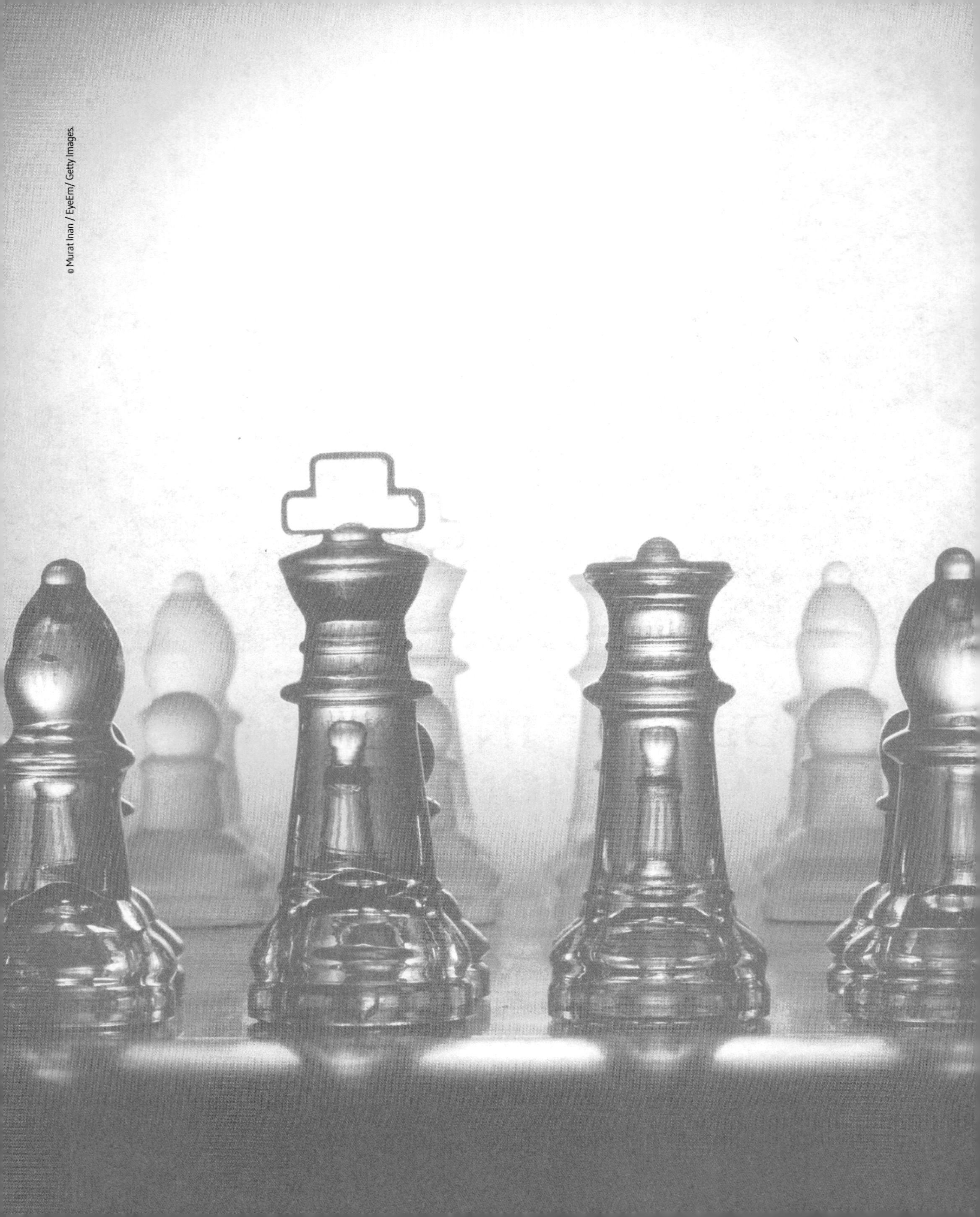

LEADERSHIP AND THE COMPLEX HEALTH ORGANIZATION: STRATEGICALLY MANAGING THE ORGANIZATIONAL ENVIRONMENT BEFORE IT MANAGES YOU

We need leadership on the fundamentals of eating right, exercising, and not smoking. I am interested in getting people to use the healthcare system at the right time, getting them to see the doctor early enough, before a small health problem turns serious.
Donna Shalala, President of the University of Miami[1]

This chapter discusses the leader's role in strategically leading the organization. Basic principles of creating and implementing a mission, vision, value, strategies, goals, objective statements, and action steps are presented. A matrix tool that assists in understanding relationships within the environment that affect organizational culture and change management is also described. In addition, the leader's self-awareness and understanding of cultural factors are emphasized in terms of their effects on organizational change. The chapter concludes with an emphasis on strategic leadership options for managing organizational culture change.

LEARNING OBJECTIVES

1. Identify the strategic direction elements of the strategic plan, identify the other elements of the strategic and operational plan, describe each of these elements in summary, and outline which internal and external environmental factors influence the strategic plan to include strategic sourcing.

2. Distinguish the levels of organizational culture, and summarize the actions and behaviors a health leader would perform to proactively and positively change organizational culture.

3. Predict how strategic planning might positively influence organizational culture and the internal environment; describe how strategy selection (e.g., competitive, adaptive) reinforces those changes to organizational culture and the internal environment and its impact on strategic sourcing.

4. Analyze how external and internal environmental factors influence the strategic plan and the organizational culture of a health organization.

5. Design a methodology to perform internal environmental scanning, monitoring, and assessment and external environmental scanning, forecasting, and monitoring for a hospital or group practice, public health organization, long-term care organization, stand-alone allied health practice, or retail pharmacy.

6. Interpret the current external environmental factors in the health industry; turn the interpretation into a critical list for action for a health organization; and appraise each element on the critical list for action as to where it should be addressed by the health organization (e.g., strategic plan, directional strategies, external or internal environment, organizational culture), noting that critical list items may affect more than one area of the health organization.

MISSION, VISION, VALUES, STRATEGIES, GOALS, OBJECTIVES, AND ACTION STEPS

Leaders in health organizations utilize a strategic system of leadership and management. Much of the literature uses the phrase "strategic management system" to describe this system. In reality, a more appropriate name for it is "strategic system of leadership and management," because people are led and resources are managed: Human resources are "managed" from the context of a strategic human resources system, considering job analysis, job design, and the like, but the people need to be led. From this context, the dynamic culture leadership (DCL) model, for example, ascribes to a strategic system of leadership and management with a heavy emphasis on organizational culture. Embedding a strategic and operational planning structure and process, with feedback loops, into the organizational culture is paramount for organizations if they hope to survive in dynamic conditions. Regardless of organizational type, or industry, or size, strategic systems are required. Indeed,

as complexity increases, these systems become even more critical, as long as the leadership holds to a consistent application of the system and organizational values.

Health organizations are complex and are of varying sizes. Sizes range from small solo physician practices, to a town pharmacy, to an integrated group practice, to a rehabilitation company, to a stand-alone hospital, to a large integrated health system. Regardless of the size of the health organization, the speed of change, the complexity of the health industry, and the expectations of perfection by society, all health organizations require leaders' wise use of mission, vision, values, strategies, goals, objectives, and action steps to steer their course. Health leaders use these elements to guide the organization; develop and maintain an effective, efficient, and efficacious organizational culture; and focus the collective energy of the health organization where people are led and resources are managed. The health leadership team most likely will utilize a strategic and operational planning process to formally develop an organization's mission, vision, strategies, goals, objectives, and action steps. As part of this effort, each element of strategic and operational planning will be discussed in rational groupings.

Mission, vision, and values are guideposts[2] that leaders use to focus the health organization's collective energy and resources. "Mission, vision, values, and strategic goals are appropriately called directional strategies because they guide strategists when they make key organizational decisions."[3] A health organization's mission is tied to its purpose. Purpose is what the organization does every day to meet the needs and demands of the external environment (patients, customers, and stakeholders) and to deliver its outputs to a community in some competitive way (effective, efficient, efficacious, and available). Stakeholders include those individuals, groups, community members (individual and collective), and companies that interact with the organization, such as patients, customers, staff members, suppliers, and the community. Stakeholders can directly and indirectly influence the success of the organization.

An extension of purpose is the health organization's mission. Mission is why the organization exists, which business it is in, who it serves, and where it provides its products or services. Swayne, Duncan, and Ginter defined characteristics of mission statements as follows:

1. Mission statements are broadly defined statements of purpose;
2. Mission statements are enduring;
3. Mission statements should underscore the uniqueness of the organization; and
4. Mission statements should identify the scope of operations in terms of service and market.[4]

Vision is an aspiration for what the organization intends to become—that is, the shared image of the future organization that places the organization in a better position to perform its mission and fulfill its purpose. In essence, vision is the dream of what the organization can become. Values are the beliefs and attitudes that an organization holds that guide day-to-day decision making, behavior, and actions. Health leaders "acquire vision from an appreciation of the history of the organization, a perception of the opportunities present in the environment, and an understanding of the strategic capacity of the organization to take advantage of these opportunities. These factors work together to form an organization's hope for the future."[5]

The purpose of a vision statement is to provide a group, organization, or community with a shared image of its direction over the long term. It catalyzes a group's efforts and focuses decisions. Vision statements should:

1. Describe an organization's big picture and project its future;
2. Be grounded in sound knowledge of the business;
3. Be concrete and as specific as practical;
4. Contrast the present and the future;

5. Stretch the imaginations and creative energies of people in the organization;
6. Have a sense of significance; and they should matter.[6,7]

Leaders must be ever cognizant of the need to be consistent in the development of a mission statement and a vision statement and the need to embrace the values that the health organization holds as important. Yukl suggests using the mission and vision development process as a means for leaders to transform organizations by developing a strategic vision in consultation with the senior leadership team, articulating a clear and appealing vision, developing (senior leadership ownership required) a strategy or strategies to attain the vision, and focusing on the core mission(s) of the organization.[8] Schein argues that mission, vision, and strategies are essential for external adaptation—that is, for conforming with the expectations of the external environment—for organizations.[9] Senior leadership must be committed to and involved in the process of mission and vision statement development, but also involve its subordinates and staff in the process as well.[10]

Morris and Senge call strategists (in this case, health organization strategists) "pathfinders" in that they provide a vision, determine the approaches the organization will take to realize the vision, and provide a clear methodology to implement the plan and succeed.[11,12] Where there is no vision, the people perish.[13] Health leaders are clearly in the "pathfinder" role for their organizations. "Strategic processes encompass a wide range of topics including analysis, planning, decision making and many aspects of an organization's culture, vision and value system."[14]

Strategies, goals, and objectives are the sequential building blocks of planning to successfully achieve the mission, but also for striving to achieve the vision of the health organization. "Strategic goals are those over-arching end results that the organization pursues to accomplish its mission and achieve its vision."[15] Strategies follow "a decision logic of development."[16] Directional strategies lead to adaptive strategies, market entry strategies, and competitive strategies; each of these strategies should also have its own implementation strategy.[17] **Figure 9-1** summarizes the types, scope, and role of strategy.

Goals translate the broad strategies of the vision into specific statements for organizational action by focusing the organizational resources to achieve the strategy and build the vision. Goals are broader statements—sometimes aspirations—that are hierarchically above objectives. Objectives align organizational resources to meet the stated goals. Objectives should be measurable, assigned to a responsible person (agent or owner), have time lines for completion, and be frequently reviewed by the health organization leadership

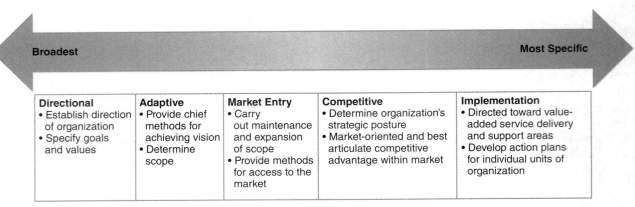

FIGURE 9-1 Strategy taxonomy, scope, and roles.

Swayne, L. E., Duncan, W. J., & Ginter, P. M. (2006). *Strategic management of health care organizations* (5th ed.). Malden, MA: Blackwell, p. 229, Exhibit 6-3.

for progress and resource sufficiency. Action steps (or action plans) are created to produce a step-by-step or task-level implementation sequence for each objective. Each task in the action steps (or plan) has a responsible person (or owner) and a time range for accomplishment, and some tasks may have a measurable variable as well. Action step owners "report" to the objective owner, who "reports" to the goal owner, who ultimately reports to the leadership team; the senior leadership team directs the organization at the strategy level.

Mission, vision, values, strategies, goals, objectives, and action steps are essential components of the strategic system of leadership and management. Health leaders utilize the strategic system's tools, such as planning (strategic and operational), to transform, guide, and develop organizational culture, thereby focusing the collective energy and resources of the health organization to effectively, efficiently, and efficaciously serve its purpose. "Strategy-making processes are organizational-level phenomena involving key decisions made on behalf of the entire organization."[18] Vital to strategic thinking, planning, and implementation, understanding the internal environment of the health organization is of paramount concern for the health leader; in fact, Roney suggests that internal assessment is a basic component of any comprehensive plan.[19]

UNDERSTANDING THE INTERNAL ENVIRONMENT

Internal scanning, monitoring, and assessment of the health organization are vital leadership activities. It is well known that effective leaders are effective internal organization scanners, monitors, and assessors. Research on internal organizational scanning, monitoring, and assessment consistently

points to active and ongoing leadership emphasis in this arena. In 1986, Komaki reported that leaders and managers who did more monitoring were more effective; in 1990, Yukl found that school principals who monitored internal activity well had higher scholastic achievement in their schools; and in 1987, Jenster noted that successful firms that monitored the progress of their strategic plans performed much better than their competitors.[20]

The most important elements of understanding the internal health organization's environment should focus on systems such as the human resources management system, supply chain system, technological system, information system, and culture and subcultures. The salient theme is one of integrated synergy among all the health organization's systems. Specific areas of scanning, monitoring, and assessing for the health leader include the following issues:

- Competitive advantage and the unique or distinctive competencies the organization possesses (e.g., centers of excellence)
- Strengths and weaknesses of the organization
- Functional strategies for implementation of strategies that are supported by goals, objectives, and action steps
- Operational effectiveness, efficiency, and efficacy
- Organizational culture (Is the culture aligned with the organization's direction?)

Health leaders must create a well-thought-out approach to internal scanning, monitoring, and assessing of the organization against the current strategic and operational plans (which focus effort toward the organization's vision and mission) and the fit with the external environment. How the health leader conducts these processes depends on the viewpoint (or paradigm or context). Leaders develop assumptions and constraints that are internally oriented to achieve understanding of the internal environment. Assumptions in this context are internal (rooted in organizational circumstances) and characterized by a situation or state that exists now or will exist in the future and guides thinking. Constraints include any current conditions that may prevent strategies or goals from being pursued in striving to meet the organizational vision. Constraints are rooted in existing rules, traditions, habits, policies, social norms, or laws that set parameters on what an organization or individual can do.

The remainder of this section discusses topics involved in understanding the internal organizational environment; organizational culture is discussed later in this chapter.

INSTITUTIONAL FACTORS

Institutional organizations and environments highlight the importance of social, political, and psychological aspects of organizational dynamics. There is really no mystery why so many health organizations are so similar when looking at basic processes and policies. According to Powell and DiMaggio, the creation of a field of organizations triggers a paradox—namely, that rational actors make the organizations similar as they simultaneously try to change the organizations.[21,22]

An understanding of what constitutes a field is useful in understanding the constructs of institutional theory. Organizations are considered to be in a field if they are institutionally defined and dependent on structural equivalence—that is, if there is a need for an organization to meet certain established competencies that prevent competing organizations from becoming too dissimilar. This situation is an example of the "walks like a duck, looks like a duck, and quacks like a duck" phenomenon: Then it must be a duck. It is important for health leaders to appreciate the fact that a successful CEO in one health organization will likely be successful in another health organization due to the basic organizational similarities found across the field. Much of this success derives from leaders' mastery of "run" stage competencies and thorough understanding of the context of health. The process of defining institutional organizations and environments can be judged based on four dynamics:[23–25]

- An increase in the interaction among organizations in a particular group
- Emergence of interorganizational structures, domination, and patterns of coalition
- An increase in the information load that an organization must address
- A mutual "awareness" among participants in a set or organizations that they are involved in a common enterprise

Institutional Factors vs. Institutionalization

Leaders must make a distinction and be aware of the benefits of an institutional view versus becoming institutionalized within thought and actions. As noted, an institutional view is helpful in establishing norms in the field, communicating standards of practice, and creating benchmarks that others can view as examples of excellence. An institutional view also can assist leaders in maintaining effectiveness within the profession. However, leaders who take on an institutional view without recognizing important changes in culture, climate, and environment can become extremely ineffective as well. Leaders who become resistant to change find their opinions so rooted in arrogance that they often become positions of pride rather than evidence. Such is the case with distance learning education and some outside stakeholder organizations. Although the U.S. Department of Education has found "… on average, students in online learning conditions performed modestly better than those receiving face-to-face instruction,"[26] leaders in some accrediting, professional, traditional, and fixed facility organizations still have a baseless bias against distance learning education. This institutionalized and unsupported opinion will ultimately lead to a loss of market share, talent recruiting, and productivity for those institutionalized organizations (or leaders) over time.

The Institutional View

The institutional view, in essence, is an assessment of the organization's situation compared with a health leader's predetermined standard, benchmark, or expectations relative to competitors.[27] In this context, organizational strengths and weaknesses are determined, unique organizational competencies are compiled, and functional-level implementation strategies are assessed.

Part of this effort involves listing the organization's strengths and weaknesses. Strengths are what the organization does well, which elements create a competitive advantage, and what makes the organization uniquely appealing to the external environment. Conversely, weaknesses are those elements that the organization does not do well or lacks and that make the organization appear less desirable in the external environment. Health leaders must make difficult decisions to lessen or remove weaknesses in their organization, whereas strengths are highlighted and used as building blocks for future expansion.

Unique health organization competencies are focused to create competitive advantage. Competencies merge with resources and processes (or systems—that is, a group of processes) to create capabilities; the assessment of capabilities determines the level of competitive advantage a specific capability confers upon the health organization. Once strengths and weaknesses are determined, how the health organization compares to its competitors and to relevant standards (such as the professional or national standard of care) enables an honest assessment of the organization's competitive advantage. What the organization does—its purpose—is assessed. The assessment should be performed on the patient or customer flow process of preservice (what exists and is accomplished before caring for a patient), point of service (the patient care process and experience), and after service (patient interaction and organizational activity after the care process); it should also be performed on the organizational culture, structure, and strategic resources (e.g., technology, supply chain, human resources, information systems). The results may then be compared to competitors' performance, with competitive advantage being defined in terms of those organizational characteristics that are evaluated as valuable, rare, imitable, and sustainable.[28] From this assessment, advantages and disadvantages can be discerned. Of equal importance, implementation strategies must be scanned, monitored, and assessed.

Understanding the implementation of strategies in a health organization can be complex. Nevertheless, with a thorough plan and teamwork, implementation strategies can be assessed effectively. Implementation of any strategy is key to success; a strategy in and of itself does nothing if it is not put into practice. Given that many health organizations have similar competencies and enjoy only subtle competitive advantages relative to their competitors, implementation is a very essential organizational "skill" that health leaders must build into their organizations. In fact, effective implementation may be the best competitive advantage a health organization possesses. Implementation strategies are also called functional strategies and operational strategies: Do not let the terminology confuse you—implementation is concerned with putting a strategy into practice, utilizing the strategy, and gaining from the strategy.

In implementation, vertical and horizontal fit are important aspects of assessment. *Vertical fit* comprises the congruence, interoperability, and seamlessness between *different* organizational levels in putting a strategy into practice. In vertical fit assessment and strategic implementation, the following leadership concerns are vital:

- Organizational coupling (adherence to rules, policies, procedures, and norms)
- Interdependence between organizational units (interdependence creates uncertainty)
- Similarity in work functions between units (similarity in work units creates ambiguity)

- Quality control and in-progress reviews
- Communication

An assessment of these concerns to reduce weak points and flaws, the appropriate allocation of resources, leadership communication of expectations, goal setting, frequent communication between team members, and appropriate leadership intervention, guidance, and rewards during the process is essential.

Horizontal fit is the coordination and integration of different actions, tasks, functions, or processes performed at the same organizational level. Health leaders should consider this assessment from a coordination (sequencing, serial, or parallel processing) perspective; however, similar concerns exist as in assessment of vertical fit.

Institutional organizations focus on the reproduction of organizational activities and routines in response to external pressures, expectations of professionals in the industry, and collective norms of the institutional environment. In this manner, organizations hold themselves hostage to coercive (outside stakeholders telling them what to do), normative (making efforts to benchmark against like organizations in the same field), and mimetic mechanisms (copying the best practices and procedures of similar organizations despite the fact that the organization may or may not have a structure that supports the practice). These behaviors continue to make the organization more similar to other like organizations without necessarily making it more efficient. Health leaders in highly institutional organizations would be wise to become rapidly familiar with the environmental pressures of coercion, mimicry, and other normative external pressures.

Institutional Environments

Overall, institutional environments are preoccupied with ensuring that the correct and appropriate structures and processes are used to pursue organizational goals and objectives. Institutional constraints consist of elaborate rules and regulations to which organizations must conform if they are to receive support and gain legitimacy. Institutional organizations tend to be tightly coupled across all policies, procedures, and cultural norms. In this environment, the leader may be bound to policies so massive that even the simplest new actions and changes require more effort than they are worth.[29] The only way to uncouple this kind of binding to an institutional environment is to reengineer the organization. Entire departments, many personnel, and a wealth of practices may need to be eliminated and new ones established in their place to alter this tightly coupled situation.

Most often, health organizations are a hybrid of institutional and technical environments. Technical environments exist where there is a need for interdisciplinary teamwork and varied skill sets that enable organizations to manage, control, and coordinate work processes effectively, while buffering them from environmental institutional disturbances. Technical environments are characterized by barriers to entry into the industry due to the vastness of knowledge, skills, and abilities of professionals in that environment as well as the high cost of the technology required to produce the products and services of the industry. The medical care sector, for example, seems to combine relatively strong institutional and technical environmental forces.[30] In a very real sense, the "environment" is linked to the organizational culture of that particular organization. "Culture gives people a sense of who they are, of belonging, of how they should behave, and of what they should be doing. Culture impacts behavior, morale, and productivity at work, and includes values and patterns that influence company attitudes and actions. Culture is dynamic. Cultures change ... but slowly."[31]

The structural contingency theory[32] (SCT) is an organizational theory that includes the environment as a major associating factor. The basis of this theory involves three points: there is no one "best" way to organize actions, not all ways are equal in effectiveness, and the "better" ways depend on the organizational environment. Larger organizations have an advantage when it comes to SCT because these organizations are abundant in power and resources and are able to try out new strategies without fear of serious adverse reactions in times of environmental change.

The SCT emphasizes that there is no universal best organizational structure. Instead, an organizational structure must be carefully planned and executed based on the environment. That being said, the environment will change and successful organizations should be able to adapt to alteration quickly and efficiently. SCT states that the survival of the organization depends on its ability to adapt to the surrounding environment.

RESOURCE DEPENDENCY

The resource-dependent organization desires to maintain autonomy and remain relatively independent of its environment. At the same time, organizations also recognize the need to form coalitions to bring together resources to help reduce transaction costs. If the environment is unstable, organizations may be less likely to rely on other organizations for support. The stability of the environment may be evaluated by assessing the number and types of organizations, the munificence of those organizations (maturity and

size), and the interconnectedness of those organizations (competition and complexity of relationships).

Resource-dependent organizations also assume that leaders can actively increase an organization's effectiveness and influence the environment. *Effectiveness* is defined as the ability to create acceptable outcomes and actions as perceived by outside organizations and agents.[33] In the health arena, the supply chain component of the organization, and of the industry for that matter, may fit best within this typological category.

One of the basic propositions governing the resource-dependent organization is that leaders must be aware that the most efficient or effective organizations do not always survive. Rather—and perhaps not surprisingly—the organizations with the most power survive. Power is defined as the ability to secure and maintain the most stable and most respected networks of resource chains. Key steps in maintaining power include preparing contingency plans for potential environmental shifts, building redundant networks, and establishing an efficient value chain. As in the supply chain example, volume of purchases and extensiveness of supplier networks act as the power behind efficient and effective supply chain operations in health.

For example, in a stable and healthy environment, resource chains may be several levels deep and have many redundant alternatives. In this milieu, an organization's power may be affected by the introduction of more influential organizations into the environment or by the scarcity of resources and resource levels in periods of environmental famine. Organizations are vulnerable if vital resources are controlled by other organizations, such as manufacturers and distributors of medical equipment, supplies, and pharmaceuticals. Thus organizations purposefully engage in networks of interorganizational relationships to obtain the needed resources and improve their survival chances. In the end, the organization with the best access to suppliers, customers, regulators, and competitors holds the most power in the market and has the greatest survival potential.[34]

The resource-dependent view is also an inventory of the health organization within the context of how it serves its purpose in the external environment. In this paradigm, the health organization's resources, capabilities, competencies, core competencies, and distinctive competencies are assessed.[35] "Resources are the stocks of human and nonhuman factors that are available for use in producing goods and services. Resources may be tangible, as in the case of land, labor, and capital, or they may be intangible, as in the case of intellectual property [includes business and care processes], reputation, and goodwill."[36] Similar to the institutional view, the organization's list of resources and competencies is assessed to determine their value, rareness, imitability, durability, and ultimate importance to the organization.

Definition of these terms in this context is appropriate. *Value* is the subjective worth of the organization's resources in the practice of "purpose" as it delivers its services and products to the external environment; surrogate measures of value can be market share, lives saved, procedures successfully performed, number and percentage of patients successfully treated, percentage of return patients or customers, and financial statements (considered subjective in this context because a financial statement is temporal). *Rareness* reflects how likely one would be able to find the services, products, and processes in the external environment; rareness would denote that one would not find a similar set of services or products or processes. (Of course, a health organization can be rare but of little or marginal value.) *Imitability* describes the speed with which the health organization's resources, processes, and capabilities can be duplicated or copied by other health organizations. *Durability* indicates the speed with which a health organization's resources, processes, and capabilities become obsolete or unusable; this issue is especially important considering the expected standard of care in the health industry.

Health leaders should continuously build and improve the resource and competencies list in this view as assessed by the directional strategies and strategic goals of the organization. A strengths and weaknesses assessment, as discussed previously within the institutional view, is a valuable tool in this context as well. A five-step approach to strategy analysis in this paradigm follows:

1. Identify and classify resources.
2. Combine strengths and turn them into capabilities.
3. Appraise the profit (margin, for nonprofit organizations) potential of capabilities.
4. Select the strategy that best serves the organization given the macro and micro external environmental factors.
5. Identify resource gaps and invest in weaknesses.[37]

Resource-Dependent Environments

In a resource-dependent environment, the organization requires resources to gain and maintain power and, therefore, must (sometimes reluctantly) interact with the environment.[38] At the same time, a resource-dependent organization conceptualizes the environment in terms of other organizations with which the focal organization engages in exchange relationships. The closed-panel health maintenance organization (HMO) is an example of this type of environment. In this situation, leaders want total control of empanelled providers, enrolled beneficiaries, referrals,

and practice plans; they want to dictate the types of services provided and have governance over all other practices and procedures. Today, closed-panel HMOs—at least under the original model developed by Kaiser Permanente—cannot expect to survive for long periods of time in the free market. Leaders who try to maintain a hermetically sealed organization and operation fail to achieve economies of scale and scope and often lose competitive advantage.[39]

CONTINGENCY

Contingent organizations are more flexible and rely less on rigid policies and practices. These organizations utilize more loosely established internal best practices; hence they are described as "loosely coupled." Within this type of organization, a leader's success is based on a unique amalgamation of internal and external factors—that is, organizational and environmental factors are contingent on one another. Leaders of contingent organizations base many of their assumptions on the fact that many aspects of organizational survival are dependent on factors beyond the organization's control. For the organization to achieve a "good fit" and survive, internal and external demands on the organization must be balanced effectively given the environment. The leadership approach is always based on the organization's current situation in this model. Leaders of this type of organization know that what makes an organization successful today may not keep it successful tomorrow.[40]

The underlying assumptions of contingent organizations are based on the premise that organizational structures are open and are not organizationally egalitarian: There is no one best way to organize, and any one way of organizing is not equally effective in another organization. In keeping with this last postulate, what might work in one organization with one set of particular environmental conditions and employees may not work in a similar organization with its own set of conditions and employees, regardless of the similarity of the organizations.[41]

The contingent view utilizes a scenario-based methodology. Health leaders use an institutional, resource-dependent, or combined approach to scan, monitor, and assess the internal organizational environment, create various likely scenarios for the organization (possible futures in which the organization would survive and thrive), and assess the internal organization's strengths, weaknesses, competencies, patient or customer processes (preservice, point of service, and after service), and implementation strategies against those scenarios. Each scenario requires the internal organization to be evaluated in terms of its value, rareness, imitability, sustainability, durability, vertical and horizontal fit of strategy implementation, and impact on and congruence with organizational culture. Assessment as compared to competitors, potential competitors, and macro- and micro-environmental changes should be conducted routinely. A method for evaluating internal health organizations is provided in **Table 9-1**; multiple contingent scenarios can be evaluated by scoring each scenario against the others.

Leaders operating an organization that practices a contingent strategy need to be aware that the organization's growth may not always support the contingent strategy. *Size* refers to the scale and scope of an organization, especially the number of individuals to be organized. Contingent organizations suggest that size is positively correlated with increasing levels of bureaucratic scale

within organizations. Child provided empirical evidence that size and bureaucratic structure are related to organizational performance: As organizational size increases, a higher degree of routinization is required (i.e., more policies, procedures, and tighter coupling).[42] Furthermore, larger organizations tend to be more highly diverse in terms of organizational structure, be more vertical (more levels of hierarchy), and have greater horizontal differentiation (more divisions and a greater span of control). As a result, growth of contingent organizations suggests a need for a wide variety of specialized tasks; these include larger administrative components, in terms of both the number of hierarchical levels and the number of internal support personnel required.[43]

Table 9-1 Internal Health Organization Assessment

Current Institutional Resource	Value (1–10, where 10 is best)	Rareness (1–10, where 10 is best)	Imitability (1–10, where 10 is best)	Sustainability (1–10, where 10 is best)	Durability (1–10, where 10 is best)	Fit (Vertical and/or Horizontal) (1–10, where 10 is best)	Organizational Culture (1–10, where 10 is best)
Strengths (list and score each)							
Weaknesses (list and score each as a 1–10 negative number to show how weak each item is)							
Competencies (list and score each)							
Capabilities (list and score each)							
Implementation strategies (list and score each)							
Patient or customer flow process (list [preservice, point of service, and after service] and score each)							
Organizational culture							

Contingent Environments

An important factor for a leader operating an organization in a contingent environment is that as the environment becomes more uncertain, organizations respond by employing strategies that change structural characteristics of the organization.[44] Furthermore, organizations tend to cope with uncertainty from the environment by buffering their technical core and protecting the main revenue generation processes of the organization from outside influences. For example, pharmaceutical companies threatened by the expiration of patents and the possible introduction of generic drugs that threaten their profits and market share may develop a similar product line in which the same pill needs to be taken only once a week instead of daily. By doing so, the organization protects its technical core under a fallacy of daily dosage quality. Leaders in this type of organization use symbolic and political messages more often in times of uncertainty and ambiguity than structural or human resources–oriented pronouncements.

MATRIX ASSESSMENT

An assessment tool can be a good starting point to assess the internal environment. Taking internal environmental scanning, assessing, and monitoring into account, the successful health leader will create a system, method, or set of tools with which to understand the internal situation. Table 9-1 shows an example of this kind of tool.

As in the contingent health organization, scenarios are developed as possible future states for the organization. Using the tool in Table 9-1, each scenario is scored and ranked. Each scenario should be ranked regarding the likelihood of its being fulfilled or realized; then the table rankings and scenarios are compared.

The next phase envisions how to transform the health organization to serve its purpose, fulfill its mission, and achieve its vision in the external environment. What would be required to change weaknesses into strengths (or at least render the factor neutral) for the health organization? What should be changed to improve or change competencies that can be translated into needed or demanded capabilities? Which revisions or resources would be necessary to improve implementation strategies, and which changes would be needed to develop a more appropriate organizational culture? **Table 9-2** can serve as a catalyst for this thought process.

A thorough and continuous internal health organization scanning, monitoring, and assessment system will serve leaders, managers, and the organization as a whole very well. Understanding "who" and "what" the health organization is as part of its current status or "state of nature" is a critical element to leading people and managing resources. Internal assessment is a tangible method for understanding the integration of all of the various resources and capabilities of a complex health organization. How the health organization fits with and serves its purpose in the community is of utmost importance to the leader and leadership team. Understanding the external environment—the topic of the next section—is the next major challenge.

Table 9-2 Improvement of Internal Health Organization							
Internal Component (State for each component)	Goal (State in simple terms)	Expectation (State in simple terms what is expected from this effort)	Tangible Resources Required (List land, labor, and capital)	Intangible Resources Required (List processes, intellectual property, reputation, and goodwill)	Expected Cost of Resources (List each resource needed and its approximate cost, and sum the costs)	Time Range to Complete (Provide a starting date and an ending date)	Importance Rank (Rank each item by importance to the organization considering the scenario scores)
Weaknesses							
Competencies and capabilities							
Implementation strategies							
Organizational culture							

UNDERSTANDING THE EXTERNAL ENVIRONMENT

Understanding the external environment focuses on scanning, monitoring, forecasting, and assessing the macro and micro forces of the external environment. *Scanning* involves identifying the subtle to dramatic signals of macro and micro forces as they change. Environmental scanning is defined as "a process of gathering, analyzing, and dispensing information for tactical or strategic purposes; success in today's [achievement-oriented] business environment depends, to a large extent on the ability of the firm to gather and process information and the amount of relevant information used in the planning process."[45] *Monitoring* focuses on deriving meaning from a pattern of observations obtained from scanning macro and micro forces. *Forecasting* is the active development of projections and likely scenarios based on the patterns identified through monitoring. *Assessing* entails prioritizing and quantifying the effects of changes in the macro and micro forces' external environment, with scenario forecasts being incorporated into that valuation. "External environmental analysis attempts to identify, aggregate, and interpret environmental issues as well as provide information for the analysis of the internal [organizational] environment."[46]

The critical reason for understanding the external environment is to determine how to best situate the health organization to serve its purpose in the short term, yet still be able to adapt and survive in the long term. Rakich, Longest, and Darr provide categories that give leaders a structure through which to scan (environmental scanning), monitor, forecast, and assess a dynamic health industry:

1. Macro-Environmental Forces
   a. Legal [regulatory, executive orders, and case law] and ethical forces
   b. Political (including government policy) forces
   c. Cultural and sociological (including values [beliefs and attitudes]) forces
   d. Public expectations (including community, interest groups, and media)
   e. Economic forces
   f. Ecological forces
2. Health Care Environmental Forces [also called Micro-Environmental Forces]
   a. Planning and public policy (regulation, licensure, and accreditation) forces
   b. Competitive forces
   c. Health care financing (third-party payers, both public and private, and financial risk)
   d. Technology (equipment, material, and supply entities) forces
   e. Health research and education

   f. Health status and health promotion (wellness and disease)
   g. [Integration with other health disciplines and organizations'] public health (e.g., sanitation, environmental protection) forces[47]

The Rand Corporation suggests that the immense pressure of cost containment is the leading factor for change in the health industry at this time.[48] Multiple forces, however, cumulatively contribute to change in the health industry. Professional associations and societies, the scholarly literature, and professional journals are all sources in which to look for external environmental information.

An evaluation of threats and opportunities of the external environment is essential for the health organization. Threats and opportunities (externally focused) are married to strengths and weaknesses (internally focused) to complete the SWOT analysis used in many strategic planning models and processes. Threats comprise issues, events, or changes that affect the organization negatively and serve as barriers to mission accomplishment and vision attainment. Opportunities are potentially positive issues, events, or changes that, with planning, resourcing, and implementation, can have positive effects on the health organization.

Another aspect of external analysis, particularly regarding forecasting, is the development of assumptions and constraints. *Assumptions* are perspectives on a condition or state of nature that are supposed to be true or are taken for granted. Assumptions in this context are external (rooted in macro- or micro-environmental factors) and suggest a situation or state that exists now or will exist in the future that guides thinking. *Constraints* are current conditions that may prevent strategies or goals from being pursued in striving to meet the organizational vision. Constraints are rooted in existing rules, traditions, habits, policies, social norms, or laws that set limits on what an organization or individual can do or plans to do.

Using federally mandated programs on emergency preparedness as examples, the Public Health Emergency Preparedness (PHEP) cooperative agreement, managed by the Centers for Disease Control and Prevention (CDC), and the Hospital Preparedness Program (HPP), managed by the Assistant Secretary for Preparedness and Response, are required to be aligned. (Both are subordinate to the U.S. Department of Health and Human Services.) An illustration of planning at a programmatic level is provided in **Figure 9–2**. The assessment of the jurisdiction (county, district, city, etc.) provides the environmental assessment and situational analysis with which the improvement planning is facilitated. The GREaT Assessment System (General information, Resource Elements, and Tasks) provides the basis for the required assessment of 15 capabilities and

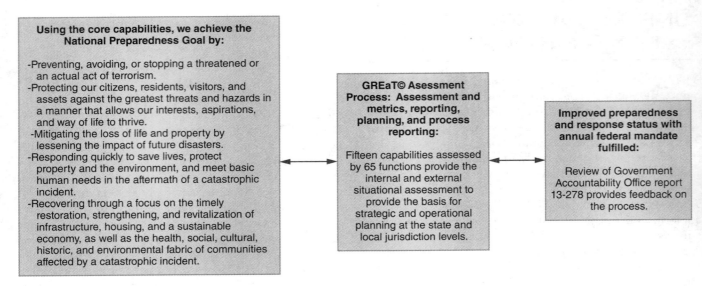

Using the core capabilities, we achieve the National Preparedness Goal by:

-Preventing, avoiding, or stopping a threatened or an actual act of terrorism.
-Protecting our citizens, residents, visitors, and assets against the greatest threats and hazards in a manner that allows our interests, aspirations, and way of life to thrive.
-Mitigating the loss of life and property by lessening the impact of future disasters.
-Responding quickly to save lives, protect property and the environment, and meet basic human needs in the aftermath of a catastrophic incident.
-Recovering through a focus on the timely restoration, strengthening, and revitalization of infrastructure, housing, and a sustainable economy, as well as the health, social, cultural, historic, and environmental fabric of communities affected by a catastrophic incident.

GREaT© Asessment Process: Assessment and metrics, reporting, planning, and process reporting:

Fifteen capabilities assessed by 65 functions provide the internal and external situational assessment to provide the basis for strategic and operational planning at the state and local jurisdiction levels.

Improved preparedness and response status with annual federal mandate fulfilled:

Review of Government Accountability Office report 13-278 provides feedback on the process.

FIGURE 9-2 Public health preparedness assessment.

65 functions for the PHEP and 8 capabilities and 29 functions for the HPP.

EXAMPLE OF SITUATIONAL ASSESSMENT

Figure 9-2 shows an example of the strategic process and requirements of the public health emergency preparedness program utilized by all states and territories as directed by the CDC's Office of Public Health Preparedness and Response. The assessment is an example of a situational assessment that links to a strategic and operational planning process aimed at preparedness improvement. The PHEP guidelines provide the basis for assessment of capabilities and functions for public health. The HPP guidelines provide the basis for assessment of capabilities and functions for healthcare delivery organizations and hospitals. These programs are funded and managed separately but now require alignment and integration to provide a better picture of preparedness.

Creating a planning culture allows leaders and their organizations to utilize the planning concepts and tools across multiple contexts and programs. An overview of horizontal, vertical, and dynamic external environmental considerations is provided for discussion in the next section. Leaders need to understand how various linkages and relationships influence their organization, especially as it relates to situational assessment and environmental influences.

HORIZONTAL FACTORS

One of the most difficult leadership skills for health executives to master is viewing the health organization as a horizontal organization. Horizontal organizations have cooperative relationships, affiliations, or ownership rights with multiple outside agents and actors. A *health actor* is any individual, group, or organization that exerts influence on an entity. An *agent* is a principal lobbyist or representative of a health actor who is trusted with making decisions or statements on behalf of the actor. When poor relationships are in place, actors and agents working in concert can exert so much pressure on the organization that the organization is placed in a position where it must accede to the will of outside parties rather than acting in its own interest. Given this possibility, it is the goal of every healthcare executive to ensure that harmonious and affable relationships are maintained within the horizontal structure.[49]

From a reductionist point of view, horizontal organizations seek to maintain a level of homeostasis with all elements internal and external to the establishment. In horizontal organizations, it is not possible to operate and survive without forming cooperative relationships with multiple outside actors and agents. As a result, horizontal organizations must maintain a careful balance between mutually exclusive organizational needs and the needs of external stakeholders. Failing to balance these simultaneous priorities may lead to organizational failure or loss of competitiveness (i.e., loss of market share or market penetration).

For example, a health organization that views health only from a business-driven perspective (defined as concentrating on rates of return and profit or margin as the primary goal) may find over time that it has lost competitive advantage relative to other organizations in the same industry and could lose the trust and confidence of customers. Such was the perception of the health industry by the U.S. population in the 1980s and early 1990s. The introduction of managed care principles, such as gatekeeper access, specialty care referral, and preauthorization, caused consumers to perceive that health organizations were large, uncaring companies that were more concerned with keeping people away than providing high-quality care for the ill and injured.

A more recent organizational example can be found among the big oil companies in 2005, 2006, and 2007. Increases of more than 100% in fuel prices in less than 1 year (and even higher increases in some areas) created distrust for these organizations among consumers. Compounding this perception were reports of record-breaking, billion-dollar profits for these companies as well as exorbitant salaries and bonuses for their executives. At the same time, customers were forced to pay record-breaking prices for gasoline at the pump. These outcomes caused consumers to perceive oil companies as focused on greed and self-fulfillment, and resulted in the Democratic-led Congress of 2007 revoking certain tax incentives for these organizations.

Despite these negative examples, health organizations cannot afford to become too altruistic and empathetic. For example, engaging in an abundance of uncompensated and charity care may fail to promote organizational survival, prosperity, and growth. Clearly, balance is necessary in a health organization participating in a horizontal environment.

VERTICAL FACTORS

The horizontal organization stands in stark contrast to the vertical organization. The vertical organization builds a monument unto itself and seeks to minimize its reliance on any and all outside stakeholders and actors. In terms of organizational dynamics, there are actually very few truly vertical organizations. Thus, when we speak of vertical organizations, we refer to those organizations that attempt to control the environment first, rather than living in the environment and becoming a participatory member within the community.

Vertical considerations include health providers, possible competitors, suppliers, patients, customers, and other stakeholders associated with health services and goods that are above or below the organization within the continuum of care. For example, a hospital would have vertical considerations at the primary care level (e.g., physician offices and group practices) and above its level in tertiary care (e.g., a large medical center), rehabilitative care, or hospice care. Developing solid relationships and coordination are the keys to success in this scenario, which explains why many of these organizations work to become vertically integrated.

Vertical integration in the health industry is the ability, through ownership, affiliation, or alliance, to offer products and services that span the continuum of care. A vertically integrated health system may offer primary care, secondary care, tertiary care, long-term care, and hospice care services under its umbrella; likewise, it may include academic medical centers (e.g., in-house education and practice for physicians and surgeons, nurse education and training, allied health education and training), a group purchasing organization and distribution operation (for controlling the supply chain, as described in "The Non-Intermediated or Vertically Integrated Health Supply Chain," where the health organization internally performs many of the distributor functions of the supply chain[50]), and a research and development operation. This broad span of operations differs significantly from that of a horizontally integrated health organization. Large horizontally integrated health organizations encompass several like organizations across a large area; for example, a health system may include 25 hospitals located across 5 states. Some large health systems are both vertically and horizontally integrated. The degree of integration in each dimension plays a role in determining whether the organization assumes a horizontal or vertical internal "stance" and influences the organizational culture.

One of the last, great vertical organizations was the Ford Motor Company of the early twentieth century. Henry Ford not only built cars, but also owned dealerships, transportation companies, steel mills, oil refineries, rubber plantations, tire manufacturing warehouses, fuel companies, and leather and tanning industries. Put simply, he attempted to control all aspects of automobile manufacturing. This philosophy eventually failed for Ford; however, many organizations still try to minimize their reliance on outside environmental actors and agents.

Some early health organizations, such as the initial Kaiser closed-panel HMO model of the early 1940s, attempted to replicate the vertical organization structure. In today's dynamic health environment, few organizations can be mutually exclusive and simultaneously rely on no outside influences.

DYNAMIC FACTORS

Dynamic organizations are those that do not qualify as either vertical or horizontal organizations. They also do not fit nicely into a model of being an open or closed organization. Nevertheless, many dynamic organizations may be described as having an open and horizontal architecture as opposed to a closed and vertical persona. Open and closed systems can exist in either horizontal or vertical organizations, depending on the organization's size and complexity.

In an open system, organizations are a smaller part of a larger system. Consequently, the environment has a central role in determining organizational survival. Additionally, in an open system model, the system interacts with and adapts to the environment; thus the situation may be described as dynamic. Inherent to open systems are feedback loops and adaptation to the external environment. Open systems do not negate prediction entirely; rather, through control over and understanding of the influences, outcomes are presumed. In such a case, the leader realizes that the environment is defined as the sum of the political, economic, social, and regulatory forces that exert influence on the organization; the organization itself is viewed as an organic living system within the environment. In this regard, no organization is entirely self-contained. As a result, the organization is dependent to some extent on the environment.

Standing in opposition to the open system is the closed system approach to organizational life cycle analysis. In this design, the leader must be aware that the organization is guided by internal governance. In other words, the sum total of work of the organization is split within internal staff. Additionally, the leadership is hierarchical, probably more technically competent than conceptually driven, and the work of the organization is carried out impersonally and autocratically. In the closed system, the leader and the organization operate in isolation from environmental influences as much as possible. The effects are entirely predictable, because a finite number of variables affect the outcome. Such systems are not the rule, however, but the exception.[51-54]

When unpredictable open and horizontal systems actively interact with one another, it takes an accomplished leader to steady the organization in view of the higher levels of complexity. A complex system exists in the dynamic environment when large numbers of interacting organizations and elements begin to establish patterns and relationships that are new and unique. This dynamic can result in rapid and unpredictable change that follows no apparent pattern. Complexity, therefore, is an extension of the general system for which the leader must be prepared.[55]

For leaders in the modern era, effectiveness in dealing with the complex dynamics of the health industry requires a deep understanding of the relationships between evaluative and empirical properties. Management within this kind of dynamic environment is most difficult for early careerists to do before they have mastered the complexities of the "crawl" and "walk" elements of professional growth. For example, relationships may exist between segments

within the organization along an informal network that have great consequences for organizational outputs. The more dynamic the task environment, the greater are the contingencies presented to the organization.

It can be an intimidating task to forecast the future in a dynamic environment. Different possibilities in the environmental characteristics constantly require the creation of new and different ways of positioning the organization for success. Leaders must produce and determine contingencies that can quickly be put in place for countless future scenarios that may evolve. As Daft has suggested, in such an environment, both the destination and the route may turn out to be unexpected and unintended; strategy emerges spontaneously from the chaos of challenge and contradiction, through a process of real-time learning and politics.[56] "In order to achieve and maintain competitiveness and sustainable growth, companies have to constantly create new knowledge and pursue practical wisdom."[57]

Leaders in the current era are more likely to work in open health systems. Thus the importance of an external presence for the leader cannot be overemphasized. The leader becomes the calming voice on behalf of the organization in an otherwise turbulent and uncertain environment to countless stakeholders, upon many of whom the leader has no direct influence, other than through the power of his or her organization.

ORGANIZATIONAL CULTURE

From a broad perspective, health leaders assess the external and internal environments of the organization, determine which organizational culture will best meet the needs of the external environment, and then design, develop, implement, and refine the organizational culture. From this "big picture" view, leadership seems simple—yet accomplishing the task of organizational alignment with the external environment requires a focused, clear, appealing vision that is well communicated, combined with leadership and management team actions that are consistent with that vision. From this standpoint, leaders must be knowledgeable and competent about organizational dynamics, culture, communication, assessment and analysis, and change management. All of these areas are important, yet culture is the fabric that weaves all of these components together.

Health leaders can forge a new, better-fitting organization by devising a new culture that meets the needs of a dynamic environment using the best of science and art. If a supportive and confirming communication organizational environment, a planning and accountability emphasis, a push-down decision-making strategy that focuses on appropriate employee empowerment, and a learning and knowledge management–oriented operation are characteristics of the organizational culture needed to best provide health services and products, then the health leader needs an implementation plan or concept. To begin moving an organizational culture toward change, the health leader should take the following guidelines to heart:

- Model the behavior you expect yourself.
- Communicate expectations and train other leaders, managers, and staff.
- Revise structures and reporting relationships.
- Conduct team-based planning and policy development.
- Use primary and secondary mechanisms[58] (discussed later in this chapter).
- Be consistent and communicate often to the organization.
- Continue to scan, monitor, and assess the internal health organization environment while you scan, monitor, forecast, and assess the external environment.

DEFINING ORGANIZATIONAL CULTURE

Organizational culture is a complex construct that incorporates many concepts and multitudes of variables. It encompasses a large set of largely ignored or invisible assumptions that deal with how group members interpret both their external relationships (external environment) and their internal relationships with one another. Culture is an outcome of group learning. As people solve problems together successfully, a condition for culture formation exists. Health organizational survival is intimately linked to meeting the needs of the external environment (the community that the organization serves). This goal is accomplished by effectively, efficiently, and efficaciously (high quality) developing organizational integration of resources, capabilities, and systems (developing synergy) to produce services and goods that satisfy marketplace demands and expectations.

Each organization deals with external adaptation and internal integration in its own way. The "way" the health organization adapts and integrates forms its collective organizational culture.

Schein gives an excellent summary of the various issues related to external adaptation and internal integration:

External Adaptation Issues[59]

- Mission and strategy: Obtaining a shared understanding of core mission, primary tasks, and organizational functions (both manifest and latent).

- Goals: Developing consensus on goals, as derived from the core mission.
- Means: Developing consensus on the means to be used to attain the goals, such as the organizational structure, division of labor, reward system, and authority system.
- Measurement: Developing consensus on the criteria to be used in measuring how well the group is doing in fulfilling its goals, such as the information and control systems.
- Correction: Developing consensus on the appropriate remedial or repair strategies to be used if goals are not being met.

Internal Integration Issues[60]

- Common language and conceptual categories: If members cannot communicate with and understand one another, a group is impossible by definition. Consider healthcare jargon as an example.
- Group boundaries and criteria for membership inclusion and exclusion.
- Power and status: Consensus in this area is crucial as to who has power and status.
- Intimacy, friendship, and love: What are the rules of the game for peer relationships?
- Rewards and punishments: What are heroic and sinful behaviors?
- Ideology and "religion": How are unexplainable and inexplicable events given meaning?

As you read about and reflect on organizational culture in the remainder of this chapter, note which similarities the research and information presented here share with research and models of leadership such as the omnibus leadership model, the dynamic culture leadership model, and the reframing organizational leadership model from authors Coppola, Ledlow, and Bolman and Deal. Can you integrate the concepts?

Edgar Schein, who is recognized as the "father of organizational culture," defines culture as a pattern of basic assumptions that are invented, discovered, or developed by a given group as it learns to cope with its problems of external adaptation and integration; these assumptions have worked well enough to be considered valid and, therefore, are taught to new members as the correct way to perceive, think, and feel in relation to their problems, challenges, and opportunities.[61] Sathe defines culture as the "set of important understandings (often unstated) that members of a community share in common."[62] Louis suggests that organizational culture is "a set of understandings or meanings shared by a group of people; the meanings are largely tacit among the members, are clearly relevant to the particular group, and are distinctive to the group."[63] Consider healthcare marketing and advertising in today's very competitive environment: Thirty years ago, very little "health care" was advertised (and thus became part of the culture); today, competition is intense and marketing and advertising are essential for survival. Marketing, customer service, entertainment during the care process, and advertising are now key parts of the culture that help ensure health organizational survival.

At the heart of organizational culture are questions about values, beliefs, and attitudes that become translated into behaviors, norms, and social expectations within the health workplace. Culture consists of ideational elements, such as beliefs and values, that explain and reinforce the foundation of the organization.[64] Which values, beliefs, and attitudes do you hold? How do they differ from your organizational experiences?

> An *attitude* is a learned predisposition to respond to a person, object, or idea in a favorable, neutral, or unfavorable way. A *belief* is the way you structure what is true and false, and a *value* is an enduring conception of good and bad.[65]

Layered like an onion (as depicted graphically in **Figure 9-3**), values power beliefs, and beliefs greatly influence attitudes. Behaviors are linked to attitudes. Behaviors are easier to change than attitudes, and attitudes easier to change than beliefs and values.

Where can you see, hear, or touch organizational culture?

> Manifestations of culture include rituals, stories, humor, jargon, physical arrangements, and formal structures and policies, as well as informal norms and practices. Content themes (such as values or basic assumptions) are used to capture and show relationships among interpretations of the meanings of these manifestations. These are the building blocks needed for you to understand the theoretical assumptions underlying a culture study, summarize the content of any cultural

portrait, and if you wish, develop your own answers to the questions: What is culture? What is not culture?[66]

Schein provides insight into the tangible and intangible components of organizational culture. According to this theorist, three levels of culture interact to form the fabric of culture. Notably, organizational culture cannot be assessed and "known" in a short time or by walking through the corridors and reading policy documents; rather, it is discerned by observing, interviewing, and interacting with the full spectrum of these three levels.[67]

- *Level 1: Artifacts and creations*: These elements are the most readily visible components of culture and include the organization's constructed social and physical environment. This level includes technology, art, visible and audible behavior patterns (visible but often not decipherable) such as written and spoken language, overt behaviors, and the ways in which members demonstrate status.
- *Level 2: Values*: Values are testable in the physical environment, but are testable only by social consensus (such as taking care of patients). Central values provide the day-to-day operating principles that the members of the culture use to guide their behavior. As values are taken for granted, they gradually become beliefs and drop out of consciousness, just as habits become unconscious and automatic.
- *Level 3: Basic underlying assumptions*: Level 3 elements include the relationship to the environment; the nature of reality, time, and space; the nature of human nature; the nature of human activity; and the nature of human relationships (taken for granted, invisible, preconscious). These implicit assumptions tell group members how to perceive, think about, and feel about things. These assumptions are taken for granted; members would find behavior based on any other premise inconceivable.[68]

Martin also recommends four types of formal practices, of interest to culture researchers, that should be evaluated to begin to understand organizational culture: (1) organizational structure and hierarchy (reporting relationships and locations), (2) tasks and technologies (what employees do to produce goods and services), (3) rules and procedures, and (4) financial controls (authority to commit, audit, and forecast financial resources).[69] Informal practices that should be evaluated (if possible) are not written down, but rather take the form of social rules and norms ("how things really work around here"). Often, these unwritten rules are inconsistent with formal policies and procedures.[70]

Organizational climate is a temporal phenomenon that changes quickly based on the current situation and

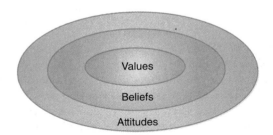

Rokeach's Model

FIGURE 9-3 Values, beliefs, and attitudes.

Data from Beebe, S. A., & Masterson, J. T. (1997). *Communicating in small groups: Principles and practices* (5th ed.). New York: Addison-Wesley Educational, p. 174.

influences. Climate is a snapshot in time and is dynamic, whereas culture remains stable over a longer time span. In essence, a simple explanation comprises a long series of organizational climate snapshots, strung together over time, that depict a large part of organizational culture; this is especially true in explaining the feeling of the workplace.

Climate can be changed quickly. For example, how would your subordinates and the work climate change if you announced a 5% pay reduction to support a budget cut? The next day, you announce that the pay reduction was an error and each employee will actually receive a 5% pay increase: Would the climate change? What would happen if you greeted and talked with each employee for a few minutes each morning to check on that person and his or her family and interests, and you followed this routine consistently over several weeks, but then one day you came in with a sad or frowning face, walked into your office, and closed the door, not coming out to greet everyone? How would the climate change?

Health leaders can affect climate on a daily basis. With consistent application of behaviors, training, expectations and goal setting, reinforcement, and communication, over time climate influences culture.

ORGANIZATIONAL CULTURE TYPOLOGIES

Several different typologies of organizational culture exist. A typology is a categorization and description system that attempts to make sense of differing "states of nature" with regard, in this case, to organizational culture. The following subsections describe some of these typologies.

Interpersonal Interaction Model[71]

The interpersonal interaction model categorizes organizational cultures into one of four types:

- *Power culture*: Strong leaders are needed to distribute resources. Leaders are firm, but fair and generous to loyal followers. If the organization is badly led, there is rule by fear, abuse of power for personal gain, and political intrigue.
- *Achievement culture*: Results are rewarded, but not unproductive efforts. Work teams are self-directed. Rules and structure serve the system, but are not an end unto themselves. A possible downside is sustaining energy and enthusiasm over time.
- *Support culture*: Employees are valued both as people and as workers. Employee harmony is important. The weakness is a possible internal commitment without an external task focus.
- *Role culture*: There is a rule of law that outlines clear responsibilities; reward systems are clear, with tight coupling to responsibilities. This type provides stability, justice, and efficiency. Its weakness lies in the impersonal operating procedures and a stifling of creativity and innovation.

Gordon and DiTomaso's Typology

Gordon and DiTomaso's typology of organizational culture is based on the persona of the organization. **Table 9-3** describes this typology.

Table 9-3 Gordon and DiTomaso's Typology

Cultural Practices	Description/Scale
Aggressiveness/action orientation	Emphasis is placed on getting things done, on being a pacesetter rather than a follower.
Innovation	This type indicates the extent to which individual managers are encouraged to take risks and innovate.
Confrontation	This type involves addressing issues openly instead of burying them.
Planning orientation	This element emphasizes managing in a proactive (planning) manner and avoiding surprises.
Results orientation	Emphasis is placed on holding people accountable for and demanding clear end results.
People orientation	A strong emphasis is placed on concern for growth of current employees.
Team orientation	This type refers to the extent that people are encouraged to cooperate and coordinate within and across units.
Communication	This type involves an openness to communicate in other areas of the company that might affect how a job is done.

Data from Gordon, G. G., & DiTomaso, N. (1992). Predicting corporate performance from organizational culture. *Journal of Management Studies, 29*(6), 783–797.

Table 9-4 Daft's Organizational Culture Typology

Cultures	Description
Adaptability/entrepreneurial	The organization is characterized by a strategic focus on the external environment through flexibility and change to meet customer needs. The organization actively creates change. Innovation and risk taking are rewarded.
Mission	The organization places major importance on a clear vision of organizational purpose. This type is appropriate for organizations concerned with serving specific customers in the external environment, but without the need for rapid change.
Clan	The organization has a primary focus on the involvement and participation of the organization's members and on rapidly changing expectations from the external environment.
Bureaucratic	The organization has an internal focus and a consistency orientation for a stable environment. There are high levels of consistency, conformity, and collaboration among members.

Data from Daft, R. L. (2000). *Organization theory and design*. Mason, OH: South Western College Publishing.

Daft's Typology

Daft's typology categorizes organizational cultures based on external and internal behaviors and actions. **Table 9–4** describes this typology.

Societal Expression Cultures

There are different types of culture, just as there are different types of personality. Researcher Jeffrey Sonnenfeld identified four types of cultures:[72]

- *Academy culture*: Employees are highly skilled and tend to stay in the organization, while working their way up the ranks. The organization provides a stable environment for employees to develop and exercise their skills. Examples include universities, hospitals, and large corporations.
- *Baseball team culture*: Employees are "free agents" who have highly prized skills. They are in high demand and can easily get jobs elsewhere. This type of culture exists in fast-paced, high-risk organizations, such as investment banking and advertising.
- *Club culture*: The most important requirement for employees in this culture is to fit into the group. Usually employees start at the bottom and stay with the organization. The organization promotes from within and highly values seniority. Examples include the military and some law firms.
- *Fortress culture*: Employees do not know if they will be laid off. These organizations often undergo massive reorganization. There are many opportunities for those with timely, specialized skills. Examples include savings and loan companies and large car companies.

DEFINING LEADERSHIP FROM AN ORGANIZATIONAL CULTURE CONTEXT

Many studies have attempted to elucidate the relationship between the leader and the group and to determine the effect of a leader's personality and style on group formation as highly relevant to the understanding of how cultures form and evolve. Most group and leadership theories develop distinctions parallel to the internal and external task-oriented leadership functions and the internal group-oriented leadership functions. Schein's well-established paradigm of leadership is an excellent example of implied scientific and artistic practice. Schein views the unique and important function of leadership, as contrasted with management or administration, as the conceptualization, creation, and management of organizational culture.[73] Culture is a learned and evolved system of knowledge, behavior, attitudes, beliefs, values, and norms that is shared by a group of people.

> Leaders go beyond a narrow focus on power and control in periods of organizational change. They create commitment and energy among stakeholders to make the change work. They create a sense of direction, then nurture and support others who can make the new organization a success.[74]

Health leaders lead people and manage resources within a framework of organizational culture.

CHANGING AND ADAPTING ORGANIZATIONAL CULTURE

How do health leaders implement their proposals and recommendations? How do they communicate the assumptions underlying these proposed solutions and embed them in the health organization's thought processes? Most often, leaders use an approach that does not consider the contemporary realities of organizational life:

> The problem is simple: we are using a mechanistic model, first applied to managing physical work, and superimposing it onto the new mental model of today's knowledge organization. We keep breaking change into small pieces and then manage the pieces. But with change, the task is to manage [lead] the dynamic, not the pieces.[75]

When leadership scholars describe the importance of the leader "articulating a vision" for the group, they are referring to this same set of issues—that is, to the development of organizational culture.[76] In fact, the strength of the social norms associated with an organizational culture influences the perception of the effectiveness of the leadership team.[77] The next two subsections describe essential concerns for health leaders who want to succeed in developing, changing, and maintaining organizational culture. In the dynamic environment of the health industry, the leader's ability to assess the changing situation (externally and internally) and revise the organization's culture is a vital competence whose successful use requires a set of skills and abilities grounded in these mechanisms. The following subsections provide guidelines with which to measure your leadership effectiveness with regard to organizational culture; these areas—primary embedding mechanisms and secondary articulation and reinforcement mechanisms—are where you, the leader, change, maintain, reengineer, and alter organizational culture.

Primary Embedding Mechanisms[78]

Health leaders have a set of powerful tools, behaviors, and mechanisms at their disposal with which to develop, refine, maintain, or change organizational culture. The importance of these mechanisms cannot be overstated. The primary embedding mechanisms are as follows:

- What leaders pay attention to, measure, and control
- Leader reactions to critical incidents and organizational crises
- Deliberate role modeling, teaching, and coaching by leaders
- Criteria for allocation of rewards and status
- Criteria for recruitment, selection, promotion, retirement, and excommunication

Schein strongly states that leaders communicate both explicitly and implicitly the assumptions they really hold. If they are conflicted, their conflicts and inconsistencies are also communicated and become part of the culture. Consistency is the key; health leaders must predetermine where and how to guide the organization and stay on task. The secondary set of mechanisms (profiled next) support the primary set.

Secondary Articulation and Reinforcement Mechanisms[79]

The secondary articulation and reinforcement mechanisms reinforce the primary embedding mechanisms. The following are of the greatest importance:

- The organization's design and structure
- Organizational systems and procedures
- Design of physical space, facades, and buildings
- Stories, legends, myths, and parables about important events and people
- Formal statements of organizational philosophy, creeds, and charters

Schein calls these mechanisms "secondary" because they work only if they are consistent with the primary mechanisms. They are less powerful, more ambiguous, and more difficult to control than the primary mechanisms, yet they can be powerful reinforcements of the primary messages if the leader is able to control them. The important point is that all of these mechanisms communicate culture content to newcomers and current staff.

Health leaders do not have a choice about whether to communicate, only about how much to manage what they communicate through words, actions, or neglect: Leaders cannot not communicate. Organizations differ in the degree to which the cultural messages are consistent and clear, and this variation in cultural clarity is a reflection of the clarity and consistency of the assumptions of the leaders.[80]

CHALLENGES OF CHANGE

As Morrison points out, there are significant challenges to health reform in the United States. Health leaders should be cognizant of the following challenges as they work to positively change the culture of their health organizations, the culture of the health industry, and the expectations of the nation as a whole:[81]

- Recognizing the political, structural, and resource distribution tension between health and health care; understanding that medical care is not the only factor behind health status
- Developing health policies beyond managed competition

- Finding ways to make community-based healthcare systems work
- Clarifying the fuzzy boundaries between for-profit and nonprofit health care
- Dealing with regional diversity in such a large and diverse country

STRATEGIC RELATIONSHIPS AS A SYSTEM FOR LEADERSHIP CONCERN

This section of the chapter was co-authored with Dr. Karl Manrodt. Dr. Manrodt (see **Figure 9-4**) serves as a professor in the Department of Marketing and Logistics at Georgia Southern University, located in Statesboro, Georgia. He is also the director of the Southern Center for Logistics and Intermodal Transportation, and he has co-authored 5 books and over 100 academic articles and reports. Dr. Manrodt is the architect and primary force behind the International Supply Chain Metric Project, a multi decade effort for the Warehouse Education and Research Cooperative (WERC).

FIGURE 9-4 Karl Manrodt, PhD.
Courtesy of Karl Manrodt, PhD.

All organizations, especially health organizations, require strategies to survive in the competitive health industry. Leaders must evaluate, build, and maintain strategic relationships with other organizations, such as suppliers, personnel companies, and federal and state agencies, as well as other organizations. In one significant area of leadership—where situational assessment, environmental analyses, organizational culture, planning and strategy, and goal achievement interact—evaluation, selection, and relationship building with strategic partners (other organizations such as suppliers of equipment, medical/surgical supplies, or pharmaceuticals) are a critical set of competencies.

Important research by the International Association for Contract and Commercial Management shows that most companies operate under conventional transaction-based models that are constrained by a formal, legally oriented, risk-averse, and liability-based culture.[82] There is growing awareness that transactional-based approaches do not always give each party the intended results. Alternative sourcing business models are a viable alternative to the conventional transactional methods. Outcome-based approaches are gathering momentum as senior leaders see positive results from carefully crafted collaborative agreements. The CAAVE model (Competitive, Avoiding, Adaptive, Vested, and Empathetic styles of strategic partnership positioning) offers one method to evaluate and develop strategic partners; in addition, the Compatibility and Trust (CaT) Assessment evaluates relationship dynamics, market dynamics, and compatibility (organizational culture is a major aspect of compatibility) of those strategic relationships. These partnerships take multiple forms, ranging from conventional transaction-based models to equity partnerships. A continuum of these relationships can be found in Vitasek, Crawford, Nyden, and Kawamoto's book, *The Vested Outsourcing Manual*.[83]

In order to better understand the environment firms operate within, this section of the chapter outlines seven sourcing business models that fall into three categories (**Table 9-5**). Each model differs from a risk/reward perspective and should be evaluated in the context of what is being procured. The characteristics and attributes for each of these approaches are reviewed in detail. This is followed by a discussion of the CAAVE Model and the CaT Assessment.

TRANSACTION-BASED MODELS

Many companies use transaction-based business models for their commercial agreements when they make a "buy" decision. Conventional approaches to transaction-based models keep service providers at arm's length. Three types of transaction-based sourcing relationships have changed over time as businesses struggle with how to create service provider relationships that are better suited for more complex business requirements.

The economics for each of these types of supplier relationships are similar in that the supplier gets paid per

Table 9-5 Sourcing Models*			
Sourcing Business Models	**Sourcing Business Model Categories**		
	Transaction Based	**Outcome Based**	**Investment Based**
Simple transaction provider	X		
Approved provider	X		
Preferred provider	X		
Performance-based relationship		X	
Vested relationship		X	X
Shared services (internal)			X
Equitable partner (external)			X

*This section is based on "Unpacking Sourcing Business Models: 21st Century Solutions for Sourcing Services" by Kate Vitasek, Bonnie Keith, Jim Eckler, Dawn Evans, in collaboration with Jacqui Crawford, Karl Manrodt, Katherine Kawamoto, and Srinivas Krishna.

Reproduced from Vitasek, K., Keith, B., Eckler, J., & Evans, D. (n.d.). Unpacking sourcing business models: 21st century solutions for sourcing services. Retrieved from http://www.vestedway.com/wp-content/uploads/2012/09/Unpacking-Sourcing.pdf.

transaction. There is typically a predefined rate for each transaction, or unit of service. For instance, a third-party logistics service provider would get paid each month for the number of pallets stored, the number of units picked, and the number of orders shipped. Or a call center service provider would get paid a price per call or a price per minute.

Transaction-based business models are best suited when a supplier is supplying a standardized service with stable specifications that are easily measured through a commonly agreed to set of metrics. Payment can be triggered based on successful transactions completed.

The three types of transaction-based providers can be described as simple transaction provider, approved provider, and preferred provider.

Simple Transaction Provider

A simple transaction provider is a supplier who is one of many available in the marketplace, typically providing a low-cost, repetitive service. The services provided by this type of provider are often competitively bid, frequently with no interruption of service or impact to the buyer's business. A purchase order often triggers these transactions, which signals that the buying company agrees to buy a set quantity of goods or tasks (or hours) outlined in the purchase order. The supplier relationship is based solely on a review of the supplier's performance against standard metrics (did the supplier work that many hours or provide the good or service in the quantities purchased?).

Approved Provider

An approved provider is one who has been identified as offering a unique differentiation from other transactional suppliers and provides an efficiency or cost advantage for the client company. The differentiation could come in the form of a geographical location advantage, a cost or quality advantage, or being a small disadvantaged business that is ultimately approved to assist with meeting the client company's minority and women business enterprise (MWBE) goals. An approved provider is identified as a prequalified option in the pool of transactional suppliers and has fulfilled preconditions for specified service. Procurement professionals routinely turn to approved suppliers as regularly solicited sources of supply when bidding is conducted. An approved supplier may or may not operate under a master services agreement (MSA)—an overarching contract with the buying company. Approved suppliers may or may not also have volume thresholds to receive an approved status. Finally, approved suppliers may or may not participate in supplier management reviews.

Preferred Provider

A preferred provider is a supplier that has been qualified, may have a unique differentiator, and has had demonstrated acceptable performance with the buying company. Typically, these conditions include:

- Previous experiences
- Supplier performance rating (if the client company has a rating system)

- Previous contracts compliance performance
- Evidence of an external certification (e.g., International Organization for Standardization [ISO] certification)

Buying companies frequently seek to do business with a preferred provider in an effort to streamline their buying process and build relationships with key suppliers. Buying companies often enter into a longer-term contract using an MSA that allows the companies to do repeat business more efficiently. It is common for preferred providers to work under a blanket purchase order (PO) with predefined rates for work or services performed. For example, a labor-staffing firm may have a "rate card" that has the hourly rate established for various types of staffing needs. The buying company can request staffing support from the preferred provider using the predetermined blanket PO and rate card. Another example would be a facilities management firm having a pre-agreed rate of a certain price per square foot to manage a company's buildings. Often companies will work with a preferred provider using a supplier relationship management plan in which both companies agree on improvement or other opportunities.

It is worth noting that a preferred provider is still engaged in a transactional business model, but the nature

and efficiencies for how the companies work together go beyond a simple PO.

Table 9-6 outlines typical characteristics of each of the transaction-based business model approaches frequently used today.

OUTCOME-BASED BUSINESS MODELS

An outcome-based business model pays a service provider for the realization of a defined set of business outcomes or business results, or achievement of agreed-on performance indicators. Historically, outcome-based approaches are used most widely in the aerospace and defense industries. In this setting they are referred to as performance-based logistics because they couple maintenance and support with the procurement of the product. Rolls-Royce was the first known firm to explore outcome-based approaches in the 1960s. However, outcome-based business models did not gain traction until around the year 2000, and even then their use was limited. What is an outcome-based business model? A good example is when an airline pays its outsourced ground crew for achieving a short 20-minute turnaround time after the plane has been parked at the gate. In basic form, the service provider does not get paid if it does not deliver results. An outcome-based business model

Table 9-6 Attributes of Transaction-Based Business Models					
Sourcing Relationship	Focus	Interaction	Cooperation Level	Required Trust Level	Characterized By
Simple transaction provider	Cost and efficiency	Standard terms, fixed price	Low: Automated where possible	Minimal: Single transaction	Abundant and easy to resource, no need for a relationship
Approved provider	Economies of scale, ease of transactions	Blanket, negotiated terms, pricing agreements	Medium: Based on pricing or specifications	Medium: Common terms and price agreement	Managed by category locally and across business sector, purchases bundled for economies of scale
Preferred provider	Capability, capacity, and technology transactions	Contract, SOW, pricing agreement, possible gain sharing, SLAs	High: Set out in long-term service contract	High: Defined by contract, high spend zone	Integral supply across business units, delivering added value and capability, not so abundant, a pain to resource

Key: SOW = statement of work; SLA = service level agreement

typically shifts some or all risk for achieving the desired outcome to the service provider.

Outcome-based business models have gained in popularity as more companies outside of the aerospace industry have adopted the concepts and have expanded the thinking to pure outsourced service deals. A well-structured outcome-based agreement compensates a service provider's higher risk with a higher reward. Unfortunately, some companies wrongfully structure deals around "all risk, no reward"; in these cases, a supplier or service provider that does not meet the desired results is penalized.

There are two types of outcome-based business models: a performance-based agreement and a vested outsourcing agreement.

Performance-Based Agreements

The relationship with suppliers under a performance-based agreement is different than with transactional providers because these agreements begin to shift the thinking away from activities to outcomes. However, they usually still pay a supplier using transaction-based pricing triggers. These contracts are often called "pay for performance" because they have an incentive or a penalty tied to specific service-level agreements (SLAs) outlined in the contract.

For instance, a company outsourcing its call center will likely still pay a cost per transaction (most often a cost per call or cost per minute); however, it creates incentives or penalties if the service provider does not hit a metric, such as answering 80% of the calls within 20 seconds. (It is the authors' opinion that incentives work better than penalties and create a more positive working relationship with service providers.)

Performance-based agreements usually require a higher level of interface between the service provider and a buying company in order to review performance against objectives and determine the reward or penalty options that are typically embedded in the contract. These reviews are periodically scheduled and generally include representatives from the service provider and the client company contracting resources.

On some occasions, the buying company's service user(s) participate in the reviews; however, in these relationships there is a tendency for the client company to solely make the reward determination. If this is not done

properly and fairly, it can cause the buyer–supplier relationship to become more adversarial in nature.

The length of time covered by the agreement in a performance-based relationship is also typically longer than in transaction-based agreements. It is not uncommon to see agreements spanning 3 to 5 years, with some even longer; however, the contract language may allow for termination at the client company's determination (termination for convenience) within 30, 60, or 90 days.

Vested Outsourcing

Vested outsourcing or the vested approach is a highly collaborative outsourcing business model in which both the client and service provider have a vested economic interest in each other's success. An excellent example is Microsoft and Accenture's relationship, called OneFinance. Both parties entered into a 7-year agreement in which Accenture was challenged to transform Microsoft's back office procure-to-pay processes. The agreement is structured so that the more successful Accenture is at achieving Microsoft's goals and transforming the work, the more successful Accenture becomes itself. (For more information and case studies on vested outsourcing, see Vitasek, Manrodt, & Kling, *Vested: How P&G, McDonald's, and Microsoft Are Redefining Winning in Business Relationships*.)

The term *vested outsourcing* was originally coined by University of Tennessee researchers to describe highly successful outcome-based outsourcing agreements that the researchers studied as part of a significant research project funded by the U.S. Air Force. Research showed that vested outsourcing agreements combined an outcome-based model with the Nobel Prize–winning concepts of behavioral economics[†] and the principles of shared value.[‡] Using these concepts, companies enter into highly collaborative arrangements designed to create value for everyone involved above and beyond the conventional buy–sell economics of a transaction-based agreement.

The vested outsourcing model is best used when a company has transformational or innovation objectives that it cannot achieve itself or by using conventional transaction-based or performance-based approaches. These transformational or innovation objectives are referred to as *desired outcomes*; it is these desired outcomes that form the foundation of the agreement. A desired outcome can be defined as a *measurable*

[†]Behavioral economics is the study of the quantified impact of individual behavior or of the decision makers within an organization. The study of behavioral economics is evolving more broadly into the concept of relational economics, which proposes that economic value can be expanded through positive relationships with mutual advantage (win–win) thinking rather than adversarial relationships (win–lose or lose–lose).

[‡]Shared value thinking involves entities working together to bring innovations that benefit the parties—with a conscious effort that the parties gain (or share) in the rewards. Two advocates are Harvard Business School's Michael Porter and Mark Kramer, who profiled their "big idea" in the January–February 2011 *Harvard Business Review*. The article states that shared value creation will drive the next wave of innovation and productivity growth in the global economy. Porter is renowned for his Five Forces model of competitive advantage. Due to his prominence, it is likely that his take on shared value, although focused on society, will cause practitioners to embrace shared value approaches.

business objective that focuses on what will be accomplished as a result of the work performed. A desired outcome is not a task-oriented SLA utilized in a conventional statement of work or performance-based agreement; rather, it is a mutually agreed upon, objective, and measurable set of deliverables for which the service provider will be rewarded—even if some of the accountability is shared with the company that is outsourcing. A desired outcome is generally categorized as an improvement to cost, schedule, market share, revenue, customer service levels, customer satisfaction levels, or performance.

Another great example of a vested outsourcing agreement is one between Jaguar and Unipart. Unipart was inherently incentivized under its 10-year agreement to make significant investments that would increase dealer support and ultimately improve customer loyalty for service parts management effectiveness and efficiency. Under the agreement, Unipart helped Jaguar move from number 9 in JD Power's customer loyalty ranking to number 1 by leveraging vested thinking.[84] Together, the companies were able to reduce the number of cars waiting on warranty parts by 98%, while at the same time reducing inventory levels by 35%. (Inventory costs money to hold, store, manage, and maintain; thus, less inventory on hand costs less.)

Table 9–7 summarizes the typical characteristics of performance-based and vested-based approaches.

INVESTMENT-BASED MODEL (INSOURCING)

The investment-based approach, also known as insourcing, provides an option for organizations to "make" or produce the needed functions, services, or products within their organization. This is opposed to outsourcing where the organization contracts or "buys" needed functions, services, or products from another organization.

Shared Services

Companies that struggle to meet complex business requirements using conventional transaction-based or outcome-based approaches usually invest to develop capabilities themselves (or insource). In these cases, many companies have chosen to adopt what is commonly referred to as a "shared services" structure, which is the establishment of an internal organization modeled on an arms-length outsourcing arrangement. Using this method, processes are typically centralized into a shared services organization and departments are cross-charged for the services used.

A key driver when building a shared services organization or a joint venture structure is to centralize and standardize operations that improve operational efficiencies. The results can be significant. American Productivity and Quality Center (APQC) research shows a direct correlation between low procurement cost and shared services or centralized procurement function. Specifically, companies with centralized and shared services procurement functions experience procurement costs almost one-third of those of companies that have decentralized functions.[85] The chart in **Figure 9–5** shows the procurement cost performance of centralized, shared, and decentralized procurement structures.

A vested outsourcing business model seeks to align the interests of the company with the interests of the service provider by following five rules of the vested approach for

Table 9-7 Attributes of Outcome-Based Business Models					
Sourcing Relationship	Focus	Interaction	Cooperation Level	Required Trust Level	Characterized By
Outcome-based/ performance-based relationship	Outcomes or performance	SRM governance, performance incentives, fees at risk	Integrated	Integrated	Longer-term relationship
Vested outsourcing relationship	Mutual gain, shared outcomes	Vested agreement, vested governance framework, performance incentives, margin matching	Integrated: cooperative, win–win	Integrated: Behave as single entity	Interdependent outcomes, aligned, mutual gain, managed performance, long-term relationship
Key: SRM = strategic resource management					

Reproduced from Vitasek, K., Keith, B., Eckler, J., & Evans, D. (n.d.). Unpacking sourcing business models: 21st century solutions for sourcing services. Retrieved from http://www.vestedway.com/wp-content/uploads/2012/09/Unpacking-Sourcing.pdf.

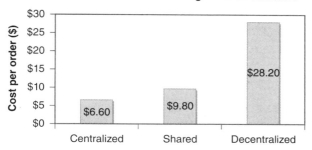

**Cost of Purchase Orders
Based on Procurement Organization Structure**

FIGURE 9-5 Procurement cost performance.

Reproduced from Vitasek, K., Keith, B., Eckler, J., & Evans, D. (n.d.). Unpacking sourcing business models: 21st century solutions for sourcing services. Retrieved from http://www.vestedway.com/wp-content/uploads/2012/09/Unpacking-Sourcing.pdf.

structuring the buyer–supplier relationship. These rules, when followed by shared services organizations, will better align the interests of internal shared services organizations with their internal customers.

Although many shared services organizations are set up to naturally follow some of the vested rules, most shared services do not follow all five rules. Yet, research shows that doing so would create a tighter alignment and further drive efficiencies for the provider.[86] Specifically, shared services organizations and joint ventures could benefit by applying the lessons of a vested approach. **Table 9-8** provides the authors' viewpoint with regard to the maturity of shared services in applying vested principles.

Equity Partner

Some companies decide they do not have the internal capabilities necessary for the work, yet they do not want to outsource for a variety of reasons. In these cases, companies may opt to develop a joint venture or other legal form in an effort to acquire and assure mission-critical goods and services. These equity partnerships can take many different legal forms, from buying a service provider, to becoming a subsidiary, to equity-sharing joint ventures. These partnerships may require the strategic interweaving of infrastructure and heavy co-investment. Equity partnerships, by default, bring costs "in house" and create a fixed cost burden. Because of this, equity partnerships often conflict with the desires of many organizations to create more variable and flexible cost structures on their balance sheets. **Table 9–9** outlines the typical characteristics of both shared services– and joint venture–type investment-based sourcing relationships.

RELATING CAAVE TO STRATEGIC RELATIONSHIPS

How does this relate to CAAVE and to strategic relationships? Managers have to first determine which approach to utilize. Should the relationship remain transactional in nature, or should it be more strategic? How critical is alignment between their providers? What is the potential for value creation?

Considering the current evidence, the CAAVE approach incorporates contemporary constructs necessary for thorough evaluation of strategic relationships in a parsimonious framework. The CAAVE model rests on four quadrants (see **Figure 9-6**) while integrating relationship dynamics as well as firm compatibility based on assessment of the constructs of each set of axes. These four quadrants provide basic outcomes of the relationship (transactional as well as strategic) and the styles or behaviors that would need to be practiced by both parties to maximize the potential of the relationship. Each of these four quadrants is discussed

Table 9-8 Application of Vested Principles in Shared Services Business Models	
Vested Rule	**Level of Shared Services Adoption**
Outcome-based vs. transaction-based	Low
Focus on the what, not the how	Medium
Clearly defined and measurable desired outcomes	Medium
Pricing model with incentives that optimize for cost/service trade-offs	Low
Insight vs. oversight governance	Medium

Reproduced from Vitasek, K., Keith, B., Eckler, J., & Evans, D. (n.d.). Unpacking sourcing business models: 21st century solutions for sourcing services. Retrieved from http://www.vestedway.com/wp-content/uploads/2012/09/Unpacking-Sourcing.pdf.

Table 9-9 Attributes of Investment-Based Business Models

Sourcing Relationship	Focus	Interaction	Cooperation Level	Required Trust Level	Characterized By
Shared services	Leveraging cost and investments	Cross-company services, may include multicompany service	Integrated: Cooperative, win–win	Integrated: Dictated by equity sharing	Formal charter, intercompany governance structure, interdependent outcomes, aligned goals and objectives, managed performance, win–win relationship
Equity partner	Equity sharing	Joint venture asset-based governance framework	Integrated: Cooperative, interrelated structure	Integrated: Dictated by equity sharing	Legally bound, formal strategic partnerships, mergers and acquisitions, asset sharing/holding

Reproduced from Vitasek, K., Keith, B., Eckler, J., & Evans, D. (n.d.). Unpacking sourcing business models: 21st century solutions for sourcing services. Retrieved from http://www.vestedway.com/wp-content/uploads/2012/09/Unpacking-Sourcing.pdf.

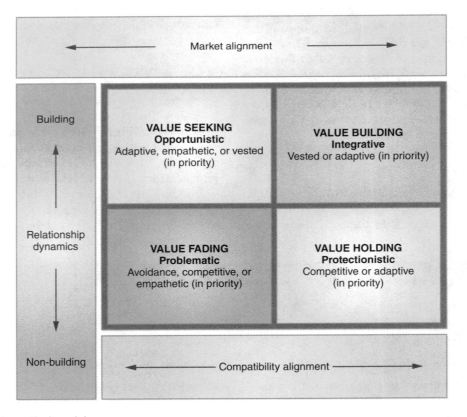

FIGURE 9-6 CAAVE theoretical model.

Reproduced from Ledlow, G., Manrodt, K., & Stephens, J. (2012). Measuring compatibility gaps in strategic relationships. In N. Delener, et al. (Eds.), *Mapping the global future: Evolution through innovation and excellence* (pp. 420–431). New York: Global Business and Technology Association.

in the following list, followed by a discussion of each of the five styles in the CAAVE model:

- *Value fading*: Indicative of behaviors that destroy relationship trust and of incompatible cultures. For instance, the entities may have worked well together in the past, but economic circumstances changed and now they fight for resources.
- *Value holding*: Typified by one party exerting its "power" to hold onto an unequal portion of the value in the relationship. In marketing literature, these firms are referred to as "channel captains" in that they hold the power and ability to dictate how suppliers will perform. This performance could be tied to new demands on packaging, shipping, or the like.
- *Value seeking*: Characterized by one party taking a passive role, giving up value in hopes that the other party will be fair. In this instance there is a level of trust and a desire to work together. It is not enlightened, because one party could take advantage of the other.
- *Value building*: Characterized by a balanced relationship in which both parties work under the concept "What's in it for we?" (WIIFWe) to grow *and share value* created by the relationship. In this case, all of the partners share value from the relationship. It is characterized by innovation and cost reduction for the buyer, while at the same time the provider receives revenue or margin increases due to efficiencies and/or more opportunities to expand business with the buyer.

Within each of the four quadrants are five basic ways, or styles, that firms can adopt. Each of these is explained here.

1. Competitive
   - When quick, decisive action is vital to the organization (e.g., emergency situations such as a disaster or terrorism incident or accident)
   - On important issues where unpopular actions need implementing (e.g., cost cutting, enforcing unpopular rules, discipline)
   - On issues vital to company welfare and survival when you know you are right
   - Against people who take advantage of noncompetitive behavior
2. Avoidance
   - When an issue is trivial or more important issues are pressing
   - When you perceive no chance of satisfying your needs
   - When potential disruption outweighs the benefits of resolution

- To let people cool down and regain perspective
- When gathering information supersedes making an immediate decision
- When the relationship could be damaging to the organization and is not critical
- When partnering or contracting seems rushed or pushed as a result of other issues; short-term strategy to buy time

3. Adaptive
   - When goals are important, but not worth the effort or potential disruption of competing because the situation does not allow a collaborative approach
   - When opponents with equal power are committed to mutually exclusive goals; adapting to the contract/partnership situation and creating the most advantageous position
   - To achieve temporary settlements to complex issues
   - To arrive at expedient solutions under time pressure
   - As a backup when a vested or competitive style is unsuccessful
4. Vested
   - May not always work (takes two to make this style work) and requires trust between parties
   - Requires the identification of a broader range of strategies, transaction costs, and longer-term goals
   - To find an integrative solution when both sets of concerns are too important to be compromised
   - When your objective is to learn and mutually benefit from the relationship
   - To merge insights from people with different perspectives
   - To gain commitment by incorporating concerns into a consensus
   - To work through organizational issues, like transaction costs, service levels, and the like that could harm a relationship
5. Empathetic
   - When you find you are wrong; to allow a better position to be heard, to learn, and to show your reasonableness
   - When issues are more important to others than to you; to satisfy others and maintain cooperation
   - To build social capital for later issues
   - To minimize loss when you are outmatched and lack any competitive advantage

- When harmony and stability are especially important; when you are building up a weaker partner in the market
- To allow subordinates to develop by learning from their mistakes

However, it is necessary to validate the inclusion of organizational theory, human dynamics, communication, and leadership into the genre of outsourcing as firms strategically seek relationships for purposes of contracts and partnerships. Williamson supports that strategic relationships need development and evolution to incorporate relationship constructs. "James Buchanan advises that economics as a science of contract is underdeveloped and that this should be rectified"[87] and "… additional gains can be realized if order-preserving mechanisms are devised that enable the parties to preserve cooperation during contract execution."[88] Carter and Easton support the inclusion of constructs of strategy (sustainability), organizational culture, and transparency (stakeholder engagement) with the goal of sustainability into the evolution of the method supported by the CAAVE model.[89] The strongest guidance offered by Williamson follows:

Interestingly, both the economist Friedrich Hayek and the organization theorist Chester Barnard were in agreement on this point, albeit with differences. Hayek (1945, pp. 526–527) focused on the adaptation of economic actors who adjust spontaneously to changes in the market. Upon looking "at the price system as … a mechanism for communication information," the marvel of the market resides in "how little the individual participants need to know to be able to take the right action." By contrast, Barnard (1938, p. 9) featured coordinated adaptation among economic actors working through administration (hierarchy). The latter is accomplished not spontaneously but in a "conscious, deliberate, purposeful" way with the use of administration. Thus, economic theory meets organizational theory in the real world.[90]

So, as a leader, how do you apply a style for specific strategic relationships? An overview and application context of the CAAVE model styles follows. These five styles are competitive, avoidance, adaptive, vested, and empathetic (see **Figure 9-7**). The CAAVE model enables assessment, initially based on market dynamics (includes consideration of transaction cost economics [TCE]) and basic relationship dynamics. This assessment offers recommendations of styles for firms to utilize within the buyer–supplier relationship.

Integrating the CAAVE model styles with Williamson's styles within the quadrants (with suggested styles for each quadrant) is the next focus of the model (see **Figure 9-8**). Style migration within quadrants is expected in the model. It is important to note that Nash's Win–Win model integrates the CAAVE model only in the upper-right corner of the model (specifically, the Value Building quadrant).

The CAAVE model integrates Nash's and Williamson's concepts within a flexible framework. Once firms assess their strategic outsourcing relationship considering their compatibility or alignment between styles, then assessments can be conducted for deeper relationship dynamics and compatibility, as well as trust. As firms are assessed either in the Value Building quadrant or close to that quadrant, the integration of Nash's Win–Win situation is realized. You can utilize the appropriate style based on the quadrants you assess your strategic partner (or potential partner) to be in. The goal is to move strategic partnerships into the Value Building quadrant or area, which focuses on the vested style to build strategic relationships.

SITUATIONAL ASSESSMENT PREFERRED STYLE:	Style		Score (higher score preferred)	
	Competitive	C	✗	5
	Avoidance	A	✗	4
	Adaptive	A	!	9
	Vested	V	✓	13
	Empathetic	E	!	9

FIGURE 9-7 Style selection for CAAVE based on market (TCE included) and relationship dynamics.

Reproduced from Ledlow, G., Manrodt, K., & Stephens, J. (2012). Measuring compatibility gaps in strategic relationships. In N. Delener, et al. (Eds.), *Mapping the global future: Evolution through innovation and excellence* (pp. 420–431). New York: Global Business and Technology Association.

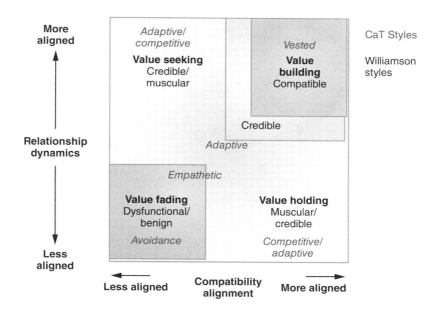

FIGURE 9-8 Evolution of CAAVE model with Williamson styles and CAAVE (CaT) styles.

© 2011 Jerry Ledlow, PhD, & Karl Manrodt, PhD. Used with permission.

Considering the previous evidence, relationship dynamics, compatibility between firms, and trust can be parsimoniously measured by subconstructs of trust, innovation, communication, team orientation, and focus, as these constructs best measure organizations within a successful strategic relationship. *Trust* is performing as promised and meeting commitments. Without performance, trust cannot exist. Strong and trusting relationships allow the parties to innovate by sharing risks and rewards, investing in each other's capabilities, and collaborating to achieve common goals. *Communication* refers to the open and timely sharing of all information that is relevant to a partner's decision-making ability. With *team orientation*, both sides of a relationship must believe in the relationship. Efforts are made to view decisions from the partner's perspective to mitigate opportunism and promote collaboration. Finally, the dimension of *focus* means that there is common purpose and direction on both sides. When the five dimensions of compatibility and trust are cultivated, relationships can prosper due to greater collaboration and better performance. See **Table 9-10** for an example of a CaT assessment.

The compatibility for a successful, vested-style, win–win long-term strategic relationship is measured by key stakeholders of the dyadic (or triadic or quadratic) relationship through an interactive survey tool that examines the key constructs from multiple angles. Table 9-10 shows an example for a large-firm buyer and large-firm supplier.

Cousins and Spekman strongly suggest that relationship assessment and development include assessment of constructs, in order to include service fulfillment and financial concerns within the realm of performance measurement for strategic relationships.[91] "Unquestionably, the supplier's side should be included in any strategic thinking on the field of purchasing and supply management."[92] Unfortunately, more leaders have fallen back to qualitative methods of supplier selection (for lack of a better approach).[93] "Key to this research would be placing meaningful measurements on the effect of relationships on a company."[94] (See **Figure 9-9**.)

The firms' assessment is plotted on the CAAVE model quadrants to evaluate the potential success of a vested-style and long-term strategic relationship. The beginnings of a compatibility index for firms can be derived from this assessment. This illustrates the integration of relationship dynamics and compatibility between firms with market dynamics, TCE, and win–win situations. Once firms engage in strategic partnerships, performance is added to the equation with ongoing relationship dynamics and compatibility assessments.

As outsourcing and strategic partnerships become more critical to the success of the organization, it will become imperative to select the right firm with which to partner. Failure to do so could lead to reduced service levels, increased costs, and lost market share and profitability. In many cases, selecting the right strategic partner has led to

Compatibility Dimensions	Buyer	Buyer Perception of Supplier	Supplier	Supplier Perception of Buyer
Focus	85%	61%	75%	72%
Team orientation	83%	64%	83%	67%
Communication	77%	66%	74%	72%
Innovation	83%	70%	75%	75%
Trust	78%	66%	81%	66%

Table 9-10 CaT Assessment Example: Measuring Two Firms' Compatibility and Perceptions of Each Other

increased innovation, along with lower costs and increased service, market share, or profitability.

Returning to the Microsoft/Accenture partnership described earlier in this chapter, Microsoft outsourced all of its procure-to-pay processes for 95 countries to Accenture. As a result of this relationship, Microsoft has achieved significant cost reductions and process standardizations. When asked how it was possible for Microsoft to trust Accenture so much, the Microsoft response was "How can I not trust them?"

These relationships also thrive when there are compatible goals, beliefs, and objectives. Managers should work to determine the level of compatibility between organizations, because this enables a joint commitment to a shared vision and to a set of desired outcomes. Compatibility improves your ability to have empathy for your partner and builds trust. This, then, gives each party comfort to invest in transformational work and grow the size and number of opportunities both firms can obtain together.

With support and evidence, the CAAVE model offers a contemporary approach to evaluation of strategic partnerships. From the literature, it was necessary to develop the relationship dynamics view of strategic partnerships while integrating cooperative game theory, transaction cost economics, and market dynamics into the package of constructs with regard to strategic agreements and partnerships among firms. How can health leaders use this approach—integrating organizational culture, situational assessment, and strategic relationship evaluation into a system to improve the organization?

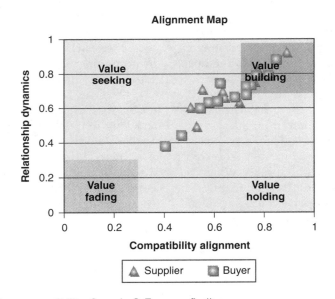

FIGURE 9-9 Measuring and plotting compatibility: Sample CaT survey findings.

Reproduced from Ledlow, G., Manrodt, K., & Stephens, J. (2012). Measuring compatibility gaps in strategic relationships. In N. Delener, et al. (Eds.), *Mapping the global future: Evolution through innovation and excellence* (pp. 420–431). New York: Global Business and Technology Association.

SUMMARY

This chapter discussed the leader's role in strategically leading the health organization. Basic principles of creating and implementing mission, vision, values, strategies, goals, objective statements, and action steps were presented. A matrix tool was described that assists in understanding the various relationships within the environment that affect organizational culture and change management. The leader's self-awareness and understanding of cultural factors are key considerations in the leader's ability to effect change within the organization, which may either narrow or expand the strategic leadership options available for managing organizational culture change. The CAAVE model, vested outsourcing, and the CaT assessment were utilized to offer a leadership system to apply to strategic relationships where situational assessment, organizational culture, and strategy integrate within the health organization.

DISCUSSION QUESTIONS

1. What are the strategic direction elements of the strategic plan? What are the other elements of the strategic and operational plan? What are the various challenges a health leader faces in institutional, resource-dependent, and contingent environments? Which strategies might you suggest that the leader could implement to obtain successful outcomes to include strategic sourcing?
2. Discuss the levels of organizational culture. Summarize the actions and behaviors a health leader would perform to proactively and positively change organizational culture.
3. Can you predict how strategic planning might positively influence organizational culture and the internal environment? How does strategy selection (e.g., competitive, adaptive) reinforce those changes to organizational culture and the internal environment?
4. How might external and internal environmental factors influence the strategic plan and the organizational culture of a health organization? In your answer, highlight the basic differences between vertical and horizontal external environments compared to internal institutional, resource-dependent, and contingent environments. Which strategies might a health leader operating in these environments leverage to ensure success?
5. Discuss a methodology to perform internal environmental scanning, monitoring, and assessment and external environmental scanning, forecasting, and monitoring for a hospital or group practice, public health organization, long-term care organization, stand-alone allied health practice, or retail pharmacy.
6. Explain how you would interpret the current external environmental factors in the health industry; translate your interpretation into a critical list of action items for a health organization. How would you appraise each element on this list in terms of where it should be addressed by the health organization (e.g., strategic plan, directional strategies, external or internal environment, organizational culture), noting that critical list items may affect more than one area of the health organization?

EXERCISES

1. Identify the different challenges a health leader faces in institutional, resource-dependent, and contingent environments. Which strategies should a health leader implement for successful outcomes to include strategic sourcing? Your answer should take the form of a one- to two-page paper.
2. In a one- to two-page paper, summarize the levels of organizational culture and predict the actions and behaviors a health leader would perform to proactively and positively change organizational culture.
3. In a one- to two-page paper, explain how strategic planning can positively influence organizational culture and the internal environment. In your paper, describe how strategy selection (e.g., competitive, adaptive) reinforces those changes to organizational culture and the internal environment.
4. Analyze how external and internal environmental factors influence the strategic plan and the organizational culture of a health organization, highlighting the basic differences between vertical and

horizontal external environments compared to internal institutional, resource-dependent, and contingent environments. Which strategies might a health leader operating in these environments be able to leverage to ensure success? Your answer should take the form of a two- to three-page paper.

5. In a one- to two-page paper, outline a methodology to perform internal environmental scanning, monitoring, and assessment and external environmental scanning, forecasting, and monitoring for a hospital or group practice, public health organization,

long-term care organization, stand-alone allied health practice, or retail pharmacy.

6. Evaluate and interpret the current external environmental factors in the health industry; translate your interpretation into a list of critical action items for a health organization. How could you appraise each element on this list in terms of how it should be addressed by the health organization (e.g., strategic plan, directional strategies, external or internal environment, organizational culture), noting that critical list items may affect more than one area of the health organization?

REFERENCES

1. *U.S. News and World Report.* (2005, Oct. 22). America's best leaders: Q&A with Donna Shalala, President of the University of Miami. Retrieved from http://www.usnews.com/usnews/news/articles/051022/22shalala.htm.
2. Ledlow, G., Cwiek, M., & Johnson, J. (2002). Dynamic culture leadership: Effective leader as both scientist and artist. In N. Delener & C-n. Chao (Eds.), *Proceedings of Global Business and Technology Association International Conference; Beyond Boundaries: Challenges of Leadership, Innovation, Integration and Technology* (pp. 694–740). New York: Global Business and Technology Association.
3. Swayne, L. E., Duncan, W. J., & Ginter, P. M. (2006). *Strategic management of health care organizations* (5th ed.). Malden, MA: Blackwell, p. 187.
4. Swayne et al., note 3, pp. 191–192.
5. Swayne et al., note 3, p. 198.
6. Lerner, H. (2003, November). Vision statements. *Beyond Numbers*, 9.
7. Lerner, H. (2003). Vision statements. *Principal's Report, 3*(12), 2. Also appears in Swayne et al., note 3, p. 200.
8. Yukl, G. (1994). *Leadership in organizations* (3rd ed.). Englewood Cliffs, NJ: Prentice Hall.
9. Schein, E. H. (1999). *The corporate culture survival guide: Sense and nonsense about culture change.* San Francisco, CA: Jossey-Bass.
10. Swayne et al., note 3.
11. Morris, G. B. (1988). The executive: A pathfinder. *Organizational Dynamics, 16*(2), 62–77.
12. Senge, P. (1998). The leader's new work. In G. Hickman (Ed.), *Leading organizations: Perspectives for a new era* (pp. 439–457). Thousand Oaks, CA: Sage.
13. Proverbs 29:18.
14. Hart, S. (1992). An integrative framework for strategy-making processes. *Academy of Management Review, 17,* 327–351.
15. Swayne et al., note 3, p. 187.
16. Swayne et al., note 3, p. 227.
17. Swayne et al., note 3, p. 227, Exhibit 6-2.
18. Dess, G. G., & Lumpkin, G. T. (2005). Emerging issues in strategy process research. In M. A. Hitt, R. E. Freeman, & J. S. Harrison (Eds.), *The Blackwell handbook of strategic management* (p. 3). Malden, MA: Blackwell.
19. Roney, C. W. (2004). *Strategic management methodology: Generally accepted principles for practitioners.* Westport, CT: Praeger, p. 44.
20. Yukl, note 8, pp. 103–104.
21. DiMaggio, P. J., & Powell, W. W. (1991). Introduction. In W. W. Powell & P. J. DiMaggio (Eds.), *The new institutionalism in organizational analysis* (pp. 1–38). Chicago: University of Chicago Press.
22. Tolbert, P. S., & Zucker, L. G. (1996). The institutionalization of institutional theory. In S. R. Clegg, C. Hardy, & W. R. Nord (Eds.), *The handbook of organization studies* (pp. 175–190). London: Sage.
23. DiMaggio, P. J., & Powell, W. W. (1983). The iron cage revisited: Institutional isomorphism and collective rationality in organizational fields. *American Sociological Review, 48,* 147–160.
24. DiMaggio & Powell, note 23.
25. Meyer, J. W., & Rowan, B. (1977). Institutionalized organizations: Formal structure as myth and ceremony. *American Journal of Sociology, 83*(2), 340–363.
26. Means, B., Toyama, Y., Murphy, R., Bakia, M., & Jones, K. (2009). Evaluation of evidence-based practices in online learning: A meta-analysis and review

of online learning studies. U.S. Department of Education. Retrieved from http://www2.ed.gov/rschstat/eval/tech/evidence-based-practices/finalreport.pdf.

27. Van Wijngaarden, J. D. H., Scholten, G. R. M., & Van Wijk, K. P. (2012). Strategic analysis for health care organizations: The suitability of the SWOT analysis. *The International Journal of Health Planning and Management, 27*(1), 34–49.

28. Swayne et al., note 3, p. 159, Exhibit 4-3.

29. DiMaggio & Powell, note 23.

30. Meyer & Rowan, note 25.

31. Moran, R. T., Abramson, N. R., & Moran, S. V. (2014). *Managing cultural differences* (9th ed.). New York: Routledge. Retrieved from http://books.google.com/books?hl=en&lr=&id=zrbpAgAAQBAJ&oi=fnd&pg=PP1&dq=organizational+culture+in+healthcare+management&ots=ugMqtJP4Pn&sig=OmXzDZXifXxX-KWcvxXSO9qhjPY#v=onepage&q&f=false, p. 11.

32. Farnsworth Mick, S. S., & Shay, P. D. (2014). A primer of organization theories in health care. In S. S. Farnsworth Mick & P. D. Shay (Eds.), *Advances in Health Care Organization Theory* (pp. 25–47). San Francisco, CA: Wiley. Retrieved from http://books.google.com/books?hl=en&lr=&id=GenoAwAAQBAJ&oi=fnd&pg=PA25&dq=contingency+theory+in+healthcare&ots=tpzdkkves0&sig=5f3WWEm6OlHoI836xxKgA9t2oss#v=onepage&q=contingency%20theory%20in%20healthcare&f=false.

33. Pfeffer, J., & Salancik, G. (1978). *The external control of organizations: A resource dependence perspective.* New York: Harper and Row.

34. Coppola, M. N., Hudak, R., & Gidwani, P. (2002). A theoretical perspective utilizing resource dependency to predict issues with the repatriation of Medicare eligible military beneficiaries back into TRICARE. *Military Medicine, 167*(9), 726–731.

35. Wheelen, T. L., & Hunger, J. D. (2006). Internal scanning: Organizational analysis. In T. L. Wheelen & J. D. Hunger (Eds.), *Strategic management and business policy* (10th ed., pp. 104–136). Englewood Cliffs, NJ: Prentice Hall.

36. Swayne et al., note 3, p. 162.

37. Wheelen & Hunger, note 35.

38. Pfeffer & Salancik, note 33.

39. Schein, E. H. (1993). Defining organizational culture. In J. M. Shafritz, J. S. Ott, & Y. S. Jang (Eds.), *Classics of organization theory* (6th ed., pp. 372–398). London: Thomson.

40. Lawrence, P. R., & Lorsch, J. W. (1967). *Organizations and environment.* Boston: Harvard Business School Press.

41. Itzkowitz, G. (1996). *Contingency theory.* Washington, D.C.: University Press.

42. Child, J. (1972). Organization structure, environment and performance: The role of strategic choice. *Sociology, 6,* 1–22.

43. Child, note 42.

44. Tosi, H. L., & Slocum, J. W. (1984). Contingency theory: Some suggested directions. *Journal of Management, 10*(1), 9–26.

45. Khan, R. M. (2014). The relationship between environmental scanning sources of information and new service development performance: A case of Bangkok Hospital, Thailand. *Second Global Conference on Business Management* (pp. 50–93). Singapore: Asia Pacific International Academy.

46. Swayne et al., note 3, p. 57.

47. Rakich, J., Longest, B., & Darr, K. (1992). *Managing health services organizations.* Baltimore, MD: Health Professions Press, p. 17

48. Brook, R. H. (n.d.). Changes in the healthcare system: Goals, forces, solutions. Retrieved from http://www.rand.org/cgi-bin/health/showab.cgi?key=1998_77&year=1998.

49. Coppola, M. N., Erckenbrack, D., & Ledlow, G. R. (2008). Stakeholder dynamics. In J. A. Johnson (Ed.), *Health organizations: Theory, behavior, and development* (pp. 255–278). Sudbury, MA: Jones & Bartlett.

50. Ledlow, G., Corry, A., & Cwiek, M. (2007). *Optimize your healthcare supply chain performance: A strategic approach.* Chicago: Health Administration Press.

51. Weber, M. (1964/1925). *Basic concepts of sociology* (H. P. Secher, Trans.). New York: Citadel Press.

52. Weber, M. (1948/1921). Bureaucracy. In H. H. Gerthand & C. W. Mills (Eds.), *From Max Weber* (pp. 196–244). London: Routledge Kegan Paul.

53. Parsons, T. (1960/1957). The distribution of power in American society. In T. Parsons (Ed.), *Structure and process in modern society* (pp. 199–225). New York: The Free Press.

54. Morcol, G. (2005). Phenomenology of complexity theory and cognitive science: Implications for developing an embodied knowledge of public administration and policy. *Administrative Theory & Praxis, 27*(1), 1–23.

55. Miller, K. (1998). Nurses at the edge of chaos: The application of "new science" concepts to

organizational systems. *Management Communication Quarterly*, *12*(1), 112–127.

56. Daft, R. L. (2003). *Organization theory and design* (8th ed.). Cincinnati, OH: South Western College.

57. Nonaka, I., Kodama, M., Hirose, A., & Kohlbacher, F. (2014). Dynamic fractal organizations for promoting knowledge-based transformation: A new paradigm for organizational theory. *European Management Journal*, *32*, 137–146. Retrieved from http://144.76.219.46/mojtaba /Elsevier/European%20Management%20Journal /Issue%201/1-s2.0-S026323731300025X-main .pdf, p. 137.

58. Schein, note 9.

59. Schein, note 9.

60. Schein, note 9.

61. Schein, note 9.

62. Sathe, V. (1985). *Culture and related corporate realities: Text, cases, and readings on organizational entry, establishment, and change.* Homewood, IL: Irwin, p. 6.

63. Louis, M. (1985). An investigator's guide to workplace culture. In P. Frost, L. Moore, M. Louis, C. Lunberg, & J. Martin (Eds.), *Organizational culture* (p. 74). Beverly Hills, CA: Sage.

64. Martin, J. (2002). *Organizational culture: Mapping the terrain.* Thousand Oaks, CA: Sage, p. 59.

65. Beebe, S. A., & Masterson, J. T. (1997). *Communicating in small groups: Principles and practices* (5th ed.). New York: Addison-Wesley Educational, pp. 173–174.

66. Martin, note 64, pp. 55–56.

67. Schein, note 9.

68. Schein, note 9.

69. Martin, note 64, p. 86.

70. Martin, note 64, p. 87.

71. Wirth, R. A. (2010). Business culture. Retrieved from http://www.entarga.com/stratplan/culture.htm.

72. Office of Minority Health, United States Department of Health and Human Services. (2013). What is cultural competence? Retrieved from http://minorityhealth.hhs.gov/templates/browse .aspx?lvl=2&lvlID=11.

73. Schein, note 9.

74. Kent, T., Johnson, J. A., & Graber, D. A. (1996). Leadership in the formation of new health care environments. *Health Care Supervisor*, *15*(2), 28–29.

75. Duck, J. D. (1998). Managing change: The art of balancing. In *Harvard Business Review on change* (p. 56). Boston: Harvard Business School Press.

76. Bennis, W., Parikh, J., & Lessem, R. (1996). *Beyond leadership: Balancing economics, ethics, and ecology* (rev. ed.). Cambridge, MA: Blackwell.

77. Aktas, M., Gelfand, M. J., & Hanges, P. J. (2016, February). Cultural tightness–looseness and perceptions of effective leadership. *Journal of Cross-Cultural Psychology*, *47*, 294–309, first published on September 22, 2015. doi:10.1177/0022022115606802

78. Schein, note 9.

79. Schein, note 9.

80. Schein, note 9.

81. Morrison, I. (2000). *Health care in the new millennium.* San Francisco: Jossey-Bass.

82. International Association of Contracting and Commercial Management. (2010, April/May). Contract negotiations continue to undermine value. In *2010 Top Terms in Negotiation*. Special Issue, International Association for Contract and Commercial Management.

83. Vitasek, K., Crawford, J., Nyden, J., & Kawamoto, K. (2011). *The vested outsourcing manual.* New York: Palgrave Macmillan.

84. JD Power and Associates. (2010). 2010 sales satisfaction index study. Retrieved from http://autos .jdpower.com/content/study-auto/7mEkcsf/2010 -sales-satisfaction-index-study.htm.

85. Vitasek, K., Keith, B., Eckler, J., Evans, D., Crawford, J., Manrodt, K., & Kawamoto, K. Unpacking sourcing business models: 21st century solutions for sourcing services. Benchmark statistics courtesy of the American Productivity and Quality Center.

86. Dubois, A., & Pedersen, A.-C. (2002). Why relationships do not fit into purchasing portfolio models: A comparison between the portfolio and industrial network approaches. *European Journal of Purchasing and Supply Management*, *8*, 35–42.

87. Williamson, O. E. (2008). Outsourcing: Transaction cost economics and supply chain management. *Journal of Supply Chain Management* 44(2), 5–27.

88. Williamson, note 87, p. 6.

89. Carter, C. R., & Easton, P. L. (2011). Sustainable supply chain management: Evolution and future directions. *International Journal of Physical Distribution & Logistics Management*, *41*(1), 46–62.

90. Williamson, note 87, p. 7.

91. Cousins, P. D., & Spekman, R. (2003). Strategic supply and the management of inter- and intra-organizational relationships. *Journal of Purchasing and Supply Management*, *9*, 19–29.

92. Gelderman, C. J., & Van Weele, A. (2003). Handling measurement issues and strategic directions in Kraljic's purchasing portfolio model. *Journal of Purchasing and Supply Management, 9,* 207–216.

93. Luo, X., Wu, C., Rosenberg, D., & Barnes, D. (2009). Supplier selection in agile supply chains: An information-processing model and an illustration. *Journal of Purchasing and Supply Management, 15,* 249–262.

94. Parry, G., Graves, A., & James-Moore, M. (2006). The threat to core competence posed by developing closer supply chain relationships. *International Journal of Logistics, Research and Applications, 9*(3), 295–305.

Note: The GREaT Assessment System for PHEP and HPP is used in this chapter by permission of Health Supply Analytics, LLC. For more information contact support@healthsupplyanalytics.com.

ETHICS IN HEALTH LEADERSHIP

Healthcare executives should view ethics as a special charge and responsibility to the patient, client, or others served, the organization and its personnel, themselves and the profession, and, ultimately, but less directly, to society.
American College of Healthcare Executives, 2009

In recent years, the United States has seen the near-collapse of much of its banking system. In hindsight, the chaos was largely attributable to unethical practices and procedures enacted by a few unscrupulous, greedy members of the industry. With the collapse of WorldCom and Enron—both companies that manipulated the stock market and defrauded investors—and the conviction of Bernard Madoff, the mastermind behind a record-setting Ponzi scheme, higher education is realizing the essential need to study ethics and to incorporate those ethical principles and moral practices into the development schema of the next generation of business and health leaders. In support of this view, a review of the top 50 master of business administration (MBA) and master of health administration (MHA) programs in the United States over the last 5 years, as profiled by *U.S. News and World Report*, suggests that many graduate programs are incorporating ethics-based courses into their curricula. Clearly, it is critical for nascent health leaders to study health ethics so that they can develop a sound foundation upon which to base decisions, allocate resources, and develop organizational culture. The need for health ethics is magnified as healthcare organizations (HCOs) join together to leverage economies of scope and scale. The lack of ethical guidance for large HCOs has forced many organizations to rely on generalizations to resolve ethical issues arising in specific contexts.[1]

This chapter presents the ethical responsibilities of health leaders from an organizational perspective. Several ethical theories and frameworks are presented as structures to open up the discussion of ethics. In addition, regulatory compliance, which is essential to organizational morality, is presented from the aspect of a health organization. The chapter also discusses professional, educational, and contractual relationships affecting the operation of the health organization.

LEARNING OBJECTIVES

1. Define *distributive justice, ethics, morals, values, promise keeping,* and *leadership bankruptcy.* Describe how they are used by leaders in decision making based in an ethical framework.

2. Explain four ethical principles and four statutes or regulations that guide decision making associated with patient care.

3. Apply at least two ethical frameworks or distributive justice theories, with examples of moral practice of a leader, to an ethical issue in a health organization.

4. Analyze arguments and make a recommendation for health leaders to adopt utilitarian or deontological postures in their organization, and differentiate potential decisions leaders would make between the two frameworks to support your analysis and recommendation.

5. Compile a list of options that a leader in a health organization has to develop for an integrated system of ethics and moral practice, and summarize the potential impact of each option regarding appropriate ethical adaptation across the organization.

6. Compare and contrast at least three ethical frameworks or distributive justice theories for the topics of patient autonomy, beneficence, nonmaleficence, and justice, and interpret the moral practice associated with those frameworks (at least three) for a right-to-life issue and for the practice of euthanasia.

INTRODUCTION

Defining ethics can be difficult. According to Pozgar, ethics is a moral philosophy about concepts of right and wrong behaviors. Pozgar suggests that ethics "deals with values relating to human conduct with respect to the rightness and wrongness of actions and the goodness and badness of motives and ends."[2] In the context of the health leader, ethics refers to a set of moral guidelines, principles, and suggested standards of conduct for health professionals. All health leaders, regardless of their status as patient care providers, encounter ethical dilemmas or challenges.[3]

The ethical tone and moral expectations in any organization are set by the leader. Unethical leaders set the stage for harmful activities and outcomes that will eventually affect all people and all stakeholders in the organization. It may be said that ethical leaders have a moral responsibility to treat their followers with dignity and respect and that they must act in ways that promote the welfare of others—most immediately, the welfare of their followers. This consideration is of particular importance for health leaders who rely on actions that involve intrinsic aspects of an individual's values and behaviors to achieve motivational and goal-directed outcomes that support organizational success. Health ethicists have suggested that health organizations have an ethical and moral obligation to provide care that is not only of high quality, but also ethically driven and managed.[4]

Too often, ethics, ethical practice, and discussions of ethics are placed in a legal context of liability reduction and "legalism." In fact, the ethical component of many U.S. educational degree programs, both undergraduate and graduate, is embedded in some sort of "legal" or "law" course; the practice of ethics in a profession is likewise relegated to a "legal counsel office." This reality is based on the litigious environment of the health industry; lawsuits and settlements for breaches of ethical expectations and errors in health services delivery run rampant in today's world.

Health leaders model the behavior expected in the organization, including being a moral actor—a visible moral actor—in the health organization. Remember, leaders "do the right thing." Sometimes doing the right thing does not always agree with actions that limit the organization's legal liability, but that has to be the leader's decision. By the end of this chapter, you should be able to answer a key question in this arena: How will you balance "legalism" and "leadership practice" with regard to ethics and moral practice?

WHAT IS ETHICS?

Professional organizations and prospective employers frequently suggest that they are looking for ethical leaders. In response, we might ask ourselves, "What is ethics?" Within the literature, ethics is defined as a moral philosophy that focuses on concepts of right and wrong behaviors as linked to resource allocation. It deals with values relating to human conduct with respect to the rightness and wrongness of actions and the "goodness" and "badness" of motives. Ethics in the health field can be further defined as a set of moral principles and rules of conduct for health professionals to follow.[5,6]

Ethics can, at times, be culturally defined. What may be considered ethically and morally appropriate by one culture may be seen as inappropriate and immoral by another culture. For example, the triage and medical treatment of persons by gender, race, and age may be unethical, if not illegal, in the United States. In the United States, providers may find it extremely unethical to make medical decisions based on a patient's age. In fact, Americans may find it extremely distasteful that some countries with socialized medicine and national healthcare systems ration medical care for certain ailments for patients who have passed a certain age.[7] Americans find this form of triage "unethical" or, more simply, "not the right thing to do."

At a general and broad level, however, the United States holds to a system where medical triage is based on a patient's ability to pay. In many ways, persons who have health insurance coverage have access to the entire continuum of care, whereas those without coverage are severely limited in their ability to access the appropriate services within the continuum of care. Many democratic nations find the practice of basing medical care on remuneration "unethical," and not in keeping with the practice of "goodness." This practice, they suggest, violates a sense of beneficence and distributive justice attributed to health services. Clearly, ethics may not only be culturally driven, but also nationally recognized and lawfully upheld based on the beliefs and cultural norms advocated by a national government.[8]

Despite the ineffable and difficult-to-understand nature of ethics, health leaders should study ethics so that they can better understand the human condition and better appreciate the differing points of view presented in the environment. Areas in health where ethics may assist in decision making are highly eclectic. For example, the study of ethics can assist in decision making associated with finance, risk management, resource allocation, customer advocacy, law, and organizational standing policies, to name only a few areas. A health leader in possession of a wider point of view of the dynamic field is better able to handle the complex and challenging issues presented to him or her. This chapter covers some of the areas from which both an early careerist and a seasoned professional may base ethical decision making.

THE DIFFERENCE BETWEEN ETHICS, VALUES, AND MORALS

Ethics is the practice of "goodness and rightness" over "wrongness and badness" within a system of resource allocation and preferences. These principles are based on several factors gleaned from myriad experiences, which include, but are not limited to, constructs of values and morals. Societal norms and mores greatly influence ethical frameworks and moral practice; those norms and mores are embedded in the beliefs and values held by the members of that society.

Values are enduring beliefs based on some early form of indoctrination and experience. They are learned from parents, the community, school, peers, professional organizations, and personal self-development, to name only a few areas. Values inform beliefs; beliefs facilitate the development of attitudes; and attitudes contribute to behaviors. Changing attitudes is easier than changing beliefs; in turn, changing beliefs is easier than changing values. A health leader's values provide a basis from which to make decisions and establish preferences. For example, one controversial health debate centered on values focuses on a fetus's *right to life*. Health leaders who have embraced a belief from their own personal experience that life begins at conception may question the "ethics" of abortion. Such an early belief may be based on spiritual experiences or parental teachings. These enduring beliefs are difficult to change and are rarely modified within an individual's lifetime. All values are based on some internalized experience or learned behavior.

To unlearn and reorient values is difficult; value change is a complex issue for any individual.

Morals are applied practices derived from an ethical framework that is based on values and beliefs. These practices are based on behaviors learned through experience and internalized principles. Different from values, morals comprise the principles on which decision making is based. Morality is the level of compliance to an ethical framework. One way of conceptualizing morality is to think of it as a yardstick that measures each action, decision, or distribution of resources from the standpoint of the accepted ethical framework of a society, organization, community, group, or individual.

Principles are those immutable characteristics of value-based decision making that are broken down into mutually exclusive categories (nominal data) of outcomes or answers such as "yes/no" or "I strongly agree/agree/disagree/strongly disagree" (ordinal data). A principle may be a screening behavior upon which a decision is based. For example, one principle may be the belief, "All those who break the law need to be punished." Once this screening criterion is put into place (yes/no, I agree/disagree), the second step in the process may be acted upon. The progenitor step is to take action and to continue with the consequences of that principle based on an action; in this case, the action is to determine the degree of the punishment. In this second stage, more values-based and evaluative criteria are put into place based on the circumstances and factors associated with the actual breaking of the law. Because values are evaluative and subject to interpretation, a values-driven behavior of providing a "second chance" may result in no punishment for the law breaker or a larger consequence and penalty if forgiveness is not an option in the evaluative process.

Following this discussion, we can simply say that morals are the actions and outcomes of the human condition processed over time as evaluated against the ethical framework based on values and resource allocation principles. They arise when values, principles, and preferences (and other factors) are generally internalized through lived experiences. In reality, these lived experiences may take years to compile and practice. Because morals are so difficult to embrace without lived experiences, they are generally taught through storytelling and lessons.

Consequently, we learn about the lived experiences of populations in communities, groups in the organizations, and individual experiences in one's own life through the sharing of moral tales. One such example is the moral tale of the *Grasshopper and the Ants* from Aesop's fables.

In Aesop's fable, the ants diligently work through the warm summer days preparing for winter by constructing a summer nest and stockpiling food. During the period of time when the ants are working hard, the grasshopper plays the days away singing (**Figure 10-1**). When winter finally comes, and no food or shelter can be foraged above ground, the grasshopper finds itself starving and cold, while the ants are warm and well fed below ground. It is then that the grasshopper states the lesson of the story: "It is best to prepare for the days of necessity."[9] As an analogy, a health leader might simply suggest that eating right and taking care of your body and mind today ensures a higher quality of life tomorrow.

The "moral" of this story is that it is always best to prepare for one's future in the face of the uncertainty of the environment. However, because this "lived experience" may take an individual's entire lifetime to learn, the experience is shared through the lived experience of others through moral tales. Similar to propositional statements, morals can be statements of opinion presented as if they were true. As a result, they become the "moral compass" by which some leaders conduct their lives in both the personal and professional spheres.

SETTING AN ETHICAL STANDARD IN THE HEALTH ORGANIZATION

Health leaders face ethical dilemmas in their daily work of delivering health services and products within the health organization. This stands in contrast to the experiences of their "strictly business"-oriented peers in the nonhealth, for-profit environment. In respect to patient care options, the ethical considerations of the health leader may often be tied to those of the physician, but not always. The physician's ethical duty derives from the Hippocratic Oath and (for many) Section 5 of the Code of Ethics of the American Medical Association, which states that in an emergency physicians should do their best to render service to the

FIGURE 10-1 *The Grasshopper and the Ants.*

Reproduced from *The Aesop for children with pictures by Milo Winter.* Copyright © 1919, by Rand McNally & Company.

patient, despite prejudice of any kind. By comparison, the health leader of an organization may have less of an ethical and legal duty to provide care that exceeds the standing policies and procedures established by the governing board. Health leaders may often find themselves torn between owing allegiance to the financial stability of the organization and the charitable nature of the health profession. As a result, the health organization's policies, screening criteria, and guidelines for services (such as preadmission procedures in a hospital) often may come into conflict with the health of the patient and the patient's compensatory reimbursement potential.

Many hospitals attempt to overcome this dilemma by achieving a balance between the business aspect of operating a health facility and the social aspect of caring for the indigent through the establishment of ethics committees within their managed care organization.[10–12]

Another critical element is the incorporation of stakeholders' ethical expectations for the health organization. Stakeholder expectations are expressed and integrated into the organization in the following ways: through the board of directors or board of trustees membership, which represents the communities served; through advocacy on behalf of stakeholder expectations carried out by senior leadership of the health entity; and within internal committee structures of the organization, such as with the ethics committee. Establishing an ethics committee, in particular, is a necessary element in health organization operations and strategy.

The ethics committee has three main purposes: education, consultation, and policy review. Challenges faced by the members of this committee include conflicting internal organizational principles, values contradiction, leadership team decision making, and community and industry ethical attitudinal changes. Other challenges include targeted education, proactive initiatives, and accreditation. Finally, it should be noted that the ethics committee seeks to assess implications for stakeholders during its review of policies. Stakeholders may include the institution and its culture, patients, individuals who receive training in the institution, volunteers, and other health providers in the region.[13,14]

To aid in the establishment of an ethical organization, the health organization should have an individual on staff appointed as the resident ethicist to assist in decision and policy making. The establishment of an ethics committee that meets on a regular and recurring basis can likewise keep the leadership informed of relevant and legitimate ethical issues confronting the health organization.

The health leader may partner with outside stakeholders and agencies to ensure it is meeting certain ethical norms and standards within the environmental setting.[15]

Moreover, the organization can seek guidance from ethical policy statements and positions published by such organizations as the American College of Healthcare Executives (ACHE), the American Hospital Association (AHA), the Medical Group Management Association (MGMA), the Association of University Programs in Health Administration (AUPHA), the Joint Commission, state organizations, and other regional quasi-government organizations. Health leaders who are leading a well-rounded organization made up of participatory stakeholders and consumers will ensure that the organization's posture on policies and principles regarding ethics is maintained consistently.[16]

A health leader must remember that it will never be enough to have an organization that just claims that it is an ethical entity; rather, it must behave, advocate, and have systems that foster moral action, such as having recognized committees or boards that separately address clinical and/or research ethics. One such committee is the institutional review board (IRB), the entity that reviews and approves research within a health organization; its role is especially important in the review and strict adherence to human subject laws, policies, and procedures. These ethically associated committees or bodies must have the power and the ability to act and foster change.[17] Unfortunately, according to national polls, 50% of health ethics committee chairs feel inadequately prepared to address issues in the health environment.[18] To overcome this problem, a wise health leadership team will invest in professional education and training for the organization's chief ethicist, as well as the members of the committees that make up any advisory panels within the faculty. This investment may offer future dividends in complex leadership dilemmas.

Example: When Actions and Ethics Collide

During the financial collapse of many U.S.-based organizations in the fall of 2008, Congress reacted by providing more than $700 billion to organizations that had run themselves into the ground through bad business practices and risky financial behaviors. It was later learned that the CEOs of many of these financially insolvent organizations would receive annual bonus checks of as much as $620,000.[19] The public was outraged that the leaders of these mammoth financial institutions could be rewarded for their incompetency that ruined the financial health of their own organizations and sent hundreds of employees to the unemployment line.

Many industry leaders replied by stating the bonuses that were received were contractually legal. Taxpayers countered by suggesting that although the bonuses may have been legally provided, it was unethical to receive such bonuses when so many people were out of work and when so many outside stakeholders, including taxpayers, had assumed financial responsibility for the corporate mess.

In an effort to establish a new leadership and ethical tone during the financial collapse of 2008–2009, and in response to taxpayer outrage, one financial organization, American International Group (AIG), made an attempt to change the message. AIG's CEO, Edward M. Liddy, stated, "I have asked the employees of AIG Financial Products to step up and do the right thing. Specifically, I have asked those who received retention payments of $100,000 or more to return at least half of those payments."[20] In response to his request, 15 of AIG's 20 executives receiving the highest bonuses later agreed to return the money. This good faith, ethical gesture helped AIG to reclaim some of the public's trust in the banking industry.

Common Ethical Dilemmas in Health Organizations

Ethical dilemmas in health organizations generally arise out of professional or values-based conflicts of interest. According to the American College of Healthcare Executives, a conflict of interest occurs when a person has conflicting duties or responsibilities and meeting one of them makes it impossible to meet the other. The classic example occurs when a decision maker for one organization is also a decision maker or influencer for another organization with which business is transacted. Often, the potential conflict of interest becomes an actual conflict of interest because the decision maker cannot meet the duty of fidelity (loyalty) to both organizations when a decision that impacts both is needed.[21]

Relationship Morality

Ethical dilemmas in the health organization are inevitable. In the field of health leadership, such dilemmas occur at three levels: micro, macro, and meso.

The micro level involves individual issues, such as relationships between individuals and leaders. An example of a micro-level ethical dilemma in the health setting is the reduced decision-making power accorded to some health professionals, such as a physician being forced to order a cheaper test with less diagnostic power. The micro level of management usually is dyadic, occurring on a person-to-person basis. It is exemplified by health professionals who work directly with patients and face a number of ethical dilemmas in a provider-agent role.

Health leaders should remember to praise in public and correct in private. All positive actions, behaviors, or performance and, especially, all negative actions, behaviors, or performance (extra emphasis on ethical breaches) should be documented regarding subordinates, staff, and peers. If you observe an ethical breach by a superior leader, privately discuss the issue with the individual and ask the person to correct the situation and report the issue to his or her superior leader. If the individual refuses or does not comply, it is your duty to discuss the ethical breach with that person's superior leader. This is tremendously difficult to do—but it is the right thing to do. Always confront the leader who has committed an ethical breach immediately and, at first, privately; always document the scenario in a confidential memorandum that you keep in a secured location in case you need to provide evidence to senior leadership at a later time. You cannot let ethical breaches go without confronting the person who committed the ethical error; you cannot let the ethical breach go uncorrected and unreported. If you do, you are modeling a negative behavior—namely, corruption and ethical cover-up. Although the choice is sometimes difficult, it is up to you to decide to be moral (or not). This decision-making process includes not only your actions and behaviors, but also, as a leader, the actions and behaviors you observe in others.

The macro level of ethical dilemmas involves societal or community issues that reflect governmental actions or social policies. These dilemmas are typically culturally based. For example, closing down a hospital's emergency department when it may be the only source of entry into the health system for the uninsured may be a prudent business decision, but the lack of consideration shown for the impoverished by this decision may violate the value of the health organization's responsibility to provide care.

The meso level involves organizational or professional issues. A restrictive agreement between health organizations and managed care organizations, such as the use and contractual arrangement for durable medical equipment, is an example of a meso-level ethical dilemma.[22]

Business and Financial Ethics

Business and financial ethics has been acutely observed since the Enron and other scandals began to erupt at the beginning of the twenty-first century. The Sarbanes-Oxley Act, which requires a firm's senior leader to validate and confirm financial statements and performance, is a governmental reaction to the public outrage over unethical business and financial behavior by organizations. Health leaders need to deal fairly and honestly in business and financial matters. In the health business, telling the truth is paramount. Of course, telling every financial or business secret and breaking confidentiality are neither reasonable nor moral. If you cannot tell the truth, it is better to say nothing. The golden rule applies to business and financial operations of the health enterprise: "Do unto others as you would have them do unto you." Avoid and acknowledge conflicts of interest; remove yourself from situations where conflicts of interest might compromise your ability to make decisions fairly. Follow the law, regulatory requirements, accreditation recommendations, and good business practices. Never leverage "good" for "bad" intentions.

Build systems that are efficient, effective, and efficacious while treating people with respect, dignity, and honesty. Apply those same principles to the moral application of day-to-day business activities. This is never more important than when you are in discussions with bond raters; those organizations decide your organization's bond rating (e.g., AAA, B, C), which has a direct correspondence with the interest rates charged on your organization's loans. Tell the truth, and act according to that truth. A good bond rating, for example, does not get better if trust is broken; a poor bond rating does not get better with broken trust. These ratings do improve, however, if trust is the basis of discussions and interactions.

In addition, health organizations must have regular external audits of their financial records, flow of funds, and policy compliance, conducted by a firm with a solid reputation. Especially important is the audit of financial information and systems of claims and reimbursement to taxpayer-funded programs such as Medicare and Medicaid. If errors or systemic problems are found, either by the external audit firm or by internal staff, immediate communication with the appropriate fiscal intermediaries and government agencies must occur. As an ethical health organization, application of this process is also appropriate with any commercial payer or for any contract with an outside entity.

Contracts and Negotiations

Ethical standards regarding negotiations and contracts are of particular interest and importance. Whenever a health organization is engaged in a negotiation or contract process, the organization is most likely working with some external entity. A successful negotiation usually concludes with a contract; this contract may be written or verbal and should specify terms, conditions of performance, payment, liability conditions, and outcomes if either party breaches the contract (i.e., does not perform its agreed-upon actions to the level of quality stated). Representing the health organization honestly by stating the needs and conditions of a particular negotiation or contract event, the elements of performance, the payment, and the commitment to comply with the ultimate terms is paramount in this type of negotiation.

A successfully completed negotiation and signed or verbally agreed-to contract must be complied with; when compliance may be at risk, communication with the other party or parties must occur in a timely fashion. Negotiations and contracts should include involvement of the health organization's legal counsel to ensure compliance with all applicable laws and regulations and to ensure a reasonable amount of liability protection. All negotiations and contract processes should consist of well-thought-out elements that adhere to the values and ethical expectations of the organization.

Health leaders must not engage in negotiations or contracts that are inherently illegal—for example, making inappropriate payments. This is the professional ethical expectation for all negotiations and contracts.

Right-to-Life Issues

It is not possible for a health leader, especially a CEO, of a large and munificent health organization to avoid policy discussions on right-to-life issues. The term *right to life* has transcended boundaries in the recent era and is no longer associated with only abortion-related issues. Health leaders will find themselves faced with a variety of right-to-life issues that include abortion, the death penalty, and euthanasia.

Despite the increased number of situations associated with the generalization of right-to-life issues, health leaders in government, secular, nonsecular, for-profit, and non-profit health organizations alike will be faced with decisions brought to their attention regarding abortion issues from the medical staff, stakeholders, and patients. In response, they may have to issue a policy statement on abortion procedures in the facility or provide institutional guidance on the practice. In doing so, health leaders must balance their personal views and organizational goals simultaneously and perhaps select one value and principle over the other if the personal and professional dilemmas related to abortion procedures cannot be reconciled.

For health leaders who have very specific and partisan views regarding abortion, the selection of a health organization as an employer may need to be carefully evaluated. For example, if you believe that abortion is wrong and immoral, seeking a position in a health organization that refuses to abort a fetus should be your focus. Many religious-based health organizations, such as Catholic-, Lutheran-, Baptist-, and Methodist-based or value-founding organizations, will not perform procedures that go against their values regarding right to life.

The famous *Roe v. Wade* decision is an example worth noting regarding the contradiction of values within a society. These contradictions in values in a society, especially as health is concerned, are at the heart of ethical challenges faced by health leaders. As health leaders progress up the ladder of responsibility and accountability, the ethical issues encountered become both more frequent and more challenging.

Roe v. Wade

The following excerpt was adapted from Harris's *Contemporary Issues in Healthcare Law and Ethics*:[23]

> In 1973, the U.S. Supreme Court delivered a decision in the case of *Roe v. Wade* based on a woman fictitiously named Jane Roe who sought an abortion in the state of Texas but did not "fit within the sole exception" as a medical necessity to save the life of the mother. The ruling gave women the right to abort a fetus for any reason up until the fetus became viable. The term viable was defined as a fetus brought to 28 weeks of gestational age, or a fetus that could live on its own outside the womb with reasonable medical aid. Women were still given the option to pursue an abortion after 29 weeks if there was/is substantial cause to protect the life of the mother.
>
> The Court further ruled that the Texas abortion statute violated the constitutional right of personal privacy and it "emphasized the physician's right to practice medicine without interference by the state." The ruling additionally gave states opportunities for placing more regulations and statutes to protect maternal health and potential life.
>
> In 1992, the U.S. Supreme Court ruled on the case of *Planned Parenthood of Southeastern Pennsylvania v. Casey*, in which the court upheld the ruling of *Roe v. Wade* [stating that] a woman had the right to terminate a pregnancy prior to the point of viability, but the court rejected the trimester framework as previously ruled in *Roe v. Wade*. However, the court left open the interpretation of "point of viability" to future medical developments.
>
> In 2000, the Supreme Court ruled that a statute banning partial-birth abortions in Nebraska was unconstitutional as it contained an exception to "preserve the life of the mother," but not an exception to "preserve the health of the mother." In 2002, President George W. Bush signed into law the *Born-Alive Infants Protection Act*, which treats every infant who is born alive, including those as a result of abortion, as a "person." The debate continues.

Euthanasia

Euthanasia can be defined as the active termination of an otherwise viable human life in a painless manner. It can also be defined as a passive methodology in which life-sustaining treatment is withheld or withdrawn. Euthanasia issues are generally grouped with right-to-life issues in health facilities and provide similar dilemmas for leaders to ponder.

Euthanasia is becoming an acceptable alternative to heroic medical care as some patients are securing *advanced directives* that state life support should not be provided to them under certain medical conditions. Research also suggests that hospice and palliative care may actually increase the incidence of euthanasia requests, because individuals who seek out these services are more accepting of their condition and may be more likely to "plan" for their deaths. Additionally, the concept of the "slippery slope" may be justified in the argument against legislation of voluntary euthanasia for elderly individuals who are pressured to "opt for death when they perceive themselves to be a burden for loved ones."[24]

THE ETHICS OF POLICY MAKING AND TREATMENT IN THE UNITED STATES

The first thing U.S. healthcare leaders need to understand is that our view of healthcare ethics in regard to medical treatment and healthcare access is very different from that of many other countries. Healthcare ethics is defined very differently by other nations. We also need to know that ethics in health care can, at times, be culturally defined. What may be considered ethically and morally appropriate for one culture or one nation may seem to be inappropriate and immoral to another culture or nation.

As mentioned earlier in the chapter, the triage for medical treatment of persons by gender, race, and age may be unethical, if not illegal, in the United States. In the United States, we find it extremely unethical to make medical decisions based on a patient's age, gender, or race. In fact, Americans may find it extremely distasteful that some countries with socialized medicine and national healthcare systems do ration medical care for certain ailments for patients who have passed a certain age. Americans find this form of triage "unethical," or, simply, "not the right thing to do."

However, the United States has a system in place where medical triage is based (in some cases) on a patient's ability to pay. Many nations outside the United States find the practice of basing medical care on remuneration "unethical" and not in keeping with the practice of "goodness." To some cultures and nations, the U.S. healthcare policy of basing care on payment violates a sense of beneficence and distributive justice.

Unique to the U.S. healthcare system is the availability of healthcare treatment and access through a variety of financial-based structures, such as for-profit, not-for-profit, county, state, and government entities (to name the major actors in the field). However, each entity will have unique stakeholder dynamics guiding its views and policies regarding reimbursements, uncompensated care, and unfinanced requirements for quality initiatives. Financial morality and trust are critical. "Trust is essential in finance, but finance ethics is about far more than trust. Finance consists of an array of activities that involve the handling of financial assets—usually those of other people. Not only does the welfare of everyone depend on the safeguarding and deployment of these assets, but billions of financial transactions take place each day with a high level of integrity. With this large volume of financial activities, there are ample opportunities for some people to gain at other's expense."[25]

ETHICS AND ADVOCACY

The definition of *advocacy* in the legal sense is the act of pleading for, supporting, or recommending; however, in the health professions, the application of this perspective is problematic because health providers must consider whether advocating for one patient will in any way compromise the health of this individual or of others. In the current structure of the U.S. health system, professionals also must often weigh the quality of care versus the cost of that care. Additionally, advocacy is an effort that must contribute positively to the exercise of self-determination. It is the effort to help patients become clear about what they want in a situation, and to assist them in discerning and clarifying their values and examining available options in light of those values. A patient's right to self-determination is often a source of moral contention, because this fundamental right is constrained by the patient's limited knowledge of his or her health issues and inexperience with the healthcare system. As a result, patient advocacy is not an optional activity for health professionals; however, most professional organizational codes lack a discussion of how health professionals can best apply advocacy in practice.[26,27]

UNDERSTANDING THE PATIENT'S SPIRITUALITY BASE IN DECISION MAKING

Despite the Joint Commission's 2010 publication, *Advancing Effective Communication, Cultural Competence, and Patient- and Family-Centered Care*, which specifically identifies the importance of understanding spiritual beliefs and practices as part of the domain for provision of care, healthcare executives and providers are hesitant to openly discuss spirituality in their organizations. However, it is well known that spiritual principles are the basis for many decisions made by consumers in today's healthcare environment. Furthermore, policies and procedures currently in place in many healthcare organizations may already be linked to spiritual principals—albeit they are presented as ethical, cultural competence, clinical, and/or bioethical practices.

Within the health and general leadership environment, the topic of spirituality in leadership is often considered taboo and may even be a career-ending conversation for executives and practitioners. This stance is beginning to soften in society; spirituality in leadership is beginning to be discussed more openly in more organizations. At the same time, it is well known that spiritual principles are the basis for many values and enduring beliefs that guide the moral and ethical development of health leadership practices in our society.[28,29] Therefore, spirituality as a construct of discussion and examination in health leadership practice should not be overlooked in future research examining leadership theory.

A national survey of spirituality conducted by Baylor University in 2011 reaffirmed that over 85% of the U.S. population consider themselves religious. Furthermore, this same study suggested that over 75% of the U.S. population believes that God has a purpose for their lives. Certainly, spirituality plays an important role in the decision to use, and consume, health resources.

A similar study of Canadians found that 72% claimed to have spiritual needs, and 70% believed in miraculous healing. These factors have tremendous implications for health professionals in terms of meeting the physical, emotional, and personal needs of their patients and their patients' families. As Pesut has suggested, "professionals are now expected to play a role that was once borne by the institutional church, which may include helping individuals to reconcile spiritual beliefs with their health care decisions."[30]

Within the study of leadership theory, it has been suggested that the distinct absence of the study of spirituality in ethics and leadership results in a gap in the process that seeks to understand the decisions ultimately reached by patients in regard to end-of-life decisions. End-of-life decisions, do-not-resuscitate requests, cord blood recovery, stem cell studies, pregnancy termination, sexual abstinence, organ donation, and volunteering for human subjects research are only some of the relevant issues faced by patients and families for which spiritual teachings (spanning a variety of religious affiliations) are known to influence decision making. Healthcare executives and providers are similarly faced with issues in decision making, healthcare policy interpretation, and ethics for which both judgment and course of action selection are influenced by those enduring beliefs learned through spiritual teachings. Unfortunately, spirituality is often directly omitted from these important conversations regardless of known influence. As a result, the concept of spirituality in leadership should not be overlooked when discussing ethical decisions in the modern health environment.[31–33]

To adjust to the spiritual needs of patients entering the health system, leaders should strive to be aware of the diverse beliefs within their organization and foster a high degree of sensitivity and respect for those beliefs. Specific beliefs and practices to consider include, but are not limited to, the following:

- Healing rituals
- Dying, death, and care of dead bodies
- Harvesting and transplanting organs
- End-of-life and right-to-life decisions
- Use of reproductive technologies

In an article published in 2009 titled "Incorporating Patients' Spirituality into Care Using Gadow's Ethical Framework,"[34] Pesut suggests that there is a growing need to address spirituality in client care. In addition, Pesut notes that several health professional organizations are now addressing spirituality as an ethical obligation to care. She further states that in many situations, spiritual values and beliefs provide a source of encouragement as patients endure experiences of suffering.

One challenge of addressing spirituality in health is the use of language and narratives that may be foreign to health professionals outside of a specific faith. Language and terminology that are consistent and easily understood by one faith-based group of individuals may be misunderstood or misconstrued by an individual unfamiliar with that faith-based group's tradition. As an elementary example, if we describe our friend Pat as a "religious person," are we operationalizing "religious" as someone who is simply spiritual, or as someone who is Christian, Confucianist, Mormon, or Muslim in that they are in good concordance with that particular mindset and belief system?

In conclusion, although understanding faith-based beliefs is important for health professionals so that they will be sensitive to and respectful of those beliefs, the leader should be careful when asked to provide faith-based advice.

ETHICAL CODES ADOPTED BY THE HEALTH INDUSTRY

Over the last 100-plus years, guidelines, codes, and other regulations have been created to help guide the conduct of research involving human participants. Some of these guidelines were created in response to ethical lapses in judgment committed by individuals or organizations. Other guidelines have evolved in an attempt to provide answers to new problems and challenges created by the ever-changing research environment. Finally, some guidelines and laws are currently being addressed in order to better serve the changing world of research, including issues such as cloning. Regardless of how ethical principles and frameworks have arrived, it is imperative for health leaders to be aware of the current environment and history of research ethics if the healthcare system is going to continue to be a ready and relevant force of community service and political direction in the future. This section discusses some of the philosophical viewpoints associated with ethical decision making. Understanding these values-driven points of view may assist you in your own decision-making process in future ethical events where your individual judgment will have to be exercised. It is prudent to remember that not all individuals exercise ethical decision making in the same way or even consistently over time. In understanding both his or her own personality dynamic and the various perspectives from which health professionals make decisions, the health leader will have an advantage in elucidating the dynamics of the patients and human resources in the organization.

The philosophies or ethical frameworks discussed here are distributive justice, utilitarianism, egalitarianism, libertarianism, deontology, and pluralism.

DISTRIBUTIVE JUSTICE

At the foundation of ethics is distributive justice. This set of theories or ideologies attempts to instill a set of values, ideals of fairness based on those values, and beliefs in the allocation of resources (e.g., food, water, housing, wealth/money, opportunities, materials) throughout a society. At its roots, ethics is a framework that is based on a distributive justice theory or combination of those theories; ethics is an extension of resource allocation and the methods of that allocation, whereas morality or morals are the level of congruence to that ethical framework. "Principles of distributive justice are normative principles designed to guide the allocation of the benefits and burdens of economic activity."[35] *Distributive injustice* occurs when the costs outweigh the rewards.[36]

Taken individually, distributive justice theories are neither right nor wrong in and of themselves. Instead, situations, contingencies, and values must be considered in the selection (creating an ethical framework) and application (level of morality) of the distribution of resources. Would the distribution of resources be the same in a mass-casualty situation in an emergency room, such as an influx of patients from a bus accident, as when conducting choles-terol checks at a health fair in the community? Of course not. The tough part of selecting an ethical framework based on values and beliefs and the application of that framework (morality) comes down to one simple truth: Resources are scarce in society, in health organizations, in departments, in units, in families, and for individuals.

Resource scarcity—the reality responsible for cre-ation of disciplines such as economics, political science, and distributive justice/ethics—is the catalyst that requires a method for resource distribution. If all resources were abun-dant, how many conflicts, political maneuvers, or crimes would society have to deal with or resolve? Selection of a distributive justice theory based on the values and beliefs of a society, organization, group, or individual; developing an ethical framework from that theory; and applying that framework are responsible for some of the cultural con-flicts, group tensions, and individual conflicts in the world, society, organization, or group. If two groups are strongly attached to their different ethical frameworks, resource dis-tribution that fosters "fairness" for both groups can be dif-ficult; that is one reason why negotiation is a valued skill. Lastly, avarice or greed may play into the scenario; scarcity can motivate greed and motivate competition. (In ancient Greece, avarice or greed was considered one of the seven deadly sins.)

In health, social justice and market justice discussions are integrated as part of the selection of resource distribu-tion mechanisms. Social justice advocates that:

[I]n a just society, minimal levels of basic needs like income, housing, education, and health should be pro-vided to all citizens as fundamental rights. These basic needs are usually provided through various forms of social insurance; while market justice supports that the inexorable logic of supply and demand operating within the economic marketplace are key to determin-ing the optimal outcomes of health care resources (with minimal or no intervention by government).[37]

These issues muddy the waters surrounding distribu-tion of resources, especially in the health industry. Some of the well-known distributive justice theories are presented here in summary. What theories work best in health orga-nizations? Does one theory fit all health situations?

Utilitarianism

Utilitarianism, as a theory, aims to maximize the possible happiness of society as a whole. This goal requires that it be ascertained what makes every individual in that society happy and how to satisfy the greatest number of them. A policy that makes the highest number of people happy—or

at least dissatisfies the fewest—is the correct option to choose according to the dictates of this theory.[38] Utilitari-anism thus seeks to maximize utility (usefulness) from the distribution of resources in a society. This theory would balance social and market justice.

Egalitarianism

Egalitarianism is a set of closely related theories that ... advocate the thesis that all members of a society should have exactly equal amounts of resources. Sim-pler theories of this kind are satisfied with the claim that everyone should be given, at all costs, completely equal quantities of certain crucial material goods, like money.[39]

John Rawls, in *A Theory of Justice* (1971),[40] posited a supplementary position to egalitarianism known as the *dif-ference principle*. In essence, egalitarianism negatively affects those who are less fortunate, such as the disabled and mentally challenged; based on this reality, more resources should be allocated to those who are less capable of per-forming productive work. This theory is more aligned with social justice.

Libertarianism

Libertarianism suggests that the market or market forces should determine the distribution of resources in a society. The Nobel Prize–winning economist Milton Friedman, who died in 2006 at the age of 94, was the best-known advocate on behalf of modern market forces as the key fac-tors in an economy; he joined a long line of economists associated with this model, including the major historical figures Adam Smith and John Keynes. According to this perspective, market justice is the force that controls distri-bution. No pattern or criteria are important in the distri-bution of resources in a market-based approach; instead, those persons who work diligently and intelligently should receive the fruits of their labor. Market justice is strongly associated with libertarianism.

Deontology

Deontology is the opposite of utilitarianism. It is an ethical framework and philosophy of resource allocation that sug-gests actions should be judged right or wrong based on their own values and principle-driven characteristics. Within this theory, there is no planning for the consequences of an action. As a result, the preponderance of the masses is not a major consideration, and the needs of the one can out-weigh the needs of the many. In many ways, deontology is a case-by-case or individual-based framework for resource allocation considering the factors associated with that individual. Social and market justice are both considered valid considerations in this framework.

Pluralism

> Pluralists hold that goods which are normally distributed in any society are too different to be distributed according to only one criterion.... To be just, a criterion which holds in one sphere should not be applied in another one. For instance, rewards and punishments should be distributed according to performance, jobs according to ability, political positions according to [election results], medical care according to needs, income according to success on the market, and the like.[41]

Both social and market justice are applicable in a pluralistic view.

SOCIETAL APPLICATION OF DISTRIBUTIVE JUSTICE THEORIES

How does a society justly distribute resources? Resources include goods, materials, technologies, and funding/money—but also time and effort. As a health leader, the cost, quality, and access paradigm should be considered along with distributive justice considerations. Because health organizations are a scarce resource in a community, how resources are allocated and to whom are particularly salient issues and can be thorny points for health leaders. Does everyone get all the health services they need? How do you know? Does everyone get all of the services they want? How do you know? Has your organization done needs assessments and other analyses to determine these needs and wants?

An example of the application of distributive justice theories can be found straight out the window of the health organization's facility. Look at the parking lot. Parking in many places is a scarce resource. How are parking spaces allocated by your health organization, by your university or college, your clinic, your agency, or your association? In most health organizations, spots close to entries of the facility are reserved for disabled patrons, customers, patients and family members, and expecting or recent mothers (deontology); these are prime parking spaces that often remain empty. Other spaces may be reserved for surgeons, physicians, nurses, pharmacists, administrators, emergency room staff, and possibly others (utilitarianism) so that those professionals can get to work and start performing their various missions in the facility in order to do the greatest good, using scarce skills, for the greatest number of patients.

Other spaces may be reserved by payment of a lease for the parking space (or valet parking) for those persons who do not want to hunt for a parking space (libertarianism); spaces more advantageous or closer to the facility usually cost more in terms of the monthly lease payment. The rest of the spaces are open on a first come, first served basis, so that everyone has an equal chance at the space (egalitarianism). In the totality of the parking lot situation, pluralism is used to allocate this scarce resource. Thus distributive justice theories are the foundation of the ethical framework used to allocate parking spaces in a manner that society can justify within the norms and mores of that society. Surely you can see how resources are distributed in other areas of society and which distributive justice theory or theories would apply to those areas.

SELECTED APPLICATION OF PHILOSOPHIES

Distributive justice theories can serve as ethical frameworks that may assist a health leader in framing his or her decision-making policies, systems, and processes. Two of these theories are presented in this section as contrasting frameworks for discussion: utilitarianism and deontology. Not all health organizations use only utilitarianism or deontological frameworks; for example, a health department's immunization program most likely uses an egalitarian framework. Issues surrounding patient rights of autonomy, beneficence, nonmaleficence, and justice are addressed here as well. The selected ethical codes or frameworks should be integrated with the cost, quality, and access paradigm after considering any changes to the health system or resource allocation of health resources. Although these topics could take several chapters of discussion, we address them here for consistency and familiarization within the leadership framework.

Health Leader Framework: Utilitarianism

Utilitarianism is the view that an action is deemed morally acceptable because it produces the greatest balance of good over evil, taking into account all individuals affected. This theory posits that the needs of the many outweigh the needs of the few. It also suggests that the end results and outcomes outweigh the process and the procedure used to reach those results and outcomes. The ultimate goal with utilitarianism is "mass happiness," or the bringing of the greatest good to the preponderance of the people. Due to the end-results focus of this methodology for decision making, the outcomes are often viewed as justifiable measures despite the consequences of the process. Under this

THE ETHICS OF HUMAN SUBJECT RESEARCH: A BRIEF HISTORY

The ethical issues in human subject research have received increasing attention from health leaders over the last 50 years. Several ethical issues usually arise when designing research that will involve human beings. Among these are issues such as safety of the participant, informed consent, privacy, confidentiality, and adverse effects. Along with ethical issues, there are also ethical principles that govern research. Three primary ethical principles, which are traditionally cited as originating in the *Belmont Report*, are autonomy, which deals with a participant making an informed decision regarding participation in a research study; beneficence, which refers to maximizing benefits and minimizing risk of harm to the individual; and justice, which demands equitable selection of participants and equality in distribution of benefits and burdens.

Nuremberg Code: The history of research on unwilling and uninformed subjects is long and tragic. One of the main historical events that had an impact on establishing federal regulations for the protection of human research subjects was the Nuremberg Trial. This was the first high-profile case questioning medical research. The trial occurred in 1949 when Adolph Hitler's personal doctor, Karl Brandt, and 22 other doctors were accused of war crimes and crimes against humanity for conducting cruel and unusual experiments on Jews and other minorities. The Nuremberg Code, which emerged from the trial, emphasizes the importance of capacity to consent, freedom from coercion, and comprehension of the consequences of a person's involvement in medical research (informed consent). Other provisions require the minimization of risk of harm, a favorable harm/benefit ratio, qualified investigators using appropriate research designs to answer questions, and freedom for the subject to withdraw at any time. The modern era of human subject protection is routinely dated from the promulgation of the Nuremberg Code. Its standards have been accepted and expanded upon by the international research community.

Declaration of Helsinki: The World Medical Association (WMA) adopted the Declaration of Helsinki in June 1964. Its recommendations signaled the first efforts to attempt to distinguish between research that intended to directly benefit the volunteer clinically (therapeutic) and research whose primary purpose was to answer a scientific question (nontherapeutic). Emphasis was placed on the fiduciary relationship that exists between the physician and his or her patients.

"The Declaration of Geneva of the WMA binds the physician with the words, 'The health of my patient will be my first consideration,' and the International Code of Medical Ethics declares that, 'A physician shall act only in the patient's interest when providing medical care.'" According to the Declaration of Helsinki, all experimental procedures involving human subjects should be clearly formulated in an experimental protocol.

The *Belmont Report*: Another regulation to protect human subjects was established in the United States by the National Research Act of 1974, which established the National Commission for the Protection of Human Subjects of Biomedical and Behavioral Research. The Commission issued the *Belmont Report* in 1978, which contained guidelines for the conduct of research based on the applied principles of autonomy (respect for persons), beneficence (maximize benefits/minimize harms), and justice (fairness in distribution). Human research ethics rests on these three basic principles that are considered the foundation of all regulations or guidelines governing research ethics.

The Common Rule: In 1981, the Department of Health and Human Services (DHHS) and the Food and Drug Administration (FDA) published convergent regulations that were based on the Belmont principles. These mandated that members of an institutional review board (IRB) have broad backgrounds and include people who could represent community attitudes. Informed consent was required for research participants, and specific elements of information were required. The IRB is a review committee established to help protect the rights and welfare of human research subjects. Regulations require IRB review and approval for research involving human subjects if it is funded or regulated by the federal government. Most research institutions, professional organizations, and scholarly journals apply the same requirements to all human research. The jurisdiction of the IRBs includes the authority to review, disapprove, or modify research as well as to conduct reviews, observe/verify changes, and suspend or terminate approval.

perspective, the outcomes dictate the rules, and decisions are based on the predetermined desires of leaders.[42,43]

Medicare and Medicaid may be thought of as a utilitarian decision when the benefits were first introduced in 1963. The decision to redistribute the income of working persons in the United States by taking a certain percentage of every employee's wages so that other certain individuals who were older than the age of 65 or who were indigent could receive subsidized care was initially (by many) seen as a socialist movement in the United States. The policy itself, almost by definition, provides for the greater good at the expense of others.[44] These programs are different, however. Medicare is an entitlement program; most people have to pay into the program over time to become eligible for the program. In contrast, Medicaid is a welfare program, for which eligibility is based on various criteria and into which a citizen does not have to pay to become eligible. From a macro view, however, both programs could be seen as utilitarian in nature.

As the CEO of a health organization, you may someday be involved in a bond initiative where you lobby the county or local jurisdiction to increase local taxes in support of a new health venture in your local community. Your argument for this bond initiative may be based on a utilitarian effort.[45]

Health Leader Framework: Deontology

Deontology is the opposite of utilitarianism. This ethical framework and philosophy suggests that actions should be judged right or wrong based on their own values and principle-driven characteristics. Within this theory, there is no planning for the consequences of an action. As a result, the preponderance of the masses is not a major consideration in this theory, and the needs of the one can outweigh the needs of the many.

This system of thought also focuses on personal responsibility and "what one ought to do." According to this principle, the most moral decision will be reached when one follows the "rules" or "duty" without deviation.[46] Immanuel Kant introduced a deontological theory that assesses conditions from the vantage of inputs rather than outcomes. Kant's categorical imperative judges morality by examining the nature of actions and the will of agents rather than the goals achieved. Although Kant's theories are useful in making the moral judgments involved in the decision-making process, deontology holds that consequences are less important than intent.[47]

Providers of care are often the greatest users of deontology principles. In perfect and unconstrained conditions, providers of care would love to practice a more exact science of medicine in which expensive laboratory tests and consults could confirm or disconfirm the judgment and instincts of a more imperfect physical exam. This may have been the practice of medicine in the era before managed care, when preapproved specialty consults were unnecessary for access, and fee-for-service, indemnity, and open systems were the norm. Modern patient care providers are bound by capitation; gatekeeper access restrictions; and

per-member, per-month withholds on premiums. As a result, modern physicians are less likely to practice a form of deontology than their predecessors from the pre–managed care era.

Autonomy, Beneficence, Nonmaleficence, and Justice

Similar to the ethical principles of utilitarianism and deontology that guide, forecast, and help frame the discussions and actions of senior leaders in a health organization regarding policy implementation and organizational resource allocation, the patient frameworks of autonomy, beneficence, nonmaleficence, and justice help guide a health leader's agenda with respect to patient care decisions. Ethical issues surrounding patient care generally revolve around four commonly accepted and established healthcare practices:

- *Autonomy*: The patient's right to self-governance and medical decision making
- *Beneficence*: The requirement of the health organization to do "good"
- *Nonmaleficence*: The requirement for the health organization to do no harm
- *Justice*: The obligation to give each patient fair resource allocation (services and products associated with the care process)

In health organizations, the tenets of patient autonomy and justice often come into conflict with the obligations of beneficence and nonmaleficence. This potential for conflict explains why the provider of care—in most cases, the physician—is the agent for the patient who structures and delivers the correct regimen of diagnostic procedures and treatments. This point is especially salient if the patient is deliberately seeking uncompensated care or some other secondary benefit.

THE DIFFERENCE BETWEEN MEDICAL ETHICS, CLINICAL ETHICS, AND BIOETHICS

Clinical ethics refers to the ethics of the clinical practice of medicine and to ethical problems that arise in the care of patients. It includes traditional professional medical ethics, which places the patient at the center of consideration. Traditional medical ethics have proved deficient in the face of technological advances of recent years; this reality has given rise to bioethics. Bioethics' first concern was with "the intersection of ethics and the life sciences." This was later expanded to include human values.[48] Thus today's health organizations have to balance and develop systems to adhere to medical and clinical ethical standards as well as emerging bioethical standards.

GOALS OF ORGANIZATIONAL ETHICS

Today, health costs are on the rise, patients are demanding more from their health professionals, and government and third-party payers have tightened controls on reimbursement for services, length of hospital stay, and allocation of resources. In this environment, it is becoming increasingly difficult for the health professional to practice morally while meeting all other health, professional standard of care, and organizational demands. Tension between demands for health services and demands for profit/margins are imposing enormous pressures on health professionals to achieve cost reductions, increased revenues, and enhanced quality of care.[49]

Some individuals can manage to "do the right thing" in practically any situation and consistently place the needs of others above their own. Unfortunately, the individuals who achieve this feat seemingly so naturally can be difficult to locate and identify. In health organizations in general, but particularly in nursing, there is a need for the ability to learn to use increasingly complex technologies, develop a solid background in biological sciences, and yet operate with compassion and caring every day for every patient (many times with high patient loads). Few individuals innately have the ability to learn nursing's technical complexities and already have full command of ethical values to the point that they can act from a targeted decision-making perspective rather than from instinct.

Individuals' ethical values generally are built over a lifetime. Study of the old philosophers can give a voice and a rationale to active decision making that the individual can then describe and defend. For immediate guidance, values statements and codes of ethics can be used to guide decision making.[50]

HEALTH LEADERS ARE PART ETHICIST

Attention to various branches of philosophical and professional ethics assists in building and maintaining an ethical climate within the organization. Because they are knowledgeable about ethical frameworks, experienced leaders can act more mindfully of the consequences of their actions and decisions, and they are able to explain their positions to patients and external stakeholders more easily. Health leaders must incorporate an ethical framework and expectation of moral actions and behaviors from all organizational stakeholders; this is most true for internal stakeholders and

acutely important for direct subordinates. Leaders should ponder and answer the questions listed under the "A Health Leader's Challenge: Where to Start?" section later in this chapter, but should also ensure that ethical frameworks, moral practice, and regulatory compliance are inherently embedded in the health organization. To make sure that these concerns are addressed effectively, the organization can take the following steps:

- Establish and charter ethics committees with authority.
- Require staff attendance, participation, and evaluation of educational programs.
- Create a system of policy development and review.
- Seek consultation by utilizing consultants with similar values and moral practices.
- Integrate professional, clinical, and business ethical performance through leader role modeling and subordinate reinforcement (rewards and punishments).
- Foster a positive ethical climate within an open and supportive communication environment (e.g., it is acceptable to tell leadership about a mistake or error).
- Review relationships with external stakeholders, partners, and entities with which the health organization has contract relationships to evaluate ethical framework and moral practice congruence with the health organization.

A HEALTH LEADER'S CHALLENGE: WHERE TO START?

All of the dilemmas mentioned in this chapter have an ability to influence an organization's financial stability, community legitimacy, and stakeholder dynamics. Leaders in health organizations should be prepared for relationship conflicts at several levels within the health organization and strategically plan for negative consequences before they occur.[51] The following list of questions is intended to provide a model for health leaders with regard to creating a system of ethics and morality in their organizations:

1. Which values does the organization hold?
2. On which distributive justice theoretical framework should ethical decisions be based?
   - Does that framework apply to all situations? If not, when does the framework not apply and which framework takes its place?
   - How do values of the health organization get put into practice?

3. How does the health organization establish an ethical framework and moral application of principles (e.g., through planning, group discussions, professional associations, laws and regulations, community expectations, community needs)?

4. Does the health organization have an ethical statement or creed that is highly visible and accessible by all stakeholders?

5. To embed the ethical foundation and moral actions, which systems need to be in place, such as committees, policies, procedures, enforcement of those policies and procedures (e.g., should coupling be tight or loose regarding ethical frameworks and moral behavior and actions?), and leadership role modeling considering customers' and patients' expectations, business conduct and operations, negotiations, contract agreements and compliance, legal/regulation compliance, error remediation (e.g., how are errors resolved?), and health service and product delivery?

6. How can leadership decisions remain consistent with the ethical framework over time? How do you know when you are consistent?

7. How can the organizational culture incorporate the ethical framework and moral application of principles that the health organization holds important?

8. How does the health organization integrate its ethical framework and moral applications into its strategic planning, decision making, and daily operations?

9. How does the health organization communicate its ethical framework and moral application to the communities it serves and to its external stakeholders?

10. How does the health organization ensure internal staff and subordinate adaptation to the ethical framework and moral application of that framework both to long-term (e.g., training, annual updates, rewards and punishments) employees and to new employees (e.g., orientation, training)?

11. Who keeps the health leadership team accountable to the ethical framework and moral application of established principles?

12. Are the ethical framework and moral application of those principles reasonable, relevant, and realistic? How are boundaries established?

13. Who (e.g., individuals, groups, legal counsel) has the authority to initiate an ethical incident report, an ethical discussion, an ethical incident investigation, or an ethically attributed reward or punishment? Is the health organization legally or liability oriented to ethical considerations, leadership oriented, or both? (What may be legally "moral" so as to limit liability may not be leadership "moral" in terms of doing what is right.)

REGULATORY COMPLIANCE

A moral organization, and its leaders, must foster and maintain systems for health operations that comply with statutory regulations from federal, state, and local governments. Leading a health organization within a system of laws is a moral obligation as well as a legal obligation. A leader's duty is to be compliant with regulations, statutes, laws, and policies and create systems, checks, and quality control processes to ensure a system of compliance. Leaders who foster regulatory-compliant health organizations protect the ethical framework of the organization while reinforcing the moral culture of the organization; likewise, regulatory compliance reduces the legal liability, community negativity, and potential financial loss for the organization.

The text box provides an example of an application-based approach from a composite of actual health organizations regarding leading a regulatory-compliant health organization. The names of the organizations have been changed to the American Medical Center for purposes of anonymity.

AMERICAN MEDICAL CENTER† CODE OF CORPORATE COMPLIANCE

I. Policy

A. Compliance Program

American Medical Center's (the "Center") Compliance Program requires all employees, agents, independent contractors, consultants, associates, trustees, medical staff members, vendors, volunteers, or any individual who provides care or services to the Center or conducts business for or on behalf of Center (collectively "Center Representatives") to act in an

---

†Based on Dr. Ledlow's personal correspondence via email with medical directors of several corporate healthcare entities. The health organizations required anonymity for permission to use the material.

AMERICAN MEDICAL CENTER CODE OF CORPORATE COMPLIANCE (continued)

ethical and legal manner and to consistently comply with all applicable governmental and professional standards, requirements, and laws.

The Compliance Program includes as one of its essential elements the development of Compliance Policies and Procedures that address its compliance efforts as they apply to and/or affect Center Representatives. Such policies and procedures will explain in more detail what the Compliance Program requires of Center Representatives. This Code of Corporate Compliance (the "Code") contains an overview of the Center's principal Compliance Policies and Procedures.

Other key components of the Compliance Program include the appointment of a Compliance Officer and a Compliance Committee, training and education about the Compliance Program, internal and external monitoring and auditing of compliance issues and concerns, adoption of a system that allows for both open and anonymous inquiries and reports related to compliance matters and suspected compliance violations, and enforcement of Compliance Policies and Procedures.

B. Scope

The Compliance Program applies to all entities affiliated with the Center. Entities include specifically American Medical Center and its off-site facilities. Entities also include American Health Care Professionals, American Medical Properties, American Diagnostic Imaging, and American Sleep and Neurological Disorders. Entities also include any future delivery sites established by the Center or its affiliates.

The Center looks to its executives, senior managers, supervisors, and other leaders to lead by example in encouraging all Center Representatives to become familiar with and to abide by the Code and the Compliance Program. The Center expects its leaders to be role models in every respect and to ensure that their team members have the information they need to comply with applicable laws, standards, and policies, as well as the resources they need to deal with ethical dilemmas. One of these leaders' primary responsibilities is to foster a culture within the Center that advocates compliance and ethical conduct. That culture must enable all Center Representatives to ask questions and raise concerns without fear of retaliation. Leaders should maintain an "open door" policy with respect to questions of ethics or law, or any other compliance-related issues.

C. Code of Corporate Compliance

This Code is designed to support the Compliance Program. This Code demonstrates our commitment to dealing with the highest ethical, legal, and moral standards regarding all aspects of our business practices. This Code specifically addresses overall standards of conduct, organization of the Compliance Program, assessment of compliance effectiveness, and responding to government investigation.

This Code is not intended to describe all of the programs and practices of the Center that are designed to achieve integrity and compliance. The Center already maintains various integrity and Compliance Policies and Procedures documented elsewhere, which continue to be part of its overall legal and ethical compliance effort. Such policies and procedures will explain in more detail what the Compliance Program requires of Center Representatives. This Code contains an overview of the Center's principal Compliance Policies and Procedures.

D. Compliance Policies and Procedures

It is the policy of the Center to conduct its affairs in a lawful and ethical manner. Applicable laws, regulations, and standards address such subjects as certificates of need, licenses, permits, accreditation, access to treatment, consent to treatment, medical record keeping, access to medical records and confidentiality, patients' rights, terminal care decision making, medical staff membership and clinical privileges, corporate practice of medicine restrictions, and Medicare and Medicaid regulations, to name a few. The Center and Center Representatives will comply with all applicable laws, regulations, and standards.

As part of its good faith commitment to compliance, the Center expects the Center Representatives to abide by the following Compliance Policies and Procedures. For a more detailed understanding of what these policies and procedures require of Center Representatives, they should consult the Center-wide compliance policies available on the Center's intranet. Any

(continues)

AMERICAN MEDICAL CENTER CODE OF CORPORATE COMPLIANCE (continued)

Center Representative who does not have access to the Center's intranet and who would like a copy of any Center-wide compliance policy may request a copy from the Compliance Officer.

1. Acknowledgment

The Center will require all Center Representatives to sign an acknowledgment confirming that they have received a copy of this Code, as well as the Compliance Policies and Procedures, and that they understand these represent mandatory policies of the Center. New Center Representatives will be required to sign this acknowledgment as a condition of employment.

A copy of the acknowledgment form is attached as the last page of this Code. Adherence to and support of the Center's Code and participation in related activities and training will be considered in decisions regarding hiring, promotion, and compensation for all current or future Center Representatives.

E. Basis

The Center voluntarily created this Code to enable us to meet our goals, improve the quality of patient care, and do our part to reduce fraud, waste, and abuse, as well as reduce the cost of health care. The Code is based upon the seven steps of the Federal Sentencing Guidelines and upon program guidance published by the Department of Health and Human Services, Office of Inspector General. The Code will be reviewed annually by the Center's Compliance Officer and Compliance Committee to ensure that it continues to meet our needs.

II. Objectives

The objectives of the Code are to:

1. Establish ethical and legal standards and Compliance Policies and Procedures to be followed by all Center Representatives to ensure compliance with applicable federal, state, and local laws or regulations.
2. Designate a Compliance Officer, a Compliance Committee, and other Center officials responsible for directing the efforts to enhance integrity and compliance, including implementation of the Code, and maintenance and development of the Compliance Policies and Procedures.
3. Provide a means for communicating the ethical and legal standards of the Compliance Policies and Procedures that all Center Representatives are expected to know, understand, and follow.
4. Increase training of Center Representatives (including medical staff members) concerning applicable reimbursement compliance requirements and Compliance Policies and Procedures.
5. Prevent criminal conduct by ensuring that discretionary authority is given to appropriate Center Representatives who are unlikely to engage in criminal conduct.
6. Establish a system of monitoring and oversight of activities to ensure adherence to the established standards and Compliance Policies and Procedures.
7. Provide a means for reporting apparent illegal activity to appropriate authorities.
8. Provide a mechanism to investigate any alleged violations and to prevent violations in the future.
9. Provide for the enforcement of the ethical and legal standards and Compliance Policies and Procedures.
10. Document the Center's compliance efforts.
11. Provide for regular review of overall compliance efforts, including department-specific Compliance Policies and Procedures, to ensure that Compliance Policies and Procedures reflect current requirements and that other adjustments are made as needed to improve compliance.

III. Regulatory Compliance

A. General

In order for the Center to continue to prosper financially, the Center must be paid for the services and products that it provides. It is vitally important that the Center make accurate and timely requests for reimbursement or payment and that the

AMERICAN MEDICAL CENTER CODE OF CORPORATE COMPLIANCE (continued)

Center be reimbursed accurately. The process of seeking and receiving reimbursement is governed by a number of laws with which the Center must comply. Failure to obey those laws is unethical and illegal. When such a failure results in an overcharge or misbilling, it can lead to substantial civil and criminal penalties being imposed on the Center, each Center entity involved, and/or the individual(s) who participated in the delivery or billing of such services. The Center participates in the Medicare and Medicaid programs, which are government-funded healthcare programs. Providers that participate in these government-funded healthcare programs such as Medicare and Medicaid are subject to particularly strict reimbursement rules intended to combat fraud and abuse of the Medicare and Medicaid programs. Center Representatives must be familiar with the Medicare/Medicaid fraud and abuse laws that apply to them and must give those laws the utmost consideration when performing services for the Center.

Medicare/Medicaid fraud and abuse can take many forms, some of which might not seem improper unless you keep in mind that special rules govern healthcare providers who participate in the Medicare/Medicaid programs. It is important to remember that health care has become one of the most heavily regulated industries in the country today and that stopping fraud and abuse is a very high priority of the government. Many practices that are perfectly acceptable in other business contexts are *not* permitted in the healthcare context. Examples of fraud and abuse, all of which are unethical and illegal, include but are not limited to the following:

- Billing for services that are not performed or for items that are not provided
- Billing twice for the same service or item (i.e., double billing)
- Upcoding (i.e., billing for a service at a rate higher than that warranted by the service actually performed and documented)
- Billing for services or items that do not meet Medicare/Medicaid "medical necessity" criteria
- Unbundling (i.e., billing separately for services or items that should be included in a global or composite rate)
- Billing Medicare/Medicaid for services or items that are not reimbursable under those programs
- Billing Medicare patients higher charges than non-Medicare patients
- Submitting false cost reports
- Failing to refund credit balances
- Giving or paying to, or soliciting or accepting from, potential referral sources (e.g., physicians, nursing homes, other providers and suppliers) incentives for referrals (this can violate the federal Anti-Kickback Statute and/or the federal Stark Law)

Center Representatives are expected to recognize that these practices are improper, and must not knowingly participate in any such practice. Any Center Representative who knows or suspects that any of these activities is occurring is obligated to report that to his or her supervisor and/or to the Corporate Compliance Officer either directly or through the Compliance Hotline through the voicemail extension "XXXX" or 5555 or dial (555) 555-5555 from outside the Center. Knowing participation in any fraudulent or abusive activity and/or failure to report any such known or suspected activity will result in disciplinary action up to and including termination.

Proactively, the Center will make every reasonable effort to ensure that its billings to government and private insurance payers are accurate and conform to applicable laws and regulations. The Center prohibits its Center Representatives from knowingly or recklessly presenting or causing to be presented any false, fictitious, or fraudulent claim for payment or approval. The Center will take reasonable steps to verify that claims are submitted only for services that are actually provided and that those services are billed as provided. Critical to such verification is complete and accurate documentation of services provided. Accordingly, Center Representatives are responsible for maintaining current, complete, and accurate medical records. You may contact the Compliance Officer with questions concerning proper Medicare/Medicaid billing.

The Center will take reasonable steps to make sure that any subcontractors it engages to perform coding or billing services have appropriate skills, quality assurance processes, systems, and procedures to bill government and commercial insurance programs. The Compliance Officer or legal counsel should be consulted before third-party billing entities, contractors, or vendors are engaged to perform coding or billing services for the Center. Results of all audits are reported to the Compliance Committee.

(continues)

AMERICAN MEDICAL CENTER CODE OF CORPORATE COMPLIANCE (continued)

B. Summary of Applicable Laws

More specifically, among the federal Medicare/Medicaid fraud and abuse laws and tax laws of which most Center Representatives need to be aware are the following statutes:

- The Federal False Claims Act (FCA): http://www.cms.hhs.gov/smdl/downloads/SMD032207Att2.pdf
- The Medicare/Medicaid Anti-Kickback Statute (AKS): http://oig.hhs.gov/fraud/docs/safeharborregulations/012389.htm
- The Stark Law: http://oig.hhs.gov/fraud/docs/safeharborregulations/safefs.htm
- The Health Insurance Portability and Accountability Act (HIPAA): http://www.dol.gov/ebsa/newsroom/fshipaa.html#content
- The Civil Monetary Penalties statute (CMP): http://www.sec.gov/rules/final/33-7946.htm
- The Mail Fraud and Wire Fraud statutes: http://www.usdoj.gov/usao/eousa/foia_reading_room/usam/title9/43mcrm.htm
- The Emergency Medical Treatment and Active Labor Act (EMTALA): http://www.cms.gov/Regulations-and-Guidance/-Legislation/EMTALA/index.html
- The Internal Revenue Service (IRS) Intermediate Sanctions regulations: http://www.irs.gov/pub/irs-tege/eotopice03.pdf

Together, these laws prohibit intentional false billing and other forms of fraud and abuse.

Center Representatives should bear in mind that there are additional state laws and regulations not described in the following sections that prohibit conduct similar to that which is prohibited by the statutes listed above and discussed below. A summary description of these principal laws follows.

1. The False Claims Act

Under the federal False Claims Act, it is a felony to make or present to the United States or any United States agency a claim for payment when you know (or should know) that the claim is false, fictitious, or fraudulent. Violations of the False Claims Act are punishable by prison terms of up to 5 years and substantial criminal fines. Civil damage suits are also possible under the civil False Claims Act and can result in multimillion-dollar judgments against the offending entities and individuals involved.

False, fictitious, or fraudulent claims made in the course of seeking Medicare or Medicaid reimbursement are punishable under the False Claims Act.

The Medicare program is made up of two parts of reimbursement for the Medical Center (although Part C, Medigap, and Part D, Pharmacy program, are also part of Medicare but are at the patient's discretion): Medicare Part A and Medicare Part B. Medicare Part A pays for certain inpatient hospital services and certain posthospital services. Medicare Part B pays for certain physician services and certain outpatient services. Claims are submitted to a hospital's fiscal intermediary, and physician and supplier claims are submitted to the local Medicare carrier. Many complex rules govern when it is appropriate to submit a claim for reimbursement to a Medicare fiscal intermediary or a Medicare carrier.

The rules are so numerous and complex that even intermediaries and carriers often need help in interpreting and applying the rules. To assist the intermediaries and carriers, the Centers for Medicare & Medicaid Services publishes the *Medicare Claims Processing Manual.* This manual provides the basic operating instructions for intermediaries and carriers and is a source of guidance with respect to appropriate Medicare reimbursement.

Any claim for Medicare reimbursement that is rejected by a Medicare intermediary or carrier can lead to an allegation that the claim was false, fraudulent, or fictitious in violation of the False Claims Act. In addition, violations of other Medicare requirements, such as providing false information in reports submitted to Medicare and violations of the Stark Law, discussed below, can lead to allegations of False Claims Act violations.

2. The Federal Medicare/Medicaid Anti-Kickback Statute

Because the Center and many of its Center Representatives are participating providers in the Medicare/Medicaid programs, the Center and Center Representatives are subject to the federal Medicare/Medicaid Anti-Kickback Statute. Under the

AMERICAN MEDICAL CENTER CODE OF CORPORATE COMPLIANCE (continued)

Anti-Kickback Statute, no person (an individual or entity) may offer, pay, solicit, or receive anything of value (in cash or in kind) directly or indirectly for referrals of Medicare/Medicaid business. This prohibition is very broad and covers all situations in which anything of value is provided either free of charge or at a reduced cost to any potential referral source (e.g., physicians, DME or other suppliers, nursing homes, or other providers). It also prohibits compensating referral sources or marketing personnel for arranging referrals.

A "thing of value" includes, but is not limited to, the following items or services when provided free of charge or at a discount:

- Equipment (e.g., microscopes, centrifuges, computers)
- Office space
- Personnel (e.g., nurses, phlebotomists, secretaries, etc.)
- Continuing medical education (CME; or other educational programs)
- Recruitment incentives (e.g., payment of moving expenses)
- Health benefits
- Entertainment/meals
- Many other goods or services

There are a number of "safe harbors" under the Anti-Kickback Statute. Thus, for example, it is permissible for a hospital to sell or lease something to a physician or other potential referral source if all of the applicable safe harbor requirements are met, such as if the physician (or other referral source) pays *fair market value* (FMV) for that thing and the sale or lease is documented in a written agreement between the parties. Generally, FMV means the cost of the thing as negotiated between parties at arm's length, without accounting for the value or volume of any Medicare or Medicaid business or any other business between the parties. It is often prudent for a financial consultant to conduct a market analysis to document that a negotiated price is in fact "fair market value." These safe harbors are narrow in scope and require detailed legal and financial analysis to apply correctly to any proposed arrangement. No proposed arrangement should be considered "legal or safe," unless the Corporate Compliance Office or legal counsel has reviewed the arrangement and determined that a safe harbor is met.

Persons (individuals or entities) who violate the Anti-Kickback Statute are subject to criminal penalties including fines of up to $25,000 per violation and/or prison terms of up to 5 years, and exclusion from the Medicare/Medicaid programs. Violations may also result in civil monetary penalties of up to $50,000 and damages up to three times the amount of the illegal kickback. The penalties apply to all parties involved in a prohibited transaction (e.g., a hospital, laboratory, or group practice on the one hand, and the physician or other potential referral source on the other).

It is a compliance policy of the Center that the Center shall not enter into any arrangement where anything is offered, given, or paid to, or solicited or accepted from, any physician or other potential referral source for other than FMV.

3. The Stark Law

The Stark Law (named after its sponsor, Representative Fortney "Pete" Stark [D, Calif.]) prohibits physicians from referring Medicare/Medicaid patients for certain "designated health services" (as defined below) to an entity (1) in which the physician (or a family member of the physician) has an ownership/investment interest, or (2) with which the physician or a family member of the physician has a compensation arrangement (e.g., an employment relationship, a personal services agreement, a lease agreement), unless the ownership/investment interest or compensation arrangement satisfies all requirements of the Stark Law exceptions discussed below.

For purposes of the Stark Law, "designated health services" include the following:

- Clinical laboratory services
- Physical therapy services
- Occupational therapy and speech language therapy services
- Radiology (including nuclear medicine) and certain other imaging services
- Radiation therapy services and supplies

(continues)

AMERICAN MEDICAL CENTER CODE OF CORPORATE COMPLIANCE (continued)

- Durable medical equipment and supplies
- Parenteral and enteral nutrients, equipment, and supplies
- Prosthetics, orthotics, and prosthetic devices and supplies
- Home health services
- Outpatient prescription drugs
- Inpatient and outpatient hospital services

The Stark Law determines whether a physician or facility will be reimbursed from Medicare or Medicaid. There are nuances to the law, such as if a physician is associated with a hospital and treats his or her patient at the hospital, then the physician's services will be reimbursed but not the technical services that may have been used. Ownership interests and compensation arrangements are at the heart of this bill because the physician may have a direct or indirect association with the facility to which the patient was referred.

If a physician or a physician's family member has an ownership/investment interest in, or a compensation arrangement with, an entity that does not satisfy all elements of an applicable exception, the physician *cannot* refer Medicare/Medicaid patients to that entity for any designated health services. If the physician does make such a referral, it is an *automatic* violation of the Stark Law. All inpatient and outpatient hospital services are "designated health services." This means that if a physician or a physician's family member has a financial relationship with the Center that does not satisfy a Stark Law exception, that physician *cannot* refer to the Center for *any* services. Whenever a referral is made in violation of the Stark Law, the entity receiving that referral (e.g., a hospital, laboratory, physician group) *cannot* bill Medicare/Medicaid, the patient, or any third-party payer for the services provided pursuant to the referral. If the entity does bill for those services, the entity also has violated the Stark Law.

Physician referrals are prohibited for designated health services, which include services in the area of clinical lab, physical therapy, occupational therapy, radiology and imaging services, radiation therapy and supplies, durable medical supplies, parenteral and enteral nutrients, equipment and supplies, prosthetics, home health care, outpatient prescription drugs, and inpatient and outpatient services.

There are a number of exceptions to the Stark Law. All of these exceptions require detailed legal and financial analysis to evaluate and apply correctly to any arrangement. No proposed arrangement between the Center and any physician (or physician's family member) should be considered "legal or safe," unless the Compliance Officer or legal counsel has reviewed the arrangement and determined that a Stark Law exception is satisfied.

Violations of the Stark Law can result in denial of payment or repayment obligations for an entity that billed, for services arising from a prohibited referral, civil monetary damages of up to $15,000 per claim and up to $100,000 for certain schemes designed to get around the Stark Law, as well as possible exclusion from the Medicare/Medicaid programs.

Physicians may not refer Medicare/Medicaid patients for any designated health service to an entity in which the physician or a family member of the physician has a financial interest, unless the financial interest arrangement satisfies all elements of a Stark exception. The Center and its entities will make every effort not to participate in referrals prohibited by the Stark Law. If a prohibited referral occurs, no Center entity will bill for any services provided pursuant to that prohibited referral.

4. The Health Insurance Portability and Accountability Act Fraud and Abuse Provisions

On August 21, 1996, President Clinton signed the Health Insurance Portability and Accountability Act (HIPAA) into law as Public Law 104-191. HIPAA amended the Public Health Service Act (PHS Act), the Employee Retirement Income Security Act of 1974 (ERISA), and the Internal Revenue Code of 1986.

The primary purpose of the law was largely based on clinical ethics. The law provided more guidelines to limit exclusions for preexisting conditions, prohibit discrimination against employees and dependents based on their health status, guarantee renewability and availability of health coverage to certain employers and individuals, and protect many workers who lose health coverage by providing better access to individual health insurance coverage.

AMERICAN MEDICAL CENTER CODE OF CORPORATE COMPLIANCE (continued)

The HIPAA regulations make it a federal crime to engage in certain types of fraudulent or abusive activities that involve *any* payer of healthcare benefits, whether public or private. That is, the HIPAA fraud and abuse provisions apply not only to providers who deal with government-funded healthcare payers and programs, such as Medicare and Medicaid, but also to providers who deal with private, commercial payers and programs. The five types of activities prohibited by HIPAA are:

- Knowingly or willfully defrauding a healthcare program or plan, or obtaining payment from a healthcare program or plan, by using false or fraudulent pretenses
- Engaging in theft or embezzlement
- Making false statements
- Obstructing an investigation into healthcare fraud
- Money laundering related to healthcare programs or plans

HIPAA's privacy and security provisions govern the use and disclosure of patient health information. Center Representatives are expected to comply with the Center's HIPAA privacy and security policies and procedures for patient information. The Center Privacy Office furnishes guidance about those policies and procedures.

a. The Physician's Role in Ethical HIPAA Compliance. Whether they own the practice in which they work or are remunerated employees of a larger health network, physicians are often viewed by their patients as the "captains of the ship." Executives and administrators may be responsible for enabling, processing, and archiving hundreds of physician–patient encounters on a daily basis. However, physicians maintain direct patient contact and may be the first responsible parties transmitting protected health information over a health network. To maintain creditability with patients and peers and to identify major compliance issues, physicians should play more than a cursory role in HIPAA planning and implementation. Because some clinicians may view HIPAA as another bureaucratic requirement that calls for more time away from patient care, encouraging physician involvement won't always be easy. But HIPAA compliance will not be successful without physician buy-in; thus, it is incumbent on executives to facilitate physician participation.

Penalties. HIPAA penalty provisions establish civil monetary penalties of $100 per person, per violation and not more than $25,000 per person for violations of a single standard in a calendar year. Criminal penalties for any person that knowingly uses a unique health identifier or discloses protected health information can include a maximum fine of $50,000 and/or imprisonment of up to 1 year. This increases to $100,000 and 5 years if the offense is "under false pretenses." If the offense is with intent to sell or use protected health information for commercial advantage or malicious harm, fines reach $250,000 with possible jail time of 10 years.

Violations of HIPAA can result in prison terms of up to 10 years, criminal fines, or both. HIPAA also authorizes the federal government to impose civil monetary penalties on entities or individuals who engage in a pattern or practice of presenting claims that are based on a code that the person/entity knows or should know will result in more reimbursement than is appropriate or that are for services or items that are not medically necessary. **Any false, fictitious, or fraudulent claim made in the course of seeking reimbursement from any healthcare payer or program (government or private) is punishable as a federal crime under HIPAA's fraud and abuse provisions.**

5. Civil Monetary Penalties Law
Among the activities prohibited by the federal Civil Monetary Penalties Statute (CMP) are:

- Knowingly presenting or causing to be presented false claims (specifically for services not provided, or not provided as claimed, or for upcoded claims)
- Knowingly presenting or causing to be presented claims for services that are not medically necessary (as defined by Medicare)
- Knowingly presenting or causing to be presented claims that violate a benefits assignment
- Offering or giving remuneration to Medicare or Medicaid patients as an incentive for them to receive services from the entity or individual giving the remuneration
- Contracting with or employing individuals or entities excluded from participating in a federal healthcare program

(continues)

AMERICAN MEDICAL CENTER CODE OF CORPORATE COMPLIANCE (continued)

Any false claim, claim for unnecessary services, or claim for services ordered or provided by an excluded entity or individual can give rise to CMP violations. In particular, offering or providing anything of material value to Medicare/ Medicaid patients as an incentive for them to obtain services from the entity or individual (or their agent) making the offer or gift can also give rise to CMP violations.

6. Medicare Exclusionary Statute

Physicians, other individuals, and organizations can be excluded from participation in the Medicare and Medicaid programs if convicted of fraudulent activities. In particular, the Medicare exclusionary statute prohibits providers from:

- Submitting claims for unnecessary services
- Submitting claims for excessive charges
- Submitting claims for services that fail to meet professionally recognized standards of health care
- Failing to furnish medically necessary services

In addition, no payment will be made by any federal healthcare program for any items or services furnished, or ordered, or prescribed by an excluded individual or entity, or to such person's employer or anyone contracting with an excluded individual. As required by law, it is the policy of the Center to take reasonable steps not to employ, grant medical staff membership or clinical privileges to, or otherwise do business with any individual or entity named on the Office of Inspector General's list of individuals and entities who have been excluded, debarred, suspended, or are otherwise ineligible to participate in federal or state healthcare programs.

Each Center Representative will be required to affirm that he or she is not currently excluded, debarred, suspended, or otherwise ineligible to participate in federal or state healthcare programs. All such persons shall also affirm that they have never been excluded, debarred, suspended, or made otherwise ineligible to participate in federal or state healthcare programs and that they have never been convicted of any criminal offense involving or otherwise related to any government healthcare program. Further, as a condition of employment, receiving and maintaining medical staff membership and privileges at a Center hospital, or doing business with the Center, all such persons are required to immediately inform the Compliance Officer if they receive notice or otherwise become aware that they have been excluded, debarred, suspended, or otherwise become ineligible to participate in federal or state healthcare programs for any reason.

Submitting claims for unnecessary services, submitting excessive charges, and/or failing to furnish medically necessary services can implicate the Exclusionary Statute. It is illegal to employ, grant medical staff membership or clinical privileges to, or otherwise do business with any individual or entity named on the Office of Inspector General's list of individuals and entities who are excluded, debarred, suspended, or otherwise ineligible to participate in federal or state healthcare programs.

7. Mail Fraud and Wire Fraud Statutes

The Mail Fraud and Wire Fraud statutes are favorite enforcement tools of the government in its efforts to prosecute Medicare/Medicaid fraud and abuse. Any misrepresentation that is a part of a scheme to obtain money or property by use of the mail system or a wire system (e.g., phones, computers) violates these laws. Thus, these laws are very broad in their application. For example, each claim for reimbursement that the Center mails to Medicare/Medicaid or that the Center submits to Medicare/Medicaid electronically could be subject to these laws. In addition, any time a Center Representative speaks by phone with a Medicare/Medicaid Representative or other governmental representative, that conversation could be subject to these laws. As a result, it is critical that the Center's claims and its statements be accurate and correct whenever the Center communicates with Medicare/Medicaid representatives and whenever the Center seeks reimbursement from Medicare/Medicaid. Violations of the Mail and Wire Fraud statutes can lead to criminal penalties including imprisonment and fines. **Conduct that violates the False Claims Act, the Medicare/Medicaid Anti-Kickback statute, the Stark Law, and/or the CMP law, if done using the mail system or a wire system, could also violate the Mail and/or Wire Fraud statutes.**

8. Emergency Treatment and Active Labor Act

The Center abides by the rules and regulations of the Emergency Medical Treatment and Active Labor Act (EMTALA) in providing emergency medical treatment to all patients regardless of their ability to pay. The Center does not admit or discharge patients based solely on their ability to pay. Any patient who presents to a Center hospital seeking emergency care will be screened to determine whether he or she has an emergency medical condition, or if she is in active labor. If so, the patient will be treated to stabilize the condition and either will be admitted or, once stabilized, will be discharged or transferred as is appropriate. Transfers of unstabilized patients will occur only when requested in writing by the patient (or patient's family) or when a physician certifies in writing that the medical benefits of the transfer outweigh the risks. Unstabilized patients will be transferred to the closest hospital that provides the services needed by the patient, that has available beds and staff, and that accepts the transfer. Unstabilized patients will be transferred via qualified personnel and equipment including the use of medically appropriate life support measures if necessary.

EMTALA requires that all patients who come to the hospital seeking treatment of an emergency condition receive a medical screening examination to determine whether the patient has an emergency medical condition. If so, the patient may not be transferred (includes discharge) out of the hospital until his or her emergency medical condition has been stabilized, unless one of the applicable exceptions for proper transfers of unstabilized patients applies. It is illegal to delay a medical screening exam and stabilizing treatment to inquire about a patient's financial status, insurance coverage, or ability to pay.

9. Intermediate Sanctions for Private Inurement

As a tax-exempt organization under Section 501(c)(3) of the Internal Revenue Code, the Center and its member facilities must be careful to avoid entering into arrangements that could jeopardize their tax-exempt status. The IRS rules prohibit the private inurement of the Center or its facilities' earnings to private individuals, including insider physicians and the provision of other inappropriate economic benefit to "disqualified persons," which are persons who are in a position to exercise substantial influence over the affairs of the Center or a facility. An excise tax (also known as an "intermediate sanction") may be imposed against a "disqualified person" if that person was party to an "excess benefit transaction" with the Center or a member facility. An "excess benefit transaction" is generally defined as a transaction in which a disqualified person receives an economic benefit (from the tax-exempt entity) in excess of the value of the goods or services provided by the disqualified person.

The intermediate sanctions regulations provide procedures to establish a rebuttable presumption that amounts paid are reasonable for transactions with disqualified persons. If all of the steps in the safe harbor are followed properly, there is a rebuttable presumption that the transaction does not constitute an excess benefit transaction, thus providing a defense against the intermediate sanctions and penalties. The requirements for the safe harbor are as follows:

- The business arrangement is approved in advance by the governing board of the tax-exempt corporation, or a committee of the governing board, excluding any board members who have a conflict of interest.
- Prior to making its determination, the governing board relies upon appropriate data as to comparability of value.
- The governing board adequately documents the basis for its determination concurrently with making the determination.

Entering into agreements with disqualified persons could jeopardize the Center's, and its member institutions', tax-exempt status or result in the imposition of IRS intermediate sanctions against disqualified persons. The Center and its member institutions will not enter into improper excess benefit transactions with physicians or anyone else who may be a disqualified person. All transactions with disqualified persons must meet all requirements of the safe harbor described previously.

10. Tax Exempt Bonds

The Center's bond trustee and Board of Directors will maintain proper records and perform the proper calculations to comply with all applicable Internal Revenue Codes with respect to any Center bonds.

(continues)

AMERICAN MEDICAL CENTER CODE OF CORPORATE COMPLIANCE (continued)

C. Relationships with Affiliated Physicians

Since the mid-1980s, health care has become one of the most heavily regulated industries in the nation. As a result, many transactions that used to be permissible in the healthcare arena are no longer proper. Relationships between healthcare providers and physicians have come under substantial scrutiny as part of the increasing regulation of health care. Therefore, the Center must carefully structure its business arrangements with physicians to ensure that those arrangements comply with applicable legal requirements. Because most of the laws apply to the physicians involved in these transactions as well as to the Center, compliance also benefits the physicians. In order to comply with applicable legal and ethical standards regarding referrals and admissions, the Center and Center Representatives will adhere strictly to the following two rules:

The Center does not pay for referrals. The Center accepts patient referrals and admissions based solely on a patient's medical needs and the Center's ability to meet those needs. The Center does not pay or offer to pay anyone, including, but not necessarily limited to, Center Representatives, physicians, and other health professionals, for referrals of patients. That is, the Center does not offer or give anything of value (e.g., money, discounts, goods, or services), directly or indirectly, for patient referrals. The Center does not support the practice of "most favored nations." The Center will use best efforts to identify any "most-favored nations" provision in all contracts and will have said language removed prior to engagement of contracts.

The Center does not seek or accept payments for referrals that it makes. The Center, Center Representatives, health professionals, and volunteers may not solicit or receive any money or other thing of value, directly or indirectly, in exchange for referring patients to another healthcare provider or supplier. When the Center does make patient referrals to another provider or supplier, it will not consider the volume or value of referrals that that provider or supplier makes or may make to the Center.

Violation of either of these rules regarding physicians and payment for referrals could have serious consequences for the Center and for the individuals involved in the violation, including civil and criminal penalties, as well as possible exclusion from participation in federally funded healthcare programs. Any Center Representative or health professional who is contemplating a business arrangement that could implicate either of these rules must submit the proposed arrangement to the Compliance Officer or legal counsel for review and approval prior to engaging in such arrangement.

IV. Organization of the Compliance Program

Ultimate responsibility for the Compliance Program is vested in the Center's Board of Directors and the President of the Center. The Program shall be administrated through various Center Representatives as described below. All Center Representatives are required to comply with the Compliance Program.

A. Responsibility

1. Board of Directors

The Board of Directors has ultimate responsibility for the Center's Compliance Program through their governance. Responsibilities include the following:

- Ensuring that management is accountable for carrying out the Compliance
- The program's objectives
- Overseeing the effectiveness of the Compliance Program by receiving and evaluating reports regarding the Compliance Program

2. Vice President of Finance/Compliance Officer

The Vice President of Finance/Compliance Officer is responsible for implementing and maintaining the Center's Code of Compliance. The appointment of this responsibility is subject to the approval of the President of the Center. This individual also has direct access to the Board of Directors. The Vice President of Finance/Compliance Officer's responsibilities include the following:

- Oversee the dissemination, execution, functioning, direction of investigations, follow-up, and ultimate enforcement of the Code.
- Engage legal counsel as necessary with regard to the Code.
- Determine when it is necessary to retain the use of external auditors.
- Determine when to voluntarily report suspected noncompliance to appropriate government agencies.
- Provide regular reports to the Board of Directors.
- Assist with providing staff education on integrity and compliance issues.
- Develop and assist with implementation of Compliance Policies and Procedures to facilitate regulatory compliance.
- Audit all charging and billing procedures to assure regulatory compliance.
- Review and revise policies and procedures pertaining to billing and claims submission, documentation, coding, and other reimbursement compliance issues.
- Provide a means for Center Representatives and others to report alleged illegal, unethical, fraudulent, wasteful, or abusive activities.
- Immediately report any apparent illegal, unethical, fraudulent, wasteful, or abusive conduct to the President of the Center.
- Review bulletins from governmental and other third-party payers to forward information to appropriate management staff and to assure the Center and its affiliates are in compliance with current regulations.
- Re-review CDM requests for coding accuracy and allowable charging protocols.
- Review and revise the Compliance Policies and Procedures, the Code, and the Compliance Program at least annually to assess basic elements and overall effectiveness, including a review of billing and coding error rates, identified overpayments, and audit results.

3. Department Managers

All department managers shall serve as compliance officials for their respective departments. Within their respective areas of responsibility, department managers are required to:

- Coordinate, educate, and communicate requirements of the Compliance Program to supervised staff.
- Provide staff education on integrity and compliance issues.
- Monitor the activities of supervised Center Representatives to ensure integrity and compliance.
- Audit any charging and billing procedures relevant to the respective department to assure regulatory compliance.
- Develop and assist with implementation of policies and procedures to facilitate regulatory compliance.
- Review and revise the Compliance Policies and Procedures, the Code, and the Compliance Program at least annually to assess basic elements and overall effectiveness, as applicable to their department.
- Review bulletins from governmental and other third-party payers to ensure the Center and its affiliates are in compliance with current regulations.
- Provide a means for Center Representatives to report alleged illegal, unethical, fraudulent, wasteful, or abusive activities.
- Immediately investigate any reports of apparent illegal, unethical, fraudulent, wasteful, or abusive conduct or activities.
- Report any suspicions or investigations of apparent illegal, unethical, fraudulent, wasteful, or abusive conduct or reports of such to the Vice President of Finance/Compliance Officer.

4. Compliance Committee

A Compliance Committee shall be created according to the Compliance Program Manual, hereby incorporated by reference, to assist with the implementation and review of the Code and the Compliance Policies and Procedures. The Committee will consist of certain core management staff involved in high-risk compliance areas as well as the periodic addition of other members as needed.

(continues)

AMERICAN MEDICAL CENTER CODE OF CORPORATE COMPLIANCE (continued)

5. Center Representatives

(Representatives include employees, agents, independent contractors, consultants, associates, trustees, medical staff members, vendors, volunteers, or any other individual who provides care or services to the Center or who conducts business for or on behalf of the Center.) All Center Representatives are responsible for the following:

- Carry out job responsibilities in an ethical, effective, and professional manner according to policies and procedures, such as Ethics and Conduct, and standards dictated by their respective professional organization.
- Immediately report potential compliance problems (apparent illegal, unethical, fraudulent, wasteful, or abusive conduct) to management either directly, through the hotline, or through other methods described in the Code of Compliance or the Center's Compliance Policies and Procedures.
- Policies and procedures are in place to follow all aspects of the Deficit Reduction Act

B. Communication and Reporting

All Center Representatives have a responsibility to assist in combating fraud, waste, and abuse throughout the Center. Because reporting is important, an open line of communication for all Center Representatives regarding integrity and compliance exists within the structure of the Center. Communication lines already exist for employees to contact their immediate supervisor, assistant manager, manager, or vice president for situations they feel are appropriate for such communication. As part of this Code, managers are designated as compliance officials. However, in addition to the normal lines of communication, employees are also able to contact other individuals by various methods as described below to report any suspected illegal, unethical, fraudulent, wasteful, or abusive conduct. **Individuals will not be subject to retaliation for submitting reports in good faith**.

1. Reporting

Various modes of communication are available to report any suspected illegal, unethical, fraudulent, wasteful, or abusive conduct by any of the Center Representatives. Reports can be made by anyone through the following methods:

- *Hotline*: A telephone hotline is available on a 24-hour basis through the voicemail extension "XXXX" or 5555. Dial (555) 555-5555 from outside of the Center. This is a voicemail box that takes messages.
- *Email*: Internal and external email addresses are also available on a 24-hour basis that are also answered by the Center's Compliance Officer as follows: XXXXX@XXXXXCenterXXXXXXXX.org.
- *Correspondence or mail*: Correspondence can also be sent to the Compliance Officer/Vice President of Finance either by interdepartment mail or U.S. mail at the following addresses:
  Compliance Officer/Chief Financial Officer
  Interoffice address: Administration
  U.S. mail address: 11111 North Street, Any City, Any State, 11111
- *Compliance Officer/Vice President of Finance*: The Center's Compliance Officer is available for any questions, discussion, or reporting of suspected misconduct at extension 5555 or (555) 555-5555. For personal discussion, the Compliance Officer's area is located in Administration on the Fifth Floor.

2. Anonymity

Informants are encouraged to assist the compliance efforts by providing information on how they can be contacted for additional information, but the *informant may remain anonymous*. In the event the informant chooses to remain anonymous:

- An identifying number will be assigned and the Compliance Officer will make arrangements to permit the informant to be advised of any action taken with respect to the informant's allegations.
- An informant's identity will be held in confidence as permitted or required by law.

3. Documentation

In order to ensure that appropriate follow-up is completed on all reports of suspected illegal, unethical, fraudulent, wasteful, or abusive conduct, reports made to the Compliance Officer in any form such as via mail, the hotline, email, and the like will be documented and maintained in a secure and confidential manner by the Compliance Officer for a period of at least 7 years. At no time shall a copy of any report be placed in an informant's personnel file. Documentation will include as much information as the informant will provide such as:

- The informant's name, extension or telephone number, department or address, or email address
- A summary or nature of the conduct reported
- The date and time the call was received
- A summary of the follow-up activities performed

C. Training and Education

Proper training and education with continual retraining of all Center Representatives is a significant element to ensuring effective compliance to safeguard that each Center Representative is fully capable of executing his or her role in compliance with this Code and the Center's Compliance Policies and Procedures. Department Managers are responsible for ensuring that supervised staff receives appropriate training. Training shall be both general and tailored specifically for the Center Representatives' department or unit that affects reimbursement activities.

ETHICS OF PROMISE KEEPING AND LEADERSHIP BANKRUPTCY

Promise keeping can be considered synonymous with what we think of as "giving one's word." In actuality, what this means is that we trust someone's words are sincere and honest and hold no secondary meaning or intent. We also trust that those words are binding and represent an oral agreement to follow through.

Few things in our profession can be more damaging to a leader's credibility than failing to keep one's word. Trust, followership, and credibility can easily be lost when leaders cannot follow through on their own statements and/or verbal commitments to peers, superiors, or subordinates. Once a relationship is tarnished, it may be impossible for a leader to regain any level of confidence previously held with organizational members. Unfortunately, in the complex society we live in today, it can become an easy task for a leader to mince words and suggest alternate meanings for agendas after the fact. Often this behavior is not seen by individuals as dishonest, but rather as accepted "spinning" of facts. Alarmingly, this behavior is becoming more omnipresent. Sadly, the current economic situation in the United States may be based in part on a small handful of organizations, entities, and people who simply engaged in dishonest practices and made promises they had no intention, or perhaps ability, to keep.

For example, some students in the current generation do not see cheating or plagiarism as dishonest. On the contrary, it is viewed by some as a socially accepted means of getting through a degree program. The unfortunate outcome is that millions of dollars have been spent by the university industry in developing software and new educational platforms to catch and prevent this activity. The business and health profession is not without its own ethical missteps. Fraudulent billing at the local level, and HealthSouth's accounting scandal at an organizational level, are just two examples of dishonest behavior—and an organizational intent to break promises to stakeholders.

Our profession is demanding that our leaders stay true to their word and mean what they say. Although promise keeping is not a measure of any licensing, certification, or accreditation process, it may be one of the most important characteristics displayed by a leader. Stakeholder perceptions of organizational trust, value, and quality may all suffer from a leader's inability to keep promises.

The academic research surrounding leadership bankruptcy, that is, leaders who are absent of business morals, is on the rise. Sadly, the intent, or inability, of some health leaders to keep promises is escalating. As a result, implicit confidence is no longer a benefit of an individual's title or position in the industry. Trust and confidence initially must

PROMISE KEEPING IN ACTION

In West Texas, promise keeping is sometimes (and affectionately) referred to as the "West Texas handshake." In a region where individuals may still see horse hitching posts outside supermarkets for customers who arrive to the market on horseback, the concept of the West Texas handshake may mean something that is hard to describe to people from outside this region of the country.

A number of contractors, vendors, and service personnel that do business in West Texas still do so on the basis of a handshake—not a contract. As an example, in 2008, after a home builder repaired a leaking window in a recently built home in Lubbock, Texas, the builder told the homeowner if it ever leaked again, the homeowners should call him immediately so he could come out and actually see where the water was coming in from the outside when it rained.

On July 4, 2010, the homeowners had an opportunity to test this promise. Lubbock experienced over 2 inches of rain that day, and the wind gusts reached nearly 30 miles per hour. A window in the homeowner's breakfast room began to leak badly, and by 10:00 PM there was a great deal of water coming in from outside. It had been over a year and a half since the builder had made that promise to the homeowners to come back and see the leak. The homeowners had no contract—and nothing in writing—but they called him anyway. True to his word, within 30 minutes of that phone call, the builder was at their home. He brought with him duct tape, several feet of plastic cover, and towels to clean the floor. He then spent the next hour taping up the window and walking in and out of the house with a flashlight trying to find the cause of the leak. He left close to midnight to go back home. He was soaking wet, but he promised (yet again) to come back the next day to clean up the temporary repair and do the final maintenance on the window, which he did.

In West Texas, the West Texas handshake has enduring value and meaning. It is anchored in an earlier period in U.S. culture that some feel is anachronistic. However, it echoes back to a day when a person's integrity was measured by reputation among other community members, and an individual's self-worth was grounded in personal honesty and promise keeping.

As adapted from the American College of Healthcare Executives Regent Newsletter for the West Texas Region, April 2012.

be earned by the leader, shepherded during the term of the relationship, and stand as a memorable benchmark of distinction when careers part.

SOCIAL MEDIA AND MORAL CONSIDERATIONS[52]

Social media is influencing the way providers and patients communicate with one another. "In a survey of patients of an outpatient family practice clinic, 56% wanted their providers to use social media for appointment setting and reminders, diagnostic test results reporting, health information sharing, prescription notifications, and answering general questions. For those patients who do not use social media, many would start if they knew that they could connect with their providers there."[53] If providers use social media to communicate with patients, certain standards would need to be utilized to promote professionalism while protecting patient information.

While patients are entitled to share their personal health with others via social media (such as Facebook and blog forums), physicians are legally bound to patient privacy by HIPAA. "The Privacy Rule, in effect since 2003, levies heavy fines and potential criminal charges on unauthorized disclosure of individually identifiable health information, also known as protected health information (PHI), by covered entities. Protected health information applies to health information in oral, paper, or electronic forms. There have been many well-publicized breaches of HIPAA involving social media; in many of these cases, disclosure was inadvertent."[54] Providers and administrators must be careful to avoid such breaches of patient information.

Some providers go even further and "friend request" or add their patients to their social media networks. "In a survey of practicing physicians, approximately one-third of physicians who use social networking reported receiving a friend request from a patient or a patient's family member; however only a small minority (5%) had ever extended the friend request themselves."[55] This small percentage proves how fearful providers are of HIPAA violations and protecting their reputations. Providers' personal pages may also present them in an unprofessional light. Even when communicating by private messages on third-party sites, it is important to remember that these communications, although private, are owned by the website and breaches have been known to occur. Posting information about patients or patient interactions may also lead to serious consequences for the reputation of the provider and the facility. Providers may also try to obtain more information about a patient from their personal profiles. Although the provider may have good intentions by doing so, some patients may view it as a compromise of trust. Consideration for the patient and his or her preferences is vital to the success of patient–provider social media interactions.

The American Medical Association (AMA) has a list of ethical and professional implications that may be used as a framework when utilizing social media in provider–patient interactions. "Medical professionalism has been defined in many ways but generally includes standards of competence and integrity, placing the patient's interest above those of the physician, and providing expert advice to society on matters of health."[56] Administrators and others working in the healthcare industry have a moral duty to report providers who appear to behave unprofessionally in their social media usage. While there are strong advocates for using social media in provider–patient communication, leaders must make the decision regarding whether or not this is advantageous to the organization, in compliance with law, and within professional standards expected of the organization.

SUMMARY

Despite its ineffable and difficult nature to understand, health leaders should study ethics in order to better understand the human condition and the differing points of views presented in the environment. Areas in health where ethics may assist in decision making are highly eclectic. The study of ethics can assist in the decision making associated with finance, risk management, resource allocation, customer advocacy, law, and organization standing policy, to name only a few areas. A health leader in possession of a wider point of view of the dynamic field is better able to handle the complex and challenging issues presented to him or her.

This chapter presented the ethical responsibilities of health leaders from an organizational perspective. Distributive justice theories, which describe the ideology of resource distribution in a society, were presented as a framework to open up a discussion of ethics. Organizational ethics consists of a process to address ethical issues associated with the business, financial, and management areas of health organizations. Professional, educational, and contractual relationships all have ethical components that can affect the operation of the health organization. Excerpts from a merger of several corporate compliance policy statements, formed from the application of several regulatory statutes, were provided as an example of one of the essential components of health organization morality and compliance. Leadership is important for organizations because leaders set the ethical standard for employees.[57]

DISCUSSION QUESTIONS

1. How do you (personally) balance legalism and leadership practice with regard to ethics?
2. Define *distributive justice*, *ethics*, *morals*, *values*, and *conflict of interest*. How are they used by health leaders in decision making?
3. Explain four ethical principles that guide decision making associated with patient care. How can leaders use these principles in decision making within a health organization?
4. How could you apply at least two ethical frameworks or distributive justice theories, with examples of moral practice of a leader, to an ethical issue in a health organization? What would be the results?
5. Should health leaders adopt utilitarian and/or deontological postures in their organization? How would you differentiate the potential decisions that leaders would make under these two frameworks? Is treatment by ability to pay moral? Are treatment decisions based on a patient's age moral? Are ability to pay or age treatment decisions more or less moral?
6. Which options does a leader in a health organization have for developing an integrated system of ethics and moral practice? What would be the potential impact of each option regarding appropriate ethical adaptation across the organization?
7. How would the utilization of at least three different ethical frameworks or distributive justice theories affect patient autonomy, beneficence, nonmaleficence, and justice? How would the application of moral practice associated with those frameworks (at least three) be different for a right-to-life issue and for the practice of euthanasia?

EXERCISES

1. In a one-page paper, define *distributive justice*, *ethics*, *morals*, and *values*, and describe how they are used by leaders in decision making.
2. In a one-page paper, explain four ethical principles that guide decision making associated with patient care.
3. In a two-page paper, apply at least two ethical frameworks or distributive justice theories, with examples of moral practice of a leader, to an ethical issue in a health organization.
4. In a two- to three-page paper, analyze arguments and make a recommendation for health leaders to adopt utilitarian and/or deontological postures in their organization; differentiate potential decisions leaders would make in the two frameworks to support your analysis and recommendation.
5. Compile a list of options that a leader in a health organization has to develop an integrated system

of ethics and moral practice. In a one- to two-page paper, summarize the potential impact of each option regarding appropriate ethical adaptation across the organization.
6. Read "The Case Study of the Transferred Employee" and answer the following questions in a two- to three-page paper:
   a. What do you do?
   b. Do you change the documents?
   c. Do you go back and confront your supervisor?
   d. What is your decision, and why did you make it?
   e. What is your next course of action?
   f. Which other factors do you consider, and which other actions do you take?
   g. Which ethical framework or distributive justice theory best supports your decisions regarding the case, and why?

THE CASE STUDY OF THE TRANSFERRED EMPLOYEE

You are an administrator of a department in a health organization that has recently been reorganized. Personnel from other units have been permanently transferred into your department so that your department can take on additional tasks in support of the mission of the health organization.

After 2 months have passed, one of your new employees comes to you asking for you to complete his annual job performance appraisal. You are surprised because all annual performance appraisals were supposed to have been completed by the supervisors of the departments losing the personnel before they were transferred into your department. Because you do not feel you know the new employee well enough to do an annual performance appraisal, you call the former supervisor and ask that she complete the performance evaluation herself on the employee. The losing supervisor refuses, saying that the issue is now your problem. The losing supervisor further states that no one from the human resources department told her that she was supposed to do a performance appraisal on the employee before the employee left her division. The losing supervisor also confides that writing a performance appraisal 90 days after it is due will trigger a "red flag" with human resources, which may reflect negatively on the losing supervisor's management and the supervisory effectiveness of her department.

Frustrated with the situation, you approach your supervisor and ask for his guidance. He suggests that you change the date on the employee's internal transfer documents, making it seem as if the employee arrived in your department yesterday. Your supervisor also says that he will talk to the other department leader and make sure she did an evaluation for 12 months on the employee, and not just for 9 months. He also suggests that you could provide some input on the evaluation because the employee did work for you for the last 60 days. Your supervisor says, "This happens all the time." He continues by stating, "It is easily corrected by creating a new set of documents." He assures you that there is nothing illegal about this practice and that this methodology is used frequently to correct otherwise careless administrative actions in the facility.

Your supervisor then tells you to go back to your office, retrieve the transfer documents already in place, and replace them with new ones containing the dates you and he just talked about. As you walk back to your office, you begin to feel uncomfortable with the prospect of taking an administratively correct set of documents, destroying them, and then replacing them with some newly created documents that do not represent the actual dates of the transfer. You believe that this practice provides further support for an otherwise ineffective human resources system. However, as a new department head, you are uncomfortable losing favor with the boss who controls your future in the organization.

THE CASE STUDY OF THE TRANSFERRED EMPLOYEE (continued)

To protect yourself, you call the organization's legal counsel to get some advice on an informal basis. Legal counsel tells you that your supervisor is, indeed, correct; it is not illegal to change the documents if changing them results in a correction to a previously made administrative error. You counter by telling legal counsel that this may not have been a human resources or administrative error as much as it is an attempt to avoid a negative human resources action. Legal counsel suggests you go back and discuss the issues with your supervisor if you are uncomfortable doing anything regarding this matter. This suggestion makes you even more uncomfortable, because your boss is not an individual who enjoys repeating himself or being challenged or questioned by his employees. Such events are perceived by your boss as the actions of disloyal employees. You are certain that going back to your supervisor will result in an uncomfortable event for you.

REFERENCES

1. Mantel, J. (2015). Ethical integrity in health care organizations: Currents in contemporary bioethics. *The Journal of Law, Medicine & Ethics, 43*(3), 661–665.
2. Pozgar, G. D. (2004). *Legal aspects of health care administration* (9th ed.). Sudbury, MA: Jones & Bartlett, p. 2.
3. Pozgar, note 2.
4. Joseph, A. M. (2007). The impact of nursing on patient and organizational outcomes. *Nursing Economics, 25*, 30–34.
5. Pozgar, note 2.
6. Hewitt-Taylor, J. (2003). Issues involved in promoting patient autonomy in health care. *British Journal of Nursing, 12*(22), 1323–1330.
7. Johnson, J. A. (2009). *Comparative health systems.* Sudbury, MA: Jones & Bartlett.
8. Coppola, M. N., Croft, T., & Leo, L. (1997). Understanding the uninsured dilemma: A necessity for managed care survival. *Medical Group Management Journal, 44*(5), 72–82, 100.
9. Gibbs, L. (Trans.). (2002). Aesop's fable of the grasshopper and the ants. *Aesop's fables.* Oxford: Oxford University Press.
10. Coppola et al., note 8.
11. Southwick, A. (1988). *The law of hospital and health care administration.* Chicago, IL: Health Administration Press.
12. Beauchamp, T. L., & Childress, J. F. (2008). *Principles of biomedical ethics.* Princeton, NJ: Oxford University Press.
13. McDonald, F., Simpson, C., & O'Brien, F. (2008). Including organizational ethics in policy review processes in healthcare institutions: A view from Canada. *HEC Forum, 20*(2), 137–153.
14. Emmanuel, L. (2000). Ethics and the structures of healthcare. *Cambridge Quarterly of Healthcare Ethics, 9,* 151–168.
15. Povar, G. J., Blumen, H., Daniel, J., Daub, S., Evans, L., Holm, R. P., et al. (2004). Ethics in practice: Managed care and the changing health care environment. *Annals of Internal Medicine, 141*(2), 131–137.
16. Reiser, S. J. (1994). The ethical life of health care organizations. *Hastings Centre Report, 24*(6), 28.
17. McGee, G., Spanogle, J. P., Caplan, A. L., & Asch, D. A. (2001). A national study of ethics committees. *American Journal of Bioethics, 1*(4), 60–64.
18. McGee et al., note 17.
19. Muir, D. (2008, Oct. 30). Congress speaks out about CEO bonuses. ABC News Online. Retrieved from http://abcnews.go.com/Business/story?id=6150746&page=1.
20. Stout, D. (2009, March 18). A.I.G. chief asks bonus recipients to give back half. *New York Times.* Retrieved from http://www.nytimes.com/2009/03/19/business/19web-aig.html.
21. American College of HealthCare Executives. (2005). *Board of Governors' certification exam study guide.* Chicago, IL: Health Administration Press.
22. Peer, K. S., & Rakich, J. S. (1999). Ethical decision making in healthcare management. *Hospital Topics, 77*(4), 7–13.
23. Harris, D. M. (2003). *Contemporary issues in healthcare law and ethics.* Chicago, IL: Health Administration Press.
24. Leathard, A., & Goodinson-McLaren, S. (2007). *Ethics: Contemporary challenges in health and social care.* Bristol, UK: Policy Press.

25. Boatright, J. R. (2013). *Ethics in finance* (3rd ed.). West Sussex, UK: Wiley & Sons, Inc. Retrieved October 3, 2015 from http://books.google.com/books?hl=en&lr=&id=DgNgAgAAQBAJ&oi=fnd&pg=PP1&dq=ethics+of+leadership+bankruptcy&ots=C_syOg8m9n&sig=BGkYiSuJm_PaDXXpwEUBf-6YQMU#v=onepage&q=ethics%20of%20leadership%20bankruptcy&f=false, p. 1.

26. Grace, P. J. (2001). Professional advocacy: Widening the scope of accountability. *Nursing Philosophy*, 2(2), 151–162

27. MacDonald, H. (2007). Relational ethics and advocacy in nursing: Literature review. *Journal of Advanced Nursing*, 57(2), 119–126.

28. Coppola, M. N., & Ledlow, J. R. (2009). *A scholarly discussion of spirituality in healthcare leadership: Why not?* American College of Healthcare Executive (ACHE) abstract (unpublished), West Texas Region.

29. Pesut, B. (2009). Incorporating patients' spirituality into care using Gadow's ethical framework. *Nursing Ethics*, 16(4), 418–428.

30. Pesut, note 29.

31. Baylor University, Institute for Studies of Religion. (2008). Baylor religion survey. Waco, TX: Baylor University.

32. Coppola & Ledlow, note 28.

33. Giesler, N. L. (1981). *Options in contemporary Christian ethics*. Grand Rapids, MI: Baker Book House.

34. Pesut, note 29.

35. Lamont, J., & Favor, C. (2013). Distributive justice. Retrieved from http://plato.stanford.edu/entries/justice-distributive/.

36. Greenberg, J., & Colquitt, J. A. (2013). *Handbook of organizational justice*. East Sussex, U.K: Psychology Press. Retrieved December 3, 2015 from http://books.google.com/books?hl=en&lr=&id=-ui-8tN6EtAC&oi=fnd&pg=PR3&dq=organization+distributive+justice+theories&ots=hGEaOgBd4b&sig=VNCc_dQHHwXysftOH4uzuXWBR_4#v=onepage&q=organization%20distributive%20justice%20theories&f=false.

37. Matthews, J. R. (2006, Nov. 17). Social justice v. market incentive. Retrieved from http://medicalethics.suite101.com/article.cfm/social_justice_v__market_incentive.

38. Distributive Justice. (n.d.). Utilitarianism. Retrieved from http://www.distributive-justice.com/theory/p-utilitarism-en.htm.

39. Distributive Justice. (n.d.). Strict egalitarianism. Retrieved from http://www.distributive-justice.com/theory/p-strict-egalit-en.htm.

40. Rawls, J. (1971). *A theory of justice*. Boston: The Belknap Press of Harvard University Press.

41. Distributive Justice. (n.d.). Pluralism. Retrieved from http://www.distributive-justice.com/theory/p-pluralism-en.htm.

42. Kovner, A. (1995). *Jonas's health care delivery in the United States* (5th ed.). New York: Springer.

43. Giesler, note 33.

44. Crisp, J., Potter, P. A., Taylor, C., & Griffin Perry, A. (2008). *Potter and Perry's fundamentals of nursing* (7th ed.). St. Louis: Mosby.

45. Ven, V., Poole, H. W., & Scott. M. (1995). Explaining development and change in organizations. *Management Review*, 20(3), 510–540.

46. Kovner, A., & Jonas, S. (1999). *Jonas and Kovner's health care delivery in the United States* (6th ed.). New York: Springer.

47. Kay, C. D. (1997, Jan. 20). Notes on deontology. Retrieved from http://webs.wofford.edu/kaycd/ethics/deon.htm.

48. Spencer, E. M., Mills, A. E., Rorty, M. V., & Werhane, P. H. (2000). *Organization ethics in health care*. New York: Oxford University Press.

49. Proenca, E. J. (2004). Ethics orientation as a mediator of organizational integrity in health services organizations. *Health Care Management Review*, 29(1), 40–51.

50. Spencer et al., note 48.

51. Curtin, L., & Flaherty, M. J. (1982). *Nursing ethics: Theories and pragmatics*. Bowie, MD: Robert J. Brady.

52. Chretien, K. C., & Kind, T. (2013). Social media as a tool in medicine: Ethical, professional, and social implications. The American Heart Association. Retrieved from http://circ.ahajournals.org/content/127/13/1413.full.

53. Chretien, note 52, p. 1413.

54. Chretien, note 52, p. 1415.

55. Chretien, note 52, p. 1414.

56. Chretien, note 52, p. 1414.

57. Zhang, X., Walumbwa, F. O., Aryee, S., & Chen, Z. X. (2013). Ethical leadership, employee citizenship and work withdrawal behaviors: Examining mediating and moderating processes. *The Leadership Quarterly*, 24(1), 284–297. Retrieved from http://www.sciencedirect.com/science/article/pii/S1048984312001233.

CHAPTER 11

MEASURING THE OUTCOMES OF LEADERSHIP INITIATIVES

While the sage advice "you can't manage what you can't measure" is still very much true, in an e-business environment it is also true that "you can't measure what you can't monitor."

Peter Drucker[1]

This chapter discusses how leaders can measure and assess the impact and progress of their leadership efforts within the health organization. We have all heard the phrase, "If you can't measure it, you can't manage it." Measurement and assessment of health leadership is one of the more underrepresented aspects within the health industry. This chapter defines common issues related to this consideration for health leaders and recommends ways in which to measure outcomes. A distinction is made between measuring leader efficiency, effectiveness, performance, organizational efficacy, and the leader's goal, with these elements being combined to create a composite quality leadership outcome assessment such as the Baldrige National Quality Award Program. Several frameworks or models of assessment, including Baldrige, are presented.

LEARNING OBJECTIVES

1. Describe how health leaders measure and capture information (i.e., use metrics) related to efficiency, effectiveness, performance, efficacy, and quality in health organizations.

2. Explain the importance of measurement and developing criteria for efficiency, effectiveness, performance, efficacy, and quality in health organizations.

3. Demonstrate applicable models and tools that represent the constructs of efficiency, effectiveness, performance, and quality in health organizations.

4. Compare and contrast two or more models of health leader assessment and evaluation and analyze the process of capturing metrics for this assessment and evaluation within a health organization.

5. Compile and categorize health leader measures/metrics for assessment and evaluation of effectiveness, efficiency, performance, efficacy, and quality; compile and categorize measures/metrics for assessment and evaluation of the health organization; and finally, relate the two lists.

6. Appraise, evaluate, and justify the use of performance and quality measures/metrics for a specific type of health organization (e.g., hospital, group practice, rehabilitation center).

INTRODUCTION

This is a very important chapter for health leaders to embrace and understand within the context of leadership practice. In this chapter, we discuss the important duties a leader has with regard to managing his or her facility from perspectives of efficiency, effectiveness, efficacy, performance and productivity, benchmarking, optimization, and quality. How do you know you are leading the health organization well considering the complexity and multifaceted environment of the health industry? This chapter will assist you in answering that critically important question. As a leader, you will be scrutinized on a daily basis on organizational performance, your competence, and your integrity.

The trend in the U.S. health industry is for leaders to become more efficient, effective, and efficacious in leading people and managing resources, while simultaneously achieving high performance and quality outcomes within their organization. To keep up with this trend, measurement and assessment has become a necessary competency for leaders. However, before any leader can become skilled in this area, he or she must understand the difference between the constructs of efficiency, effectiveness, efficacy, performance, and quality and identify how the operationalization of salient variables for these constructs can assist in leading highly successful organizations.[2]

Terms such as *efficiency* and *effectiveness* are called constructs. Constructs are those things that lack identification through one of the five senses. As a result, to maximize opportunities for achieving highly effective, efficient, efficacious, performing, and quality organizations, it is incumbent on the health leader to recognize the differences between these constructs (as they are generally understood in the health arena) and be able to use common indicators (e.g., variables) that are also understood by internal and external stakeholders. Failing to use appropriate terminology (e.g., constructs and variables) that is universally understood and applied consistently within and outside the organization may result in conflicting messages. For this reason, it is incumbent upon the leader to "stay on message," adhere to industry standards in terms of the definition and use of commonly accepted and widely employed health terminology, and measure these variables consistently.

EARLY EFFORTS OF THE U.S. HEALTH SYSTEM IN MEASUREMENT

Measuring organizational and leader performance has always been uniquely important within the health industry. In the early part of the twentieth century, a convergent evolution was occurring within the U.S. healthcare industry that sought to benchmark and measure the performance of organization and leadership efforts. During this time, medical societies, private health organizations, and many health leaders collectively adopted as a goal the improvement of the quality and delivery of health services and products. In fact, Abraham Flexner wrote one of the earliest works on hospital performance, called *Medical Education in the United States and Canada*.[3] This early work on standards and measures led to improvement in the scientific method and also to improved curriculum and standards in medical education. Nevertheless, despite these policy changes and the widespread acceptance of Flexner's work, leaders of early U.S. hospitals and health systems remained largely reluctant to change traditional practices and procedures.

Despite Flexner's recommended innovations, a review of the early archives of leadership and management of hospitals from the early 1900s suggests that studies of hospital performance were viewed as bothersome. Although he wrote one of the earliest published works on hospital efforts to improve hospital efficiency, Dr. Ernest Codman of Massachusetts General Hospital noted that "the carrying out of comparative studies is troublesome, difficult, and time-consuming and may point to the desirability of making changes in procedure in organizations which are bothersome, to say the least."[4]

Nonetheless, capitalizing on the growing trend in U.S. medicine in the early twentieth century to deliver higher quality and more productive care, the American College of Surgeons instituted an efficiency program of its own during that time. In 1918, this organization launched a program geared toward standardizing hospital procedures and organization. More than any other single factor, the masterful implementation of these standards has been responsible for the most constructive changes in the efficiency of hospital operations in the United States; the legacy of this effort continues to influence leaders in health organizations today. Since 1918, standards, processes, and procedures for health leaders have grown from the simplistic and finite to the dramatically complex and seemingly infinite.

CONSTRUCTS, VARIABLES, AND TOOLS TO MEASURE HEALTH LEADERS AND THEIR ORGANIZATIONS

How can you evaluate a health leader's performance and the performance of the health organization? Numerous tools and methods, comprising various constructs and variables, are available to assist with assessment and evaluation of leadership and the organization as a whole. This chapter summarizes several of these organizational and individual methods, although many more approaches to evaluation exist.

It is extremely difficult to separate leadership performance and evaluation from organizational performance and evaluation because leadership, in its broadest definition, exists to enable and facilitate a health organization in performing well and fulfilling its purpose effectively, efficiently, and efficaciously. Health leaders should develop an assessment and evaluation system for the health organization, for the leadership and management group within the organization, for groups categorized appropriately within the organization, and at the individual level. This system of assessment and evaluation is closely related to internal and external organizational processes of assessment, monitoring, forecasting, and evaluation, although the focus in this context is on improving group and individual leadership competencies, outcomes, and processes. As in program evaluation, when assessing leadership as part of a strategic system that goes down to the individual health leader, eight constructs are salient. According to Veney and Kaluzny, evaluation must contain methods and measures of relevance, adequacy, progress, effectiveness, impact, efficiency, and sustainability;[5] efficacy is the eighth consideration.

Why is health leadership assessment and evaluation important? A key justification is that success in improving organizational performance and outcomes rests primarily in the competent leadership of the health organization. Also, promoting competent leaders to higher levels of responsibility in the health organization is of utmost concern. Consider the following points made by the National Center for Healthcare Leadership (NCHL):

- The attrition rate for senior-level health executives could reach 40% in the next decade.[6]
- The cost of turnover for a middle- to senior-level leader in the health industry is approximately $250,000.[7]*
- Sixty-six percent of health organizations fail to provide formal leadership training to prepare the next generation of leaders.[8]

Health leaders who show competence at lower levels of the health organization should, over time, be given greater levels of responsibility, accountability, and authority. As a person gains experience and masters leadership at lower and middle organizational levels, opportunities for senior-level

---

*Industry estimate: 2.5 times annual salary, based on $100,000 annual salary.

leadership should be visible on the horizon. To reach senior leadership and perform well at entry and middle leadership levels, the health leader's ability to honestly and objectively assess and evaluate his or her own performance is critical. From a theoretical perspective, emotional maturity or emotional intelligence is a prerequisite for honest self-evaluation.

EMOTIONAL INTELLIGENCE[9] AND SELF-EFFICACY

Knowing oneself is absolutely essential. Emotional intelligence constructs support the self-monitoring and adaptation of the dynamic culture leader fairly well. "It [emotional intelligence] doesn't measure how well you did in school or what your GMAT scores were, but rather, how well you handle yourself and your relationships."[10] It used to be said, "It doesn't matter what you know, but who you know." Today, a new rule applies: "It matters what you know, and who you know, and perhaps most importantly, what you know about yourself."

The four basic constructs of the emotional intelligence model are (1) self-awareness, (2) self-management, (3) social awareness, and (4) social skills.[11] These constructs are slanted toward the art of leadership. Even so, they can and should merge to form a secondary level of "intelligence" that monitors the technical and relationship orientations of the leader on an ongoing basis. Thinking about when to emphasize science or art, as in the dynamic culture leadership model, or even better, how to merge the two, should become an intuitive exercise within the subconscious processes of the health leader. Conscious engagement and mastery lead to subconscious implementation. This is the internal gyroscope that many successful health leaders learn to depend on:

> Those who use the emotional intelligence framework to guide their thoughts and actions may find it easier to create trust in relationships, harness energy under pressure, and sharpen their ability to make sound decisions—in other words, they increase their potential for success in the workplace.[12]

The health leader connects the four emotional intelligence constructs with this "internal gyroscope" to analyze both him- or herself and the organization and to merge the appropriate levels of leadership science and art in creating an organizational culture that can withstand the ever-changing environmental challenges. The more emotionally intelligent and mature the health leader is, the better he or she will be able to assess and evaluate his or her own, the leadership group's, and the organization's performance

honestly and objectively. The health leader's level of self-efficacy, coupled with emotional intelligence, is worthy of discussion as well.

A high level of self-efficacy is important for the health leader. Self-efficacy is an individual's capability to produce a desired effect:

> Perceived self-efficacy is defined as people's beliefs about their capabilities to produce designated levels of performance that exercise influence over events that affect their lives. Self-efficacy beliefs determine how people feel, think, motivate themselves and behave.[13]

Rotter's internalizer/externalizer-based theory, which focuses on the locus of control, intuitively supports leadership capabilities and high levels of self-efficacy. Internalizers, it would seem, have higher levels of self-efficacy. Health leaders need to be self-efficacious in their capability to lead people and manage resources, but they must also instill a sense and organizational culture of efficacy for excellence in patient care. Only in this way can subordinates be directed to accomplish the mission, goals, and objectives of the organization and to improve the health status of the community as a whole.

Developing a system to assess and evaluate your leadership capabilities at the individual through the organizational levels is vital to your growth and development as a health leader; seeking to improve and lead better on a continuous basis should be a long-term career goal. To assist in developing your assessment and evaluation system, the next section outlines the strategic system of leadership and management—specifically, fulfillment of the strategic plan—within the context of evaluation.

STRATEGIC PLAN

At a basic level, strategic planning addresses the following question: Has the organization been or is the organization now fulfilling and achieving its mission and vision? Using directional strategies, such as mission and vision, an evaluation of leadership, the strategic system of leadership and management, and the organization can be undertaken. This evaluation is rather subjective in a broad sense, but can be very specific at the objective level, where measures should be employed. A more objective view—that is, a more measurement-based approach in evaluating strategic plans and strategies—is to assess the progress made toward accomplishing action step tasks, objectives, and goals that are linked to specific strategies. Objectives are evaluated by variables of interest that are inherently integrated into the objective itself. Are action step tasks associated with each objective being accomplished? Is the variable of interest for the objective moving toward (or has it reached) the desired level? This combination of subjective and objective assessment should be conducted several times throughout any given year (such as on a quarterly basis).

From a strategic system of leadership and management, leadership and the organization as a whole can be evaluated by the leadership team, the board of directors (or trustees), shareholders (if the organization is a publically traded company), the corporate organization, or the community at large (stakeholders). In this assessment, strategies and goals contain constructs important to the organization, and objectives contain measurable variables.

MARKET SHARE/GROWTH

Another high-level construct that assesses a health organization's performance is market share rate and the trend of that rate. In other words, how much of the geographical-bound percentage of qualified and available customers or patients come to the organization for care? Market share is a percentage, such as 50% or 70%. The more market share an organization possesses, the more power it wields in the community. Patient or customer satisfaction rates are associated to a certain extent with market share and with the level of repeat or return business (i.e., when a patient returns to the organization for additional or different health care in the future).

The direction of the organization's market share is important. If you evaluate the market share of a health organization during a single time period, you cannot assess much. If you assess trends in the organization's market share over multiple years, however, then you have a much better basis for making judgments about organizational performance. Growth, decline, and maintenance of market share and the organization's performance are subjective and relative. Health organizations that strategically want or need to grow should realize that market share growth occurs over time; they also should recognize that leaders in the organization should be held accountable for a predetermined evolution of market share growth. Conversely, if a growth strategy results in a decline in the organization's market share, the leadership team, strategies, and goals should be reevaluated within the context of the external environment. If the environment is extremely competitive, with new competitors entering the marketplace, that factor should weigh into the evaluation. This high-level method of evaluation must consider the environment and the unique circumstances of the health organization.

BENCHMARKING

Benchmarking is a critical tool for leaders to understand and embrace as a method for tracking programs and performance in the health organization. Benchmarking is a continuous process of measuring performance and services against best-in-class cases or organizations; it is an ongoing process of gathering information from peers and competitors in the industry and applying that information to internal performance assessment. It is not a linear or one-time process for hospital or group practice administrators. Health leaders must continually measure their organization's performance against its peers in the industry to establish benchmarks for meeting the current and future needs of patients, stakeholders, the community, and beneficiaries (if in insurance).

Similar to internal assessment, benchmarking is an eight-step process:

1. Determine which independent and dependent variables to benchmark.
2. Plan the process.
3. Collect internal data.
4. Collect external data.
5. Analyze differences.
6. Transform the data into information and then into knowledge (information that is actionable).
7. Plan the action.
8. Reassess the situation (periodic reassessment).

Determining what to benchmark and analyzing differences between outcomes to determine whether there are relevant and incremental differences in processes may be the two most important steps in determining a benchmarking scheme for the health leader. The key point to recognize in the process of benchmarking is that benchmarking is not a linear process, despite the sequential and procedural list of steps associated with implementing the program. Often, when evaluating benchmarking schemes, it will be necessary to reevaluate the plan or revisit the interpretation of the data collected. By continually refining the process and encouraging group participation and interaction, health leaders can hone in on a relevant benchmarking decision.[14]

Performance Variables in Benchmarking

Benchmarking performance variables (also called indicators) measure the organization's performance against other similar organizations or similar groups of organizations, based on size, geographic location, or other criteria. Benchmarking data can be purchased or acquired through professional associations and societies, firms specializing in benchmarking and health data/information, some consulting firms, and state associations (e.g., state hospital associations). These data and information may include a variety of constructs and associated variables—for example, financial performance; patient care mortality and morbidity by service line (e.g., cardiac care, cancer care, pediatrics), diagnosis-related groups (DRG), or International Classification of Disease, ninth or tenth revision (ICD-9 or ICD-10) category; and measures of efficiency, effectiveness, and efficacy ranging from patient satisfaction rates to staff satisfaction, pay scales, turnover rates, and market share. Benchmarking data are invaluable in comparing the effectiveness, efficiency, and efficacy of leadership performance and organizational performance against those of similar organizations. Many health organizations use "dashboards" to conduct ongoing assessments of their organization's performance, from the construct level down to the variable level.

ORGANIZATIONAL SATISFACTION, ABSENTEEISM, AND TURNOVER

Internal organization performance and outcomes can provide a method to assess and evaluate health leadership. Although many internal performance and outcome measures exist, the three major constructs for performance and outcome evaluation are organization employee/staff satisfaction, employee absenteeism, and turnover. Organization employee/staff and physician satisfaction is the employees' or staff's perception of the level of approval they have for the direction and approaches utilized by the health organization, the fulfillment they experience in performing their responsibilities, the contentment they have with the work environment, and the agreement (trust) they have with equitable treatment. Satisfaction from this perspective is significantly correlated with leadership and leader performance. This level of satisfaction should be assessed over time (i.e., as a trend) to determine leadership effectiveness in terms of this construct because satisfaction is relatively temporal and dynamic (similar to organizational climate). Higher levels of satisfaction are preferable, but some dynamic tension is desirable and expected. (Perfect satisfaction is rare and may not be conducive to productivity.)

Absenteeism—missing scheduled work due to illness or social loafing—is usually a result of less-than-satisfied employees or staff members. Poor work conditions, lack of clarity in responsibilities, mistreatment, inequitable application of rewards and punishment, less than competitive pay and benefits packages, decision and policy inconsistency, and lack of perceived appreciation from the employees' perspective are root causes of the symptom of absenteeism. Acute absenteeism is a real problem for health organizations given their patient care processes and standards. Moderate to high levels of absenteeism usually are attributed to poor or inattentive leadership and management.

Excessive turnover is a result of similar prolonged problems. Turnover is the cumulative resignation (quitting their jobs) of employees, staff, and physicians over time. High turnover rates correspond directly to inconsistent leadership and management practices and have root causes similar to those associated with high absenteeism. High turnover rates are the ultimate action of employees, staff, or physicians in expressing their dissatisfaction with the health organization. A low to moderate level of turnover is expected in a dynamic and transient world, but high turnover is a leadership problem; this problem is most usually reflective of poor or inconsistent leadership and management.

NATIONAL-LEVEL SYSTEMS

Groups or organizations utilize systems of performance and quality evaluation. Many health systems, integrated health systems (systems with insurance plans), and health insurance plans, for example, use the National Committee for Quality Assurance's (NCQA's) Healthcare Effectiveness Data and Information Set (HEDIS)[15] report card and Quality Compass system:

> HEDIS is a tool used by more than 90 percent of America's health plans to measure performance on important dimensions of care and service. Altogether, HEDIS consists of 71 measures [variables] across 8 domains [constructs] of care. Because so many plans collect HEDIS data, and because the measures are so specifically defined, HEDIS makes it possible to compare the performance of health plans on an "apples-to-apples" basis. Health plans also use HEDIS results themselves to see where they need to focus their improvement efforts.[16]

Constructs and variables, along with an integrated *State of Health Care Quality* report, are essential tools for health leaders.[17]

At the highest level, a national strategic plan for health prevention and promotion is embodied in the Healthy People 2020 initiative; Healthy People 2000 and 2010 were earlier versions of the current plan:

> Healthy People 2020 provides a framework for prevention for the Nation. It is a statement of national health objectives designed to identify the most significant preventable threats to health and to establish national goals to reduce these threats.[18]

This plan incorporates several health constructs (called leading indicators) and variables to measure progress toward the desired goal (such as reducing deaths from colorectal cancer).[19]

Health leaders must determine which constructs and variables they want to improve at the organization; how they will perform group benchmarking against peers; which group performance and quality they will seek, such as inclusion in health plan HEDIS indicators; and at the national level, how those indicators relate to and integrate with their particular health organization's mission and vision. A physician group practice in a rural area would not include constructs and variables outside its scope of practice as part of its self-assessment, but would strive to improve the variables relevant to their practice, such as immunization rates, cancer screening for their patients, and improvements to administration of their practice.

Next, individual leadership assessment and evaluation tools are described. This discussion is followed by examples of health leader development process and competency models and, finally, organization performance measures.

HEALTH LEADER COMPETENCY MODEL REVISITED

The complex and multifaceted nature of the health industry, and the organizations that comprise the industry, at first glance may seem daunting to "measure" for leadership performance. Let us reconsider the macro model representing today's health leadership challenges (**Figure 11-1**).

From this model, leadership competencies emerge (**Figure 11-2**). Keeping the challenges of today in mind,

leaders must be competent, moral, and performance-oriented in this dynamic industry. Figure 11-2 represents the modern competency health leader model. That the challenges of today require healthcare leadership is supported by several development and competency domains developed by Drs. Ledlow and Stephens.

The chapter sections that follow provide tools, concepts, and structures to measure individual leader performance in health organizations today. Developing competence in each competency domain is essential, and mastering these competencies should be the goal.

TOOLS TO MEASURE LEADERSHIP OUTCOMES AND COMPETENCIES

Health leaders are assessed and evaluated in many ways. These methods range from organizational performance and outcomes to individual performance, outcomes, and mastery of competencies. In this section, individual leadership

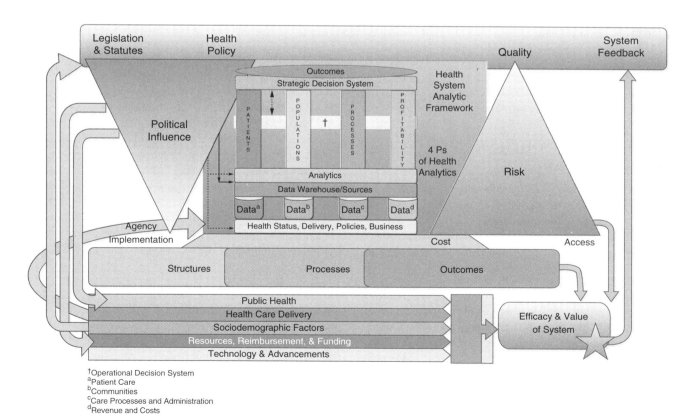

†Operational Decision System
aPatient Care
bCommunities
cCare Processes and Administration
dRevenue and Costs

FIGURE 11-1 Today's health leadership challenges.

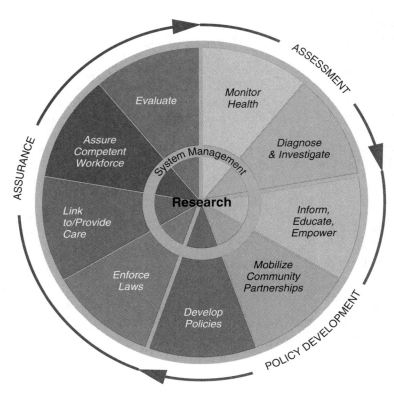

FIGURE 11-2 Major contemporary leadership development and competency domains.

outcomes and competencies are described as sources of individual leadership improvement that lead, in turn, to improved organizational performance and outcomes.

COMPETENCIES FOR ASSESSMENT AND EVALUATION

A recent collaboration of five professional associations has created five domains that include a total of 300 competencies for the health leader and manager.

OBJECTIVES

Health leaders can be assessed and evaluated by objectives. Using goal-setting theory applications, the health leader and her or his supervisor (another leader or board member) should establish specific yet challenging goals for a specified time period (e.g., quarter, year, 2 years). These goals, for which the health leader is held accountable, can target the individual, group, section/divisional, or organizational levels. They may also contain group goals, wherein a group (leaders, or leaders and subordinates) as a whole is responsible for achieving the objective. Even though health leaders may have multiple goals across the spectrum just described,

these goals should be consistent and aligned with the organizational mission, vision, strategies, and goals.

The health leader's goals should have a good vertical and horizontal fit with other goals established by the organization, meaning that they should not conflict or contradict with the goals of others. Measureable variables, such as organizational satisfaction rates, absenteeism, turnover rates, productivity rates, and market share, should be associated with each goal. Some goals may have several variables linked to the goal. Rather than having 20 goals, 5 to 10 well-devised, important goals that are challenging and for which adequate resources are available are preferable.

SURVEYS

A health leader can be assessed and evaluated by a survey of his or her subordinates; the survey may be distributed to the leader's peers as well. The survey should elicit the respondent's assessment of the leader's attention to and accomplishment of organizational objectives and goals, work environment variables (those similar to satisfaction and/or organizational climate), communication ability, and the appropriate competencies described previously. Survey results should be validated and standardized to other leaders' results; national or regional leadership assessment and evaluation surveys are used by many health organizations for this purpose. Simply developing a survey without experience, internal assessment, and validation of the instrument is not advised. Surveys should be used only in conjunction with other leader performance and outcome information.

360-DEGREE EVALUATION

A 360-degree evaluation is a survey that is given to all those in the organization who work with and work for the leader under assessment. In this approach, superiors, subordinates, and peers assess the health leader. As stated previously, survey results should be validated and standardized to other leaders' results; national or regional leadership assessment and evaluation surveys are used by many health organizations for this purpose. Simply developing a survey without experience, internal assessment, and validation of the instrument is not advised. Like surveys, 360-degree evaluations should be used only in conjunction with other leader performance and outcome information.

MODELS FOR LEADERSHIP ASSESSMENT AND EVALUATION

This section presents three models for review and reflection—namely, models provided by the National Center for Healthcare Leadership (NCHL), General Electric (GE)

Healthcare Performance Solutions, and the National Public Health Leadership Institute (NPHLI). When studying these models (**Figures 11-3**, **11-4**, and **11-5**), consider the leadership theories, models, knowledge, skills and abilities, and subsequent competencies a health leader should possess, understand, discern, apply, and master. Then review the leadership competencies provided by the five professional associations listed in this chapter. Do you see an integration of multiple constructs? Which variables would you measure to assess and evaluate your own leadership capabilities? Do you see constructs or elements that are familiar to you? Can you list leader constructs and variables to assess performance? What would you measure?

In Figures 11-3, 11-4, and 11-5, would you add other constructs (such as a strategic supply-chain system) for leader evaluation? Can you prioritize the constructs by importance? Which variables would you measure, and how would you measure them for constructs that are important?

Health leaders do their jobs, seek continuous improvement of their leadership capabilities, and use moral approaches to ensure that their health organizations survive and thrive, while providing excellent patient care services or products. It takes every leader, throughout the organization, to focus the collective energy of the health organization to serve its community and fulfill its purpose. Health leaders develop the organizational culture, select the strategies, and lead people and manage resources to consistently improve health services, care practices, and the health status of their communities. The capability to perform these

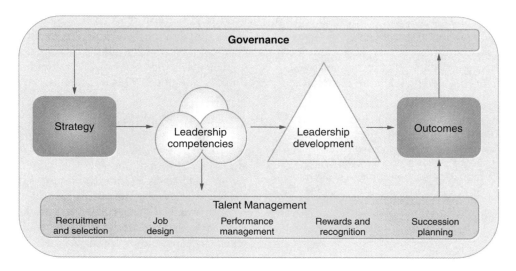

FIGURE 11-3   National Center for Healthcare Leadership and GE Institute for Transformational Leadership development construct model.

National Center for Healthcare Leadership (NCHL) & General Electric Institute for Transformational Leadership. (n.d.). Preparing leaders to achieve organizational excellence, p. 5. Retrieved from http://www.nchl.org/ns/calendar/NCHL_Overview_1.08.pdf.

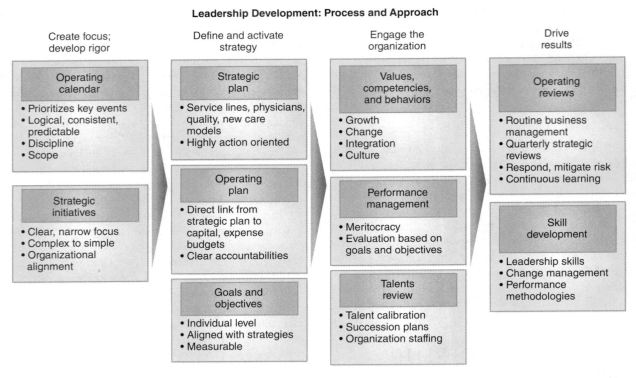

FIGURE 11-4   GE Institute for Transformational Leadership development variable and process model.

Data from National Center for Healthcare Leadership (NCHL) & General Electric Institute for Transformational Leadership. (n.d.). Preparing leaders to achieve organizational excellence, p. 8. Retrieved from http://www.nchl.org/ns/calendar/NCHL_Overview_1.08.pdf.

essential leadership tasks is grounded in the health leader's ability to assess, evaluate, and develop leadership knowledge, skills, abilities, and subsequent competencies and, ultimately, to translate them into practice.

Next, this chapter continues with a discussion of efficiency, effectiveness, performance, efficacy, and quality. Many times, effectiveness and efficiency are confused:

> Organizational effectiveness has an external orientation and suggests that the organization is well positioned to accomplish its mission and realize its vision and goals. Efficiency, on the other hand, has an internal orientation and suggests that economies can be realized in the use of capital, personnel, or physical plant.[20]

Effectiveness is "doing the right thing," whereas efficiency is "doing things right."[21,22]

HEALTH EFFICIENCY

Defining health efficiency is very important. *Efficiency* is defined as a Pareto optimal allocation of resources. An allocation is "Pareto optimal" or "Pareto efficient" if production and distribution cannot be reorganized to increase the utility of one or more units without decreasing the utility of other units. This concept is also referred to as technical efficiency, because the outcome will always be improved based on economic performance measures without reference to subjective weights or comparisons. Efficiency is further measured in terms of the productivity of selected outputs and inputs. This measure can be stated in the form of a ratio:

Efficiency = Outputs/Inputs (subject to constraints)

In layperson's terms, one can think of efficiency as analogous to a triathlon, where an individual is expected to swim, cycle, and run for great distances. Now think of the sequence of events. Between the arduous swimming and running events is the cycling event. Studies have been done to validate that the fastest scores in triathlons are achieved when the three events are structured with a swim, a cycle, and then a run; reversing the order results in slower times. The most "efficient" way to sequence the three events—the one that results in the least amount of time for the overall triathlon—is to conduct them in the following order: swimming, cycling, and running.

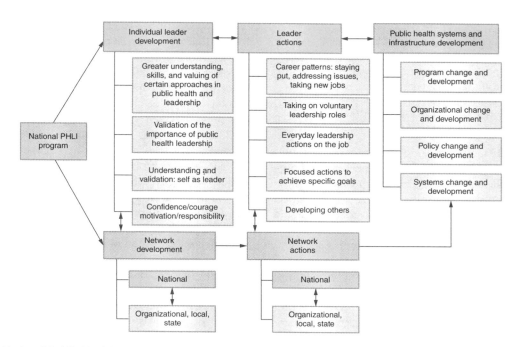

FIGURE 11-5 National Public Health Leadership Institute model of leadership evaluation.

Reproduced from Umble, K., Diehl, S., Gunn, A., & Haws, S. (2008). Developing leaders, building networks: An evaluation of the National Public Health Leadership Institute 1991–2006. National Public Health Leadership Institute, Gillings School of Global Public Health, University of North Carolina, p. 28. Retrieved from http://www.phli.org.

In a similar fashion, task organization and careful planning can make a health leader more "efficient" in his or her job. Efficiency in this case results in the ability to accomplish the same tasks within shorter periods of time or to accomplish more tasks in a given workday. Obviously, efficiency is extremely important to a health leader from an individual perspective; it is also important from an organizational perspective, given that hundreds or thousands of simultaneous activities may be occurring during the course of a normal day of operations.

To illustrate how efficiency plays out in the health arena, here is an example. Is it possible to increase patient visits to a clinic by 25% without adding providers to the clinic to examine those patients? From an efficiency standpoint, think of acute care and the physician office visit sequence of events. Usually the patient makes an appointment, arrives at the clinic or practice, and sees the physician. The physician then orders some diagnostic tests to be performed on the patient (e.g., a blood test, culture, or urinalysis). Next, the physician makes a preliminary diagnosis (many times without the diagnostic test results), writes a prescription or treatment regimen for the patient, and follows up with the patient after the diagnostic test results are provided to the physician. If the diagnostic test result is different than the physician expected, the patient may have to return for additional examinations or may need different treatments.

How inefficient is this traditional process? If you create a system for prescreening and assessment (i.e., an algorithm or protocol), have the patient receive the diagnostic test based on that prescreening process, and make the diagnostic test results available before the physician examines the patient, the efficiency for both patient and physician is enhanced. By changing this traditional process, efficiency can be enhanced by as much as 25% for the physician; as a consequence, the physician can see more patients and have more confidence in the diagnosis and treatment regimen.

> Efficiency refers to whether program results [organizational results] could be obtained less expensively. Questions of efficiency concern the relationship between the results obtained from a specific program and the resources expended to maintain the program.[23]

Efficiency has an internal orientation and focuses on those resources, including time, required to achieve a desired outcome or result. Efficient operation, as in the context of organizational performance, can be understood as "(1) effective operation as measured by a comparison of production with cost (as in energy, time, and money); and (2) the ratio of the useful energy delivered by a dynamic system to the energy supplied to it."[24]

To economists, efficiency is a relationship between ends and means. When we call a situation inefficient, we are claiming that we could achieve the desired ends with less means, or that the means employed could produce more of the ends desired. "Less" and "more" in this context necessarily refer to less and more value. Thus, economic efficiency is measured not by the relationship between the physical quantities of ends and means, but by the relationship between the value of the ends and the value of the means.[25]

Selecting and operationalizing the appropriate inputs and outputs to measure (variables) are critical steps in producing the best efficiency analysis for health leaders. Failure to use the best available measures may lead to inadequate representation of efficiency for the organization. It should also be noted that within the health industry, the term *productivity* is sometimes used interchangeably with *efficiency*. It is not uncommon to see these terms used haphazardly in organizational parlance. Finally, it is important to recognize that several different kinds of efficiency measures may exist in a health organization. The tables in the next section present snapshots of the different types and definitions of efficiency.

Defining and Measuring Efficiency

The important thing to know about efficiency that makes it different from all other terms is that efficiency is a quantitative term expressed as a ratio. More so than with any other term used in health, the definition of efficiency must include a numerator and a denominator expressed as a ratio. For example, from a reductionist point of view, if your car is supposed to get 100 miles/gallon of gas, but after you drive it for a week, you average only 95 miles/gallon, your car's efficiency can be measured as a function of outputs divided by inputs: 95/100 = 95% efficiency. **Table 11–1** summarizes the calculation of an efficiency ratio.

A variety of health efficiency measures are available to leaders that are universally understood and applied in health organizations. Basic ratio analysis (i.e., efficiency) is the cornerstone of U.S. health system metrics. An example is the percentage of occupied bed–days, where the result is the ratio of patient-occupied beds to total beds. Other ratios can be used as well, such as infection rates per total patients seen, and morbidity and mortality rates for overall patient encounters. Most health service research over the last 50 years has emphasized ratio analysis to discern the contributions of single input or output variables. Once meaningful and prudent ratios are calculated, they can be compared against those from previous years and from other organizations for benchmarking purposes. Ratios can provide useful information on how an item of interest has performed in the past and may perform in the future. They can provide quick and easily understandable information to health leaders, and they should be one of the first calculations performed in any new organization.[26] In the examples in **Table 11–2**, note that all of the measures can be subjected to ratio analysis once the correct variables are selected for manipulation.

Examples of Best Practices in Industry[27]

In the 1990s the healthcare supply chain found at Sisters of Mercy Health System was much like those at many other organizations. The fragmented and duplicative systems across Mercy were dependent on six different information technology (IT) materials management software solutions, were unable to negotiate the maximal supplier discounts, and were relying heavily on outside vendors to help facilitate the management of the health system's supply chains.

The decentralized work found in the mimicking of similar processes at each health system was not managed for

---

Table 11-1 Efficiency Calculation

Efficiency is a quantitative term. It is derived through a process of dividing outputs by inputs: E = O/I.
Inputs can be defined based on *design capacity*.
Design capacity is determined through predetermined structures and processes. For example, a clinic might be designed to see 220 patients per day based on available full-time employees (FTEs) and treatment rooms.
Outputs are defined based on outcomes.
Outcomes are captured from actual data generated by the organization. For example, outputs are the actual number of patients seen per day. In this case, suppose 180 patients were seen by the facility:

Efficiency calculation: E = O/I
E = 180/220
E = 82%

The health leader can see that his or her new clinic is operating at only 82% efficiency. Two possible areas to investigate are immediately evident:
1. The facility is not meeting its operational capacity.
2. The facility's design capacity was originally miscalculated or forecasted erroneously.

Table 11-2 Types of Efficiency Measures in Health from a Leader Perspective

- **Cost efficiency** focuses on the optimal distribution of funds to meet daily activities in the health setting.
- **Productivity**, or process efficiency, measures the work expended to produce healthcare products.
- **Economic efficiency** measures the resources consumed per unit of service output.
- **Response efficiency** refers to how quickly a system reacts to a request for service.
- **Technical efficiency** focuses on optimizing inputs to create outputs in such a way that no other reorganization could use resources more fully.
- **Operational efficiency** is defined as achieving the full potential for all resources available. It differs from technical efficiency in that there is emphasis on avoiding waste.

process efficiency or cost savings at the enterprise level. This realization created a new organization at the system level, with the intent to create an integrated supply chain that better utilized available technologies for inventory management and implemented supply chain best practices from inside and outside the industry. With the creation of a new centralized supply chain, departmental data could be shared across the system, and Mercy's reliance on outside vendor information was dramatically lessened (**Figure 11-6**).

The creation of resource optimization and innovation (ROI) helped to consolidate the supply chain throughout Mercy at the corporate level, align major processes utilizing

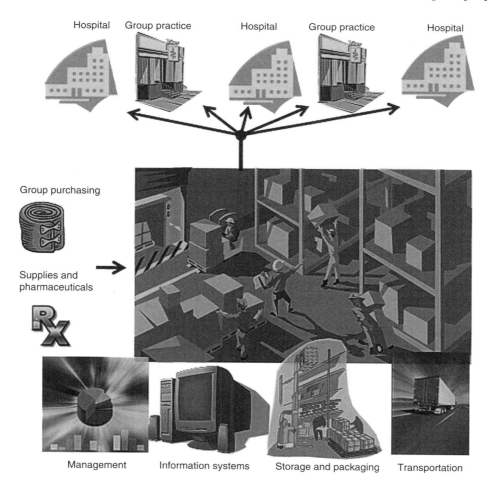

FIGURE 11-6   What is a consolidated services center?

a shared materials management software solution, create an internal group purchasing organization, and allow for the enterprise-wide management of supply chain distribution and repackaging processes within Mercy. The creation of an internally owned and managed repackaging and distribution facility, the consolidated services center (CSC), permitted improved supply chain responsiveness by better catering to customer hospitals, improving fill rates over the 85% to 90% that other distributors achieved, streamlining the receiving process, and reducing complexity by 70% through combined deliveries of medical/surgical supplies and pharmaceuticals; created standard inventory management metrics such as fill rate percentage to measure departmental and centralized performance; permitted more timely deliveries to facilities (with an internal truck fleet), improving cost savings by eliminating third-party markup fees (approximately $3 million annually) and by purchasing directly from manufacturers; and permitted bulk purchasing and contracting for economies of scope and scale. With these efficiency improvements and by taking advantage of economies of scope and scale, the Sisters of Mercy supply chain now returns $6 for every $1 invested in this core business function.

Leading the operation of the supply chain requires technical and artful skill. As a leader, how would you lead people and manage resources in the supply chain of your organization? How would you measure success?

Optimization

Optimization is sometimes used as a synonym for efficiency. In reality, this term refers to an isolated case of efficiency in which the ratio of outputs to inputs is 1 (or 100%). Most times, optimization is something to be strived for, rather than actually achieved.

Optimization is defined as achieving perfect efficiency goals. It results from maximizing the outputs for the design capacity for the unit under study. When something is optimized, it is operating at 100% efficiency; thus, there can be no greater output based on designed inputs than that which has resulted from the process of generating those results. Process optimization should identify and consistently maintain the best combination of manufacturing conditions, operating procedures, and technologies to consistently achieve the highest level of long-term outputs.[28]

HEALTH EFFECTIVENESS

Effectiveness differs from the concept of efficiency insofar as it may be a qualitative variable and not always a quantitative variable.[29] New treatments may be cost-effective on the individual level but the demand for treatment, or lack thereof, can make development of new treatments for rare

conditions difficult.[30] Additionally, the concept of effectiveness is subjective and may be based on emotion- and value-driven behaviors. For example, the concept of efficiency will always have a ratio associated with it so that the metric can be calculated. Effectiveness, in contrast, may not always be a quantitative term. It may simply be stated in terms of the ability to create outcomes and actions that are perceived as acceptable by outside stakeholders. Such outside perceptions may be subjective and may not always be generalizable outside of the context under assessment. Care must be taken to generalize effectiveness to the entire population because effectiveness is strongly rooted in the perceptions of the individual.[31]

Think of the current presidential administration trying to craft a new policy. Although the new policy may not have been implemented yet, or have any metrics associated with it such as costs and numbers of persons served, there is always a perception of approval or disapproval of the concept based on individual values, enduring beliefs, and other personal factors. Effectiveness is (or can be) a highly opinionated assessment, not supported by any creditable argument for satisfaction or dissatisfaction other than the opinion of the person (or group of individuals) making the evaluation of the item under discussion.

As far as health items are concerned, the cliché that "Beauty is in the eye of the beholder" is a reasonable metaphor for forecasting effective outcomes. Positive and empirical outcomes may be one way to judge a health leader.[32] However, if the population at large does not place the same value on the outcomes as the health leader does, then the leader may be judged to be ineffective despite the otherwise positive metrics he or she is producing.

Defining and Measuring Effectiveness

Defining and measuring health effectiveness is difficult due to the ineffable nature of the values of the people who are making the decisions on the behavior under study. In this regard, the effectiveness of a health leader may be based on a variety of factors, including both empirical variables (such as outcomes measures) and latent variables (such as employee satisfaction). As a result, effectiveness becomes the sum of quantitative and qualitative factors that are individually interpreted by stakeholders.[33]

$$\text{Effectiveness} = \text{Degree of}$$
$$(\text{Qualitative} + \text{Quantitative factors})$$
$$(\text{interpreted by stakeholders})$$

For example, a physician who is producing high volumes of output for the organization—that is, seeing a large number of patients per day—could make a cogent argument that he or she is contributing greatly to the organization in terms of revenue generation. However, if the physician has a poor bedside manner that ultimately results in some patients complaining about the physician–patient encounter, then the outcomes of number of patients seen per day must be evaluated in the context of patient satisfaction measures. Over time, a profile for each patient care visit per provider can be collected and matched against satisfaction rates for that provider. In this scenario, effectiveness becomes a factor of both average number of patient visits and average number of complaints per patient. Thus the senior health leader has both metrics and a method with which to evaluate the overall effectiveness of the physician.[34]

The situation becomes more problematic when tangible outcome measures for effectiveness (e.g., patient satisfaction scores or number of complaints) are not available. Consider, for example, the collegiality or manners associated with an employee in an organization. Perhaps the employee is highly regarded by his or her patients and also produces good outcomes for the organization in the form of high numbers of visits, high patient satisfaction ratings, and low secondary incidence rates. Now suppose this same employee does not get along well with his or her fellow employees, is disruptive or institutionalized in regard to organization change, and is viewed as a general malcontent by his or her superiors. Despite the good outcomes this employee generates for the organization, when asked by the senior leadership if the employee is "effective," the answer may be "no" based on the intangibles surrounding the employee.

As these examples demonstrate, the concept of effectiveness can be highly subjective. For this reason, the young health leader should be cognizant of his or her persona and impressions made when interacting with internal and external stakeholders.[35]

Other ways to measure health effectiveness may be more tangible. For example, health organization effectiveness should be defined and measured in terms of the unique situation of the organization and the community or stakeholders whom it serves. A survey consisting of a series of questions may be the best method for assessing effectiveness; although these answers might seem subjective at the surface, objective measures can be incorporated in the instrument to assess the overall effectiveness of the health organization. It may be difficult to answer each question from the standpoint of the entire health organization, so service line or product line assessments should be performed and then evaluated in total to provide a better, more precise picture of health organization effectiveness. Critical questions included on such a survey would include the following:

- Are the health organization's mission and vision statements grounded and informed by a community or stakeholder assessment of needs and future needs

(forecasts)? (This assessment question is closely linked to external environment scanning, monitoring, forecasting, and assessment.)
- How has the health organization served its purpose and accomplished its stated mission?
- How well have the services and products of the health organization been perceived, adopted, or utilized by patients, customers, and stakeholders? (Measures such as patient satisfaction rates, mortality and morbidity rates, market share percentages, and return business/customers/patients rates can be used as a proxy evaluation set.)
- Are standards of care or practice being met or exceeded in the health organization?

Examples of Best Practices in Industry

Example 1: The Genesis Project[36]

Sisters of Mercy, a four-state system based in St. Louis, includes 19 hospitals along with outpatient care, physician practices, and a health plan; has 4,122 licensed beds. With over 26,000 employees, the Mercy system embarked on a $260 million project that will encompass technology upgrades throughout the system in clinical, patient access, revenue, resource planning, and supply chain areas. The supply chain operation began its movement to consolidation several years ago with the implementation of one shared materials management system, McKesson's Pathways Material Management. The Genesis Project enhances an integrated approach to that evolution for further standardization of supply chain practices and the initial standardization of clinical, revenue, and ERP (enterprise resource planning) practices and technologies.

The Genesis Project is an ambitious effort for the system that was launched in 2004, addressing six daunting challenges facing today's healthcare organizations: concerns about quality and outcomes; higher expectations of patients; shortages of clinical personnel; capacity issues; financial pressures; and abilities to have physicians and institutions operate as a team.

> In response to compelling environmental factors and based on a belief that through innovation we can positively impact the lives of our customers and communities, the Sisters of Mercy Health System is committed to improving patient safety, simplifying work processes, and enabling communication flow among patients and their families, coworkers, and physicians.[37]

The Genesis Supply Chain Management (SCM) team supported improved patient safety outcomes (such as utilizing critical inventory levels and ensuring product availability) and service by enhancing the supply chain/procurement process to provide seamless, accurate, and efficient access to supplies for patients, caregivers, and coworkers.

> Exercising leadership requires distinguishing between leadership and authority and between technical and adaptive/operational work. Clarifying these two distinctions enables us to understand why so many people in top authority positions fail to lead: they commit the classic error of treating adaptive challenges as if they were technical problems.[38]

The Genesis Project is not simply a technologically based upgrade of information systems, but a thorough assessment and standardization of business processes and flows to better meet the needs of the communities served. Among other major changes in processes and responsibility throughout the enterprise health system, Genesis will bring about a huge shift from "home-grown" health system–defined and –designed processes, to new standardized, corporate, consolidated processes and management of resources. By standardizing metrics, naming conventions, functional area processes, documentation practices, role definitions, and charging practices management, true enterprise-level management of system resources, promotion of best practices, and accurate information management will become possible.

Example 2: The American College of Surgeons' Standards

The roots of some of the United States' early quality control organizations demonstrate how values and opinions informed perceived judgments and outcomes associated with effectiveness criteria. In 1917, the American College of Surgeons (ACS) developed a set of *Minimum Standards for Hospitals*. The ACS used these standards to conduct on-site hospital inspections. The following year, after surveying 692 hospitals, only 89 of the hospitals were found to meet the ACS standards. Although these results were intended for public release, the ACS burned this list of deficient hospitals at midnight in the furnace of the Waldorf Astoria Hotel in New York. This cover-up prevented both the media and the general public from discovering that some of the most prestigious hospitals in the country did not meet the standards as set forth by the ACS.[39]

Although the burning of the list may be seen as unethical and self-serving, the intent of the leaders (at the time) was to maintain the perception of high hospital effectiveness in the United States. The introduction of this one metric into an otherwise highly regarded and trusted population of hospitals may have done more harm than good. As suggested earlier, effectiveness may be in the eye of the beholder, but it also may be based on an appropriately selected group of metrics and values.

HEALTH PERFORMANCE

The health literature to date reveals no single, universally accepted methodology for the measurement of performance in organizations for leaders to guide their strategy and vision.[40] Consequently, health leaders are faced with another very complicated construct that must be defined and measured based on other variables and metrics in the environment. Here, we offer one solution that incorporates the use of efficiency and effectiveness criteria upon which health leaders can base policy and decision making when dealing with performance constructs.[41]

As previously noted, effectiveness is a values-based term that is derived from qualitative and quantitative measures. Ultimately, it is defined as the achievement of outcomes acceptable to stakeholders. Efficiency, by comparison, is an empirical concept, defined by the statistical interpretation of outputs achieved by organizing inputs and outputs. How, then, do we interpret health organization performance?

One way to look at this complicated construct is to define performance based on the constructs of efficiency and effectiveness. The concept of performance in health organizations weds the empirical concept of efficiency with the stakeholder concept of effectiveness, thereby creating a new, measurable latent variable called performance:[42]

Performance = (Effectiveness criteria + Efficiency ratios)

Defining and Measuring Performance

For a health leader, the most important definitional issue in measuring organizational performance is capturing the correct measures to make organizational decisions. Various performance measures are available depending on the perspective being used to conceptualize performance. Once captured, these measures may highlight the potentially conflicting features of performance in an organizational system. In selecting organizational performance variables, it is critically important to stay focused on the domain of activity. For example, once a general framework or model has been selected to guide the performance measure to capture, it is necessary to determine which particular functions or activities will be evaluated on a continual basis. Most complex organizations serve a variety of aims and objectives. There is no simple measure of overall effectiveness of a health organization, which explains why several domains of activity (e.g., staffing turnover, organization full-time equivalents [FTEs], services offered) need to be captured and evaluated. There is always room to continuously improve at least some aspect of organizational performance—something for the leader to consider. A second consideration in the process is the level of analysis. An organization may wish to gather information at the clinic, department, or organizational level; having this echelon of information captured at different chokepoints in the organization provides an opportunity for the leader to effect change and engage in policy making.[43]

Examples of Best Practices in Industry

Because performance measures will differ based on the type of organization (for-profit or nonprofit; hospital, clinic, or retail pharmacy) and the product being produced by the organization, measures of performance will vary greatly between and within similar populations of organizations. High-performing for-profit hospitals will certainly look at revenue generation as a metric of performance, because this aspect is important to members of the hospital board; similarly, the employed persons in the organization may look at high revenue generation as a metric for job security. A nonprofit hospital may place more emphasis on the number of persons served and the degree of services offered to the population simultaneously as indicators of performance. Because the mission of the nonprofit organization is to provide services to the indigent or to increase the services offered to a rural community, this metric may be viewed as a performance measure. Local and regional professional organizations and internal and external stakeholders will all have different views on the achievement of performance criteria for organizations under study; leaders should quickly familiarize themselves with those measures.

Health Efficacy

Efficacy suggests possession of a special quality or virtue that gives effective power.[44] Efficacy is "the power to produce an effect."[45] Efficacy, as related to health and health care, is defined as the resources of the care process (continuum of care related to prevention, promotion, diagnosis, treatment, rehabilitation, and palliative care) that are attributed to realizing a desired or improved outcome for the patient and his or her family within an environment of respect and dignity. This is an individual patient perspective, whereas a community view of efficacy related to health and health care would be defined as the resources of the care process (continuum of care related to prevention, promotion, diagnosis, treatment, rehabilitation, and palliative care) that are attributed to realizing a desired or improved health status for the community that adds value to improve production and quality of life of its members.

Seemingly the opposite of efficacy is *maleficence*, which is defined as the "act of committing harm or evil";[46] health organizations are duty bound to not do harm. "Efficacy and effectiveness relate to one of the most important questions in medicine—does a particular intervention work or not?"[47] Basically, efficacy is the value of health organizations in maintaining, restoring, and improving health and providing appropriate palliative care to those who desire health services. These definitions are different from self-efficacy, discussed earlier in this chapter.

Defining and Measuring Efficacy

Health organizations are expected to provide error-free services and products; in essence, high levels of efficacy are expected by all stakeholders. This charge is rooted deeply in the values of health professionals and in cultural paradigms of health organizations. This expectation requires health leaders and their organizations to consider and apply strategies that bring efficacy concerns and realities to the top of the list of priorities. Health leaders must balance effectiveness and efficiency but cannot compromise on efficacy. This aspect of their operation is vital for the health organization's survival and the perception of the health organization in the community and industry.

Measuring health organization efficacy focuses on outcomes that are clinically and administratively based. Using the professional or national standard of care and standards of practice, what are the health organization's outcomes relative to national, regional, or similar organizations' benchmark statistics? Quality is highly associated with health efficacy.

Examples of Best Practices in Industry[48]

The Sisters of Mercy Health System (Mercy) has launched the "Mercy Meds" medication administration program, which will bring bedside barcoding and other medication safety features to more than 3,000 patient beds in 10 hospitals. In addition to ensuring the safest, most reliable delivery of medication by using advanced barcode technology, the Mercy Meds program enables nurses and hospital pharmacists to spend more time with patients. Because of its multiple safety components and coordinated approach, the Mercy Meds program represents one of the most comprehensive patient safety initiatives to be implemented by a healthcare system.

> The 2006 Institute of Medicine report that cited 1.5 million people are harmed annually by medication errors, takes into account not only the incorrect administration of medication, but also the failure to prescribe or administer medication. Technology can solve a majority of the problems linked to medication errors by reducing variation and ensuring compliance.

Some of the main reasons errors occur include nurse and pharmacy staffing shortages, high patient acuity, [poor] handwriting, and medication distribution process problems. Barcodes and radio-frequency identification are the mainstays of medication administration improvements among hospitals.[49]

From the time a doctor prescribes a medication to the time it is dispensed by the pharmacy and administered to the patient, Mercy has documented more than 70 steps in the process. Mercy Meds simplifies the process by eliminating unnecessary steps and implementing technology where possible to help identify potential medication issues.

With Mercy Meds, hospital pharmacists review patients' medication orders and enter prescription information into a computer. When giving medication to a patient, nurses wheel a computer to the patient's bedside that accesses information regarding the patient's medication regimen. Nurses use a handheld scanner to scan their own ID badge, the patient's barcoded ID wrist badge, and the barcode on the medication to verify accuracy. The computerized system also prompts nurses to check for potential medication issues, such as the patient's blood pressure and diet, before giving the medication. By using the barcode technology, the medication administration is automatically and accurately documented in the patient's electronic medication record.

Less than 5% of the nation's 5,000 hospitals currently use barcode systems, partly because only 35% of pharmaceutical doses come with barcodes. The Mercy Meds program is unique because the Mercy health system has become its own pharmaceutical distributor, allowing it to store, repackage, barcode, and distribute all medications used across Mercy, eliminating potential safety gaps that stem from using pharmaceuticals without barcodes. In addition, the Mercy Meds program includes the use of computer-controlled medication storage cabinets on the nursing unit. The cabinets enable nurses to access medications in an easy and timely manner and provide another safety check in the medication process.

In February 2004, the U.S. Food and Drug Administration (FDA) issued a final rule that [required] drug manufacturers to barcode prescription drugs by 2006. In addition, consumer advocacy groups such as the National Quality Forum (NQF) and The Leapfrog Group have endorsed several medication "safe practices" that should be used universally in clinical settings to improve patient safety. The Mercy Meds program surpasses both the FDA rule and the NQF/Leapfrog safe practices in both timing and scope by combining unit-dose, barcoded medications with bedside barcode scanning technology, and increasing nursing and pharmacist participation in medication safety. "Mercy is committed to ensuring an exceptional level of patient safety," said Ron Ashworth, the former president and chief executive officer of the Sisters of Mercy Health System. "We believe the benefits of Mercy Meds are essential in today's increasingly complex healthcare environment."

A primary goal of the initiative is to increase nurses' time at patients' bedsides, which will result in better hospital experiences and better health outcomes. Mercy Meds also positions hospital pharmacists as integral members of the collaborative patient care team, bringing their unique medication expertise and insight directly to the hospital floor.

"Mercy Meds allows Mercy to capitalize on our technical and clinical expertise, but most importantly, it helps us bring an increased level of comfort and peace of mind to our patients and their loved ones," said Kelly Turner, manager of pharmacy services at Sisters of Mercy Health System.

HEALTH QUALITY

There may be no construct more important to health leaders than the ability to define, operationalize, and measure quality in the organization.[50] Quality is a very complicated construct that has different meanings considering the myriad stakeholders. Stakeholders of interest in the defining of quality include patients, providers, employers, and payers. Each of these stakeholders will have different (and competing) concepts of organizational quality. The leader of any health organization will not be successful unless he or she is aware of these stakeholder interests and perceptions of quality and is prepared to meet these demands in the delivery and organization of health services and products.[51]

Similar to the definition of leadership itself, health quality has several definitions with no one universal frame for application among the populations of health organizations in the United States. As a base of reference, the authors of this text suggest quality is absolute and universally recognizable by all stakeholders. According to Coppola, quality is a mark of uncompromising standards and the accomplishment of high achievement. It is also the process of continuous improvement that is systematically evaluated against stakeholder demands and environmental requirements. Quality is the conformity to certain specifications set forth by stakeholders so that the equifinality and totality of the organization outputs satisfy both stated implicit needs and the implied and expected desires of all stakeholders. From a reductionist point of view, quality is the sum of organizational performance metrics plus stakeholder factors and expectations and meeting (or exceeding) the professional standards of care:[52]

Quality = Performance + Stakeholder factors and expectations + Professional standards of care

Defining and Measuring Quality

Several organizations are acutely interested in health quality. The National Quality Forum, for example, focuses on health quality: "The mission of the National Quality Forum is to improve the quality of American healthcare by setting national priorities and goals for performance improvement, endorsing national consensus standards for measuring and publicly reporting on performance, and promoting the attainment of national goals through education and outreach programs."[53] The Agency for Healthcare Research and Quality (AHRQ) is the federal organization charged with monitoring and improving health quality in the United States: "AHRQ is the lead federal agency charged with improving the quality, safety, efficiency, and effectiveness of health care for all Americans. As one of 12 agencies within the Department of Health and Human Services, AHRQ supports health services research that will improve the quality of health care and promote evidence-based decision making."[54]

Quality is the perceived and actual value that a service or product delivers to the receiver of the service or product:

> There are many issues to consider when selecting a quality measure. The first step in selecting measures is to identify the measurement purpose and intended use of the measure. Quality measurement can be used to drive performance improvement. The quality improvement process is often iterative and therefore measurement may be repeated over time.[55]

Depending on the area assessed for quality, the measure and how to measure will differ from area to area. A good explanation, examples, and lists of measures and comparisons of measures can be found on the AHRQ website.[56]

In 1966, Donabedian proposed an observational methodology for evaluating quality based on the constructs of structure, process, and outcome as necessary precursors to measuring quality. This model of health quality has since become the industry standard. Donabedian's original treatise on measuring and evaluating quality contained few guidelines for empirical measurement; rather, Donabedian recommended classifications of reviewing procedures. Successful review was based on the effective application of merit-based approaches and on normative and accepted practices in the field (stakeholder dynamics). Donabedian stated that experts on the subject matter and also panels should evaluate structure, process, and outcome variables.

Since 1966, the empirical literature has identified methods and methodologies capable of measuring quality, given appropriate data. Building on Donabedian's framework and earlier methodologies developed by other authors, the framework shown in **Figure 11-7** is proposed.[57,58]

- *Structure*: Structure criteria and measures assess the context, or system, in which care or service is provided. These criteria are frequently generated from federal and state regulatory or accreditation organizations and include individual and organizational licensure, compliance to safety codes, the Joint Commission standards, and NCQA standards, to name a few. Structure can also include the resources required to deliver care, the environment in which care is delivered, the facilities, the equipment (e.g., bandages, linen, drugs), and the documentation of procedures, policies, and guidance to staff.
- *Process*: Process measures assess the way in which care or services are provided. Examples of process measures include numbers of referrals and health screening rates. These measures also encompass the actual procedures and practices implemented by staff in their prescription, delivery, and evaluation of care, and the monitoring, evaluation, and actions to adjust the provision of care.
- *Outcomes*: Outcome measures assess the end result of a care or service process. Traditional outcome measures include mortality, morbidity, and infection rates. They may also include the effects of care received by patients as a result of health service intervention, the benefits to staff as a consequence of providing this care, and the costs to the organization of providing care.

Examples of Best Practices in Industry

Like performance constructs, quality can be a difficult and complex construct for leaders to define, let alone measure. A plethora of metrics, measures, and stakeholder dynamics come into play when attempting to universally define a complex construct such as quality and apply it in a consistent manner to health organizations.

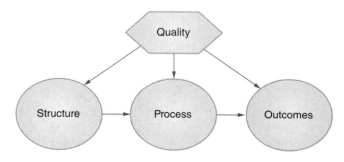

FIGURE 11-7 Quality perspective from the Donabedian model.

Starting in 1990, *U.S. News and World Report* began to publish an annual survey of "America's Best Hospitals" that has remained a standard for profiling and ranking hospitals in the United States for over 20 years. This model uses constructs of structure, process, and outcomes defined by a set of uniform variables that collectively make up a system of Likert-scale survey questions that are sent out to various key and influential stakeholders across the country. The survey also takes into account the reputation of the hospital (effectiveness criteria) as well as the evaluation of certain DRG groupings (efficiency criteria).[59]

Although the results are not perfect (and are disputed by some), the *U.S. News and World Report*'s attempt to improve on the earlier American College of Surgeons' survey conducted in 1917 is certainly successful in many ways. The improvement is that structure, process, and outcomes composite scores are reported with—and without—scores for reputation. The score for a facility's reputation (effectiveness criteria) is included as a stand-alone metric; it is also included in calculations of the overall scores for the top hospitals. In this regard, it is possible for hospitals to have highly regarded effective criteria as measured by key and influential stakeholders, as well as in terms of the operationalized metrics of the raw survey scores themselves. Although not all leaders approve of survey results serving as indices of their organization's quality performance, leaders need to be aware of their existence, and their impact on the overall perceived quality of the facility, whether warranted or not.

BALDRIGE NATIONAL QUALITY AWARD[60]

From an organizational perspective, in congruence with the leadership definition of creating an organizational culture and systems of excellence for health organizations, the Malcolm Baldrige National Quality Award is one externally directed "mark of excellence." (The healthcare organizational criteria can be found at www.nist.gov/baldrige/publications/upload/2009_2010_HealthCare_Criteria.pdf.) From the health organization criteria, key systems, an organizational culture of improvement, and patient care excellence are linked with strong evidence of leadership. Clearly, leadership, performance, and quality results are paramount. Leadership is the "action" required to be successful in the Baldrige National Quality Award Program. **Tables 11-3** through **11-6** provide the essence of the evaluation criteria, based on the major topics, associated with the Baldrige National Quality Award. How would your organization score using these criteria?

Table 11-3 Baldrige Evaluation Criteria Domains

Sections	Required Evaluative Criteria
Leadership	1.1 Leadership: Senior Leadership 1.2 Leadership: Governance and Societal Responsibilities 2.1 Strategic Planning: Strategy Development 2.2 Strategic Planning: Strategy Implementation 3.1 Customer Focus: Voice of the Customer (Stakeholder/Patient Engagement) 3.2 Customer Focus: Customer Engagement (Stakeholder/Using Patient Information)
Performance	4.1 (Performance Improvement) 4.2 (Performance Improvement/Knowledge Management) 5.1 Workforce Focus: Workforce Engagement 5.2 Workforce Focus: Workforce Environment (Workforce Capability) 6.1 Process Management: Work Systems 6.2 Process Management: Work Processes (Design, Manage, and Improve Work Processes)
Results	7.1 Results: Health Care Outcomes 7.2 Results: Customer-Focused Outcomes 7.3 Results: Financial and Market Outcomes 7.4 Results: Workforce-Focused Outcomes 7.5 Results: Process Effectiveness Outcomes 7.6 Results: Leadership Outcomes

Data from Baldrige National Quality Program. (2009). *2009–2010 health care criteria for performance excellence.* Gaithersburg, MD: National Institute of Standards and Technology.

Table 11-4 Baldrige Template for Leadership

	Element	Scoring Band % Table	Points Table	Score	Narrative Explanation for Score (100–200 words for each element in paragraph form)
			Scoring Band % × Points		
1.1	Senior Leadership		70		
1.2	Governance and Societal Responsibilities		50		
2.1	Strategy Development		40		
2.2	Strategy Implementation		45		
3.1	Voice of the Customer		40		
3.2	Customer Engagement		45		

Data from Baldrige National Quality Program. (2009). *2009–2010 health care criteria for performance excellence.* Gaithersburg, MD: National Institute of Standards and Technology.

Table 11-5 Baldrige Project Template Performance and Results

	Element	Scoring Band % Table	Points Table	Score	Narrative Explanation for Score (2–4 paragraphs for each element)
			Scoring Band % × Points		
4.1	Performance Improvement		45		
4.2	Performance Improvement/ Knowledge Management		45		
5.1	Workforce Engagement		45		
5.2	Workforce Capability		40		
6.1	Work Systems Design		35		
6.2	Design, Manage, and Improve Work Processes		50		
7.1	Health Care Services Results		100		
7.2	Patient and Stakeholder Satisfaction Results		70		
7.3	Financial and Market Results		70		
7.4	Workforce Performance Results		70		
7.5	Process Effectiveness Results		70		
7.6	Leadership and Social Responsibility Results		70		

Data from Baldrige National Quality Program. (2009). *2009–2010 health care criteria for performance excellence.* Gaithersburg, MD: National Institute of Standards and Technology.

Table 11-6 Baldrige Project Template Results					
	Element	Scoring Band % Table	Points Table	Score	Narrative Explanation for Score (2–4 paragraphs for each element)
			Scoring Band % × Points		
1.1	Senior Leadership		70		
1.2	Governance and Societal Responsibilities		50		
2.1	Strategy Development		40		
2.2	Strategy Implementation		45		
3.1	Voice of the Customer		40		
3.2	Customer Engagement		45		
4.1	Performance Improvement		45		
4.2	Performance Improvement/ Knowledge Management		45		
5.1	Workforce Engagement		45		
5.2	Workforce Capability		40		
6.1	Work Systems Design		35		
6.2	Design, Manage, and Improve Work Processes		50		
7.1	Health Care Services Results		100		
7.2	Patient and Stakeholder Satisfaction Results		70		
7.3	Financial and Market Results		70		
7.4	Workforce Performance Results		70		
7.5	Process Effectiveness Results		70		
7.6	Leadership and Social Responsibility Results		70		

Data from Baldrige National Quality Program. (2009). *2009–2010 health care criteria for performance excellence.* Gaithersburg, MD: National Institute of Standards and Technology.

SUMMARY

This chapter discussed how leaders can measure and assess the impact and progress of their leadership efforts within the health organization. Measurement and assessment of health leadership initiatives is one of the more under-represented facets of the health industry. This chapter defined common issues encountered by health leaders who undertake such measurements and recommended ways in which to measure outcomes. Distinctions were made among measuring leader efficiency, effectiveness, performance, and organizational efficacy. The health leader's goal is to combine these elements to create a composite quality leadership outcome assessment, such as that provided by the Baldrige National Quality Award Program.

Table 11-7 summarizes these terms as a take-away message for readers.

Table 11-7	Summary of Measurement-Related Terms	
Term	**Definition**	**Function**
Benchmarking	Benchmarking is a continuous process of measuring performance and services against best-in-class cases or organizations.	Compare item A to best-in-class item B
Efficiency	Efficiency is a quantitative term expressed as a ratio. It is derived through the process of dividing outputs by inputs.	E = Outputs/Inputs
Optimization	Optimization is defined as achieving perfect efficiency.	E = Outputs/Inputs, such that E = 100%
Effectiveness	Effectiveness is the sum of both quantitative and qualitative factors that are individually interpreted by stakeholders.	Effectiveness = Degree of (Qualitative + Quantitative factors), as interpreted by stakeholders
Performance	Performance in healthcare organizations weds the empirical concept of efficiency and the stakeholder concept of effectiveness, thereby forming a new, measurable latent variable.	Performance = (Effectiveness criteria + Efficiency ratios)
Quality	Quality is absolute and universally recognizable by all stakeholders.	Quality = (Performance + Stakeholder factors)

Reproduced from Coppola, M. N. (2013). *Quantitative analysis coursepack.* Lubbock, TX: Texas Tech University Health Sciences Center.

DISCUSSION QUESTIONS

1. How do health leaders measure and capture information (metrics) of efficiency, effectiveness, performance, efficacy, and quality in health organizations? Where are stakeholders' expectations important to this process?

2. Can you explain the importance of measurement and developing criteria for efficiency, effectiveness, performance, efficacy, and quality in health organizations? Why is this important to health leader evaluation?

3. Which types of applicable models and tools represent constructs of efficiency, effectiveness, performance, and quality in health organizations? Are some better than others?

4. Compare and contrast two or more models of health leader assessment and evaluation, and analyze the process of capturing metrics for this assessment and evaluation within a health organization. Which models seem most appropriate and why?

5. List health leader measures/metrics for assessment and evaluation for effectiveness, efficiency, performance, efficacy, and quality. List measures/metrics for assessment and evaluation of the health organization. How are the two lists similar and different? Do benchmarks fit into this discussion? Why or why not?

6. How would you appraise, evaluate, and justify the use of performance and quality measures/metrics for a specific type of health organization (e.g., hospital, group practice, rehabilitation center)?

EXERCISES

1. In a one- to two-page paper, describe how health leaders measure and capture information (metrics) of efficiency, effectiveness, performance, efficacy, and quality in health organizations.

2. In a one-page paper, explain the importance of measurement and developing criteria for efficiency, effectiveness, performance, efficacy, and quality in health organizations.

3. The CEO of your health organization comes to your office and states that she is not happy with the efficiency of the new ambulatory care clinic; she does not believe that the new clinic is being effective. Come

up with three different measures for efficiency and three different measures of effectiveness that you feel are uniform and applicable to ambulatory care clinics.

　a. Develop a construct representing "patient satisfaction with ambulatory care" that includes two variables and four measures based on the metrics you developed for this exercise.

　b. Based on the metrics you developed for this exercise, develop a dashboard for each metric that will provide the CEO with a snapshot of the performance items you have already suggested are important.

4. In a one- to two-page paper, compare and contrast two or more models of health leader assessment and evaluation, and analyze the process of capturing metrics for this assessment and evaluation within a health organization.

5. Compile and categorize health leader measures/metrics for assessment and evaluation for effectiveness, efficiency, performance, efficacy, and quality; and compile and categorize measures/metrics for assessment and evaluation of the health organization. In a two- to three-page paper describe and compare the two categorized lists.

6. Appraise, evaluate, and justify the use of performance and quality measures/metrics for a specific type of health organization (e.g., hospital, group practice, rehabilitation center).

REFERENCES

1. Drucker, P. (1993). *The practice of management* (reissue ed.). New York: Harper Business.

2. Aday, L. A. (1998). Introduction to health service research and policy analysis. In L. A. Aday, C. E. Begley, D. R. Lairson, & R. Balkrishnan (Eds.), *Evaluating the healthcare system: Effectiveness, efficiency, and equity* (pp. 45–172). Ann Arbor, MI: Health Administration Press.

3. Flexner, A. (1910). *Medical education in the United States and Canada*. Boston: Merrymount Press.

4. Codman, E. A. (1917/1996). *A study in hospital efficiency: As demonstrated by the case report of the first five years of a private hospital*. Oakbrook Terrace, IL: Joint Commission on Accreditation of Healthcare Organizations.

5. Veney, J. E., & Kaluzny, A. D. (2004). *Evaluation and decision making for health services* (3rd ed.). Washington, D.C.: Beard Books.

6. Beeson, J. (2004). Building bench strength: A tool kit for executive development. *Business Horizons, 47*(6), 3–9. Also in NCHL & GE Institute for Transformational Leadership. (n.d.). Preparing leaders to achieve organizational excellence. Retrieved from http://www.nchl.org/static.asp?path=3542,3552.

7. NCHL & GE Institute for Transformational Leadership. (n.d.). Preparing leaders to achieve organizational excellence. Retrieved from http://www.nchl.org/static.asp?path=3542,3552.

8. Collinson, D., Bryman, A., Collinson, D., Grint, K., & Jackson, B. (2011). Critical leadership studies. In *The Sage Handbook of Leadership* (pp. 179–192). London: Sage.

9. Ledlow, G., & Cwiek, M. (2005, July). The process of leading: Assessment and comparison of leadership team style, operating climate and expectation of the external environment. *Proceedings of the Global Business and Technology Association*. Lisbon, Portugal.

10. Lanser, E. G. (2000). Why you should care about your emotional intelligence: Strategies for honing important emotional competencies. *Healthcare Executive, 15*(6), 7.

11. Lanser, note 10, p. 7.

12. Lanser, note 10, p. 9.

13. Aday, L. A. (2009). *Evaluating the healthcare system: Effectiveness, efficiency, and equity*. Chicago: Health Administration Press.

14. Coppola, M. N. (1998). The hidden value of managing worker's compensation costs in the hospital setting. In J. Burns & M. Sipkoff (Eds.), *1999 hospital strategies in managed care* (pp. 227–255). New York: Faulkner and Gray.

15. Agency for Healthcare Research and Quality, National Committee for Quality Assurance. (n.d.). HEDIS & performance measurement. Retrieved from http://www.ncqa.org/tabid/59/Default.aspx.

16. Agency for Healthcare Research and Quality, National Committee for Quality Assurance. (n.d.). Features and announcements. Retrieved from http://www.ncqa.org/tabid/187/Default.aspx.

17. Agency for Healthcare Research and Quality, National Committee for Quality Assurance. (n.d.). Media/industry studies. Retrieved from http://www.ncqa.org/Default.aspx?tabid=136.

18. HealthyPeople.gov. (n.d.). Retrieved from http://www.healthypeople.gov.

19. HealthyPeople.gov. (n.d.). Retrieved from http://www.healthypeople.gov; and Collinson, D. L. (2000).

Strategies of resistance: Power, knowledge and subjectivity in the workplace. In K. Grint (Ed.), *Work and society: A reader* (pp. 163–198). Cambridge, UK: Polity Press.

20. Swayne, L. E., Duncan, W. J., & Ginter, P. M. (2006). *Strategic management of health care organizations* (5th ed.). Malden, MA: Blackwell, p. 56.
21. Swayne et al., note 20, p. 56.
22. Veney & Kaluzny, note 5.
23. Veney & Kaluzny, note 5, pp. 5–6.
24. Merriam-Webster. (n.d.). Efficiency. Retrieved from http://www.merriam-webster.com/dictionary /efficiency.
25. Heyne, P. (n.d.). The concise encyclopedia of economics: Efficiency. Retrieved from http://www .econlib.org/library/Enc/Efficiency.html.
26. Coppola, M. N. (2003). *Correlates of military medical treatment facility (MTF) performance: Measuring technical efficiency with the structural adaptation to regain fit (SARFIT) model and data envelopment analysis (DEA).* Doctoral thesis, Medical College of Virginia Campus, Virginia Commonwealth University, Richmond, VA.
27. This section is excerpted from the following source: Corry, A., Ledlow, G., & Shockley, S. (2005). Designing the standard for a healthy supply chain. In *Achieving supply chain excellence through technology (ASCET)* (Vol. 6, pp. 199–202). San Francisco, CA: Montgomery Research.
28. Coppola, M. N. (2013). *Quantitative analysis coursepack.* Lubbock, TX: Texas Tech University Health Sciences Center.
29. Coppola, note 28.
30. Rein, D. B., Wittenborn, J. S., Smith, B. D., Liffmann, D. K., & Ward, J. W. (2015). Editor's choice: The cost-effectiveness, health benefits, and financial costs of new antiviral treatments for hepatitis C virus. *Clinical Infectious Diseases, 61*(2), 157–168. First published online March 16, 2015. doi:10.1093 /cid/civ220.
31. Coppola, note 28.
32. Starfield, B. (1992). *Primary care: Concept, evaluation, and policy.* New York: Oxford University Press.
33. Coppola, note 28.
34. Coppola, note 28.
35. Coppola, note 28.
36. The first example was taken from Corry et al., note 27.
37. Sisters of Mercy Health System. (2004, April). *The Genesis Project: Background paper.* St. Louis, MO: Sisters of Mercy Health System.
38. Conger, J., Speitzer, G., & Lawler, E. III. (1999). *The leader's change handbook: An essential guide to setting direction and taking action.* San Francisco, CA: Jossey-Bass, p. 56.
39. Roberts, J. S., Coale, J. G., & Redman, R. R. (1987). A history of the Joint Commission on Accreditation of Hospitals. *Journal of the American Medical Association, 258*(7), 936–940.
40. Coppola, M. N., Ozcan, Y. A., & Bogacki, R. (2003). Evaluation of performance of dental providers on posterior restorations using amalgam or composite material: Does experience matter? A data envelopment analysis (DEA) approach. *Journal of Medical Systems, 27*(5), 447–458.
41. Coppola, note 28.
42. Coppola, note 28.
43. Coppola, note 28.
44. Merriam-Webster. (n.d.). Effective. Retrieved from http://www.merriam-webster.com/dictionary /effectiveness.
45. Merriam-Webster. (n.d.). Efficacy. Retrieved from http://www.merriam-webster.com/dictionary /efficacy.
46. Merriam-Webster. (n.d.). Maleficence. Retrieved from http://www.merriam-webster.com/dictionary /maleficence.
47. Cole, B. (2011). *How to win friends and influence people in the digital age.* New York: Simon & Schuster.
48. Woehrmann, K. (2012). Mercy/ROi, BD to collaborate to improve quality, reduce costs. Retrieved from http://www.mercy.net/newsroom/2012-01-19 /mercyroi-bd-collaborate-to-improve-quality -reduce-costs.
49. Ganguly, I. (2009). Effective medication administration. *Advance for Health Information Executives, 13*(6), 21.
50. Coppola, note 28.
51. Coppola, M. N., Harrison, J., Kerr, B., & Erckenbrack, D. (2007). The military managed care health system. In P. Kongstvedt (Ed.), *Essentials of managed care* (5th ed., pp. 633–655). Sudbury, MA: Jones & Bartlett.
52. Coppola, note 28.
53. National Quality Forum. (n.d.). What we do. Retrieved from http://www.qualityforum.org/Home _New/What_we_do.aspx
54. U.S. Department of Health and Human Services, Agency for Healthcare Research and Quality. (n.d.). AHRQ at a glance. Retrieved from http://www .ahrq.gov/about/ataglance.htm.
55. U.S. Department of Health and Human Services, Agency for Healthcare Research and Quality. (n.d.).

Measuring performance. Retrieved from http://www.qualitymeasures.ahrq.gov/browse/by-topic.aspx.

56. U.S. Department of Health and Human Services, note 55.

57. Donabedian, A. (1966). Evaluating the quality of medical care. *Milbank Memorial Fund Quarterly, 44,* 166–206.

58. Coppola, M. N. (2008). Anatomy and physiology of theory. In J. A. Johnson (Ed.), *Health organizations: Theory, behavior, and development* (pp. 9–29). Sudbury, MA: Jones & Bartlett.

59. McFarlane, E., Murphy, J., Olmsted, M. G., Drozd, E. M., & Hill, C. (2008). America's best hospital methodology. Retrieved from http://www.usnews.com/usnews/health/best-hospitals/methodology/ABH_Methodology_2008.pdf.

60. Baldrige National Quality Program. (2010). 2009–2010 health care criteria for performance excellence. Retrieved from http://www.nist.gov/baldrige/publications/upload/2009_2010_HealthCare_Criteria.pdf.

© Murat Inan / EyeEm / Getty Images.

UNDERSTANDING THE EXECUTIVE ROLES OF HEALTH LEADERSHIP

Necessity does the work of courage.
George Eliot, *Romola*

This chapter examines the complex cycle of relationships within health organizations. The needs and desires of nurses, physicians, administrators, and medical function leaders are presented. This chapter also places special emphasis on the relationships between major stakeholders within health entities. For the purpose of this discussion, we designate major health organization stakeholders as payers, providers, patients, and organizational entities. We additionally elaborate on the complexities of stakeholder relationships as they are concerned with cost, quality, and access issues. Finally, the chapter presents a conceptual model called the "parity of health care" that combines stakeholders and stakeholder issues into one schematic that assists in explaining and forecasting relationships in the dynamic world of the health industry.

LEARNING OBJECTIVES

1. Identify the steps, characteristics, and behaviors a health leader should employ to build relationships with internal, "interface," and external stakeholders.

2. Explain the Parity of Health Care model and its usefulness to health leaders.

3. Construct a health organization stakeholder list and predict at least two motivations of each stakeholder considering cost, quality, and access to health services and products.

4. Compare and contrast internal health organization stakeholder motivations and issues.

5. Combine two or more theories or models into a practical stakeholder management and relationship development model.

6. Evaluate internal and external health organization stakeholders, and justify their motivations, needs, and aspirations with regard to health services and products.

LEADERSHIP FOR PHYSICIANS, NURSES, ADMINISTRATORS, AND MEDICAL FUNCTION DIRECTORS

Health leadership is situational and contextual, influenced by cultural constructs, and moderated by relational factors. The myriad internal stakeholders and their differences are complex in both breadth and depth. In simple terms, health leaders need to lead people and manage resources to direct the collective energy of the organization toward successfully achieving the mission of the organization. This mission is always to serve patients and the community. This idea may be simple to state, but it is difficult to realize in practice. Similar to a conductor leading an orchestra, health leaders must ensure a seamless and harmonious operation such that all participants are collectively moving forward to accomplish the mission of the organization simultaneously. To do so, leaders must understand and motivate the various stakeholders in different ways while staying true to the organization's preferred strategies, goals, and objectives. Stakeholders hold differing views, have differing incentives and motivations, and serve differing roles in the health organization; leaders understand these differences and integrate the value and efforts of stakeholders to achieve the mission and aspire to reach the vision of the organization.

PHYSICIAN LEADERS

Health leaders need physicians to diagnose, treat, and refer patients to their organization. Without physicians, health

organizations would not receive reimbursements or other revenues for the patient care process. With this point in mind, health leaders need to create a symbiotic, trusting, and integrity-based relationship with physicians. This is especially true of physician leadership. Health leaders should visit and know all physicians who practice and refer patients to their organization; these visits should be regular events that occur at times when physicians are not engaged in patient care. Health leaders should seek input from physician leadership on important decisions within the organization and provide frequent feedback on the decision process as well. The relationship a health executive builds with the physician leadership is critical.

It is always very important to respect a physician's education, background, decision-making priorities, and skills. A health leader should constantly be communicating the organization's vision, strategies, goals, and objectives in a clear and consistent manner while weaving the value of physician involvement and work into the discussion. Health executives should also try to maximize physicians' time to diagnose, treat, prescribe, and refer patients by creating or reengineering processes and systems that focus on their skills.

One of the greatest fears that physicians have with regard to any proposed "national healthcare" system is that they might lose control of their clinical practice autonomy. Physicians believe that any time spent away from direct patient care on additional bureaucratic requirements lowers patient care quality. Additionally, providers view decreased patient contact as inhibiting access to patients. Organizations can alleviate some of this fear by continuing to solicit physician input in all policy analyses and decision making that affect the care process or the logistics of the care process. For example, provider participation in policy making and strategic planning are essential to program success. To discount physician involvement and influence in health policy will ultimately doom policy implementation. Include physicians in all health and care delivery policy decisions that might affect their day-to-day autonomy or decision making.

NURSE LEADERS

Nurse leaders are important to the health organization in that they provide care for patients on an ongoing basis. In most health organizations, nurses account for the largest personnel expense for the entity as a whole. Nurses are needed to "staff" hospital beds, work in health programs, provide home health services, and perform any number of other jobs in health entities. Nurse leaders, like physician leaders, want to be respected, trusted, and sought out for input into decisions affecting the care process. Nurses want good work environments, with reasonable patient care loads (usually four to six patients per nurse per shift for average-acuity patients); to be treated with respect by administrators, physicians, and other medical staff personnel; and to have some level of self-governance (e.g., nurse education, scheduling). Common characteristics of exemplary nurse leaders include: a passion for nursing, a sense of optimism, the ability to form personal connections with their staff, excellent role modeling and mentorship, and the ability to manage a crisis while being well guided by a set of moral principles.[1]

Building a solid relationship with nurse leaders is like building a relationship with anyone else—trust, respect, and honesty form the foundation for interaction. As with physicians, health leaders should meet with nurse leaders and ask how to best build great relationships. Most nurses will respect the health leader's courage and intent to build a good relationship within the organization.

ADMINISTRATIVE LEADERS AND MEDICAL FUNCTION LEADERS/ DEPARTMENT HEADS

Building professional and effective relationships with administrators and medical function leaders (e.g., pharmacists, laboratory staff) is important in building a cohesive team of superiors, peers, and subordinates. Relationships with these leaders should be built on trust, respect, and honesty. However, different leaders will have different foci and motivations. For example, the finance leader is concerned with the bottom line and efficient use of resources. The

pharmacist may be interested in error-free operations and streamlining supply chain logistical tasks. The laboratory leader may be focused on acquiring new capital equipment to keep up with the technology diffusion in this field. As this discussion suggests, the "wish lists" of administrators and medical function leaders are both dynamic and nearly endless. As a result, managing these competing interests and priorities is challenging for any health leader. Even so, regardless of their job and organizational placement within the facility, it is important to listen to, respect, and understand the needs of these stakeholders.

STAKEHOLDER DYNAMICS

Stakeholder dynamics are critically important for leaders of health organizations. This reality becomes more salient as leaders rise to positions of greater responsibility within the health organization. Key stakeholders in any health entity will include groups, individuals, and associations. Within these three classifications, stakeholders can further be defined as internal, interface, and external stakeholders.

In a health organization, internal stakeholders operate within the organization and consist of management and professional and nonprofessional staff. Interface stakeholders function both internally and externally to the organization; they include medical staff, the governing body, and, if applicable, stockholders. External stakeholders include patients and their families, suppliers, third-party payers, competitors, special-interest groups, regulatory and accrediting agencies, local communities, and labor organizations.[2,3] All of these stakeholders exert an influence on every issue and must be recognized and evaluated for their potential to support or threaten the organization and its competitive goals.[4,5]

Health organizations have a particularly complex set of stakeholders. They include patients and families; payers; buyers (employers); regulatory agencies, such as The Joint Commission; community groups, such as public health departments, local employers, churches, and civic organizations; providers, including medical staff members, employees, and volunteers; suppliers and financing agencies; associate organizations, such as physician professional organizations; and other providers, including competing organizations and agencies whose service lines may be either competing or complementary, such as home care agencies and primary care clinics.[6]

Key stakeholders are those most important to health organizations. These stakeholders directly or indirectly control reimbursement, information, approvals, or other resources valued by the organization, or are in a position to impose costs on the organization.[7] Stakeholder dynamics are a key factor that explains why the healthcare industry is so complex. The industry requires stakeholder cooperation and balance in order to run smoothly; however, this is easer stated than done.[8] Healthcare administrators sometimes have to make a choice between which key stakeholder to make happy and which to disappoint (not everyone is going to agree with all policies); healthcare administrators (leaders) must decide which key stakeholder or stakeholders are most important to the success of the organization (although ideally one would want satisfaction for all stakeholders).[9]

Although the number of stakeholders in health organizations may be high, four main types of stakeholders should be considered in any healthcare decision making: patients, payers, employers, and providers. These four stakeholder groups have recently been labeled with a new term in managed care—the *managed care quaternion*.[10] Collectively, the stakeholders in the managed care quaternion affect all aspects of health organizational life, including patient care, payment, reimbursement arrangements, external costs, and other policy affecting organization survivability. Patients, payers, employers, and providers all play a vital role in the operations of any health organization. If any one of the four major stakeholders of the managed care quaternion is omitted in the decision-making process for a healthcare entity, failure at some level is highly probable.

THE MANAGED CARE QUATERNION AND THE IRON TRIANGLE

The managed care quaternion (MCQ) model was developed in the early part of 2003 by Coppola.[11] It has since gained popular support within governmental organizations, as well as within some state Medicaid agencies, as an aid to health planning and policy making. It has also been used to forecast future healthcare needs. Furthermore, the MCQ concept is slowly working its way into the mainstream of health education. It will be an important model for health leaders to become familiar with as a tool for decision making in the next decade. However, the MCQ model alone cannot be used as a basis for policy or decision making. Instead, it is more beneficial to view this model in concert with the Iron Triangle of health care.

The concept of the Iron Triangle was developed by Kissick in the early 1990s during the managed care revolution in the United States.[12] Kissick coined the term *Iron Triangle* to demonstrate the difficulty in selecting priorities for health as they relate to healthcare costs, quality, and access. Kissick suggested that an understanding of these resource elements would assist managed care organizations in establishing their logistical priorities.

For example, Kissick recognized that cost is only one important resource for the healthcare industry. In the Iron Triangle, costs form one angle of the three points, with quality and access being the other two resource priorities. These three factors together are kept in balance by the expectations, cultural goals, and economics of the society that supports the industry. Any angle (or construct) in the triangle can be increased, but only at the expense of the other two. For instance, quality in the U.S. health industry can be improved through large expenditures for additional technology or in training allied health providers; however, the increased expenditures may result in restricted access of this improved health care to only those persons who can pay for the higher quality of care. Put simply, the normal increase in one construct may adversely affect some combination of equifinality of the other two.

Health leaders have used the concept of the Iron Triangle for more than a decade to guide development of strategic plans, organizational vision, and mission statements. Furthermore, this notion has become a staple and core competency in most health and business programs in the United States. Every young graduate student in this country should be familiar with the Iron Triangle and be able to relate it to resource priorities in organizational analysis.

Kissick's model is a vital tool for health leaders; however, the model itself fails to take into account outside actors and agents. In this regard, it is incomplete as a means for conducting dynamic organizational analysis. When the Iron Triangle and the MCQ model are combined, they form a dynamic model called the *Parity of Health Care*. This model describes, explains, and can forecast competing issues and organizational dynamics in the healthcare arena (**Figure 12-1**). The Parity of Health Care model is explained in more detail later in this chapter; we present it here for visual stimulation. Readers should refer back to this illustration as the various components of the model are described later in this chapter.

Optimally, it will be every health leader's goal to deliver high-quality care, services, or products, while simultaneously increasing access to services or products and lowering costs. Unfortunately, as health leaders try to make improvements in one area, there is often a tradeoff consideration in another area. For instance, increasing access to pharmacy benefits by opening an after-hours pharmacy window may improve access and be seen as a quality initiative, but this service may not generate enough new revenue to pay for itself. If the pharmacy window continues to draw scarce resources from other areas in the health facility, its growing drain on the overall fitness of the organization may negatively influence other areas—perhaps professional development and training opportunities, for example. In this case, the decreased opportunities for continuing health and medical education may translate into lower-quality

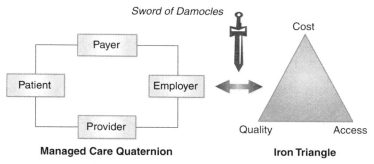

FIGURE 12-1 The Parity of Health Care model.

outcomes for customers. The decrease in quality outcomes may be the result of the organization failing to take advantage of industry best practices that peer organizations have implemented due to their emphasis on professional development and training.

This complicated relationship forces health leaders to think conceptually and in nonlinear approaches. As a result, they must perform careful analyses of new policy ideas or agendas to ensure that the organization will maintain an effective balance between health costs, quality, and access. The cost, quality, and access tradeoffs associated with the interrelationships among actors must be considered.

The following sections provide an overview of the key stakeholders of the MCQ model, relating them to various dynamics of the Iron Triangle. The goal here is to illuminate the complicated and delicate nature of health dynamics.

Payers

Payers are a key stakeholder group because they provide reimbursement for services and products provided by health organizations. This group of stakeholders includes patients (who may pay for at least some, if not all, of their expenses on an out-of-pocket basis); governmental insurance programs, including Medicare and Medicaid; and private health insurers. Payer organizations attempt to keep the cost of care as low as possible and, more recently, have begun their own efforts to improve the quality and safety of care.[13]

Payers seek the lowest costs possible for health services and products and are usually willing to sacrifice the time costs of patients to achieve that goal. Accordingly, access is a secondary issue to the cost of care; the quality tradeoff is only marginally discussed after the cost of care. Although risk management issues certainly come into play with large-scale health-based plans, the payer will, unfortunately, often go with the lowest physician bidder who can validate equally effective health outcomes in an

environment of acceptable access. Such is the paradox and dilemma of being a large-scale health payer.

Leaders of health organizations need to be aware that large insurance companies may be more interested in health costs as opposed to outcomes of health services or products. This tendency is somewhat due to the migration of beneficiaries from plan to plan over short time periods; most health insurance plans are focused on medical expense ratios and maintaining a profit margin because long-term prevention and outcomes linked to beneficiaries are rarely beneficial to the health insurance plan in which the beneficiary is enrolled at the time. Furthermore, although interested in health policy as a vehicle to lowering costs, the legislation that surrounds policy making is only a means to an end when it comes to cost controls. However, purchasers of health care may see reasonable price controls as a quality indicator and demand to see comparative data from different organizations. Such has been the case lately with many car insurance companies, which freely offer their prices for automobile insurance to consumers, allowing them to compare these prices against those offered by competitors. This transparent and open system of pricing not only translates into an imprimatur of honesty and candidness for the organization, but also can be perceived as an effort to promote a partnership in the insurance industry rather than advocate for a cost-driven industry.

Accordingly, leaders of health organizations in the current decade may be placed in situations where they are forced to provide comparative data. Comparative data in health may include information to assist the purchaser to distinguish between health organizations' quality outcomes and services delivered. The payer, if not an individual patient, may also be concerned about the total cost per employer per year and acuity-adjusted disability periods if economies of scale are achieved to negotiate large-scale discounts on fees for services. As a result, health organizations need a strategy that allows them to know ahead of time how to implement a partnership with outside purchasers that is seen as a cooperative relationship rather than a utilitarian, profit-driven liaison.

Importance of Medicare and Medicaid

Two of the largest payers that both early career health leaders and established leaders will deal with most commonly today in the United States are Medicare and Medicaid. Many issues play a role in the development of policy, payment decision making, and resource management for these payer organizations.

Medicare

Medicare is an entitlement program where beneficiaries are required to "pay into" the system to be entitled to Medicare coverage once eligibility criteria are met. Medicare is administered through a series of intermediaries. Organizations such as Trail Blazers, Blue Cross and Blue Shield, and Aetna act as Medicare agents in determining interpretations of Medicare law and case management of patients. This system allows individual health organizations to work with one primary organization for funding and regulation compliance rather than having all organizations going through one central Medicare supplier in Washington, D.C. The downside to having a larger number of agencies administering this program is that each agency has its own interpretation of the Medicare law, and this results in some lack of consistency across the nation.

Medicare has gone through many permutations over the past four decades. The Balanced Budget Act of 1997 brought Medicare, the federally funded healthcare payer, to this point in history: Medicare has 43 million beneficiaries and is the United States' largest health insurance program. With estimated costs of $430 billion per year, spending is growing more rapidly than revenue. If current trends continue, the program will be unable to pay for all medical bills by 2018.[14] Leaders need to keep this point in mind in any analysis that incorporates the payer cost mix within the organization.

The Medicare system is under constant construction and renovation, with the most recent efforts being directed at the Medicare disability programs. This portion of Medicare provides health services for Americans who are declared disabled through the Social Security Administration. With the reelection of President Barack Obama, lawmakers and more than 75 disability advocacy groups have begun lobbying Congress to decrease the wait time for Medicare's disability benefits to take effect.[15]

Medicaid

Medicare is the federally funded insurance plan for Americans age 65 or older as well as some other groups, such as people with kidney failure. In contrast to Medicare, Medicaid services are provided through individual states and supplemented with federal dollars through a block grant program. Medicaid is a welfare program that requires beneficiaries to meet state-based criteria for coverage. Leaders of local state-funded hospitals need to remain keenly aware of the varying payments and restrictions that are found in their state.

Medicaid funds are geared toward low-income individuals and often pay for basic health service and product needs. The one exception is children younger than age 18, who often receive dental and vision care as well as the standard medical care through Medicaid and/or the Children's Health Insurance Program (CHIP). Medicaid programs are often difficult to navigate for leaders of health organizations, health providers, and patients alike. The bureaucracy limits options for services due to the difficult requirements for becoming part of the system. Many physicians do not accept assignment for services because of low reimbursements and slow payment for services provided. As part of current legislative efforts, policy makers have been focusing on increasing reimbursement rates as a means of encouraging provider participation and building a more extensive provider network for beneficiaries. Also, many states have moved to Medicaid managed care plans in an effort to rein in costs and stabilize quality.

Patients

Ironically, the term *patient* was derived from a Latin verb meaning *to suffer*. It is used to describe those persons who are recipients of care. The patient is an individual who will use some part of the health system in a facility for reasons known only to that person and his or her caretakers. Patient needs, interests, and expectations vary depending on the problem and the patient's past experiences. Understanding patients is important to health leaders because they are the ones who use the facilities and ultimately pay for services and products.[16,17]

Traditionally, health patients have been more interested in the indicators of satisfaction, access to care, facility accommodations, and service quality rather than how an organization is structured to provide that care. This is especially true if the patient has insurance that results in little to no out-of-pocket cost; moral hazard is a phenomenon that explains the increase in health services and product utilization noted when the patient incurs few financial demands at the time of service or product delivery. Now, however, a new era of health consumerism exists. Patients, who have learned to expect more from the products and services they purchase, are beginning to benchmark their health services against similar services they receive from the best organizations outside the health industry. In this growing era of patient autonomy, they are using their experiences and observations to ask pointed questions. For example, if a package shipping company can answer calls in one ring, why can't the insurance claim center meet the same standard? If an investment advisor can offer a convenient after-hours appointment within a week, why can't a physician do so? If a company will accept without question the return of a product that does not fit properly, why won't the triage center trust a consumer who shares information about medical symptoms?

The health industry has not kept pace with the expectations of increasingly demanding patients. Complaints about quality and access to care are common. Making convenient appointments with the "right" practitioner remains a challenge for the average patient. Administrative minutiae have become more time consuming than the actual delivery of health services, and stories of medication errors and the lack of patient safety in different settings are increasingly prevalent. In the midst of this turbulence, organizations known for health excellence, such as Harvard Pilgrim Health Care and many Blue Cross and Blue Shield plans, are falling on hard financial times. As a result of these trends, health leaders who do not control costs while simultaneously managing patients' expectations of quality and access will fail to receive the confidence of their patients, and their organizations may find themselves facing the problems of financial instability and lower revenues. To quell this possibility, health leaders must manage patient expectations of access and quality, all the while controlling costs, if they want to compete and survive in this highly competitive, dynamic health environment.[18]

Hospitals spend countless hours creating surveys, working on process improvement issues, and studying best-practice alternatives. The information gained through these efforts is then used to identify what a patient actually needs to have in order to be processed through the service line comfortably and effectively. A patient's wants and needs are important to identify within the realm of the hospital's community. For instance, a hospital located within an oil-producing area should have the capability of dealing with the problems commonly experienced in this area—this is a need. An example of a want would be fresh flowers in an inpatient room every day or covered parking for all patient and guest vehicles. These concerns are important to patients, and patients realize that major changes will affect the cost of health services and products. Therefore, a patient's wants and needs must be carefully analyzed and implemented to benefit the needs of the patient, while simultaneously maintaining or exceeding the professional standard of care.

As previously stated, patients have traditionally been more interested in access to care and quality than in how an organization is structured to provide that care. Today, these issues are still important to patients, but now patients are requesting a voice in how their local organizations are run. This voice and input may include demands for services not currently offered and extended hours. Patients also want to be treated as individuals; the health industry needs to respect their cultures.[19] Leaders also need to know that many patients are surfing the Internet for published service and product benchmarks. One survey found that Internet users were successful in locating many of the hospital benchmarks they were interested in with regard to certain health issues in less than 6 minutes.[20] Given the ready access patients have to this information, health leaders need to be aware of what is written about their organizations and what is publically available.

Health leaders are always striving to provide the necessities that patients require. One important necessity is the role that hospitals have in treating patients as individuals. Treating patients as individuals, and not just as a medical record numbers, means that facilities must respect the values, privacy, and cultures of all patients. Culture refers to a cohesive body of learned behaviors, taught from one generation to the next. One's culture constitutes one's rationale and rules for living; it makes experiences meaningful. Cultures are not simply a hodgepodge of disparate habits.[21,22]

Providing cultural satisfaction is a complex issue because all patients have cultural views that may or may not be congruent with those of the health organization's staff. Ultimately, it is important for the leader to set aside cultural differences and to accommodate and incorporate cultural satisfaction into his or her health organization; after all, to maximize a patient's recovery is to make the patient as comfortable as possible.

Patients' Views on Costs

Patients today are concerned with their out-of-pocket costs, health insurance premium costs, and pharmaceutical costs. Health expenditures have become a major concern for most Americans. Many view the rising costs of health services and products as a sign of a failing health system. Within the past decade, several debates have dealt with the issues of universal health care, electronic medical records, and insurance reform. As a consequence, the new patient now typically views the health organization not only as a place for medical care, but also as a business that does not care about the financial concerns of the patient stakeholder group.

It is incumbent upon every health organization to create a vision that will benefit its community. This vision usually becomes a reality if costs and the objectives of patients come together to form a broad picture. Patient objectives are items that patients would like to have accomplished as part of their interaction with the health organization. These objectives can be personal or they can belong to a group of stakeholders. An example of a personal objective would be satisfying the itinerary that a therapist sets at the beginning of treatment. An example of a group objective would be petitioning the hospital to provide more handicap access routes for easier maneuverability. Objectives can be considered goals; however, objectives are generally items that need to be accomplished. Goals, by comparison, are items that the organization wants to reach, but for which there are no deleterious effects if they are not attained. Objectives are very important to cost analysis when dealing with patient care.

Patients' Views on Quality

The Institute of Medicine (IOM) defines quality as follows: "the degree to which health services for individuals and populations increase the likelihood of desired health outcomes and are consistent with current professional standards."[23] Patients are motivated to participate in their care when they receive quality care. The patient is the key to how a health organization scores regarding quality. Patients who become motivated to care for themselves first do so by recognizing what quality means to them, then by measuring the performance of the health professionals, and finally, by assessing the organization's ability to meet patient needs. Patients' views of quality reflect their perceptions of their treatment while in the health organization, hospital, clinic, or doctor's office; the service provided; and the competency of the staff. These views are collected by the organization through patient surveys, questionnaires, and discharge interviews. Information is then analyzed, and performance improvements or performance initiatives are implemented within the health system. Health leaders should maximize these opportunities when possible.

Patients' Views on Access

Several factors affect access to health services and products: cultural and linguistic barriers, inability to get through by telephone, long wait times in the physician's office, inability to secure appointments, physician office hours that are not convenient for patients, lack of transportation, and being uninsured or underinsured. In a study conducted by the National Health Interview Survey (NHIS), a survey of 23,413 participants concluded that even when adults have a regular source for medical care, such as a personal physician, various problems in accessing care from their primary care physician—long waiting times in the office, limited availability of appointments, lack of transportation, or difficulty reaching the physician by telephone—can increase the use of the hospital emergency department, which acts as a surrogate to primary care with the personal physician. This diminishes the benefits of having a regular source of primary care. Solutions that might improve access to medical care, such as implementing open access scheduling, can not only benefit patients, but also can benefit health policy related to cost-effective healthcare delivery systems and relieve overcrowding in emergency department waiting rooms.[24]

Health leaders know that the largest obstacle standing in the way of access to care is actually the inability to pay for health insurance or healthcare services. According to the U.S. Census Bureau, 45.7 million Americans are uninsured.[25] Insurance coverage greatly increases the probability of accessing and potential to access health services and products. Lack of health insurance and inability to pay for health services is a huge problem. For many Americans, it has grim consequences, because uninsured people often put off necessary care until an illness or disease has escalated to either a difficult situation that is challenging to treat. Because of their lack of access, these patients typically seek treatment through the emergency department of a local hospital or institution as a last resort. As this trend continues (and is affected by the Emergency Medical Treatment and Active Labor Act [EMTALA]) and results in more patients who cannot fully pay for services or cannot pay at all, hospitals will face serious debt that must either be written off or funded by taxpayers. This reality of uncompensated care can have long-term negative effects for the health organization and its leadership.

Providers

Providers, sometimes referred to as practitioners, are key stakeholders in a health organization. Most people think of providers as the physicians and surgeons who treat the patients. In reality, nurses, physical and occupational therapists, technicians, and other clinical staff are also providers. They all play critical roles in the healthcare process.

There are two categories of providers: primary and secondary. Primary providers include hospitals, health departments, long-term care facilities, nursing facilities, health maintenance organizations (HMOs), ambulatory care institutions, and home healthcare institutions.[26] Secondary providers include educational institutes such as medical schools, organizations that pay for care, and pharmaceutical and drug supply companies. Essentially, providers are both the individuals and the organizations involved with providing health services and products.

The primary interest of providers is the best treatment for the patient; primary, secondary, and individual providers share this interest. Hospitals, health departments, and other participants in providing care also want to provide the best care for those in need of health services and products. Medical school interests are to educate students to their fullest potential so they may then care for and treat the sick. Pharmaceutical companies are working around the clock to develop new and improved medicines to improve patients' health and cure illnesses. All providers want to offer the best care possible, but that best care is not always available—thus the problem of access is an important consideration.

Cultural and Ethnic Impacts on Providers

At one time, treating a population was a fairly straightforward process. The U.S. population seeking care at hospitals was mainly white, and most doctors (and nurses) were white. Ethnic minorities sought treatment along ethnic lines and stayed among themselves. Less than 100 years after segregation in health treatment was the norm, the United States has evolved into a true melting pot in which "minorities" are projected to be the "majority" by 2050. Any person of color can now walk into any doctor's office and any hospital and expect the same treatment as his or her white counterpart.

But is that really true? The problem when it comes to people of color and today's health system is that there continues to be latent bias and disparity when it comes to health providers and their treatment of these patients. There is still a large difference in the treatment of people of color and ethnic minorities that goes beyond language; there is a cultural divide as well.

The Impact of Cost, Quality, and Access on Providers

Many factors affect providers regarding cost, quality, and access. When looking at the cost issue, providers are forced to balance the costs of care with the costs of maintaining the organization in a financially viable situation; from a systems perspective, if the cost of care exceeds the health organization's ability to survive, where will patients receive care if the health organization closes? There are several reasons for cost increases over time: Improved equipment costs more, improved practitioners with better skills cost more, and increased use of information technology costs more. In fact, information technology has been one of the largest factors contributing to the rising costs of health care.[27]

Access also has been affected by these trends. Because of the higher costs to provide care, higher out-of-pocket costs for patients, and staff shortages, access to health services has declined. Many rural and urban areas lack health providers and have been designated by government as health professions shortage areas (HPSAs) and/or medically underserved areas (MUAs). There is an ongoing shortage of health professionals such as nurses, medical technicians, and physicians working in certain specialties. Many hospitals, health organizations, and even medical schools have closed because of lack of funds or the inability to implement new technologies.[28] Moreover, the cost of malpractice insurance continues to increase, adding yet another cost into the system—one that providers pass along to the patients, payers, and employers.

With higher costs, it might be assumed that quality and access would also increase. Unfortunately, the relationship between these variables is quite the opposite. As Chaudhry and Harris point out, many of the technological improvements being implemented in health care are not affecting the overall quality of care. At the same time, there are continuous advances being made in the treatment and care of patients. Providers are implementing new surgical procedures and tools, such as minimally invasive procedures; new pharmaceuticals are being introduced daily; and new and improved ways of treating illnesses are constantly being updated. It is apparent that plenty of quality improvements are being made within health organizations, but at what cost?[29] With the increasing emphasis on quality of care, there are an increasing number of studies analyzing the hidden costs of low healthcare quality, such as patient dissatisfaction[30] and high readmission rates.

Employers

Employers, especially large employers, are the largest stakeholder group purchaser or payer of health services and products in today's complex world of health delivery. Employers are more often the conduit to a health plan that ultimately reimburses for the cost of care; this reality is based on health insurance as an employment benefit—an enticement to employment for potential employees. Employers tend to pay between 60% and 80% of insurance premiums; the employee pays the balance of the premium from his or her pay or salary. In this regard, the health leader needs to understand that health care is a prospective commodity that is paid for in advance. Reflecting this view, employers may focus on health care as a means of ensuring continued productivity in the workforce (keeping the workforce healthy, treating illness quickly to return workers to work) and emphasize the quality and timeliness of care; employers want to see a return on investment for the health insurance they pay for in prepaid premiums.

An example of employer constituent group efforts to improve and justify health outcomes to employer inputs (efficiency measure based on health outcomes [productivity of workforce] as compared to employer insurance premiums paid) is The Leapfrog Group. The Leapfrog Group serves as a forum for airing employer concerns. It also develops initiatives, such as those aimed at reducing adverse drug events, to improve the value of health services from the perspective of the employer. Similarly, both federal and state governments are large employers that attempt to improve their value proposition with regard to health services.

Employers face many challenges in today's business world. In the current era of complex managed care and potential national health care, organizational entities may find themselves between "a rock and a hard place" due to their inability to manage health costs at one extreme and their choice to give up healthcare benefits altogether at the other extreme.[31] Employers' healthcare costs are large and growing, with little hope of relief in sight. The overwhelming costs associated with employers' health benefits have prompted some employers to drop healthcare benefits for their employees. Many leaders of large organizations find it more cost effective to hire part-time employees who work fewer than 40 hours per week, thereby making them ineligible for benefits such as health insurance coverage, which is provided only to full-time workers. (A full-time worker, also known as a full-time equivalent [FTE], typically works approximately 2,080 hours per year, whereas a part-time worker works less than full time, usually 16 to 24 hours per week or 832 to 1,248 hours per year.) Currently, the proportion of the U.S. gross domestic product (GDP, the summed value of all goods and services produced in the United States in a year) attributed to health costs is approximately 16 to 17%, which means that 16 to 17% of the costs of all products and services made or delivered in the United States are attributable to healthcare costs. Considering that the world is rapidly merging into a global economy, can U.S. employers compete with a product or service made in another country that devotes only 8 or 10% of its GDP to health care?

Today, the majority of large health organizations do not support establishment of a national health plan. A recent survey of more than 450 health organizations found that almost 85% did not want a national health policy in place of the current system. This strong consensus indicates that there is a need to look at alternative options to assist employers with their health benefits. As Ted Nussbaum states, "Most large companies believe they have a fairly good understanding of how they should manage their health care and how it impacts their workforce."[32]

Employers' Perspective Concerning Cost, Quality, and Access

Employers' perspective on healthcare cost, quality, and access over the last two decades has been overshadowed by the increased costs of health in the United States. Employer-sponsored health insurance is the primary source of medical benefits for Americans who do not qualify for Medicare or other government-run programs. Employers provide health insurance benefits primarily to attract and retain employees. Nevertheless, faced with the rising costs of health services and products, many businesses, both small and large, have begun reconsidering their decisions to provide health insurance benefits. Employers have been faced with many uncertainties and modifications because of the increasing costs of providing health benefits to their employees. They have used many new strategies to decrease their costs such as cost shifting or cost sharing methods, consumer-directed health plans, high-deductible plans, and/or prevention or disease management plans.

Cost sharing and cost shifting have become widely accepted methods for attempting to reduce employer health costs. These initiatives ask employees to "share a higher portion of their health costs" by paying larger shares of the premium or assuming higher deductibles and/or copayments. The coinsurance initiative was introduced in the 1970s and 1980s as a method to reduce employer health costs; with this approach, employees are required to "pay a percentage of the actual cost of the healthcare services provided."[33]

Employers have also adopted consumer-directed health plans (CDHPs) to help reduce the rising costs of providing health services and products to their employees. CDHPs place more responsibility on employees and allow employees to "manage their health care spending and to make informed choices about the use of health care."[34] These plans usually come with high deductibles and consumer-controlled health savings accounts. Employers offer two primary types of health savings accounts: health savings accounts (HSAs) and health reimbursement accounts (HRAs). HSAs are employee-owned healthcare accounts that can be funded by employers and employees and used for qualified medical expenses. HRAs are employer-established and funded accounts that "provide non-taxed funds that employees can use for medical expenses."[35] Employers have turned to CDHPs as a means to facilitate cutting healthcare costs by asking employees to consider costs when making decisions about their health. Health leaders must understand and navigate these complex issues while building relationships with employer stakeholders.

Employers have also created prevention and disease management programs to assist with reducing the costs of providing health benefits to their employees. With these programs, employers focus on disease prevention and disease management as means to avoid onset or progression of disease, with the ultimate goal being to have better-managed diseases, resulting in less absenteeism and more productive employees. Employers have faced challenges when trying to implement these prevention and disease management programs, however, namely because of the lack of short-term cost cuts the programs offer and the generally low rates of employee utilization.[36]

Employers continually face challenges related to escalating costs as they seek the best way to provide quality health services and products to their employees. If they hope to flourish over the long term, employers also must attract and keep quality employees, who typically expect health coverage as a benefit of employment. Cost-effective benefit programs are crucial for employers to compete in the job market and obtain and retain beneficial employees. Thus, along with analyzing costs, employers must also keep in mind the quality of health benefits that their health plans provide.

Quality is an attribute that must be at the forefront for employers when making decisions about the type of health benefits to offer employees. Employers need to provide good, quality health services and product coverage to boost their probability of having healthy and productive employees. As discussed previously, many of the current trends in health design are aimed at increasing employees' power in managing their own health, a trend known as consumerism. At the same time, employers seek to provide employees with the education they need to obtain necessary, high-quality, cost-effective care and services and, in turn, become less likely to participate in treatments and services that are "unnecessary and ineffective from either a quality or cost perspective."[37]

Employers have been petitioning to have more price and quality transparency in health care so that employees can make more informed decisions. Employees currently have difficulty in identifying high-quality, efficient treatment centers because of the lack of information available about quality and price. Employers have begun promoting the use of agencies such as the National Data Cooperative and Quest Analytics to provide employees with information concerning quality and price of health services, thereby enabling patients to make informed, responsible decisions. Ideally, the widespread availability of quality and price information will assist employees with making prudent choices for their health decisions and, in turn, save employers money.[38]

Cost and quality are two very important elements for employers to consider when choosing health benefits, but access is also critical for successful health benefit programs. Employers must provide access to the most up-to-date medicine and medical advances to help their employees manage acute and chronic illnesses; this move is intended to ensure that their workforce is as healthy and as productive

as possible. One new concern related to recent medical advancements stems from the use of biotechnology medications, which may delay the onset of some conditions and are used to treat many high-cost diseases such as cancer. Employers have struggled with the dilemma of whether they should offer their employees access to these often exorbitantly expensive biotechnology medicines. Pitney Bowes, a large *Fortune* 500 company, found that improving employees' access to biotechnology medicines resulted in fewer acute cases, fewer hospitalizations, and less absenteeism. Therefore, it may be a profitable investment for employers to adjust their health benefits and allow employees access to biotechnology medicines and other medical advancements and technologies.[39]

Regarding access to health services and products, employers continue to search for methods of cost containment. Some have chosen not to provide any health benefits—that is, they provide no access at all. One increasingly popular way to cut back on employers' costs involves restricting or cutting health benefits for retired employees. Galvin and Delbanco report that "offering health coverage to retirees has less payback for employers," and employers can find "short-term and long-term cost savings" by taking away these benefits. Strategists suggest that this type of restriction may be just the first step for employers seeking an exit strategy. According to Galvin and Delbanco, many employers feel incapable of finding the answer to the challenge of decreasing the costs of providing health coverage to employees and believe that they would be better off getting out of the business of providing health benefits to all employees. Clearly, employers are faced with a tough challenge ahead of them in deciding whether to provide access to health services and products through employer-based insurance benefits and, if they choose to do so, in determining the most cost-effective and high-quality benefits that can be offered.[40]

PARITY OF HEALTH CARE

The Parity of Health Care is a unique model that juxtaposes two mutually exclusive models in an interrelated medium that allows leaders to forecast the impact of new policy decisions on the organization. As previously discussed, the Parity of Health Care model incorporates the MCQ and the Iron Triangle. Refer back to Figure 12-1 as this model is discussed here.

Perhaps the most significant issue the U.S. health system has grappled with since the inception of managed care, and the adoption of a public option healthcare plan under the Obama administration, is the balance between the business and financial priorities of care and stakeholder needs. These relationships can be conceptually viewed in the Parity of Health Care model. For example, the MCQ model helps to explain the complex interactions among employers, patients, providers, and payers in regard to partisan and competing views about health. Moreover, these health stakeholders have dissimilar views and preferences when overlaid with Kissick's Iron Triangle. The triangle comprises logistical factors of cost, quality, and access. Because each MCQ stakeholder may have different views associated with Kissick's cost, quality, and access options, the potential number of outcomes can be difficult to negotiate.

Table 12-1 demonstrates the complexity of this reality and assists in explaining why sustained consensus is difficult in developing health policy. For example, if one stakeholder (say, the payer) prioritizes cost–quality–access concerns as wanting the lowest out-of-pocket costs first, places receiving the highest quality of care possible during that low-cost visit second, and positions immediate access for that care third, it may have trouble finding a provider stakeholder with identical priorities. As Table 12-1 makes clear, stakeholders can be demanding; however, they rarely have all three priorities sequenced in a manner that will meet a competing stakeholder's priorities. As can be seen in Table 12-1, even a slight variation in the prioritization of Iron Triangle options results in myriad interrelated and intrarelated competing priorities that can be difficult for even the stakeholders to

resolve themselves, let alone in tandem with all of the other stakeholders along the continuum of care.

The challenge for health professionals regarding employers, patients, providers, and payers is to maintain high satisfaction with each stakeholder along the continuum of care in relation to aspects of cost, quality, and access. For example, a primary care clinic without extended and weekend office hours may be regarded as low quality by the patient and the employer, but high quality by the payers and by the providers who work in the clinic. However, if employers and patients continue to perceive lack of extended and weekend office hours as equivalent to low quality, dissatisfaction with the overall health plan may result. In a worst-case scenario, that factor might result in the termination of the health contract. Thus health professionals are in a constant struggle to maintain high satisfaction with all elements of the MCQ model.

As an example of the complexity of multiple-construct propositional phrases, consider the phrase "the right to bear arms." For more than 200 years, the greatest scholars and minds in the United States have debated on the true meaning of the founding fathers' objective in granting "the right to bear arms" to the American people. However, as we can see if we further deconstruct the propositional phrase "the right to bear arms," we can easily see that this phrase has three related propositional constructs applied to one unit of analysis. That one unit of analysis is "people," and because people have differing opinions of priorities, meanings, terminology, and

Table 12-1 Parity of Health Care Model: Competing Priorities of Stakeholders	
Payer	**Patient**
Cost–quality–access	Access–cost–quality
Access–cost–quality	Quality–access–cost
Quality–access–cost	Quality–cost–access
Quality–cost–access	Access–quality–cost
Access–quality–cost	Cost–access–quality
Cost–access–quality	Cost–quality–access
Employer	**Provider**
Access–quality–cost	Quality–cost–access
Cost–access–quality	Access–quality–cost
Cost–quality–access	Cost–access–quality
Access–cost–quality	Cost–quality–access
Quality–access–cost	Access–cost–quality
Quality–cost–access	Quality–access–cost

application, we can begin to see why the phrase "the right to bear arms" is so complex. By comparison, understanding and applying the Parity of the Health Care model is many more times as complex, due to the addition of four distinct units of analysis competing over three different logistical priorities. The factorial nature of competing priorities within this model results in more than 500 potential combinations of echelon rankings among all stakeholders—now that is complexity! Given this complexity associated with forecasting only one stakeholder's priorities over a sustained period of time, it becomes clear why it is so challenging for health leaders to accurately predict all future needs for all stakeholders.

THE SWORD OF DAMOCLES

For understanding the difficult nature of the relationships between the Iron Triangle and the managed care quaternion, we offer a metaphor from classical literature called the *Sword of Damocles*. In Greek mythology, the Sword of Damocles represents ever-present peril. It is also used as a metaphor to suggest a frailty in existing relationships. For example, in the Parity of Health Care model, the Sword of Damocles represents an inability of any one stakeholder to reach sustained consensus on the priorities assigned to healthcare cost, quality, and access.

With health priorities constantly changing due to environmental demands, it is no wonder why agreements on health policy are difficult to reach. However, an understanding of the Parity of Health Care model can be helpful to health leaders for strategically forecasting threats to relationships amid stakeholders, while also balancing priorities among those stakeholders. If anything is apparent, it is that continuous external and internal assessment and evaluation and relationship building among stakeholders are critical to leadership success.

Health planners must be cognizant that solutions developed to solve health problems in the current environment may not be valid solutions to the issues of tomorrow. As environmental demands continue to place pressures on the relationships within the Parity of Health Care, health leaders must renegotiate priorities. Health planners and leaders should be aware of this fact and view change as a new opportunity for success and not simply a problem of the dynamic environment. Always consider that the Sword of Damocles represents the frailty of established relationships among stakeholders and that constant maintenance and attention are required to ensure that these relationships remain healthy.

THE NEW CHIEF EXECUTIVE OFFICER

When considering the transformation of hospital systems shifting to the new organizational structures of an integrated health system, while focusing on ambulatory care facilities and financial risk of value-based payment, now is the time for the development of a new and different chief executive officer (CEO). The constant changes in the health industry illustrate the urgent requirement for healthcare executives to acquire new experiences and executive skills in order to lead their organizations successfully. The new healthcare CEO will need to have a full understanding of the continuum of care, whether it is from inpatient to physician offices, to ancillary services, to home health, nursing homes, and providing quality care at an acceptable cost.

The growing progress toward population health management and accountable care organizations appears to be one of the major factors for the high CEO turnover rates—20% for 2013 and averaging greater than 17% over the past 5 years. "The continuing trend of consolidation among organizations, the increasing demand on chief executives to lead in a complex and rapidly changing environment, and the retiring of leaders from the baby boomers era may all be contributing to this continuing higher level of change in the senior leadership of hospitals," says Deborah J. Bowen, President and CEO of the American College of Healthcare Executives.[41] She further states, "The findings also serve as a reminder for healthcare organizations to continue to ensure they have appropriate strategies in place, including robust succession planning to successfully manage senior leadership changes."[42]

Although experience and skills are necessary, healthcare leaders must incorporate enthusiasm for change and the possibilities of a transformed health system for improving patient's health. Suggested by Larkin, the characteristics and qualities for the new CEO to succeed in a complex healthcare industry may include the following:[43]

- *Skill—Change Champion*: Developing change management as a core executive competency is required, along with innovative thinking and critical thinking/strategic planning.
- *Skill—Data Driver*: The most significant change in the healthcare industry is that buyers and patients have hospital/physician performance data available to them for contracting and purchasing decisions. Understanding what the data mean in strategic contracting is considered a skill hospital CEOs lack. Health insurers and self-insured analyzers have access to analytics and models that indicate inefficient and inappropriate care. The new CEO must understand how to use these data to develop performance improvement and implement strategic decisions. Because of the major capital requested to deploy, as well as the clinical and administrative structures and practices impacted by the changes, the CEO must initiate this change.

- *Skill—Motivated Executive*: The new CEO must be motivated to do what is needed and necessary. Sometimes this means changing people, because a transformational leader cannot always build a new organizational structure by developing others within it. An organizational strategy should be developed focusing on what needs to be accomplished by a specific time and having the skills and motivation to do it.
- *Skill—Financially Focused*: Improving efficiency through productivity and effective financial management is a strategic priority. Declining Medicaid payments and the demands of the Affordable Care Act have placed many hospitals in an immediate financial bind. Value-based payment has created an important new level of complexity that requires the new CEO to think about efficiency across the entire spectrum of care. As with clinical leadership, the new CEO does not need to be a chief financial officer, but does need to have a strong understanding of how changing reimbursements and financing affect the system's ability to transform into an integrated network. Certainly, reimbursement has strategic and operational issues that must have the new CEO's full attention.
- *Skill—Matrix Managers*: Because of the development of large, regional, and national health systems, the new CEO must be able to function in an environment of collaborative decision making with peers, in addition to reporting relationships to system experts in such areas as clinical quality, finance, supply chain, and operation. The new CEO operating within larger systems needs to recognize that the boundaries in which they operate can vary greatly. Some systems give local CEOs broad

goals to achieve. However, most health systems are creating a matrix management structure where multiple disciplines within the system work together to accomplish complex prospects. The health systems may have executive roles at the national, regional, or market levels. The regional health system CEO is responsible for building the entire continuum of care, including hospitals, outpatient services, and physician networks. This person usually reports to the national CEO. The market CEO is responsible for a hospital's operation to increase the effectiveness of care delivery and population health management, as well as for representing the system in the local community. They all report to the regional CEO.

- *Skill—Agile Learner*: Learning agility may be considered the leading predictor of success in the new CEO leadership role. This is the ability to assess a situation quickly and adapt with responses that did not previously exist. The skill is especially important for dealing with technology, which is an ever-changing factor in the healthcare industry. CEOs with experience in new system start-ups or organizational turnarounds are attractive candidates to health systems looking for new leaders.
- *Skill—Strategic Visionary*: Critical thinking and strategic planning are the top skills needed by the new CEO to lead the new health system of the future. The new CEO must be able to articulate a vision of a better organization and to inspire others to accept and work toward accomplishing it. The task of the new CEO will be the integration of different healthcare structures of care into a seamless system for patient medical needs.

SUMMARY

Organizations and organizational leaders cannot be successful if they do not understand the wide-ranging impact of stakeholder influence. All too often in health policy making and strategy analysis organizations become overly concerned with isolating themselves (i.e., the organization) as the principal actor around which all other factors revolve. Such was the case with Enron and WorldCom, which viewed customers, allies, employees, and investors as tertiary catalysts and insignificant stakeholders in the quest for growth and wealth. Health organizations are no different, regardless of whether they have for-profit or not-for-profit status (IRS 501(c)(3) status). Stakeholder dynamics

are critically important for organizational survival and success. To be successful in the competitive economy of the twenty-first century, health leaders must be cognizant of stakeholder dynamics and appreciate how the principal actors and components of each interrelate and influence one another. Health leader success will be in large part determined by developing and maintaining relationships with stakeholders and by aligning the health organization based on external and internal assessment and evaluation. In addition, an overview of the "new CEO" paradigm was provided within the context of executive roles of leadership in health organizations.

DISCUSSION QUESTIONS

1. What steps, characteristics, and behaviors should a health leader employ to build relationships with internal, "interface," and external stakeholders?

2. What is the Parity of Health Care model? Explain its usefulness to health leaders. Select a health organization stakeholder and predict at least two motivations of that stakeholder considering cost, quality, and access to health services and products. Are the stakeholder's issues justified?

3. Which issues arise when you compare and contrast the motivations and issues of at least two internal health organization stakeholders? How does a health leader empathize with those stakeholders to build a relationship?

4. Using previously discussed theories and models, which two or more theories or models would you use to construct a practical stakeholder management and relationship development model? Which constructs make those theories or models useful in stakeholder management?

5. Which theory or model would you use to evaluate internal and external health organization stakeholders? How do those theories or models justify stakeholder motivations, needs, and aspirations with regard to health services and products?

6. Why was the Parity of Health model developed? What utility, advantages, and strengths does it offer for forecasting stakeholder dynamics in health care?

EXERCISES

1. In a one- to two-page paper, identify the steps, characteristics, and behaviors a health leader should employ to build relationships with internal, "interface," and external stakeholders.

2. In a one-page paper, explain the Parity of Health Care model and describe its usefulness to health leaders.

3. Construct a health organization stakeholder list. In a two-page paper, predict at least two motivations of each stakeholder, considering cost, quality, and access to health services and products.

4. In a one- to two-page paper, compare and contrast the motivations and issues of internal health organization stakeholders.

5. In a three-page paper, combine two or more theories or models into a practical stakeholder management and relationship development model.

6. In a two-page paper, evaluate an internal health organization stakeholder and an external health organization stakeholder, and justify their motivations, needs, and aspirations with regard to health services and products.

REFERENCES

1. Anonson, J., Walker, M. E., Arries, E., Maposa, S., Telford, P., & Berry, L. (2014). Qualities of exemplary nurse leaders: Perspectives of frontline nurses. *Journal of Nursing Management, 22*(1), 127–136. Retrieved from http://onlinelibrary.wiley.com/doi/10.1111/jonm.12092/full.

2. Griffith, J. R., & White, K. R. (2007). *The well-managed healthcare organization* (6th ed.). Chicago: Health Administration Press.

3. Young, A. E., Wasiak, R., Roessler, R. T., McPherson, K. M., Anema, J. R., & van Poppel, M. N. M. (2005). Return-to-work outcomes following work disability: Stakeholder motivation, interests and concerns. *Journal of Occupational Rehabilitation, 15*(4), 543–556.

4. Franche, R. L., Baril, R., Shaw, W., Nicholas, M., & Loisel, P. (2005). Workplace-based return-to-work interventions: Optimizing the role of stakeholders in implementation and research. *Journal of Occupational Rehabilitation, 15*(4), 525–542.

5. Blair, J. D., & Fottler, M. D. (1998). *Strategic leadership for medical groups: Navigating your strategic web.* San Francisco: Jossey-Bass.

6. Griffith & White, note 2.

7. Blair & Fottler, note 5.

8. Niles, N. J. (2015). *Basics of the U.S. health care system* (2nd ed.). Burlington, MA: Jones & Bartlett Learning, pp. 53–100. Retrieved from http://books.google.com/books?hl=en&lr=&id=A0UoAwAAQBAJ&oi=fnd&pg=PR1&dq=US+healthcare+stakeholders&ots=A4htTIN7pV&sig=r3i0fmI5NDOwMFhKidEnIm4fkYA#v=onepage&q=US%20healthcare%20stakeholders&f=false.

9. Niles, note 8.

10. Coppola, M. N., Erckenbrack, D., & Ledlow, G. R. (2008). Stakeholder dynamics. In J. A. Johnson (Ed.), *Health organizations: Theory, behavior, and development* (pp. 255–275). Sudbury, MA: Jones & Bartlett.

11. Coppola, M. N., Harrison, J., Kerr, B., & Erckenbrack, D. (2007). The military managed care health system. In P. R. Kongstvedt (Ed.), *Essentials of managed care* (5th ed., pp. 633–655). Sudbury, MA: Jones & Bartlett.

12. Kissick, W. L. (1994). The past is prologue. In *Medicine's dilemmas: Infinite needs versus finite resources* (pp. 75–86). New Haven, CT: Yale University Press.

13. Griffith & White, note 2.

14. Antos, J. (2007, April 10). Saving Medicare from a fiscal breakdown. Retrieved from http://www.realclearpolitics.com/-articles/2007/04/saving_medicare_from_a_fiscal.html.

15. Antos, note 14.

16. Smeltzer, S. C., & Bare, B. G. (2004). *Medical surgical nursing* (10th ed.). Philadelphia: Lippincott.

17. Coppola et al., note 10.

18. Smeltzer & Bare, note 16.

19. Smeltzer & Bare, note 16.

20. Collinson, D., Bryman, A., Collinson, D., Grint, K., & Jackson, B. (2011). Critical leadership studies. In D. Collinson (Ed.), *The Sage handbook of leadership* (pp. 179–192). London: Sage.

21. Press, I. (2006). *Patient satisfaction: Understanding and managing the experience of care* (2nd ed.). Chicago: Health Administration Press.

22. Press, note 21.

23. Institute of Medicine. (2006, July 20). Crossing the quality chasm: The IOM health care initiative. Retrieved from http://www.iom.edu/˜/media/Files/Report%20Files/2001/Crossing-the-Quality-Chasm/Quality%20Chasm%202001%20%20report%20brief.pdf.

24. Rust, G., Ye, J., Baltrus, P., Daniels, E., Adesunloye, B., & Fryer, G. E. (2008). Practical barriers to timely primary care access: Impact on adult use of emergency department services. *Archives of Internal Medicine, 168*(15), 1705–1710.

25. Fairhurst, G., Bryman, A., Collinson, D., Grint, K., & Jackson, B. (2011). Discursive approaches to leadership. In D. Collinson (Ed.), *The Sage handbook of leadership* (pp. 495–507). London: Sage.

26. Bodenheimer, T. (2005). High and rising health care costs. Part 3: The role of health care providers. *Annals of Internal Medicine, 142*, 996–1002.

27. Chaudhry, B., Wang, J., Wu, S., Maglione, M., Mojica, W., Roth, E., et al. (2006). Systematic review: Impact of health information technology on quality, efficiency, and costs of medical care. *Annals of Internal Medicine, 144*, E12–E22.

28. Harris, K. M. (2002). Can high quality overcome consumer resistance to restricted provider access? Evidence from a health plan choice experiment. *Health Services Research, 37*(3), 551–571.

29. Rosenthal, M. B., Fernandopulle, R., Song, H. R., & Landon, B. (2004). Paying for quality: Providers' incentives for quality improvements. *Health Affairs, 23*(2), 127–141.

30. Gao, N.-N., & Zhang, Y. (2016). Healthcare service hidden quality cost estimation based on the SERVQUAL and QFD method. In E. Qi, J. Shen, & R Dou (Eds.), *Proceedings of the 22nd International Conference on Industrial Engineering and Engineering Management 2015* (pp. 417–426). Atlantis Press. Retrieved from http://link.springer.com/chapter/10.2991/978-94-6239-180-2_41.

31. Galvin, R., & Delbanco, S. (2006). Between a rock and a hard place: Understanding the employer mind-set. *Health Affairs, 25*(6), 1548–1555.

32. Bruno, M. (2008, April 23). Employers almost universally against universal healthcare. Retrieved from http://financialweek.com/apps/pbcs.dll/article?AID=/20080423/REG/210997508/1008/HUMANRESOURCES.

33. Hodge, B., & Martin, M. (2008). Benefit design critical to protecting out-of-pocket costs for employees. *American Journal of Managed Care, 14*(8), S246–S251.

34. Ford, J., & Harding, N. (2011). The impossibility of the true self of authentic leadership. *Leadership, 7*(4), 463–479.

35. Claxton, G. (2006). Consumer-directed health plans: Health Care Marketplace Project. Retrieved from http://www.kaiseredu.org/tutorials/CDHP/Consumer-Directed.ppt#291,1,Consumer-Directed Health Plans.

36. Claxton, note 35.

37. DiCenzo, J., & Fronstin, P. (2008). Lessons from the evolution of 401(k) retirement plans for increased consumerism in health care: An application of behavioral research. *Employee Benefit Research Institute Issue Brief, 320*(1), 3–26.

38. Griffith, J. R., & White, K. R. (2006). *The well-managed healthcare organization* (6th ed., pp. 415–465). Chicago, IL: Health Administration Press.

39. Horn, D., Mahoney, J., Wells, K., & Lednar, W. (2008). Leading employers share strategies for managing promising, high-cost biotech medications. *American Journal of Managed Care*, *14*(8), S264–S268.

40. Gardner, W., Cogliser, C., Davis, K., & Dickens, M. (2011). Authentic leadership: A critical review of the literature and research agenda. *Leadership Quarterly*, *22*(6), 1120–1145.

41. Bowen, D. J. (2014). American College of Healthcare Executives, Annual Congress, March 2014.

42. Bowen, note 41.

43. Larkin, H. (2015). What it takes to be the new CEO. *Trustee*. Retrieved from http://www.trusteemag.com /articles/947?dcrPath=/templatedata/HF_Common /NewsArticle/data/TRU/Magazine/2015/October /cover-new-health-care-CEO.

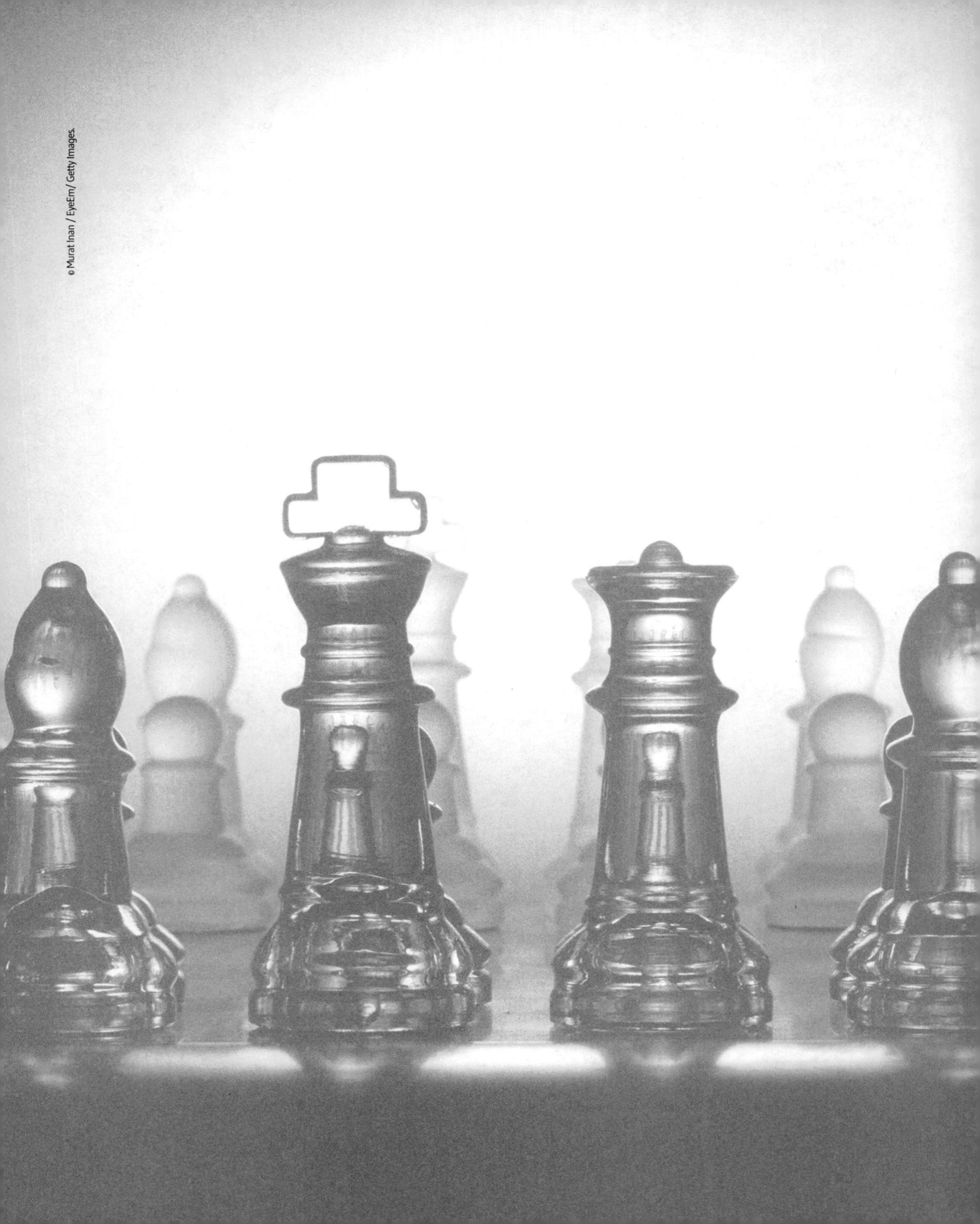

PART 4

LEADING PEOPLE AND MANAGING RESOURCES INTO THE FUTURE

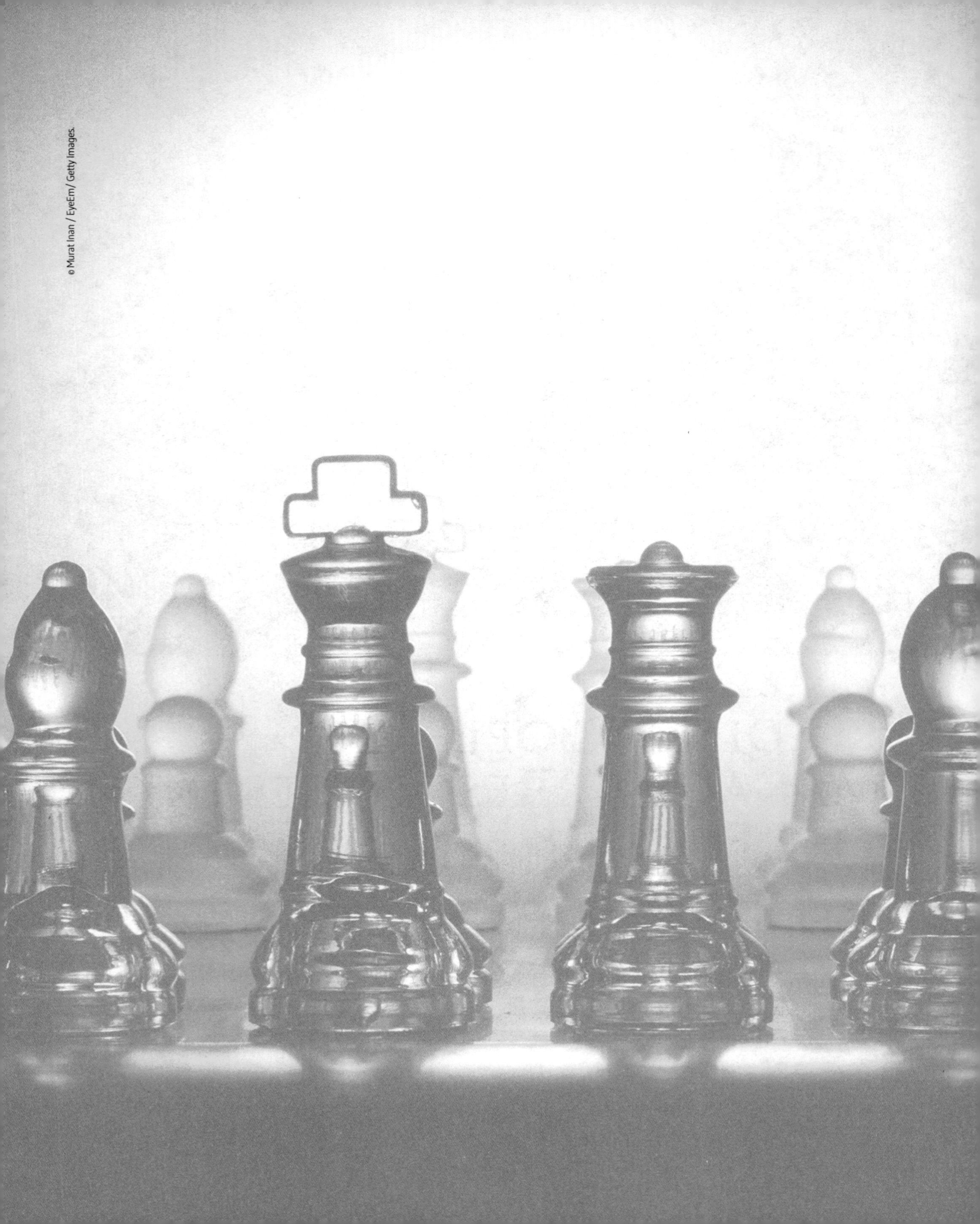

CHAPTER 13

COMPLEXITY, SPEED, AND CHANGE: LEADERSHIP CHALLENGES FOR THE NEXT DECADE

Great necessity elevates man; petty necessity casts him down.
Goethe, *Wisdom and Experience*

This chapter discusses the globalization of leadership, taking into account that many leadership theories and practices presented in many texts are based on Western ideologies. The need to leverage technology, lead through followership, and understand the basics of influence and power are addressed with respect to climate, culture change, and environment, along with suggested strategies for utilization by the health leader.

What kind of leader do you want to become and be? Leaders have an obligation to stay current and relevant in the field of leadership practice. This chapter presents issues and strategies to help leaders maintain their relevancy and credibility in the organization. In addition, the humble leader can admit to not knowing everything that occurs in a health organization; this chapter emphasizes that it is okay to say, "I don't know," when leading complex health entities.

LEARNING OBJECTIVES

1. Describe and outline issues related to globalization, power, followership, and culture change from a health leader's perspective.

2. Give examples of tools that a health leader can use to change and adapt culture in the health organization.

3. Relate global leadership style differences and similarities using appropriate constructs to transformational leadership practices.

4. Analyze a health leader's use of power as it relates to followership, culture change, and knowledge management.

5. Categorize global leadership differences according to a leader's use of power, technology, and knowledge management.

6. Evaluate approaches to knowledge management, organizational learning, and transformational leadership with health organization culture change.

CULTURAL DIFFERENCES IN LEADERSHIP

As globalization increases, health leaders need to be culturally aware, understanding, and capable of leading people from diverse backgrounds, diverse educational portfolios, and diverse outlooks. In today's global economy, it is commonplace for subordinates, peers, and superiors to be from different geographic, national, and cultural backgrounds. Likewise, patients, customers, and their families are becoming more diverse. This trend requires a culturally competent and adaptive perspective for both the health leader and the health organizational culture that the leader maintains. It adds complexity to the health leader's landscape from both internal and external environmental perspectives. In turn, this complexity lends credence to demands for a dynamic culture leadership mentality and process to create a robust organizational culture amid an environment of change—the speed of change is also increasing.

With regard to the importance of this chapter of the text, Dr. Ledlow states: "Cultural competence is inherently tied to the reservoir of social capital of the leader; social capital (that is, the goodwill the leader possesses within the organization of followers, peers, and superiors to be a facilitator for activities or results) is closely related, if not a catalyst, to improvements, change, and performance in the organization. This reality modifies, either toward success or toward failure, the health leader's ability and future potential in the organization."

Globalization causes concern when discussing differing perceptions across cultures:[1]

- Individualist (self-oriented) and collectivist (team oriented) cultures will have significantly different perceptions of work and performance.
- Power distance (higher power means more physical space): High-power cultures tend to be authoritarian, whereas power is more equally distributed in low-power cultures.
- Uncertainty avoidance (risk taking and plan implementation without all information and organizational coupling) is thick with rules and guidelines.
- Gender equality: Assertive, material, and competitive cultures tend to be masculine, whereas collaborative, harmonious, and nurturing cultures take on a feminine persona.
- High-context communication cultures transfer meaning with more emphasis on the situation, whereas low-context communication cultures emphasize the sender's responsibility to transfer communication meaning more than the situation.[2]

Situational leadership applications fit nicely in the paradigm of a culturally competent leader considering the complexity of globalization. Leadership expectations differ depending on the culture, society, nation, or ethnic group to which leaders belong (and reside and practice). It is difficult to find much in the literature on leadership outside the Western perspective, for example. The Western perspective in the literature is predominately based on research conducted in the United States, the

United Kingdom, Australia, or Europe. "To date [as of 2004] more than 90% of the organizational behavior [including leadership] literature reflects U.S.-based research and theory."[3]

In an attempt to bridge Western and Eastern thought on leadership, the new paradigm of "thinkers" in an interconnected world has evolved. Health leaders who are successful have many of the characteristics encompassed by this new paradigm:

- Thinking in open systems in contrast with fixed, ideal states
- Integration of multicultural characteristics into decision making
- Viewing things globally (acting locally)
- Global distribution
- Use of technology to scan the environment
- A full toolbox and knowledge of how to use all of the tools
- Personal characteristics of resourcefulness, fearlessness, toughness, competence, humor, and playfulness[4]

With this introduction, the most recent worldwide study on leadership, the GLOBE Study, is presented.

GLOBE LEADERSHIP STUDY[5,6]

The most comprehensive global assessment of leadership styles, propensities, and expectations is an ongoing project called the GLOBE Study; to date, 170 researchers from 62 cultures have worked on this project.[7] Many of the GLOBE Study cultural constructs were derived from the previous work of Hofstede.[8] The following constructs used in the study pertain to cultural variation:

- Performance orientation (How aggressive is task accomplishment?)
- Assertiveness (How forceful and firm is the leader?)
- Future orientation (Is tomorrow more important than yesterday or today?)
- Humane orientation (People oriented, compassionate, and empathetic?)
- Institutional collectivism (Is the total organization a "team"?)
- In-group collectivism (Is there a small-group orientation?)
- Gender egalitarianism (Are males and females equal in respect, reward, and punishment?)
- Power distance (How much physical space is normal based on the leader's or person's perceived power?)
- Uncertainty avoidance (How risk averse is the leader? Does implementation of a plan or task proceed without all information? How intuitive is the leader?)[9]

In the study, each construct embodied a set of variables pertinent to the construct. Findings were based on each construct. Although a summary and highlights are presented in this chapter, it is recommended that health leaders read and study the findings of the entire GLOBE Study;[10] the research can be found at the webpage cited in the references.

The cultural dimension termed *performance orientation* emerged from the research as exceptionally important. It "reflects the extent to which a community encourages and rewards innovation, high standards, excellence, and performance improvement."[11] High performance orientation societies value the following:

- Training
- Competitiveness and materialism
- Direct communication and formal feedback

High performance orientation societies place emphasis on what a person does rather than who that person is. In contrast, low performance orientation societies emphasize who a person is rather than what that person does, and in general these societies favor the following:

- Societal and family relationships
- Environmental harmony
- Indirect communication and informal feedback

The cultural dimension termed *uncertainty avoidance* also emerged from the research as very important; it is "the extent to which a society, organization, or group relies on social norms, rules, and procedures to alleviate the unpredictability of future events."[12] "An alternative way of thinking about uncertainty avoidance is that it's about the extent to which ambiguous situations are felt as threatening (about the extent to which deliberate measures such as making and enforcing rules and procedures are taken to reduce ambiguity)."[13] Societies that avoid high uncertainty feature the following characteristics:

- Resist change
- Depend on clear policies and procedures
- Take only deliberate risks
- Are orderly and keep meticulous records
- Emphasize formality in interactions

In contrast, societies with low uncertainty avoidance behave in the following ways:

- Display only moderate resistance to change
- Utilize informal norms in most situations
- Take risks with less premeditation
- Are less orderly and maintain fewer records
- Allow greater informality in interactions

As for leadership styles, 21 constructs, each having a set of variables that were measured, were found valid in

Table 13-1 The Six Global Leadership Groupings/Styles and Associated Constructs in the GLOBE Study[15]	
Charismatic/value based	Team oriented
Participative	Humane oriented
Self-protective	Autonomous

Adapted from House, R. J., Hanges, P. J., Javidan, M., Dorfman, P. W., & Gupta, V. (Eds.). (2004). *Culture, leadership and organizations: The GLOBE Study of 62 societies.* Thousand Oaks, CA: Sage, p. 676, Table 21.1; and Grovewell, LLC. Retrieved June 6, 2009, from http://www.grovewell.com/pub-GLOBE-dimensions.html. Reprinted with permission.

interpreting leadership style and performance across all 62 societies, which were clustered in 10 societal groups. Leadership styles were categorized and measured by 6 groupings of the 21 constructs:

- Charismatic/value based
- Team oriented
- Participative
- Autonomous
- Humane
- Self-protective[14]

From the associated constructs or traits (**Table 13–1**), each leadership grouping or style can be "defined" for the purpose of making comparisons between the styles. There is considerable overlap in some of the styles. Can you develop a continuum of preferred/desirable to less preferred/undesirable leadership styles based on the constructs?

Much of the analysis in the book [and webpage] is focused on explaining how the nine cultural dimensions (e.g., "performance orientation," "assertiveness," and seven others) as independent variables relate to the six culturally endorsed leadership theory dimensions (e.g., "charismatic/value based," "team oriented," and four others) as dependent variables across the 10 societal clusters.[16]

A summary of each style used in the GLOBE Study is provided in **Table 13–2**; the cultural constructs are listed in priority for each style as either positively related (+) or negatively related (−). Can you relate this aspect of the GLOBE Study to other leadership behavior–based studies, such as the Michigan or Ohio State leadership studies? Which other leadership theories or models can be integrated with the GLOBE Study? How do the constructs or traits that define or describe each leadership style in Table 13-1 connect to the cultural constructs?

Table 13-2 GLOBE Study Cultural Constructs Associated with Leadership Style	Charismatic/ Value Based	Team Oriented	Participative	Humane Oriented	Autonomous	Self-Protective
Performance orientation	+	+	+	+	+	−
Uncertainty avoidance		+	−	+		+
Humane orientation	+	+	+	+	−	
Power distance	−		−			+
In-group collectivism	+	+				−
Gender egalitarianism	+		+			−
Assertiveness			−	+		
Future orientation	+	+		+		
Institutional collectivism					−	

Key:
+ = Positively associated with leadership style; − = Negatively associated with leadership style

Adapted from House, R. J., Hanges, P. J., Javidan, M., Dorfman, P. W., & Gupta, V. (Eds.). (2004). *Culture, leadership and organizations: The GLOBE Study of 62 societies.* Thousand Oaks, CA: Sage, pp. 47–48.

This charismatic/value-based style, which is employed by leaders who are inspiring, visionary, self-sacrificing, and performance oriented, was universally considered the most desirable style.[17] The team-oriented leadership style and the participative leadership style were nearly universally desirable as styles, albeit not in all societal clusters.[18] Autonomous and humane-oriented (modest and compassionate) leadership styles were neither desirable nor undesirable in most societal cultures and clusters.[19] The self-protective leadership style (self-centered, status conscious, and conflict inducer) was undesirable.[20] "Attributes that facilitate, such as decisiveness, and inhibit, such as irritability, outstanding leadership"[21] were consistent across the study.

Highlights of the GLOBE Study by societal groups show the diversity in leadership style preferences, expectations, and societal norms. Ten societal clusters were identified in the study, but some of these clusters will be combined for purposes of their review in this chapter.

CULTURAL COMPETENCE

There is a strong connection among leadership, organizational culture, and organizational success. As we discussed earlier, competencies for health leaders are of utmost importance. Given opportunities for education and development, certain competencies will be strengthened whereas others will be focused on less. These competencies will greatly mold the role each healthcare administrator fills within his or her organization. Paramount to understanding these concepts is, first, to be aware of cultural competence. Cultural competency in healthcare administration is critical to achieving better health outcomes for the multicultural and vulnerable populations being served. Creating a culture of leadership throughout the organization goes hand in hand with developing values, norms, and practices that exemplify leadership and forward thinking, in line with the organization's mission and goals.

Recently, cultural competence has gained attention from healthcare policy makers, providers, insurers, and educators as a strategy to improve quality and eliminate racial/ethnic disparities in health care. The goal of cultural competence, however, is to create a healthcare system and workforce that are capable of delivering the highest-quality care to every patient regardless of race, ethnicity, culture, or language proficiency. Cultural competence has emerged as an important issue for three practical reasons. First, as the United States becomes more diverse, clinicians will increasingly see patients with a broad range of perspectives regarding health, often influenced by their social or cultural backgrounds. For instance, patients may present their symptoms quite differently from the way they are presented in medical textbooks. They may have limited English proficiency, different thresholds for seeking care or expectations about their care, and unfamiliar beliefs that influence whether they adhere to providers' recommendations. Second, research has shown that provider–patient communication is linked to patient satisfaction, adherence to medical instructions, and health outcomes. Thus, poorer health outcomes may result when sociocultural differences between patients and providers are not reconciled in the clinical encounter. Third, cultural competence is a tangible expression of "concern for people," or empathy for others, and assists in building relationships. Ultimately, these barriers apply not only to minority groups but may simply be more pronounced in all areas of health care.[22,23]

WESTERN PERSPECTIVE[24]

The Western perspective of leadership styles, for this summary, includes Germanic Europe, Anglo, and Nordic Europe clusters. For these Western clusters, charismatic/value-based leadership was the most preferred and desirable leadership style, followed by the team-oriented leadership style. Very close in preference to the team-oriented style was the participative leadership style. Significantly less preferred and less desirable was the human-oriented leadership style. The autonomous and self-protective leadership styles were not preferred and not desired for this perspective. Thus, in priority of preference, the Western perspective favored the charismatic/value-based style, team-oriented style, and participative style of leadership. The humane-oriented style was preferred or desired to only a minor degree, whereas the autonomous and self-protected styles were not preferred or desired.

Translating the Western perspective into modern leadership theories and models, transformational leadership, the omnibus leadership model, and the dynamic culture leadership model are readily integrated into this perspective. In balancing leadership emphasis among performance (mission accomplishment) and concern for people, having a team orientation, looking toward the future (vision achievement), and understanding a dynamic environment, there is considerable congruence between these models and the Western perspective of leadership style preference. Are there other leadership theories, models, principles, or competencies that integrate well with, or support, this perspective?

ASIAN PERSPECTIVE[25]

The Asian perspective of leadership styles includes the Confucian Asia (China, close neighbors of China, Japan, and close neighbors of Japan) and Southern Asia (from Afghanistan to Vietnam, including the southern belt of Asian countries) clusters. For these Asian clusters, charismatic/value-based leadership was the most preferred and desirable leadership style, followed by the team-oriented leadership style. Next in preference to the team-oriented style was the humane-oriented leadership style. Significantly less preferred and less desirable was the participative leadership style. The autonomous and self-protective leadership styles were not preferred and not desired for this perspective, yet were more readily tolerated than in the Western perspective. Thus, in priority of preference, the Asian perspective favored the charismatic/value-based style, team-oriented style, and humane-oriented style of leadership. The participative style was preferred or desired to only a moderate degree. The autonomous and self-protected styles were not preferred or desired, but were more readily tolerated by the Asian perspective than by the Western perspective.

Modern leadership theories and models salient for the Asian perspective could include transformational leadership, the "reframing organizational leadership" model, the omnibus leadership model, the dynamic culture leadership model, and an older theory, Theory Y (from behavioral leadership models). Can you match and integrate these contemporary leadership theories and models to the Asian perspective based on the GLOBE Study findings?

MIDDLE EASTERN PERSPECTIVE[26]

For the Middle Eastern perspective of preferred leadership styles, the cluster includes the land mass from southern Turkey to Iran to northwest Africa to the Mediterranean Sea. In this societal cluster, team-oriented leadership, followed by charismatic/value-based leadership, was the most preferred style. Participative and humane-oriented leadership styles were moderately preferred, whereas self-protective and autonomous leadership styles were least preferred. Tolerance for the self-protective leadership style mimicked the Asian perspective, whereas autonomous leadership was the least desired leadership style.

Modern leadership theories and models that integrate well with the Middle Eastern perspective would include the dynamic culture leadership model, transformational leadership, and the omnibus leadership model. Can you match and integrate these contemporary leadership theories and models to the Middle Eastern perspective based on the GLOBE Study findings?

LATIN PERSPECTIVE[27]

In terms of the Latin perspective of preferred leadership styles, the cluster includes Latin America and Latin Europe

(southern Europe bordering the Mediterranean Sea). In this group, charismatic/value-based leadership was the most preferred and desirable leadership style, followed by the team-oriented leadership style. Next in preference to the team-oriented style was the participative leadership style. Significantly less preferred and less desirable was the human-oriented leadership style. The autonomous and self-protective leadership styles were not preferred and not desired for this perspective. The Latin and Western perspectives are very similar based on the results of this study.

Which leadership theories and models can you relate to the Latin leadership perspective? Can you list the characteristics of the theories and models in terms of the preferred leadership styles of the Latin societal cluster?

AFRICAN PERSPECTIVE[28]

The African perspective covers sub-Saharan Africa. It is similar to the Western and Latin perspectives, although the humane-oriented leadership style was more preferred in African cultures than in Western or Latin cultures. Charismatic/value-based leadership was the most preferred and desirable leadership style, followed by the team-oriented leadership style. Next in preference to the team-oriented style was the participative leadership style. Slightly less preferred and less desirable was the human-oriented leadership style. The autonomous and self-protective leadership styles were not preferred and not desired for this perspective.

EASTERN EUROPEAN PERSPECTIVE[29]

The Eastern European perspective includes eastern Germany (former East Germany) to Russia and south to the Balkans (in essence, countries in the former Eastern European Bloc or Communist Bloc). This perspective is similar to the Middle Eastern perspective, where team-oriented leadership, followed by charismatic/value-based leadership, was the most preferred style. Participative and humane-oriented leadership styles were moderately preferred, whereas the self-protective leadership style was least preferred. Tolerance for the autonomous leadership style was the greatest in the Eastern European perspective compared with all other societal groups; this style was not preferred but would be considered a more neutral style.

GLOBE SUMMARY

The major theme that health leaders need to understand, apply, and synthesize from the international research on leadership is that charisma, values, team orientation, and performance matter. Health leaders should focus on accomplishing the mission, striving for the vision of the organization, leading people and managing resources, and mastering and applying sound practices of leadership (leadership competencies); these demands are vitally important for leaders across the globe.

This section reviews the constructs or traits that are highly prized and accepted across the world. Culturally sensitive health leaders should strive to have the following characteristics:

- Charismatic and visionary
- Charismatic and inspirational
- Charismatic and self-sacrificing
- Consistently able to lead with integrity
- Decisive
- Performance oriented
- Team collaborative
- Team integrative
- Diplomatic
- Benevolent
- Administratively competent

As a health leader, it is inevitable that you will lead and work with people from different countries, from different societies, and from different backgrounds. To demonstrate cultural competence, respect and understanding of different ways of doing things, different expectations, and different perspectives is essential. The leadership challenge is to integrate these differences into the group and organization while focusing on the mission (performance orientation), striving for the vision (future orientation), communicating well (visionary and integrating people into the mission and vision), leading people well and genuinely (charisma and humane orientation), managing resources effectively (administrative competence), building teams (team orientation), and being diplomatic, yet decisive.

The health leader needs to accomplish these tasks—a big set of tasks—within a solid moral framework built on truth, honesty, and integrity. Without morality, integrity, and honesty, regardless of cultural perspective, the leader's work is meaningless. In simple terms, the health leader must develop and maintain an organizational culture that fulfills the mission and vision while incorporating the vast diversity and complexity that the world holds within a sound ethical framework. The health leader must accomplish this feat in an environment of dynamic change while meeting and exceeding the professional standards of care and health administration.

LEVERAGING TECHNOLOGY

Leveraging technology in a health organization, like the practice of leadership itself, creates competitive advantage, that is, providing more effectiveness, efficiency, and efficacy, in the practice of medicine, in the clinical environment of care, in patient outcomes, and in the administration of the enterprise. In the health context, technology is anything that is utilized in the practice of medicine, in patient care processes, and in the leading of people and management of resources. Examples of technology, in an attempt to cover the enormity of the term, include chairs, computers, harmonic scalpels, MRIs, patient beds, knowledge of and the process of budgeting, computer software, a forklift, an intercom system, pagers, cell phones, knowledge of and the process of diagnosing disease, and utilization of media richness theory for improved communication. Technology is encompassed in the following definitions: the practical application of knowledge, especially in a particular area; a manner of accomplishing a task, especially using technical processes, methods, or knowledge; and a capability given by the practical application of knowledge.[30]

Technology, especially networked computer technology, can be leveraged by the health leader and the leadership team to facilitate communication to better lead people; to scan and monitor the efficiency, effectiveness, and efficacy of the organization; and to manage resources. True individual health leader technology leverage comes when the leader can allocate more time to interpersonal relationship building, both internal and external to the organization; exercise "leadership by purposefully walking" around and talking to subordinates, peers, and superiors; and establish a balance in the leader's religious, professional, social, and personal life.

Technology is constantly evolving, increasing the complexity and speed of change. "The nature of the work or technology is changing and subordinates need to learn new skills and procedures."[31] Yukl and Fiedler consider technology to be an important situational variable in their respective leadership models, the multiple linkage model[32] and the contingency leadership model.[33] Likewise, technology is a critical situational variable—one that affects ambiguity—in the garbage can model of decision making.[34] Schein identifies technology as an element in the category of artifact and creation of culture (a level 1 element).[35]

Health leaders should be cognizant of putting sound clinical and business practices into place, focusing on both the human and technological elements, to leverage technology most effectively.

Exercising leadership requires distinguishing between leadership and authority and between technical and adaptive/operational work. Clarifying these two distinctions enables us to understand why so many people in top authority positions fail to lead: they commit the classic error of treating adaptive challenges as if they were technical problems.[36]

Simply put, fixing a problem by changing or increasing the technology most likely will not work, but rather will further confound the problem. Human adaption to quality clinical and business processes, linked to organizational culture, needs to be effective, efficient, and efficacious so that technology can be leveraged to complement and merge as seamlessly as possible with the people the health leader leads.

> Health organization structure and control systems can no longer be depicted as tools that mechanically determine subordinates' and team members' behaviors. Health leaders must shift their thinking about organizations away from the organization as an entity, to subordinates' choice and understanding.[37]

How subordinates and team members fit into the processes and work with the technology needs to be communicated, documented, trained for, and continuously improved. Health leaders in this environment cannot assume that "cookie-cutter" methods will suffice, but instead must learn and become effective in developing teams of professionals within dynamic cultures. To appreciate the dynamic nature of organizations today, one need simply consider the realities of human diversity, information overload, the evolution of technology, the sophistication of the consumer, and e-commerce; many of these changes are rooted in technological advances.

Creating a health organization culture in which subordinates, team members, and leaders alike keep current with technological advances and best practices in clinical and administrative arenas is paramount. In their assessment of great groups or teams, Bennis and Biederman suggest that teams whose members want to excel desire new technology. Technology is embraced—the newer and the better—because creating the future is exciting.[38] Health leaders can leverage this excitement and enthusiasm by creating a conducive culture aligned with the organization's mission and vision, communicating how people fit in with the technology employed, fostering a continuous learning emphasis, and developing systems of learning and knowledge management.

LEADERS AS FOLLOWERS

Every health leader was, most likely, a follower at some point. In fact, a health leader is likely to be simultaneously a leader and a follower. Knowing what role you are in within a given situation and context is clearly important. The most successful health leaders were, and are, great followers. As a health leader, which traits, attitudes, and characteristics do you like to see in a follower? Good followers have a great attitude; commit to their responsibilities; complete their assigned (and

at times unassigned) tasks; communicate to superiors, peers, and subordinates well and often; are loyal; and focus on the mission and vision of the organization using the appropriate strategies, goals, objectives, and action steps within their purview. Great followers are honest, are moral, and put the organization's success ahead of their own interests. In many ways, great followers have attributes of great leaders.

Being a "transformational follower" means you are positively contagious to others as a role model. Transformational followers have a service "charisma," focus on the leader or leadership's organizational agenda and work to achieve it, communicate and follow up with all connected to their responsibilities and work, are loyal to leadership and the organization, stay appropriately coupled to the organizational norms and expectations, and deliver quality performance within a moral foundation.

The best method to understand how a health leader can be a great follower is to ask your superior, your leader, what his or her expectations for you are regarding followership. Leadership requires followership; followership requires leadership. Many of the same attributes of leadership pertain to followership, except that the leader sets the agenda and tempo for the follower's work and work environment. Being a great health follower goes hand in hand with being a great health leader.

POWER, INFLUENCE, AND THE BASIS OF POWER

Power is the capacity of a leader or agent to influence the values, beliefs, attitudes, and behaviors of another person, group, or organization. Using power to influence a change of behaviors is less difficult than changing attitudes; attitudes are less difficult to change than either beliefs or values. Power and influence can be characterized in several ways; the two methods presented here are the most universal.

Power can be discussed in terms of Kelman's social influence theory[39,40] and the process of social influence. Power and influence, serving as a catalyst, prompt three responses to varying degrees; that is, the subordinate or target of a leader's power- and influence-based request or requirement may demonstrate instrumental compliance, internalization, and/or identification.

- *Instrumental compliance* is defined as a subordinate's or target person's fulfillment of the leader's requested action for the purpose of obtaining a tangible reward or avoiding a punishment controlled by the agent. This is an example of transactional leadership in action from a foundation of the social exchange theory.

- *Internalization* is defined as a subordinate or target person's commitment to support and implement requests (and actions required to fulfill the requests) made by the leader because they are perceived to be intrinsically desirable and correct in relation to the target's values, beliefs, attitudes, and self-image. In this response, the request or proposal becomes integrated with the target person's underlying values and beliefs. It is an example of transformational leadership in action.
- *Identification* is defined as a subordinate's or target person's imitation of the leader's behavior and/or adoption of the same attitudes to please the leader. This is an example of social learning theory in action, closely linked to role modeling.

Another way of thinking about or considering the use of power and influence on subordinates, peers, stakeholders, and possibly superiors, results in three possibilities: commitment, compliance, or resistance.

- *Commitment* occurs when the person, group members, or organizational members who are the focus of power and influence from the leader internally agree with a decision or request from the leader; they then implement an approach to fulfill the request or implement the decision effectively, efficiently, and efficaciously. Commitment implies attitude change in the subordinates.
- *Compliance* occurs when the person, group members, or organizational members are willing to do what the leader desires but in a mechanical or apathetic manner, applying only moderate to minimal effort. Compliance implies that the subordinate's behavior, but not his or her attitude, has changed due to the leader's influence.
- *Resistance* happens when organizational members are opposed to the leader's request and actively avoid carrying it out, perhaps even taking steps to block actions to fulfill the leader's request.

Of course, there are varying degrees of commitment, compliance, and resistance. When using power and influence, health leaders should assess the organizational culture and the individual team member's personal impact and perception, such as with the coordinated management of meaning model, and should plan accordingly. Obviously, health leaders want commitment, or at least compliance, while eliminating resistance.

The most recognized basis of power and influence comes from French and Raven's power taxonomy. **Table 13-3** is presented in tandem with Kelman's model for purposes of synthesis and comparison.

Agenda power—the authority and control of agenda items—is similar to information power but can be recognized as a source of power as well: Consider the secretary's or assistant's control of meeting agenda items on behalf of the leader (superior). Moreover, health leaders have power from legitimate or formal power, also called position power: "Position power includes potential influence derived from legitimate authority, control over resources and rewards, control over punishments, control over information, and control over the organization of the work and the physical work environment."[41]

Table 13-3 French and Raven's Power Taxonomy and Kelman's Power and Influence Outcomes

French and Raven's Power Taxonomy	Description	Kelman's Influence Processes
Reward	Person complies to obtain rewards controlled by the agent	Instrumental compliance
Coercive	Person complies to avoid punishment by the agent	Instrumental compliance
Legitimate (also called formal)	Person complies because the agent has the right to make the request; person is under the chain of authority	Instrumental compliance, internalization, and identification
Expert	Person complies because the agent has special knowledge	Internalization
Referent	Person complies because he or she admires or identifies with the agent and wants the agent's approval	Identification
Information*	Control of information by agent is source of power	

*Added by Yukl.

Data from French, J. R. P., & Raven, B. H. (1959). The bases of social power. In D. Cartwright (Ed.), *Studies of social power* (pp. 150–167). Ann Arbor, MI: Institute for Social Research; Kelman, H. C. (1958). Compliance, identification and internalization: Three processes of attitude change. *Journal of Conflict Resolution, 2,* 51–56; Kelman, H. C. (1974). Further thoughts on the process of compliance, identification, and internalization. In J. T. Tedeschi (Ed.), *Perspectives on social power* (pp. 125–171). Chicago: Aldine; Yukl, G. (1994). *Leadership in organizations* (3rd ed.). Englewood Cliffs, NJ: Prentice Hall, p. 202.

Power is maintained, if not increased, by wise use of power. The use of power is particularly important in organizational culture; who controls resources, who receives those resources, and how resources are used contribute to the cultural disposition of the organization. Bolman and Deal, in their reframing organizational leadership model (specifically, under the "political" construct), overtly suggest that leaders must use power and resource distribution wisely. Again, consistent and predetermined leadership actions, when using power and distributing resources, are paramount to ensure leader success.

Power and influence, and the basis of power, change in all organizations. "Power is not static; it changes over time due to changing conditions and the actions of individuals and coalitions."[42] Subcultures in health organizations have also been shown to create and build resistance to power, influence, and change.[43] Controlling your emotions is "power's crucial foundation"[44] across all professional situations. Health leaders who control their emotional "self," are cognizant of their sources and level of power, and are sensitive to subcultures in the organization and to sources and level of power in others will best navigate amid coalitions and groups in moving the health organization forward in a positive direction.

EMPOWERMENT AND POWER

Empowerment is, in essence, the delegation of power, influence, and authority to another person—usually to a subordinate from a superior. Empowerment does not mean delegation of responsibility, although some responsibility rests in the subordinate that has delegated authority.

> All the [leadership] models suggest that these leaders use empowerment rather than control strategies in order to achieve transformational influence over their followers. They in essence advocate the transformational influence of leaders where the main goal is to change followers' core attitudes, beliefs, and values rather than to induce only compliance behavior in them. Again they all agree that these forms of leadership lead to attitudinal changes among followers characterized by identification with the leader and internalization of values embedded in the leader's vision and ideology.[45]

Empowerment involves the matching of an employee's knowledge, skills, and abilities to appropriate tasks, levels of authority, and levels of power and influence. Once the assignment is made, the health leader forgoes command over that task or authority until it is completed; again, this statement does not mean that responsibility is delegated. Oversight, mentoring, and guidance are advised in accordance

with the capabilities of the subordinate employee. Empowering subordinates and team members conveys trust and individualized consideration, which fosters ownership. This practice encourages employees to achieve their maximum potential throughout their careers, allowing an organization to develop leadership from within.

Empowerment is about providing motivation, developing subordinates, and appropriately aligning the decision-making processes in the health organization. Health leaders and leadership teams that understand what motivates subordinates and team members will know how to keep them satisfied, productive, and fulfilled in the workplace.

In 1959, psychologist Fredric Herzberg described a two-factor theory of motivation that aligns well with empowerment. Herzberg's theory distinguished between intrinsic (from the work itself) and extrinsic (outside of the actual work) motivators. Essentially, intrinsic factors are needed to motivate an employee to higher performance, and extrinsic motivators are needed to ensure an employee is not dissatisfied. Intrinsic and extrinsic motivational constructs are called "satisfiers" and "dis-satisfiers," respectively. In summary, the two-factor theory of motivation consists of intrinsic motivators—challenging work, recognition, responsibility, effectiveness, personal growth, and achievement—and extrinsic motivators—salary, work conditions, company policies, job security, status, and administration. Health leaders who appropriately (with regard to individualized consideration of the subordinates they lead) enhance and increase intrinsic factors and maintain or enhance extrinsic factors, according to the industry market norms, will most likely have motivated subordinates. Empowerment is a large key to this positive situation.

ENDURING ORGANIZATIONAL VALUES AND BELIEFS

Every health organization has a foundation of values and beliefs that its holds dear and that form the essence of the organizational culture. The values and beliefs of health organizations focus on the relationship with patient care amid the pressures of the external environment, business expectations, and survival/longevity of the organization. These values and beliefs cause health leaders to decide on a strategy that may be less efficient but is more efficacious for the patients and communities they serve. Both values and beliefs are closely linked to societal norms and mores, although increased globalization can loosen these attachments and open up new possibilities to the society. Values tend to remain very stable over time and help organizations make sense of where they are and how they serve their purpose in the community. Beliefs are stable as well and should focus on excellent patient care, effective and efficient operations, and teamwork in the health organization. How health leaders influence values and beliefs that foster attitudes and behaviors is the focus of this section.

VALUES, BELIEFS, ATTITUDES, AND BEHAVIORS

Transformational health leaders have an advantage in solidifying or changing values, beliefs, attitudes, and behaviors in the organization. "Charismatic leaders have insight into the needs, hopes, and values of followers and are able to motivate commitment to proposals and strategies for change."[46] Values and beliefs are expressed in strategic plans, organizational charters, and statements. Attitudes are the perceptions and opinions of members of the health organization that describe how they perceive the world around them. Behaviors are observed in actions. Health leaders should frequently express expectations about values, beliefs, attitudes, and behaviors to subordinates and other organizational stakeholders. Knowing your team members and subordinates also assists in knowing which values, beliefs, attitudes, and behaviors are consistent or inconsistent with the organization's expressed values, mission, and vision.

Health leadership styles can influence followers' values, beliefs, attitudes, and behaviors. Transactional leadership focuses on behaviors: Changing, motivating, and directing the behaviors and actions of subordinates based on social exchange are the essence of transaction-based leadership. It is possible that transactional leadership can alter attitudes; once the social exchange catalyst is removed or changed, however, it is highly likely that attitudes will return, at least somewhat, to their original state. Transformational leadership focuses on attitudes that lead to desired behaviors by changing the individual subordinate's or subordinate group's understanding, feeling, and connectedness with the health organization's mission, vision, or task at hand. Indirectly, transformational leadership can influence subordinates' beliefs over time and again, over time, shape the health organization's culture. Transformational leadership can also influence subordinate values, although such changes tend to occur only over a longer time horizon and are linked to the intensity and capabilities of the leader and the level of leader loyalty from subordinates.

Change means adjusting, revising, and redirecting effort and actions (behaviors), including how subordinates envision and feel about their place in the organization (attitudes), to a new course. This type of change is more typical of organizational change. Less frequently, change may modify the beliefs and values of subordinates in the health organization.

For the health leader, it is important to reflect on the interconnected nature of values, beliefs, attitudes, and behaviors of individuals in the organization with organizational culture and the collective values, beliefs, attitudes, and behaviors with organizational culture; these constructs may either reinforce or conflict with one another in a dynamic way. Temporal (one point in time) assessment of these constructs can be accomplished much like organizational climate can be assessed. Over time (many temporal points in time in a sequence), values, beliefs, attitudes, and behaviors influence the organizational culture. Health leaders with consistent focus and direction can change, modify, and redirect individual and collective values, beliefs, attitudes, and behaviors as part of the macro–organizational culture development process. Edgar Schein's primary embedding and secondary reinforcement mechanisms are an excellent approach to accomplish this aspect of organizational culture development for health leaders. Transformational leadership principles in practice are likewise both important and productive.

LEADERSHIP AND CHANGE

Health leaders who understand and are competent in applying transformational leadership principles (charisma is a component of transformational leadership) are best poised to create positive change in the health organization. Those who master transformational leadership principles and applications are best suited for initiating positive change.

To accomplish this goal, the transformational leader must be a competent communicator. Transformational leadership in action is best seen when several elements synergize to change the culture and improve the organization. "Transformational leadership refers to the process of building commitment to the organization's [mission, vision, strategies, goals and] objectives and empowering followers to accomplish these objectives."[47]

An early conception of transformational leadership was developed by Burns in 1978 from descriptive research on political leaders: "[L]eaders and followers raise one another to higher levels of morality and motivation."[48] Expectation and goal setting, empowerment, and increased use of appropriate media channels for communication can combine to focus a team, thereby enabling its members to accomplish significant tasks in system improvement.[49]

Transformational leadership is different from simple charismatic leadership in several respects (an idea attributed to Bernard Bass). Although charisma is a necessary component for transformational leadership, by itself it is not sufficient to account for transformation:

> Transformational leaders influence followers by arousing strong emotions and identification with the leader,

but they may also transform followers by serving as a coach, teacher, and mentor. Transformational leaders seek to empower and elevate followers, whereas in charismatic leadership the opposite sometimes occurs. That is, many charismatic leaders seek to keep followers weak and dependent and to instill personal loyalty rather than commitment to ideals.[50]

Schein's primary embedding mechanisms and secondary reinforcement mechanisms to develop and maintain culture are salient within the context of change; transformational health leaders who use these mechanisms with a conscious and predetermined vision for a health organizational culture are best equipped to effect positive change. When this synthesized strategy is used consistently and morally, change can be accomplished more quickly, deliver greater benefits, and enhance the health leader's status within the organization.

STRATEGIES IN CREATING A CULTURE OF CHANGE

Health leaders can use transformational leadership strategies,[51] primary embedding and secondary reinforcement mechanisms,[52] and the dynamic culture leadership (DCL) model[53] processes to develop and synthesize a model to serve as a strategy for creating a culture of change in the health organization. A review of transformational leadership is presented here, followed by a discussion of the various culture change mechanisms and the DCL process.

Bernard Bass, building on work by Burns, developed the theory of transformational leadership.[54] This model measures the leader's influence on followers. A health transformational leader would create trust, admiration, loyalty, and respect in the followers through his or her actions, behaviors, and persona.[55] Followers are motivated by the leader to do more than expected, as the leader makes followers more aware of the importance of task outcomes, induces them to transcend their own self-interest for the sake of the team, and activates their higher-order needs.[56] To do so, the leader uses the following transformational behaviors and actions:

- *Charisma*: Leader influences followers by arousing strong emotions and identification with the leader.
- *Intellectual stimulation*: Leader increases follower awareness of problems and influences followers' view of problems from a new perspective.
- *Individualized consideration*: Leader provides support, encouragement, and developmental experiences for followers.
- *Inspirational motivation*: Leader communicates an appealing vision using symbols to focus subordinate

effort and model (role modeling; Bandura's social learning theory) appropriate behavior.[57]

Primary embedding mechanisms[58] are a set of powerful tools, behaviors, and mechanisms that a health leader can use to develop, refine, maintain, or change organizational culture:

- What leaders pay attention to, measure, and control
- Leader reactions to critical incidents and organizational crises
- Deliberate role modeling, teaching, and coaching by leaders
- Criteria for allocation of rewards and status
- Criteria for recruitment, selection, promotion, retirement, and excommunication

Schein strongly states that leaders communicate both explicitly and implicitly the assumptions they really hold. If they are conflicted, their conflicts and inconsistencies are also communicated and become part of the culture. Consistency is the key: Health leaders must predetermine where and how to guide the organization and stay on task.

Another set of mechanisms support the primary set and are called secondary reinforcement mechanisms.[59] The secondary articulation and reinforcement mechanisms reinforce the primary embedding mechanisms. The following are of greatest importance to the health leader:

- The organization's design and structure
- Organizational systems and procedures
- Design of physical space, facades, and buildings
- Stories, legends, myths, and parables about important events and people
- Formal statements of organizational philosophy, creeds, and charters

Schein calls these "secondary" because they work only if they are consistent with the primary mechanisms. The secondary mechanisms are less powerful than primary mechanisms, more ambiguous, and more difficult to control, yet can be powerful reinforcements of the primary messages if the leader is able to control them.

The important point is that all of these mechanisms communicate culture content to newcomers and current staff. Together, they represent a rich set of tools, behaviors, decisions, and mechanisms that a health leader can use to develop and maintain organizational culture. Health leaders must be consistent and conscious of how and when they utilize these mechanisms.

The DCL model[60] process suggests prescriptive elements that include assessing and aligning a robust leadership and management team to ensure that all of these individuals can utilize a broad range of knowledge, skills, abilities, and perspectives while being consistent in developing and maintaining an appropriate organizational culture. The leader's use of the sequential and building elements of the model's process constructs facilitates the development of the predetermined organizational culture desired. Process constructs include the following elements:

- *Communication improvement* is the leadership's and management team's predetermined modeling, training, rewarding, and assimilation of the communication environment into the organization in the manner that best contributes to an effective organizational culture. In health organizations, a confirming and supportive communication environment that is cognizant of media richness of communication channels and competent in conflict management should be the most effective, efficient, and efficacious.
- *Strategic planning* (which includes operational planning) is the structured, inclusive process of planning to determine mission, vision, strategies, goals, objectives, and action steps that are consistent with organizational values and that meet the external environment's expectations of the organization. Subordinate, internal, and external stakeholders should be included, as appropriate to their level and responsibilities, in the planning process. Continuous, "living" planning is a cultural imperative in dynamic environments.
- *Decision-making alignment* involves aligning decisions with the strategic and operational plan while understanding reality-based decision making (pushing down decisions appropriately and using policies and standard operating procedures for routine and consistent decisions).
- *Employee enhancement* is the assessment of employee knowledge, skills, abilities, experience, and trustworthiness and the practice of increasing or reducing responsibilities (such as making decisions) appropriately of the unit, group, and individual, in line with the organizational culture in development and the strategic and operational plans.
- *Knowledge management and organizational learning* involve capturing what the organization knows and what it has learned, so that improvements to effectiveness, efficiency, and efficacy can be achieved.
- *Evaluating, reflecting, and retooling* are the leadership and management team's honest assessment of the DCL model cycle and understanding of how to perform the cycle better in the next repetition.

Using this process consistently not only improves the organization's ability to use these processes and leads to the development of an organizational culture that reflects the leadership's vision, but also enables the organization to maneuver effectively in dynamic situations. Process repetition and consistency are foundational to success in this model.

From these three integrated aspects of leadership, a strategy for creating positive change in the organization can be realized. By scanning, monitoring, forecasting (for the external environment), and assessing the health organization (internal) and its setting, context, and location in the environment (external), the health leader and/or leadership team needs to develop a predetermined direction, a preliminary vision, and a picture of the best organizational culture that can achieve that direction and vision while attending to the health organization's current mission. This process and the decisions it produces should be documented and planned over time. Health leader actions must then be planned to achieve the better future envisioned for the health organization. Health leaders must plan, practice, and hold themselves and other leaders accountable for consistency to realize the desired outcomes of the plan.

To turn the desired future into reality, change will most likely be required in the health organization and among its stakeholders. Active situational leadership—that is, selecting the appropriate mix of transformational and transactional leadership, frequent quality communication to subordinates and stakeholders, appropriately inclusive planning, decision-making alignment, empowerment, and organizational learning and knowledge management—should merge with an appealing vision of the future of the health organization so that the organization can achieve success. Can you integrate the concepts, actions, behaviors, and aspects from this section to develop an initial model of leading change? Are some elements particularly important in this respect? **Table 13-4** summarizes one model for leader-facilitated positive health organizational change.

CHANGE, CONFLICT, AND TRANSITION PLANNING

At the macro level of analysis, transformational leadership involves shaping, expressing, and mediating conflict among groups of people in addition to motivating individuals.[61] Any time there is change, there is conflict. Managing this conflict is necessary for two reasons: (1) Conflict is inevitable and (2) it can create positive results. By being consistent in their delivery of the message of change and the organizational vision, health leaders can continuously reinforce the change while calming nervous tension or anxiety in the organization. Each step of the transition through change should be planned, with subordinates and team members included, as appropriate, in developing aspects of the change and transition plan. Including

Table 13-4 Leadership-Facilitated Organizational Change: Application of Theories and Models				
Predetermined Organizational Culture to Develop	**Individual Leader Actions and Behaviors**	**Leadership Team Actions and Behaviors**	**Organizational Actions and Behaviors by Leaders and Subordinates**	**Organizational Outcomes**
Vision predetermined and culture changes predetermined by leadership team	Transformational leadership characteristics: • Charisma • Intellectual stimulation • Individualized consideration • Inspirational motivation • Performance orientation • Decisiveness • Team integration and collaboration • Being diplomatic • Being benevolent • Being administratively competent • Transactional leadership (reward for performance) where appropriate	Primary embedding mechanisms: • What leaders pay attention to, measure, and control • Leader reactions to critical incidents and organizational crises • Deliberate role modeling, teaching, and coaching by leaders • Criteria for allocation of rewards and status • Criteria for recruitment, selection, promotion, retirement, and excommunication Secondary reinforcement and articulation mechanisms: • Design and creation of the organization's design and structure • Design and creation of the organizational systems and procedures • Design of physical space, facades, and buildings • Creating and telling of stories, legends, myths, and parables about important events and people • Developing and publishing formal statements of organizational philosophy, creeds, and charters	Dynamic culture leadership process: • Leadership alignment • Communication improvement • Strategic and operational planning • Decision-making alignment • Employee enhancement • Knowledge management and organizational learning • Evaluation, reflecting and retooling, and repeating the process	Predetermined vision and organizational culture incrementally transformed and realized

internal and external stakeholders in organizational changes that will affect them is a great method for moving through the transitions and changes with less turbulence. Nevertheless, smooth change is rare—so expect some turbulence and resistance. Frequent supportive, descriptive, yet firm communication is a great tool for health leaders; media-rich channels of communication (e.g., face-to-face with individuals and groups) are recommended for communicating change.

Another change in health organizations that is inevitable involves leadership position changes. If transitional planning and succession planning has occurred, this transition tends to go more smoothly. Succession planning—the

deliberate development and placement of internal leadership and management over time—should be a part of every health organization's culture.

Maintaining a Culture of Adaptive Change

Once a culture of change is established in a health organization, it is important to nourish and maintain that culture:

> The organizational culture is a learned pattern of behavior, shared from one generation to the next. It

includes the values and an assumption shared by members about what is right, what is good and what is important. Since demands on most organizations are unlikely to be steady and stable, only cultures that can adapt and change will be associated with superior performance over long periods of time.[62]

Health leaders can and should develop a predetermined organizational culture focused on transformation, continuous improvement, and the ability to thrive in a dynamic environment. A transformational culture for health organizations facilitates adaption and change over time.

Transactional cultures exhibit the following attributes:

- Concentrate on explicit and implicit contractual relationships.
- Job assignments include statements about rules, benefits, and disciplinary codes.
- Jargon/values/assumptions usually set or imply a price or reward for doing anything.
- Rewards are contingent on performance.
- Management by exception is commonly practiced.
- Employees work individually.
- Employees do not identify with the organization, its vision, or its mission.
- Leaders are negotiators and resource allocators.
- Innovation and risk taking are discouraged.

Transformational cultures exhibit the following attributes:

- Express a sincere sense of purpose and feeling of family.
- Commitments are long-term.
- Mutual interests are shared along with a sense of shared fates and interdependence.
- Leaders serve as role models, mentors, and coaches.
- Leaders work to socialize new members into the organization.
- Shared norms are adaptive.
- Organizational purposes, visions, and missions are emphasized, not threats.
- Norms change with changes in the organization's environment.[63]

In thinking about the concepts covered in this chapter, can you incorporate leadership competencies regarding diversity, power, and changing and transforming organizations into an initial application model? After engaging in reflection, can you construct a leadership model that you can use in leading people and managing resources in a

health organization? To assist in this effort of developing a leadership model to positively change a health organization, reflect on the following suggestions:

- Model the behavior you expect of others.
- Communicate expectations and train other leaders, managers, and staff.
- Revise structures and reporting relationships.
- Conduct team-based planning and policy development.
- Use primary embedding and secondary reinforcement mechanisms.
- Utilize the DCL model sequential processes.
- Be consistent and communicate often to the organization.
- Continue to scan, monitor, and assess the internal health organization environment while you scan, monitor, forecast, and assess the external environment to guide the health organization appropriately.

Which elements are clearest to you? Can you list the leadership elements that are important for realizing change in a health organization?

KNOWLEDGE MANAGEMENT AND A LEARNING ORGANIZATION*

Learning organizations are living, open, robust systems.[64] Knowledge management in and of itself is an innovative strategy of change, adaption, and evolution. This process involves accumulating and creating knowledge and facilitating the sharing of knowledge throughout the organization. "The ability for a healthcare organization to develop systems to manage knowledge directly impacts the level of institutional knowledge and organizational learning."[65] Knowledge management empowers the organization to fulfill its mission and vision. The ability to reach the vision of the organization, in turn, provides a greater ability to compete in a dynamic environment. If knowledge is created, captured, and managed appropriately in a consistent manner over time, a culture of learning is created. To manage knowledge effectively within the organization, it is first important to create a working definition of knowledge and to define what knowledge is not.

Clear distinctions can be made among data, information, and knowledge. *Data* comprise a set of objective facts

---

*Much of this section was completed in collaboration with Kelley Chester, doctoral candidate, Georgia Southern University, 2007–2009.

about certain objects, events, people, or observations. Data become information when these facts are used to inform or convey a relevant message to the receiver. Information is capable of yielding knowledge, but is not synonymous with knowledge. *Information* becomes knowledge when decision makers determine how to take advantage of the information to further health organizational goals or as part of the decision-making process. *Knowledge* is "actionable" information. It conveys understanding as it applies to a particular problem.

In creating a practical working definition of knowledge, the organization should understand and emphasize these differences. A working definition of knowledge offered by Davenport and Prusak states that knowledge is a dynamic mix of contextually based experiences, values, contextual information, and insights that provide a framework for evaluating and incorporating new experiences and information.[66] In creating a system of knowledge management for the health organization, there are three processes of importance: knowledge accumulation, knowledge creation, and knowledge sharing.

ACCUMULATING KNOWLEDGE

To learn, a health organization must have data, information, and knowledge to draw from. Essential data and information that are critical to the mission and core systems and processes of the health organization must be identified. Because knowledge management is an organizational phenomenon, the health organization should first identify and clarify the organization's mission, vision, and core values. Identifying these organizational concepts provides an understanding of the current state of the organization, which will influence how priorities and boundaries for capturing and creating knowledge are set. The next step in accumulating knowledge is to discover existing knowledge and put it into a health organizational context. This step involves gathering and organizing knowledge to make it useful to others. If the intent of knowledge is to inform and influence decision making, then its focus must be on the future. Allowing for discussion and frequent debate is a vehicle to accumulate existing knowledge.

CREATING KNOWLEDGE

Knowledge generation and usage is a never-ending work in progress. The health organization must continually acquire and create new knowledge. Experiments are crucial to the creation of new knowledge because they provide data and information; employees learn by taking chances and, sometimes, by making mistakes. Unintended mistakes should be viewed as opportunities to learn and improve patient care and business processes; they should be acceptable in the organization. At the same time, patient care should always strive to be error free (although mistakes do occur at times). People learn from mistakes and then push the answers out to others.

According to Nonaka, two types of knowledge—tacit and explicit—are important to the knowledge creation process.[67] *Explicit knowledge* is knowledge that is transferable by the use of language. It is something that we can say or tell someone. *Tacit knowledge* is much more difficult to convey, because it is the result of subjective and experiential learning and, therefore, may not always be documented. Tacit knowledge is the means by which explicit knowledge is captured, assimilated, created, and disseminated.

SHARING KNOWLEDGE

Capturing and storing knowledge are the cornerstones of knowledge management. Although knowledge is stored in many ways in a health organization, the most popular approach combines a database form with the use of a technology-related platform. Once knowledge is stored properly, it can be disseminated throughout the organization and applied to specific situations and the decision-making process.

Knowledge databases should be broad in scope to provide for greater usability. Leaders must be obsessive about noting and correcting errors in their stock of knowledge. What do they know or think they know? How does what they know or do not know affect specific decisions? Which errors reside in their knowledge and what are the consequences of those errors? Once errors are identified, a plan to rectify those errors must be developed.

For knowledge to be usable, the target audience of the knowledge database must be clear. Organizations today can deliver knowledge via a variety of technology platforms. Technology is a means to access information and knowledge but is no substitute for interaction. Put simply, communication and the learning process are inherently types of personal dialogue.[68]

SUMMARY OF KNOWLEDGE MANAGEMENT AND ORGANIZATIONAL LEARNING

Based on the concepts of knowledge accumulation, knowledge creation, and knowledge sharing, a five-step approach to knowledge management is proposed:[†]

1. Identify what is critical to the organization.
2. Discover existing knowledge and put it into an organizational context.

---

†This model is from the unpublished work of Kelley Chester, Dr. PH, Georgia Southern University, 2007–2009.

3. Acquire or create new knowledge.
4. Establish knowledge databases.
5. Distribute knowledge to the appropriate audience.

Building a culture of learning within the health organization to foster the development and sharing of knowledge is an essential element in establishing and maintaining an effective, efficient, and efficacious knowledge management system. As the acceptance of evidence-based medicine and administrative practice grows, establishing and maintaining a knowledge management system within a culture of organizational learning will be critical to ensuring the success of both the health organization and its leadership team.

WHAT KIND OF LEADER DO YOU WANT TO BE?

This is a serious question: What kind of leader are you? For many people who are just starting their careers, this question may be rephrased: What kind of leader do you want to become? Armed with what was learned from the behavioral phase and the situational phase of leadership thought, can you learn, practice, and develop leadership knowledge, skills, abilities, and competencies starting today, and continue that development throughout your lifetime? One definition of leadership is: *Leadership* is the *dynamic* and *active* creation and maintenance of an organizational *culture* and *strategic systems* that focus the collective energy of both *leading people and managing resources* toward *meeting the needs of the external environment*, while utilizing the most efficient, effective, and efficacious methods possible by moral means. To become the kind of leader you want to be, you will need to be active in your approach to the art and science of leadership. The process of "practicing the art of leadership" is discussed in more detail in this chapter. However, one characteristic you will have to embrace is the process of internalizing leadership as a continuous process if you want to be a leader who always gets better, always stays credible, and always wants to be the best.

The desire to be a great leader comes from within. For example, Fairholm summarizes several principles of "inner leadership." Inner leadership is based on many of the principles of empowerment. Empowerment engages the inner leader in the kinds of actions necessary to internalize leadership as a constant process. By doing this, the leader becomes capable of assuming the following responsibilities:

- Goal setting
- Delegating to followers
- Encouraging participation
- Encouraging self-reliance

- Challenging followers
- Focusing on workers
- Specifying followers' roles[69]

When looking at this series of inner leadership principles, how many theories and models come to mind that can be applied to them? How many could be put into practice? Which theories and models would work well together, and which ones might contradict one another? For purposes of synergy of theories and models, reflect on **Table 13-5**, which shows a few of the linkages. Many more connections are also possible: Could more linkages to theories and models be listed?

A leader's predisposition toward a certain mental hardwiring might lend itself to a natural tendency to emulate some of the many leadership styles discussed in this text. Looking at Table 13-5, which theories and leadership methods best fit with your experiences and natural talents? Although this process may seem somewhat mechanical and prescriptive, without an understanding of his or her own style and natural tendencies, a leader cannot emphasize strengths and work on weaknesses. With practice and over time, a leader should be able to seamlessly incorporate personal style and abilities into a blended practice of leadership.

You should be able to list other connections and links to theories and models. Again, it is important to create a vision for yourself of what kind of leader you want to be. Because it is important to communicate a clear and appealing vision to your subordinates, you need to develop a personal leadership vision. You will need to sell that vision of your leadership to potential employers in job interviews and in your performance in the job:

> Today, senior leaders of major organizations consistently rank leadership development as their number one concern. Leaders and the art they perfect is not bestowed on those, it is developed over time and with great effort; good leaders are not born but are produced over time and with great effort.[70]

IT'S OKAY TO SAY, "I DON'T KNOW"

Leaders of health organizations are probably at a greater disadvantage than leaders of any other large organizations. Their unique challenges stem from the complexity of health organizations and the lack of understanding of what goes on in the health facility. To outsiders and less informed individuals, a physician is a physician, a nurse is a nurse, and any one administrator is equally as competent as the next. The complexities, competencies, skills, and specializations among administrators, physicians, nurses, and other allied health personnel and employees are lost on the layperson.

Leaders of health organizations not only have to be aware of the same accounting, marketing, logistical, human resources, and compliance regulations as their manufacturing and service industry peers, but also the challenges of managing Food and Drug Administration (FDA)–designated controlled substances, licensing and certification issues, innovation and technology, and the rapidly changing multispecialty best practices in areas of medicine or patient care. Moreover, this feat must be achieved in an environment of near perfection when it comes to patient care.

In addition, the leader in a health organization may have absolutely no experience or professional education related to many of the daily activities that go on in the health facility. For example, in popular fast-food franchises, the list of menu items is finite and can be generalized. With few colloquial exceptions, the same items on the menu of one fast-food restaurant will be identical to the menu items at the same franchise restaurant across town. Managers of these local restaurants are required to be keenly aware of the ordering, processing, and delivery of all food items on the menu, as well as the intimate details of how everyone in that franchise does his or her job. This is never the case with the health leader, who must rely on the competence, honesty, and reporting of those who work for him or her in the organizational hierarchy over and above firsthand knowledge.[71-73]

For example, in many manufacturing organizations, the leader must know the skills and duties of those persons who work underneath him or her in the organizational hierarchy. This is a difficult task for the leader of a health organization. A leader in a multispecialty, primary, secondary, or tertiary health organization will never be as competent at doing the individual tasks of any two individuals across specialties within the organization. In almost all cases with leaders who rise to positions of greater responsibility in health organizations, there will be dozens, even hundreds, of people in the organization who know more about their own jobs than the leader does. More so in health organizations than any other manufacturing- or service-driven organization, the leader must be comfortable with the prospect of not knowing the inner complexities of the organization that he or she is running. At the same time, the health leader must be able to develop and employ systems and processes that create an efficient, effective, and efficacious healthcare environment. The leader must be comfortable with a personal and professional

Table 13-5 Inner Leadership Principles Linked to Theories and Models

Inner Leadership Principle	Link to Other Leadership or Related Theory or Model (1)	Link to Other Leadership or Related Theory or Model (2)	Link to Other Leadership or Related Theory or Model (3)
Goal setting	Goal-setting theory (Locke and Latham)	Expectancy theory (Vroom) and path–goal model (House)	Dynamic culture leadership; planning, and specifically, objectives (Ledlow)
Delegating to followers	Garbage can model of decision making (March and Weisinger-Baylon)	Motivation by empowerment (several models: Bolman and Deal's reframing organizations and Ledlow's dynamic culture leadership)	Kaizen, total quality management, continuous quality management, and process improvement
Encouraging participation	Situational leadership model (Hersey and Blanchard)	Kelman's model (instrumental) and the model of influence considering commitment, compliance, and resistance	Reframing leadership and management in organizations (Bolman and Deal)
Encouraging self-reliance	Transformational leadership model (Burns and Bass) and locus of control (Rotter)	Dynamic culture leadership (specifically, knowledge management and organizational learning)	Organizational culture primary and secondary mechanisms (Schein)
Challenging followers	Competency-based leadership (Bennis)	Transformational leadership (Burns and Bass)	Communication environment, conflict management, and media richness theory (Daft and Lengel)
Focusing on workers	Transformational leadership (Burns and Bass)	Cultural competence	Coordinated management of meaning (Pearce and Cronen)
Specifying followers' roles	Shutz's theory of affiliation	Communication clarity	Tuckman's model of group dynamics

posture of admitting to him- or herself that he or she does not know everything that goes on in the organization. Leaders who try to know everything, manage everything, and control everything are destined for personal frustration, professional disappointment, and, ultimately, leader failure.

MAINTAINING RELEVANCY AND CREDIBILITY

In becoming comfortable stating, "I don't know," within a health organization, the next logical question a leader has to ask him- or herself is this: How do I maintain relevancy and credibility with my peers and colleagues? These critical self-assessment issues must be constantly addressed and evaluated by the leader, at least on an annual basis. Additionally, both relevancy and credibility are mutually exclusive issues the leader must pursue through individual strategies.[74,75]

CREDIBILITY

Credibility is a complex construct that can be measured through experience, outcomes, and employee trust. A leader with little previous experience in the day-to-day operations of the health organization may not be perceived as credible. However, the defining of experience becomes even more complex when discussing the specific nature of the experience of the individual. For example, nurses may not be perceived as having credible experience in leading health organizations if their 20-year familiarity with leading people in health organizations has been restricted to leading only other nurses. Similarly, professional administrative leaders without clinical degrees may look at a physician leader with skepticism if the physician has risen to a position of authority based on his or her medical and clinical prowess rather than by taking on administrative and management developmental activities. The circle may continue if physicians view the administrator with only a master's degree as an individual without experience to know enough about hands-on patient care to manage physicians.

As this discussion suggests, credibility is highly wedded to trust. Although professional rivalries and professional competition are part and parcel of leading complex health organizations, the leader should never lose focus on maintaining and instilling positive relationships with peers and staff.[76] Without gaining the trust of those in the organization, the leader will not be effective in his or her job. Consequently, trust is also highly wedded to outcomes all along the continuum and process of daily operations.[77,78] Likewise, building a trusting relationship with peers and colleagues is a key element in achieving credibility and positive outcomes.

OUTCOMES

Outcomes in regard to credibility are not restricted to financial, logistical, and morbidity/mortality metrics. Perhaps most importantly, they are related to outcomes with human resources. Organizational satisfaction, leader and employee development opportunities, and formation and maintenance of positive relationships with stakeholders are some of the most critical factors for a leader to consider. How a leader treats employees in regard to acknowledging input, respecting candor, protecting employee autonomy, and maintaining a positive leader climate are some of the most important factors that any leader can focus on in his or her organization.[79] The loss of trust of even a single person, considering that person's influence in the organization, can begin a professional downturn for the leader. In fact, President Lyndon Johnson once said he had lost the trust of America because he lost the trust of one man: Walter Cronkite, the famous *CBS Evening News* anchorman. Cronkite said in 1968 during the evening newscast that he thought the Vietnam War could not be won. President Johnson was later quoted as saying, "If I've lost Cronkite, I've lost Middle America."

RELEVANCY

Relevancy is an easier behavior trait for a leader to maintain. Relevancy is defined as a leader's ability to maintain a position of continued and sustained contribution to the organization's success. All other factors are antecedent to this ability.[80] Relevancy may be one of the most important hierarchical dispositions of the leader in any health organization. If the organization is growing its market share, increasing its local or national prominence, and improving in terms of other quality factors measured on a regular basis, these changes can be indicators of the relevancy of the leader of the organization. However, an organization that achieves high outcomes while discounting employee satisfaction is a weak model of leader effectiveness.[81,82] As a result, credibility and relevancy are partnered elements of success. The path to achieving high outcomes in both of these areas is multifaceted and revolves around four key areas: joining professional organizations, service, continuing education, and personal professional development.

Professional Organizations

Membership in professional organizations is critical to establish a leader's credibility and relevancy. For the sake of fairness, we will not identify any one organization in this chapter as the panacea for professional success. Rather, the selection of a professional organization in which to seek membership is a personal issue, and this decision should be tied to a leader's current work environment. For example, a leader who was previously vested in a professional organization specializing in hospice care may no longer find the organization "relevant" if he or she decides to seek a leadership position within a multispecialty group practice. The goals of the two health organizations are not parallel. Outside stakeholders will clearly see that the leader has failed to maintain relevancy by not vesting him- or herself in a more creditable professional entity.

The greatest benefit offered by any professional organization is the opportunity to network and collaborate with peers from similar organizations. Despite the competitive nature of the business of health care, professional organizations seek to share best practices between and within similar organizations along the continuum of care. Professional organizations are also multidirectional warehouses where topical information from the environment is captured and then disseminated to leaders and organizational entities. For instance, professional organizations were seen as the leading entities for the dissemination of Health Insurance Portability and Accountability Act (HIPAA) information when these regulations and compliance standards were introduced in the latter part of the 1990s and early 2000s, over and above the information provided by governmental agencies.[83]

Professional organizations also provide opportunities for mentoring and networking. Young leaders who become fully vested in professional organizations that are willing to share information and best practices will find the favor returned in later years when new policies, practices, or procedures need to be developed quickly with minimal resources. Many health leaders will freely share and contribute knowledge to peers within professional organizations out of professional courtesy and respect for the common organization they share. Failing to join, contribute to, and maintain a presence in a professional organization of choice will surely decrease opportunities for both organizational and personal growth.

Service

Professional service can be defined in a variety of ways. It is suggested that health professionals consider service from a volunteer perspective that involves contributing to their own organizational entity, their community, and their personal professional organization of choice.

Leading by example and volunteering are critical parts of any leader's success. For instance, through his volunteer work as a reading tutor, which continued nearly up until the time of his death, Senator Edward Kennedy spent many hours around Washington, D.C., working with elementary school–aged children.[84] His leading by example resulted in

the development of a district-wide volunteer initiative that resulted in hundreds of school-aged children in the nation's capital having an adult mentor to read to them. Similarly, the health leader should be aware that if he or she wants the organization's employees to demonstrate organizational citizenship behavior (OCB)—that is, doing extra work for the organization that benefits the organization, albeit without compensation—the leader must model this behavior him- or herself and lead by example.

Many organizations thrive on the OCB initiatives of their employees. Simple activities such as sponsoring the department's annual Christmas party or starting a before-work exercise program demonstrate an individual's potential to the organization beyond those qualities documented in annual performance reports. Likewise, service to the community by volunteering to sit on after-hours community boards or participating in charitable outreach programs not only establishes an individual as a leader outside the organization, but also provides positive marketing for the organization itself. Service to professional organizations can also be rewarding in many ways that benefit both the individual and the organizational entity if the professional is able to rise, or become elected, to a national position of prominence. As a result, the service to the organization, service to the community, and service to the profession will collectively result in increased opportunities for both personal growth and organizational success.

Continuing Education

A few years ago, the authors of this book participated in a seminar where the speaker was discussing strategies to pass a Joint Commission accreditation site visit. The speaker was very well known to the group and had achieved a level of national prominence and the respect of his peers. However, this particular speaker had not worked in the practical world of health care for several years. After a very brief period of time, it became clear to a few members of the audience that the speaker was addressing old standards and procedures that were no longer applicable to more recent initiatives in accreditation site visits. Many in the audience were not aware of the subtle outdated information that was presented; however, a few people did get up and walk out of the room. It was clear that the speaker had not maintained credibility and relevancy in regard to his personal continuing education since he had left his CEO position in a major facility.

Continuing education (CE) is different for practicing patient providers and administrators. The elements of CE are generally described as twofold: (1) continuing health education (CHE), or nonclinical education, and (2) continuing medical education (CME), or clinical education.

Other variations exist; however, these two are the prevalent forms of CE in the health field.

For clinical professionals, the need for CME is immediately evident. New pharmaceuticals, procedures, and materials are constantly being introduced and changing in ways that may affect patient care. Medical professionals who do not keep abreast of these changes place both themselves and the organization in professional peril.

For nonclinical professionals, the need for CHE may be less mandated by state and national licensing agencies. Nevertheless, failure to seek out CHE is progressive, noticeable, and professionally and organizationally damaging for a professional. A leader who is unaware of how national policy affects billing, organizational strategy, and compliance issues can place the organization at risk or, as in the seminar speaker example, expose the organization to a loss of reputation.

CE opportunities are generally widely available to a leader in the modern era. Webcasts, podcasts, computer-based training, online seminars, and teleconferences have made CE readily available to those serving in both rural and urban communities. A leader who seeks to maintain both personal and organizational relevancy and legitimacy will seek out those CE opportunities best suited to the organizational needs on a continual basis.

Mentoring and Professional Development

No individual is ever too old or experienced for mentoring and additional professional development. Self-proclaiming that a level of personal success has been reached such that there is no one individual left to role model best practices or act as a benchmark for achievement can be both a narcissistic act and a fatally flawed methodology for achieving personal and organizational success. It is incumbent upon the leader to become a mentor to the next generation of health leaders.[85] Often, a 30-year-old employee with 5 to 7 years of experience under his or her belt may be a more effective role model to a new employee than a more seasoned and (possibly) intimidating senior leader who is much older.

Seek out a mentor, ask questions, and follow the example of those leaders you find successful. You have a world of possible informal mentors to observe, including those who perform well and those who do not; seek out those who perform at a high level and are moral leaders. If a mentor cannot be found in your current organization, seek a mentor (through a professional organization or association) from another organization; this is not a rare situation.

Professional development is a necessary component of staying relevant within the industry. Leaders all along the health continuum should seek opportunities to attend seminars and presentations on a continual basis. Additionally, staying current with the public and professional literature is important. Associations, topical publications, and top-tier news organizations provide a myriad of material to enhance a leader's knowledge base. A leader should allow for at least 30 to 60 minutes of professional reading each day to maintain a sense of relevancy with events in his or her environment. Quality books on leadership, management, systems, leading people, managing resources, and the like should be read as well.

Which book did you read last month and what are you reading this month? Try to finish a quality leadership and/or management book at least once a month.

DEVELOPMENT OF SYSTEMS TO LEAD PEOPLE AND MANAGE RESOURCES

As a health leader, you are responsible for leading people and managing resources. (Has that been said often enough?) To accomplish these essential and broad tasks, leaders must develop, refine, evaluate, and implement systems that facilitate leading people and managing resources. Nearly all of the theories and models in this book, and many of the applications of these theories and models, have provided a foundation for developing these systems. We encourage health leaders to put the dynamic culture leadership (DCL) model into practice as a basis of a system to lead people and manage resources. Yes, we are biased toward our model, but it is a solid starting point. (Other methods exist and can be used equally effectively, of course.) Personally, you as a health leader must plug into the systems you create. As a continuously developing situational and moral leader, your style, behaviors, and actions must be consistent with the organizational culture, values, strategies, and goals.

There are many systems in place in most health organizations, such as the human resources system, revenue management system, financial system, patient care system, and supply chain system. Considering these systems from a leadership perspective, are the systems and their associated processes aligned and consistent with the organizational culture required to succeed in the external environment? How do you keep these systems aligned and consistent? How would you use the DCL model to improve and integrate, with consistency, these systems? Remember, health leaders lead people and manage resources.

TAKE CARE OF PEOPLE

The most important resources in any organization are the human resources. Individuals in any health organization will always be the most significant component of organizational success. Leaders will be wise to keep this fact close and personal. Without skilled, dedicated, and competent individuals to do the work of the organization in an ongoing manner, the organization is sure to fail. Always remember that the employees whom the leader directs will reflect the values and goals of the organization as well as communicate those goals and values to the customers whom the organization serves. Taking care of people is not only based on monetary and work environment factors, but also on moral grounds.[86]

Leaders should also recognize the importance of taking advantage of the diversity in the workforce. It is a well-known fact that workforce diversity lends itself to achieving a higher degree of technical quality and organizational efficiency. Diversity increases the personnel resource pool available to the leader, which in turn tends to eliminate groupthink and increase differentiation. An increase in differentiation allows the organization to pursue new and innovative concepts that will increase its ability to survive—and thrive—over the long term.[87]

Take Care of Resources

Resources are the materials and technologies that the leader needs to perform the business of the organization. Resources, in turn, are used as the inputs for the organization to process its outputs. This is true regardless of whether the organization has a service or manufacturing orientation. It is incumbent upon the leader to provide appropriate resources to the employees of the organization so that they can carry out the business of the entity. The leader must also stay abreast of emerging technologies that can aid employees in becoming more productive in the performance of their jobs. As a fiduciary agent of the health organization, the leader who can manage and take care of resources is better able to lead people. Managing resources tends to be easier than leading people; however, leaders must be competent at both aspects of leadership.

As a leader, you should develop and maintain a list of all resources under your management. This list should identify where the resource is housed, who uses it, how and when it is maintained (in-house, under warranty, or by contract), and, if appropriate, its calibration or performance quality assurance record. All resources (the tangible ones) should be on a maintenance schedule and checked according to the standards of practice for that resource; this is especially critical for resources that are used on, near, in, or with patients, providers, and staff. Also, all resources should be inventoried routinely (at least once a year) by you or your trusted representative; you should see and compare serial numbers

for resources in use compared to your list of resources. This inventory can be done with a quick check of 8 to 9% of resources on a monthly basis. During this inventory, verify if routine maintenance has been accomplished on the resource, if necessary supplies are available for use with the resource, and if the resource is in good working order.

As for intangible resources (such as dollars in a budget), leaders should keep track of committed and obligated funds. Leaders should meet routinely with the controller and/or financial officer of the health organization. It is suggested that young leaders meet with the financial officer once a month for the first 6 months of employment and then quarterly (at a minimum) thereafter to ensure fiscal responsibilities are being met and managed properly.

Pay Attention to Details

There is a careful balance in leadership between micromanagement and being detail oriented. In assessing the effectiveness of the work of the leader, the leader's communication of vision, mission, values, and goal statements should be explicit. Implicit communication will be effective only if there are ingrained values and norms in the organization that clearly support ambiguity in direction and goal orientation. For example, a leader looking to relax dress standards for "casual Fridays" away from a coat and tie to something like khakis and three-button shirts would be incorrect in assuming that all employees consider casual dress to include polo shirts and items featured in *GQ* magazine. As the leader, ensure that you communicate your expectations explicitly. Additionally, attend to the details of the organization without micromanaging the process of work. Finally, if you are not predisposed to paying attention to details, you can develop that skill and learn by consistency and perseverance. Set a goal to be detail oriented.

Attend to the Communities Served by the Organization

Health leaders are expected to be knowledgeable about the community in which they operate. Even more importantly, health leaders are expected to become involved in the communities that their organizations serve. Community assessments to identify health improvement opportunities, as well as preparedness (consider the public health and healthcare/hospital preparedness programs) assessments and improvements, must be accomplished within the fabric of the community.

The reality of the modern business of health is that large organizations and individual populations of providers will tend to do business with the leaders of the organizations with which they have a personal relationship.[88,89] Although the

Stark laws[90] prevent physicians from referring patients only to those facilities in which they have a financial interest, organizations, populations of physicians, and other entities will be more likely to do business with organizations with which they have an existing personal relationship. Without violating the parameters of ethics, the reality of the environment is that trust remains a major factor in doing business in the health field.

Leaders can establish and maintain trust with organizations, populations of providers, and outside stakeholders by becoming involved with and integrated into the community rather than isolating their personal and professional practices. To truly "live" in the community, the health leader will be expected to become a part of the process and participate in activities (or minimally support activities) along both horizontal and vertical community bridges. An effective leader will see being involved and becoming part of the community as a natural direction of organizational outreach. Those leaders who find this interaction to be too much of a chore might be advised to rethink whether the dynamic role of health leadership is truly their professional calling.[91,92]

SHARE YOUR KNOWLEDGE

Health leaders are some of the most open, knowledge-sharing, and innovative industry leaders operating in the global community. The health community contains hundreds of health-related journals, industry trade publications, magazines, newspapers, and websites where best practices and innovative techniques are freely shared. Authors of these articles vigorously promote their ideas and personal success stories as benchmarks for success for peer organizations and affiliated professionals to adopt so that (often competing) organizations can improve their effectiveness. This behavior stands in stark contrast to that observed in nonhealth professions, such as the fast-food and soft drink industries, where simple cola formulas and food recipes are regarded as top-secret property.

As a health leader, you have an obligation to contribute to the body of knowledge of the profession.[93] Leaders should personally author, or provide support and opportunity for those in the organization to author, descriptions of best practices and methods that increase outcomes along the continuum of care. Publishing, speaking at local and national conferences, and sharing information and knowledge not only will increase the leader's personal credibility and relevancy in the community, but

also act as a proxy for increasing the recognition of the organization.

PARTNER WITH COMMUNITY LEADERS

The "Henry Ford," resource-dependent model of vertical integration, which attempts to control every aspect of production and throughput in an organization, has long since been cast aside. It is no longer possible to control every employee involved in sales and revenue generation connected to organizational survivability in the health industry. Joint ventures are becoming more common in the healthcare field as organizational entities try to achieve economies of scope and scale. Physician practice plans, sharing of administrative third-party entities, and contracting with part-time employees are models of success for future health organizations. As a result of these ventures, leaders will have to partner with other health leaders who are effective in their own specialty niche, such as technology or billing. In many cases, a leader may belong to an invisible network of suppliers, administrative personnel, record keepers, and human resources. Problems with simple one-item elements, such as a decrease in the availability of blood products from a single-source supplier, can threaten an organization's credibility and survivability in this environment if backup plans and collegial networks of support are not in place to assist the organization when it faces lean, changing, and turbid environments. Today's savvy health leader is aware that the leader of a perceived rival organization today may be the organization's rescuer tomorrow in resource-restricted environments if positive relationships have been maintained.

INTEGRITY

In this chapter, we have presented issues revolving around relevancy and credibility. The end result of consistency in practice and awareness by stakeholders of this genuine predisposition to care is a construct recognized by outside agents as integrity.‡[94,95]

Integrity may be defined as the consistency of actions over time.[96] Lack of integrity is impossible to disguise for long periods. True integrity may be demonstrated through a leader's ability to lead by example, becoming a "Do as I do" leader, and taking responsibility for actions. If an early careerist can embrace these life rules as a compass for daily

---

‡On page 242 of reference 93, Carter credits influence, to some extent, by the fine discussion of integrity in Martin Benjamin's book, *Splitting the Difference: Compromise and Integrity in Ethics and Politics* (Lawrence, KS: Lawrence University Press of Kansas, 1990).

activities, he or she certainly has a high chance of achieving enviable professional development and success.

RELATIONSHIP BUILDING AND COMMUNICATION

The ability to build and maintain relationships is critical for successful health leaders. Highly competent communication skills are also a health leader imperative for success. This section reiterates the foundations of relationships and communication. Read it while you keep all health organization stakeholders in mind, such as physicians, nurses, allied health staff, administrators, other leaders, community members, and patients. Can you visualize what you would do to build relationships and communicate with key stakeholder groups?

Factors to Strengthen Relationships

Relationships refer to the feelings, roles, norms, status, and trust that both affect and reflect the quality of communication between members of a group.[97] Relational communication theorists assert that every message has both a content and relationship dimension, where

- Content contains specific information conveyed to someone.
- Relationship messages cue or provide hints about whether the sender/receiver likes or dislikes the other person.

Communicating with someone in a manner that provides both content and positive relationship information is important. Language, tone, and nonverbal communication work together to provide communicative meaning that is interpreted by another person. In particular, care must be taken with nonverbal communication.[98,99]

- Nonverbal communication is more prevalent than verbal communication. It consists of
  - Eye contact
  - Facial expressions
  - Body posture
  - Movement
- People believe nonverbal communication more than verbal communication: Sixty-five percent of meaning is derived from nonverbal communication.
- People communicate emotions primarily through nonverbal communication: Ninety-three percent of emotions are communicated nonverbally.

Frequency of communication that is timely, useful, accurate, and in reasonable quantity must be considered to reinforce and validate the relationship. One important factor in this regard is *quality communication of sufficient and desired frequency*, which enhances the likelihood of developing quality interpersonal relationships.

Another key factor is disclosure. Disclosure relates to the type of information you and the other person in the relationship share with each other; disclosure is one factor that can help you "measure" or evaluate the depth and breadth of a relationship. The "deeper" the information disclosed, the closer the bond of the relationship. Broader topics of information and experience sharing (e.g., family activities, work, fishing together, or playing golf) suggest a closer bond within the relationship as well.

Self-disclosure can be categorized and measured. In the following model, level 5 illustrates a weak relationship bond whereas level 1 shows a strong relationship bond. Disclosure or self-disclosure is strongly and positively correlated with trust (i.e., connected such that more trust means more disclosure), and trust starts with quality communication. Shown are Powell's self-disclosure levels:[100]

- *Level 5*: Cliché communication
- *Level 4*: Facts and biographical information
- *Level 3*: Personal attitudes and ideas
- *Level 2*: Personal feelings
- *Level 1*: Peak communication (rare; usually with family or close friends)

In summary, self-disclosure can be described as follows:[101]

- A function of ongoing relationships
- Reciprocal
- Timed to what is happening in the relationship (contextual/situational/relational)
- Relevant to what is happening among people present
- Usually moves by small increments

A third factor in establishing effective relationships is trust. Trust is built and earned over time through honest interaction (communication and experiences). Honesty, inclusion, and sincerity are directly linked to building trust. Trust is an essential component of a quality, positive relationship. Honesty is being truthful and open concerning important pieces of information that you share with another person. Inclusion focuses on including the other person in the relationship in activities and experiences that are important to both of you. Inclusion is also about making sure the other person is part of the "group" in the organization. Sincerity is meaning what you say, meaning what you do, and not keeping a record or account of the relationship (not keeping score). Over time, if honesty, inclusion, and sincerity are the basis of your interaction with others, positive and quality relationships will begin to grow.

The fourth factor in relationship building is cultural competence. This factor is based not only on ethnic or national dimensions, but also on socioeconomic factors. For instance, consider the cultural differences in surgeons versus nurses versus facility technicians or linen staff or consultants. Every stakeholder group, and every individual, has a unique culture. Understanding those cultural issues, or "walking a mile in someone else's shoes," is a factor important to building solid interpersonal relationships. Understanding and modifying your approach to relationship building and enhancement based on cultural differences will serve you well in leadership positions.

HAVE FUN

Leaders of health organizations can endure only if they are having fun in pursuit of productive and results-driven efforts. Managing complex issues on a continuous problem-solving cycle[102] can lead to burnout and leader turnover. Those leaders who endure in the profession truly see the art and science of leading complex health organizations as a pseudo-hobby and as an extension of their own personality. If this is you, you have the potential to have a long and productive career in the health field.

SUMMARY

This chapter discussed the globalization of leadership, taking into account that many of the leadership theories and practices presented in this book are based on Western ideologies. The need to leverage technology, lead through followership, and understand the basics of influence and power are important with respect to climate, culture change, and environment. Knowledge management and organizational learning are also keys to keeping the health organization attuned to its dynamic environment and flexible enough to embrace change when necessary. As part of this effort, the health leader may use a variety of integrative models as the basis for fostering change, including change in the culture, within the organization. Lastly, what kind of leader do you want to be? What kind of leader will you be? What will your organization accomplish because of your efforts, initiatives, motivation, and leadership ability?

DISCUSSION QUESTIONS

1. Describe and outline issues related to globalization, power, followership, and culture change from a health leader's perspective.
2. Which tools can a health leader use to change and adapt culture in the health organization? Are some tools better than others? Why?
3. What are the major global leadership style differences and similarities (based on appropriate constructs)? Do leaders from certain cultures seem to be able to use transformational leadership practices more effectively than leaders from other cultures? Why or why not?
4. How can a health leader use power? Which kind of power works best in the setting of followership, culture change, technology, and knowledge management?
5. Can you categorize global leadership differences according to a leader's use of power, technology, and knowledge management? Which leaders from various cultures would use each type of power most successfully? Which leaders from various cultures would lead culture change efforts best? Why?
6. What are the best approaches to knowledge management, organizational learning, and transformational leadership within health organizations? How can a health leader facilitate culture change using transformational leadership practices, tools, and processes?

EXERCISES

1. In a one- to two-page paper, describe and outline issues related to globalization, power, followership, and culture change from a health leader's perspective.
2. In a one- to two-page paper, give examples of tools a health leader can use to change and adapt culture in the health organization.

3. In a two- to three-page paper, relate global leadership style differences and similarities using appropriate constructs for transformational leadership practices.

4. In a two-page paper, analyze a health leader's use of power as it relates to followership, culture change, and knowledge management.

5. In a two- to three-page paper, categorize global leadership differences according to a leader's use of power, technology, and knowledge management.

6. In a four-page paper, evaluate approaches to knowledge management, organizational learning, and transformational leadership in relation to health organization culture change.

REFERENCES

1. Friedman, J. (2015). Globalization, class and culture in global systems. *Journal of World-Systems Research*, *6*(3), 636–656. doi:http://dx.doi.org/10.5195/jwsr .2000.198

2. Harris, T. E., & Nelson, M. D. (2008). *Applied organizational communication: Theory and practice in a global environment* (3rd ed.). New York: Lawrence Erlbaum Associates, Chapter 2.

3. House, R. (2004). Preface. In R. J. House, P. J. Hanges, M. Javidan, P. W. Dorfman, & V. Gupta (Eds.), *Culture, leadership and organizations: The GLOBE Study of 62 societies* (p. xxv). Thousand Oaks, CA: Sage.

4. Bennis, W., Parikh, J., & Lessem, R. (1994). *Beyond leadership: Balancing economics, ethics and ecology* (2nd ed.). Oxford, UK: Blackwell, p. 23.

5. House, R. J., Hanges, P. J., Javidan, M., Dorfman, P. W., & Gupta, V. (Eds.). (2004). *Culture, leadership and organizations: The GLOBE Study of 62 societies*. Thousand Oaks, CA: Sage.

6. Grove, N. D. (n.d.). Worldwide differences in business values and practices: Overview of GLOBE research findings. Retrieved from http://www .grovewell.com/pub-GLOBE-dimensions.html.

7. Triandis, H. C. (2004). Foreword. In R. J. House, P. J. Hanges, M. Javidan, P. W. Dorfman, & V. Gupta (Eds.), *Culture, leadership and organizations: The GLOBE Study of 62 societies* (p. xv). Thousand Oaks, CA: Sage.

8. Hofstede, G. (1980). *Culture's consequences: International differences in work-related values*. London: Sage.

9. Triandis, note 7.

10. Grove, note 6.

11. House et al., note 5, pp. 20, 239; Grove, note 6.

12. Sharma, A., & Grant, D. (2011). Narrative, drama and charismatic leadership: The case of Apple's Steve Jobs. *Leadership 7*(1): 3–26.

13. House et al., note 5; Grove, note 6.

14. Triandis, note 7.

15. House et al., note 5, p. 676, Table 21.1; Grove, note 6.

16. Grove, note 6.

17. Triandis, note 7, p. xvii.

18. Triandis, note 7, p. xvii.

19. Rogers, J., Van Buskirk, A., & Zechman, S. (2011). Disclosure tone and shareholder litigation. *Accounting Review*, *86*(6), 2155–2183.

20. Triandis, note 7, p. xviii.

21. Triandis, note 7, p. xvii.

22. Srivastava, R. (2008). The ABC (and DE) of cultural competence in clinical care. *Ethnicity and Inequalities in Health and Social Care*, *1*(1), 27–33.

23. Van Os, J., & Triffaux, J. M. (2008). Evidence that the two-way communication checklist identifies patient–doctor needs discordance resulting in better 6-month outcome. *Acta Psychiatrica Scandinavica*, *118*(4), 322–326.

24. House, R. (2004). Introduction. In R. J. House, P. J. Hanges, M. Javidan, P. W. Dorfman, & V. Gupta (Eds.), *Culture, leadership and organizations: The GLOBE Study of 62 societies* (pp. 42–45). Thousand Oaks, CA: Sage

25. House, note 24.

26. House, note 24.

27. House, note 24.

28. House, note 24.

29. House, note 24.

30. Merriam-Webster. (n.d.). Technology. Retrieved from http://www.merriam-webster.com/dictionary /technology.

31. Yukl, G. (1994). *Leadership in organizations* (3rd ed.). Englewood Cliffs, NJ: Prentice Hall, p. 91.

32. Yukl, note 31.

33. Ledlow, G., & Coppola, N. (2008). Leadership theory and influence. In J. A. Johnson (Ed.), *Organizational theory, behavior, and development* (pp. 167–192). Sudbury, MA: Jones & Bartlett.

34. March, J. G., & Weisinger-Baylon, R. (1986). *Ambiguity and command: Organizational perspectives on military decision making*. Marshfield, MA: Pitman.

35. Schein, E. H. (1999). *The corporate culture survival guide: Sense and nonsense about culture change.* San Francisco, CA: Jossey-Bass.

36. Conger, J., Speitzer, G., & Lawler, E. III. (1999). *The leader's change handbook: An essential guide to setting direction and taking action.* San Francisco, CA: Jossey-Bass, p. 56.

37. Jelinek, M., & Litterer, J. A. (1995). Toward entrepreneurial organizations: Meeting ambiguity with engagement. *Entrepreneurship: Theory and Practice, 19*(3), 137–169.

38. Bennis, W., & Biederman, P. W. (1997). *Organizing genius: The secret of creative collaboration.* New York: Perseus.

39. Kelman, H. C. (1958). Compliance, identification and internalization: Three processes of attitude change. *Journal of Conflict Resolution, 2,* 51–56.

40. Kelman, H. C. (1974). Further thoughts on the process of compliance, identification, and internalization. In J. T. Tedeschi (Ed.), *Perspectives on social power* (pp. 125–171). Chicago, IL: Aldine.

41. Yukl, note 31, p. 197.

42. Yukl, note 31, p. 209.

43. Jermier, J. M., Slocum, J. W. Jr., Fry, L. W., & Gaines, J. (1991). Organizational subcultures in a soft bureaucracy: Resistance behind the myth and façade of an official culture. *Organization Science, 2*(2), 170–194.

44. Greene, R. (1998). *The 48 laws of power.* New York: Penguin, p. xix.

45. Conger, J. A. (1999). Charismatic and transformational leadership in organizations: An insider's perspective on these developing streams of research. *Leadership Quarterly, 10*(2), 157.

46. Yukl, note 31, p. 207.

47. Yukl, note 31, p. 350.

48. Yukl, note 31, p. 350.

49. Ledlow, G. R., Bradshaw, D. M., & Shockley, C. (2000). Primary care access improvement: An empowerment–interaction model. *Military Medicine, 165*(2), 390–395.

50. Yukl, note 31, p. 353.

51. Yukl, note 31.

52. Schein, note 35.

53. Ledlow, G., Cwiek, M., & Johnson, J. (2002). Dynamic culture leadership: Effective leader as both scientist and artist. In N. Delener & C-n. Chao (Eds.), *Global Business and Technology Association (GBATA) International Conference: Beyond boundaries: Challenges of leadership, innovation, integration and technology* (pp. 694–740), New York: GBATA.

54. Bass, B. (1998). *Transformational leadership: Industrial, military, and educational impact.* Mahwah, NJ: Lawrence Erlbaum Associates.

55. Yukl, note 31.

56. Yukl, note 31.

57. Yukl, note 31, pp. 352–353.

58. Schein, note 35.

59. Schein, note 35.

60. Ledlow et al., note 53.

61. Yukl, note 31, p. 351.

62. Bass, note 54, p. 62.

63. Bass, note 54, pp. 64–65.

64. Bennis et al., note 4.

65. Johnson, J., Ledlow, G., & Kerr, B. (2005). Organizational development, training and knowledge management. In B. Fried, J. Johnson, & M. Fottler (Eds.), *Managing human resources in healthcare organizations* (2nd ed., pp. 202–222). Chicago, IL: Health Administration Press.

66. Davenport, T. H., & Prusak, L. (2000). *Working knowledge: How organizations manage what they know.* Boston: Harvard Business School Press.

67. Nonaka, I. (1994). A dynamic theory of organizational knowledge creation. *Organization Science, 5*(1), 14–37.

68. Fahey, L., & Prusak, L. (1998). The eleven deadliest sins of knowledge management. *California Management Review, 40*(3), 14–37.

69. Fairholm, G. (2003). *The techniques of inner leadership: Making inner leadership work.* Westport, CT: Praeger.

70. Murphy, E. C., & Murphy, M. A. (2002). *Leading on the edge of chaos: The 10 critical elements for success in volatile times.* Paramus, NJ: Prentice-Hall, p. 54.

71. Walsh, A., & Borkowski, S. (1995). Differences in factors affecting health care administration development. *Hospital and Health Services Administration, 40,* 263–277.

72. Ulrich, D., Zenger, J., & Smallwood, N. (1999). *Results-based leadership.* Boston: Harvard Business School Press.

73. Welch, R. L. (2000). Training a new generation of leaders. *Journal of Leadership Studies, 7*(1), 70–81.

74. Metzger, M. J., Flanagin, A. J., Eyal, K., Lemus, D. R., & McCann, R. (2003). Credibility in the 21st century: Integrating perspectives on source, message, and media credibility in the contemporary media environment. In P. Kalbfleisch (Ed.), *Communication yearbook* (Vol. *27,* pp. 293–335). Mahwah, NJ: Lawrence Erlbaum Associates.

75. Sperber, D., & Wilson, D. (1986/1995). *Relevance: Communication and cognition* (2nd ed.). Oxford, UK: Blackwell.

76. Volk, M., & Lucas, M. (1991). Relationship of management style and anticipated turnover. *Dimensions of Critical Care Nursing, 10*(1), 35–40.

77. Dunham, N. C., Kindig, D. A, & Schulz, R. (1994, Fall). The value of the physician executive role to organizational effectiveness and performance. *Health Care Management Review, 19*, 56–63.

78. Morrison, R., Jones, L., & Fuller, B. (1997). The relation between leadership style and empowerment on job satisfaction of nurses. *Journal of Nursing Administration, 27*(5), 27–34.

79. Kouzes, J., & Posner, B. (1995). *The leadership challenge: How to keep getting extraordinary things done in organizations.* San Francisco, CA: Jossey-Bass.

80. Burns, J. (1978). *Leadership.* New York: Harper and Row.

81. Grinspun, D. (2000). Taking care of the bottom line: Shifting paradigms in hospital management. In D. L. Gustafson (Ed.), *Care and consequences* (pp. 22–24). Halifax, NS: Fernwood.

82. Upenieks, V. (2003). What constitutes effective leadership? *Journal of Nursing Administration, 33*(9), 456–467.

83. Coppola, M. N, Burke, D., Dianna, M., & Rangappa, S. (2002). Physician practice awareness and preparedness for HIPAA: A national survey. *Group Practice Journal, 51*(5), 13–19.

84. Corporation for National and Community Service. (n.d.). Edward M. Kennedy Serve America Act of 2009. Retrieved from http://www.nationalservice.gov/about/serveamerica/index.asp.

85. Prather, J. (2009, Winter). Soldiering on: Baylor Army grad mentors the next generation. *Baylor Line Magazine.* Retrieved from http://www.bayloralumniassociation.com/baylor_line/past_issues/win09_soldiering_on.asp.

86. Cole, M. (1999). Become the leader followers want to follow. *Supervision, 60*(12), 9–11.

87. Gillert, A., & Chuzischvili, G. (2004). Dealing with diversity: A matter of beliefs. *Industrial and Commercial Training, 36*(40), 166–170.

88. Six, F. E. (2004, June 24.). Trust and trouble: Building interpersonal trust within organizations [Doctoral thesis]. Retrieved from http://hdl.handle.net/1765/1271.

89. Hamel, G., & Prahalad, C. K. (1994). *Competing for the future.* Boston: Harvard Business School Press.

90. Social Security Act Amendments of 1994 (P.L. 103-432).

91. Laschinger, H., Finegan, J., Shamian, J., & Casier, S. (2000). Organizational trust and empowerment in restructured health care settings: Effects on staff nurse commitment. *Journal of Nursing Administration, 30*(9), 413–425.

92. Wheatley, M. (2002). *Turning to one another: Simple conversations to restore hope to the future.* San Francisco, CA: Berrett-Koehler.

93. Hansen, M., Nohria, N., & Tierney, T. (1999). What's your strategy for managing knowledge? *Harvard Business Review, 77*(2), 106–116.

94. Carter, S. L. (1996). *Integrity.* New York: Basic Books/HarperCollins, pp. 7, 10.

95. Lewicki, R., & Bunker, B. (1996). Developing and maintaining trust in work relationships. In R. N. Kramer & T. R. Tyler (Eds.), *Trust in organizations: Frontiers in theory and research* (pp. 114–139). Thousand Oaks, CA: Sage.

96. Storr, L. (2004). Leading with integrity: A qualitative research study. *Journal of Health Organization and Management, 18*, 415–434.

97. Beebe, S. A., & Masterson, J. T. (1997). *Communicating in small groups: Principles and practices* (5th ed.). New York: Addison-Wesley Educational, p. 71.

98. O'Hair, D., Friedrich, G. W., Wiemann, J. M., & Wiemann, M. O. (1997). *Competent communication* (2nd ed.). New York: St. Martin's Press.

99. Beebe & Masterson, note 97.

100. Beebe & Masterson, note 97.

101. Beebe & Masterson, note 97.

102. Coppola, M. N. (1997, July/August). The four horsemen of the problem solving apocalypse. *Army Medical Department Journal, PB 8-97-7/8*, 20–27.

LEADERSHIP: A CRITICAL FACTOR FOR THE FUTURE SUCCESS OF THE INDUSTRY

The first step to leadership is servanthood.
John Maxwell

This chapter focuses on the technical side of leadership, considering the systems perspective of the leadership definition for health organizations. Intended to highlight the need for leaders to learn, understand, and master complex systems in health organizations, this chapter is not comprehensive but provides information most students in health programs are not exposed to before entering their career. The complex nature of integrated systems in health care must be learned and understood by leaders to maximize the efficiency, effectiveness, and, most importantly, efficacy of the care process.

Competence to lead people and manage the resources of complex and integrated systems, considering both the human business practice(s) and the information systems element that reinforces and supports the business practice(s), requires knowledge, comprehension, and the ability to apply leadership principles to operating the system. A complex and integrated system, the supply chain as integrated with the revenue management system, is highlighted to serve as an example of how leaders need technical competence to evaluate, improve, and reassess systems that provide for, support, and influence the operation of the health organization. Additionally, knowledge required to lead this and other systems, such as budgeting, reimbursement, insurance integration, and other components, is highlighted at the end of the chapter to illustrate the complexity of essential health organization business elements. This is important because all areas within a healthcare organization and all healthcare leaders are dependent on this type of support and collaboration to lead people successfully and manage resources efficiently.

LEARNING OBJECTIVES

1. Describe the basics of the supply chain and revenue management systems in a health organization.

2. Explain the attributes of an efficient supply chain and revenue management system.

3. Relate leadership, leading people, and managing resources to efficient, effective, and efficacious direction of the supply chain and revenue management systems.

4. Identify and assess the key principles of leadership, leading people, and managing resources that apply to developing and improving health systems.

5. Combine three leadership theories or models with actions that assist in leading health systems.

6. Appraise and defend what quality supply chain and revenue management systems would be and summarize a leadership plan to accomplish your ideal systems.

HEALTH SYSTEMS AND LEADERSHIP

Creating, improving, and maintaining efficient, effective, and efficacious systems to deliver and support health and patient care to communities are leader responsibilities. As in the definition of leadership, *systems* support the work of the health industry, but also facilitate an organizational culture of excellence, service, and quality outcomes. For many leaders, the health systems prevalent in the modern health organization are complex and highly integrated, which makes leading people and managing resources in those systems difficult. Without knowledge, comprehension, the ability to apply knowledge, the ability to analyze and synthesize, and the ability to evaluate those systems, how can leaders do their job, improve the systems, or develop the organizational culture necessary to foster excellence in the organization?

Leaders have to be innovators and search out ways to make improvements for the organization. Leaders cannot know every aspect of every system in the organization, but they are expected to have the desire and drive to seek out information and determine ways in which process improvements can be implemented. It is easy to work within the silo of an individual department, but an important and necessary step is to begin to understand how other systems operate and how those systems integrate. To highlight the necessity for leadership to understand systems and how systems work together, consider the Comprehensive Care for Joint Replacement Model, the Final Ruling, which requires bundled pricing for reimbursement (Comprehensive Care for Joint Replacement Model, Final Ruling; http://federalregister.gov/a/2015-29438). Given that 30 to 45% of the expense for these procedures is attributed to the supply chain, understanding this system is critical for successful leaders. In the future, additional service lines in health care will move to bundled pricing (i.e., one set, bundled price for an entire episode of care) under federal programs such as Medicare. Historically, commercial insurance markets have followed in the steps of the federal pricing model in short order, so expect to see bundled pricing as a pervasive method of reimbursement in the future for high-priced service lines and associated procedures. Health leaders must have knowledge of and understand the healthcare supply chain and other systems to improve the viability and longevity of the health organization and the providers of care associated with that enterprise.

To provide a brief and integrative overview for leaders, a supply chain integrated with revenue management within a context of information systems is presented in the following section. These systems, supply chain and revenue management, are two of the least understood and often overlooked systems in the industry, but offer some of the greatest improvement possibilities. How can leaders develop and improve these systems to further the results/outcomes of quality and excellence? How can leaders improve the financial situation of the health organization considering these systems? The hope is that leaders can begin to have a better capability to lead people and manage resources as improvements to these systems become realized from leadership direction, effort, motivation, and understanding. A significant strategy for health organizations today is to improve the efficiency, effectiveness, and efficacy of the supply chain and revenue management systems. As a leader, would this strategy offer competitive advantage for your health organization? As a leader, how can you make a positive influence on the performance of the system? How can you influence quality outcomes? Read and reflect on this chapter from a system perspective and determine how you can utilize your leadership style(s) and plan(s) to enhance these systems.

HEALTHCARE SUPPLY CHAIN

The products brought to the care process by the supply chain system provide the technology that enables the diagnosis, treatment, and care of patients. These products include equipment (such as imaging machines, IV stands, desks, chairs, anesthesia machines, and endoscopy sets), medical and surgical supplies (such as sutures, bandages, gauze, and splints), scientific supplies (such as laboratory testing reagents used for patient specimen testing), pharmaceuticals (such as medications, ointments, and IV solutions), and general supplies (such as office paper, pencils, and cleaning materials). Without these products, the educated and highly trained healthcare professionals could not deliver patient care and other health services. Consuming approximately 30 to 40% of annual operating expenses for a typical hospital, the supply chain comprises many different components, actions, and processes all working together to deliver a product from a raw material to the final product used by the customer.[1] A strong and successful supply chain depends on the quality and success of supply chain management practices, which include "communication within an organization, support for the supply chain management processes and effort, information systems for data collection, analysis and sharing measurement systems to assess total supply chain cost and performance."[2]

Health organizations must acquire necessary equipment and supplies from relationships with other organizations. Cutting-edge health organizations consider

acquisition of these materials to be a strategic imperative called *strategic sourcing*. The CAAVE model and Compatibility and Trust (CaT) assessments provide a framework to lead the strategic sourcing and relationship component of the supply chain system. Brent Johnson, vice president of supply chain at Intermountain Healthcare, defined strategic sourcing as "a disciplined, systematic process of analyzing corporate expenditures and developing strategies to reduce the total costs of externally purchased material and services."[3] A lot of effort and work go into strategic sourcing; it starts with "opportunity assessment and spend analysis, category analysis including specification development, market research that may or may not include a request for information and with all this information available, developing a strategy to approach spending."[4] Once materials are sourced, the aspect of materials management within the supply chain becomes salient. It is not as simple as finding "any" vendor to provide supplies and equipment, but rather, a true leader creates systems that seek value-oriented relationships in strategic partnership and vendor relationships while considering the total cost of the transactions that bring supplies and equipment into the health organization. Strategic sourcing is a subsystem of great importance to health organizations and adds complexity to the equation exponentially. Effective leadership and management of the supply chain requires effective strategic sourcing of the technologies required to provide care, keep communities healthy, and improve the productivity of community residents through efficacious health practices.

THE SUPPLY CHAIN AND SUPPLY CHAIN MANAGEMENT

Although the term *supply chain management* (SCM) may be new to you, it traces its roots back at least 30 years. It was not until the 1990s that SCM captured the attention of most executives in the business community, and it was another decade until some of the key concepts started to appear in health care.

Yet SCM is not really a new concept. From the beginning of time people have thought about and used two key components of SCM in their lives—logistics and transportation. Farmers looked for ways to store their produce and take it to market. Ships sailed to all parts of the world trading spices, silk, cotton, coffee, and other goods. Even military campaigns depend on the success or failure of logistics and transportation.

The modern supply chain has its roots in the industrial revolution of the 1800s. One of the first examples of a supply chain commonly cited is that of the Ford Motor

Company, which introduced the Model T in 1908. To increase production of the Model T, Henry Ford installed the first moving assembly line in 1913. This innovation was important for the development of the supply chain, because as materials were used more quickly, the ability to resupply the required materials became critical.

Supply chain management is the integration of the flows of products, information, services, and finances from the point of origin to the final customer. This includes the transport and storage of raw materials, work in progress, and finished goods from production to the point of usage. A supply chain is an interconnected network of people and organizations that are involved in the production of products and services (see **Figure 14-1**). Every organization is part of a supply chain, whether they produce a product or a service.

MATERIALS MANAGEMENT

Medical and surgical supplies, scientific supplies, pharmaceuticals, and equipment are the technology acquired from strategic sourcing that enables the delivery of healthcare services. These technologies couple with clinician knowledge and expertise within an appropriate healthcare facility to provide efficacious services to patients who need or demand care through the clinician credentials review and privileging process. **Figure 14-2** shows examples of the technologies associated with materials management. Materials management in health care is the storage, inventory control, delivery, quality control, and operational management of supplies, pharmaceuticals, equipment, and other items used in the delivery of patient care or the management of the patient care system. Materials management is a subset of the larger function of SCM; the supply chain also includes the logistics or movement of those materials to caregiving facilities and organizations. For greater understanding of the healthcare supply chain, a visual representation can be found in the reference cited.[5]

The acquisition, logistics, and management of materials in health care are complex and require a sophisticated information system to provide effective, efficient, and efficacious materials at the right time, at the right place, with the right type of material, and in sufficient quantity. All are critical in providing patient care. Materials management and departmental managers have to communicate and work together to ensure periodic automatic replenishment (par) levels and that places where supplies are stored and replenished are appropriate. Par levels set too high will create waste and prove to be costly, considering the cost of storage and cost of the supplies; however, par levels set

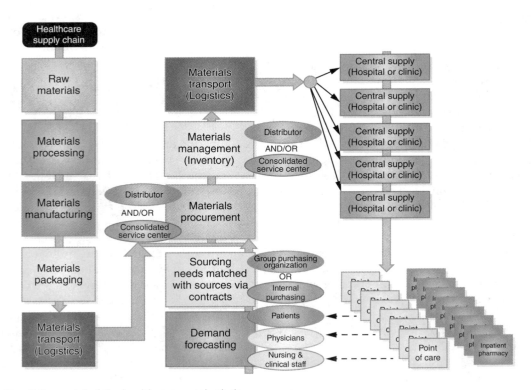

FIGURE 14-1 Simplistic model of the healthcare supply chain.

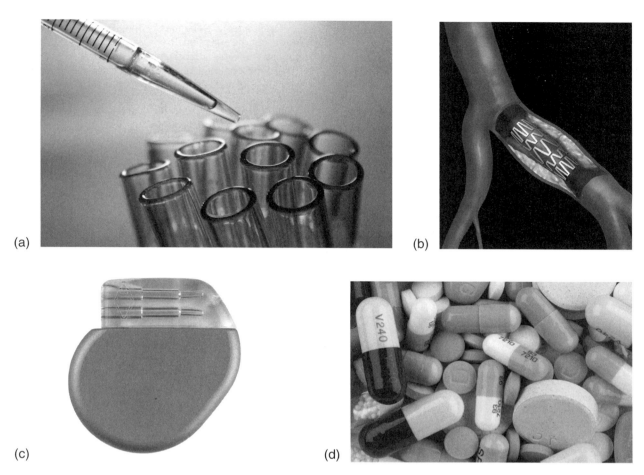

FIGURE 14-2 Technologies supported by the supply chain: (a) patient testing, (b) stent, (c) pacemaker, and (d) pharmaceuticals.
(a) © Cre8tive Images/Shutterstock; (b) © Alexonline/Shutterstock; (c) © Carolina K. Smith, MD/Shutterstock; (d) © Mitar/Shutterstock.

too low can create a situation where there are not adequate supplies available when necessary for patient care and other patient support activities.

The past two decades have seen tremendous change that contributes to the sophistication of the supply chain. The advances in electronic catalogs, information systems such as enterprise resource planning (ERP) systems like Lawson, Infor,[6] or McKesson,[7] warehousing and inventory control systems such as TecSys[8] and Manhattan Associates,[9] exchanges such as Global Health Exchange[10] (GHX), and integration with other systems such as clinical, revenue management, and finance have provided the environment for improved supply chain performance and management in health care. Although advances are readily available, opportunities to improve current supply chain operations in health care still exist. The healthcare supply chain is an untapped resource of financial savings

opportunities (and revenue enhancement opportunities).[11] Information system vendors such as Lawson also recognize efficiency and financial improvement opportunities as keys to selling and marketing their systems and platforms.[12] Additional support for improvement is strongly advocated by the Healthcare Information and Management Systems Society (HIMSS). In a 2007 white paper, HIMSS noted that enormous changes in the healthcare industry necessitated serious changes in both the value chain and in the ability of providers to deliver quality clinical care. Those organizations unable to meet market demands were expected to encounter financial difficulties or even financial ruin due to a confluence of factors, including information overload, a skilled labor shortage, an increase in supply costs, and decreased Medicare reimbursements. One way to avoid these problems would be through enterprise technological solutions, which could serve as tools to increase quality and safety. SCM and ERP have become increasingly important to health organizations, with ERP software for the industry expected to grow 8.7% in North America and 8.8% worldwide through 2009. As the white paper indicated:

> Providers need to have enhanced solutions and technological innovation to meet their annual objectives and long-term strategies. It should not take an 18-month re-implementation of their ERP and SCM systems to do

so. Quick and agile changes by the users should be the norm, not the exception. To enable the intended outcome requires executive support, trained resources, dedicated cross-functional teams, and an effective relationship with the ERP and SCM IS [information system] vendors.[13]

When contemplating the complexity of the healthcare supply chain environment, for example, how do you begin to serve the operating suite or emergency room suite (see **Figure 14–3**) with equipment, scientific supplies,

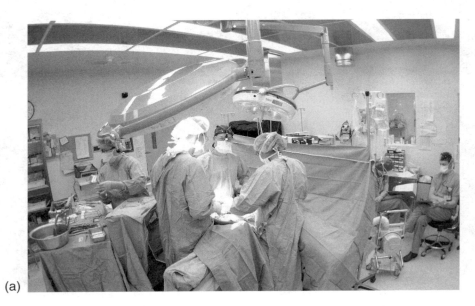

(a)

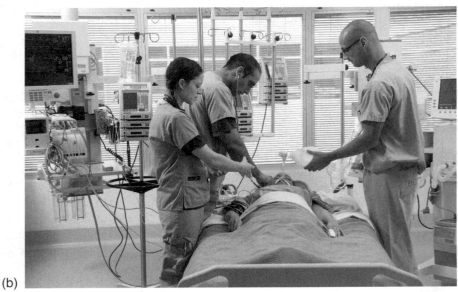

(b)

FIGURE 14-3 (a) Typical operating suite. (b) Typical emergency room suite.

(a) © AbleStock; (b) © iStockphoto.com/LifesizeImages

pharmaceuticals, and medical and/or surgical supplies? Consider the acquisition, logistics, and materials management function of the healthcare supply chain.

The importance of enterprise-wide information systems and the technology associated with those systems, such as barcode scanners and electronic medicinal cabinets (such as Omnicell[14] or Pyxis[15]), should be apparent based on understanding some of the interaction of the operational and management components of the supply chain. To highlight the necessity for integration of the healthcare supply chain, let us examine some basic components: the supply item master file, the charge description master file, the vendor master file, and the transaction history file (**Figure 14-4**).

- *The supply item master file* is a list of all items used in the delivery of care for a health organization that can be requested by healthcare services providers and managers. This file typically contains from 30,000 to 100,000 items.
- *The charge description master file* is a list of all prices for services (diagnosis-related groups [DRGs], Healthcare Common Procedure Coding System [HCPCS], Current Procedural Terminology 4 [CPT-4s], for example) or goods provided to patients, and it serves as the basis for billing.
- *The vendor master file* is a list of all manufacturers or distributors (vendors) who provide the materials needed for the healthcare organization and contains the associated contract terms and prices for specific items. This file typically contains between 200 and 500 different vendors/suppliers.

- *The transaction history file* is a running log of all material transactions of the healthcare organization.

These four basic files, although there are other important files as well, must be integrated and connected to each other to support the operations and management of the supply chain. In a typical health system with 25 hospitals and 75 stand-alone clinics, 3,800 internal customers (those who order from the supply chain operation to provide services to patients or manage healthcare operations) who order a combined $2.4 billion in material and create thousands of transactions from hundreds of vendors would be commonplace. This is the epitome of a system in need of the technological sophistication of an information system. The integration necessary in the modern healthcare organization is illustrated in the wire diagram of interfaces (data stream connections between information systems) across supply chain, clinical, and financial systems shown in **Figure 14-5**.[16]

Technological advances are enabling organizations to more efficiently and consistently manage supply chain operations, billing practices, and compliance while providing flexibility for different processes within the system of care.[17] "In all industries, not just health care, three out of four chief executive officers consider their supply chains to be essential to gaining competitive advantage within their markets."[18,19] According to Vance Moore, CEO of ROi (the supply chain entity within the Sisters of Mercy Health System based in St. Louis, Missouri), in a 2008 presentation he gave in Chicago, the trend in the cost of the healthcare supply chain continues to grow; if the trend continues, the supply chain could equal labor cost in annual operating

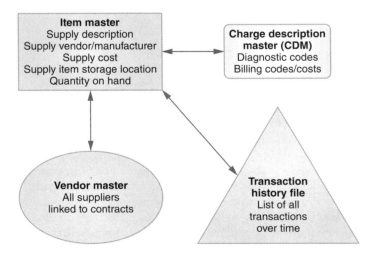

FIGURE 14-4 Integration of master, vendor master, charge description master, and transaction history files.

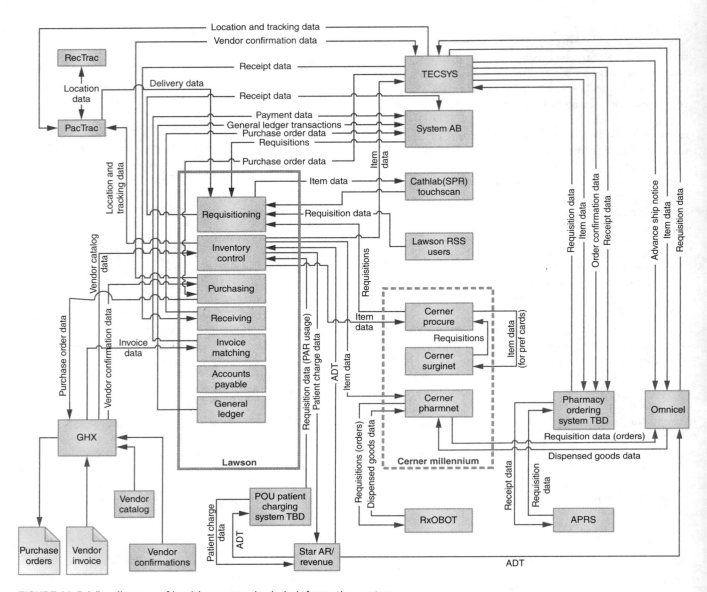

FIGURE 14-5 Wire diagram of healthcare supply chain information systems.

expenses for hospitals and health systems between the years 2020 and 2025.[20] Clearly, maximizing the efficiency of the healthcare supply chain is an increasing concern. For this reason, leaders have to evaluate how processes can be made more efficient. In today's economy and with the changes in health care, health programs, and health-related activities, organizations are facing a more austere payment environment for services provided. This, in turn, puts a larger strain on the organization to become more efficient; however, efficiency cannot be improved at the cost of patient safety, efficacy, and morality.

Consider supply charge capture where patient-specific supplies are ordered for the care of a patient; these supply items are each billed separately to the patient. From an analysis of charges for fiscal year 2003, approximately 36% of inpatient nursing floor unit supply charge capture items were actually being charged correctly.[21] Much of this lost efficiency can be attributed to lack of standard processes and lack or inefficient use of information system technology. In addition, clinical staff who provide patient care are sometimes not informed regarding the downstream effect of not capturing charges correctly. This is not their main focus—their focus is on patient care. Leaders have the responsibility for educating staff to understand the loss that occurs when supplies are not accounted for correctly. Additionally, there has to be education and importance placed on reducing waste and only using what is truly needed for patient care. This type of education is basic and can assist with understanding; however, in order to be successful, emphasis needs to be placed on innovation and technology. Improving business processes and implementing complementary technology can be catalysts for efficiency improvement. Data, such as the supply item master and charge description master (CDM), must be maintained. This is where the supply chain and revenue management system clearly integrate. Accuracy in the hospital's CDM (and item master as well) is essential to efficient supply charge capture.[22] "It is a common problem. Every year, hospitals lose millions of dollars when items used in the course of a patient's care somehow slip through the system without ever being charged or reimbursed."[23]

Typically materials management, also known as central supply (CS), in the hospital bears the burden of having the right item at the right place at the right time.[24] As a starting point, the following concepts, coupled with a solid information system platform, should be applied to improve SCM and materials management.[25–27]

Process Standardization in Conjunction with Utilization of an Information System

Develop standardized (or *more standardized*) processes for:

- Item master and CDM maintenance and synchronization
- Supply stock selection, reduction, compression, and management
- Supply charge item capture (accurate and timely)
- Accountability measures for central supply and clinical units
- Clinical/floor stocked supplies replenishment
- Daily reconciliation of pharmaceuticals and medical/surgical supply items, especially supply charge capture items

Process Standardization in Process Improvement: Balancing Tradeoffs

Competing goals exist among various stakeholder groups; tradeoffs will be required to find the proper balance that best meets all needs.

- Clinician goals
  - Do not impede caregivers or patient care delivery
  - Minimize rework
  - Right supplies, right place, right time

- Supply chain managers/central supply goals
  - Improve accuracy for supplies consumed
  - Improve timeliness for supply consumption
  - Efficient use of labor
- Revenue and cost avoidance goals
  - Procure and acquire material wisely with contracted compliance goals
  - Efficient management of materials considering utilization rates, preferences, expiration dates, and Food and Drug Administration requirements
  - Reduce number of supply charge capture items
  - Improve accuracy for charge capture
  - Improve timeliness for charge capture
  - Improve charge capture rate

Operating and managing a supply chain in health care requires competent and efficient business processes, utilization of a complementary information system that is integrated with clinical and financial systems, and a set of goals and priorities that allow clinicians to provide care to patients. In the final analysis, it is all about getting the right items to the right clinicians at the right time to care for people that entrust their care, life, and well-being to us, the healthcare team.

Overall, the supply chain integrates with every aspect of the organization's mission and tasks across the operation. To provide additional background on elements that connect to the supply chain and are essential to the revenue management system, a quick overview of key elements important to those integrated systems is presented.

One of the first considerations a leader faces in managing resources of the supply chain for their area of responsibility is budgeting. Budgeting will be overviewed briefly as an important skill of leading systems in health organizations.

BUDGETING TECHNIQUES

Zero-based budgeting is an approach to budgeting that continually questions both the need for existing programs and their level of funding, as well as the need for new programs.

Incremental budgeting is an approach to budgeting that starts with an existing budget to plan future budgets. This approach gives a slight increase, no change, or slight decrease to various line items, programs, or departments. In some cases, all programs may receive an equal increase or decrease. In other instances, management may differentially give increases or decreases.

Program budgeting is an extension of the line item budget, which shows revenues and expenses by category, such as labor and supplies. The program budget instead shows revenues and expenses by program or service lines.

Cash flow is concerned with "Where did cash come from and where did it go?" Changes in cash position are categorized as either sources of cash flow (receipts) or uses of cash flow (disbursements). Sources of cash include collection of accounts receivable, cash sales, investment income, sale of assets, financing, and capital contributions. Uses of cash include payments to employees, payments to suppliers, payments to lenders for interest and principle, purchases of fixed assets, and investments.

The primary factor affecting the validity of the cash budget is the accuracy of the forecasts for individual cash flow categories. The greater the degree of possible variation between actual and forecasted cash flow, the higher the liquidity needs of the firm. Firms that cannot predict cash flow with much certainty should increase their cash balances or negotiate lines of credit to escape the possibility of severe cash insolvency problems.

The *operating margin* is a profitability ratio. It is computed by dividing operating income (total operating revenues minus total operating expenses) by total operating revenues. The margin indicates the proportion of profit earned for each dollar of operating revenue.

$$\text{Operating margin} = \frac{\text{Operating income}}{\text{Total operating revenues}}$$

The purpose of a profitability ratio is to determine whether the firm is making money, and to what extent. It affects the organization's flexibility and its ability to survive. This ratio is of special interest to boards, owners (present and potential), and long-term lenders. Higher is better for all profitability ratios. As budgeting is the "cost" side of leading a system, reimbursement is the "revenue" side of the equation. A brief overview of reimbursement methods is provided next.

REIMBURSEMENT METHODS

There are several ways in which organizational entities control pricing. There is no general "one-size-fits-all" approach to creating revenue scales; however, the following methodologies are the most common in the industry.

Per Diem

The phrase *per diem* is Latin for *per day*, and it is often used when referring to daily employee expenses or reimbursements. The provider is paid a fixed amount for each day that service is provided, regardless of the nature of the services. The provider bears the risk for any costs that exceed the daily (per diem) rate.

Diagnosis-Related Group (DRG)

Diagnosis-related group (DRG) is an inpatient classification system used by the U.S. Department of Health and Human Services, Centers for Medicare and Medicaid Services (CMS) to determine hospital reimbursement for Medicare patients. The DRG system categorizes patients with similar medical diagnoses, treatment patterns, and statistically comparable lengths of stay in a hospital and attaches a reimbursement rate to each DRG. Some managed care plans use the DRG payment method for setting payment rates and selecting providers. The provider is paid based on the patient's diagnosis. Medicare's DRGs are used as the basis for determining the patient's diagnosis. The provider is at risk for the portion of the care that exceeds the allowable amount for the DRG.

Capitated Method

The capitated method uses a fixed dollar amount for each month the patient remains under contract. This requires an explicit selection of a provider by the patient, even though the patient may not seek care at all. The provider is paid a fixed amount per enrollee per period (usually a year). The enrollees can access the system as often as needed during this period. The provider, usually a hospital–physician group combination, accepts full risk for managing the patient's care. Capitation has proven unattractive to physicians and patients alike. Of all payment systems, this one is the most risky for the provider.

Under a capitated form of reimbursement, the total amount of reimbursement is a function of the number of subscribers, not the volume of services provided. Once the coverage period starts, the number of subscribers is fixed; therefore, the total revenue curve is flat (i.e., does not increase with volume).

Whoever accepts the capitated rate is responsible for any overutilization of health services that exceeds the premium paid. All providers, third-party payers, and insurance companies can also be paid on a capitated basis, but it is up to the initial organization receiving the premium to negotiate the method of reimbursement to the providers actually providing the care.

Cost Based

In the cost-based method, the provider is paid for the cost of providing care. Generally the payer and provider negotiate over the costs that will be reimbursed. There are two approaches to cost-based reimbursement:

1. *Retrospective*: The provider is reimbursed for the allowable costs as they happen and receives a final settlement when the care is complete.

2. *Prospective*: The payer knows how much they will reimburse for each category of care provided. If costs exceed the predetermined amount, sometimes the payer will upwardly adjust the reimbursement. Where cost and revenue are planned, leaders must understand a pro forma and how costs and revenues come together in various budget models. The basics of essential budgets are provided.

Cash Budget

A cash budget is a forecast of estimated cash receipts and disbursements for a specified period of time. It identifies required cash balances throughout the year. The cash budget uses the capital budget to determine what capital items will be purchased in the current year. The cash budget must be structured such that required cash balances are available when needed to purchase capital items. Effective cash budgeting means an organization holds the minimum acceptable cash balance at all times. Too much cash means lost opportunity for investment. Too little cash means the organization cannot purchase necessary items.

Revenue

This is the total amount of money received by a company for goods sold or services provided during a certain time period. It also includes all net sales, exchange of assets, interest, and any other increase in owner's equity, and it is calculated before any expenses are subtracted. Net income can be calculated by subtracting expenses from revenue. In terms of reporting revenue in a company's financial statements, different companies consider revenue to be received, or "recognized," in different ways. For example, revenue could be recognized when a deal is signed, when the money is received, when the services are provided, or at other times. There are rules specifying when revenue should be recognized in different situations for companies using different accounting methods, such as cash basis or accrual basis.

Operating Budget

The operating budget (revenues and expenses) outlines when money will come to the organization in the form of revenues and leave the organization in the form of expenses. The cash budget uses the operating budget projections to project cash balances at each point throughout the year. The operating budget is used to identify only those revenues and expenses that will occur in the coming year.

Budget

The capital budget is one of the four major types of budgets (the other three being cash, revenue, and operating). It summarizes the anticipated purchases for the year. Typically, to be included, all items in this budget must have a minimum purchase price, such as $500, and a plan to finance long-term outlays, such as for fixed assets like facilities and equipment. There are two major parts of the capital budgeting process. The first involves determining whether the capital project meets the financial and nonfinancial cutoff points of the organization. The second involves ranking the projects that meet the initial screening criteria, which is capital rationing.

COMPLEXITY OF INTEGRATED SYSTEMS

So, given the previous short list of items that were overviewed, how complex are the integrated systems outlined in this chapter? How do you lead people and manage resources amid the operations of these systems? Seek out knowledge to understand how these systems operate on a daily basis and then on a strategic basis. If anything prompts your response as a leader, use this chapter as a catalyst for seeking more knowledge and understanding so you can lead these essential and technically rich systems. Can you build a mental picture of the integration of the elements discussed in this chapter?

OVERVIEW OF REVENUE MANAGEMENT

The revenue management function is based on the tasks associated with claims processing and the management of those activities. An integrated information system, connected to the clinical, supply chain, financial, and human resources systems, is necessary to operate a revenue management system. Previously, we highlighted the connection of supply chain operations with charge capture. Imagine the number of insurance organizations (third-party payers) that interact with a typical health organization; there could be dozens. To make the situation more complex, each of these payer organizations/insurers may have several plans or benefit packages for its beneficiaries. Each benefit package has different rules, pays different amounts (reimbursement), and has different copays, deductibles, and "carve-outs" (services or items not covered or paid for in the benefit package). Some patients are covered by governmental plans and others by private insurance or charity care. Some have no insurance coverage, making them a private pay patient. The system must be able to keep each of the payer types separate, know the requirements of how to bill the claims and who to bill with the balances, and know whether the balances need to be written off and not billed to anyone. Collections can be very challenging to manage for the typical health organization. Many new standards have been adopted for claims processing, but there are still many different options and variables associated with the multitude of insurance organizations/payers/insurers. The key to revenue management is to capture the work of the health organization that is reimbursable; that is, services and supplies that can be charged to an insurance organization/payer/insurer for payment to the health organization. Essential to this effort is the "clean claim."

Sending clean claims is vital to quick payment/reimbursement. The health organization needs to receive the payment/reimbursement as quickly as possible in order to meet the financial obligations in its disbursements and accounts payable functions. Being paid is usually a high priority for most employees, so collecting the money is crucial. Clearly, gathering the claims, including supply items that can be charged to a patient for their care, is of paramount concern. The claims processing system needs to be able to review the claim before it is submitted to make sure all necessary fields are complete and accurate. If the claim does not go out clean, it will be denied, creating even more of a delay in receiving the payment for the service provided.

Denial management is an essential element of revenue management. The information system needs to be able to prevent denials from the insurance companies in a variety of ways. For example, the request by clinical personnel for the patient to stay an additional day in their current patient status (i.e., observation, inpatient) may be denied. The submitted insurance claim for a patient's stay may also be denied for improper coding or missing information. When the denial occurs, the information system needs to be able to track the update and progress on getting the denial reversed. Just because a claim or request was denied initially does not mean the decision cannot be reversed. Persistence and proper documentation can be the deciding factor on the reversal. As Cruze points out,[28] documentation must be detailed and able to be included with the denial reversal request in order to be effective. In addition, the communications that took place between each area of patient care must be maintained together in an orderly manner for the proof of the claim to be shown.

LEADING EVALUATION OF SYSTEMS

The ability for leaders in health organizations to create, improve, and maintain systems, such as the supply chain management system, requires understanding of the system, but also an understanding of methods used to evaluate the system. Benchmarking your system against other health organizations is essential; this key element requires a list of important measures or metrics that are standardized and then compared to determine what areas of the system need improvement. Also remember, the system links to other systems, such as the linkage between the supply chain and the revenue management systems, so a thorough understanding and assessment are required before improvements are made to any system in the health organization. **Table 14-1** is an excerpt of metrics that can assist evaluation efforts of the supply chain system. In addition to understanding metrics, there has to be an overall understanding of the supply chain system and the needs of each department as a customer.

A manager in the operating room, pharmacy, or laboratory is not going to have an understanding of the processes within the supply chain system, just as the supply chain system manager is not going to understand the processes within various clinical departments. This is not unusual; even though these departments work closely together they are not in tune with each other. To have success with improving processes, an overall understanding has to be accomplished before improvements can be made. Communication is important in this situation. Managers need to work together to outline their processes for each other as well as outline how their individual processes are affected by the other department(s). Once they have an overall understanding, managers can work together to determine where areas for improvement exist. This can be accomplished through basic communication and taking the time to work together. Meetings with management from each department to understand each other's processes are key. By taking this basic step, leaders can move much further in improvement.

Often there is a basic misunderstanding of processes that inhibits decisions and improvements from being implemented. In addition to open communication to understand processes, leaders must also communicate to implement improvements that will be long lasting. Without the proper knowledge and the right individuals around the table to discuss improvements, it is likely that only quick fixes will be implemented. There is also the risk of implementing changes or process improvements that may have a positive impact on one department, but end up having a negative impact on another department. These types of issues are all a result of a lack of understanding and a lack of communication between departments.

It is never too late to open the doors to this type of communication and bring about a culture of understanding and working together instead of working in separate silos. Leadership is a team operation of managing the integration of systems.

Table 14-1 Excerpt of Healthcare Supply Chain Metrics

Healthcare Supply Chain Metric	Numeric	Calculation/ Formula	Target	Variance (add and subtract to target for range)	Definition	Importance
Inventory Turnover Rate	#	Total annual expense on stock items ÷ Average inventory value in stock	> 15	Range: +8 to −2	Measures the capital invested in storing goods and in the value of those goods; should be evaluated in the context of reordering and restocking and the risk of being out of stock	Inventory is an asset that should be utilized often because dollars tied up in inventory represent funds not available for other purposes.
Contract Utilization Rate	%	Amount of dollar value in purchases using a valid contract ÷ Amount of total dollar value of all purchases × 100	> 79%	Range: +11 to −4%	Measures the percentage of supply chain item spending for contracted items as compared to total supply chain purchases	Supplies purchased utilizing a valid contract from a vendor promote standardization, typically cost less, and promote contract compliance and may impact contract compliance discounts or rebates and contract satisfaction.
Total Supply Cost per Adjusted Case Mix Indexed Discharge	$	Total supply cost ÷ Total number of adjusted discharges (CMI weighted)	$853.37	$507.98	Measures the medical/surgical, pharmaceutical, and other supplies' cost per adjusted patient discharge weighted by case mix index	This metric establishes the nonlabor expense by cost per adjusted patient discharge as weighted by all-payer case mix index, and represents price, utilization, and technology impacts on nonlabor costs of care.
Medical/ Surgical Supply Cost per Adjusted Case Mix Indexed Discharge	$	Medical/surgical supply cost ÷ Total number of adjusted discharges (CMI weighted)	$108.00	$82.00	Measures the medical/surgical supplies' cost per adjusted patient discharge weighted by case mix index	This metric establishes the nonlabor expense attributed to medical/surgical supplies by cost per adjusted patient discharge as weighted by all-payer case mix index, and represents price, utilization, and technology impacts on nonlabor costs of care.
Pharmaceutical Supply Cost per Adjusted Case Mix Indexed Discharge	$	Pharmaceutical supply cost ÷ Total number of adjusted discharges (CMI weighted)	$744.14	$425.00	Measures the pharmaceutical supplies' cost per adjusted patient discharge weighted by case mix index	This metric establishes the nonlabor expense attributed to pharmaceuticals by cost per adjusted patient discharge as weighted by all-payer case mix index, and represents price, utilization, and technology impacts on nonlabor costs of care.

(continues)

Table 14-1 Excerpt of Healthcare Supply Chain Metrics (continued)

Healthcare Supply Chain Metric	Numeric	Calculation/ Formula	Target	Variance (add and subtract to target for range)	Definition	Importance
Other Supply Cost per Adjusted Case Mix Indexed Discharge	$	Other supply cost ÷ Total number of adjusted discharges (CMI weighted)	$1.22	$0.98	Measures the other supplies' cost per adjusted patient discharge weighted by case mix index	This metric establishes the nonlabor expense attributed to other supplies by cost per adjusted patient discharge as weighted by all-payer case mix index, and represents price, utilization, and technology impacts on nonlabor costs of care.
Supply Charge Capture Rate	%	Total dollar value of supplies charged to a patient ÷ Total dollar value of all supplies purchased × 100	Organization specific	Organization specific	Measures the percentage of supply dollars captured in a patient charge as compared to total supply dollars purchased	This ratio measures the effectiveness of supply charge capture processes.
Supply Attribution Value (SAV)	$	(Standard supply cost per DRG × Number of patients in each DRG) ÷ Total number of inpatients in all DRGs	Must establish BM	Based on BM	Measures the supply cost intensity for the patient population of a particular hospital (using supply costs as weighting similar to CMI weighting)	This metric indicates the intensity of supplies a facility is using and is then used to create better benchmark groupings. Additionally, the same standard supply costs per DRG that are used to calculate the SAV are used to calculate a predicted total supply spend.
Stock Inventory Fill Rate	%	Number of stock item requisition lines filled completely the first time ÷ Number of total stock item requisitions × 100	> 96%	2%	Measures the stock inventory (item master, stock, and standard item) fill rate for each supply location	This ratio measures the level of customer service provided by a stock inventory location; a higher fill rate ratio indicates a higher level of service with a tradeoff of either a higher stock inventory value and storage cost, higher management cost, or more intense management of time sequencing of the stock line.
Pharmacy Inventory Fill Rate	%	Number of pharmaceutical stock item requisition lines filled completely the first time ÷ Number of total pharmaceutical stock item requisitions × 100	> 97%	1%	Measures the pharmaceutical stock inventory (item master, stock, and standard item) fill rate for each supply location	This ratio measures the level of customer service provided by a pharmaceutical stock inventory location; a higher fill rate ratio indicates a higher level of service with a tradeoff of either a higher pharmaceutical stock inventory value and storage cost, higher management cost, or more intense management of time sequencing of the stock line.

Table 14-1 Excerpt of Healthcare Supply Chain Metrics (continued)

Healthcare Supply Chain Metric	Numeric	Calculation/ Formula	Target	Variance (add and subtract to target for range)	Definition	Importance
Delivery Date Accuracy	%	Number of purchase order line delivery date item deliveries on or before expected delivery date ÷ Total number of purchase order delivery lines × 100	> 85%	2%	Measures the item delivery performance to customers on time or before time as compared to the required or expected delivery date as compared by line level on purchase orders	This ratio measures the vendor delivery performance for on-time or before-time deliveries of items by comparing the actual delivery date of a purchase order line to the required or expected delivery date.
Purchase Order Accuracy	%	Number of discrepant purchase order lines ÷ Total number of purchase order lines × 100	< 3%	1%	Measures the percentage of discrepant purchase order lines (lines with errors or that are noncompliant) as compared to total invoiced purchase order lines. Most discrepancies are a result of pricing, missing data, or receiving error problems.	This ratio is used to assess the success of matching invoices to the proper purchase order, compliance with contract pricing in the item master and vendor master files, and the accuracy of receiving processes.
Catalog Purchase Order Rate	%	Number of purchase order lines generated via catalog ÷ Total number of purchase order lines generated × 100	> 89%	2%	Measures the percentage of purchase order lines created by the electronic catalog for regular items	A noncatalog item is a special order item that is not in inventory or available in the item master, resulting in more intervention and effort by the requester and buyer; this can negatively impact contract compliance.
Par or Cart Stock Out Rate	%	Total number of stock outs at par or cart level ÷ Total number of replenishments × 100	> 3%	1%	Measures the ability to get the right supply to the right location for patient care purposes	This metric maintains emphasis on supply chain support of the patient care system.

Table 14-1 Excerpt of Healthcare Supply Chain Metrics (continued)						
Healthcare Supply Chain Metric	Numeric	Calculation/ Formula	Target	Variance (add and subtract to target for range)	Definition	Importance
Par or Cart Fill Rate	%	Number of stock items replenished at the par or cart level ÷ Total number of items ordered by an end user customer × 100	> 97%	1%	Measures the supply chain operation's ability to support the clinician and the patient care mission for stock items	This measure focuses on meeting patient and clinician needs and demands for stock items.
Annual Purchase Order Cost	$	Annual operating expense for supply chain operation and management ÷ Total number of annual purchase orders	Estimated BM	Based on BM	Measures the efficiency of the supply chain operation and management by the number of purchase orders	This cost maintains focus on supply chain operation and management efficiency.
Average Lines per Purchase Order	#	Total number of purchase order lines issued ÷ Total number of purchase orders	20	5	Measures the purchasing process efficiency and can impact number of invoices processed	This measure intends to improve the efficiency of the purchase order process and reduce the number of invoices by increasing the number of purchase order lines for purchase order and per invoice.
Electronic Requisitions Rate	%	Number of requisitions electronically sent to purchasing function ÷ Total number of requisitions × 100	Estimated BM	Based on BM	Measures the use of internal information systems to leverage efficiencies	This metric focuses on the time spent processing requisitions manually.
Electronic Purchase Order Rate	%	Number of purchase orders sent electronically ÷ Total number of purchase orders × 100	Estimated BM	Based on BM	Measures the electronic purchase order rate for purposes of efficiency	This measure assesses the use of information systems in the purchasing function, with the intent of reducing purchasing process costs for both the supply chain and suppliers or vendors.
Electronic Funds Transfer (EFT) Paid Invoices Rate	%	Number of invoices paid electronically ÷ Total number of invoices × 100	Estimated BM	Based on BM	Measures the utilization of information systems and EFT for supply transactions with suppliers and vendors	This metric intends to illustrate improvement to supplier relationships and reduction of costs associated with paying invoices while improving cash flow management.

Key: BM = Benchmark; CMI = Case mix index; DRG = Diagnosis-related group

Table 14-2 Baldrige Evaluation Criteria Domains

Section	Required Evaluative Criteria
Leadership	1.1 Leadership: Senior Leadership 1.2 Leadership: Governance and Societal Responsibilities 2.1 Strategic Planning: Strategy Development 2.2 Strategic Planning: Strategy Implementation 3.1 Customer Focus: Voice of the Customer (Stakeholder/Patient Engagement) 3.2 Customer Focus: Customer Engagement (Stakeholder/Using Patient Information)
Performance	4.1 (Performance Improvement) 4.2 (Performance Improvement/Knowledge Management) 5.1 Workforce Focus: Workforce Engagement 5.2 Workforce Focus: Workforce Environment (Workforce Capability) 6.1 Process Management: Work Systems 6.2 Process Management: Work Processes (Design, Manage, and Improve Work Processes)
Results	7.1 Results: Health Care Outcomes 7.2 Results: Customer-Focused Outcomes 7.3 Results: Financial and Market Outcomes 7.4 Results: Workforce-Focused Outcomes 7.5 Results: Process Effectiveness Outcomes 7.6 Results: Leadership Outcomes

Modified from Baldrige National Quality Program. (2009). *2009–2010 health care criteria for performance excellence.* Gaithersburg, MD: National Institute of Standards and Technology.

Additionally, leaders must assess and evaluate how specific systems integrate and contribute to the whole organization's performance and results or outcomes. In the example, shown in **Table 14-2**, the Baldrige National Quality Award Program is reiterated. Review the table to imagine how the supply chain management system, with its links to other systems, fits into the total schema of the health organization's performance and results.

MEANING FOR LEADERS

What does the supply chain, revenue management, evaluation, and improvement of these integrated systems mean for health leaders? Based on the overview of the supply chain and its integration with revenue management, and from the standpoint of charge capture operations, health leaders have several needs that must be fulfilled to continue down a successful path of creating, improving, and maintaining efficient, effective, and efficacious systems.

- Need to stay current
- Need to stay technically competent
- Need to stay artfully competent
- Need to thoroughly understand systems that provide and support health delivery
- Need to thoroughly understand how these systems integrate to create the whole
- Need to have a method or system (yes, another system) to evaluate, improve, and link back to strategic planning
- Need to link to your plan of leadership to lead people and manage resources
- Need to continuously reevaluate the system(s) and how your leadership makes a positive difference to the organization
- Need to consistently look for ways to influence those around you and those in other departments to seek processes that make sense
- Need to encourage and help staff develop in their understanding of process improvement

SUMMARY

Leaders in health organizations must have capability in both the art and science of leadership. Competence to lead people, help them to understand the larger picture, and help them have buy-in regarding how processes can improve, as well as to manage resources of complex and integrated systems, considering both the human business practices element and the information system element that reinforces and supports the business practices, requires several needs to be met, of which fully understanding the system(s) is of primary concern. A technical, complex, and integrated system, the supply chain, as integrated with the revenue management system, was highlighted to serve as an example of how leaders need technical competence to evaluate, improve, and reassess systems that provide, support, and influence the operation of the health organization.

DISCUSSION QUESTIONS

1. Describe the technically competent leader you want to become and be in a health organization. What is unique about your description?
2. What are the attributes of a technically astute, successful health leader in the industry today?
3. What are three leadership and leadership-oriented theories and models that would assist you in leading people and managing resources of the supply chain or revenue management systems?
4. What are the key principles of the supply chain, and how do those principles interact in your plan and style of leadership?
5. Combine three or more methods to evaluate technical systems in health organizations.
6. Appraise and defend a "perfect" health leader of technical systems by explaining the knowledge, skills, abilities, and competencies of the "perfect" leader. Is this similar to the type of leader you want to be? Why or why not?

EXERCISES

1. In a one-page paper, describe the technical leader you want to become and be in a health organization.
2. In a one- to two-page paper, explain the attributes of a technically successful health leader in the industry today.
3. In a one- to two-page paper, relate leadership and leadership-oriented theories and models to attributes, behaviors, and actions of technically successful health leaders.
4. In a two- to three-page paper, identify and assess the key principles of the supply chain and/or revenue management systems (for leading people and managing resources). Describe how your leadership plan and style work with those principles.
5. In a two-page paper, combine three or more leadership-oriented theories or models with principles of evaluation of technical systems such as the supply chain.
6. In a three-page paper, appraise and defend a "perfect" technical system health leader by explaining the knowledge, skills, abilities, and competencies of the "perfect" leader.

REFERENCES

1. Callender, S. E. (2010, December 1). Barriers and best practices for material management in the healthcare sector. *Engineering Management Journal*, 11–19.
2. Callender, note 1, p. 11.
3. Kaczmarek, D. S. (2010). Tightening up strategic sourcing efforts. *Healthcare Purchasing News*, *34*(1), 56.
4. Kaczmarek, note 3.
5. Lawson. (2011). Lawson supply chain management for healthcare: Imagine achieving increased efficiency and reduced healthcare procurement costs [White paper]. Retrieved from http://www.lawson.com.
6. Infor. (n.d.). Infor healthcare. Retrieved from http://www.lawson.com/Industries/Healthcare/.
7. McKesson. (n.d.). Home page. Retrieved from http://www.mckesson.com/en_us/McKesson.com/.

8. Tecsys. (n.d.). Home page. Retrieved from http://www.tecsys.com.

9. Manhattan Associates. (n.d.). Distribution management: "Managing your warehouse is a lot like playing chess." Retrieved from http://www.manh.com/solutions/distribution-management.

10. GHX. (n.d.). Home page. Retrieved from http://www.ghx.com.

11. Roark, D. C. (2005). Managing the healthcare supply chain. *Nursing Management, 36*(2), 36–40.

12. Lawson, note 5.

13. Healthcare Information and Management Systems Society, Enterprise Information Systems Steering Committee. (2007). Healthcare ERP and SCM information systems: Strategies and solutions [White paper]. Washington, D.C.: Healthcare Information and Management Systems Society.

14. Omnicell. (n.d.). Home page. Retrieved from http://www.omnicell.com.

15. CareFusion. (n.d.). Pyxis MedStation system. Retrieved from http://www.carefusion.com/medical-products/medication–management/-medication-technologies/pyxis-medstation–system.aspx.

16. Achieving Supply Chain Excellence Through Technology (ASCET). (2005). *Designing the standard for a healthy supply chain*. Birmingham, AL: Montgomery Research Institute, Chapter 6.

17. ASCET, note 16.

18. Ledlow, G., Corry, A., & Cwiek, M. (2007). *Optimize your healthcare supply chain performance: A strategic approach*. Chicago, IL: Health Administration Press, p. 2.

19. Poirier, C., & Quinn, F. (2003). A survey of supply chain progress. *Supply Chain Management Review*, September/October.

20. Moore, V. (2008, March). Clinical supply chain. Presentation at the American College of Healthcare Executives National Congress, Chicago, IL.

21. Bacon, S., & Pexton, C. (2010). Improving patient charge capture at Yale-New Haven. Retrieved from http://www.isixsigma.com/index.php?option=com_k2&view=item&id=997:&Itemid=49.

22. Barrett, M. J. (1993, January). Improving charge capture to increase net revenue. *Healthcare Financial Management*. Retrieved from http://www.highbeam.com/doc/1G1-13522480.html.

23. Bacon & Pexton, note 21, p. 1.

24. Burns, L. (2002). *The healthcare chain*. San Francisco: Jossey-Bass, p. 14.

25. Evahan Technology. (2005, March). Point of use technology in the supply chain. Retrieved from http://www.ferret.com.au/c/Evahan/Point-of-use-technology-in-the-supply-chain-n698823.

26. Ledlow et al., note 18.

27. Ledlow, J. R., Stephens, J. H., & Fowler, H. H. (2011). Sticker shock: An exploration of supply charge capture outcomes. *Hospital Topics, 89*(1), 9.

28. Cruze, G. (2008). The myths of benchmarking healthcare IT spending. *Healthcare Financial Management, 62*(2), 84–89.

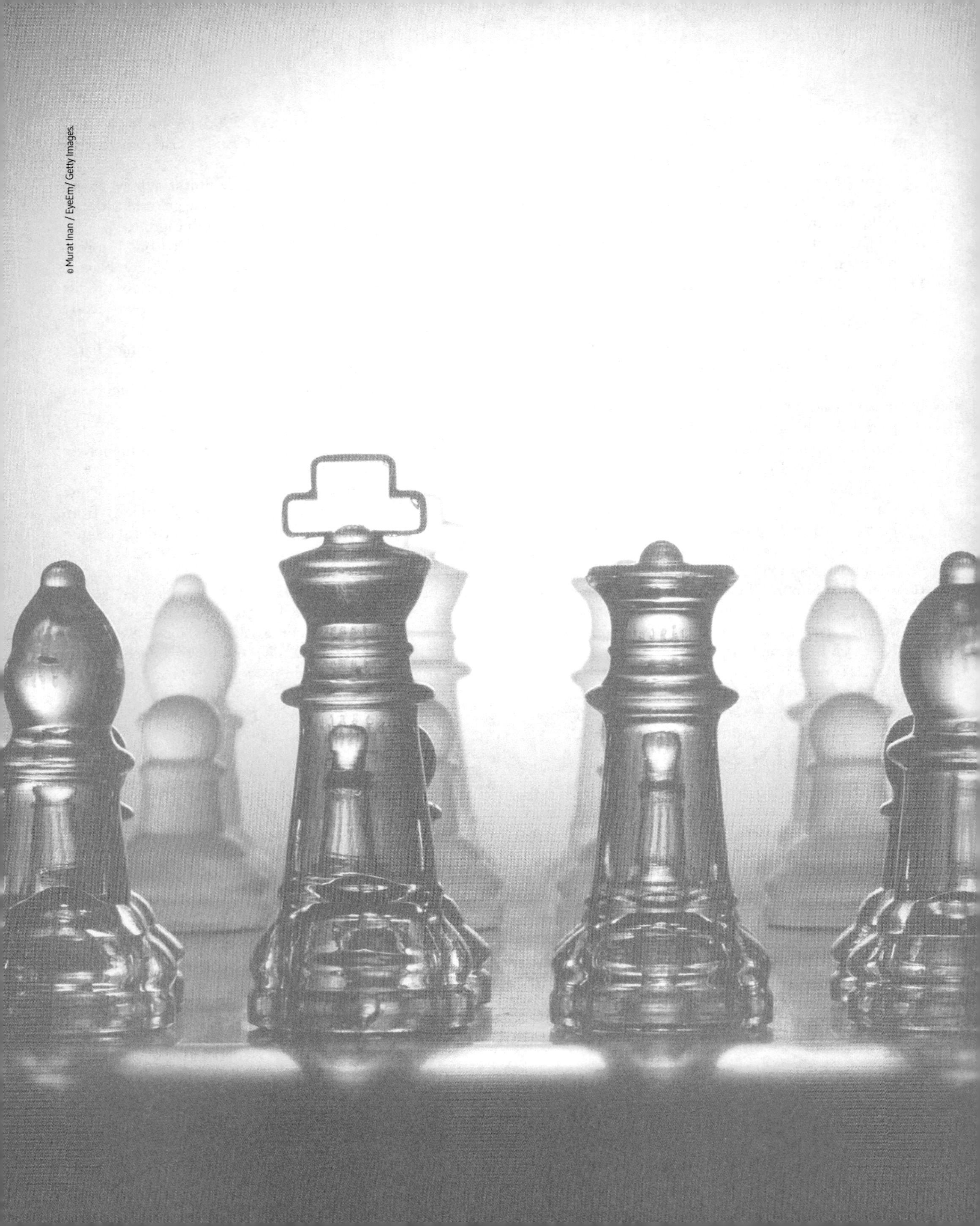

Leading Nonperforming Employees: Leadership Responsibility

Accountable work has consequences: rewards for work well done and sanctions for work that is not well done.
Brian Dive, *The Accountable Leader*

This chapter discusses the role leaders have in health organizations when confronted with nonperforming employees. Positive aspects and opportunities for reiterating and defining standards of performance are addressed and articulated. Readers are encouraged always to see nonperforming employees in a positive light and to look for opportunities to coach, nurture, educate, and mentor these employees. Nonperforming employees can be viewed as opportunities to create and inspire personal loyalty and to create organizational loyalty, too. When all else fails, last-resort options and consequences of risk management and termination may be necessary. In the end, leaders must reinforce the culture of productivity and excellence required in the health industry.

LEARNING OBJECTIVES

1. Describe the importance of dealing with nonperforming employees in the workplace.

2. Distinguish between the different types of nonperforming employees in the organization.

3. Relate progressive strategies for moving nonperforming employees toward a more productive posture within the organization and predict outcomes of each strategy.

4. Diagram and differentiate the steps—that is, the progressive actions from initial recognition of the problem to termination—a leader should take when confronting nonperforming employees.

5. Categorize and summarize methods for implementing continuing education in the organization.

6. Evaluate the risk management issues associated with dismissing employees and/or asking them to engage in performance improvement plans.

INTRODUCTION

People are the most important "resources" in the health organization. Human resources must be managed to meet the needs of the organization; however, people are led. Human resource systems provide the framework to manage the professionals who represent the "people" in the health organization. Without dedicated and high-performing employees, no organization can be a success. A health organization is only as good as the people who work in it, including the leader. Working alongside dedicated, autonomous, and hard-working employees can be a sincere pleasure for any leader. Unfortunately, the opposite may be true when leading nonperforming employees. In addition to all of the other responsibilities of leadership the person in charge has to perform, there may be no task more difficult than working with nonperforming employees.[1] Let us consider some factually influenced opinions. First, disruptive behavior between physicians and nurses can have far-reaching consequences on patient care.[2] Second, retaining counterproductive employees is a serious detriment to any health organization.[3] As a test of the proposition that dealing with nonperforming employees is a major leadership issue, we challenge you to ask any leader you know what his or her top three leadership challenges were in a current or past leadership job. Typically, the replies of most leaders will revolve around communication challenges, the health industry environment, and the difficulties of leading nonperforming employees and what to do about those employees.

At a keynote address to a university in Washington, D.C., former Secretary of State and Army General Colin

Powell suggested that it is a leader's responsibility to lead not only the performing employees in an organization, but also the nonperforming employees. He stated that the entire organization will be watching the leader and how he or she leads these individuals.[4]

For the purpose of this chapter, we classify nonperforming employees into two categories: the unproductive employee and the employee who seeks to avoid work. Both types can pose a variety of complex challenges to the leader. Unfortunately, dealing with nonperforming employees cannot be delegated by the leader to a subordinate; this is true in most cases. It will always remain the personal responsibility of the leader to remedy the issues surrounding those who are not contributing to the workplace and to the health organization's mission. These situations are reminiscent of McGregor's Theory X and Theory Y employees; nonperforming employees would fall in the Theory X category.

UNPRODUCTIVE EMPLOYEES

The unproductive employee may be an employee who lacks the appropriate motivation or education needed to maintain productivity in the workplace. These employees may be willing to perform the work of the organization; however, they may not have enough foundational or continuing education to actually "do" the work the job requires. Employees who were hired years ago with special skills and talents may find themselves working in organizations where those skills, tools, and abilities are no longer relevant. For example, an employee who is negligent in maintaining currency with innovation in medical informatics may gradually begin to become less productive in the workplace if this lack of currency results in an inability to complete daily work. This specific aspect of nonperformance—an employee's lack of knowledge, skills, and abilities—will be addressed later in this chapter.

On the other end of the spectrum of unproductive employees are those who may no longer be inspired by the organization's leadership, policies, or mission to perform diligently on the job. Reflect on Herzberg's two-factor theory of intrinsic and extrinsic factors: Intrinsically, the employee may not be committed to the mission of the health organization; extrinsically, the employee may not be satisfied with new norms, policies, or pay or reward systems. For instance, an employee who is accustomed to receiving praise, additional responsibility, and being thought of as the "go-to" person in the organization under the supervision of one leader may become less productive in the organization if supervised by a different leader whose style differs from that of his or her predecessor. Other factors may affect the reality of employees becoming unproductive in the workplace. It will be incumbent upon the leader to discover the cause of these outcomes before trying to effect change. Using Herzberg's two-factor theory to identify potential intrinsic and extrinsic causes of an employee's lack of motivation to perform is a solid method of determining causes or catalysts that have led to nonperformance.

Regardless of the cause of the subpar performance, the leader needs to be aware that employees who are unable to perform the work of the organization on a continual basis affect other employees in the business.[5] For instance, other employees in the work unit may be forced to pick up the slack for the unproductive employee. This practice results in one or more employees having to do more tasks just to maintain the organization's effectiveness. Shouldering this extra burden for long periods of time will result in high employee dissatisfaction with the leader's effectiveness at remediating unproductive employees as well as a lack of desire to continue the work of the organization. Fortunately, strategies for improving the behavior and outcomes of unproductive employees are generally simple and easy to implement in the organization; ultimately, if the employee continues to be unproductive, dismissal may be the solution if the health leader has the will to move to that stage of progressive action.

WORK AVOIDANCE EMPLOYEES

The second type of nonperforming employee is more troublesome. These employees are work avoiders (also known as malingerers). Malingerers attempt to avoid the work of the organization altogether, either for some personal reason or for secondary gain. Malingerers are employees who,

for whatever reason, are no longer willing to perform the work of the organization on a daily basis. They feel entitled to continue to draw a paycheck from the health organization without delivering the requisite work productivity. This feeling of entitlement may have nothing to do with the employees' current work (or output) contributions to the workplace. As a result, employees who have adopted a work avoidance or malingering attitude toward the daily activities of work in the organization will affect the bottom line of the organization. Nonperforming employees such as these are similar to what Locke, as part of his goal-setting theory, deemed "social loafers." This situation should never be tolerated because it can create a new organizational culture characterized by entitlement and low productivity. This negative organizational culture may also lead to patient care errors, financial errors, and fraud.

Evidence of the leader becoming weak in handling malingerers will ultimately create a distrustful environment for all employees in the organization. The employees will eventually come to see the leader as ineffective, easily manipulated, and frail. Some employees may abandon their personal goal of achieving excellence in the workplace, allowing mediocrity and apathy to run rampant in the organization. Unfortunately, strategies for managing malingerers are more complex and time consuming than those used for managing unproductive employees and can be both physically and emotionally draining. However, it is a leader's responsibility to lead not only the high performers in the organization, but also the low performers.

A RESPONSIBILITY

A leader who allows nonperforming employees to continue along this path in the organization is not doing his or her job as a leader—it is as simple as that. Concomitant with successfully building teams and creating a positive work environment, the leader must take center stage in improving the work of nonperforming employees or dismissing these employees from the health organization. Both of these options are the most difficult job of leadership, regardless of the industry in which the leader works.

Verbally reprimanding or dismissing a nonperforming employee can invite a host of unpleasant consequences. At a minimum, it can create discomfort in the workplace if informal relationships are tightly interconnected in professional organizational reporting chains. In more complex situations, the nonperforming employee may retaliate and file a complaint with any number of organizations, either internal or external to the organization. In this case, the leader places both the organization and him- or herself in a position of professional peril if appropriate documentation does not support verbal or other actions that confirm the lack of productivity of the employee and the steps initiated to remedy the lack of performance. Furthermore (and often even more troublesome), the result of any complaint filed against the leader by an employee may be viewed (incorrectly) by outside stakeholders as circumstantial evidence of a leader's inability to lead people in the organization. As a result, some leaders may become "gun-shy" about the potential for such employee retaliation. The outcome may be an inappropriate decision by the leader to do nothing or to take easy action over more difficult action and avoid the employee rather than confront the poor behavior.

In the worst-case scenario, steps taken to deal with non-performing employees may lead to litigation. The unfortunate reality of defending against frivolous and nuisance employee complaints is that it often results in the organization expending significant financial and leadership resources in responding to these allegations. Thus, concurrently with taking legitimate action against nonperforming employees, the leader must ensure that his or her actions are supported by local laws, senior leadership, and internal policy. The leader must also ensure that the process is thoroughly documented.[6]

LEADER ASSESSMENT OF NONPERFORMING PERSONNEL

As with all human endeavors, problems may arise that hinder, block, or eliminate the health organization's efforts to fulfill its mission and reach its vision state. People, employees, subordinates, peers, and, sometimes, superiors may be the catalysts or root of the problem. Even when the organization has a thoroughly vetted hiring system, including a multilevel and multiple-approach interviewing process, some employees may not perform to the level required to meet the standards of the health organization. Sometimes organizational change creates a situation where employees can no longer perform to the level expected. When employees are not performing up to expectations, it is a health leader's duty and responsibility to intervene to remedy the situation.

Leader intervention in this situation takes courage, integrity, communication, and documentation; alignment with organizational values, direction, mission, vision, strategies, and goals; and compassion for the nonperforming employee. The leader at the closest level to the nonperforming employee should be the one to start the process of intervention, although more senior leaders may play a role if the situation dictates their involvement. Health leaders who do not intervene with nonperformers are simply reinforcing and modeling behaviors that are at odds with the leadership's predetermined organizational mission, vision, strategies, goals, objectives, and, ultimately, the culture

needed for the organization to thrive in the health industry. As with all aspects of leadership, consistency is critical in intervening with nonperformers.

Given the two main categories of nonperforming employees, several approaches may be taken to evaluate nonperforming employees. Three approaches of evaluation are discussed in this section. First is evaluation of the lack of employee commitment or compliance or employee resistance to organizational norms, standards, policies, and procedures; this is an example of loose coupling by the employee when the organization requires a tighter level of coupling. In this modality, employee motivation is critical. Second is evaluation of the lack of knowledge, skills, or abilities or lack of competency of skills and abilities that create a nonperformance situation on the part of the employee; this can also incorporate the lack of the required licensures, certifications, or education/training. Third, evaluation may address whether the employee is inconsistent or unreliable in commitment or compliance with the health organization's norms, standards, policies, and procedures or inconsistent in job or task performance; that is, the employee may not fit into the culture of the organization. These situations are examples that link back directly to the model of commitment, compliance, or resistance. An individual's personality plays a major role in a leader's understanding of that employee.

Personality, as a construct, can assist in understanding the individual employee. "People like to believe that their behavior is sensible and rational, as opposed to foolish and irrational."[7] Personality is a complex and constantly evolving and adapting system of mental structures, mental processes (such as needs, wants, memories, and self-image), and the way in which individuals see themselves in relation to their environment.[8,9] An employee's personality changes over time to adapt to the situation, as well as to his or her activity level, development, education and training, occupation, marital status, health, and socioeconomic status.[10] Employees' self-image—in essence, the values and beliefs they see in themselves and how they portray that image in the environment where they live and work—does remain relatively stable, however. For example, "the achievement-oriented person will continue to seek success, the conscientious person will continue to be reliable and the aggressive person will continue to be combative over time and across situations."[11]

Health leaders are increasingly interested in selecting, hiring, promoting, and sustaining employees who are able to adapt to changing situations; stay loyal to the organizational mission, vision, strategies, goals, and objectives; and perform their duties well. Likewise, employees who are not able to adapt to change, have questionable loyalty, and demonstrate marginal performance are not selected, not hired, and not promoted and may face removal or punishment.

Health leaders must foster hiring, rewarding, promoting, and resourcing of subordinates and other employees who can adapt to change, are organizationally loyal, and perform their duties well. When leaders do less than reward and credit subordinates with organizationally complementary and supportive personalities, then they are essentially reinforcing personalities and behaviors that go against the organizational direction, the organizational culture, and the leadership as a whole.

Reward those subordinates who exhibit the personalities and behaviors you want, and redirect those who do not meet your expectations. This simple fact is directly tied to the process of developing organizational culture through Schein's primary embedding mechanisms. The next section presents several methods to intervene with the nonperforming employee in hopes of enhancing his or her performance and value to the organization.

REITERATION, ADAPTATION, AND COMMITMENT TO ORGANIZATIONAL NORMS AND STANDARDS

The health marketplace is a highly competitive environment. Employees who have successfully made it through a set of screening criteria based on their education and experience as depicted on a resume, and later evaluative criteria based on personal interviews, have demonstrated that they are skilled and competent when applying for a job. No employer hires any employee with the preordained knowledge that the employee will be terminated within months or a few years after initial employment. The slow creep away from a position of performance may be gradual. The actual slip into nonperformance may even go unnoticed until negative outcomes emerge. In such cases, initial strategies for the leader are clear and simple.

Health leaders, when confronted with nonperforming subordinates, should reiterate organizational expectations, norms, and performance standards. Frequent communication of expectations should be verbalized, modeled, and documented to all subordinates and employees across the organization. Nevertheless, nonperforming employees may need explicit counseling for each expectation, norm, and performance standard. As in transformational leadership, individualized consideration and intellectual stimulation are key considerations when dealing with nonperformers; the leader must express how that nonperforming individual fits into the scheme of the organization and meshes with the organization's mission, vision, strategies, and goals.

Many times in health organizations, change results in the need to become more organizationally efficient and cost-conscious. In these situations, the leadership may change the requirements of compliance using policies and procedures. The requirement to be consistent and compliant with organizational policies, standards, and norms can be explained in terms of a construct called organizational coupling; both loose and tight coupling are possible, along with many degrees in between. When tighter organizational coupling becomes the new norm, some employees may find it difficult to adapt to the new culture. The strength of communication feedback loops determines organizational coupling; stronger feedback loops imply tighter coupling, whereas weaker loops suggest loose coupling.[12] Jelinek and Litterer suggest four criteria for determining the coupling status in organizations:

1. *Formal rules*: The more closely the rules are followed, the tighter the coupling.
2. *Agreement on rules*: The greater the employee congruence with the rules, the tighter the coupling.
3. *Feedback*: The closer the feedback in time, the tighter the coupling.
4. *Attention*: Empowered individuals allocate energy and time to prioritized areas in their "area" (participation, competence, and empowerment foster focused attention to areas of responsibility).[13]

To meet organizational norms, especially in compliance with policies, the health leader should facilitate frequent norm- and standards-oriented communication with the nonperforming employee to reinforce the new norm. Rewarding the performance of those employees in compliance with the norms and punishing those employees not in compliance are both part of a leader's duty in reinforcing and solidifying the organizational norm.

The leader should be aware that the creep into nonperformance may not be intentional or readily evident to the employee under discussion. An employee who has always managed medical records the same way for years may be unaware of new compliance regulations governing the disposition of these records. In a similar fashion, an employee who has worked for several years in an environment where subtle errors in internal memos or spreadsheets were tolerated may find him- or herself at odds with a new leader who has higher standards for the same information. The health leader should take opportunities whenever possible to reiterate workplace standards that reflect the positive aspects of committing to organizational standards rather than the negative aspects. For example, an employee who turns in a flawless report without spelling or mathematical errors should be publically praised so that the other employees are aware of benchmarks.[14] Examples of standards should be readily available to all employees; this is an example of how an organizational cultural artifact may be used as a model. This practice also helps to reemphasize the leader's performance standards and expectations of other employees without singling out noncompliant employees in the organization.

The passive role-modeling approach may not work for employees who are too tightly wedded to their workplace habits. In such situations, it will be incumbent upon the leader to call the employee in for a positive, reassuring, and coaching/mentoring discussion where workplace standards are clearly presented simultaneously with the employee's efforts in meeting those standards. The employee's efforts should be praised, and the employee should be made to feel reassured and valued. This approach is critical in the process of reiterating standards. A leader who comes across too strong, in an admonishing or overly critical manner, may not only lose the loyalty of that employee for the remainder of the time that they continue to work together, but may also create a perceived environment of intolerance in which the employee is not comfortable taking risks or engaging in organizational citizenship behavior. A careful balance must be maintained. An experienced leader will become comfortable and proactive in this strategy. The ideal outcome is the employee understanding the leader's vision and embracing it as his or her own.

The choice of whether to document these types of informal or verbal coaching sessions will be an individual decision made by the leader. The preponderance of employees will reflect on the conversation positively and improve their efforts toward meeting the organization's standards. This verbal, unrecorded, and unwritten exchange may be the only action necessary. However, should subsequent conversations need to take place regarding similar actions within a brief period of time, the leader may adopt a strategy of following up the conversation with a friendly and nonthreatening (no attribution) note or email that documents the conversation and the items discussed. This step will become important only if the leader believes that the employee will not take positive and individual steps to improve performance. It also begins the process of documentation to protect the organization at a later time should levels of nonperformance escalate.

STRATEGIES FOR COACHING, MENTORING, PEER MENTORING, AND EDUCATING NONPERFORMERS

Coaching, mentoring, peer mentoring, and educating nonperforming employees are other methods of transforming the employee into a performer. These techniques have varying levels of time commitment and formality and are associated with potentially different outcomes. For example, coaching, as a central function, facilitates change and development.[15] Coaching, in the context of the nonperforming employee, is instructing, guiding, correcting, and challenging the employee to perform to expectations.

COACHING

Leader coaching is a continual process that goes beyond task accomplishment. It is a constant process of trying to improve task accomplishment through encouraging and valuing the employee. Coaching involves evaluating an employee's current efforts, motivating him or her to achieve greater outcomes on subsequent projects, and instilling a sense of pride and commitment to the organization. Leaders should constantly seek coaching opportunities in daily activities of work. These techniques can range from a simple visit to an employee's workstation to discuss organizational progress, to more complex engagements where a leader shares his or her experience doing similar projects through demonstration. Leaders should be careful not to remove themselves from the direct coaching of employees in the organization; leaders must be "available" and "aware" of the activities they are responsible for and the people engaged under them in this work. Coaching, like leading itself, cannot be delegated.

It is difficult[16]—and perhaps impossible—to coach someone via email or memo (although weaker leaders may try to do so). Coaching is often a face-to-face reality of doing business in the modern health organization. However, these coaching techniques can also take place with groups of individuals in larger sessions addressing common points of productivity for all employees. Coaching is based on transformational leadership constructs, such as individualized consideration, intellectual stimulation, and performance expectations for the employee. Personal, face-to-face, frequent, and planned actions are necessary to be a coach. Coaching in a professional sense is usually specific to a set of activities, work processes, or tool utilization within a specific time period.

MENTORING

Leader mentoring has a similar yet slightly different role than coaching. Mentoring tends to be of broader scope (career oriented rather than specific to activities or projects or tool utilization) and requires a longer time commitment compared to coaching, although the leader actions and behaviors used in coaching are often similar to those used in mentoring.

Mentoring nonperforming employees can be frustrating at first. The nonperforming employee may see mentoring as targeted behavior and feel that he or she is being singled out unfairly. The nonperforming employee may not look favorably on the leader's increased attention. Nevertheless, mentoring nonperforming employees should be considered one of the many leadership options available for improving performance.

Professional mentoring usually requires a longer commitment—several months to a year or more—so it can result in a professionally intimate relationship.[17] Mentoring is the practice of coaching, coupled with instruction on the subtle elements of the profession, while securing increasingly more challenging opportunities for the mentee by the mentor. Health leaders are, inherently, coaches and mentors. Both roles, subtly different, are performed to improve the future career of the employee and, therefore, the outlook for the organization as a whole. Both roles are also future oriented.

Similar to leader role modeling that is imbued with transformational leadership characteristics, coaching and mentoring complement the leadership persona. Hudson suggests that coaches and mentors follow these guidelines:

- "Model mastery in professional areas that others want to obtain
- Guide others to high performance in emerging scenarios
- Advocate, criticize, and extend corporate [organizational] culture [to include culture change] and wisdom
- Endorse and sponsor others without using [or needing to use] power or having control over them
- Facilitate professional development and organizational system development"[18]

Deeprose recommends team coaching and mentoring, in which the coach facilitates communication, conducts long-range planning, supports career development of team members, mediates or resolves conflicts, and measures performance.[19]

PEER MENTORING

Peer mentoring differs from mentoring in several important ways. Peer mentoring occurs when information between two peers is freely shared without leader supervision or intervention. Peer mentoring can result in several positive benefits to the organization and those who participate in it. These benefits include opportunities for leader development at lower levels of the organization, opportunities for employees to improve the collegiality of their relationships

with one another, and increased overall organizational efficiency.[20] In the context of managing nonperforming employees, peer mentoring provides for a semiformal process of aligning a well-performing employee or subordinate with a nonperforming or marginal-performing employee or subordinate. Many of the same coaching and mentoring concepts apply, but role modeling and knowledge, skills, and abilities transfer in the process of the work environment are especially pronounced in this context. Many employees label peer mentoring as "on-the-job-training." Although it is training on the job, it also entails purposefully matching an excellent performer with a lower-performing employee.

Peer mentoring is an effective way to facilitate the creation and sharing of knowledge, through its intentional linking of high performers and low performers.[21] Peer mentoring is also an old and time-honored tradition in organizations. Successful organizations have found ways to promote and leverage this behavior for centuries. One such example can be found in the *Wilson & Company Employee Handbook* from 1919. The employee handbook states [*sic*]:

> Older employees can do a single service by giving new employees the benefit of their experience. Appoint yourself a Committee of One to take the new employee in your Department in tow. Point out the things he or she should know. You may be sure that your efforts will be appreciated. Remember too, the power and the responsibility of Example.

Although this example specifically addresses new employees, the same philosophy can be applied to a nonperforming employee in any organization in the modern era.

It would be wonderful if all employees in the health organization were so conscientious and forward thinking about the leadership of new or nonperforming employees. Organizations that have employees within their walls who see peer mentoring as an obligation of employment to the entity are truly rare and unique. In cases where this philosophy does exist, there may be little evidence of nonperforming employees in the organization at all. If this is not your organization (and likely so), it may be incumbent on you as a leader to ask high-performing employees to "adopt" nonperformers as a method of improving overall organizational performance. This method serves three main purposes: (1) it frees the leader's time to focus attention on other priorities of interest in the organization, (2) it provides an opportunity for leadership development of junior employees, and (3) it improves organizational effectiveness. A good leader leverages the resources available to him or her in the organization. If you are able to leverage your own employees in the task of improving nonperforming employee performance, do it!

Education and Training

Education and training are formal, objective-based periods of instruction that explicitly set learning objectives and detail expected mastery of knowledge, skills, abilities, and behaviors. Education is a formal process, such as the path followed while earning a degree. In contrast, training is usually a workplace-oriented activity. Both education and training can enhance the knowledge, skills, and abilities of a nonperforming employee; education and training can also positively influence behaviors, attitudes, and, to some degree, values and beliefs. The longer the learning time, the more potential impact the effort will have for the employee.

No industry in the United States is under more scrutiny in terms of the need for continuing education (CE) than the health professions. Unfortunately, the same high degree of CE that is offered to medical and allied health professionals may not be freely available to administrative, management, and general workers of the health organization. Although it may be cost-prohibitive to send all employees to 1- and 2-day conferences on an annual basis, the organization should provide educational and training opportunities for all employees on a frequent and cyclical basis. Education and training must complement, enhance, or enable the organizational culture envisioned by the leadership of the health organization.

The leader must be cognizant that CE is vital to the survival of the health organization. Education of all employees begins with their basic orientation in the health organization after being hired and ideally should continue throughout their tenure in the organization. A health organization cannot be recognized as "high performing" unless it continuously ensures that its employees are exposed to opportunities that enable them to update their skills with modern medical procedures and equipment, administrative techniques, and technologies. For the health leader, creating such opportunities can be challenging; however, significant effort must be made to ensure that health practitioners and administrative personnel maintain appropriate and up-to-date levels of professional competence. This competence directly contributes to the development of high-performing employees. Depending on the health professional specialty, CE may be required to maintain licensure, credentials, or status in professional associations as well as privileges to practice in the health organization.

Workshops

Workshops are closely associated with training and can assist nonperformers in correcting behaviors and actions—that is, moving them toward those behaviors and actions desired by the leadership. Both workshops and training need to be well planned, delivered, and logistically supported to achieve the expected outcomes of the activities. Gordon, Morgan, and Ponticell, as well as Blanchard and Thacker, advise leaders who are providing retraining, workshops, or other education to subordinates, and especially to nonperformers, to consider nine principles before and during any such initiative:

1. Identify the types of individual learning strengths and problems, and tailor the training around them.
2. Align learning objectives to organizational goals.
3. Clearly define program goals and objectives at the start.
4. Actively engage the trainee, thus maximizing attention, expectations, and memory.
5. Use a systematic, logically connected sequencing of learning activities so that trainees have mastered lower levels of learning before moving onto higher levels.
6. Use a variety of training methods (such as auditory, visual-verbal, visual-nonverbal, and kinesthetic methods).
7. Use realistic, job-relevant training materials.
8. Allow trainees to work together and share experiences.
9. Provide constant feedback and reinforcement while encouraging self-assessment.[22,23]

Learning

Even with nonperforming employees, effective health leaders must find the proper balance of education and training to assist them in developing the skills they need to perform their primary job, make sound decisions, and uncover underlying connections to deal with more general issues in the workplace. They are encouraged to work closely with professional educators and trainers so that education programs will be aligned with expected outcomes and provide realistic experiences that will produce the competencies essential to effective performance. As in most institutions, the fundamental forms of employee education in health settings materialize through the use of passive, active, and experiential learning techniques.

In *passive learning* (the most basic form), the employee simply sits quietly while receiving the information. Lectures are the classic illustration of this style of learning. If not necessarily the most enjoyable technique, reading manuals is another traditional form of passive education. More sophisticated techniques include demonstrations, videos, and self-taught or self-paced course materials. In addition, some large health organizations are putting training materials, which may include sophisticated graphics and video, on their intranets.[24] This type of learning uses visual–verbal (text), visual–nonverbal (graphics, pictures, and videos), and auditory learning modalities.

Active learning techniques include anything that the employee does in a classroom setting other than merely passively listening to a lecture. They encompass everything from listening, where the students/employees absorb what they hear; to short writing exercises, in which students/employees react to lecture material; to complex group exercises, in which students/employees apply course material to real-life situations and new problems.[25] This form of learning uses a combination of visual–verbal (text), visual–nonverbal (graphics, pictures, and videos), auditory (listening), and kinesthetic (doing) learning modalities.

Somewhere in between the activity levels of the passive and active learning alternatives is *experiential learning*, which involves learning through the work process. Basic on-the-job training of a new employee is the most common example. Another is rotation, in which an employee is temporarily placed in a different job setting so that he or she can acquire new knowledge and practice new techniques used by that unit.[26] The primary learning modality in experiential learning is kinesthetic.

PERFORMANCE APPRAISALS

The performance appraisal is the assessment of the individual employee. In this activity, the health leader truly and honestly assesses an employee's performance across the spectrum of expectations. This process is a component of the health organization's performance management system. Performance appraisals are conducted periodically, such as annually, semiannually, or quarterly. With nonperforming employees, more frequent appraisals—quarterly or monthly—may be prudent until the salient issues of nonperformance are resolved. Performance appraisals are the end of a performance assessment cycle. Setting expectations, such as by using the goal-setting model from Locke and Latham's goal-setting theory, and measuring performance are critical components of this process. The assessment cycle should follow a logical sequence of "setting performance goals and development plans with the employee, monitoring the employee's progress toward achieving objectives and goals, providing continual coaching, training and education as appropriate, conducting periodic performance reviews using measurable goals and development plans as guides, and establishing the next cycle's plan and goals."[27]

Health leaders should set aside significant time—perhaps an hour to 90 minutes—to conduct a face-to-face performance review with each employee; again, this step is especially critical with nonperforming employees. Using a media-rich communication channel, such as face-to-face meetings, will foster feedback and a sense of urgency, and it better enables the leader to express expectations to the employee. Fried recommends that performance reviews be reserved for the following situations:

- "Giving employees the opportunity to discuss performance and performance standards
- Addressing employee strengths and weaknesses
- Identifying and recommending strategies for improving employee performance
- Discussing personnel decisions, such as compensation, promotion, and termination
- Defining a variety of regulatory requirements that deal with employee performance, and discussing compliance [and commitment] methods"[28]

Successful health leaders use performance management systems to assess organizational, group, section, or team performance while evaluating individuals within those structures. Taking time to develop, revise, and utilize this system not only sets expectations and standards, but also transfers culture and cultural meaning to others, and it sets measurable goals and objectives for everyone to commit to for moving the organization forward to reach its vision.

Performance appraisals should reflect the actual work of the employee in the health organization. They should be based on performance metrics, output, and organizational potential. Unfortunately, many performance appraisals overrate employees' performance. In many cases, appraisals are used as tools to maintain harmony or professional collegiality in the workplace; however, this is not the purpose of the evaluation. Moreover, failing to maintain accurate and thoughtful reporting on the evaluation can reflect poorly on the leader's ability to manage the workforce.[29]

Lenient evaluations can become even more problematic when the upwardly mobile leader advances within the organization, or seeks a position outside the organization, and leaves a satisfactory performance history on nonperforming employees that makes it difficult for the next leader to take any form of corrective action. This self-serving bias negatively affects the performance of the organization and everyone in it.[30] Put simply, performance appraisals should never be used to maintain relationships, build professional bridges, or avoid the difficult task of confronting an employee's weak performance.

MODELING

There is a time-honored quote related to leadership that cannot be attributed to any one source. It is often repeated and highly cited in leadership, management, and organizational behavior literature as a panacea for success:

>Do as I do.

No individual in the organization is watched more closely than the leader, and no one's actions are analyzed more intensely than those of the leader. From the time the health leader arrives at the organization to the time he or she departs, subordinate employees will form judgments and opinions in regard to the leader's actions, words, and deeds. In particular, the chronically nonperforming employee may seek to leverage his or her own erratic behavior by pointing out the leader's shortcomings. A leader who has become too comfortable and relaxed in his or her job may informally signal to employees that this behavior may be emulated in the workplace. Any performance improvement in any employee must start with the leader role modeling the behavior expected in the health organization.

For example, health leaders should always model the behavior they expect of subordinates, peers, and superiors (yes, even superiors—they are watching you as well). Modeling is contagious, and it becomes even more so when you are in a leadership position. Everyone watches leaders, and their actions set the tone by modeling appropriate and desired behaviors. According to social learning theory[31] (which is mostly attributed to Albert Bandura), the desired result or outcome of modeling is the mimicking of observed behavior by others. Leaders model behaviors and actions all the time, even when they do not realize it. Conscious modeling sets the expectation for behaviors and actions for all employees in the organization. For nonperforming employees, modeling can greatly assist in their learning. The more employees around the nonperformer who model the desired behavior, the more peer pressure builds to create adaption in the nonperformer.

RECOGNIZING THAT EMPLOYEE FAILURE CAN BE A FAILURE OF LEADERSHIP

Nonperforming subordinates are not solely to blame for their predicament; their nonperformance is also a failure of leadership. A health leader's ability to intervene positively and change a nonperformer into a performer is at the heart of this reality. The health leader should do all that is possible, such as creating an intervention plan for the nonperforming subordinate (based on the suggestions in this chapter), to turn around an employee so that he or she becomes a valuable part of the organization. Most people want to do a good job, be valuable, and contribute to the health organization's mission; this is a Theory Y perspective. Health leaders should do all they can to positively intervene when nonperformance is *first recognized* because there is a positive relationship between leadership style and employee productivity.[32]

BE SENSITIVE TO PERSONAL ISSUES AS THE CAUSES OF NONPERFORMANCE

Abraham Lincoln once said, "Most folks are about as happy as they make their minds up to be." If his statement is accurate, then a successful health leader would benefit greatly from learning to recognize and understand the problems that arise when leading employees, because there will be instances when employee problems that are carried from home into the workplace significantly affect an employee's ability to perform his or her job.

The majority of employees with personal problems will share those problems outright with their leader if he or she takes the time to listen. At other times, the leader needs to pay closer attention to an employee's mood or performance to identify personal problems that are cause for concern. Poor performance is typically a good early indication of trouble. If employees are going through a really tough time, their personal issue will almost always affect their performance. The most common signs that may indicate an employee needs help include (but are not limited to) coming in late frequently, avoidance of other employees, repeated absences, complaints about finances, argumentativeness, lack of concentration, and missed deadlines.

Initially, the health leader may choose to ignore the problem or wait until it goes away. Although this technique sometimes works, a successful leader must not let problems drag on longer than necessary. On the contrary, a health leader should not choose to ignore poor performance or behavior just because he or she is aware of an employee who is experiencing a problem. The leader has a right to expect adequate performance from all of his or her employees. Continue to coach, counsel, and discipline as needed.

If reasonable accommodations can be made to reduce the stress or personal issues faced by the employee, then try to implement the accommodations. Many personal problems are short lived; if the personal problem is long term or significant, referring the employee to counseling is a prudent step for the health leader. If the health leader senses that the personal issue of the employee could escalate, refer the employee to counseling and inform the human resources department of the health organization based on established procedures.

Be sensitive yet firm about your expectations; be reasonable, but set boundaries. Comply with the health organization's policies (if you do not know them, ask the human resources department) with regard to employee personal issues that have affected or could affect either the employee's performance or the health organization's reputation.

TRANSFORMATIONAL, TRANSACTIONAL, AND SITUATIONAL LEADERSHIP OPPORTUNITIES

As a health leader, you should recognize that many aspects of leadership discussed in this chapter mirror aspects of the transformational, transactional, and other situational leadership models. Using transformational characteristics (emphasized in coaching and mentoring, for example) and transactional characteristics (for example, setting goals and outlining rewards and punishments, such as termination) and recognizing other situational leadership characteristics (such as the in-group and out-group concepts detailed in Fiedler's contingency theory) can greatly assist the health leader in intervention with the nonperforming subordinate or employee. Even with the "optimal" leadership style and behavior, there is always potential for subordinates to resist or fail to comply with cultural norms of the organization, rules, policies, and process standards. In these cases, leaders must utilize concepts of correction or discipline to ensure a productive, fair, and moral atmosphere in the workplace.

OPTIONS FOR DISCIPLINE

PRAISE IN PUBLIC AND ADMONISH IN PRIVATE

A good leadership maxim is always to praise in public and to admonish in private. Younger leaders and early careerists may not be aware of the potential to bring harm on themselves by reprimanding an employee in public. Not only may the early careerist make him- or herself a potential defendant in a human resources complaint for potential issues of harassment, but it will also demonstrate to peers that the early careerist is not mature and emotionally self-aware of the disadvantages of admonishing employees in a public venue. No one likes to see the boss be rude in public. On the other hand, more respect will be given to leaders who show mutual respect and a restrained approach when unprofessional behavior occurs in public. A simple, "Mr. Smith, please see me in my office," is more than enough to establish to employees that you are in charge and are handling the situation. In regard to praise, the opposite may be true.

Employees generally like to receive public acknowledgment for a job well done in the presence of coworkers. Doing so can build significant political capital for the leader over time.

Many disciplinary options may be used with nonperforming employees. From reducing authority, responsibility, and salary or pay, to demotion, to termination, the health leader has many ways to leverage transactional leadership in hopes of improving an employee's performance. The idea that "the punishment should fit the crime" is important, however. Small defects in employee performance should not engender large punishment actions by the leader. Likewise, gross violations of performance and behaviors should be subject to more severe punishment and leadership actions. Remember, others are watching how leaders deal with nonperformers or violators of policies and procedures; fair and equitable treatment is always correct. Initially giving the employee the benefit of the doubt is a good rule as well.

The more severe the punishment for nonperformance, the more responsibility the health leader has to measure performance accurately, document expectations thoroughly, and engage in counseling of the nonperformer. In health organizations, considering the complexity of the organization, everyone should know and understand those behaviors and actions that are heavily frowned upon by leadership. At the same time, they should know that second chances are given. Some leader mercy will assist in creating a less stressful workplace. The leader should always keep a record of all nonperformance, indicating times, dates, activities, and locations where nonperformance is noticed.

VERBAL AND WRITTEN WARNINGS

Once nonperformance is noticed, the health leader should start with verbal warnings and discussion with the nonperforming employee. Written warnings and documentation should follow if the nonperformance is not corrected. Health leaders should also report their actions regarding written warnings and documentation to their superiors, so that the chain of leadership stays informed about the problem and can reinforce the direct leader's efforts.

PROGRESSIVE CORRECTIVE ACTION

Progressive corrective action is usually effective in remedying employee performance problems. All too often, a health leader tolerates an employee's unacceptable performance for as long as possible without taking disciplinary action. When the employee's conduct finally becomes intolerable, the health leader then tends to overreact and recommend action whose severity exceeds the severity of the actual infraction. By using a sequential progressive process, it is hoped that many employee problems can be corrected at an early stage, thereby benefiting both the health organization and the employee.

To achieve the most effective use of progressive corrective action for nonperforming employees, health leaders should become familiar with their health organization's human resources policies and departmental regulations. This ensures that infractions can be quickly and accurately identified and dealt with appropriately. Similarly, it is extremely important that good judgment be used in determining the degree of corrective action that is warranted in each employee's case. It is always a great idea to consult with the director of human resources prior to taking any action toward an employee. Also, in all instances where corrective action is required, it is the responsibility of the immediate health leader to initiate the action. In other words, sometimes you need to be the "bad guy" in the eye of the nonperforming employee before you enlist any assistance from senior leaders. The high-performing employees will see you as a leader for their unit if your actions are warranted and appropriate given the violations committed by the nonperforming employee.

Progressive corrective action will generally result in one of four measures: (1) documented verbal warning, (2) documented written warning with improvement plan of action, (3) suspension, or (4) dismissal, depending on the severity of the employee's performance issues and the number of times the individual has been counseled. You should ask for, read, and retain a copy of your health organization's progressive corrective action policy from the human resources department. If the policy or an aspect of the policy is not clear or does not seem to be appropriate for the situation, meet with the human resources leader and health organization legal counsel for guidance prior to initiating the process identified in the policy with the nonperforming employee.

Verbal Warning

The health leader uses a verbal warning to single out the employee's exact performance or behavior problem. It is important to always provide the employee with an opportunity to explain his or her perspective of the situation. Follow up with a request for a specific positive and measurable change, and confirm with the employee his or her understanding of what is expected. Always advise the employee that the verbal warning will be documented and that a copy of the documentation of the discussion will be provided for the employee (as well as placed in his or her personnel file). Likewise, it is highly suggested that an acknowledgment of

receipt of the warning be signed and dated by the employee prior to conclusion of the meeting.

Written Warning

The health leader begins the written warning process much like the verbal warning process. However, after requesting a specific change and achieving confirmation from the employee that he or she understands what has occurred, the leader proceeds to explain to the employee the importance of positive performance standards for the organization's employees. This discussion tends to go much more smoothly when the health leader expresses a desire and willingness to help the employee remain employed. This message is further reinforced with the creation of a written performance improvement plan. Even so, the health leader should advise the employee of the written warning and explain that a copy of the documentation of the discussion will be provided for the employee (and placed in his or her personnel file). Correspondingly, it is always helpful to have the employee demonstrate an understanding of the desired behavior by signing and dating an organizational form of acknowledgment stating that disciplinary action could occur should there be a reoccurrence of the behavior.

Suspension

With suspension, the health leader initiates a counseling session similar to that used in the verbal and written warning phases. However, after providing the employee with an opportunity to explain the situation and advising him or her that the previous discussions/actions have been ineffective in modifying his or her behavior and performance, the health leader suspends the individual without pay for a specific number of days based on organizational policy. As with verbal and written corrective actions, the health leader has the employee sign and date an acknowledgment form for the corrective action, and the employee is informed that a copy of the acknowledgment will be placed in his or her personnel file.

Dismissal

Dismissal is the health leader's option of last resort. An employee who does not correct problems identified during the earlier phases of the progressive corrective action process is indicating an inability or unwillingness to change his or her behavior. That is, the employee clearly does not wish to work to reach satisfactory performance standards. It is during this time that the health leader must do what is best for both the organization and the employee. Indeed, discharge may well be the best solution for both parties.[33]

Before a dismissal action is undertaken, the health leader should have exhausted efforts to rehabilitate the nonperforming employee, and the health organization's human resources department, senior leaders, and legal counsel should have been aware of the situation for some time. Of course, according to health organization policy, some actions and behaviors of employees warrant immediate dismissal from the organization. In these situations, the health leader should immediately contact the senior leader (the health leader's superior), the human resources department, and legal counsel and follow their guidance regarding the procedure to dismiss an employee based on a specific action, behavior, or event.

EMPLOYEE IMPROVEMENT PROGRAMS

Employee improvement programs are systematic methods to enhance performance of not just nonperformers, but also marginal performers. Leader identification and employee matriculation into such a program start with a person analysis based on a series (a trend) of performance appraisals, documented counseling sessions, and verbal performance discussions:

> The person analysis identifies individuals who are not meeting the desired performance requirements or goals. The expected performance compared to the actual performance provides a performance discrepancy from which the training intervention can be designed. Data sources for the person analysis include supervisor ratings, performance appraisals, observation, interviews, questionnaires, tests, attitude surveys, checklists, rating scales, in-basket exercises and simulations, and self ratings, and assessment centers.[34]

In essence, an employee improvement program is a professional "boot camp" focused on performance building, behavior change (such as termination of alcohol or drug abuse), and cultural adaptation. These programs can be semiformal to formal in nature, may be held on-site at the workplace or off-site, and can be of either short-term or long-term duration.

PERFORMANCE IMPROVEMENT PLANS

The performance improvement plan is designed to facilitate constructive discussion between a health leader and an underperforming employee. This discussion focuses on clarifying the work performance to be improved. Performance improvement plans are implemented at the discretion of the health leader when it becomes necessary to help an employee improve his or her performance. The plan should always be developed with input from the affected employee as a means to gain the employee's commitment to achieve the desired level of performance.

If a formal performance improvement plan is developed and documented, the employee should receive a copy of it; another copy should be placed in the employee's personnel file. In the event that the documented issues lead to more severe disciplinary actions, such as suspension or dismissal, the plan is signed by the employee and the leader or manager. Be aware that many employees will refuse to sign this type of document, especially when they dispute the evaluation. In this case, the health leader should document the employee's refusal to sign the plan. The employee's refusal to sign does not change the requirement for the employee to follow the improvement plan.[35]

RESPONSIBILITIES TO DOCUMENT NONPERFORMANCE

Health leaders are duty-bound to document employees' failure or refusal to perform to standards or comply with organizational policies, standards, or norms. What the leader does with this documentation depends on the length of nonperformance of the employee, the severity of the nonperformance, and the motivation of the employee to correct, adapt, or adjust the undesirable behaviors and actions to meet expectations. Due process is the sequence of leader actions of identifying the problem, documenting the problem, counseling the nonperformer, remediating the situation, and providing enough time for the nonperforming employee to correct the behaviors and actions so that they align with organizational expectations. Due process is required for public-sector employees[36] by law, but it is a good system for all other employees (called "at-will" employees, because they can be dismissed without cause) to deal with nonperformance.

When all attempts fail to correct performance, termination is the usual remedy. Termination should be a near-to-last or last resort, undertaken only after exhausting the due process policy and all other options for intervention with the nonperforming employee. Termination is expensive because the hiring process to replace the nonperformer can be costly in dollars, time, and (potentially) legal liability. Of course, paying for nonperformance over time can also be expensive. Rubin and Fried cite four basic reasons for termination or dismissal for cause of a nonperforming employee:

- Misconduct, including fraud, embezzlement, and commission of a criminal act
- Violation of corporate policy or practice

- Material failure to perform employment obligations
- For professionals, loss of license[37]

Termination or dismissal of an employee is a serious matter. Health leaders should put the following recommendations into action concerning employee termination or dismissal:

- Analyze the risk before terminating the employee, including all documentation pertaining to the employee.
- Avoid procrastination.
- Strategically select the date to terminate the employee by avoiding Fridays or significant personal dates of the employee.
- Consult human resources personnel (and legal counsel, if necessary).
- Act.[38]

It is the responsibility of the health leader, the human resources department, and the organization as a whole to assess risk and legal liability concerning any action, but most especially a negative action such as dismissal, that affects a subordinate or employee.

RISK MANAGEMENT AND LEGAL LIABILITY ASSOCIATED WITH CREATING EMPLOYEE IMPROVEMENT PROGRAMS AND TERMINATION

Risk and legal liability issues arise when steps such as creating employee improvement programs and terminating employees are undertaken. Anyone, for nearly any reason, can file a civil lawsuit against a health organization. For example, a suit may be filed if an employee who is targeted for intervention (e.g., with an employee improvement program) or an employee who has been terminated believes that he or she was treated unfairly, inconsistently (based on precedents set by the organization's dealings with other employees), or abruptly. The best countermeasures for these risks are health leader documentation, documented (with the employee's signature) counseling with the nonperforming employee, informing senior leaders in the organization about the situation of nonperformance, and early and ongoing counsel from the health organization's legal counsel or legal team.

Today's society is very litigious, so following published organizational policies and procedures regarding nonperformance, documentation, fair warning, and remedial intervention for the employee, along with continuous advice from in-house or retained legal experts, are key responsibilities of the successful and prudent health leader. Health leaders must train and guide subordinate leaders and managers in

this process as well. In essence, health leaders need to build a documented and supportable case to negatively change the subordinate's status in the organization; this pertains to demotion, loss of bonus(es), termination or dismissal, or any other action that affects the employee negatively.

DISRUPTIVE PHYSICIAN BEHAVIOR: ANOTHER ASPECT OF NONPERFORMANCE

Disruptive behavior is another aspect of nonperformance and is particularly sensitive and damaging when involving physicians. According to Pfifferling, "disruptive behavior causes stress, anxiety, frustration, and anger, which can impede communication and collaboration, which can result in avoidable medical errors, adverse events, and other compromises in quality of care."[39] Healthcare human resource departments and the organization's leadership, from the CEO to frontline leaders, must be aware of such circumstances and must develop policies, standards, and procedures to effectively deal with this very serious and complicated issue. Gaining a better understanding of what contributes to physician disruptive behavior will help organizations provide the appropriate education, training, organizational culture reinforcement, and reiteration of expected norms to help decrease disruptive behavior episodes. The overall consequences of physician disruptive behavior include the threat of patient errors, poor employee morale, nursing shortages, and potential legal liability against the health organization. Having systems and structures in place to address this issue will help promote an efficient, effective, and efficacious work environment.

A healthy work environment is one that promotes interaction and communication among all professionals. In the healthcare setting, the nurse–physician relationship is highly critical because they manage patient care together, which requires constant communication. Disruptive physician behavior in health care is on a steady incline and making headlines in newspapers.[40] Physicians can consciously or unconsciously participate in disruptive behavior in the workplace; these actions are felt by others to represent anger, intimidation, and the threat of harm. Common behaviors of the disruptive physician are intimidation, anger, abusive language, blaming or shaming others for adverse outcomes, unnecessary sarcasm, sexual harassment, racial slurs, lack of respect for others, and threats of violence.[41] Staff relationships and how staff work together to enhance patient continuity is an important element in the healthcare delivery system. Having strong communication and collaboration, the right number of staff members, and the optimal staff mix tremendously affects the overall outcomes in the healthcare system. Disruptive physician behavior is by far one of the most important influences on the quality of staff relationships.[42] This is a serious and complicated leadership and human resource issue for health organizations.

Rosenstein and O'Daniel discussed a survey on the impact of disruptive behaviors and communication conducted by VHA West Coast and published in the Joint Commission *Journal on Quality and Patient Safety*.[43] The survey consisted of 22 questions and was distributed to physicians, nurses, and administrative executives of the 388 member hospitals; 102 hospitals actually participated, a 26% response rate. There were 4,530 participants; 2,846 had nursing titles, 944 were physicians, 40 were administrative executives, and 700 chose not to identify their titles.[44] The results demonstrated that 77% of the respondents (88% of the nurses and 51% of the physicians) reported that physician disruptive behavior had been witnessed in the organization. In addition, 67% of the respondents agreed that the act of disruptive behavior was linked with adverse events in the organization, which included 71% resulting in medical errors and 72% causing patient mortality.

Nurse and staff members fear working with certain physicians due to disruptive behavior, and they may therefore withhold pertinent information that could be detrimental to the patient's condition. This behavior clearly leads to potentially preventable adverse events, patient mortality, patient errors, and safety compromises. Strategies must be in place within the organization to address such behavior. This is surely a leadership issue that requires action.

Until recently, many health organizations did not have policies, procedures, or guidelines to assist them when faced with a physician's alleged unprofessional behavior. There is also a conflict of interest when the decision to take disciplinary action depends on whether the physician significantly contributes to the organization's bottom line, has a special relationship with administration, or is affiliated with major physician groups who have power.[45] As of January 1, 2009, the Joint Commission requires all accredited health organizations to develop policies and procedures to address disruptive physician behavior in the workplace. The new leadership standard, LD.03.01.01, from the Joint Commission requires that:

- The hospital has a code of conduct that states clearly the requirements around disruptive and inappropriate behaviors.
- Leadership implements a process for managing disruptive and inappropriate behaviors.

In addition, the Joint Commission recommends policies and procedures for guidance, which include:

- Zero tolerance for gross misconduct behavior such as intimidation and assault

- Ways to address intimidating behavior of physicians toward staff
- Provisions to protect the employees who report disruptive behavior
- Methods of responding to patients and family members who may have witnessed disruptive behavior
- Direction on how and when to begin disciplinary action for disruptive behavior

For leaders, early intervention by setting clear expectations through policies, procedures, and an organization code of conduct and by setting an example can help prevent disruptive physician behavior. From a human resource perspective, a physician disruptive behavior policy must be implemented that identifies the specific acts associated with disruptive behavior. The same processes for working with nonperforming employees can be utilized; however, the medical director or senior medical leader should be involved in the situation and in correcting the disruptive behavior. According to Iwrey, the following is an example of a clearly written physician disruptive behavior policy:[46]

"Disruptive conduct" by a medical staff member is defined as conduct that adversely affects the hospital's ability to accomplish its objectives defined above and includes but is not necessarily limited to the following actions toward colleagues, hospital personnel, patients, or visitors: (1) hostile, angry, or aggressive confrontational voice or body language; (2) attacks (verbal or physical) that go beyond the bounds of fair professional conduct; (3) inappropriate expressions of anger such as destruction of property or throwing items; (4) abusive language or criticism directed at the recipient in such a way as to ridicule, humiliate, intimidate, undermine confidence, or belittle; (5) derogatory comments that go beyond differences of opinion that are made to patients or patients' families about caregivers (this is not intended to prohibit comments that deal constructively with the care given); (6) writing of malicious, arbitrary, or inappropriate comments/notes in the medical record; and (7) sexual harassment.

It is important for leaders to actively intervene in physician disruptive behavior situations. This is another aspect of leading people and managing resources.

LEARNING FROM LEADERS WHO FAIL US

Within the health professions, the discussion of nonperformance usually centers on nonperforming employees; however, what if it is the leader who is failing his or her employees in a supervisory or employment perspective?

These situations can become more tenuous when the senior leader in the unit has failed to maintain competence in the profession, acts unethically, or simply does not lead. These are uncomfortable and precarious situations in the health profession, and they occur more often than we think.

THE UNETHICAL LEADER

The unethical leader may be the easiest one to address. Whenever a subordinate employee witnesses a senior leader committing an unethical act, it should be discussed with the appropriate alternate leader in the organization. In some cases this may mean that the junior employee makes a meeting for the purposes of information gathering with the local human resources (HR), Equal Employment Opportunity (EEO), or some other authoritative office in the organization. An employee should never be afraid to hold an information-gathering meeting with a local HR office. HR offices exist to help and to safeguard the organization, and they should be used by all employees when appropriate.

Always remember that an ethical leader will be the one standing at the end of the day when admonishments, reprimands, and/or other disciplinary actions (such as termination) are executed by the senior leadership. Always be part of the solution—not the problem. Also, know that a complicit employee who is knowledgeable of wrongdoings may be viewed as lacking leadership skills him- or herself when allegations become investigative realities. Never be afraid to do the right thing and (minimally) discuss your perceptions of unethical behavior with HR or EEO offices within your entity.

THE INCOMPETENT LEADER

The incompetent leader is a more difficult situation to engage. Perhaps this leader was at one time a highly regarded and respected figure in the health profession. However, over time, and due to a failure to maintain competence or continuing education in the field, the leader may no longer occupy a position of *expert* authority within the profession. Such may be the case with a leader who last served in a hospital environment when the Joint Commission was referred to as JCAHO, or perhaps a clinical person with no administrative background was promoted above his or her competence into a managerial profession for which he or she has no education, training, or experience. This latter situation is more common in the health professions where wonderful and exceptionally performing clinical personnel are promoted too rapidly outside their clinical area of expertise. So, what can be done? The forward-thinking employee should try to partner with the senior leader and offer guidance and assistance in a manner that is not politically insulting or insubordinate. For example, if there is an issue with third-party payers and uncompensated care, and it is clear that the new leader is far less familiar with these areas of finance than his or her predecessor, then the subordinate employee's offer to help may both assist in the productivity of the organization and assist in on-the-job education for the new leader. Generally leaders will appreciate the altruistic assistance provided to them as they transition into a new job. It will additionally send a message to the leader that everyone wants to "stay on the team" and work together for the benefit of the organization.

THE NONLEADING LEADER

The leader who will not lead is (perhaps) the most frustrating example of a leader who fails his or her employees. These outcomes can be caused by a variety of situations that stem from the leader's own boredom with his or her job, a complete inability to do the job in the current environment, or simply because the leader has moved from a position of Theory Y (enthusiastic and self-motivated leadership) to a Theory X (nonproductive leadership) position of leadership in his or her current stage of life. This last example is often the case with leaders who have successfully risen up the corporate ladder to positions of success over a great period of time only to find themselves burned out and bored. They no longer have the energy and enthusiasm they once had that made them success driven. A leader who is truly burned out (or just bored in his or her job) will be hard to reignite. And if (for some reason) the organization wants to allow this person to stay in their position for an extended period of time, personal decisions on employment within that organization may have to be made by those under his or her supervision. Few things can be more frustrating in the health profession than working for a leader who will no longer engage in the process of change or the process of improvement cycles. If this is your boss, it may be time for you to move on.

THE NONPERFORMING LEADER WHO GOT THE JOB BASED ON FRIENDSHIP AND/OR PAYBACK

It would be naïve to think that all leadership positions in the health profession are based on merit, performance, and potential. The sad reality is that as senior personnel advance in the health profession they may be likely to advance subordinates with them that they have known and trusted for a long time. Rather than advancing personnel based on merit or potential, the nonperforming leader who was advanced based on a personal relationship with the boss may be likely to advance his or her own friends within the organization, too. On face value, this may make sense to the nonperforming leader who was advanced based on sycophancy over merit. After all, an unknown applicant who has demonstrated performance and potential over a sustained period of time in another organization may still be an unknown quantity in the eyes of the leader who makes decisions based on friendship and payback over competence and performance.

This outcome is observed less in the for-profit arena. Such outcomes of promotion based on friendships are more likely in family businesses, federal sector organizations, state employee services, and certain areas of the nonprofit field. In these entities, an informal network, friendships, and connections can often be important considerations in the hiring and promotion process, especially when revenue generation is not always a top priority for the organization. For example, in these latter organizations it is possible that an advancing executive may want to pay back sustained service and loyalty to lesser qualified personnel who have not demonstrated leadership potential, but have "taken care of the boss" over a period of time. So what can one do when the boss is nonperforming—but liked by his or her own boss, and clearly not moving?

As we suggested in the previous situation, a capable employee caught in an environment where nonperformance is rewarded for various internal organizational causes may have to reevaluate his or her future in the organization. Departing the organization may be the only option in this case. However, if the employee believes in the mission of the organization, has contributions to the entity that are valued by external and internal stakeholders, and feels the job that he or she is in is value added, then making the best of a bad situation may be the only option. If this is the case, then it is best to role model positive behaviors so that personnel in the informal network of the organization continue to see your sustained leadership. Employees in the organization who see you continue to do the right things, at the right time, despite the lack of merit demonstrated by the

promoted employee, will gain trust and confidence in the organization through your leading by following. Honorable leadership is sometimes viewed by no one but yourself. At the end of the day, you have to do the right thing for the organization because it benefits patients, fellow employees, the organization, or the community. Gain satisfaction by being the one your peers see as the competent leader, and be proud of the work that is accomplished despite the more junior level. Your time will come. Continue to lead from a distance and lead when no one is looking, because at some point, they might be!

As hard as it is to imagine, it is possible to see personnel advance in the profession who simply do not know what they are doing with regard to the basic elements of leadership. More frustrating are those who get promoted but are simply unable to perform the job. Personal experience suggests these outcomes are more prevalent in state, government, and not-for-profit organizations. In these organizations, factors that may not have as much to do with job qualifications may be looked at with greater interest than a history of performance. For example, some government and federal jobs may give preference to military retirees (or spouses of veterans) over candidates who may have more direct experience and ability to do the job. In other cases, leadership positions in some not-for-profit organizations may be filled with close friends and networking colleagues over more qualified candidates. In the very worst cases, leaders in the most senior of positions may make decisions on vacant positions in the company based along lines of friendship and "paybacks" for years of otherwise loyal personal support that may have little to do with merit or performance. In some cases, even these non–merit-based employment opportunities can be addressed with local or state EEO offices. And if the opportunity allows, frustrated employees should engage in exploratory conversations with these agencies as well. However, if it seems clear that an organization has a vested interest in keeping an incompetent, nonperforming, and nonleading leader in a position of authority, then the only choice may be for the early careerist to make personal decisions to move his or her employment and career elsewhere.

SUMMARY

This chapter discussed the role leaders have in health organizations when confronted with nonperforming employees. Positive aspects and opportunities for reiterating and defining standards of performance were addressed and articulated. Health leaders are encouraged to always see nonperforming employees in a positive light and to look for opportunities to coach, nurture, educate, and mentor these individuals. They should also see nonperforming employees as opportunities to create and inspire personal loyalty and to create organizational loyalty. Leadership is also required in situations involving disruptive behavior by physicians. When all else fails, last-resort options may become necessary, in which case the consequences of risk management and termination must be assessed carefully.

This required corrective action is also needed when leaders do not perform (nonperforming leaders) in the workplace.

DISCUSSION QUESTIONS

1. Using your gender as a starting point, outline how you would admonish and reprimand a same-sex employee. Would this process be different than one used with an opposite-sex employee? Why or why not?

2. Dealing with nonperforming employees is as unique as an individual's leadership style. How would you begin to inform an employee about his or her nonperforming behavior? Why would you start this way? How does the initiation of your leader actions work with your preferred leadership style? How are your perceptions different from those of other members of the class? Do your initial findings support the theory that internal hardwiring affects your leadership decision making with regard to nonperforming employees? Can you distinguish differences between different leadership styles?

3. How many verbal and undocumented warnings should an employee get before the formal process of written documentation starts? At what point do you think you would "give up" on coaching and mentoring an employee and move toward dismissal?

How would you apply progressive action steps to nonperformance?

4. How would documentation of your attempts to make a nonperforming employee aware of his or her nonperformance assist you in risk management situations later on if the employee filed a complaint? How do your leader actions set a new standard or reinforce an existing standard for the organization, division, branch, or section? Analyze and infer how leader actions can set new standards or reinforce existing standards.

5. Discuss the differences and similarities between coaching, mentoring, and conducting a performance improvement plan. Do the techniques support one another, or are they mutually exclusive? Why? Devise a general plan for a "generic" nonperforming employee.

6. Discuss special circumstances in which the admonishment and reprimanding of an employee can be delegated to someone other than the employee's immediate supervisor. Justify when delegation in these cases is appropriate.

EXERCISES

1. In a one-page paper, describe the importance of dealing with nonperforming employees in the workplace.

2. In a one-page paper, distinguish between the different types of nonperforming employees in an organization.

3. In a two-page paper, describe progressive strategies for moving nonperforming employees toward a more productive posture within the organization and predict outcomes of each strategy.

4. In a two-page paper, diagram and differentiate the steps in the progressive action sequence, from initial

warnings to termination, that a leader should take when confronting nonperforming employees.

5. In a one-page paper, categorize and summarize methods for implementing continuing education in the health organization.

6. In a two- to three-page paper, evaluate the risk management issues associated with dismissing an employee or asking an employee to comply with a performance improvement plan.

REFERENCES

1. Dive, B. (2007). *The accountable leader.* London: Kogan Page.

2. Brooks, A. M. T., Polis, N., & Phillips, E. (2014). The new healthcare landscape: Disruptive behaviors influence work environment, safety, and clinical outcomes. *Nurse Leader, 12*(1), 39–44.

3. Self, D. R., & Self, T. B. (2014). Negligent retention of counterproductive employees. *International*

Journal of Law and Management, 56(3), 216–230. doi:10.1108/IJLMA-07-2012-0021

4. Powell, C. (2009, Oct. 24). Keynote address at Capella University Colloquium, Arlington, VA.

5. Srisupatpongsa, K., & Jones, G. (2001). Action to be taken with a non-performing employee decision model implementation [White paper]. Developed by Saint-Gobain Crystals and Detectors, Houston, TX. Retrieved from http://professorforman.com /Forman/GSmodels/Employee%20Action.pdf.

6. Eyres, P. (2005). Avoid successful lawsuits by non-performing employees. *Connections.* Retrieved from http://www.furninfo.com/Furniture%20World %20Archives/4738.

7. James, L. R., & Mazerolle, M. D. (2002). *Personality in work organizations.* Thousand Oaks, CA: Sage, p. 9.

8. Allport, G. W. (1937). *Personality: A psychological interpretation.* New York: Holt.

9. Millon, T. (1990). The disorders of personality. In L. A. Pervin (Ed.), *Handbook of personality: Theory and research* (pp. 339–370). New York: Guilford.

10. James & Mazerolle, note 7.

11. James & Mazerolle, note 7, p. 1.

12. Van de Ven, A. H., & Poole, M. S. (1995). Explaining development and change in organizations. *Academy of Management Review, 20*(3), 510–541.

13. Jelinek, M., & Litterer, J. A. (1995). Toward entrepreneurial organizations: Meeting ambiguity with engagement. *Entrepreneurship: Theory and Practice, 19*(3), 137–169.

14. Branham, L. (2005). *The 7 hidden reasons employees leave: How to recognize the subtle signs and act before it's too late.* New York: AMACOM.

15. Hudson, F. M. (1999). *The handbook of coaching: A comprehensive resource guide for managers, executives, consultants, and human resource professionals.* New York: Jossey-Bass, p. 3.

16. Cahill, M., & Payne, G. (2006). Online mentoring: ANNA connections. *Nephrology Nursing Journal, 33*(6), 695–697.

17. Hudson, note 15, p. 6.

18. Ciulla, J. B., & Forsyth, J. (2011). Leadership ethics. In A. Bryman, D. Collinson, K. Grint, B. Jackson, & M. Uhl-Bein (Eds.), *Sage handbook of leadership* (pp. 227–239). Thousand Oaks, CA: Sage.

19. Deeprose, D. (1995). *The team coach: Vital new skills for supervisors and managers in a team environment.* New York: AMACOM.

20. Bryant, S. E., & Terborg, J. R. (2008). Impact of peer mentor training on creating and sharing organizational knowledge. *Journal of Managerial Issues, 20*(1), 11–31.

21. Olivier, A. (2011). Phenomenology of the human condition. *South African Journal of Philosophy, 30*(2), 94–106.

22. Gordon, E., Morgan, E., & Ponticell, J. (1995, September). The individualized training alternative. *Training and Development,* 52–60.

23. Blanchard, P. N., & Thacker, J. W. (1999). *Effective training systems, strategies, and practices.* Upper Saddle River, NJ: Prentice Hall.

24. Austin, C., & Boxerman, S. (2002). *Information systems for healthcare management.* Ann Arbor, MI: AUPHA Press/Health Administration Press.

25. Paulson, D. R., & Faust, J. L. (2009). Active learning for the college classroom. Retrieved from http://www.calstatela.edu/dept/chem/chem2 /Active/#authors.

26. Shi, L. (2007). *Managing human resources in health care organizations.* Sudbury, MA: Jones and Bartlett.

27. Fried, B. J. (2008). Performance management. In B. J. Fried & M. D. Fottler (Eds.), *Human resources in healthcare: Managing for success* (p. 261). Chicago, IL: Health Administration Press.

28. Fried, note 27, p. 262.

29. Holmes, B. (2003, June). The lenient evaluator is hurting your organization. *HR Magazine,* 11–14.

30. Greenberg, J. (1991, March). Motivation to inflate performance ratings: Perceptual bias or response bias? *Journal of Motivation and Emotion, 15*(1), 81–97.

31. Greenberg, note 30.

32. Henker, N., Sonnentag, S., & Unger, D. (2014). Transformational leadership and employee creativity: The mediating role of promotion focus and creative process engagement. *Journal of Business and Psychology, 30*(2), 235–247. doi:10.1007 /s10869-014-9348-7

33. Harvard Business School Press. (2007). *Dismissing an employee.* Boston: Harvard Business Review Press.

34. Johnson, J., Ledlow, G., & Kerr, B. (2005). Organizational development, training and knowledge management. In B. Fried, J. Johnson, & M. Fottler (Eds.), *Human resources in healthcare: Managing for success* (2nd ed., p. 213). Chicago, IL: Health Administration Press.

35. Flynn, W. J., Mathis, R. L., & Jackson, J. H. (2007). *Healthcare human resource management* (2nd ed.). Mason, OH: Thomson South-Western.

36. Rubin, B. L., & Fried, B. J. (2008). The legal environment of human resources. In B. J. Fried & M. D. Fottler (Eds.), *Human resources in healthcare: Managing*

for success (p. 135). Chicago, IL: Health Administration Press.

37. Rubin & Fried, note 36, p. 134.
38. Rubin & Fried, note 36, pp. 133–134.
39. Pfifferling, J. (1999). The disruptive physician. *Physician Executive*, *25*(2), 56. Retrieved from Business Source Complete.
40. Porto, G., & Lauve, R. (2006, July/Aug.). Disruptive clinician behavior: A persistent threat to patient safety. Retrieved from http://www.psqh.com/julaug06/disruptive.html.
41. Pfifferling, note 39.

42. Rosenstein, A., & O'Daniel, M. (2008). Invited article: Managing disruptive physician behavior: Impact on staff relationships and patient care. *Neurology*, *70*(17), 1564–1570. Retrieved from Medline.
43. Rosenstein & O'Daniel, note 42.
44. Rosenstein & O'Daniel, note 42.
45. Iwrey, R. S. (2009). Physician disruptive behavior policies require a measured approach. *MedStaff News*, *8*(2). Retrieved from http://www.healthlawyers.org/Members/PracticeGroups/MSCPR/Documents/MedStaffNews_Sep09.pdf.
46. Iwrey, note 45, p. 2.

THE HEALTH LEADER, INFORMATION, DECISIONS, AND CREATING A KNOWLEDGE CULTURE: THE 4 PS OF HEALTH ANALYTICS ADOPTION

Start by doing what is necessary; then do what is possible; and suddenly you are doing the impossible!
Saint Francis of Assisi

Political and socioeconomic trends, advocated by public health professionals, are moving population health closer to health-care delivery operations and strategies. The movement is a positive and important change to reduce costs, improve quality, and improve access to care for communities that are served by the health industry. The technological element of care and the use of data for decision making are growing in the industry as well. The models and ideas presented in this chapter merge the changes of increased technology and data with the integration of population health and healthcare delivery to spur critical thinking and improvement of health status across the communities of our nation. This chapter was authored by Dr. Gerald Ledlow, Dr. Dave Schott, and Mr. Tyler Croft.

LEARNING OBJECTIVES

1. Describe the significant changes in the health industry that prompt an integrated approach for utilizing health information from multiple areas to make good decisions for health services delivery and improved health status of communities.

2. Explain how health industry reform and policy changes impact the rate of health analytics adoption within health organizations and what changes require analytics adoption within the health industry.

3. Demonstrate how applicable models associated with health information and technology improve efficiency, effectiveness, performance, and efficacy of health services and healthcare delivery.

4. Compare and contrast methods to effectively use analytic models to integrate raw data and develop knowledge to improve health system performance and equity within a community.

5. Categorize health organizations in technology adoption, analytics adoption (information utilization), and information integration using the integration of the Health Information Management and Systems Society (HIMSS) DELTA model and the 4 Ps of Health Analytics model and provide examples.

6. Appraise and evaluate the integration of population, patient, process, and profitability (net margin for nonprofits) information in solving community health challenges and/or strategic planning for a health organization.

INTRODUCTION

Health leaders need information to effectively guide and direct their organizations. Starting with raw data gathered from various operational, governmental, and other systems, how do health leaders create an organizational culture based on knowledge utilization? How do health leaders take data, place them in context, integrate information from multiple domains, take action based on the information, and have the organization learn from those actions in order to improve the strategies and operations of the health organization? With the changes in the health industry that require closer connections to the communities that health organizations serve and more assumption of risk for the health status of those communities, what model can health leaders utilize to achieve a knowledge-based organization? Complicated ideas are often shown as a model. A *model* is a simplified substitute for an event or situation that is being studied or predicted. Models can be used in multiple ways. The most common ways are describing a situation or prescribing a course of action. A *descriptive* model *describes* how a system should function according to the model. A *prescriptive* model *shows* how to make a system function according to the model. The most useful type of model is a combination of the two concepts, a model that is both prescriptive and descriptive. Models of this type describe both how something works and how to make it work as described.

Due to the complex nature of the health industry, there are many models regarding the operation of health organizations. This is true of health analytics, or health information for analysis and decision making, because it is an exciting, rapidly evolving field—even by health industry standards. The implication of change is relevant; the health industry is a dynamic industry. Recent changes resulting from healthcare reform, policy changes, and the need to demonstrate value in health services delivery have created an environment where new models of health analytics, health information utilization, and health technology are required. In this chapter we will discuss the need, basis, creation, and usage of the 4 Ps of Health Analytics. The 4 Ps of Health Analytics model integrates well with the knowledge management and learning organization construct and with the strategic planning process construct of the dynamic culture leadership model. The 4 Ps of Health Analytics model, a model concerned with how information is efficiently, effectively, and efficaciously utilized in an integrated manner, describes conceptually *how* data flow and from what data domain within a health organization, and prescribes integration of data from crucial domains to develop knowledge in the health organization. Health leaders need to be competent in the philosophy and utilization of information as it is developed into useful knowledge. This chapter explains this process within the 4 Ps of Health Analytics model and how to achieve success. Combined with other valuable models, the integrated model is the 4 Ps of Health Analytics adoption model. Success is defined as coupling technology with integrated information to build knowledge that improves strategic and operational planning, health outcomes, health equity, and community health status.

SITUATIONAL ANALYSIS: CATALYST TO INTEGRATED INFORMATION NECESSITY

PATIENT PROTECTION AND AFFORDABLE CARE ACT

The Patient Protection and Affordable Care Act of 2010 is commonly referred to as the Affordable Care Act (ACA) or "Obamacare," after President Barack Obama, who signed the bill into law on March 23, 2010. The ACA is the largest and most significant change to the U.S. healthcare system since the passage of Medicare and Medicaid in 1965 with the Social Security Amendments 18 and 19. The ACA is still very controversial, with multiple challenges waiting to be heard by the Supreme Court. Additionally, operational challenges within the health industry will require changes to the law, to the system, and for the leaders of health organizations.

The ACA places a greater focus on prevention and on cost-effective care, while increasing the number of insured individuals through mandatory insurance coverage. Health insurance can be purchased directly from private companies, or the purchase can be facilitated by the federal government or state governments through health insurance exchanges or marketplaces. *Health insurance marketplaces* are exchanges for consumers to buy health insurance plans that meet ACA guidelines. These exchanges have been set up by both state governments and the federal government.

ACA-compliant healthcare plans must meet certain standards set by the federal government. These plans are rated according to the "metal" system: Bronze, Silver, Gold, and Platinum. Companies offering plans on the health exchanges must provide plans that meet at least the Silver and Gold level. The reason for this is to give consumers choice in their health insurance. Individuals that earn between 138% and 400% of the federal poverty level are eligible for subsidies of their health insurance premiums; below this level an individual is eligible for Medicaid. The *federal poverty level* is the level below which an individual is said to be living in poverty. As of 2014, this is $11,600 for an individual or $23,850 for a family of four.[1] The Silver plan is considered the standard for calculating which subsidies will be available to individual beneficiaries.[2] Purchasing

insurance plans through the healthcare marketplace is done during a period of open enrollment. *Open enrollment* is a period of time during which an individual is able to apply for or change their current health insurance plan. For the qualified health plans in the marketplace this time period is from November 15th through February 15th each year.[3]

Individuals are required to show that they have health insurance when they file their taxes; if they do not, they must pay a fine. The fine will gradually increase from 1% of an individual's annual household income or $94 dollars per person, to 2% of household income or $695 per person, whichever is greater. Individuals earning less than $10,150 per year do not have to pay a penalty. Under the income percentage method, the maximum penalty is roughly the same as the national average premium for a Bronze plan.[4] This policy was enacted to encourage people to purchase health insurance through the exchanges.

In addition to requiring individuals to purchase health insurance, the ACA has provisions aimed at improving the quality of care provided. One of these provisions calls for the meaningful use of electronic health records (EHRs). *Meaningful use* is defined as the use of EHRs to improve quality, safety, efficiency, and to reduce health disparities. The meaningful use requirements include a reward/penalty system to compel hospital compliance. The payment adjustments associated with the meaningful use of EHRs begins in federal fiscal year 2015. This grace period of a few years from the passage of the ACA was intended to allow hospitals the opportunity to implement an EHR system and avoid a penalty.[5] The meaningful use requirement is a strong incentive to install an EHR system for health organizations that have not yet moved to at least a partial electronic system. For those facilities that already have electronic medical records (EMRs), the program, along with other ACA provisions, provides encouragement to improve EMR systems. Whether installing, maintaining, or upgrading an EHR system, there is a need to measure the effectiveness of the EHR system. As mentioned in the introduction, this measurement is best done through the use of a model. With a large increase in the number of insured individuals, many without a history of insurance coverage, how do health organizations gain insight into the services needed by this newly insured group? Considering the disease profiles, cultural differences, and health system understanding levels of the newly insured, how do health organizations deliver quality care and needed services to improve community health status, improve patient care outcomes, and serve those who, historically, have been medically underserved? How does a health organization provide outreach, education, and screening for health indicators to a group of individuals without established access to care? How do health organizations provide demonstrated value to existing patients and to new patients? Will these answers mitigate and allow health organizations to manage risk effectively?

AMERICAN HOSPITAL ASSOCIATION PERSPECTIVES

YOUR HOSPITAL'S PATH TO THE SECOND CURVE FRAMEWORK: INTEGRATION AND TRANSFORMATION

In response to regulatory and environmental factors, payment systems, and changing demographics, health organizations have begun to transition from volume-based systems to value-based systems. *Volume-based systems* involve providing more services to a greater population with little focus on outcomes. *Value-based systems* focus on maximizing outcomes while reducing costs. Hospitals that use volume-based systems are considered to be on the "first curve."[6] Hospitals that have undergone organizational transformation and utilize a value-based system are considered to be on the "second curve."[7] Many hospitals are currently located in the gap between the two curves as they try to evolve under the pressure of dynamic change. It is necessary for leaders of these healthcare systems to develop strategies to reach the second curve. To reach the second curve requires swift movement toward acquiring greater clinical, financial, operational, and cultural integration.[8] Waiting to evolve is a very dangerous approach for health systems, given the changing landscape of the industry. Developing the capacity to take risks is necessary for healthcare systems to survive "life in the gap." Healthcare leaders need to consider the following key issues:[9]

- Health care is moving to new performance models in which organizations are integrating financial risk and care delivery.
- There is no one-size-fits-all model; provider capabilities and community needs are different everywhere.
- The status quo is not a viable strategy because the environment is changing rapidly.
- Each hospital and care system can consider multiple paths.
- Each path has its own distinct risks and rewards.[10]

As these organizations make short-term and long-term plans, the changing landscape, environment, and trends must be identified and analyzed thoroughly. Health leaders will need to be aware of the following pressures:[11]

- Patient demographics will shift significantly throughout the next decade.

- Enhancing care coordination during hospital-to-home transitions has consistently shown beneficial effects on cost reduction and care quality; this requires hospital leaders to focus on care after patients leave the hospital.
- Political and regulatory pressures are compelling hospitals and care systems to provide efficient and optimal patient care and address market volatility.
- Hospitals need to serve multiple patient populations effectively.[12]

PATHS TO TRANSFORMATIONAL CHANGE

Organizational transformation can be a daunting task for many health organizations; however, there are five transformational paths that can be used:[13]

1. *Redefine* to a different care delivery system.
2. *Partner* with a care delivery system or health plan for greater horizontal or vertical reach, efficiency, and resources for at-risk contracting.
3. *Integrate* by developing a health insurance function or services across the continuum.
4. *Experiment* with new payment and care delivery models.
5. *Specialize* to become a higher performing and essential provider.[14]

There is not one specific path to which health organizations must adhere; instead, a combination of these paths can be used. The paths chosen must best fit the needs and goals of the health organization.

HEALTH EQUITY: AHA EQUITY CARE REPORT

Value-based health organizations will need to work to improve the quality of care to patients and patient populations by improving and refining data collection and assessment. Risk management is also greatly enhanced by thorough and quality data collection and assessment. It is projected that by the year 2043, racial and ethnic minorities will account for the majority of the population in the United States. Successful health organizations must adapt to accommodate these changes and must begin collecting and analyzing race, ethnicity, and language data, also referred to as REAL data.[15] The REAL data can "identify high-cost drivers, develop interventions to improve care for vulnerable populations and, as a result, appropriately deploy resources."[16] Despite the usefulness of REAL data, only about 14–25% of hospitals and health systems are utilizing these data to improve the quality of care and care outcomes. There are four steps that should be followed when using REAL data:[17]

1. Determine appropriate data categories by acquiring census data, distributing surveys, forming focus groups with important community organizations, and utilizing data that have already been acquired.
2. Develop a methodology for data collection by deciding who collects the data, how often, processes, and methodology standardization; monitoring data collection progress; and assigning accountability.[18]
3. Train staff members on methodology for data collection.
4. Assign accountability and monitor progress of data collection efforts. Identify appropriate measures, reference points, risk adjustments, and sample size.

Organizations that utilize this four-step approach will clearly identify where disparities exist, allocate resources, and create effective and efficient interventions. Benefits of collecting and using REAL data include: "reducing costs, reducing disparities in health outcomes, reducing hospital readmissions, receiving incentive payments, and meeting PCMH [patient-centered medical home] certification requirements."[19] Effective collection and use of REAL data will position hospitals and care systems for success in an environment where regulators, payers, employers, and, most importantly, patients are looking for more differentiated and individualized health care.[20]

ONE SIZE DOES NOT FIT ALL: MEETING THE HEALTHCARE NEEDS OF DIVERSE POPULATIONS

Effective data collection will allow health organizations to better assess and analyze information related to diverse populations. Demographic data will provide a greater understanding of the population and lead to better resource allocation, identification of health inequities, and greater communication and community interaction.[21] Demographic data include race, language, socioeconomic status, gender, and age. Identifying unique and different populations will allow organizations to respond to changing demographics, health needs, and market-based demands and be able to forecast future service needs.[22] Once these data have been thoroughly evaluated, the organization can begin implementing policies tailored to suit the needs of the populations it serves.

Accommodating the needs of specific populations includes promoting staff awareness through training and dialogue to support cultural competence, enhancing the hospital's physical space, adapting services to address cultural beliefs, and helping patients to manage their care.[23] Staff members are given incentives to be culturally sensitive in order to accommodate the patient populations they serve, which includes compensation for cultural training. The development of cultural competence among staff requires ongoing training, which is tailored to patient needs.[24]

The fourth theme discusses the need to establish internal and external collaborations.[25] *Internal collaborations* include different stakeholders being brought together to develop, implement, evaluate, and improve initiatives aimed at meeting the needs of diverse patients.[26] Additionally, the stakeholders of the health organization should be as diverse as the populations they serve; thus, organizations should include individuals from different departments, ethnic backgrounds, positions, and professional levels.[27] Stakeholders are also excellent sources for data associated with the community that may otherwise be unattainable. *External collaborations* can be with other hospitals, health organizations, governmental agencies, and community groups that have the same patient needs, patient base, and educational institution affiliations.[28] External collaborations will be important to address challenges, such as limited resources and high costs of developing new materials. The health organizations can share information and materials to reduce expenses. The community collaboration strategy should include community leaders, educational institutions, health-related governmental officials, and patients. Including patients and community members is important to bring a more diverse perspective while increasing the likelihood of bridging cultural barriers, thus allowing the health organization to become more active in the community.[29]

THE JOINT COMMISSION PERSPECTIVES

THE JOINT COMMISSION ROAD MAP

Through data collection and research, it has been discovered that nonclinical needs of patients can shape how patients view, receive, and participate with health organizations.[30] Health organizations must integrate effective communication, cultural competence, and patient- and family-centered care practices into their core activities.[31] As discussed earlier, each health organization is unique and no one-size-fits-all solution exists. Developed by The Joint Commission, *A Roadmap for Hospitals* was created to assist health organizations, specifically hospitals, in deciding which directions and methods should be used to meet the specific needs of their patients. The Joint Commission uses the *care continuum* to illustrate changes that must be made to patient care to better connect and serve communities.[32] Hospitals should address the following components of the care continuum:[33]

- Admission
- Assessment
- Treatment
- End-of-life care
- Discharge and transfer
- Organization readiness

The admission phase of the care continuum offers opportunities to identify the needs of each patient during both emergencies and scheduled appointments.[34] Patients and their families share information regarding their background, physical requirements, and family history that can be accessible to all departments in the hospital.[35] Assessments are often collected during the admission process to help staff members address sensitive issues.[36] Some of these issues include the patient's health literacy level, mobility, sexual orientation, and gender identity and expression, as well as cultural, religious, spiritual, lifestyle, or dietary needs.[37] It is crucial to address the needs of the patient during admission and during assessment. However, it also is important for hospitals to address the needs of their patients while providing appropriate diagnostic services, care, treatment, and other services.[38]

Treatment-stage hospitals should integrate communication and cultural competence with patient- and family-centered care in order to address treatment options, risks, and alternatives for patients.[39] The initial treatment for the patient should address any communication barriers, such as language, culture, or sensory impairments (ear or eye), through patients' medical records.[40] Consent can be given only if the patient fully understands the information provided. Alternative communication resources (translator or interpreter) should be provided, if necessary.[41] The interpreter should be someone who is not affiliated with the patient or family to reduce the potential for miscommunication.[42] Materials should be modified so that patients can understand them regardless of their educational level. Addressing a patient's cultural, religious, or spiritual beliefs and practices is another large part of the treatment process; as best as possible, these beliefs should not be violated during treatment.[43] Dietary needs or restrictions should be noted.[44] The last aspect of the treatment process is to make sure all of the needs of the patient are directly communicated to the entire care team.[45] This requires integration of data, in the context of the patient, to provide actionable information to the care team members across the care continuum.

Supportive care should be given to the patient during the final stages of life. It is essential that patient communication needs be addressed and any communication barriers noted.[46] Changes in the patient's ability to communicate also should be addressed during each stage of health so that appropriate communication methods can be sought and employed.[47] Additionally, involving the decision maker, noting mobility needs, and recognizing religious or cultural beliefs should be noted and incorporated into the care plan and processes.[48] This element also requires integrated and actionable information.

During the discharge and transfer process, there is a concern that patients and their families feel overwhelmed by the amount of healthcare information included in the discharge and transfer plan.[49] When hospitals plan to transfer or provide referrals for follow-up care and treatment, appropriate providers should be identified.[50] Nurses and other discharge planners must deal efficiently with the discharge planning services, and nurses must be the cornerstones for in-home healthcare services.[51] It is increasingly evident that effective hospital discharges can be achieved only when there is quality collaboration between the care providers, primary care providers, and others involved in the care of the patient, including a clear understanding of the respective services required after institutional care.[52] Without this, the diverse needs of local communities and individuals cannot be met.[53] This element also requires integration and access to information across the care continuum. There are five domains for organization readiness to serve diverse patient groups: leadership; data collection and use; workforce commitment; provision of care, treatment, and services; and patient, family, and community engagement.[54]

- *The leadership domain* discusses how leaders must clearly articulate a hospital's commitment to meet the unique needs of its patients in order to establish an organizational culture that values effective communication, cultural competence, and patient- and family-centered care.[55]
- *The data collection and use domain* discusses how the hospital must define what types of data to collect, how to collect the data, and how to use the data for service planning and resource allocation to advance effective communication, cultural competence, and patient- and family-centered care.[56]
- *The workforce domain* discusses how the hospital and its staff, including the medical staff, must commit

to meeting the unique needs of the patients they serve.[57]

- *The provision of care domain* discusses how the hospital, in striving to meet the individual needs of each patient, must embed the concepts of effective communication, cultural competence, and patient- and family-centered care into the core activities of its care delivery system.[58]
- *The patient, family, and community engagement domain* discusses how the hospital must be prepared to respond to the changing needs and demographics of patients, families, and the community served. The hospital can identify the need for new or modified services by being involved and contributing to the overall engagement of patients.[59]

Each domain represents a key area that health organizations, specifically hospitals, should address to make sure necessary systems and processes exist to meet the unique needs of each patient. The hospital can use the domains as a framework for exploring the organization's readiness to address patient needs throughout the care continuum. Recommendations for increasing the readiness of health organizations for innovation should include key organizational strategies for embedding innovation: development of incentives, sophisticated knowledge management, interfunctional and interorganizational coordination and collaboration, and development of an innovation infrastructure.[60]

GOVERNMENTAL IMPERATIVES

INTERNAL REVENUE SERVICE POLICY GUIDANCE

The Internal Revenue Service (IRS), in its oversight of not-for-profit organizations with IRS code section 501(c)(3) status, has revised its policy guidance. The guidance change reflects the requirement that not-for-profit health organizations improve service and connection with the communities they serve. One major element is the requirement for not-for-profit health organizations to conduct community health needs assessments, integrate the findings of those assessments into the strategic decision making of the organization, and monitor effectiveness of community health needs initiatives. The organization must write and publish a fee assistance policy, a policy for actions taken in emergency medical conditions, and perform a community needs assessment once every 3 years.[61] These requirements require resources to establish but will

become part of the culture and, eventually, can be administered seamlessly.[62]

This movement toward more community connection requires the integration of community and population data into the flow of information that leads to actionable information and knowledge within the health organization.

CENTERS FOR MEDICARE AND MEDICAID SERVICES: MEDICARE VALUE-BASED PURCHASING

Value-based purchasing (VBP) is an initiative from the Centers for Medicare and Medicaid Services (CMS) designed to reward acute care hospitals with incentive payments for providing high-quality care to people insured by Medicare. It is important to note that historically, commercial health insurance providers have followed the federal government's example of implementing quality improvement programs within a few months to a few years of federal program implementation. CMS measures the quality of care provided based on how well the facility enhances the patient experience during his or her hospital stay and how closely clinical best practices are followed. This is a change from previous systems that simply paid based on the number of procedures performed. The VBP program was established with the passage of the ACA and was initiated with payments starting October 1, 2012. The launch of the program included 2,985 hospitals across the country.

Through the VBP program, incentive payments are made based on:

- How well a facility performs on a given measure
- The amount of improvement in performance on each measure compared to the baseline time period, 2 years prior (for example, 2015 vs. 2013)

The categories of performance measures under VBP are clinical process of care, patient experience of care, outcomes, and efficiency. Under each category are standard practices, such as stopping certain medications related to a surgical procedure at the correct time, doctor communication, and reporting of key measures, such as mortality due to heart failure. Hospitals are given a score based on their results in these categories, with patient experience of care and outcomes being weighted most heavily.

The VBP program is funded by reimbursement payments withheld from hospitals for care provided to Medicare patients. When the program started in 2013, the bonus money available was 1% of Medicare payments, and when the program is in full effect, in 2017, the applicable percentage will be 2% of Medicare payments.[63] Hospitals that fail to improve under VBP lose their applicable percentage from Medicare payments. Through this mechanism, the VBP system is cost neutral in terms of payments; the "reward" payments given to high performers are covered by the payments withheld from low performers.

Hospital Compare

Hospital Compare is a website, launched in 2005, that has information about the quality of care provided at over 4,000 Medicare-certified hospitals across the United States. The system can be used, as the name suggests, to find and compare the quality of care provided at different hospitals. The information on Hospital Compare is provided in an easy-to-use format targeted to consumers.[64]

Physician Compare

The *Physician Compare* website displays information on physicians and other healthcare practitioners who participate in the program. The Physician Compare system includes information on physician practices as well as on individual physicians.[65]

In addition to comparing physicians and hospitals, CMS also collects data on nursing homes, home health, and dialysis facilities. These websites are interconnected for ease of use. However, ranking services, such as these provided by CMS, are not unique; there are many other similar services run by professional groups, private companies, or industry watchdog groups. You may have seen advertisements for hospitals proudly announcing, "one of the best hospitals in the country is just around the corner." The ranking of hospitals is typically not consistent between various "best hospital" lists, and this also holds true for data in the Hospital Compare system; however, over time the data and consistency of those data should improve. A likely cause of discordant ranking between the myriad quality indicator-based systems is the different methods used by each ranking service, constructs used, and the use of geographic and volume modifiers with the analyses; the variance in these rankings can lead to confusion for consumers.[66]

INTEGRATED INFORMATION REQUIRED: NEED FOR TECHNOLOGY AND INFORMATICS SOLUTIONS

Health is a rapidly evolving industry. Perhaps due to the rapid changes within the health industry itself, the industry has been slow to adopt advances pioneered in other fields such as information technology. The use of EMR began in the early 1970s as computer systems became sophisticated enough to perform the tasks required. From the start, the use of EMR was controversial. Originally, the concern about the adoption of EMR was due to resistance to change (EMR was different from current or older systems).[67] Even though the technology has been available for nearly 50 years, many facilities are slow to adopt EMR systems. Most of the concern around implementing EMR today stems from the cost associated with the systems and concerns about return on investment.[68] However, the use of EMR has increased quickly due to a requirement by the federal government that medical facilities demonstrate meaningful use of EMR by 2015 or face a 1% penalty on their Medicare reimbursement; this penalty will increase over time.[69]

As health organizations begin to transition to EMR in ever-increasing numbers, the need for effective and reliable methods of measuring the level of utility that health institutions are receiving from their EMR implementation is evident. As mentioned in the introduction, effectively measuring how something is used or implemented is best done through a model.

HEALTH INFORMATION MANAGEMENT AND SYSTEMS SOCIETY (HIMSS) DELTA MODEL

Originally, the HIMSS DELTA model was a five-level model that categorized the maturity level of a health organization's analytics system.[70,71] *Analytics* is the use of information (actionable information) resulting from the analysis of data. The data, in this case, are the data elements or components of the EMR, as well as any supporting information stored within a health organization's computer systems.

The five categories for organizations within the HIMSS DELTA model, based on how they use analytics, were admittedly very broad, but the model collected a wide range of data in order to make the categorization. The HIMSS DELTA model was a technology oriented model. The assessment could be thought of as a "first step" in developing an analytics adoption and optimization plan for an organization. The assessment for the DELTA model measured the usage of analytics over five core competences: **d**ata, **e**nterprise, **l**eadership, **t**argets, and **a**nalysts.

Regarding *data*, the depth and breadth of the data available was critical to the effective use of analytics. If limited or fragmented data were available, then the usefulness of the analytical solution was limited, because the data may not have been reliable.

Enterprise consistsed of the approach to managing the data and whether the team managing the system had the appropriate support structure in place.

STAGE	HIMSS Analytics AMAM Adoption Model for Analytics Maturity Cumulative Capabilities
7	Personalized medicine & prescriptive analytics
6	Clinical risk intervention & predictive analytics
5	Enhancing quality of care, population health, and understanding the economics of care
4	Measuring & managing evidence based care, care variability, and waste reduction
3	Efficient, consistent internal and external report production and agility
2	Core data warehouse workout: centralized database with an analytics competency center
1	Foundation building: data aggregation and initial data governance
0	Fragmented point solutions

FIGURE 16-1 Health Information Management & Systems Society's updated analytics model, based on the DELTA model.

Reproduced from Health Information Management & Systems Society. (2013). HIMSS Analytics – DELTA Powered™ Analytics Maturity Suite. Retrieved from http://www.himssanalytics.org/delta.

Leadership measured the passion and commitment of the leaders in an organization toward the implementation of an analytic solution. If the leadership was not passionate about the implementation of an analytic solution, the project would be given lower priority, and it was likely that the implementation would be slow, sloppy, or incomplete.

Targets measured the appropriateness of the goals associated with the implementation and usage of the analytical system. Appropriate goals, according to HIMSS, needed to be first deep, then broad. The purpose behind this was to ensure that the details behind the use and implementation of analytics were not overlooked due to the large scope of an analytics project.

Analysts were an incredibly important piece of the analytical puzzle. Analysts served as the interface between the data contained in an analytical system and the end users—the decision makers who use the information.

HIMSS has upgraded their model to an eight-stage model that can be used as discussed in the chapter (see **Figure 16-1**). Note that the higher levels of "attainment" in the model can only be attributed to higher levels of integration and performance by the health organization.

The 4 Ps of Health Analytics: An Informatics Framework

The 4 Ps of Health Analytics is a descriptive model of how data are used within a health system. It is also a prescriptive model; this will be discussed later in the chapter. Unlike the HIMSS DELTA model, the 4 Ps breaks data into four categories that are depicted in the following figure (**Figure 16-2**).

The 4 Ps of Health Analytics describes the interconnections between the four major categories of data found in health organizations: patients, populations, processes, and profitability (net margin in not-for-profit organizations).

Traditionally, these four types of information have been used separately. When data are not easily accessed or integrated with those from complementary domains, the data are referred to as being in an *information silo*. As computer systems evolved, it became possible to store data in an electronic database which, when properly implemented, allows information that was previously in a silo to be used with other data sources. Another term for these electronic databases is a data warehouse or enterprise data warehouse. A *data warehouse* is a system that creates a central repository of data and makes those data available for reporting and analysis.

While the HIMSS DELTA model was oriented toward technology, the 4 Ps model is oriented toward information. To reduce complexity, the 4 Ps model is presented in its component parts and by what is included in each type of data, before explaining the interconnectivity within the model. The component parts are as follows:

- *Patient data* are data pertaining directly to the demographic information, history, diagnostics, treatment, care plans, and outcomes of care of the patient; these data are contained in the EMR system.

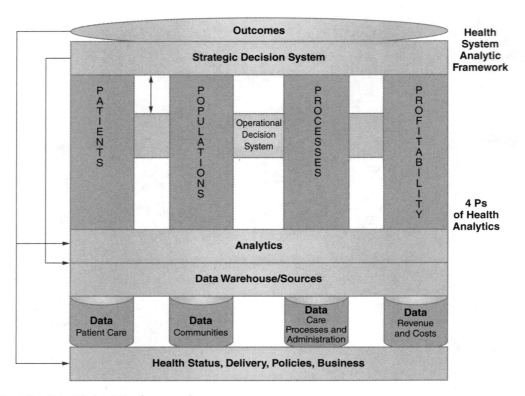

FIGURE 16-2 The 4 Ps of Health Analytics framework.

- *Population data* refer to the communities where health organizations are located. The data in this category are related to improving community health status, and to the health and well-being of the community as a whole.
- *Process data* include information on the way business is conducted within the health organization; these data (or elements of the data) can be found in enterprise resource planning (ERP) systems and organizational documents.
- *Profitability data* (net margin for not-for-profit health organizations) include data on the ability of a health organization to generate income, such as cost of services, amount billed, and expected reimbursement along with expenses; these data can be found in ERP systems and organizational documents.

PROFITABILITY

Ensuring profitability (another way to consider this is ensuring financial viability) requires organizations to properly measure and continuously assess all of the financial components. Financial ratios such as operating margins, days cash on hand, operating margins, debt to capitalization, and capital spending are some important metrics that can be pulled from a health organization's financial statement to measure profitability, liquidity, and capital structure.[72] The transition to VBP, narrowing margins, and focus on reducing costs will require health organizations to look further into operations, expenses, and reimbursement to maintain profitability or net margin. The Health Research & Educational Trust, in partnership with the American Hospital Association (AHA), published metrics for high priority strategies for evolving to the second curve. As previously noted, one of the top four strategies is improving efficiency through productivity and financial management; this is crucial to profitability.[73]

The first metric is expense per episode for each care setting established by analysis with a broad range of episodes of care (volume of patients). These data give insight and understanding to the true cost of care for specific episodes by service line (cardiology, labor and delivery, etc.), which is necessary for financial planning and improvement strategies. Metrics should be in place to measure, manage, model, and predict risk, using a broad set of historical data from multiple sources.[74] Measuring risk is necessary when entering into partnerships with payers, and it can be assessed with possible financial gains and savings.[75]

Cost-reduction goals can be created for specific departments or services, in order to increase profitability, and still meet the needs of patients. Organizations must use these metrics to establish specific yet attainable goals.[76] Similarly, results from quality improvement initiatives and process reengineering should be measurable.[77] In order to meet these goals and assess profitability, these changes must be demonstrated and monitored through a series of metrics. Lastly, the impact of managing future Medicare payment levels must be considered. Projecting the financial impact is necessary to cut costs in order to manage the organization at the forecasted reimbursement level for all payments while monitoring expenses.[78]

Effective financial management requires more comprehensive data sources, integrated information, and appropriate analytical methods for assessment and evaluation. Implementing appropriate technology, coupled with an informatics framework, facilitates metrics to be utilized in cutting costs, increasing efficiency, and boosting revenues.[79]

The profitability of a health organization is critical to the continued operation of the organization. A hospital may provide the best care in the country, with superior outcomes in patient care and high levels of satisfaction, but if the staff salaries and bills cannot be paid, the doors will close. Health organizations want the latest medical technology and the most highly qualified physicians and staff. Having these will attract patients, but this achievement is unreachable without the availability of financial resources. However, not-for-profit health organizations, considering the IRS policy guidance, may lose tax-exempt status if the culture becomes overly focused on reputation and profit while ignoring the community.

An indicator of a financially healthy organization is its ability to earn a profit or net margin and achieve a return on its investments. The financial stability of health organizations is measured by gross profit margin. The *gross profit margin* is defined as the percentage of money remaining after goods and services have been paid for. Focusing on a healthy or high gross profit margin will reflect favorable potential earnings. This, in turn, mirrors profitability. A net profit margin highlights pricing, cost structure, and efficiency of the organization. All three of these components dictate the success and future direction of any organization. When money is spent, however, costs must be managed as well. An organization must be efficient in order to gain the most from purchases of labor, equipment, facilities, and supplies. Inefficiency can reduce the ability to transform costs into productive activity that leads to profitability.

Whether or not an entity is making adequate use of its resources can be measured by looking at the return on assets. Every resource is valuable. Not using an available resource to its highest efficacy is a waste and a drain on the potential improvement. Before taking on any new ventures or investments, an organization should take the additional measure of conducting a review of the organization's return on equity.[80] This allows the health organization to see the returns, if any, gained on the investments that were made previously.[81] The healthcare organization must also track return on investments to determine whether or not resources should remain allocated to a particular aspect of the operation.[82] Positive returns on an investment may control decisions on future investments. A decrease in profitability will result in a decline in the return on assets and return on equity. Each of the previous measures is important to sustain a financially healthy status.[83]

In order to sustain profitability, health organization revenue must be safeguarded. This can be achieved through internal audits.[84] Internal audits can mitigate the potential for revenue loss through denied or recovered payments.[85] Changes in coding and qualified bundle payments will only increase the number of denied claims.[86] Through an internal audit, mistakes can be caught before a loss of time and money ensues or prolongs. This, in turn, allows health organizations to improve billing and coding.[87] As a result, the health organization can seek entitled revenue, knowing its system is above reproach even during payer audits.[88]

Profitability is a key element in maintaining the state-of-the-art technology needed to attract and retain highly trained healthcare professionals.[89] Profitability is also a crucial component to providing high-quality care for patients. For-profit hospitals can raise equity by issuing shares; in order to retain not-for-profit status for tax purposes, a not-for-profit hospital cannot issue shares.[90] It can, however, build equity on internal operations, supplemented with donations and gifts to manage financial investments.[91] Singh's study looks at the relationship between patient revenue in relation to assets and the time it takes to collect patient revenue.[92] Other important factors include financial performance indicators: operating and total profit margins, free cash flow, and equity capital of the health organization. Managing the patient revenue cycle successfully can lead to increased profitability. Of course, higher patient revenue amounts per total assets and quicker collection times are associated with improved operating and profit margins.[93] The research noted faster collections reduced the balance in accounts receivable, and, as a result, the health organization's need for short-term financing, reducing interest expenses.[94] Effective revenue cycle management also allowed for higher free cash flows. This facilitated an increase in cash flow from operations.[95] The study provides firsthand evidence that significant improvements can be achieved in each health organization's revenue cycle performance.[96]

Likewise, effective financial management, expense management, and productivity, coupled with quality revenue management, are imperatives for health organizations and directly linked to their survival. Integrated, multidomain information is required to achieve this level of leadership.

Patients

At the heart of the health industry is the patient and his or her family. Several data sources and metrics should be used to evaluate the patient domain: readmissions, patient satisfaction surveys, awards, occupancy rates, and average length of stay.[97] Readmissions are important because these numbers can help determine whether or not appropriate care was provided to the patient in a previous visit to the health organization within a 30-day period and the effectiveness of discharge plans.[98] This metric evaluates whether treatment methods were effective or not. Patient satisfaction surveys determine whether the medical staff communicated appropriately with the patient when providing care. Awards are a way of determining the effectiveness of patient care compared with other medical facilities. They also provide feedback for health organization performance.[99] Another way of measuring patient care is through occupancy rates, which indicate the health organization's census.[100] Patient satisfaction can be measured through occupancy rates; for example, if the census of the health organization remains high, perhaps it is an indication of success and/or quality throughout the organization.[101] Finally, the average length of stay (AVLOS) is the fifth metric used to measure patients; it determines the types of patient treated in the hospital.[102] For example, if most AVLOS are high, it shows a greater number of patients with severe illnesses, higher acuity, or patients with more complex or multiple procedures per episode of care.[103] Patient outcomes and satisfaction are essential to understand before a leader can develop a knowledge culture; integrated information is required to firmly grasp patient outcomes and satisfaction levels.

Populations

A population can be measured in various ways, but understanding the overall population, groups within the population, and special groups within the population is the basis for community linkage and serving that community. How can you best understand a community's population? Some of the metrics that can be used to measure the population include census information, school data, state and federal health data sources, focus groups with important community organizations, and surveys, as well as the use of REAL data.[104] These metrics can be utilized to acquire reliable, accurate, and useful information on the surrounding community.[105] As previously stated, assessing the needs of the population can help deliver not only a higher quality of care but the type of care that is needed.

EHRs contain a considerable amount of health information. EHRs, once data are separated from individual patient records, can provide insight into health needs and may offer solutions to improving population health. EHRs can be used for research integration and patient care.[106] Realizing this potential will require understanding of what EHRs can realistically offer in efforts to improve population health, the requirements for obtaining useful information from EHRs, and a plan for addressing these requirements.[107] Potential contributions of EHRs for improving population health include better understanding of the level and distribution of disease, function, and well-being within populations.[108] Being able to effectively utilize EHRs allows for better understanding of the patient and how to assess patient needs, while providing insight into improving services.[109]

With the advancement of EHRs, population health will become a high priority for health information management (HIM) and for HIM professionals. A shift in population health management must occur in the near future, as medicine becomes the spotlight for managing the long-term health effects of patient populations.[110]

> Population health management (PHM) lowers costs by refocusing healthcare on not just the sick but also the well. The goal of PHM is to keep a patient population as healthy as possible and reduce the need for expensive interventions like tests, emergency department visits, hospitalizations, and procedures. While most healthcare providers see the critical importance of PHM, they do not have the information technology, the required understanding of PHM, or the data management skills and resources that are required to successfully utilize population health management. Some of the first things that must be understood when launching a PHM program is what a population of healthy people looks like, how clinical risk is defined, how financial risk is measured, and what will be the metrics used to analyze how sick patients with chronic disease do and do not get sicker. PHM programs also track and trend inpatient, ambulatory, and emergency department patients.[111]

Understanding the usage of PHM and all of its functions is important in addressing all of the risks related to a population of nonhealthy people versus healthy people.[112] PHM makes use of patient data registries and data banks to create a portrait of a certain population, analyze trends to find solutions to problematic behaviors, and connect care gaps that may leave certain segments chronically underserved.[113] Using population health data to their fullest extent and achieving complete data integration will "redesign the way providers approach and deliver care" while taking advantage of existing health IT initiatives, such as EHRs and health information exchanges (HIEs) that represent huge investments for hospitals and physicians.[114] Drawing from recent data and analytics, HIM professionals must be the trendsetters in quality data analytics by gathering proper information; maintaining the integrity of clinical documentation, HIE governance, and EHRs; and effectively analyzing data to improve the way patients in diverse populations are perceived and treated.[115]

PROCESSES

Previous studies show that medical errors due to lack of communication among medical staff are estimated to be the chief cause of death for between 44,000 and 98,000 patients every year. Therefore, the productivity of health organizations and improvement of patient health rests upon the implementation of health information technology (HIT) in health organizations. Defining HIT can be challenging because it can be composed of multiple administrative and clinical applications that may vary across different organizations and medical settings. HIT is not an application that can be applied to the health organization and be expected to run smoothly by itself; HIT needs the commitment of the leadership and staff of the organization for it to work effectively and efficiently.[116] Focusing only on the technology and not on the reasons for the technology—to provide information that is actionable to develop a knowledge culture—would be unwise. Why you have the technology, what you get from that technology, and how you use the output (in this case, information) is critical.

Health leaders are the spearhead of this operation and, therefore, must advocate for the implementation of HIT into their organizations.[117] Health leaders must focus on what HIT provides—information. Of equal importance, leaders must understand that HIT implementation is a process, and it may take years to have an optimal and operational system.[118] Thus, the loss of productivity in the "project" years should be expected and taken into consideration.[119] Moreover, having a successful operating HIT not only helps productivity within the organization, but it also helps the organization's profitability and improves the patient's quality of care (outcomes), processes, and population health.[120] Along with all the pros of HIT adoption, there are also cons. The cons include cost and loss of productivity in the project phase due to learning and adjustment processes.[121] Health leaders must keep their eyes on the reason for HIT, the actionable and integrated information that can inform high-quality decisions across the organization in pursuit of a knowledge culture.

HIT will increase productivity after the initial 2 years of implementation by allowing smoother communication with supply chain management, accounting, and billing.[122] It will also reduce transaction costs and improve resource allocation.[123] The rising cost of health care and the presence of inefficiencies in health organizations can lead to loss of resources (dollars, time, high-quality physicians and staff, and opportunities). HIT can satisfy many functions including monitoring physician behavior and how resources are allocated;[124] a clinical information monitoring system can be used to identify any overuse of laboratory and radiology resources, for example.[125] This reduction in transaction costs attributed to inefficiency of production and resource allocation will increase overall profitability, improve patient care outcomes (to include increased safety), and enhance processes and community health status by allowing the health organizations to keep more of their profits or net margin[126] and use those funds for improvements. This requires integrated and actionable information.

HIT, such as EMRs, will also improve patients' quality of care by allowing better communication between physicians and staff throughout the health organization and its external support structures.[127] Patient care requires coordination of many activities across multiple and various departments in which communication among the staff is critical; human errors can be costly to both the organization and its patients.[128] HIT implementation allows for a reduction of redundancy of treatment and communication errors among medical staff.[129] This improves patient care by allowing patients to manage their health alongside the physician.[130]

The main deterrent to the adoption of HIT is cost. Many inefficient health organizations struggle to survive; having to adapt to a brand new clinical and administrative HIT system may seem daunting.[131] Productivity in the overall operation can be increased due to HIT, such as when EMRs are introduced (once the learning curve is overcome), with the benefits likely outweighing the costs of adoption.[132] Moreover, improving health through the process of HIT requires more than just integrating the technology into the organization's system;[133] the technology must provide pertinent information to realize these desires. Training is an important part of HIT implementation; more importantly, making postimplementation maintenance training available to the staff is critical.[134]

HIMSS ANALYTICS DELTA POWERED MATURITY MODEL

There are several constructs related to the DELTA model that fall under the category of analytics maturity models. An analytics maturity model offers a more detailed description of an organization at each level of analytics usage. Of particular interest for our purposes is the electronic medical record adoption model (EMRAM). The EMRAM categorizes analytics maturity based on the capabilities of the EMR system utilized by the organization. HIMSS Analytics has conducted several studies using the EMRAM in the United States and Canada that revealed interesting results that are summarized in **Tables 16–1 to 16–4**.

As can be seen from the results, high levels of analytics adoption are rare in the sample from the United States and nonexistent in the Canadian sample. When the results were repeated in 2014 Q2, the adoption rates had not changed from Q1 in Canada, while there was moderate improvement among U.S. health organizations.

The survey reveals that there is great potential for improvement with regard to the use of analytics in health organizations across the United States and Canada. Additionally, the increasing levels of EMR utilization in the United States shows that EMR adoption and system improvement is an issue important to U.S.-based health systems today. The reasons for this improvement could be related to the ACA requirements, the timeliness of the technology, or competitive factors. Regardless of the reason, health organizations will need to adapt and grow their EMR systems to keep pace with industry-wide adoption of the technology.

The EMRAM can be used for other types of data as well, not just EMR or patient-related data. If this type of scale is used to measure the effectiveness of all four information types, it can provide a score for how all data types are utilized. Although EMRAM does an excellent job of categorizing the utilization of analytics, it does not address the actionable information, knowledge, or meaningful use components.

INTEGRATION OF 4 PS, HIMSS ANALYTICS DELTA, AND EMRAM MODELS

EFFICIENCY, EFFECTIVENESS, AND EFFICACY

The efficiency, effectiveness, and efficacy of a model are important considerations to take into account when selecting a method to pursue in the domain of informatics. *Efficiency* is how much time, effort, or resources are required to implement the model divided by the output or utility of the model. *Effectiveness*, in this context, is how well the model works to achieve a set of goals or objectives in real-world

Table 16-1 U.S. Electronic Medical Record Adoption Model[135]

	U.S. EMR Adoption Model[SM]		
Stage	**Cumulative Capabilities**	**2013 Q4**	**2014 Q1**
Stage 7	Complete EMR; CCD transactions to share data; Data warehousing; Data continuity with ED, ambulatory, OP	2.9%	3.1%
Stage 6	Physician documentation (structured templates), full CDSS (variance and compliance), full R-PACS	12.5%	13.3%
Stage 5	Closed loop medication administration	22.0%	24.2%
Stage 4	CPOE, Clinical decision support (clinical protocols)	15.5%	15.7%
Stage 3	Nursing/clinical documentation (flow sheets), CDSS (error checking), PACS available outside radiology	30.3%	27.7%
Stage 2	CDR, Controlled medical vocabulary, CDS, may have document imaging; HIE capable	7.6%	7.2%
Stage 1	Ancillaries: lab, rad, pharmacy all installed	3.3%	3.2%
Stage 0	All three ancillaries not installed	5.8%	5.6%

Data from HIMSS Analytics® Database ©2014.
Reproduced from US EMR Adoption Model. Retrieved from https://app.himssanalytics.org/stagesGraph.asp.

Table 16-2 Canada Electronic Medical Record Adoption Model[136]

	Canada EMR Adoption Model[SM]			
Stage	Cumulative Capabilities	2013 Q4	2014 Q1
Stage 7	Complete EMR; CCD transactions to share data; Data warehousing; Data continuity with ED, ambulatory, OP	0.0%	0.0%
Stage 6	Physician documentation (structured templates), full CDSS (variance and compliance), full R-PACS	0.6%	0.6%
Stage 5	Closed loop medication administration	0.0%	0.5%
Stage 4	CPOE, Clinical decision support (clinical protocols)	3.8%	3.6%
Stage 3	Nursing/clinical documentation (flow sheets), CDSS (error checking), PACS available outside radiology	32.2%	32.5%
Stage 2	CDR, Controlled medical vocabulary, CDS, may have document imaging; HIE capable	29.1%	28.9%
Stage 1	Ancillaries: lab, rad, pharmacy all installed	14.5%	14.5%
Stage 0	All three ancillaries not installed	19.8%	19.4%

Reproduced from Canada EMR Adoption Model. Retrieved from https://app.himssanalytics.org/stagesGraph.asp.

Table 16-3 U.S. EMR Adoption Cumulative Capabilities[137]

	U.S. EMR Adoption Model[SM]			
Stage	Cumulative Capabilities	2014 Q1	2014 Q2
Stage 7	Complete EMR; CCD transactions to share data; Data warehousing; Data continuity with ED, ambulatory, OP	3.1%	3.2%
Stage 6	Physician documentation (structured templates), full CDSS (variance and compliance), full R-PACS	13.3%	15.0%
Stage 5	Closed loop medication administration	24.2%	27.5%
Stage 4	CPOE, Clinical decision support (clinical protocols)	15.7%	15.3%
Stage 3	Nursing/clinical documentation (flow sheets), CDSS (error checking), PACS available outside radiology	27.7%	25.4%
Stage 2	CDR, Controlled medical vocabulary, CDS, may have document imaging; HIE capable	7.2%	5.9%
Stage 1	Ancillaries: lab, rad, pharmacy all installed	3.2%	2.8%
Stage 0	All three ancillaries not installed	5.6%	4.9%

Reproduced from US EMR Adoption Cumulative Capabilities Model. Retrieved from https://app.himssanalytics.org/stagesGraph.asp.

Table 16-4 Canada EMR Adoption Cumulative Capabilites[138]			
Canada EMR Adoption Model^(SM)			
Stage	**Cumulative Capabilities**	**2014 Q1**	**2014 Q2**
Stage 7	Complete EMR; CCD transactions to share data; Data warehousing; Data continuity with ED, ambulatory, OP	0.0%	0.0%
Stage 6	Physician documentation (structured templates), full CDSS (variance and compliance), full R-PACS	0.6%	0.6%
Stage 5	Closed loop medication administration	0.5%	0.5%
Stage 4	CPOE, Clinical decision support (clinical protocols)	3.6%	3.6%
Stage 3	Nursing/clinical documentation (flow sheets), CDSS (error checking), PACS available outside radiology	32.5%	32.5%
Stage 2	CDR, Controlled medical vocabulary, CDS, may have document imaging; HIE capable	28.9%	28.9%
Stage 1	Ancillaries: lab, rad, pharmacy all installed	14.5%	14.5%
Stage 0	All three ancillaries not installed	19.4%	19.4%

Reproduced from Canadian EMR Adoption Cumulative Capabilities Model. Retrieved from https://app.himssanalytics.org/stagesGraph.asp.

situations. *Efficacy* is how much value or "good" the model brings to the problem or improvement effort; in essence, what positive outcomes can you attribute to using a particular model? At first glance, it may appear that effectiveness and efficacy are measuring the same attribute; this is a common point of confusion. Models with high efficacy must be effective when applied to real-world situations. Regardless of the efficacy and effectiveness of a model, if it is not efficient to use, the model will be less useful in the fast-paced environment of health organizations. Let us explore some models.

For illustration purposes, each of the models, EMRAM, DELTA, and the 4 Ps, describes a different aspect of an EMR system. Because each model emphasizes a different important element of the EMR, combining the models allows a more comprehensive picture to emerge concerning EMR; actually, the combination of the models will create a more robust picture of any technologically enabled informatics situation. Used in conjunction, or integrated, all of these models are effective, efficient, and have high efficacy.

INTEGRATION

By combining the 4 Ps, DELTA, and EMRAM, a new model that is both prescriptive and descriptive emerges.

The 4 Ps model describes the type of data and how the four types of data in each domain (patients, populations, processes, and profitability) work together. The HIMSS DELTA model ranks the utilization of data analytics. The HIMSS EMRAM gives an in depth description of each level of utilization. Combining the three models creates a complete picture of how data should be used at each stage of analytics adoption and gives a roadmap for improvement. The combined model, for purposes of discussion, is the 4 Ps of Health Analytics *adoption*.

4 PS OF HEALTH ANALYTICS ADOPTION

The 4 Ps of Health Analytics adoption is both a prescriptive and descriptive model that is an extension of the 4 Ps of Health Analytics model and incorporates the valuable HIMSS Analytics DELTA Powered™ Analytics Maturity Model and EMR Adoption Model (see **Figure 16-3**). At each level of analytics utilization, data are unified through the data warehouse. The extent of this utilization is what determines the effectiveness and efficacy of the data; this combined effectiveness and efficacy is quantified by a score

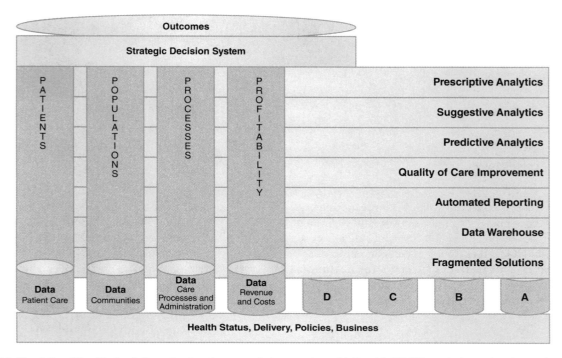

FIGURE 16-3 The 4 Ps of Health Analytics adoption framework, integration of 4 Ps with HIMSS analytics technology adoption levels.

in the model. The utilization levels are loosely based on the scores associated with the EMRAM, developed by HIMSS Analytics.

Data used incorrectly, even if the electronic systems are fully utilized, will not help an organization and can actually negatively impact organizational decisions. To measure the effectiveness at which the data provided by analytical systems are converted into knowledge, the 4 Ps of Health Analytics adoption assigns a letter grade, the same as one would expect to receive in a class. The knowledge scale in the 4 Ps of Health Analytics adoption model consists of a four-letter range: A, B, C, D. Note that a high knowledge score is essentially measuring the meaningful use of the electronic systems and EMR, combined with continuous learning and feedback loops using the information. When the score is combined with the knowledge score, a matrix of possible values can be created. As an example, this point is illustrated in **Table 16-5**.

While an "X" in Table 16-5 is the most common score, any value within the table is possible, although much less likely to occur. The reasoning behind this becomes apparent when the extreme scores of "1A" and "7D" are examined. A score of "1A" means that only fragmented bits of information are available and what is available is converted to high levels of knowledge spanning the patient, the population in which they live, the processes that support their

treatment, and the financial implications. A score of "7D" is also unlikely to occur. A score of "7D" would be assigned to an organization that has full utilization of all possible analytic solutions and adoptive technologies but is unable to use those systems to generate anything beyond raw data. With this framework, individual scoring can be explored.

WHAT DOES MY KNOWLEDGE SCORE MEAN?

The knowledge score is a single letter grade between "A" and "D" and shows the transition from raw data to knowledge.

- A = Knowledge; actionable and integrated information used for improvement in a continuous feedback loop. Knowledge-based organizational cultures operate in this environment for most strategic and operational decisions.
- B = Actionable information is integrated across the 4 Ps and prompts action.
- C = Data are in context or information that is minimally integrated across the 4 Ps.
- D = Raw data without integration; data remain in their "silo."

It is noteworthy that raw data could be further broken down into incomplete, fragmented, and clean. The reason

Table 16-5 The 4 Ps of Health Analytics Adoption and HIMSS Analytics DELTA-Powered Analytics Maturity Model Integration						
A				X	X	X	X
B			X	X	X	X	X
C	X	X	X	X	X	
D	X	X	X			
Information score (4 Ps)/Technology adoption score (HIMSS Analytics)	1	2	3	4	5	6	7

the 4 P model does not do this is because it is not relevant to what the 4 Ps are describing. The purpose of the model is to move organizations to higher levels of utilization so, while it is acknowledged that further categorization of raw data is possible, moving past this state of informatics utilization is prudent since most health organizations are beyond this state of development regarding informatics.

WHAT DOES MY UTILIZATION SCORE MEAN?

The utilization score is a number between 1 and 7 and describes the adoption of analytical tools within a health organization. The integration of the knowledge scores with the utilization scores becomes clear with the explanation that follows:

1. Fragmented data with multiple sources available
   - A score of 1 means that an organization is in the planning stages of adopting analytical tools. At this stage, data are most likely stored in separate systems with no integration or unified fields. Any available data are likely to be fragmented with multiple versions of "the truth" available at any one time.
2. Data warehouse with patient, population, process, and profitability data stored in a standardized system
   - The standardization of the system is important because this is what allows the data from multiple sources to be utilized in a meaningful way. If the data were simply stored in a single system without standardization, they still would be effectively in an information silo.
3. Automated internal dashboards and external reporting using the data available from the data warehouse
   - Dashboards and scorecards define modern business. In health organizations these tools are used, some would say overused, every day. By automating the creation of these tools, analysts are able to

spend their time analyzing data instead of building reports. As a result, it is possible to have more effective meetings and allow decision making to keep pace with the healthcare environment.
4. Waste reduction and quality of care improvement
   - The reduction of waste and quality of care improvement can be accomplished through streamlining the supply chain based on analysis of supply usage. By understanding how much is used when, inventory on hand can be reduced, and space that was once used for storage can be converted to patient care areas.
5. Predictive analytics to manage clinical outcomes
   - Predictive analytics to manage clinical outcomes takes into account how patients behave in their communities. Predicting how patients will behave once they leave the facility allows case managers to effectively manage risks for readmission and other target areas.
6. Suggestive analytics to manage population health
   - Suggestive analytics go beyond what is offered by predictive analytics in that they suggest potential treatment options to providers based on patterns in existing information.
7. Prescriptive analytics to personalize medicine
   - This is the ultimate goal of analytics in health care. Prescriptive analytics do not necessarily translate to a knowledge score of "A." Having such an analytics system and not fully understanding it would result in a score less than an "A."

WHEN SHOULD MY ORGANIZATION WORK TO INCREASE OUR UTILIZATION LEVEL?

A health organization and its leadership team will receive the most benefit of an increase in the level of analytics utilization if the knowledge score for the current level is maximized. Increasing utilization before the knowledge score is maximized will most likely result in no change to the knowledge score without improvements to the adaptive (human ways of using information) processes and organizational culture. The reason behind this is that the addition of new systems when the current ones are underutilized shines a light on business processes and adaptive/human issues. This can be countered through additional training on existing systems and providing intensive training on new features as they are added. It can also be beneficial to provide periodic review courses for essential team members to create understanding of why information is needed and how it is utilized.

EXAMPLES OF 4 PS OF HEALTH ANALYTICS ADOPTION MODEL IN PRACTICE

Next, we will look at some examples of how the 4 Ps can be used in common situations within a health system. The examples used are simple, yet they demonstrate the initial basic assessment that using the 4 Ps Health Analytics adoption model can provide without a large investment in time or other resources. Our first example is a small rural hospital, and the second is within the context of a large health system.

Example 1: Using the 4 Ps in a Small Rural Hospital to Determine the Need for an Analytics Solution

As the CEO of a critical access hospital, your organization is struggling to make payroll, and investment in new capital equipment is not possible at this time. With the EMR meaningful use requirements looming on the horizon, VBP increasingly causing stress, and net margin narrow, you must act quickly so that your Medicare reimbursement is not affected. This is especially important to your organization, because Medicare comprises nearly 40% of your payer mix and you are dependent on Medicare reimbursement payments to pay your employees. Many vendors want to install an EMR system in your hospital, but you are not sure which product is the correct choice for your hospital. Additionally, you want to make sure that your staff is effectively using its available analytics resources.

The 4 Ps of Health Analytics adoption is the perfect model to use in this situation because it accounts for the needs of small facilities as well as large. Under the 4 Ps model a utilization score of 7 is not necessarily the "best." Rather, the usage of the information available is the most important factor, and whether that information gives you

the decision support you need to operate and lead successfully. A small facility may have its analytics needs met at a score of 3B, 4B, or 4A, for example.

Armed with this knowledge, you and your team complete the 4 Ps assessment process and find that your current score is 2B. This score shows that actionable information is available, and the available information is being utilized rather effectively at a utilization level of 2. This result, combined with other research, gives you the confidence to select an EMR system that would move your utilization to a 3 or 4 level with the option to expand capabilities in the future. In this example, you know that your facility is ready for the basic EMR system because the information available was already being highly utilized; advancing the technology utilization level and increasing the level of information available will most likely be the best choice to improve your organization. The investment in EMR will most likely result in a positive return on investment. Let us assume, for example, that the 4 Ps assessment returned a score of 1D for this small hospital. This score would inform the CEO that additional basic comprehensive training on the use of the current information systems is needed before and during the EMR implementation process and that an update of the business processes of the organization must be made prior to that implementation. If this update of business practices (adaptive changes) and training does not occur, the EMR system would be severely underutilized, and for a hospital on a tight budget, this will likely be a wasted investment.

Example 2: Using the 4 Ps in a Large Health System with an Existing EMR and Data Warehouse System

Imagine that you are the CIO of a large healthcare system. Your organization has been using an EMR system with an associated data warehouse for about 10 years. Overall, physicians with whom you speak are happy with the current EMR system and operational leaders/managers feel that they have the tools they need to assess the risks of patients, improve processes in the operation, and connect better with the populations in the community. Your organization is growing at a rapid pace; there is a need for expanded technological and informatics systems. Due to the cost associated with changes or additions to the information systems, you want to see how well the current systems are being utilized. Your team completes the utilization and knowledge assessments and presents the findings. Under the 4 Ps of Health Analytics adoption model, your health system received a score of 4C. This score means that while your health system has advanced analytics capabilities to automate reporting, improve some operational processes, and streamline the supply chain with electronic data interchange (EDI) transaction processing, the data available within your systems are not being effectively converted to integrated actionable information, not to mention consistently achieving the knowledge level. Because the current systems are not being fully utilized, an expansion of the information system may not be as effective without enhanced training, improvements to business operations, utilization of metrics, and professional analysts to interpret and use the data correctly.

Based on the results of the 4 Ps of Health Analytics adoption model assessment, a business process reengineering and update process was initiated, a training program on utilizing data/information/knowledge for improved operations and services was begun, and a thorough assessment of business and clinical analyst needs was launched. These efforts were started before expanding the information systems at your organization. When the 4 Ps of Health Analytics adoption model assessment was completed again 18 months later, your organization received the score of 5B showing a growth in utilization and knowledge. Because the 4 Ps of Health Analytics adoption model is a prescriptive and assessment model, this reevaluation has also shown areas for further growth.

SUMMARY

In this time of rapid change and the absolute necessity for health leaders to understand how information and technology can evolve health organizations, one way for health organizations to continue to advance is to adopt technological advancements such as EMRs and other clinical and administrative HIT systems. This is especially important given recent reform, policy guidance, and reimbursement changes, along with new expectations placed on health systems by patients and the community. Managing risk and serving the needs of a population are very new requirements for health services delivery organizations; this challenge is a leadership responsibility to migrate the culture to a knowledge-enabled organization. A health leader must be able to make informed decisions with integrated information in the patient, process, population, and profitability domains. To assess current utilization of analytics and other tools that create knowledge from raw data, a model such as the 4 Ps of Health Analytics adoption is a starting point.

The 4 Ps of Health Analytics is a descriptive model that describes the ideal use of mission-critical data into actionable information with an emphasis on creating a knowledge-based culture. With the valuable HIMSS models integrated with the 4 Ps of Health Analytics model, the 4 Ps of Health Analytics *adoption* model is both a prescriptive and descriptive model; it describes and assesses the current state of utilization of technology and knowledge in information systems, coupled with business practices. Successful health leadership requires selecting the correct model to inform, guide, and improve health organizations. With the industry rapidly evolving, knowledge from the four basic domains will equip the health organization to embrace challenges and improve health status both one patient at a time *and* among the entire population of the communities that the organization serves.

DISCUSSION QUESTIONS

1. Describe the significant changes in the health industry that prompt an integrated approach for utilizing health information from multiple areas to make good decisions for health services delivery and improved health status of communities.
2. Explain how health industry reform and policy changes impact the rate of health analytics adoption within health organizations and what changes require analytics adoption within the health industry.
3. Demonstrate how applicable models associated with health information and technology tools improve efficiency, effectiveness, performance, and efficacy of health services and healthcare delivery.
4. Compare and contrast methods to effectively use analytic models to integrate raw data and develop knowledge to improve health system performance and equity within a community.
5. Categorize health organizations in technology adoption, analytics adoption (information utilization), and information integration using the integration of the HIMSS DELTA model and the 4 Ps of Health Analytics models, and provide examples.
6. Appraise and evaluate the integration of population, patient, process, and profitability (net margin for nonprofits) information in solving community health challenges and/or strategic planning for a health organization.

EXERCISES

1. In one page or less, describe the significant changes in the health industry that prompt an integrated approach for utilizing health information from multiple areas to make good decisions for health services delivery and improved health status of communities.

2. Explain how health industry reform and policy changes, based on the American Hospital Association and other associations, impact the rate of health analytics adoption within health organizations and what changes require analytics adoption in the health industry.

3. Demonstrate how applicable models associated with the health information and technology tools improve efficiency, effectiveness, performance, and efficacy of health services and healthcare delivery (visit http://svi.cdc.org). How can the 4 Ps of Health Analytics adoption model be used with social and vulnerable populations using the SVI Index?

4. Compare and contrast methods to effectively use analytic models to integrate raw data and develop knowledge to improve health system performance and equity within a community.

5. Categorize health organizations in technology adoption, analytics adoption (information utilization), and information integration using the integration of the HIMSS DELTA model and the 4 Ps of Health Analytics models, and provide examples.

6. Appraise and evaluate the integration of population, patient, process, and profitability (net margin for nonprofits) information in solving community health challenges and/or strategic planning for a health organization. Utilize the 4 Ps of Health Analytics adoption model as if you were working for one of the organizations used in Example 1 or 2 from the text, and discuss your results.

ADDITIONAL RESOURCES

Health Research & Educational Trust. (2013, August). *Reducing healthcare disparities: Collection and use of race, ethnicity and language data.* Chicago, IL: Health Research & Educational Trust. Retrieved from http://www.hpoe.org/EOC-real-data.

O'Donnell, O., van Doorslaer, E., Wagstaff, A., & Lindelow, M. (2007). *Analyzing health equity using household survey data: A guide to techniques and their implementation.* Washington, D.C.: World Bank Group. Retrieved from http://documents.worldbank.org/curated/en/2008/01/9007641/analyzing-health-equity-using-household-survey-data-guide-techniques-implementation.

U.S. Office of the Federal Register. (2012). *Additional requirements for charitable hospitals.* Retrieved from https://federalregister.gov/a/2012-15537.

The Joint Commission. (2010). *Advancing effective communication, cultural competence, and patient- and family-centered care: A roadmap for hospitals.* Oakbrook Terrace, IL: The Joint Commission. Retrieved from http://www.jointcommission.org/roadmap_for_hospitals/.

Wilson-Stronks, A., Lee, K. K., Cordero, C. L., Kopp, A. L., & Galvez, E. (2008). *One size does not fit all: Meeting the health care needs of diverse populations.* Oakbrook Terrace, IL: The Joint Commission. Retrieved from http://www.jointcommission.org/assets/1/6/HLCOneSizeFinal.pdf.

American Hospital Association, Committee on Research. (2014, January). *Your hospital's path to the second curve: Integration and transformation.* Chicago, IL: Health Research & Educational Trust. Retrieved from http://www.aha.org/paths-to-second-curve.

REFERENCES

1. U.S. Department of Health and Human Services. (2014). 2014 poverty guidelines. Retrieved from http://aspe.hhs.gov/poverty/14poverty.cfm.
2. ObamaCare Facts. (2013). ObamaCare subsidies—ObamaCare facts. Retrieved from http://obamacarefacts.com/obamacare-subsidies.php.
3. HealthCare.gov. (2013). Open enrollment period. Retrieved from https://www.healthcare.gov/glossary/open-enrollment-period/.
4. HealthCare.gov. (2014). The fee you pay if you don't have health coverage. Retrieved from https://www.healthcare.gov/what-if-i-dont-have-health-coverage/.

5. Centers for Medicare and Medicaid Services (CMS). (2012). Meaningful use stage 1 requirements, pp. 29–30. Retrieved from https://www.cms.gov/Regulations-and-Guidance/Legislation/EHRIncentivePrograms/downloads/MU_Stage1_ReqOverview.pdf.

6. American Hospital Association, Committee on Research (AHA). (2014, January). *Your hospital's path to the second curve: Integration and transformation.* Chicago, IL: Health Research & Educational Trust, p. 4.

7. AHA, note 6, p. 4.

8. AHA, note 6, p. 4.

9. AHA, note 6, p. 4.

10. AHA, note 6, p. 4.

11. AHA, note 6, p. 6.

12. AHA, note 6, p. 6.

13. AHA, note 6, p. 16.

14. AHA, note 6, p. 16.

15. Health Research & Educational Trust. (2013, August). *Reducing healthcare disparities: Collection and use of race, ethnicity and language data.* Chicago, IL: Health Research & Educational Trust, p. 2. Retrieved from www.hpoe.org.

16. Health Research & Educational Trust, note 15, p. 2.

17. Health Research & Educational Trust, note 15, pp. 3–5.

18. Health Research & Educational Trust, note 15, pp. 3–5.

19. Health Research & Educational Trust, note 15, p. 6.

20. Health Research & Educational Trust, note 15, p. 6.

21. Wilson-Stronks, A., Lee, K. K., Cordero, C. L., Kopp, A. L., & Galvez, E. (2008). One size does not fit all: Meeting the health care needs of diverse populations, p 7. Retrieved from http://www.jointcommission.org/assets/1/6/HLCOneSizeFinal.pdf.

22. Wilson-Stronks et al., note 21, p. 7.

23. Wilson-Stronks et al., note 21, p. 8.

24. Wilson-Stronks et al., note 21, p. 8.

25. Wilson-Stronks et al., note 21, pp. 40–44.

26. Wilson-Stronks et al., note 21, pp. 40–44.

27. Wilson-Stronks et al., note 21, pp. 40–44.

28. Wilson-Stronks et al., note 21, pp. 40–44.

29. Wilson-Stronks et al., note 21, pp. 40–44.

30. The Joint Commission. (2010). Advancing effective communication, cultural competence, and patient- and family-centered care: A roadmap for hospitals, p. 3. Retrieved from http://www.jointcommission.org/assets/1/6/aroadmapforhospitalsfinalversion727.pdf.

31. The Joint Commission, note 30, p. 3.

32. The Joint Commission, note 30, p. 3.

33. The Joint Commission, note 30, p. 3.

34. The Joint Commission, note 30, p. 3.

35. The Joint Commission, note 30, p. 9.

36. The Joint Commission, note 30, p. 13.

37. The Joint Commission, note 30, p. 13.

38. The Joint Commission, note 30, p. 13.

39. The Joint Commission, note 30, p. 17.

40. The Joint Commission, note 30, pp. 18–23.

41. The Joint Commission, note 30, pp. 18–23.

42. The Joint Commission, note 30, pp. 18–23.

43. The Joint Commission, note 30, pp. 18–23.

44. The Joint Commission, note 30, pp. 18–23.

45. The Joint Commission, note 30, pp. 18–23.

46. The Joint Commission, note 30, pp. 25–26.

47. The Joint Commission, note 30, p. 26.

48. The Joint Commission, note 30, p. 26.

49. The Joint Commission, note 30, p. 29.

50. The Joint Commission, note 30, pp. 29–30.

51. The Joint Commission, note 30, pp. 29–30.

52. The Joint Commission, note 30, pp. 29–30.

53. Department of Health. (2003). Discharge from hospital: Pathway, process and practice, p. v. Retrieved from http://www.wales.nhs.uk/sitesplus/documents/829/DoH%20-%20Discharge%20Pathway%202003.PDF.

54. The Joint Commission, note 30, pp. 33–43.

55. The Joint Commission, note 30, pp. 33–43.

56. The Joint Commission, note 30, pp. 33–43.

57. The Joint Commission, note 30, pp. 33–43.

58. The Joint Commission, note 30, pp. 33–43.

59. The Joint Commission, note 30, pp. 33–43.

60. Williams, I. (2011, January 1). Organizational readiness for innovation in health care: Some lessons from the recent literature. *Health Services Management Research*, *24*(4), 213–218. Retrieved from http://www.birmingham.ac.uk/Documents/college-social-sciences/social-policy/HSMC/publications/2011/organisational-readiness-health-care.pdf.

61. Ingram, S. H. Department of the Treasury, Internal Revenue Service. (2012). *Additional requirements for charitable hospitals (2012–15537).*

62. Ingram, note 61.

63. CMS. (2012). Hospital value-based purchasing program, pp. 1–8, Retrieved from http://www.cms.gov/Outreach-and-Education/Medicare-Learning-Network-MLN/MLNProducts/downloads/Hospital_VBPurchasing_Fact_Sheet_ICN907664.pdf.

64. Medicare.gov. (2013). Medicare Hospital Compare Overview. Retrieved from http://www.medicare.gov/hospitalcompare/About/What-Is-HOS.html.

65. CMS. (2013). Medicare.gov—About the data. Retrieved from http://www.medicare.gov/physician compare/staticpages/data/aboutthedata.html.

66. Halasyamani, L. K., & Davis, M. M. (2007). Conflicting measures of hospital quality: Ratings from "Hospital Compare" versus "Best Hospitals." *Journal of Hospital Medicine*, *2*(3), 128–134.

67. Mather, B. S. (1973). Problem oriented medical record. *British Medical Journal*, *4*(5883), 49.

68. Jha, A. K., DesRoches, C. M., Campbell, E. G., Donelan, K., Rao, S. R., Ferris, et al. (2009). Use of electronic health records in US hospitals. *New England Journal of Medicine*, *360*(16), 1628–1638.

69. U. S. Congress. (2009). American Recovery and Reinvestment Act of 2009. *Public Law*, (111-5), 111.

70. HIMSS Analytics (2013). HIMSS Analytics – DELTA Powered™ Analytics Maturity Suite. Retrieved from http://www.himssanalytics.org/DELTA/.

71. HIMSS Analytics. Electronic Medical Record Adoption Model (EMRAM). Retrieved from http://www.himssanalytics.org/emram/emram.aspx.

72. Rodak, S. (2012). 5 key financial ratios healthcare providers should track. Becker's Hospital CFO. Retrieved from http://www.beckershospitalreview.com/finance/5-key-financial-ratios-healthcare-providers-should-track.html.

73. AHA, note 6, p. 18.

74. AHA, note 6, p. 2.

75. AHA, note 6, p. 2.

76. AHA, note 6, p. 5.

77. AHA, note 6, p. 6.

78. AHA, note 6, p. 2

79. L.E.K. Consulting. (2013). Hospitals adopt new strategies to boost profitability, but still face deep challenges: A new imperative for MedTech. *Executive Insights*, *15*(4), 5. Retrieved from http://www.lek.com/sites/default/files/2013_L.E.K._Hospital_Priorities_Study.pdf.

80. Benton, D. C., Gonzalez-Jurado, M. A., Beneit-Montesinos, J. V., & Fernandez, P. (2013). Use of open systems theory to describe regulatory trends. *Journal of Nursing Regulation*, *4*(3), 49–56, 51.

81. Benton et al., note 80, pp. 49–56.

82. Benton et al., note 80, pp. 49–56.

83. Benton et al., note 80, pp. 49–56.

84. Allen, B. (2013). Internal audits can safeguard hospital revenue. *Hfm (Healthcare Financial Management)*, *67*(9), 106–112, 106.

85. Allen, note 84, p. 106.

86. Allen, note 84, p. 106.

87. Allen, note 84, p. 106.

88. Allen, note 84, p. 106.

89. Rauscher Singh, S., & Wheeler, J. (2012). Hospital financial management: What is the link between revenue cycle management, profitability, and not-for-profit hospitals' ability to grow equity? *Journal of Healthcare Management*, *57*(5), 325–339, 326.

90. Rauscher Singh & Wheeler, note 89, p. 326.

91. Rauscher Singh & Wheeler, note 89, p. 326.

92. Rauscher Singh & Wheeler, note 89, p. 325.

93. Rauscher Singh & Wheeler, note 89, p. 325.

94. Rauscher Singh & Wheeler, note 89, p. 335.

95. Rauscher Singh & Wheeler, note 89, p. 333.

96. Rauscher Singh & Wheeler, note 89, p. 327.

97. Cosgrove, D., Fisher, M., Gabow, P., et al. (2012). A CEO checklist for high-value health care. Discussion paper. Washington, D.C.: Institute of Medicine. Retrieved from http://www.iom.edu/Global/Perspectives/2012/CEOChecklist.aspx.

98. Cosgrove et al., note 97.

99. Sorra, J., Famolaro, T., Yount, N. D., et al. (2014, March). Hospital survey on patient safety culture 2014 user comparative database report. (Prepared by Westat, Rockville, MD, under Contract No. HHSA 290201300003C). Rockville, MD: Agency for Healthcare Research & Quality.

100. Sorra et al., note 99.

101. Sorra et al., note 99.

102. Health Research & Educational Trust. (2011). *Improving health equity through data collection and use: A guide for hospital leaders*. Chicago: Health Research & Educational Trust, p. 2. Retrieved from http://www.hret.org/health-equity/index.shtml.

103. Health Research & Educational Trust, note 102, p. 3.

104. Health Research & Educational Trust, note 102, p. 4.

105. Health Research & Educational Trust, note 102, p. 3.

106. Friedman, D. J., Parrish, R., & Ross, D. A. (2013). Electronic health records and US public health: Current realities and future promise. *American Journal of Public Health*, *103*(9) 1560–1567, p. 1560. doi: 0.2105/AJPH.2013.301220

107. Friedman, note 106, p. 1561.

108. Bresnick, J. (2013, July 30). Population health is the new frontier for HIM, says AHIMA. *EHR Intelligence*. Retrieved from http://ehrintelligence.com/2013/07/30/population-health-is-the-new-frontier-for-him-says-ahima/.

109. Bresnick, note 108.

110. Bresnick, note 108.

111. Bresnick, note 108.
112. Bresnick, note 108.
113. Bresnick, note 108.
114. Bresnick, note 108, p. 1.
115. Bresnick, note 108, p. 1.
116. Zhang, N., Seblega, B., Wan, T., Unruh, L., Agiro, A., & Miao, L. (n.d.). Health information technology adoption in US acute care hospitals. *Journal of Medical Systems*, *37*(2), 8.
117. Zhang et al., note 116, p. 8.
118. Zhivan, N., & Diana, M. (2012). U.S. hospital efficiency and adoption of health information technology. *Health Care Management Science*, *15*(1), 37–47, 38. doi:10.1007/s10729-011-9179-2
119. Zhivan & Diana, note 118, p. 38.
120. Zhivan & Diana, note 118, p. 38.
121. Zhivan & Diana, note 118.
122. Zhivan & Diana, note 118.
123. Zhivan & Diana, note 118, p. 40.
124. Zhivan & Diana, note 118, p. 37.
125. Zhivan & Diana, note 118.
126. Zhivan & Diana, note 118, p. 45.
127. Zhivan & Diana, note 118, p. 45.
128. Zhivan & Diana, note 118, p. 42.
129. Zhivan & Diana, note 118, p 45.
130. Zhivan & Diana, note 118, p. 45.
131. Zhivan & Diana, note 118, p. 45.
132. Zhivan & Diana, note 118.
133. Zhivan & Diana, note 118.
134. Zhivan & Diana, note 118.
135. HIMSS Analytics, note 71.
136. HIMSS Analytics, note 71.
137. HIMSS Analytics. (2014). The EMR adoption model—HIMSS Analytics. Retrieved from https://www.himssanalytics.org/stagesGraph.asp.
138. HIMSS Analytics, note 71.

CHAPTER 17

© Murat Inan / EyeEm / Getty Images.

RESPONSIBILITIES OF MENTORSHIP AND SUCCESSION PLANNING

Health organizations that embrace a mentoring culture hope to cultivate leaders that remain in the organization to build trust and loyalty.
Finley, Ivanitskaya, and Kennedy[1]

In this chapter, mentoring is discussed from a historical perspective. Mentoring has been part and parcel of leadership activities for many millennia. From its historical beginnings, mentoring has evolved to the point that it can influence modern-day organizational success, survivability, and prosperity. Mentoring can increase employee satisfaction and stabilize the organization during times of turbulent change. Lastly, mentoring can influence transitions in an organization when senior leaders depart an organization and others move into new positions.

The concept of mentoring was first discussed in about 800 BCE as illustrated in Greek mythology: *The Odyssey*, written by Homer, tells the story of a king named Odysseus who went to fight in the Trojan War, leaving his son Telemachus with a trusted friend named Mentor. This chapter discusses the importance and responsibilities that leaders have in mentoring. Strategies are posited for mentoring across constructs of culture and gender. Correlations with mentoring and organizational success are documented and addressed. Ways to implement a mentoring program within the organization that supports succession planning are covered as well. The chapter ends by presenting a template to develop a leadership system for use in leadership practice.

419

LEARNING OBJECTIVES

1. Describe the importance of mentorship and succession planning to the long-term success of the health organization.

2. Distinguish between the concepts of mentee and protégé.

3. Discuss some of the barriers to establishing a mentoring program in health organizations regarding gender, ethnicity, age, and race, and apply methods to reduce those barriers.

4. Explain the steps involved in establishing a mentoring program in an organization.

5. Differentiate and list similarities between leading, mentoring, and succession planning in health organizations.

6. Combine theories and models, develop an implementation plan, and evaluate a personal leadership system for practical application in a health organization.

HISTORY OF MENTORING

The term *mentor* is derived from the character named Mentor, who was a faithful friend of the Greek hero Odysseus in Homer's epic story, *The Odyssey*. When Odysseus went off to war, he left Mentor behind to serve as a tutor to his son, Telemachus. Mentor served ably in this role, earning a reputation as being wise, sober, and loyal. It is from the relationship between these two characters that the classic understanding of the term *mentorship* has evolved. However, it was not until 1883 that the word *mentor* appeared in a dictionary. When the word first entered into the American parlance and lexicon, it was defined as "a wise and faithful counselor or monitor."[2,3] Certainly, roles and opinions of the mentor and the process of mentoring have changed over the years.

Mentoring as a distinct theory did not emerge in the modern era until 1978, when Levinson and colleagues first looked at the benefits and measures associated with the mentor's and mentee's relationship to the organization.[4] In the 1980s, books and journals solidified the understanding of mentoring as a separate behavioral process, distinct from leadership and coaching.[5,6] Several authors have found successful mentoring in the workplace to be a specific cause of success in organizations. As a result of these perceptions, mentoring eventually worked its way into organizational activities that supported both entity survival and organizational performance.[7,8]

In contemporary terms, mentoring can be either a formal or an informal relationship between two people: a mentor and a mentee. A mentor is a person of greater knowledge or wisdom who shares his or her experiences to help develop the abilities of a person junior to the mentor; the junior leader is called a mentee. However, the study of mentoring, like the study of leadership, is complex. Similar to leadership, the term *mentoring* (as found in the literature) is associated with a wide range of definitions. Words such as *guidance counselor*, *expert*, *leader*, *advisor*, and *coach* are often used in these definitions.

As originally defined, mentoring was a process where a wise and trusted advisor helped a less experienced person or professional.[9,10] Over time, this definition has evolved, with some theorists suggesting that mentoring must also be a voluntary relationship of equality, openness, and trust between the counselor and the counselee.[11] Other scholars have suggested a mentor is defined as an individual influential in the work environment who has advanced experience and knowledge and who is committed to providing upward mobility and support to a certain person's career.[12] Finally, some have suggested that mentoring is analogous to a parent–child relationship, where the best interests of the mentee are placed over and above those of the mentor.[13] Regardless of the definition selected, in health leadership development, mentoring is generally the process of developing a relationship that can be either informal or formal, that involves two or more people, and that has the goal of securing some personal or professional outcome agreeable to the parties in the activity.

WHY MENTOR?

Health organizations that embrace a mentoring culture hope to cultivate leaders who remain in the organization, thereby building trust and loyalty.[14] Mentoring has been shown to provide for greater stability of employees in an organization as well as to improve both the individual and organizational loyalty of employees. Ideally, these two benefits will ultimately result in improved organizational performance and survivability.

Health leaders should look at mentoring as a fundamental responsibility. Not only do the mentor and the mentee benefit from this exchange of ideas and information, but the organization benefits greatly as well. Consider this ancient Chinese proverb:

> If you want one year of prosperity, grow grain;
> If you want ten years of prosperity, grow trees;
> If you want one hundred years of prosperity, grow people.

The majority of health leaders would agree that leadership qualities are transferred by means of example (modeling). As such, it is important to know and understand that subordinates are always watching and learning from leaders' direct and indirect actions. For this reason, leaders need to accept the task of intentionally training those junior to them in all facets of their profession.

Additionally, it is important that subordinates learn the art and science of decision making. In this context, the goal is not necessarily for the mentee to make the decision, but rather that he or she understand the process through which the decision was made by the leader. A great by-product of such learning will be better teamwork and cohesion within the organization. For instance, once subordinates understand the central theme of a problem, they will be compelled to support decisions made by senior management, and when feasible they will be able to explain the decisions to other employees. Whether people agree or not, once they understand the issues surrounding a problem, they are less likely to gossip or cause dissension within the organization. Accurate information and communication always improve morale and team cohesion. This principle directly connects to the motivation and influence processes, especially in terms of the commitment, compliance, or resistance of subordinates regarding a leader-made decision.

THE DIFFERENCES AMONG LEADING, COACHING, AND MENTORING

Due to the very difficult nature of defining terms (i.e., constructs) in organizational behavior and leadership, it is not surprising that the terms *leading* and *mentoring* are often

thought of as being synonymous. In reality, this is not the case. Leading is a macro-organizational concept that involves the goal-directed behavior of followers toward the organizationally selected mission, vision, values, and goals. Many employees in the organization may not see their boss's boss on a monthly or quarterly basis (or even over the scope of a year). For this reason, it is the leader's responsibility to carefully direct and lead those under him or her in a manner that results in consistent, goal-directed behavior. This must be accomplished across the organization regardless of size or geographic displacement of employees.

Mentoring is quite different from this leadership activity. Mentoring is an individual process of taking a mentee "under the mentor's wing" and personally helping the individual to succeed in a professional career. The action is analogous to a mother or father bird shielding a young hatchling from the threats of the environment (**Figure 17-1**). The process requires a combination of intense face-to-face coaching, leading, educating, and parenting to ensure that the mentee is successful at his or her job. Personal time resources and costs are invested in this activity.

Many people in the field of health consider their personal adoption by high-level leaders in the organization as mentees to be a great compliment. Many mentors also fiercely protect their mentees (like a parent would) against internal politics and organizational threats (such as downsizing).

Coaching differs from both mentoring and leading. Coaching is more specific—that is, it is geared toward teaching specific skills or activities to the coached individual or trainee. It involves a transfer of skills, and a one-on-one development of the trainee's own knowledge and thought processes. It also emphasizes the development of team skills and creates a supportive environment that encourages and motivates the coached individual. The end state is that the personal qualities of the coached individual are developed in a positive way. Coaching occurs on a personal level but can also be done in groups over short periods of time.

DEFINING PROTÉGÉ AND MENTEE RELATIONSHIPS

Mentoring can be defined according to organizational factors and specific job functions. Career functions help the protégé to develop career skills, by assigning challenging assignments to the individual, and psychosocial functions, by encouraging the protégé to pursue his or her dreams.[15] When a mentee takes on specific roles and responsibilities that are specifically directed toward preparing the mentee to ultimately replace the mentor in a certain position, the relationship between mentee and mentor is better defined as one of a mentor and protégé.

FIGURE 17-1 A parent bird shielding hatchlings under its wing.
© rgaf72/Dreamstime.com.

Protégé is derived from a French verb that means "to guide and support someone younger." In the business world, the protégé is guided and advised by the mentor, who has worn the same shoes and traveled the same path. Unlike in the relationship between mentor and mentee, where success in the profession is the ultimate goal of the mentee, the protégé is carefully guided in a controlled succession of education and progressive job opportunities that may ultimately lead to the protégé replacing the mentor in the job that the mentor currently occupies. This type of behavior is most often seen in family-dominated businesses where financial control and ownership of the organization will pass from parent to child. It is also seen in the British monarchy, where certain members of Parliament (in the House of Lords) inherit their positions based on birthright.[16]

Table 17-1 summarizes the key definitions related to mentoring, distinguishing it from similar, yet different leadership, coaching, and protégé relationships.

Mentoring Across Cultural and Gender Barriers

Mentors and mentees must be matched according to their personality types and attitudes, rather than based on any

Table 17-1 Mentoring-Related Terms Defined	
Term	**Defined**
Leadership	Concerned with overall organizational success of vision, mission, and goals of the organization. The leader directs dozens of personnel, who in turn supervise and manage hundreds or thousands of other employees.
Mentoring	Concerned with the overall success of the individual within the profession. This process is personal and intimate and requires face-to-face interaction.
Mentor	A person of greater knowledge or wisdom who shares experience to help develop the abilities of a junior person.
Mentee	A person who seeks guidance or wisdom from a mentor.
Protégé	Concerned with personal succession. This process is wedded to a long-term commitment to leader development, resulting in the transfer of organizational responsibilities and organizational controls from mentor to protégé.
Coaching	Concerned with the overall success of groups of individuals in the organization. This process is personal, but not intimate, and it may not require direct contact and interaction.

cultural or demographic similarity.[17] By following this concept, the organization ensures that the resulting interpersonal relationship will strengthen the employee's creative thinking skills, while fostering a culture of respect and sharing in the workplace. The encouragement and promotion of fundamental values provide for rewards and the employee's integrative learning.[18] However, white male leaders should be aware of the potential for disproportionate mentoring opportunities: People of color and females should receive mentoring opportunities in the workplace as well. Human nature tends to focus our efforts toward those who are like us, but diversity is now a top priority for many organizations.[19] Both potential mentors and potential mentees should remain open to mentoring based on behavior, performance, and aptitude.

In support of this point, Finley, Ivanitskaya, and Kennedy found in their 2007 mentoring study of health leaders that 95% of the respondents to their survey were white, and 84% were men.[20] Two explanations for these findings are possible. First, the preponderance of health mentors who actively engaged in this role may have been white and male. Second, for some reason minorities and females did not feel it was important to engage in a study of mentoring due to possible preconceived notions of the futility of the study in changing existing organizational practices.

Regardless of the exact reason for its existence, this trend is disturbing. It may not be satisfactory for a white male in the organization to only adopt same-gender and same-race mentees. The leader should be cognizant of the disproportionate opportunities for mentoring open to nonmale, nonwhite employees and should actively be on the lookout to establish mentoring opportunities among minorities and women in the workplace. It is common for some women and minorities in organizations to feel that they do not possess the necessary competencies for success unless a culture of gender and racial diversity is embraced.[21–23]

Earlier in this chapter, it was noted that the word *mentor* came from Greek mythology and the book, *The Odyssey*. However, what we failed to mention was that Athena (a goddess in myth) presented herself as a much older man to the child Telemachus, so that he would more readily accept the old man named Mentor as a wise sage. This example illustrates that for millennia the process of mentoring was male specific. Why would a Greek goddess deem it necessary to present herself to a mortal child in male form to gain his confidence and trust? This trend may continue to this day as well. An extensive review suggests that the preponderance of the literature associated with the study of mentorship is male and nonminority-centric.[24,25]

Hezlett and Gibson found that the major factor contributing to decreased levels of employee dissatisfaction, burnout, workplace disharmony, stress, and early retirement was mentoring.[26] They suggest that these factors are within the control of the organization to effect change. Also, because the consequences of these factors are known to disrupt organizational performance, the question might be: Why not implement a mentoring program (as opposed to not starting one)? Leaders in large organizations should always promote, within their organizational culture, opportunities for employees to seek out mentors. Mentoring also supports, if not enables, an organizational learning culture and possibly a knowledge management culture. The establishment of formal mentoring programs will assist in this process.[27]

It will always be the responsibility of the top leader in the organization to establish mentoring programs and to ensure their ongoing success. Nevertheless, all leaders at all levels of the organization can do their part in mentoring when they lead by example and ensure that personnel in their chain of supervision are mentored—even if the corporate culture of the organization is not formally supportive of this process.[28]

MENTORING AS A MEANS TO FOSTER ORGANIZATIONAL SUCCESS

Mature and experienced organizations see mentoring as another method to help the entity achieve its mission, objectives, and goals. Additionally, mentoring programs can fit seamlessly into an organization's daily practice of doing business. As such, these programs do not interfere with the daily business of the entity, but complement and enhance the work activity.[29,30]

According to the CEO of the American College of Healthcare Executives (ACHE), health leaders must "confront daily challenges by developing strong healthcare executives for tomorrow."[31] Furthermore, no health organization can be successful if it lacks strong and competent leaders. Mentoring helps foster the development of these leaders.

One of the primary objectives of mentoring is to ensure that organizational skills, organizational knowledge, and organizational best practices are transferred from the mentor to the mentee. As a result of this knowledge transfer, the organization benefits through the development of more highly trained and competent employees who are loyal, more efficient, and more competent in their jobs.[32]

Most mentors report longer job tenure related to having a formal mentor. Mentoring is a tool that both leaders and health organizations can use to help foster organizational success. It is considered a path for forging long-term personal and professional relationships, for acknowledging and fulfilling the basic spiritual and psychological human needs in support of today's and tomorrow's loyal employees. The process of mentoring can be used to instruct organizational culture, pass on technical expertise, develop creative problem solving, foster critical thinking, and build interpersonal skills.

Finley, Ivanitskaya, and Kennedy suggest that mentoring has myriad benefits for health executives. In their research, these authors discovered that mentoring was associated with both primary and secondary gains for the entire organization. Elements of satisfaction, performance, and productivity were all improved when the organization supported mentoring. However, the greatest benefit to the overall process was a culture shift, such that mentoring was seen as a responsibility of all employees in the organization, and not just a duty of the CEO.[33]

A 2005 survey by Block and colleagues found that a major element in the turnover of nurses in health organizations was not having or receiving mentorship in the organization. Considering the shortage of nurses in the nursing profession and the highly competitive nature of the health industry, it is much easier for nurses to find outside or alternative employment than many of their similar, allied health peers. The job dissatisfaction experienced by nurses may be reduced by a leader-supported and organizationally based mentoring program.[34] Organizations that see the benefits to this approach and implement such a program most likely will decrease their turnover rates, increase employee and patient satisfaction, and maintain a competitive advantage in the workplace. Attempting to define an effective mentoring situation, a study that looked at mentor–mentee pairs in a nursing program concluded that eight components prevailed. These components were "(1) open communication and accessibility, (2) goals and challenges, (3) passion and inspiration, (4) caring personal relationships, (5) mutual respect and trust, (6) exchange of knowledge, (7) independence and collaboration, and (8) role modeling."[35]

STARTING A MENTORING PROGRAM

Leaders in any health organization should establish, or provide an opportunity for the creation of, a formal mentoring program. Mentoring in health organizations, like a cargo net, may go up and down or from side to side but "holds" the organization together through assimilation of institutional knowledge. For example, it goes up when a new employee mentors an experienced worker on technology matters, and it goes from side to side when employees relate common learning, knowledge, experiences, and skill sets with their coworkers within the organization.

Formal organizational mentoring programs must incorporate six critical elements to respond to the basic needs of mentees:[36,37]

1. A mentoring program must have "clear strategic goals that are established and understood by all organizational members."

2. The program must have "a method to carefully select mentors."

3. It should "provide for confidentiality between the mentor and mentee."

4. Participants must be "trained with the skills needed to be successful mentors or mentees."

5. The mentor and mentee must "understand the importance of being politically savvy."

6. There must be "someone responsible for monitoring and assessing the status of the organization's planned mentoring efforts."

Mentoring helps prepare young health professionals to assume increased responsibilities in the health organization by encouraging job competency, professional development, and higher education, as well as by serving the needs of the organization. It can cover a wide range of areas, such as guiding a young administrator through the steps of professional development and career management, clarifying an individual's understanding of health operations in various health and care settings, becoming affiliated with professional organizations, and engaging in continuing educational and training programs. In the same way, mentoring sets a leadership example for new members of the medical community. It also includes sharing knowledge of the health organization itself, including an understanding of the organization's mission, vision, and strategic imperatives. Sharing knowledge regarding techniques, procedures, and skills is an important part of the process, but taking a personal interest in the development of the individual is what separates mentoring from supervising—and is exactly what today's young health professional needs.

MENTORING AND TECHNOLOGICAL CHANGE

Telementoring is emerging as a way to pair teachers and learners with subject matter experts who can provide advice, guidance, and feedback on learning projects. Technology is also assisting mentoring in organizations, such as corporations with offices around the country and around the world, that connect mentors and protégés via email or videoconferencing.[38] In addition, telementoring is proving essential in distance learning. The isolation that often contributes to distance learners dropping out can be overcome by pairing learners with faculty telementors. Empire State College, for example, has successfully used this strategy to improve retention and completion for distance learners and adult students in individualized degree programs.[39] At Iona College, faculty mentors use telephone, written, and email interaction to guide video-based learning for adult students.[40]

The combination of digital technologies and organizational change is making individuals more responsible for their own learning and career development. Freelancing, consulting, and "portfolio work" make it more difficult for people to connect with traditional sources of mentors in organizations.[41] At the same time, telecommuting increases the worker's physical distance from the workplace and decreases the ability to acquire the tacit or craft knowledge that comes from interaction with experienced workers. For these reasons, mentoring becomes even more important for individuals who are attempting to develop an array of flexible skills and for organizations that are seeking to maintain institutional knowledge.[42]

MENTORING FROM A DISTANCE (TELEMENTORING)

Misplaced bias against the long-distance delivery of mentoring mirrors that held against distance learning education. For example, for much of the last century, the only way to attain a college degree was to attended classes that were offered from 9 AM to 5 PM, Monday to Friday. Although the first documented event of regular and reoccurring night school occurred around 1890 in the United States, the rapid growth of evening and weekend education did not occur until after World War II (WWII). During this time, our country saw military veterans, armed with the GI Bill, but often married, employed, and with children, looking for avenues to go to school. In response to this new opportunity in the marketplace, many local universities began to develop evening classes to accommodate this population. Interestingly enough (in this post-WWII period), there was a profound bias against the growing number of night school graduates in the United States. The end result was a class divide—that is, attending day school was better than attending night school. You can still see examples of this bias in movies from the 1950s. Whenever the story plot wanted to target a movie character as unintelligent, the dialogue would eventually lead to the characterization of that person as a "night school graduate."

Flash forward 60 years, and we no longer have a bias against night school graduates. Part of this is due to the cultural acceptance of night school as a legitimate manner in which to earn a degree; however (and more importantly), research and evidence-based outcomes have demonstrated there is no difference between a night school graduate and a student who went to classes during the day.

Oddly enough, many national and state professional accrediting organizations cannot keep up, and agree with the accepted forms of educational delivery in the United States, not to mention successful programs of mentorship. For example, under U.S. Department of Education guidance, a face-to-face education event can be delivered via a webinar over the Internet to synchronous personnel. However, some accrediting bodies view this as unacceptable and instead have moved toward a more colloquial expression now called "in-person" mentoring, which means the educational process must be delivered by someone physically in the same room as the learner. The same is often true with mentoring opportunities: Certain professional organizations will not recognize mentoring if it is not conducted in person. Sadly, stereotyping the delivery methodology of mentoring is becoming a commonly accepted bias in U.S. education. Fortunately for the preponderance of those involved in telementoring, the process has resulted in favorable, sustainable, and productive outcomes both personally and professionally, despite the bias and resistance of those seated heavily in traditional practices.

MENTORING AND ORGANIZATIONAL CHANGE

Organizational trends such as downsizing, restructuring, teamwork orientation, increased diversity, and individual responsibility for career development are contributing to the resurgent interest in mentoring. Downsizing has heightened the need to preserve institutional memory and to share the information and experiences that remain in the company.[43] Mentors represent continuity; as mentors, older and more experienced workers can continue contributing to their organizations and professions. The Mentoring Institute maintains that, in the past, mentoring typically "just happened" as experienced people recognized and developed new talent or as beginners sought the counsel of knowledgeable elders. Now, the institute describes a "new mentoring paradigm": Today's protégés are better educated but still need a mentor's practical know-how and wisdom (craft knowledge) that can be acquired only experientially. Therefore, many organizations are instituting formal mentoring programs as a cost-effective way to upgrade skills, enhance recruitment and retention, and increase job satisfaction.[44,45]

Many mentoring programs have been geared specifically toward women and minorities as a way of helping them break into the "good old boy network" and through the "glass ceiling." However, the value of opening these opportunities to all is being recognized. Gunn suggests that a more democratic approach to mentoring is emerging, with programs being thrown open to more employees at more levels.[46] For example, a high-level employee who is hired because of specific expertise may still need the coaching in organizational culture that mentors can provide—a form of partnership that entails a two-way transfer of skills and experience. This more inclusive mentoring strategy is seen as an alternative to the career ladders and security that organizations are no longer providing. Another democratic approach is a trend toward group mentoring, in which the mentor is a learning leader of a team or "learning group" within an organization.[47] Members of a diverse learning group can learn from one another (peer mentoring) as well as from the learning leader.

Loeb goes further by suggesting that one-on-one mentoring is becoming less viable as competition increases and people change jobs more frequently, becoming less identified with one organization. He recommends that individuals manage their own career development with the help of a "board of advisors," where multiple mentors within and outside of their organizations provide a wide range of expertise and advice about both specific organizational politics and culture as well as broader trends in a profession or field.[48] With options from single mentoring programs to group mentoring, regardless of the program structure, there are general responsibilities of the mentor and the mentee.

RESPONSIBILITIES OF THE MENTOR AND THE MENTEE

THE MENTOR

An effective mentor must, at a minimum, have a heightened awareness of or sensitivity to the needs of others and be willing to pause and listen (empathy). Formal mentoring requires dedication and commitment both to the individual and to the organization. On some occasions, a member's need for mentoring may go beyond the capabilities, time, or resources of the assigned mentor. In such cases, referral to a more appropriate resource is necessary. It is the mentor's responsibility to recognize these limitations and offer alternatives. The mentor is encouraged to set the stage by establishing a mentoring agreement with the individual to be mentored. Such an agreement defines the objectives to be achieved and time lines for accomplishment. This kind of "contract" will help ensure an effective mentoring relationship from the start.[49]

THE MENTEE

The effective mentee must be a receptive and willing participant. There must be noticeable enthusiasm on the part of the mentee to take responsibility for his or her own growth and development. Similarly, the mentee must be eager to learn and grow through new challenges and opportunities. An important aspect of the relationship for the mentee is receptiveness to feedback and sharing personal information with the mentor. In the same manner, a mentee has

to discover the mentor that is right for him or her. Also, the mentee must understand that mentorship is not necessarily a lifelong proposition. The relationship may last for only several months to several years, or it might last for the duration of either the mentor's or the mentee's career. The nature of the relationship depends on the dynamics of the relationship, the mentee's needs, and the willingness of the mentor to continue to work with the mentee.

THE MENTEE–MENTOR RELATIONSHIP MIX

The mentee and the mentor fulfill a mutually beneficial relationship while benefiting the organization. In addition to the obvious benefits already discussed in regard to organizational performance and knowledge transfer, the role of a mentor can be psychologically and personally gratifying. The mentor feels that he or she has ensured the success of the organization where the mentor has worked for years as well as that he or she has fulfilled the responsibilities of a leader by ensuring that the next generation is prepared to meet future challenges. The rewards for the mentee are more readily evident through increased abilities and opportunities.

Kelly discusses four primary elements necessary to make a mentor–mentee relationship work:[50]

- *Socialization*: The process of integrating the mentee into the organization's culture.
- *Technological assistance*: The process of acquainting the mentee with the informatics of the profession.
- *Career advancement*: Personal and specific goal-directed actions that support the mentee's growth in the organization.
- *Emotional support*: As a parent supports a child, so does the mentor take care of the mentee.

There are some downsides to mentorship. For example, there may be a perception on the part of the mentee's peers or subordinates that the mentee is receiving preferential treatment. There can be additional challenges in this regard with cross-gender mentoring relationships. Also, mentor–mentee relationships evolve over time and can terminate with negative feelings or unfulfilled expectations on the part of one or both parties.

MENTORING STORY

Dr. Nicholas Coppola was the youngest officer in the history of the Army Medical Service Corps to receive the Army's Mentoring Award. Previous recipients had all been general officers or colonels. In fact, Coppola had received a similar award, called the Peer Award, from the Medical College of Virginia Campus, Virginia Commonwealth University's graduate program, while he was there as a doctoral student.[51] When asked why he thought he had been selected for both awards, Coppola replied, "I was always more interested in the success of those around me than in my own success or accomplishments." He went on to say, "I suppose I had my own method of evaluating my own performance, and that metric was the fact that the people around me, and those who worked for me, were advancing and excelling. My own success was always secondary."

When encouraged to expand on the specific tasks he engaged in with his subordinates and peers to receive such high approbation, Coppola replied:

> It's really just a matter of freely giving your time. I never said "no" to anyone who ever came to me for help or advice. I also made it a point to get out of my office and visit with my subordinates and peers other than during the normal professional activities of work. Moreover, I never waited for my employees to come to me. I'd often offer career and professional advice without being

asked. Mentorship is really not a once-a-year activity during a performance evaluation. When you actively take a 24/7 interest in an employee's professional career, it's appreciated by your employees and becomes valued.

Coppola, however, was never one to shy away from one-time mentoring events, either. If a soldier with whom he had had little contact needed or requested some mentorship, Coppola would make sure he was available to share time with that individual.

"I was always cognizant that I might not ever see that individual again," Coppola said, "However, if I could make a favorable impression on young healthcare executives that resulted in a positive outcome in their careers down the road, that was my only personal motivation."

When prompted to sum up his mentoring philosophy, Coppola replied:

> I made sure I was not a 9 AM to 5 PM mentor. I always took an active interest in the person's family, career, and personal interests. Activities like these are not something that leaders generally get evaluated

SOLDIERING ON: BAYLOR ARMY GRAD MENTORS THE NEXT GENERATION

When Dr. Nicholas Coppola [**Figure 17-2**] retired from the U.S. Army in June 2008, he was leaving a job he loved. A 1997 graduate of Baylor's Army graduate program in health administration in San Antonio, Coppola went on to earn a PhD from the Medical College of Virginia in 2003 before returning to proudly direct Baylor's San Antonio graduate program for 5 years.

But Coppola didn't just hang up his uniform and walk away forgotten. Shortly after retiring, he learned that he had been chosen to receive both the 2008 Army Medical Service Corps (MSC) Mentor of the Year Award and the 2008 Educator of the Year Award.

While both honors are meaningful, he says he was especially humbled at receiving the Mentorship Award. Coppola was selected by junior officers all over the military system as the senior officer who demonstrated "exceptional, measurable, and visible mentorship recognizable to all members of the MSC regardless of rank or duty description" and "displayed altruistic and selfless service to MSC officers worldwide."

FIGURE 17-2 Dr. Nicholas Coppola, mentor.
Courtesy of Dr. Nicholas Coppola.

He says, "I got notice of the award about a week or so after I officially retired. After twenty-six years, I was going through some very typical self-analysis. Did I do everything I could do to assure that the next generation is prepared? I guess it's sort of like fathers sending children off to college—did I do enough?"

He has now moved to Lubbock with his wife, Susannah, and three children, where he is program director and an associate professor with the Master of Science in Clinical Practice Management program of the Texas Tech University Health Science Center.

But thanks to dedicated mentors like Coppola, other graduates from Baylor's MHA program will be equally well equipped. "As I looked at my goals and visions and objectives," he says, "I was always focused on preparing the next generation of soldiers to assume leadership in military health care."

Excerpt reprinted from Pratner, J. (2009). Soldier on: Baylor Army grad mentors the next generation. *Baylor Line*, 71(1), 17.

for—*nor should they seek recognition for*—but are simply the right things to do. Lastly, I suppose I always saw my soldiers and students as extensions of my own family. And when your subordinates know you mean this—and do this—everything else falls into place by itself.

SUCCESSION PLANNING

As emphasized throughout this chapter, mentoring the next generation of healthcare leaders is a critical component of organizational success. With an aging workforce, it is more and more incumbent on organizations to include leadership succession planning early in the life cycle model rather than later.[52]

In addition to losing skilled and highly qualified employees, the organization faces the reality of the loss of talent and institutional memory, which are even more difficult to replace. Positive relationships with outside stakeholders, collegiality with local organizations within the competitive environment, and the ability to be productive and efficient are incalculable intangibles that represent huge losses to any organization as the workforce ages.[53] An appropriate succession plan can help alleviate this dilemma.

The primary purpose of succession planning is to ensure that there is appropriate training and development of junior employees, thereby preparing them to assume more responsible positions of leadership. Succession planning, like leadership development and mentoring, is a continuous process that must start years in advance of retirements or leader transitions in the organization. According to Thurgood, "Leaders in a variety of organizations must understand the role and importance of effective leadership, leadership development and succession planning in achieving organizational success. Unfortunately, leadership and leadership development do not confine themselves to a single 'checklist,' comprehensive model, or flow chart."[54] In a 2013 study, results showed that 66% of hospitals are using succession planning today, an 11% increase over a 2007 survey in a similar study.[55]

The health industry is no more stable or resistant to the impact of the economy and stakeholder dynamics than any other organizational entity.[56] Furthermore, the unfortunate reality of some recent trends—namely, the

A MENTORING PHILOSOPHY

As a mentor I am a role model to my mentee. I am an example of what years of hard work, dedication, and discipline are to my mentee. My example sets a standard for a vision for a mentee. This vision can be in professional achievement or academic excellence. A vision is defined as the sum total of goals and objectives for a young mentee to attain.

As a mentor, I work in partnership with the mentee to help him or her establish reasonable and accomplishable tasks in completing and working toward long-term goals and objectives. A goal is defined as where the mentee wants to be, and objectives are the metrics and tasks accomplished to attain that goal.

My role is not to establish the vision for the mentee, but to work as a facilitator, coach, and motivator in assisting the mentee in developing realistic and attainable objectives of his or her own. In this process, I must be as good a listener as an orator of possibilities.

As a mentor, I must be a "do as I do" person, not a "do as I say" individual. Stated another way, I should never ask my mentee to do something I have not done, or would not do, given similar circumstances and situations.

As a mentor, I acknowledge that there is the establishment of a long-term relationship that involves time, attention, and understanding. If I am not committed to this long-term, ongoing possibility, I should excuse myself from the partnership.

As a mentor, I am committed to the success of my mentee. Failure of the mentee is not so much a reflection of the mentee as a reflection of my personal leadership efforts in motivating, encouraging, and directing the mentee toward success.

As a mentor, I take on certain reflections of a parent. I guide, offer encouragement, set standards, show disappointment (when warranted), and work toward transitioning my mentee to the professional status or goal we have agreed to work on together.

An additional benefit is to teach my mentee how to be a mentor him- or herself, so that he or she may be guided by the memory of our wisdom and time together when he or she takes on the responsibilities of mentorship one day.

discovery of unethical practices of business leaders—suggests a strong need for health organizations to engage in appropriate succession planning.[57] As Swayne, Duncan, and Ginter have suggested, the health industry must be ready at all echelons within the organizational architecture to advance and replace leaders on a moment's notice. These leaders should possess the talent, skills, and organizational knowledge to maintain the performance of the organization during times of stress.[58] Establishing a mentoring program (in addition to other sound principles of continuing education and leader development) in an organization will ensure that several levels of the organization (leader redundancy) are established and will remain stable should the primary leader or mentor suddenly depart. Cultivating a mentoring program is one methodology that ensures succession plan success.

LEADERSHIP DECISIONS FOR YOUR LEADERSHIP MODEL

How much of the material and content in this text is relevant, memorable, and useful? Ideally, your answer to this question will be "much," "a lot," or "most." In reality, all of the material and context is important; application of some of the material and context is absolutely necessary, whereas application of other material and context is situational. What is important is how you critically think about, assess, plan, determine, implement, monitor, improve, and maintain how you lead, how the organization where you lead performs, and how well you meet the needs and expectations of the communities and external environment you serve.

First, as a leader in your organization (or future organization), what vision do you have for the area (or section or department or division) you lead based on the organization's strategic plan (mission, vision, strategies, goals, objectives, and values)? How do you lead people and manage resources within the context of the strategic and operationally integrated systems of delivering health services that improve community health status? How do you enhance efficiency, effectiveness, and efficacy of systems that provide and support the care process? How do you lead people and manage resources of integrated systems that are complex? How do you provide leadership that is morally sound? Write that vision down, along with the key values your leadership system holds onto. Be aware, however, that your leadership system vision and values must fit the organization you serve. From your vision and values, which kind of organizational culture (for your area of responsibility) are you developing? Write that

statement down. Lastly, list key organizational links, such as strategies, goals, and objectives, that fall within your leadership area of responsibility (directly and indirectly). These items, vision, values, culture, and linkages form the foundation from which you can launch your leadership system, regardless of the size of your leadership area of responsibility (large or small).

This section concentrates on envisioning your leadership "system": Select those theories and models that are the most applicable, determine how you would apply those theories and models, consider whether a synthesis of theories and models would be most appropriate, and contemplate how you would evaluate your overall approach. This important exercise is very personal; these decisions have to fit you. However, this is a wonderful tool to bring to and discuss with your mentor or supervisor. To facilitate this work, a template such as the one shown below could be utilized for your leadership system. (In reality, this template could be many pages long; an example is shown in **Table 17-2**.) Once you finish filling out the template, how consistent are the different parts of your leadership system? Consistency should be evaluated and measured by scoring each construct or item of your leadership system vision.

Vision of your leadership system:

_____

_____

_____

_____

Values of your leadership system:

_____

_____

_____

_____

Organizational culture (Write a statement based on your vision and values that explains your envisioned culture.):

_____

_____

_____

_____

Organizational strategies, goals, etc. (Which organizational links influence your leadership at your level and in your area of responsibility?):

_____

_____

_____

_____

Table 17-2 Leadership System Template Example

Construct	Applicable Theories and Models (Must Fit You)	How to Apply (Single Theory or Model or a Synthesis of Theories and Models)	Evaluation (What Is Successful Utilization?)	Time Period
Leadership style(s)	Dynamic culture leadership (DCL); transformational leadership; transactional leadership; reframing organizational leadership and management	Use DCL as a sequential system to lead and manage; transformational leadership coupled with transactional leadership as a personal leadership style; and reframing organizational leadership as situational to emphasize appropriate frames in action and communication.	Plan and complete the sequence of DCL; keep a daily reflective journal of your leadership style to evaluate transformational and transactional leadership and in communication; determine the appropriate framework to emphasize in a log.	Within 18 months. Start the journal immediately and continue it for 1 year; periodically (weekly) assess the journal. Start the log immediately and assess it weekly along with the journal.
Organizational culture leadership	Edgar Schein's primary embedding mechanisms and secondary reinforcement mechanisms; coordinated management of meaning; Shutz's theory of affiliation; goal-setting theory	Integrate the primary and secondary mechanisms with your leadership style and measures of subordinate performance based on goal setting for each subordinate that focuses on team building and performance.	Determine measurement of key variables; monitor and report them for the team. Assign and monitor subordinate goals and progress toward those goals, placing equal weight on team performance goals. Maintain a behaviors and actions log that reflects the desired culture and identifies any behavior that does not match the desired culture. (Praise publically good behavior and counsel in private behavior to improve.)	Within 6 months. Integrate primary and secondary mechanisms into daily work and subordinate goals (as appropriate); monitor with performance appraisals every 6 months for 2 years. Keep the actions log and review it (not pointing fingers at anyone with "bad" log entries) with the subordinate group monthly for 1 year.
Communication environment	Confirming communication environment; media richness theory; conflict management	*How would you utilize a synthesis of these theories and models?*	*How would you evaluate this?*	*What time frame seems to be reasonable?*
Planning	*Which theories and models would you use?*	*How would you utilize a synthesis of these theories and models?*	*How would you evaluate this?*	*What time frame seems to be reasonable?*
Decision making	*Which theories and models would you use?*	*How would you utilize a synthesis of these theories and models?*	*How would you evaluate this?*	*What time frame seems to be reasonable?*
Employee enhancement	*Which theories and models would you use?*	*How would you utilize a synthesis of these theories and models?*	*How would you evaluate this?*	*What time frame seems to be reasonable?*

Table 17-2 Leadership System Template Example (continued)

Construct	Applicable Theories and Models (Must Fit You)	How to Apply (Single Theory or Model or a Synthesis of Theories and Models)	Evaluation (What Is Successful Utilization?)	Time Period
Health organization systems (supply chain, revenue management, clinical, financial, human resources)	*How do your leadership plan(s) and style(s) facilitate improvement, excellence, and quality for health systems?*	*How will you learn about these systems and create an integrative approach to leading people and managing resources for these systems?*	*How would you evaluate the performance of systems you lead?*	*What time frame seems to be reasonable?*
Health organization subsystems (healthcare preparedness program [disasters and emergencies] and community assessments)	*How do your leadership plan(s) and style(s) facilitate improvement, excellence, and quality for health systems?*	*How will you learn about these systems and create an integrative approach to leading people and managing resources for these systems?*	*How would you evaluate the performance of systems you lead?*	*What time frame seems to be reasonable?*

To assess your consistency, based on your vision, values, organizational culture, and organizational links statements and lists, score each construct (use the cell/box in Table 17-2 that lists the construct for each) for commitment to that foundation on a 10-point scale; sum the number of consistency points and divide by the number of constructs to get an average. A higher average is better, but the number should definitely be above 8.

As you can see, assessment of your leadership system is a very extensive exercise that requires considerable critical thinking—thinking about both implementation and evaluation. The necessity for leaders at all levels to conduct this exercise is simple: If you do not know where you and your organization are going, if you do not know how to get there, and if you do not know how to evaluate your progress, then how can you expect those whom you lead to know what to do? You as the leader must be clear, concise, and consistent in your expectations, implement a plan to meet your expectations, monitor its progress, and expect those whom you lead to perform.

Although you may not want to develop a personal leadership system plan for each possible construct, consider the following list of constructs as possibilities to include in your leadership system exercise. For each construct, how would you determine measureable variable(s) for it? This exercise is both a great starting point and a routine monitoring plan you can discuss with your mentor or supervisor. A summary (not expansive) construct list based on the dynamic culture leadership (DCL) model follows; note that each item listed could be expanded into more than one item:

- Leadership style
- Leadership alignment
- Leadership development
- Organizational culture
- Cultural competence
- Communication environment
- Communication improvement
- Strategic planning
- Operational planning
- Decision making
- Decision-making processes and procedures
- Employee enhancement
- Employee performance appraisal
- Employee training
- Organizational learning
- Knowledge management
- Performance evaluation
- Resource acquisition and distribution
- Management of resources
- Development, improvement, and leadership of systems (both technical/scientific and interpersonal/artistic)
- Network development
- Coalition building
- External assessment
- Internal assessment
- Ethical framework
- Patient/customer satisfaction
- Quality assurance/performance/improvement

What kind of health leader do you want to be? What kind of organization do you want to lead? Can you envision it? Determining your leadership system and plan and being consistent are critical. If you know where you are going, you are more likely to get there! Leading, especially in health organizations, is a challenging enterprise but a rewarding one; leadership in health organizations is also necessary and needed if we are to make progress as an industry.

Leader Success = Individual (Nature + Nurture)
　　　　　　　× Situational Adaptation
　　　　　　　× Organizational Culture
　　　　　　　× Personal
　　　　　　　+ Subordinate Accountability

Leadership is the *dynamic* and *active* creation and maintenance of an organizational *culture* and *strategic systems* that focus the collective energy of both *leading people and managing resources* toward *meeting the needs of the external environment* utilizing the most efficient, effective, and, most importantly, efficacious methods possible by moral means.

The health industry is different from other service and product industries. To appreciate this difference, consider that many times efficacy is more important than efficiency in health care; patient outcomes are more important than profits and margin; the "rational man" theory of economics is set aside when certain injuries or illnesses invade our families, such that chaos or irrational economic decisions prevail; and society holds the health industry to an extremely high standard—it expects perfection. Moreover, health organizations are extremely complex, run continuously, and are highly regulated and closely scrutinized. These realities create a distinctive leadership niche, that of the health leader.

ONE OF MANY CHALLENGES IN HEALTH LEADERSHIP TO PONDER

Considering the macro-industry model (described in Chapter 3), how can you as a health leader integrate the complexity, change, and societal expectations of healthy communities and healthcare delivery? Porter has discussed value as it relates to health and health care; the authors of this text strongly believe advancement of Porter's value of health equation is in order. In fact, we encourage adding

another level to Porter's concept. In that spirit, "efficacy value" is the salient metric. Efficacy value is the amount of good or improvement to health status (efficacy) beyond the expected group mean or average outcome (such as from an actuarial table) divided by resources utilized. Thus, the simple equation for efficacy value is as follows:

$$\frac{\text{Health Organization Intervention Outcome} - \text{Expected Actuarial Outcome}}{\text{Resources Utilized}} = \frac{\text{Efficacy}}{\text{Value}}$$

This equation puts a much greater burden on the health industry and may have payers of health care contemplate true "value." Actuarial analysis can predict health outcomes for a given population with a particular disease, injury, or chronic condition when considering no health intervention and, in most cases, when the patient receives a "standard" intervention (meeting the professional or national standard of care). We also have a good estimate, in most cases, of the resources required to deliver a "standard" health intervention. But how can a health organization, health program, public health program, etc. deliver value with regard to an outcome that is better or as good but with less resource utilization? That is the crux of the efficacy value equation— where "efficacy" is the amount of "good" produced for a patient, group, or community due to a health or public health intervention.

This is a high and difficult standard, but this is the standard employers/payers and governmental programs/taxpayers expect. The health industry and our communities are up for the challenge! Of course risk needs to be considered within the framework of value, efficacy, and "efficacy value." As health leaders, can you lead people and manage resources with the efficacy value equation in mind? Are new skill sets needed to augment the traditional "leadership or management" team in health organizations? Thinking about this equation may prompt discussion of new subdisciplines such as an "actuarial epidemiologist" or "interventional health analyst" or "analytical health informatician." Change is upon us and we must learn and improve our interprofessional and interindustry relationships at the individual, group, and organizational levels. We leave you with the "challenges of today" in health leadership.

We look forward to hearing from you and watching your success as a leader in our industry. Remember: People are led and resources are managed! Leadership is *your* responsibility!

SUMMARY

The concept of mentoring dates back at least to Homer's *Odyssey*; the word *mentor* was not formally introduced or

recognized in American parlance until 1883, however. For several decades, this term may have been lost, or wrongly communicated as a synonym for leadership, coaching, or advising. Finally, in the 1970s and 1980s, the concept of mentoring as a distinct and separate study from leadership and motivation became widely accepted. Since then, the formal institution of mentoring programs has resulted in decreased employee turnover, increased organizational success, and increased employee satisfaction.

Mentoring is different from leadership and coaching. Leadership is a macro concept focused on inspiring followership and completing defined tasks and objectives. Coaching is a more personal relationship that emphasizes the emulation of skills and abilities; however, it may not have any deep personal meaning to either the coach or the coached subject. In contrast, the mentee/protégé relationship is characterized by deep, personalized, and intimate interactions that are motivated by a mentor's personal desire to see the mentee/protégé succeed.

Although the concept of mentoring has been around for almost two generations, the unfortunate reality is that mentor–mentee relationships are often male dominated and race specific. More needs to be done to draw females and minorities into the fold of mentoring relationships. Health leaders should be aware that mentoring begins with setting the right example at all times and in all situations.[59] Setting the right example means taking responsibility for the preparation of future leaders so that the organization can endure tomorrow's challenges. This type of preparation is performed with a professional and caring understanding from the supervisor to the subordinate, from the mentor to the mentee. Leading by example is behavior that both influences and improves functions within the organization, including employees' job performance, career socialization, and upward mobility, as well as the preparation of future leaders.[60]

This chapter presented a method to combine, evaluate, and develop a personal leadership system for practice. Such a system can provide a framework for development of a discussion and improvement plan with your mentor or supervisor as you become a better, more efficient, more effective, more efficacious, and successful health leader. What type of leader do you aspire to be? How do you desire your organization to perform? Is integrity, excellence, and respect your calling card in your organization? How will you lead people and manage resources? Be the best leader possible. Start with a plan. Improve your scientific and artistic leadership capabilities. Lead with strong moral fiber. Enjoy your leadership role at current and future roles and positions. Make our industry better every day. People want, need, and require quality leadership.

EPILOGUE

Tedd Mitchell, MD is a past member of the President's Council for Physical Fitness, Sports and Nutrition under President George W. Bush.[61] He is currently the eighth president of the Texas Tech University Health Sciences Center. On Dr. Mitchell's desk in his office is a 2-foot-long tomahawk peace pipe. It is similar to a gift he shared with President Bush, as well as other leaders in his career. At one end of the tomahawk peace pipe is the lip for the pipe; at the other end, the ax blade and a pipe bowl. As a leadership aphorism, Dr. Mitchell suggests "It is only a warrior's willingness to use the one side that allows him to offer the other."[62]

Leaders will always be faced with multiple challenges of altruism and competition. For example, a CEO of a hospital may be seen as a nurturer and mentor to the people in his or her employ; however, to outside competitors that seek to gain market share and financial advantage over the facility, the CEO must present strength and a willingness to engage in conflict. However, at the end of the day, it is always the prudent leader that will know when it is time to offer the pipe—or use the ax.

DISCUSSION QUESTIONS

1. Describe the importance of mentorship and succession planning to the long-term success of the health organization.
2. Distinguish between the concepts of mentee and protégé.
3. Discuss some of the barriers in establishing a mentoring program in health organizations regarding gender, ethnicity, age, and race, and apply methods to reduce those barriers.
4. Explain the steps involved in establishing a mentoring program in an organization.
5. Differentiate and list similarities among leading, mentoring, and succession planning in health organizations.
6. Combine theories and models, develop an implementation plan, and evaluate a personal leadership system for practical application in a health organization.

EXERCISES

1. In a one-page paper, describe the importance of mentorship and succession planning to the long-term success of the health organization.
2. In a one-page paper, distinguish between the concepts of mentee and protégé.
3. In a two- to three-page paper, discuss some of the barriers in establishing a mentoring program in health organizations regarding gender, ethnicity, age, and race, and apply methods to reduce those barriers.
4. In a one- to two-page paper, analyze the steps in establishing a mentoring program in an organization.
5. In a one-page paper, list similarities of and differentiate between leading, mentoring, and succession planning in health organizations.
6. Combine theories and models, develop an implementation plan, and evaluate your personal leadership system for practical application in a health organization by using the leadership system template provided in this chapter.

REFERENCES

1. Finley, F. R., Ivanitskaya, L. V., & Kennedy, M. H. (2007, July/Aug.). Mentoring of junior healthcare administrators by senior executives: A description of mentoring practices in 127 U.S. hospitals. *Journal of Healthcare Management, 52*(4), 260–270.
2. Dancer, J. M. (2003). Mentoring in healthcare: Theory in search of practice? *Clinician in Management, 12,* 21–31.
3. Homer. (1996). *The odyssey* (R. Fagels, Trans.). New York: Viking.
4. Levinson, D. J., Darrow, C. N., Klein, E. B., Levinson, M. A., & McKee B. (1978). *Seasons of a man's life.* New York: Knopf.
5. Johnson, W. B., & Ridley, C. R. (2004). *The elements of mentoring.* New York: Palgrave Macmillan.
6. Finley et al., note 1.
7. Kram, K. E. (1983). Phases of the mentor relationship. *Academy of Management Journal,* 608–625.
8. Kram, K. E. (1985). *Mentoring at work: Developmental relationships in organizational life.* Glenview, IL: Scott, Foresman.
9. Cahill, M., & Payne, G. (2006). Online mentoring: ANNA connections. *Nephrology Nursing Journal, 33*(6), 695–697.
10. Clutterbuck, D. (1992). *Mentoring.* London: IPM.
11. Hafford-Letchfield, T., & Chick, N., (2006). Talking across purposes: The benefits of an interagency mentoring scheme for managers working in health and social care settings in the UK. *Work Based Learning in Primary Care, 4,* 13–24.
12. Kelly, M. J. (2001). Management mentoring in a social service organization. *Administration in Social Work, 25*(1), 17–33.
13. Pratner, J. (2009). Soldier on: Baylor Army grad mentors the next generation. *Baylor Line, 71*(1), 17.
14. Finley et al., note 1.
15. Johnson & Ridley, note 5.
16. Hester, J. P., & Setzer, R. (2013). Mentoring: Adding value to organizational culture. *The Journal of Values-Based Leadership, 6*(1). Retrieved from http://scholar.valpo.edu/jvbl/vol6/iss1/4.
17. Hankin, H. (2004). *The new workforce: Five sweeping trends that will shape your company's future.* New York: AMACOM.
18. Hankin, note 17.
19. Kets de Vries, M. F. R., Rook, C., & Engellau, E. (2016). Coaching across the gender divide—creating people-friendly organizations. In M. F. R. Kets de Vries, K. Korotov, E. Florent-Treacy, & C. Rook (Eds.), (2nd ed., pp. 241–252). London: Palgrave Macmillan UK.
20. Finley et al., note 1.
21. O'Neill, R. M., & Blake-Beard, S. D. (2002, April). Gender barriers to the female mentor–male protégé relationship. *Journal of Business Ethics, 37*(1), 51–63.
22. Linehan, M., & Walsh, J. S. (1999). Mentoring relationships and the female managerial career. *Career Development International, 4*(7), 348–352.
23. Martin, P. Y. (2004). Gender as a social institution. *Social Forces, 82,* 342–366.
24. O'Reilly, N. (2008). Women helping women: How mentoring can help your business. Retrieved from http://pdf.employmentcrossing.com/selling/150468.pdf.

25. Gibson, S. K. (2004). Mentoring in business and industry: The need for phenomenological perspective. *Mentoring and Tutoring, 12*(2), 250–275.

26. Hezlett, S. A., & Gibson, S. K. (2005). Mentoring and human resource development: Where we are and where we need to go. *Advances in Developing Human Resources, 7*(4), 446–449.

27. Kram, note 8.

28. Allen, T. D., Eby, L. T., Poteet, M. L., Lentz, E., & Lima, L. (2004). Career benefits associated with mentoring for protégés: A meta-analysis. *Journal of Applied Psychology, 89*(1), 127–136.

29. Kelly, note 12.

30. McAlearney, A. S. (2008). Using leadership development programs to improve quality and efficiency in healthcare. *Journal of Healthcare Management, 53*(5), 319–332.

31. Dolan, T. C. (2004). Mentoring at every level. *Healthcare Executive, 19*(5), 6–7.

32. Young, A. M., Cady, S., & Foxon, M. J. (2006). Demystifying gender differences in mentoring: Theoretical perspective and challenges for future research on gender and mentoring. *Human Resource Review, 5*(1), 148–175.

33. Finley et al., note 1.

34. Block, L. M., Clafrey, C., Korow, M. K., & McCaffrey, R. (2005). The value of mentoring within nursing organizations. *Nursing Forum, 40*(4), 134–141.

35. Eller, L. S., Lev, E. L., & Feurer, A. (2014). Key components of an effective mentoring relationship: A qualitative study. *Nurse Education Today, 34*, 815–820. doi: 10.1016/j.nedt.2013.07.020

36. Rigotti, M. (1997). *Mentoring of women in the United States Air Force*. Maxwell AFB, AL: Air University.

37. Oswald, P. (1996, March). *Distance learning in psychology*. Paper presented at the 10th Annual Conference on Undergraduate Teaching of Psychology, Ellenville, NY.

38. Jossi, F. (1997, August). Mentoring in changing times. *Training and Development, 51*(8), 50–54.

39. Alliance. (1995). *Celebrating excellence*. Washington, D.C.: Alliance, an Association for Alternative Degree Programs; American Council on Education.

40. Accreditation Council for Graduate Medical Education. (2011). Planning the future of graduate medical education: 2010 annual report. Retrieved from http://www.acgme.org/acgmeweb/-Portals/0/PDFs/ACGME-2010_AR_F.pdf.

41. Dyson, E. (1997). Education and jobs in the digital world. *Communications of the ACM, 40*(2), 35–36.

42. Raghuram, S. (1996). Knowledge creation in the telework context. *International Journal of Technology Management, 11*(7), 859–870.

43. Jossi, note 38.

44. Jossi, note 38.

45. Mentoring Institute. (1998). *The new mentoring paradigm*. Sidney, BC: Author. Retrieved from http://mentor.unm.edu/information/inventory.html.

46. Haggard, D. L., Dougherty, T. W., Turban, D. B., & Wilbanks, J. E. (2011). Who is a mentor? A review of evolving definitions and implications for research. *Journal of Management, 37*(1), 280–304.

47. Kaye, B., & Jacobson, B. (1996). Reframing mentoring. *Training and Development, 50*(8), 44–47.

48. Loeb, M. (1995, Nov. 27). The new mentoring. *Fortune*, p. 213.

49. Krause, M. K. (2007). ABCs of being a mentor. *Healthcare Executive, 22*(3), 62–66.

50. Kelly, D. L. (2003). *Applying quality management in healthcare: A process for improvement*. Chicago: Aupha Press.

51. Alward, D. (2005). Alumni/ae spotlight. Retrieved from http://www.had.vcu.edu/alumni/classes/Spotlights/Apr05_Coppola.html.

52. Feeg, V. D. (2008). Mentoring for leadership tomorrow: Succession today. *Pediatric Nursing, 34*(4), 277–278.

53. Lahaie, D. (2005). The impact of corporate memory loss: What happens when a senior executive leaves. *International Journal of Health Care Quality Assurance, 18*(4/5), 35–45.

54. Thurgood, K. (2008, December). *Construct for developing an integrated leadership model: Linking the correlates of effective leadership, development and succession planning*. Dissertation project submitted to the faculty of the School of Business, Capella University, Minnesota.

55. Collins, S. K., McKinnies, R. C., Matthews, E., & Collins, K. S. (2013). Succession planning: Trends regarding the perspectives of chief executive officers in US hospitals. *The Health Care Manager, 32*(3), 233–238. doi: 10.1097/HCM.0b013e31829d7386

56. Institute for the Future. (2003). *Health and healthcare 2010* (2nd ed.). San Francisco: Jossey-Bass.

57. Ncube, L. B., & Wasburn, M. H. (2006). Strategic collaboration for ethical leadership: A mentoring

framework for business and organizational decision-making. *Journal of Leadership Organizationals Studies*, *13*(1), 7–92.

58. Swayne, L. E., Duncan, W. J., & Ginter. P. M. (2006). *Strategic management of healthcare organizations* (5th ed.). Malden, MA: Blackwell.

59. Powers, R. (2008). Army commissioned officer career information: Mentoring. Retrieved from http://usmilitary.about.com/library/milinfo/arofficerinfo/blmentoring.htm.

60. Stoddard, D. A., & Tamasy, R. J. (2003). *The art of mentoring: Ten proven principles for developing people to their fullest potential*. Colorado Springs, CO: NavPress.

61. Texas Tech University Health Sciences Center. (n.d.). Experts guide: Tedd Mitchell M.D. Retrieved from http://www.ttuhsc.edu/Communications/Expert Guide/Expert/tedmitch.

62. T. Mitchell, personal communication, March 5, 2013.

APPENDIX A

LEADERSHIP IN PRACTICE: CASES AND INSIGHTS

INTRODUCTION

Health leaders utilize their knowledge, skills, and abilities in practical situations. In this important text, seven experienced, successful, and dedicated health executive leaders use real scenarios to guide your thinking and reflection about using and mastering leadership capabilities in realistic circumstances. Background on the health executive leaders is provided at the beginning of each case to help you understand the type of character, dedication, and credentials senior health leaders bring to their organizations. Lastly, consider our definition and model of leadership when reading and studying the Leadership in Practice cases:

> Leadership is the *dynamic* and *active* creation and maintenance of an organizational *culture* and *strategic systems* that focus the collective energy of both *leading people and managing resources* toward *meeting the needs of the external environment* utilizing the most efficient, effective, and, most importantly, efficacious methods possible by moral means.

> Leader Success = Individual (Nature + Nurture)
> × Situational Adaptation
> × Organizational Culture
> × Personal
> + Subordinate Accountability

The insights in the Leadership in Practice cases are important, and the background and organizational information are similarly important to provide you with an understanding of the context in which these extraordinary professionals work and produce their leadership outcomes. These health leaders are dedicated to mentoring, sharing, and fostering growth and capability in the next generation(s) of health leaders. Each health leader has prepared insights for you in his or her own style, focusing on timely and important topics.

Dr. James H. Stephens, Dr. Donald M. Bradshaw, Michael Sack, Dr. Susan Reisinger Smith, Dr. Crystal A. Riley, Dr. Paul E. Detty, and Phil Meadows—thank you for your eagerness to develop our future health leaders.

INTRODUCING THE HEALTH LEADER

JAMES H. STEPHENS, DHA, MHA, FACHE

Associate Professor and Distinguished Fellow in Healthcare Leadership
MHA Director
Jiann-Ping Hsu College of Public Health
Georgia Southern University

FIGURE A-1 Dr. James H. Stephens.
Courtesy of Dr. James H. Stephens.

Table A-1 Dr. James H. Stephens' Credentials

Degree	Institution Where Degree Was Earned	Institution Location	Year Degree Was Conferred
DHA	Central Michigan University	Mt. Pleasant, Michigan	2006
MHA	Indiana University	Indianapolis, Indiana	1974
BS	Indiana University	Bloomington, Indiana	1972

Biographical Sketch

Dr. James H. Stephens has taught at three universities for 10 years at the bachelor's, master's, and doctoral levels. He is the founding program director of the master of healthcare administration program in the Jiann-Ping Hsu College of Public Health at Georgia Southern University. The other two universities where Dr. Stephens has taught are Ohio University and University of Indianapolis.

Dr. Stephens is on his second career: Previously, he held senior executive positions at large medical centers and health systems for 25 years, including 18 years at the president and CEO level. He is a Fellow in the American College of Healthcare Executives, has been the recipient of many professional and civil awards and honors, and has been on many healthcare and community boards of directors.

What Is Your Leadership Style?

I used a combination of several leadership styles in my former executive positions. A summary of my leadership style follows.

- *Servant–Leader*: I believe it is important for leaders to think of themselves as serving others to accomplish the health organization's mission and for living its values. This style also makes you a better listener, which is a skill many leaders lack. I believe you have to learn how to follow before you ask others to follow you. A servant–leader's results will be measured beyond the organization, and the story will be told in the changed lives of others.
- *Transformational Leader*: With this style, the leader acts as a mentor to others in the organization so they can be developed into leadership positions. This is done by building trust among followers and demonstrating sincere interest in building relationships, which in turn builds healthy work environments. To be truly effective and successful, an organization will need many leaders at all levels.
- *Contingency Leadership*: This style fits the leader to the particular organization's culture by changing leadership styles, selecting leaders whose styles fit the particular situation, or changing the situation to better fit the leader's style.

What Are Your Three Biggest Leadership Challenges?

1. Building trust among the organization's key stakeholders
2. Implementing major organizational change
3. Maintaining a balance among professional, family, and personal life

Table A-2 Leadership Skills That Are Most Important to Dr. James H. Stephens

Skills	Skills	Skills
Build trust among followers.	Be a good listener.	Be decisive in decision making.
Believe in and be the main promoter of the organization's mission.	Have excellent oral and written communication skills.	Have a significant understanding of corporate finances so as to protect and appropriately utilize the organization's resources.
Have the right vision for the organization.	Be an expert in leading change.	Be competent in the corporate culture of complex organizations and operations.
Execute short- and long-range strategic plans successfully.	Have interpersonal skills to build internal and external relationships.	Be diplomatic and tactful.
Be a facilitator of a healthy and productive organizational climate and culture.	Enhance personal and professional growth of individuals.	Be socially skilled.

What Are Your Three Most Important Leadership Improvement Areas?

1. Be a better listener and communicator.
2. Understand that not all individuals wish to be effective leaders.
3. Keep up with the ever-changing state and federal regulatory requirements, policies, and laws.

LEADERSHIP IN PRACTICE: STEPHENS CASE 1

Replacing the Radiology Contract

Describe the leadership challenge of your case.

1. I was a new CEO for the health system and had not developed any relationship with the medical staff leadership (president, chief of staff, and chiefs of clinical services) or members (more than 500 physicians).
2. The previous health system CEO was aware of the many issues associated with the radiologists but had failed to address the situation.
3. The senior radiologists had been at the medical center for 20 years and had good relations with older physicians.
4. The medical center was the market leader; however, the radiology equipment was old and not state of the art.
5. The senior radiologist members were not trained in new clinical radiology treatments.
6. The radiologists were refusing to come in to the medical center at night or on weekends despite surgeons' and ER physicians' requests.
7. The medical center was in potential danger of losing market share because of a poorly performing radiology department.

Discuss how you met and dealt with the leadership challenge, and discuss the outcome or resolution of the challenge.

As a new president and CEO of a 350-bed medical center located in the Midwest, I had many organizational issues facing me upon my arrival. The medical center was a member of a national Catholic Health System, and I was the first lay CEO in the 95-year history of this medical institution. The organization was experiencing a financial downfall, employee morale was low as a result of a layoff of 100 employees, the medical staff was aging, and its main hospital rival was starting to take patient market share away from the medical center. However, the immediate problem was with the radiologist group, which had six members. In

my first 50 days on the job, I encountered a "beeline" of physicians complaining about the quality and cooperation of the radiologist group, including the president and several department chiefs of the medical staff.

The radiologist group had been at the medical center for many years and was generating significant income for each of its members. There had been a long history with this group in terms of poor working relationships with the hospital's radiology department employees and with physicians, especially with the emergency room department physicians and surgeons. The previous medical center CEO was quite aware of these issues, but refused to pursue any corrective action. I felt this situation was unacceptable, so a plan to resolve the various problems was developed. I met with the president of the medical staff, the chief of the medical staff, and the hospital management staff of the radiology department to formulate a list of major concerns to share with the radiologist group and to seek resolution. The problem list included:

- The emergency room physicians and the surgeons were having a difficult time finding a radiologist at night or on weekends. (This was a significant problem because the medical center's emergency room was the trauma center for the region.)
- Most of the radiologists left early in the afternoon, so no one was available to consult with physicians of the medical staff on specific patient medical issues.
- The radiologists had no interest in acquiring state-of-the-art radiology equipment or in enhancing their medical training for the new technology.
- There were not enough radiologists to handle the medical center patient volume, and they had no interest in recruiting additional radiologists.
- The radiologists were not meeting the 24-hour turn-around standard to interpret radiology patient films.
- The radiologists treated the department employees harshly and with no respect.
- Two of the radiologists were not board certified and had no interest in becoming certified.
- The radiologists had communication issues with other departments of the medical center.

After the problem list was finalized, I met with all of the radiologists and reviewed the list with them. During this meeting, I stated I would give them 1 year to resolve all of the issues. They were also advised that if the problem list was not resolved by the end of the year, their contract with the medical center would be cancelled. At the end of the 1-year period, the radiologist group had not resolved even a single item on the problem list. I then started to recruit a new radiologist group, which took about 5 months. The new group included nine radiologists who all were board certified and anxious for the medical center to finance an $8 million program to replace its old radiology equipment with state-of-the-art radiology equipment.

Once the new radiology group had signed a new contract and the capital funds to purchase new equipment was approved out of the budget by the governing board, I asked the members of the old radiology group to meet with me. The president of the medical staff and the chairperson of the board of trustees were informed of the meeting and the actions that I planned to take with this group. I reviewed with the radiologists that none of the items on the problem list had been resolved, which was disappointing not only to me but also to members of our medical staff and the radiology department employees. I handed each radiologist an official letter stating that his or her contract with the medical center would be cancelled within the next 90 days. Needless to say, all were quite surprised: It is highly unusual to fire an entire radiology group in a large medical center.

At the end of the 90-day period they left, albeit not very professionally, and the new group started. The old radiologist group filed a lawsuit that dragged on for 8 years; the medical center's legal fees were $700,000. The medical center did win the legal case, and the new radiologist group enhanced the radiology department revenue by an additional $1 million in the first year (i.e., $1 million more than the old radiologist group had brought in). The new radiologist group took the problem list and began to resolve every one of the items on it. The conclusion to this situation was that the medical staff and the medical center employees were very pleased with the new radiologist group and with the installation of the state-of-the-art radiology equipment. The medical center's image was enhanced both internally and externally, so that it was recognized as the medical institution with the best radiology service in the area. Once this critical issue was resolved, I began developing plans to resolve the other important issues facing our organization.

To recap this situation, as the new health system CEO, I met with the entire radiologist group to share with them the issues that had been brought to my attention by the medical staff leadership and members, as well as by the radiology department management staff. I wanted to hear their side regarding what had been said about their service and behavior. The radiologists had the attitude that the previous health system CEO did nothing about the issue and that things would be the same with me. This was a serious miscalculation. Within a month I had a second meeting with them and gave to each radiologist a list of items that they, as a group, would need to rectify in the next 12 months or I would cancel their contracts. They did not believe me,

which was their second miscalculation. During the year, I developed a strong relationship with the medical leadership. After 1 year, none of the list items had been corrected by the radiology group, so I held a meeting and gave them letters stating that their contracts would be canceled in 90 days. Before this meeting occurred, I had obtained the support of the medical staff leadership. I had also been recruiting a new radiology group, in anticipation of this outcome.

LEADERSHIP STYLES USED IN THIS CASE

I used all three leadership styles, all of which were incorporated into my leadership philosophy:

1. I used servant leadership in protecting our mission—namely, that we treat all individuals with respect and that we, as a medical center, provide the highest-quality level of health care within our means and resources.
2. I used the transformational leadership style in developing a trustworthy relationship with the medical staff leadership, who supported me when I was making a very difficult decision.
3. The contingency leadership style played a role by changing the leadership style so that I was decisive and prepared to face litigation for my actions in dealing with the radiologist group and a possible backlash from the medical staff.

LEADERSHIP SKILLS USED IN THIS CASE

1. The leader developed a trust relationship with the medical staff leadership.
2. The leader understood the long-term impact on the medical center related to changes in its market share.
3. The leader demonstrated courage in making a decision that might have strained the relationship with senior members of the medical staff and potentially spurred litigation from the radiologist group against the health system.
4. The leader demonstrated strong communication skills while presenting the medical center's case so as to win the support from the medical staff leadership.
5. The leader was effective in leading change by removing a physician group without a major uprising by the medical staff and replacing the existing radiologist group with a highly qualified and cooperative new radiology group.
6. The leader remained professional and diplomatic during the entire process, even though the old radiologist group was not professional.

OUTCOMES

The old radiology group filed a lawsuit about 60 days after their final day at the medical center. They wanted to settle the case many times but I refused. After 8 years and $700,000 in legal fees, the judge in the case dismissed it and it was over. In their first year the new radiologist group increased the radiology department revenue $1 million above what the old group had generated and performed even better in the following years. The medical staff, the radiology employees, and I were all pleased with our new group.

INTRODUCING THE HEALTH LEADER

DONALD M. BRADSHAW, MD, MPH, FAAFP, FACHE, FACPE

Senior Vice President, Defense Health Operations Manager, Health Solutions Business Unit
Science Applications International Corporation (SAIC)

FIGURE A-2 Dr. Donald M. Bradshaw.
Courtesy of Jody L. Bradshaw.

Interests

Facilitating and providing quality health care; mentoring exceptional leaders and managers; and developing innovative and creative answers to challenges, issues, and problems.

Biographical Sketch

Don Bradshaw is the senior vice president and operations manager for SAIC's Health Solutions Business Unit's Defense Health Operations (DHO).

DHO is the customer-facing organization for the support that SAIC provides to the Department of Defense's Health Affairs and TRICARE Management Agency (TMA), the Department of Veterans Affairs, and the medical elements of the Army, Navy, Air Force, and Coast Guard. SAIC has more than 1,000 personnel supporting these organizations, including staff at every military treatment facility in the United States and abroad. The team's skills and expertise center on health information technology, including full life cycle systems integration support and services, health domain expertise, supply chain management and medical logistics, workforce support services (counseling, nurse advice line, and employee assistance programs), and health administrative services (coding, claims auditing, appointing, referral management, enrollments, and third-party collections).

Bradshaw, who is a retired Brigadier General in the U.S. Army and board-certified in family medicine and medical management, manages the DHO team and also provides executive-level support on the company's health and medical initiatives.

Prior to joining SAIC, Bradshaw was a senior partner at Martin, Blanck and Associates, a leading health services consulting practice focused on federal health sector programs and services. In addition, his military service spanned more than 30 years, which included commander- and director-level experience across the entire military health organization:

- From 2005–2009, Bradshaw was the Commanding General of the Southeast Regional Medical Command, a healthcare system with five hospitals and six clinics in seven states and Puerto Rico, serving more than 750,000 patients and generating annual revenues exceeding $1 billion. Simultaneously, he was the Commanding General at Eisenhower Army Medical Center, a teaching, referral hospital in Georgia with four satellite clinics in three states and annual revenues exceeding $225 million.
- From 2003–2005, Bradshaw was the Commander (Chief Executive Officer) of the Fort Benning Hospital and Health System, which had clinics in three states, 80,000 patients, a graduate medical education program, and annual revenues exceeding $120 million.
- From 2001–2003, Bradshaw was the Medical Director and then Lead Agent of the military's TRICARE Central Region, where he managed the tri-service Military Healthcare System's integration with the TRICARE Managed Care Support Contractor, including management and operational oversight for purchased services totaling $2.3 billion supporting 1.1 million patients with 26 military hospitals and major clinics in 16 states.

In addition to his military service, Bradshaw earned his medical degree (Doctor of Medicine) from the Uniformed Services University of the Health Sciences in Bethesda, Maryland; his master's degree in Public Health from the University of Washington; and a bachelor's degree in Chemistry from Wheaton College. He is a fellow of the American Academy of Family Physicians, the American College of Healthcare Executives, and the American College of Physician Executives. He has also served as the senior advisor of the Central Savannah River Area Wounded Warrior Mentorship Program and as a member of the board of directors at the Christian Medical and Dental Associations of Central Savannah River Area. His office is located in Falls Church, Virginia, at SAIC's Skyline facility.

What Is Your Leadership Style?

My leadership is cooperative and collegial in the development of vision, mission, priorities, and resourcing. I understand that ultimate responsibility rests with me, even as I delegate authority and roles to subordinates. I then allow those subordinates freedom of action within mutually agreed-to boundaries. I ensure accountability and encourage a freedom to innovate. I underwrite well-thought-out risks and accept that not every idea or plan will be completely successful. Subordinates are expected to lead and manage their responsibilities as part of the organizational team. Simultaneously, they should be learning and growing to expand their knowledge, skills, attributes, and attitudes. They must also grow their subordinates to ensure future leaders and managers throughout the organization. I believe healthcare organizations must learn and grow while remaining focused on the patient and the highest quality care.

What Are Your Three Biggest Leadership Challenges?

1. Effectively communicating with all levels of the organization
2. Developing "middle managers" to lead, manage, understand accountability, and develop others
3. Encouraging innovation and creativity balanced with standardization and consistency throughout the organization

What Are Your Three Most Important Leadership Improvement Areas?

1. Communication, communication, communication
2. Balancing accountability with subordinates' authority and freedom of action
3. Counseling marginal or poor performers

Organizational Background

SAIC is a *Fortune* 500 scientific, engineering, and technology applications company that uses its deep domain knowledge to solve problems of vital importance to the nation and the world in national security, energy and the environment, health, and cybersecurity. The company's approximately 41,000 employees serve customers in the U.S. Department of Defense, the intelligence community, the U.S. Department of Homeland Security, other U.S. government civil agencies, and selected commercial markets. Headquartered in McLean, Virginia, SAIC had annual revenues of approximately $10.6 billion for its fiscal year ended January 31, 2012. For more information, visit www.saic.com.

LEADERSHIP IN PRACTICE: BRADSHAW CASE 1

Implementing an Information System: Electronic Health Record

Describe the leadership challenge of your case.

Our task was to implement an outpatient electronic health record (EHR) within our health system, which consisted of multiple, geographically separated clinics and a community hospital. We were part of a vertically integrated, staff-model, worldwide healthcare system; the EHR was developed by our parent organization, and the training package was centrally contracted. Because we were early in the process of implementing the EHR, important leadership roles were to capture strengths, weaknesses, and lessons learned concerning the EHR system. The greatest challenge was to use the EHR implementation to evaluate the entire care process and not just take our present processes of information flow, patient flow, and staff communication

Table A-3 Leadership Skills That Are Most Important to Dr. Donald M. Bradshaw		
Skills	**Skills**	**Skills**
Vision	Character— especially integrity	Integrity
Effective, multidimensional communication	Team building	Patient/customer focus
Ability to make, communicate, and enforce tough decisions	Subordinate development	

to the electronic record, but improve the efficiency, effectiveness, and efficacy of the care processes utilized.

Discuss how you met and dealt with the leadership challenge, and discuss the outcome or resolution of the challenge.

We addressed this challenge in several areas by utilizing a situational assessment that included an analysis of the following areas:

1. Equipment and infrastructure (e.g., computers, printers, bandwidth, classrooms).
2. Patient flow. After this analysis, we reengineered patient flow while determining the scope of practice and duties of providers and staff; we then modeled changes caused by or necessary to support EHR implementation.
3. Staffing implications for EHR implementation (not only the trainers and information management/information technology staff, but also additional support staff in clinics, appointment and admissions sections, shifting duties among present staff, dealing with labor unions, and other relevant issues).
4. Implications for reimbursement/compensation caused by decreased patient care during implementation (salary versus workload-driven compensation models).
5. Adequacy of the centrally contracted trainers compared to our organization's needs: If additional local trainers are required, how do we find, hire, and train those local trainers?

In essence, moving to an EHR across the entire system required changing our existing models of delivering care. Leadership issues in change management included the following points:

1. Developing a vision, message, and communication plan for the EHR implementation.
2. Identifying champions (physicians, nurses, support staff) for each area of the system.
3. Identifying early adopters who would stimulate change and "anchors" who were resistant to change.
4. Determining the appropriate implementation model (rapid change for the entire organization over several weeks versus clinic-by-clinic implementation over several months).
5. Determining the appropriate training model (large groups with individual follow-up versus one-on-one, over-the-shoulder, on-the-job training), structure (in groups by function versus by clinical team), and time lines. Because central contractors were deemed adequate only for the initial training, we needed additional trainers for maintenance training.

Leadership imperatives for the implementation of the EHR included the following needs:

1. Ensuring synchronization of equipment, training, and staffing
2. Ensuring adequate training, both initially and then over the long term (refresher, new employees, and revisions); scheduling; and the ability to modify training and scheduling based on individual needs and unexpected events (e.g., staff or trainer illness, system downtime, local surge in illness or demands)
3. Creating incentives for using the EHR system and publishing results
4. Developing a system to ensure rapid response to questions, suggestions, and needs
5. Celebrating success

The results of the EHR implementation were successful. Over a 9-month period, an implementation plan was developed, training was completed, and the necessary changes were implemented with a marked improvement in effectiveness and efficiency of care. After implementation, more than 95% of patients had records available at clinic visits (baseline was less than 70%), documentation vastly improved in legibility, records were linked to electronic prescriptions with improved safety, and health promotion and preventive measures were facilitated through systematic reminders and ease of tracking. Additionally, improved staff satisfaction with their new or changed roles, due to reengineering, was realized.

Over the 4 months of initial implementation, we did see 15% less productivity (e.g., more training time, slower patient flow, longer visits required, patient education) in outpatient clinics. Implementing a single EHR for primary care and specialty clinics was challenging: The EHR was developed for primary care, so specialty care applications for drawing, scanning, and other needs had to be developed. Also, EHR continues to be a challenge owing to issues related to ongoing training, accuracy of coding, and some provider dissatisfaction with movement through the electronic record (multiple screens, slow response, and multiple logins).

LEADERSHIP IN PRACTICE: BRADSHAW CASE 2

Ineffective Subordinate Leader

Describe the leadership challenge of your case.

The chief medical officer (CMO; also called the chief of medical staff) at the hospital was a nice guy, well liked by staff, but ineffective. He had limited experience in critical areas such as credentials, risk management, and project management. He could not manage the medical staff effectively.

Discuss how you met and dealt with the leadership challenge, and discuss the outcome or resolution of the challenge.

First, I had to determine how much of a knowledge deficit the chief of the medical staff had, how much was attitude, how much was personality, and if he was willing to learn and grow.

Second, I had to determine critical areas that could not wait on his growth because they might lead to loss of workload (and the corresponding funding), loss of accreditation, or loss of key medical staff members. I then had to determine possible short-term solutions for these critical deficit areas for the CMO.

Third, I had to determine which options were available to lead him:

- Could I move him or relieve him of his duties?
- Could I develop him without destroying his capabilities to lead medical staff over the long term?
- Could I work with him at all? (Was the relationship open to and capable of sustaining counseling, growth, accountability, and open communication?) If not, could someone else provide the mentoring?

Fourth, I had to develop a plan to stimulate his growth, including setting appropriate time lines and goals. At this point, I counseled him, identifying what he was accountable for in this process.

To implement the plan for his growth and improvement, the following occurred:

- The CMO's skills were assessed through a variety of tools (he had already taken several assessments including a 360-degree management-style evaluation tool) and interviews.
- New chairs of several critical committees were temporarily appointed, with the announcement that the CMO was assuming specific other duties for the 6-month period that would prevent him from providing focused leadership during this time frame.
- A plan for the CMO's development was created, including specific readings, courses, and time spent "shadowing" various experts (e.g., the credentials staff); specific targets for improvement were set.
- I counseled the CMO initially every week and then every 2 weeks, identifying specific written and verbal projects for him to complete and provide to me and the medical staff.

The results of the CMO improvement program were generally successful. This executive did complete his time as CMO; we did have a Joint Commission survey and achieved full accreditation with commendation. Other staff members developed their leadership skills as they chaired committees and led specific projects. The CMO was placed back into a full-time clinical role with minimal administrative duties and remained a productive member of the organization. However, his leadership void did result in some distress and power shifts with the COO and senior nurse executive, which required additional time from me to monitor, listen, and occasionally "referee" disagreements. Looking back on this situation, once the CMO's assessments were completed and it was clear his greatest lack was an ability to hold others accountable, I should have moved this individual back to a clinical position without leadership responsibilities earlier.

LEADERSHIP IN PRACTICE: BRADSHAW CASE 3

Values and Vision Conflicts

Describe the leadership challenge of your case.

As the CEO of a hospital within a larger system, you are faced with your higher leadership developing a plan to reorganize the reporting and accountability system within the entire organization that includes the hospital you lead. The goals of the reorganization are to streamline reporting, improve clarity of responsibilities, cut down on leaders with multiple supervisors, and hold leadership at all levels accountable for performance. You feel certain that the proposed plan will actually increase the complexity, decrease clarity, fail to decrease multiple chains of supervision, and decrease accountability. You have expressed your beliefs to leadership, but they appear not to listen, and they proceed with the proposed actions. It appears much of the weight behind their decision is political (limit loss of jobs in any one area, market it as better focus on prevention and community health, and continue to build up headquarters' centralization of control).

You are the spokesperson who must tell your hospital staff, your patients, and your community about the reorganization. As senior leader, you are charged with communicating why they should support this reorganization, why they should not be concerned for their jobs, why this change is good and meets the stated goals, and how the reorganization will be implemented at your hospital.

The following are leadership issues at the local level:

1. Do you readdress your concerns with higher leadership?
2. Do you discuss your concerns with other hospital CEOs (your peers) within the organization? If so, for what purpose or what action?

3. Do you support the "party line" when marketing this reorganization internally and externally?
4. Do you resign?
5. Do you start a job search?

Additionally, the following are topics for discussion based on the reorganization plan:

1. Loyalty to the larger organization when it conflicts with your perception of loyalty to your own staff and organization.
2. Communication within the larger organization and specifically your communication, impact, and participation in decision making.
3. Your personal integrity and reputation: How do you maintain them in various situations?
4. Your standing within the bigger organization: Should you consider the decision to go ahead with the reorganization to indicate a failure of alignment of your goals, leadership style, and purpose with those of your employer, and begin a job search for a company with better alignment?
5. Means to additional information or other (peer) input and advice without appearing disloyal, not a team player, or overly opinionated.
6. Ways to transmit the higher organizational level's messages to your staff, community, and political leaders.

Discuss how you met and dealt with the leadership challenge, and discuss the outcome or resolution of the challenge.

First verify all of your concerns. Do you understand the plan? Then go to your mentors or people you trust (preferably outside the organization); discuss your concerns to get a broader understanding and additional opinions about them, and to have others challenge your concerns. If your concerns are validated, readdress them with higher-level leadership in a nonconfrontational manner to better understand their decision-making process, develop better communication, and develop a fuller understanding of the issues.

Then you have one of several choices:

1. Support the plan and implement it to the best of your ability.
2. Find other CEOs (if any) who agree with you and go as a group to higher leadership. Be prepared to present your own plan and alternatives, not just negatives or complaints.
3. Take this rejection of your position as an indicator that this organization may not be a good long-term fit for you and begin a job search. (Continue to do your best so you leave with a positive reputation.)

You should always strive to develop ways to improve your communication with higher levels of leadership and provide your input early in change processes. An absolute imperative is that you do not complain to your staff or community leaders about upper management's decisions.

INTRODUCING THE HEALTH LEADER

MICHAEL SACK

President and CEO
Hallmark Health

FIGURE A-3 Michael Sack.
Courtesy of Hallmark Health System, Inc.

A short list of leadership characteristics that Michael Sack finds critical and valuable:

• Ethical behavior
• Enthusiasm
• Personal authenticity
• Motivation
• Discipline
• Sincerity
• Goal-oriented perspective

A short list of leadership challenges:

• Delivering a consistent message to all parties that is realistic and motivating
• Creating a culture of belief and achievement

- Selecting and building a competent, successful leadership team
- Engaging clinical practitioners in protocol assessment and constructive changes
- Ensuring operational performance effectiveness
- Developing administrative and medical leadership

Organization Background

Hallmark Health System is the premier charitable provider of vital health services to communities in the northern metropolitan Boston area. This system includes Lawrence Memorial Hospital of Medford; Melrose–Wakefield Hospital, Melrose; Hallmark Health Cancer Center, Stoneham; CHEM Center for MRI, Stoneham; CHEM Center for Radiation/Oncology, Stoneham; Hallmark Health Medical Center, Reading; Hallmark Health VNA and Hospice, Malden; Lawrence Memorial/Regis College Nursing and Radiography Programs, Medford; and Hallmark Health Medical Associates. Hallmark Health is affiliated with Massachusetts General Hospital for cardiology services and with Tufts Medical Center for neonatology services.

Mission, Vision, and Values

Hallmark Health System's mission is to provide, in a community-based setting, the highest quality health care to Boston's northern suburbs. Its vision is to be the healthcare system of choice in the region, with demonstrated service to and support from area residents and physicians.

Customers

Hallmark Health System has stated that its intention is to help anyone who is looking for high-quality service and care in a local setting. The goal is to give patients access to the same level of services and expertise found in Boston, but in a much easier to navigate community setting.

Services

Hallmark Health System provides care in a wide array of clinical categories, including internal medicine, surgery, maternal/newborn services, psychiatric care, walk-in service, and emergency services. It also offers quality-focused specialty care in the areas of cardiac and endovascular health, bone and joint replacement, bariatric surgery, and cancer care. In addition, the company offers convenient access to the latest imaging and diagnostic services, including MRI, CT scan, digital mammography, ultrasound, interventional radiology, and a full range of laboratory and physical rehabilitation services. Two outpatient medical centers and a home care agency round out the full line of services offered throughout this healthcare system.

Core Values

As a core part of its values, Hallmark Health System is committed to the communities that it serves. To help fulfill this community benefit commitment, the company has established community outreach teams. The teams help Hallmark Health System determine where its support would have the greatest impact on the health and well-being of everyone in the community. Some of these efforts include organizing more than 40 local health programs in over 8 communities, including providing more than $2 million in community service programs that include flu shot clinics, a tri-city WIC (Women, Infants, and Children) program, various health screenings and education programs, and much more. The company has also collaborated with local agencies to foster emergency preparedness programs and disaster readiness. As a system, Hallmark Health provided more than $8 million in uncompensated care in 2009 to people in the communities it serves.

Commitment to Quality

Hallmark Health System's leadership believes that quality care starts internally, by working together to build the teams, policies, and commitment necessary to deliver the level of care its patients deserve. The company then takes these internal guidelines and translates them into new, high-quality care and service for patients as measured by clinical and industry guidelines and standards. Its success to date is reflected in the recent recognition and ratings Hallmark Health System has received and the future recognition and ratings that it promises to continuously strive to obtain.

LEADERSHIP IN PRACTICE: SACK CASE 1

Physician Leadership Development

Describe the leadership challenge of your case.

Running a healthcare delivery organization requires sound, committed physician leadership. Where do you get it?

Hallmark Health System is an integrated healthcare delivery organization serving communities located at the northern edge of Boston. It was formed in 1998 by the merger of four community hospitals with some overlap in service area and in physicians, all of whom are private, independent practitioners. Because they competed with one another, and because they did not support the organizational merger, there was no established physician leadership to help guide the new organization. As a result, there were four of everything following the merger. Each meeting had to have representation from each former organization. Nothing got done in the hospitals with engaged, helpful physician input. Most concerning, decisions were stalemated; when a decision was made, generally dissatisfaction predominated.

For the first few years following the merger, the new entity's significant financial losses diverted board and management attention away from active efforts to develop medical staff unity and promote strategic harmony. In 2003, a change in administrative leadership occurred.

Among my many initial priorities, the development of a bond of trust between physicians and management was my key initiative. To do so, I recognized formal medical staff leaders and sought informal leaders with whom I could form personal and professional relationships. Finding few individuals who met these criteria among the formally oriented, typically formerly competitive individuals, I turned to the task of developing new leadership talent. I recognized the need to bridge, or transition, from the current structure to a new one.

Discuss how you met and dealt with the leadership challenge, and discuss the outcome or resolution of the challenge.

I created leadership positions for the Hallmark Health System; the people who filled those positions were appointed by me and came from outside the medical staff organizational structure. The medical executive committees held jurisdiction over all other leadership roles through medical staff elections. I did not disrupt their authority but made it quite clear that the chiefs of departments would report to these "administrative medical directors."

Goals and objectives were established for the positions. After 6 months, it became clear the administrative medical directors were helpful in terms of physician interactions and problem solving. Private attending chiefs were happy to have someone else to assist in planning, in handling operational details, and in spending time in meetings.

Simultaneously, I developed a Medical Leadership Academy for individuals desiring or selected to be medical staff leaders. This program consists of quarterly sessions in which outside faculty are present and leading discussions on topics such as organizational finance, meeting management, dealing with disruptive behavior, and collaborative problem solving. There has even been a session on self-awareness and personal style. If an individual becomes an organizational leader, he or she is required to attend at least one leadership training session per year.

As a result of these initiatives undertaken over the past 2 years, we now have new individuals who appreciate their leadership roles and who are involved more effectively in our organization. Their involvement in and guidance on strategy

decisions are helpful, and their influence on their colleagues is tremendous. The cost of the stipends for these positions and the cost of the training academy are amply offset by the more collegial atmosphere, reduction of tension, reduced opposition, and improvement in outcome measures.

LEADERSHIP IN PRACTICE: SACK CASE 2
Cultural Change

Describe the leadership challenge of your case.

Corporate mergers are rarely easy. Creating a sense of unity and mutual respect can be a challenge. First, there needs to be an understandable purpose for the merger. Second, there must be fair and committed leadership. Third, the focus that cements the formerly separate components into a seamless whole must be an attitude of accountability for results.

I have been involved in three such efforts with varying degrees of success. All have withstood challenges and have adapted over time into successful organizations.

Discuss how you met and dealt with the leadership challenge, and discuss the outcome or resolution of the challenge.

My first experience was as a junior executive involved in merging two hospitals in a small town. There were no other hospitals or places for hospital employment. Services were initially divided between the two sites, both of which were old and greatly in need of capital repairs. The compelling purpose for the merger was to avoid closure for either or both organizations. Strong community leaders joined forces and mandated that the two hospitals consolidate their operations and reduce duplication of services. New administrative leadership was brought in and tasked with rationalizing the services, generating a strong balance sheet, and ultimately developing a replacement facility. Duplicate services were consolidated, new programs were established, forums were frequently held in public town hall meetings, educational sessions were provided for physicians, and communication with employees was emphasized. Over a period of 6 years, services were "right sized," a culture of togetherness prevailed, and the cornerstone for a new replacement facility was laid. Over the past 25 years, the organization has thrived, has expanded twice, and is now a major regional tertiary care center.

My second experience was as a senior executive who was recruited to manage a smaller hospital that was taken over by a larger, nearby competing institution. This situation was a much more difficult challenge. There was no sense of togetherness, nor was such cohesion expected, because this deal was not a merger of equals—the connection was forced. Few operations were formally merged, but departmental managers from the larger organization typically became responsible for managing the corresponding department in the smaller organization. "Take over" and "mandate" were prevailing attitudes. One culture was stripped away and replaced.

Perhaps not surprisingly, tension was high and significant personnel losses occurred. With the loss of identity, there was an erosion of community support for the smaller hospital. After 6 years of effort, the smaller organization was converted into a behavioral health and (Commission on Accreditation of Rehabilitation Facilities) CARF-accredited rehabilitation facility. The larger organization was expanded to assume all acute care operations.

This organization continues to be successful, but took a dramatically different path in reaching its current state. Cultural acceptance never occurred between the two facilities. A culture did emerge, but only through the adoption of the larger organization's existing culture by new employees, new doctors, and leaders of clinical directions.

My third experience was as the chief executive officer in the merger of three competing organizations in a large suburban service area where there are other competing organizations. The merger was prompted by significant over-bedding in the area. At the point when the merger occurred, four other hospitals had already closed. The belief was that the overlap in service areas by these three organizations would facilitate economies of scale and lead to greater ease of operational integration among them.

So far, the boards and management of these three organizations have become integrated reasonably well. The wild card has been the medical staffs. Resistance among physicians to the prospect of working together has made operational consolidation and the achievement of economics of scale difficult. In fact, one of the three hospitals was eventually closed.

This merger has provided some valuable lessons. Namely, just because a name connects one organization to others, it does not guarantee that patients and doctors will make the same connection and use the affiliated hospitals. In this case, physicians' reluctant attitude made it difficult for integration to occur and the result was a drastic loss of patient volume. Services that were expanded in anticipation of increased activity went underutilized. A change in administrative leadership brought me to the organization. My goal was to develop two separate but related hospitals servicing separate populations through a single medical staff with distinct differences by campus. However, this plan created confusion among the hospital employees,

Six years later, we are focusing on creating a common culture by emphasizing a separation in purposes of various elements of Hallmark Health System. There is a corporate, business organization with a unifying oversight of business functions. There are two clinical care delivery organizations that retain their heritage and community recognition. Although this separation is working, a stagnant patient population base, the aging of facilities, and demand for new technology now require new investment and development of a new purpose. The recognition that business practices play a key role in physician payment reform, operating efficiency, and collaborative practice is gaining acceptance and bringing people together.

At this point, we are reconsidering our organizational culture and developing a new vision that will support future successes for Hallmark Health System. The loss of pride, the confusion over which organization we were, and the uncertainty of our purpose in the immediate aftermath of the merger have been replaced with a much more cohesive, enthusiastic sense of pride. Our emphasis on accountability for results and a strong return to our roots in the communities served has resulted in favorable operating performance. We have also recruited many new physicians, which is helping to minimize the competitive atmosphere. Everyone is more willing to work together for the common purpose of improving the care offered throughout the health system. New leadership—which includes some leaders recruited from the outside and some promoted from within—has helped stabilize the situation and focus on the organization's goals, promoted thoughtful dialogue, and facilitated open communication. Persistence, respect, and clear communication of purpose and results are keys to success.

INTRODUCING THE HEALTH LEADER

Susan Reisinger Smith, DHA, MSN, RN

Vice President, Clinical Practice, Research, and Education Gentiva Home Health

FIGURE A-4 Dr. Susan Reisinger Smith.
Courtesy of Ben B. Smith.

Interests

Healthcare administration, health legislation issues, chronic health issues, and informatics.

Biographical Sketch

Susan Reisinger Smith has 29 years of combined experience in administrative and managerial positions, including acute care hospital operations, long-term acute care hospital operations, acute rehabilitation, ambulatory care, and industrial health. She has been a hospital CEO for the past 5 years. Because it is important to her to develop the next generation of health professionals, she serves as an adjunct faculty member. Her continued desire is to research the chronic health issues and escalating healthcare costs caused by social, environmental, and stakeholder influences. Dr. Smith is a licensed registered nurse.

What Is Your Leadership Style?

Throughout my career, I have been able to grow and develop from a manager to a leader utilizing the theory of transformational leadership. "Transformational leadership occurs when in their interactions, people raise one another to higher levels of motivation and morality."[1] My efforts as a leader have proved effective in changing organizations by utilizing effective communication of shared values and truthfulness. I have been able to enlist others and develop a team by communicating openly successes and failures, rewarding and recognizing others, fostering empowerment, and developing a sense of ownership at all levels. I believe that leadership is not an individual act by the leader, but rather a team effort that seeks to achieve successes and overcome failures. Collaboration and a feeling of personal ownership throughout the organization are critical necessities to accomplish its goals and sustain winning strategies.

I utilize leadership evaluation tools to assist in my professional growth and in transforming organizations. I am constantly evaluating myself and others for improvement by seeking feedback and listening. Lack of communication listening skills can lead to missed opportunities, failures, and mistrust. According to Manion, it is important for leaders to speak from the heart and share their beliefs, regardless of the feeling of vulnerability.[2] Moreover, leaders should provide feedback and emphasize that every person's contributions are appreciated and valued. An employee who understands the leader's values will be less distrustful of leadership and willing to participate and be accountable in achieving organizational goals.

According to Kouzes and Posner, "You can't do it alone is the mantra of exemplary leaders . . . collaboration can be sustained only when you create a climate of trust and facilitate effective long-term relationships among your constituents."[3] My future success will depend on my ability to engage in continual learning and understanding of the organizational dynamics while understanding the influence of the systems, both internally and externally.

What Are Your Three Biggest Leadership Challenges?

1. Keeping people inspired and motivated through the "rough times"
2. Achieving sustainability over the course of healthcare reform, and continuing sustainability after the reform is complete
3. Fostering a sense of ownership throughout the organization on a continuous basis

What Are Your Three Most Important Leadership Improvement Areas?

1. Confidence in my leadership—both within the organization and in the community
2. Communication techniques in achieving goals, and setting achievable goals to foster a sense of success
3. Success at building teams

Organization Background

Regency Hospital Company is in the business of providing long-term acute care through 24 hospital locations in several states. Regency Hospital of Central Georgia is a 34-bed, long-term acute care hospital located in Macon, Georgia, which opened in April 2004. An expansion created a 60-bed facility in Macon that opened in December 2010. More information can be found at: www.regencyhospital.com/company/locations/georgia-central-georgia.aspx.

Long-term acute care hospitals are the most appropriate setting for severely ill, medically complex patients and chronically ill patients needing long-term acute care. Care for the chronically ill patient takes a highly planned and coordinated effort by a nursing, therapy, and rehabilitative team working in conjunction with physicians, as well as a case management team, to ensure the best possible outcomes are achieved for the patient and his or her family within a reasonable period of time.

LEADERSHIP IN PRACTICE: SMITH CASE 1
Evidence-Based Leadership: A Formula for Success?

Describe the leadership challenge of your case.

Will standardizing leadership through evidence-based practices enable organizations to continue to provide excellent service, outcomes, and sustainability?

Discuss how you met and dealt with the leadership challenge, and discuss the outcome or resolution of the challenge.

Many environmental changes are requiring organizations to engage in significant, systematic, and sustained change to improve outcomes and viability. Bill O'Brien, former CEO of Hanover Insurance, has stated, "The ferment in management will continue until we build organizations that are more consistent with man's higher aspirations beyond food, shelter, and belonging."[4] Most organizations have a vision, mission, and value statement, yet many organizations fail from lack of commitment and ownership. Improving an organization's performance and effectiveness requires the "vision of one who created it, and the efforts of many that make the vision come to life and survive."[5]

Evidence-based leadership is a concept that provides "best practices" regarding how to achieve successful applied leadership skills. Evidence-based leadership is defined as a philosophy based on using current "best evidence" to make decisions about what the organization needs.[6] Will standardizing leadership through evidence-based practices enable organizations to continue to provide excellent service, outcomes, and sustainability?

Applied leadership utilizes evidence-based leadership practices to develop and model leadership behaviors for organizational success and sustainability. According to Kouzes and Posner, five practices are commonly used by exemplary leaders: modeling the way, inspiring a shared vision, challenging the process, enabling others to act, and encouraging the heart.[7] Modeling the way requires leaders to demonstrate the types of behaviors that they expect of others. Successful leaders understand that their behaviors must represent the whole organization. Leaders must also inspire others to commit to the organization through motivation, enthusiasm, inspiration, and excellent communication skills. Leaders provide a vision so others can see how things could be. Exemplary leaders will not avoid challenging existing processes and will take risks in their search for opportunities to innovate, grow, and improve the organization. Successful leaders foster collaboration and build support and faith in others through teamwork, trust, and empowerment. They encourage the heart by providing support, recognition, and celebration of successes.

Many organizations have attempted to use evidence obtained through measuring outcomes, testing, and other reporting methodologies to improve their performance by eliminating variances contributing to negative outcomes. "Quick fixes" implemented to improve outcomes based on organizational data have typically led to the creation of rules and interventions, which then inevitably resulted in only short-term improvements, inconsistencies, and even failures. These interventions for achieving success generally do not take advantage of best practices that might foster team collaboration by sharing of skills and do not communicate opportunities to improve outcomes that would have long-term effects.

According to Senge, "Organizations that truly excel in the future will be the organizations that discover how to tap people's commitment and the capacity to learn at all levels" (p. 4). Improved technologies and an increasingly complex work environment are creating an increased need for organizations to become more "learningful."[8] Successful organizations promote leadership development programs to foster a culture of learning and ownership. They recognize that effective implementation of best leadership practices must reside with the user. Regardless of the level of knowledge base mastery, the challenge for the leader becomes one of applying the knowledge base to the day-to-day operation with colleagues and clients who possess various knowledge bases and whose expectations of leadership development cover a broad continuum.[9] Kouzes and Posner found that "leadership is an observable set of skills and abilities rather than an innate set of character traits. . . . effective leaders are the leaders who are constantly learning."[10]

Applied leadership development focuses on key components of successful evidence-based practices. These practices include a change in leadership from a top-down perspective to group-centered leadership, from a hierarchical mode of operations to adoption of a stewardship attitude, and a vision that is value based.[11] Leadership development requires self-development, an assessment of one's strengths and weaknesses, and an understanding of one's values, motivations, and passions.[12] Unfortunately, many leaders refrain from best practices and standardization of leadership practices. According to Studer, "leaders want standardization for others, but prefer autonomy for themselves . . . it is appropriate for leaders have their own individual style, but standardization is important for certain leadership procedures as a key to eliminate variances and achieve lasting organizational results."[13] Studer defines variance as the difference between what the results can be and what actually occurs.[14]

The National Council on Disability defines a leader as one who fosters change; is value based; recognizes that all people are potential leaders; understands that leadership is a group process; fosters continual learning, creativity, flexibility, and resilience; and has a vision.[15] Leadership is not a solo act, but rather a team effort.[16] The traditional view of "leading" others requires an evidence-based shift to shared power. Leaders must be skilled in creating a climate of trust and facilitating relationships to foster collaboration.[17] Indeed, collaboration among the members of the organization is a critical necessity to accomplish and sustain winning strategies. Given this understanding, leaders must question whether personal autonomy is more important than achieving the organization's desired results.[18]

Leadership requires the understanding of one's values. Values influence behavior on both an organizational level and an individual level. Values form the basis of how we see ourselves as individuals, how we see others, and how we interpret the world. They are used to decide between alternatives; they serve as the cornerstones of who we are and how we do things. Strong values are what is put first, defended most, and least likely to be sacrificed even when the system process requires a change. The exemplary leader must understand how to manage his or her personal values when they conflict with the organizational values.

Evidence-based leadership requires effective communicative skills, including the ability to listen in different cultural settings. Downs and Adrian state, "For organizations to perform effectively, it is essential for periodic monitoring of the communication process that is necessary for excellent organizational development."[19] Communication techniques influence how effective the process of hiring and training of employees is, how people are motivated, how instructions are received, and how interventions are handled in difficult situations. "We all come from different backgrounds and bring different experiences to the table . . . dealing with cultural differences or with messages stemming from nonverbal communication . . . barriers to effective communication can be a disruptive force."[20] Ineffective listening is a barrier to effective organizational communication. A leader who cannot listen will create gaps in interpretation. Communication techniques developed from evidence-based practices offer the value of knowledge gained through failures, successes, and measured outcomes.

Standardizing leadership through evidence-based best practices will enable organizations to continue to provide excellent service, outcomes, and sustainability. Evidence-based leadership establishes an infrastructure that provides individuals, collegial groups, and employees with the time and resources needed to analyze data, scrutinize evidence, identify areas of action and development, and be involved in action research.[21] Leaders who embrace this approach utilize a management style that encourages a constant informed interchange of professional information among colleagues.[22] Evidence-based practices enhance a person's abilities to reuse evidence to work faster, shorten learning cycles, identify new opportunities, increase quality of deliverables, and increase the volume of work on matters of priority.[23] The goal of standardization of leadership through evidence-based practices is to create a self-sustaining culture that has the energy and vision to achieve excellence.[24]

Exemplary leaders will develop an organizational culture that fosters continual leadership learning and collaborative decision making. Ultimately, the success of the organization depends on the leader's ability to apply evidence-based leadership techniques to foster ideas and motivate creative solutions that will lead to relationships built on trust and commitment. The leader must focus on a strategic plan based on learning, embracing standardized leadership best practices, and utilizing applied leadership techniques for continual success. The leader must not wait until signs of decline or negative outcomes appear to seek out leadership learning. Instead, the leader must model the way proactively, inspire a shared vision, challenge the process, enable others to act, and encourage the heart. How leaders effectively utilize evidence-based leadership standards is connected to how effectively they manage the knowledge and techniques learned. Evidence-based leadership provides leaders with the tools to effectively share the information, effectively communicate with other people, and utilize outcomes to alter and improve the organizational system's ability to sustain environmental influences. This type of leader, through standardized practices, will be able to create a lasting culture of individual accountability and a sense of ownership throughout the organization.

LEADERSHIP IN PRACTICE: SMITH CASE 2
Ownership and Accountability Culture

Describe the leadership challenge of your case.

How does a leader create a climate and sense of "ownership" in the organization?

Discuss how you met and dealt with the leadership challenge, and discuss the outcome or resolution of the challenge.

Hospitals are service organizations. The success of a hospital depends on customers' perception of the services it delivers. Health organizations are challenged to meet the demand for services universally with no untoward events; perfection in delivery of care is the norm. Over the years, each healthcare organization has likely drilled into employees the institution's standards through staff meetings and memos. These standards include those that the organization's leaders believe are necessary both to achieve success and to meet regulatory requirements.

Unfortunately, many organizations are unable to obtain "buy-in" from each and every employee regarding the importance of its standards. What is often missing in such cases is the participation of the employees in developing the organization's underlying principles that would enable it to achieve the kind of quality service that is expected by customers. Instruction is not enough; employees and leaders must be able to see and feel what is necessary to create and sustain a great organization.

Accountability is critical to the success and sustainability of an organization. People who do not work together, but rather operate in silos, lack cohesiveness, and their activities soon become fragmented. In this milieu, poor communication develops and flourishes, feelings of distrust become evident, and attaining the organization's goals becomes ever more difficult. Optimal service delivery for hospital organizations requires communication between departments, coworkers, and leadership for essential positive outcomes. A sense of "ownership" or a feeling of pride must exist among all members of the organization.

Establishing buy-in, or a sense of ownership and accountability throughout the organization, requires both extensive effort by the leader and a concerted effort to ensure transparency. For starters, it means having the employees establish the organization's standards of conduct or behaviors. This step might begin, for example, by creating the organization's principles or "credo." These principles must be established to create the foundation for achieving high-quality service and organizational goals. The behaviors must be demonstrated by all, including top-level leaders. Leaders who follow the principles signal that no one is excused from adhering to the principles.

Principles for the credo may include, but are not limited to, the following examples:

- I will wash my hands.
- I will be happy to provide assistance.
- I will reduce risks and promote safety.
- I will communicate effectively.
- I will respect privacy and confidentiality.
- I will never say, "I don't know"; instead, I will say, "Let me find out for you."
- I will never say, "It is not my job."
- I will take the initiative.
- I am committed to my colleagues.
- I will make every effort to reduce anxiety for our customers and my coworkers.

Once the credo is made, it must be made visible and placed where all employees will be reminded of it on a daily basis. All employees must sign a copy of the credo and keep it for themselves and sign a second copy to be maintained by the organization. New prospective employees should be shown a copy of the credo during their interview to disclose the organization's principles prior to any job offer. When this extra step is taken during the interview or application process, the organization can be sure that future employment seekers will have an understanding of its minimum

expectations. Periodically, the credo will need review by the employees to add new principles, tweak current ones, and provide detailed expectations related to current principles to improve understanding and compliance.

The next step toward achieving a feeling of ownership within the organization focuses on making the organization's goals part of every employee's evaluation process. This step requires the leader to define the goals to be measured to ensure organizational success. Specifically, goals must be measurable and weighted by significance. For example, a hospital must provide excellent patient satisfaction to have a positive reputation in the community and surrounding areas. Patient satisfaction survey questions can identify weak areas that require improvement to increase patient satisfaction. These weak areas might include time to answer a call light, temperature of food, communication with patients about test results, discharge instructions, and attitudes of the providers.

Financial viability is every organization's objective. Financial goals may include measurement of average length of stay, optimal discharge percentage range, readmissions, equipment replacement costs and repairs, and operating expenses per patient-day. High turnover rates among staff members are not only costly for organizations, but also can have an effect on quality, patient outcomes, and an organization's reputation. Including the staff turnover rate as part of the evaluation process encourages staff to recruit and retain existing employees, which will assist in lowering the organization's operating costs and improving its quality of care.

Nosocomial infection rates are a measurement that healthcare institutions track. The infection rate of an organization not only has an immediate effect on the patient's outcome, but also affects the cost of care, the length of stay, and the hospital's reputation. Adding nosocomial infections and other risk issues such as falls and treatment/medication errors to the evaluation process encourages staff to be more aware of their own actions as well as the actions of their coworkers.

Adding the objective evaluation piece to employees' overall evaluations encourages employees to become creative in seeking solutions to improve systems that may be hindering performance and service. Once the goals are established for the evaluations, quarterly postings on "how we are doing" can communicate to staff what is working well, what requires immediate attention, and what can be improved.

The two basic techniques discussed here are (1) employees establishing the organization's principles and (2) incorporating the organization's objective measureable goals into the individual employee evaluations; both are designed to enhance staff engagement and feelings of ownership. Ideally, their implementation will result in enhanced organizational sustainability.

Table A-4 Leadership Skills That Are Most Important to Dr. Susan Reisinger Smith		
Skills	**Skills**	**Skills**
Conduct a self-evaluation (know who you are: self-evaluation; understand your own beliefs and values: self-esteem and confidence)	Ability to build a foundation	Ability to create a vision
Ability to take risks	Transparency (excellent communication and listening skills)	Inspire commitment (building commitment in the face of controversy and conflict)
Creative thinking	Always learning: learning never ends (commitment to growth of people: mentoring)	Clear understanding of what it takes to sustain an organization; understanding of the "Iron Triangle"
Systems thinker: capacity to see the big picture	Ability to foster harmony—recognize and reward employees	Ability to empower individuals; trust
Ability to balance your personal life and work	Foster collaboration	Energize, inspire, and motivate staff
Ability to build teams	Ability to create and manage change	Purpose management skills

INTRODUCING THE HEALTH LEADER

CRYSTAL A. RILEY, PHARMD, RPH, MSHCA, CPHQ

Associate Director, Federal Relations
The Joint Commission
Six Sigma Yellow Belt

FIGURE A-5 Dr. Crystal A. Riley.
Courtesy of Martin Studio Photograph.

Biographical Sketch

Prior to joining The Joint Commission, Dr. Riley's work history consisted of clinical pharmacy work in a variety of settings, including inpatient hospital and ambulatory facilities. She gained experience in performing medication reconciliation studies in two large suburban hospitals, which ultimately led to the creation of a reconciliation tool designed to assist medication tracking throughout the patient's stay in the facility. Dr. Riley was also involved in the implementation of an electronic health record (EHR) and computerized physician order entry (CPOE) system in a 600-bed hospital, which allowed her to gain additional insight into medication management and reconciliation issues within hospital settings. She has had the opportunity to work with national consumer safety organizations and has had experience working for a large payer of healthcare services, providing drug information services, and adjudicating pharmacy claim grievances and appeals for state assistance programs. Additionally, Riley served on the medication reconciliation cluster workgroup for a large pharmacy quality alliance and participated on a committee focused on the utilization of health information technology to reduce disparities in health care. Dr. Riley earned her doctorate of pharmacy from Howard University in Washington, D.C., and a master's degree in Healthcare Administration and Business from the University of Maryland University College.

Current Position

Currently, Dr. Riley is the Associate Director, Federal Relations at The Joint Commission, where her portfolio of responsibilities includes data-driven performance measurement and quality improvement/patient safety within hospital settings, including outpatient services. On the measurement side, Dr. Riley has knowledge of issues surrounding measure development, risk adjustment, application, and data collection. In addition to acting as a drug information resource within The Joint Commission enterprise, she is actively involved in outside medication safety councils that work to reduce the prevalence of medication errors and avoidable adverse drug events. Furthermore, she monitors pharmacy-centered issues such as novel drug development and pharmacotherapy related to Centers for Medicare and Medicaid Services (CMS)-focused disease states. Recently, she had the opportunity to act as a clinical reviewer for updating nationally recognized venous thromboembolism treatment guidelines and has also served on a technical expert panel reviewing medication management measures for CMS.

Thoughts on Leader Characteristics

Early on in my career, the term *leader* seemed ridiculously straightforward. It was someone who told others what to do, and they did it. Through work experience and additional education, I came to understand that being a leader encompasses so much more than issuing directives to others. It really is more of a mindset, an attitude, and a hunger for change that will encourage others to align with you and help you achieve your end results.

My own observations have shown me some common characteristics of people I believe to be some of the most effective leaders. Chief among these traits is passion. You recognize those people who truly believe in their missions; they are dynamic when they speak, and when they fall silent, you think that you can be a part of their movement that will change the world. There is a spark in them that radiates through those that listen, and their desire to act is infectious. You feel their momentum and want to move along with them because they've made you believe.

Many of the best leaders that I have seen are also believers in transparency. They recognize that there are few to no actions that are without consequence, and they do what they can to give a global view of all considerations. They carefully outline processes, concerns as they arise, and outcomes of activities, regardless of success or failure. And they are capable of acknowledging when they have been wrong.

One of the most important characteristics that a leader can have, particularly in the healthcare arena, is a collaborative spirit. Health care itself is changing from a siloed practice model to one of integrated care; in order to keep up, leadership must follow. Leaders must recognize that they cannot make changes without engaging and working collaboratively with others. Limited support from stakeholders will almost ensure that initiatives remain stagnant and no change occurs.

Leadership in Practice: Riley Case 1
Pharmaceutical Inconsistencies

Describe the leadership challenge of your case.

During my last year of pharmacy school, I leveraged my drug information rotation into a job that I started immediately after graduating and passing my state licensing exam. As a part of my position, I would be a contracted clinical pharmacist/drug information specialist that split time between two large community hospitals that operated under the same healthcare system. Included in my daily duties were rounding with physician teams, performing IV to oral medication conversions, making dosage and medication adjustments, tracking adverse events, and providing educational services to staff. For a new graduate, it was exciting and frightening at the same time. However, I was ready to take on the challenges and was hopeful that I would find someone to guide me through the learning process.

A short time into my tenure at the two hospitals, I noticed that, in the course of reviewing patient charts, there were many inconsistencies in the manner in which patient medications were recorded and tracked throughout patients' stay in the facility. I approached pharmacy leadership with my concerns and was given the green light to start researching medication reconciliation processes within the hospital system. Health care at the time was still largely paper-based; computerized systems were extraordinarily expensive and were limited in their use. I spent the next few months examining old patient records to see exactly how patient medications were noted in patients' charts. The results were disheartening. Out of the nearly 200 records that I reviewed, only approximately 20% of them had complete reconciliation of patient medications from patients' arrival at the hospital to their discharge home or to another facility. The lapse in continuity was particularly evident during the times when patients were transitioned from one level of care to another. I presented my findings to leadership and was told to find a solution.

Issues Encountered

Although I was excited to have an opportunity to make a difference in hospital processes, my project didn't go as smoothly as I would have hoped. The information gathering process was all done by hand and recorded on paper with no backup system in place. So when I arrived at work after a weekend and retrieved my documents only to find that they had been altered and, in some areas, completely whited out, I had no recourse but to start over from the beginning.

Once I did have the results and the analysis completed, the reception to the presentation of my findings was less than warm. The meeting turned into something of a "blame game" with fingers being pointed and responsibility being shifted from one department to another and many ill feelings toward me for presumably insulting staff for not doing their jobs properly.

The intricate medication reconciliation form that I had created to be included with all patient charts received strong negative feedback, with committee members citing concerns of burden and questions on who would bear the responsibility of ensuring that the forms were completed correctly.

Resolution and Outcomes

At the end of the process, and after several revisions to the medication reconciliation document, a version was finally agreed on for integration in the patient charts. The form was quite simplistic, requiring a minimal amount of information to be provided, and the effort would be shared by the patient's caregivers. There were no additional processes put in place to ensure that the form was being filled out properly or consistently, and everyone seemed satisfied that this was a reasonable solution to the medication reconciliation process.

Lessons Learned

Looking back over the past near-decade since my foray into the medication reconciliation process, I can both appreciate and curse my naiveté during that time. I was truly excited to have the opportunity to be a part of change, something that would improve hospital systems and patient safety and care at the same time. But I forgot to consider stakeholders outside of myself and the patients. I did not have an appreciation of truly collaborative efforts or the concept of burden. Nor could I have imagined the resentment that the implications of my work could cause because of implied blame. The need for a new process was apparent and the research was sound, but there were many things that, if I had the same task to complete now, I would do much differently.

I would engage people that have the potential to be affected by my work. In this case, physicians, nurses, and pharmacists all bore responsibility in ensuring that patients' medications remained correct throughout their duration of stay. It would have been better for all involved to be aware of what I was doing and why I was doing it and for me to gain some of their insights on how the problem could be addressed. I would have framed my results in a manner that would have felt less accusatory. The outcome of the research may not have changed, but the delivery may have been accepted better if it had not seemed as though the staff were not performing their duties properly.

It was not until I was fully immersed in health care and my master's degree studies that I understood the consequences of being an ineffective leader. Dissent, resentment, and potential sabotage are all sequelae of ill-leveraged leadership, and transparency, engagement, and openness would all have served me well in the quest to better health care in my hospitals. I did not realize it then, but it has been a lesson well learned over time.

INTRODUCING THE HEALTH LEADERS

PAUL E. DETTY, MD, MHA, AND PHIL MEADOWS, MBA

Paul E. Detty, MD, MHA

Midwest Medical Center
Six Sigma Green Belt

FIGURE A-6 Dr. Paul Detty.
Courtesy of Donna Stalter.

As a seasoned physician and former executive director of a for-profit ambulatory surgical center, I have had the opportunity to be part of a dynamic, challenging, and evolving healthcare delivery system for 30 years. In order for us, as physicians and health administrators, to continue to meet the challenges facing our profession, multifunctional teams must work collaboratively to deliver quality health care while meeting cost management and sustainability goals.

My background includes 30 years managing a successful OB/GYN private practice, during which time I performed more than 7,000 deliveries. Concurrent with my responsibilities as a clinician, in 1997, I collaborated with seven other surgeons to build an ambulatory surgery center to provide patients with a dedicated, freestanding specialized outpatient surgery facility. In 2011, the surgery center was sold to the local 222-bed acute care not-for-profit community hospital. In addition to practicing as an attending gynecologic surgeon, I served as either chief executive officer or as a member of the board of managers.

The changes I have witnessed within the medical profession throughout my career—from both internal and external forces—have been profound, and today the industry bears little resemblance to the one I entered in 1981. However, I find these new challenges exciting and see great opportunity for leaders to achieve two seemingly incompatible goals: provide quality health care and meet financial objectives.

My leadership skills that have served me well include approachability, communication, respect for others, honesty, integrity, vision, being a hard worker and life-long learner, empathy, optimism, ethics, confidence, and having a willingness to assume risk and ownership.

Phil Meadows, MBA

Senior Data Analyst
Midwest Medical Center
Six Sigma Black Belt

FIGURE A-7 Phil Meadows.
Courtesy of Donna Stalter.

Phil Meadows is a healthcare leader with more than 12 years of experience in the industry. He has found a home in a 222-bed community hospital in the Midwest. It is here that he has grown to be recognized as a leader and innovator with strong influence in the organizational design, including an integrated cardiovascular institute. Other focus areas during his career with demonstrable improvements are business planning, revenue cycle operations, supply chain management, and information technology (IT) integration. Meadows's success has been founded in servant leadership, honesty and integrity, strong communication skills, relationship management, and a passion for teams, mentorship, and culture building.

LEADERSHIP IN PRACTICE: DETTY AND MEADOWS CASE 1
Data Management Processes

Describe the leadership challenge of your case.

Paul and Phil met through a Six Sigma training program at a 222-bed community hospital in the Midwest where Paul was participating in a Green Belt capacity, and Phil was a Black Belt with 6 years of experience. When the facility recognized the need to charter a project to ensure accuracy of reporting, Phil was tapped to lead the project, and Paul was asked to participate as cofacilitator to complete his Green Belt certification. The need to launch a data management project arose from a wager (a Diet Coke) made between the chief financial officer and the chief of the emergency department concerning the number of patients seen at the facility during the previous year. Both parties utilized available data to calculate the number of patients seen. There was a difference of over 4,000 patients between their individual figures, although both utilized what they considered credible institutional data.

The problem that faced the internal consultants was to study knowledge management in a facility where data and information had started at the department level, instead of through a top-down approach. A situational assessment was completed to evaluate internal and external environments affecting the institution. Ledlow and Coppola posit that a situational assessment must be unbiased, honest, and objective to identify environmental determinants capable of affecting the institution's directional strategy (mission, vision, and goals) and success.[25] According to Applebaum, a bottom-up approach is disjointed and dysfunctional. A top-down approach avoids the organization problem of multiple definitions and data stores resulting in expensive and inefficient systems.[26] This lack of planning and coordination led to competing data silos, nonstandardized analytic tools, and biased operational definitions resulting in slower than desired performance improvements. Upon initial scoping of the project, we determined that the problem extended beyond prioritized barriers and would require a complete redesign of technical infrastructure, organizational processes, and structure. However, the executive leadership team of the organization desired the project to focus on only one problem, creating standard operational definitions.

Discuss how you met and dealt with the leadership challenge and discuss the outcome or resolution of the challenge.

It was early in the scoping process that we recognized the cultural challenges that a highly relationship-driven organization can possess. Organizational culture is defined as the "implicit, invisible, intrinsic, and informed consciousness of the organization that guides the behavior of individuals and shapes itself out of their behavior."[27] If we were to change existing organizational data management, and design a new evidence-based, value-added process, it would require challenging long-held assumptions of trust and perceptions of localized expertise. The following factors were identified as leadership issues regarding change in organizations:

- Employee empowerment (high instead of low)
- Leadership style (clear direction)
- Culture at workplace (supportive and innovative, instead of bureaucratic)

Swayne, Duncan, and Ginter posit that culture change in an organization typically follows six stages:[28]

1. *Stage One: Resistance.* The first reaction to something new is to resist the change. Leaders must be capable of convincing staff that the change is beneficial and not a fad.
2. *Stage Two: Passiveness.* Effective leaders must convince staff that the change will be beneficial, will fulfill the vision for the future, and will not just go away.
3. *Stage Three: Convince Me.* Leaders must show staff that the result will be worth their time and effort.
4. *Stage Four: Hope.* Leaders must convince staff that they can make the organization better and be part of something significant.
5. *Stage Five: Involvement.* Leaders must demonstrate to staff that the organization must change and continually renew itself to remain viable.
6. *Stage Six: Advocacy.* Leaders must demonstrate optimism that change is vital and that this program can really make an important difference for the staff and the entire organization.

Hall identified communication and trust-building skills among leaders and employees as necessary components of culture change, with the realization that if the employees and low-level managers in the organization shared in assessing the problems, identifying the alternative solutions, and designing the solutions, then those same workers would work diligently to implement and refine the changes proposed.[29] Leaders should optimize communication and trust among management and employees, foster a supportive and innovative culture in the organization instead of a stressful and bureaucratic one, share the strategic plan of the organization and the planned changes with the employees in a clear manner, and involve the employees in solutions to the identified problems.[30]

Ledlow and Coppola cite the chronology of leadership study and practice.[31] We utilized a combination of transactional and transformational leadership models in which we adapted a style consistent with the circumstances at hand, specifically, the lack of an institutional data management process at the healthcare facility. The authors iterate that the "knowledge, skills, and abilities of a health leader to use transformation and transaction leadership are critical for success in today's healthcare environment."[32]

To help facilitate change, we decided on the following constructs that proved to be successful:

- *Deference to expertise*: Relationships were identified as critical factors in determining who was chosen to collect, analyze, and report data. We developed the core team around individuals who were frequently sought to perform these tasks. This would later help facilitate trust with the team members' respective department leadership, and open channels of communication and feedback for identification of the true scope of the problem and, ultimately, solutions to those issues.
- *Servant leadership and collaboration*: Although technical solutions were not initially requested by the project sponsors, collaboration with IT leaders to share a strategically timed demonstration of analytics platforms, and building proof of concepts into existing underutilized analytics tools, piqued sponsorship interest in future potential. In turn, this opened a door for furthering the scope of analysis.
- *Facilitation*: The project was structured to use the "Design for Six Sigma" (DFSS) methodology. This methodology was chosen not only due to lack of infrastructure, but also to allow for engaging the leadership team in an existing accepted format within the organization. This eliminated potential barriers that would have been present in individual stakeholder meetings. Over 75% of the leadership team participated in problem identification, critical-to-quality definition, and prioritization, in addition to solution development and evaluation.[33]
- *Charisma*: Followers were influenced by the leaders while arousing collective team spirit.

Table A-5 Leadership That Are Most Important to Dr. Paul Detty and Phil Meadows

Skills	Skills	Skills
Being a good listener	Being a lifelong learner	The ability to accept responsibility
Creating opportunities for others	The ability to motivate others	Being passionate about empowering others
The ability to communicate with others	Becoming an expert in leading change	Never forgetting that the best leaders are not necessarily the ones in front
Identifying and involving all stakeholders in decision making	Aligning the business and healthcare functions of the organization	Creating a culture that cultivates change
Promoting an ethical organizational culture	Encouraging and participating in mentoring	Being prepared for every contingency by fostering a constant state of readiness

- *Intellectual stimulation*: The leaders influenced followers' understanding of the problem and valued various and diverse team member perspectives.
- *Individualized consideration*: The leaders were supportive, encouraging, and mentoring with team members.
- *Inspirational motivation*: The leaders promoted an appealing vision to empower subordinate effort.

Outcome

Although the initial desire of sponsors was to fix the problem of multiple operational definitions, we were able to facilitate a process of organizational self-discovery to prepare for broad-based changes that allow for better alignment with directional strategies (mission, vision, and goals), the future needs of healthcare reporting, and analytics.

Leadership Takeaways

1. *Patience and diligence*: The desired time frame of a 6-month project became 1 year to simply form recommendations. Despite missed deadlines, being methodical and calculated with all stakeholders can pay huge dividends, regardless of how long it takes to meet the end goal.
2. *Courage*: When faced with initial resistance on the scope of the project, the fact remained that there was a wide gap between best practice and organizational capability. Staying the course to expand the vision of leaders is of utmost importance—especially when it is not self-serving.
3. *Humility*: In collaborating with IT leaders and deferring to the experts in departments, the reach of the project grew exponentially. Instead of the solutions being recommendations from a Six Sigma project, they had become the next logical step for the leaders of the organization. When seeking out important matters, it was proven that big things can happen if you are not concerned about receiving credit and can appreciate others' skills.

REFERENCES

1. Kouzes, J., & Posner, B. (2007). *The leadership challenge* (4th ed.). San Francisco, CA: Jossey-Bass, p. 122.
2. Manion, J. (2005). *From management to leadership: Practical strategies for health care leaders* (2nd ed.). San Francisco: Jossey-Bass, p. 77.
3. Kouzes & Posner, note 1, p. 242.
4. Senge, P. (2006). *The fifth discipline: The art and practice of the learning organization*. New York: Doubleday, p. 5.
5. Johnson, J. A. (Ed.). (2009). *Health organizations: Theory, behavior, and development*. Sudbury, MA: Jones and Bartlett, p. 109.
6. Studer, Q. (2008). *Results that last*. Hoboken, NJ: John Wiley & Sons, p. xi.
7. Kouzes & Posner, note 1, p. 14.
8. Senge, note 4, p. 4.
9. Kunkel, R. C. (1980). Toward applied leadership development: Gamblings of a rookie dean. *Journal of Teacher Education, 31*(1), 30–34.

10. Kouzes & Posner, note 1, p. 341.
11. National Council on Disability. (2001, Feb.). *Applied leadership for effective coalitions*. Washington, D.C.: Author.
12. National Council on Disability, note 11.
13. Studer, note 6, p. 81.
14. Studer, note 6, p. 81.
15. National Council on Disability, note 11.
16. Kouzes & Posner, note 1, p. 223.
17. Kouzes & Posner, note 1, p. 224.
18. Studer, note 6, p. 81.
19. Downs, C., & Adrian, A. (2004). *Assessing organizational communication: Strategic communication audits*. New York: Guilford Press, p. 2.
20. Whitehead, B. (2006, January). Identifying and overcoming barriers to effective communication. Retrieved from http://www.web-conferencing-zone .com/4106-barriers-to-effective-communication .htm.
21. Caldwell, B., & Lewis, J. (2005). Evidence-based leadership. *Educational Forum*, *69*, 182–191.
22. Caldwell & Lewis, note 21.
23. Caldwell & Lewis, note 21.
24. Studer, note 6, p. 86.
25. Ledlow, G. R., & Coppola, M. N. (2011). *Leadership for health professionals: Theory, skills, and applications*. Sudbury, MA: Jones & Bartlett, p. 98.
26. Applebaum, W. (2010). Managing the total cost of ownership of business intelligence. Retrieved from http://www.sap.com/.
27. Bower, J. L., & Gilbert, C. G. (2007). How managers' everyday decisions create or destroy your company's strategy [Supplemental material]. *Harvard Business Review*, *85*(2), 74.
28. Swayne, L. E., Duncan, W. J., & Ginter, P. M. (2011). *Strategic management of health care organizations* (6th ed.). West Sussex, England: John Wiley & Sons, pp. 299–300.
29. Hall, A. (2008). Overcoming resistance to organizational change initiatives. Retrieved from http:// www.arichall.com/academic/papers/om5216-paper .pdf.
30. Hall, note 29.
31. Ledlow & Coppola, note 25.
32. Ledlow & Coppola, note 25, p. 73.
33. General Electric. (n.d.). What is Six Sigma? Retrieved from http://www.ge.com/en/company /companyinfo/quality/whatis.htm.

APPENDIX B

UNDERSTANDING LEADERSHIP AS A THEORY

Opinion is that exercise of the human will which helps us to make a decision without information.
John Erskine, *The Complete Life*

This chapter presents students and early career executives with a sound understanding of theory. Theory is explored in terms of both anatomy (parts of the whole) and physiology (relationships with each other) to better explore the complexity of theory itself before applying it to the study of leadership. It is difficult for students of leadership to fully embrace all the nuances of leadership study if they first do not understand what a theory is and how the study of leadership theory fits in with the general dynamics of applying specific leadership theories to the practical world.

LEARNING OBJECTIVES

1. Describe why the study of theory is important in the study of leadership in health organizations.

2. Define and distinguish the basic elements and relationships of a theory.

3. Demonstrate the utility of theory in the study of leadership, leadership principles, and leadership applications.

4. Describe and compare two or more conceptual models, and discuss how the models relate to theory and support the discussion of leadership.

5. Design a simple model of leadership principles or applications (from constructs and concepts in this chapter or other literature), and summarize the relationships between the model's theoretical elements and the application of leadership principles.

6. Justify and defend the constructs in a simple model of leadership.

WHY STUDY THEORY?

Although the study of theory may seem nonessential and without practicality in a leadership course, you should ask yourself two simple questions: First, what is a theory? Second, what is leadership? If you can answer the second question without answering the first, there may be a gap in your understanding of the complexities of the art and science of leadership—and how leadership theory supports the development processes of early career executives.

The authors of this text have more than 50 years of combined experience in health leadership positions in civilian and military health organizations and in academia. We have been educated academically and trained practically in the understanding, application, synthesis, and evaluation of leadership. As a result, we feel that it may not be possible to

461

fully embrace all of the fundamentals of leadership and leadership theories without first understanding the complex relationships in theory structure and processes. Failing to understand theory may result in students of leadership not understanding what they are reading. More importantly, lack of theoretical methods knowledge could lead to misinterpretation, resulting in an inability to apply leadership knowledge, skills, and abilities in the organizational world.

Consider one of the early leadership theories posited by scholars in the mid-1800s—something called the "great man" theory. In essence, this theory suggested that to be a "great man," one had to emulate the specific "traits" of the acknowledged leaders of the time. There is overlap between great man and trait theories of leadership. What is missing is an understanding of what *great* means and how the specific traits define the word *great* for us to study. In reality, the great man theories of the early 1800s offered us no benchmark for success and no road map for others to follow. Essentially, the words *great* and *trait* were not universally understood or applied. As a result, the theory offered no utility for education or application. Simply put, the behavior of great leaders and their traits were observed and emulated without any attempt to understand the foundations of behaviors or influence of traits.

Another example is the transformational leadership theory, which was introduced in 1978.[1] This theory suggests that leaders can inspire followership by raising subordinate goals toward higher levels of motivation through developing a spirit of trust, respect, and loyalty. For example, John F. Kennedy's presidency is often characterized as inspiring the civil rights movement and a manifest destiny toward U.S. exploration of space. In support of this proposition, a janitor at NASA was once asked what he was doing cleaning a building after hours when he was not authorized to receive overtime pay for the work. His reply: "I am helping to put a man on the moon." President Kennedy was successful in transforming the perceptions of the janitor to view his job not only as a task, but also as one part of a greater vision—the U.S. quest for space exploration. Kennedy was an astute student of leadership. As a result, he was able to recognize the core values necessary to change individual behavior and form followership among the masses.[2]

Scholars of leadership theory can deconstruct Kennedy's natural abilities and provide tools, skills, and a road map for young scholars and early careerists to follow. Deconstructing "transformational theory" provides developmental insights that young executives can build on until their natural abilities associated with maturity and experience develop over time. Deconstructing theory and methods of theory building can greatly assist in this effort.

Understanding the elements of a theory, models, and the components of theories and models is critical for analyzing, synthesizing, and evaluating which elements and components of a personal leadership model would be best for you in your career, and allow you to determine how to put them into practice. As former University of Alabama football coach Paul "Bear" Bryant said, "We beat most teams because we have a plan." You need a leadership plan (your model) as well to be the best you can be in your career. The rest of this chapter starts to build the foundation for you to develop your leadership plan, your model.

WHAT IS A THEORY?

Theory is the primordial soup from which complex questions can be modeled and discussed in bounded rationality where like-minded executives can agree on issues and causality. It is important to know that there is no one accepted definition of *theory* within the organization behavior literature. In layperson's terms, a theory is an advanced form of an idea or an opinion that has some basis in the empirical world. Regardless of the definition selected, a theory must be capable of support by qualitative measures or quantitative data. If a theory is incapable of initial development based on qualitative or quantitative properties, the burgeoning theory may not have evolved past the opinion or idea phase, and it may not be valuable to the profession or the advancement of knowledge.

The term *theory* is derived from an ancient Greek word meaning to contemplate, to contemplate the divine, or to speculate. Simply put, a theory is a way to capture and represent a set of ideas, constructs, variables, and observations within a context to demonstrate how a part of the world works or could work better. A theory intends to evaluate variables that are operationally defined and measured in a dynamic world. Theories are analytical structures that seek to illustrate how linked ideas, domains, constructs, and variables perform under various conditions by using quantitative, qualitative, or combined methods. "A particular feature of science (including social science) is that it is continually evolving as a result of the scientific method which calls for a constant testing of ideas and observations of scientific facts, theories, and models."[3] Theories start out as models that have been developed using empirical thinking. Qualitative information and analysis (also known as theory building methods) such as observation and literature review start this empirical process. Quantitative analysis (also known as theory testing methodology) tests models as hypotheses to determine if the model represents the world better than what was known before. This empirical hypothesis testing can be performed as qualitative research alone in certain cases, but may also be carried out in combination with quantitative methods (a process called triangulation).

Definitions of the term *theory* support the notion that a theory provides for an integration of ideas within a context of a phenomenon. "A theory is a set of interrelated principles and definitions that present a systematic view of phenomena by specifying relationships among variables with the purpose of explaining natural phenomena."[4,5] Another definition suggests that a theory is "any set of hypotheses or principles linked by logical or mathematical arguments which is advanced to explain an area of empirical reality or type of phenomenon."[6,7] As discussed previously, the terms *model* and *hypothesis* nudge their way into the discussion; this is especially true in the study of leadership.

THEORY AS A CONCEPTUAL MODEL

In this section you will learn to visualize theory as a conceptual model. A conceptual model is a conceptual description of something abstract. It is not uncommon in business practices for executives to develop models to represent certain ideas and concepts. The model itself, like a photograph, breaks down barriers of communication, thereby making it easier for individuals to view the model and understand complex relationships. Models serve as representations of the world or phenomena around us; they are particularly useful for understanding, analyzing, and evaluating how the world works around us.

Figure B-1 shows an example of a conceptual model for a hospital. In this basic model, hospital performance is achieved as a result of an organization's inputs and outputs. In this case, the inputs are constructs (to be discussed later)

of hospital types, structural units, and the environment. The outputs in this model are the result of the previous three constructs combining to form some sort of recognized output. Finally, the performance of the hospital is based on the efficiency of those outputs being earmarked as high or low. If the output is high, there is no need for leadership to take action. If the output is low, the conceptual model guides leaders back to the relationship between constructs so that additional action can be taken.

The basic conceptual model shown in Figure B-1 helps us to evaluate hospital efficiency in a manner that is complex, yet easily understood by outside agents and stakeholders.

OVERVIEW OF THEORY

This section presents a brief overview of theory and explores how a theory can be deconstructed into constructs, variables, and measures. Readers are instructed on how to use visual and graphical tools to create a conceptual model that measures a specific outcome of leadership principles. Model building is a necessary precursor to performance-based management development, health system examination, policy formulation, and the conducting of quantitative analysis, to name only a few of its potential uses. Nevertheless, understanding the process of building empirically measurable healthcare and leadership models may be one of the more underrated aspects of leader development in today's healthcare system. This chapter places specific emphasis on creating conceptual models of leadership that can be used to measure the outcomes of various theories.

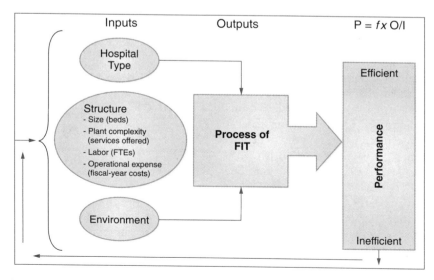

FIGURE B-1 A conceptual model.

Differentiating Between Theories and Models

The terms *theory* and *model* are used interchangeably in much of the literature. A theory is a hypothesis that has undergone scientific and practical scrutiny, albeit at various levels of intensity, to determine its value, truth, and validity. A theory does not "just happen" quickly, but rather develops over time after significant scrutiny by multiple scholars, practitioners, and researchers has proven the model is worthy of theory status. A model is a simplified abstraction of reality; it has not yet met a level of academic and practical scrutiny for scientific validation, so its value has yet to be determined. Both theories and models require ecological validity to represent and present reality well, so that scholars and practitioners can study and use them. It is more difficult to prove value, truth, and validity in the leadership discipline than it is in a basic science such as chemistry or physics. Consequently, one could argue that leadership theories and models are really hypotheses—that is, speculations about how a phenomenon actually behaves or works:

> A [social] scientific theory is a synthesis of well-tested and verified hypotheses about some aspect of the world around us. When a [social] scientific hypothesis has been confirmed repeatedly by experiment, it may become known as a [social] scientific law or scientific principle.[8]

In the leadership literature, the terms *theory* and *model* are much more prevalent than the terms *law* and *principle*, mostly due to the social requirement and nature of leadership: People's beliefs, values, attitudes, and behaviors often change, and situations are dynamic. Going back to the structure of theory, constructs, and variables, an example can explain this social sciences–based methodology.

Many leadership theories include *interpersonal relationships* as a category within their theories. Within the category of interpersonal relationships, one of the constructs is *communication*. As a construct, communication is broad and has many possible variables that can be measured. For example, *conflict management style* may be a variable within the construct of communication. Conflict management style, as a variable, can be measured using a survey to determine the leader's dominant style from six previously identified conflict management styles. Because a theory, to be useful, needs to adjust and work well in a dynamic world, recommending a conflict management style based on a particular situation would be more helpful than just relying on chance to pick the correct conflict management style out of six possibilities. Thus, in this example, a situational variable (observations from the situation) can interact with a variable from the interpersonal relationships category and communication construct, and specifically the conflict management style variable, to provide a recommended conflict management style. From a social sciences and academic perspective, this approach serves as a structure to facilitate studying, teaching, and learning about leadership. From an application viewpoint, however, the leadership theory in practice would be transformed into knowledge, skills, and abilities.

Continuing with the same example, the practicing leader understands that interpersonal relationships are important and can describe and explain why this subject is important in general, but also based on the constructs included under this category. This is an example of *knowledge*. Focusing on the communication construct and the conflict management style variable, the practicing leader can identify the type of situation at hand and apply observations from the environment to the leadership theory to reveal a recommendation for the appropriate conflict management style to use in this situation. This is an example of *ability*. Even though the recommended conflict management style may not be the leader's dominant or preferred style, the leader uses the recommended style in this particular situation. This is an example of a *skill*. If the leader can use any of the six conflict management styles dictated by the situation as appropriate, he or she would be more skillful than a leader who can use just two or three conflict management styles.

To increase the value of studying leadership, building your knowledge of theories and models is critical. Developing an ability to take apart leadership theories and models and separate them into their component domains, constructs, and variables is vital. Also, developing the ability to assess the situation or environment of leadership is important. Lastly, developing, refining, and maintaining skills associated with analyzing and using constructs and variables of leadership theories and models are paramount. As you study and master the knowledge and practice the abilities and skills of the various theories and models, your leadership acumen will improve.

THEORIES, MODELS, CONSTRUCTS, VARIABLES, AND MEASUREMENTS

History has recorded leaders' exploits for thousands of years. Anthropology, archeology, social anthropology, political science, business, communication, and other disciplines have all made valuable contributions to the basic foundations of leadership theory and practice. The health professions place leadership foundational theories and models and the practice of leadership into the complex environment of promoting health, preventing disease and injury, diagnosing and treating disease and injury, rehabilitating human bodies and functions, and facilitating dignity at the end of life. In this arena, leadership, as a complex topic, is coupled with a complex environment, the health industry, which creates a multilayered and integrative system in which the health leader must perform. To use leadership theories and models, it is important to understand the scholarly building blocks of these foundations and to extend or bridge scholarly and theoretical perspectives to the applied or practical use of leadership knowledge, skills, and abilities.

Leadership is an interdisciplinary field of study of the social sciences. Leadership is a social phenomenon: It involves individuals, groups, and populations and focuses on how those people interact given the multitude of beliefs, values, attitudes, and behaviors in society. Leadership can be simple or very complex depending on how complicated the social environment appears to both the leaders and the led. As a science (in this case, a social science), leadership is explained, taught, learned, and documented in the literature. Within this knowledge base, theories and models combine domains, constructs, and variables that can be measured to describe, prescribe, or both describe and prescribe how to think about, practice, and evaluate leadership. Given that leadership knowledge comes from several disciplines, it is important to use social sciences–based methods to provide clarity to the study of leadership. That clarity is provided through a structure that uses theories, models, constructs, variables, and measurement as a common language and guide to leadership inquiry, practice, and evaluation.

ANATOMY OF THEORY

The anatomy of theory can be broken down into specific units of analysis—namely, the theory itself, followed by sub-

ordinate constructs, variables, and operationalized measures. Surrounding these elements is the environment of discussion, an enclosure called *bounded rationality*. When discussing theoretical constructs, variables, and measures, it is first necessary to frame these elements within a plausible discussion group. By framing constructs, variables, and measures in a bounded rationality, an "out of bounds" area is revealed that helps researchers stay within certain parameters of discussion.[9]

Contained within this bounded rationality is the physiology of theory (discussed in the next section). The physiology of theory describes the interaction among constructs, variables, measures, and other elements. In this regard, the interaction of constructs within theory is helpful for developing propositional statements. This consideration is important in the early stages of qualifying theoretical relationships before quantitative data become available for testing or disconfirmation of the theory. Forming more concrete and testable relationships within the theory are the relationships between variables known as hypotheses. Propositional and hypothetical relationships are discussed in greater detail later in this chapter.

Also contained within the bounded rationality of theory are contextual factors and confounders. Contextual factors are generally known elements that exist in the same environment as constructs, variables, and measures. The interaction of contextual factors on certain constructs and variables may be known in advance and can be controlled for through awareness and intervention. Confounders are properties in the environment that are generally not known in advance and may interact with theory to produce unanticipated effects.

Figure B-2 depicts theory as a conceptual model for visual representation and understanding. A conceptual

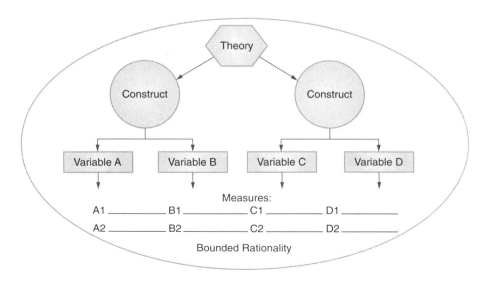

FIGURE B-2 Anatomy and physiology of a theory.

model is a "conceptual description" of the key elements of a phenomenon under study. The conceptual model should be parsimonious (simple) and offer graphic representations of theoretical elements that help outsiders understand the issue(s) being investigated at a glance. A conceptual model may include the actual theory, as well as constructs, variables, measures, confounders, and contextual factors. Some conceptual models, however, consider only specific constructs as well as certain elements specific to the unit of analysis under study.

Physiology of Theory

The physiology of theory can be described in terms of the relationships within the theoretical model. Two of these relationships are expressed in terms of hypotheses and propositions (**Figure B-3**). A proposition is a statement of opinion, based on some degree of preliminary study or heuristics, which is offered as a true or valid statement. Although the statement may not always be true or valid, it is offered as such until evidence of disconfirmation is provided. The aphorism "time is endless" is an example of a propositional statement between constructs. Another classic example of a propositional statement combining constructs is "the right to bear arms." This propositional statement is offered as a statement of fact as if it were true; however, the interpretive nature of this proposition continues to be repeatedly addressed in the United States.

A hypothesis is a testable relationship between two variables. The purpose of hypothesis testing is to discover causal relationships or associations between variables. Hypothesis statements are the foundation for all social sciences research and form the basis for the advancement of knowledge.

> The words *model, hypothesis,* and *theory* are each used quite differently in science. Their use in science is also quite different [than] in everyday language. To scientists the phrase "the *theory* of . . ." signals a particularly well-tested idea. A *hypothesis* is an idea or suggestion that has been put forward to explain a set of observations. It may be expressed in terms of a mathematical *model.* The *model* makes a number of predictions that can be tested in experiments. After many tests have been made, if the *model* can be refined to correctly describe the outcome of all experiments, it begins to have a greater status than a mere suggestion. Scientist do not use the term "the *theory* of . . ." except for those ideas that have been so thoroughly tested and developed that we know there is indeed some range of phenomena for which they give correct predictions every time. (But, language being flexible, scientists may use "a *theory*" as a synonym for "a *hypothesis,*" so listen carefully.) Today, any set of scientific ideas referred to as "the *theory* of..." is a well-tested and well-established understanding of an underlying mechanism or process. Such a *theory* can never be proved to be complete and final—that is why we no longer call it a "law." However, it is the same kind of well-tested set of rules, with an established area of applicability, as the older ideas called "laws."[10]

In essence, a theory is a representation of the world that has been confirmed to be reasonably true, valuable, and valid. Some theories (and some models) are better than others; some are very specific to particular situations, whereas others are broad or even universal. Theories and "those hoping to be theories" (i.e., models) represent an aspect of our world or a methodology to improve our world through a structured process grounded in language and approaches of the scientific method used by scholars and theorists. At the next lower level, theories (as well as models) integrate and combine constructs.

Constructs

The building blocks of theory are constructs. In our proposed conceptual model building, constructs are visualized as circles. It is critical to the study of organizational behavior to have a clear understanding of what a construct is. Failing to have a clear understanding of constructs will

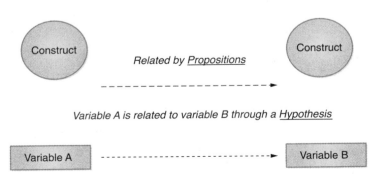

FIGURE B-3 Conceptual model of theory physiology.

result in an inability to understand many important leadership concepts.

By definition, a construct is a latent variable that lacks empiricism (taste, touch, see, smell, hear). Elements that are empirical have tangible, physical properties; for example, an apple possesses empiricism insofar as it can be tasted, touched, seen, and smelled. It does not matter that the apple does not make *noise*. Because an apple possesses attributes related to four of the five empirical senses, we can say that an apple is not a construct because it can be rationalized through empirical properties. Any physical element or property that can be described through at least one of the five senses does not qualify technically as a construct.

Said another way, a construct is an organizing device that captures a topic, subject area, or smaller and specific theory or model within a larger theory or model. For example, communication is a construct within a larger leadership theory. Constructs organize and combine multiple variables that are closely linked into one grouping or subheading within the structure of the theory or model. The critical feature of constructs derives from the term *closely linked*. Constructs must make sense in relation to the real world; thus they must have ecological validity.

Constructs, then, are the basic building blocks for grouping variables within a model or theory. It is commonplace to see the term *concept* associated with constructs. A concept is a method of organizing or categorizing an abstract topic or reality under a construct. A concept should be linked logically to the construct. A group of concepts under a construct must have cohesion that is logical or holds

true to reality (ecological validity). Concepts, in essence, are either variables or constants. Variables and constants are located at the lowest level within the organization of the construct.

Another classic example of a construct is the term *quality*. Quality is a construct that cannot be discussed without identifying it through other measurable properties or variables. The well-known statement, "Quality is in the eye of the beholder," generalizes the difficult problem we have describing quality. Other latent variables, such as health, love, happiness, pain, efficiency, effectiveness, performance, satisfaction, organizational survival, leadership, success, and motivation, are all examples of constructs. What makes constructs difficult to study is that different people may have different opinions of how to define them. Providers encounter this issue frequently when trying to understand a patient's level and tolerance for "pain." Pain is clearly a construct (or said another way, a personal concept and/or belief) that is difficult to communicate, may not be visible to another person, and clearly is perceived differently by different age groups. Although adults may have greater success in describing pain to a provider in regard to how it affects activities of daily living (ADLs), as well as frequency and duration of pain, children have less of a vocabulary and experience with describing pain. As a result, many pediatricians use a model called the pain rating scale (**Figure B-4**).[11]

As you can see, the model describes the concept of pain using a 10-point scale. Associated with the scale are emoticons. Studies have shown that children as young as

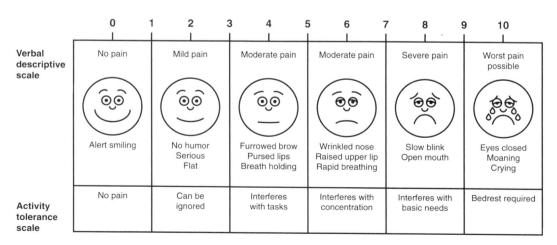

This pain assessment tool is intended to help patient care providers assess pain according to individual patient needs. Explain and use 0–10 scale for patient self-assessment. Use the faces or behavioral observations to interpret expressed pain when patient cannot communicate his/her pain intensity.

FIGURE B-4 Pain rating scale.

4 years old can associate levels of happiness and sadness using emoticons in a manner more consistent with their peers than they can using ordinary language. This example shows how the use of modeling in health care is essential for standardizing relatively simple concepts (like pain) between a patient and a provider. Unfortunately, many other communication efforts dealing with constructs in leadership are not as easily modeled and accepted. As a result, it is often necessary for health leaders to develop standardized models and measures in order to communicate exact intent.

Next we present a universal technique for communicating leadership constructs. We do this by defining constructs with empirical properties we call variables and measures.

VARIABLES

Flowing from constructs are variables. In model building we use rectangles to visually depict a variable. A variable is "a property associated with a concept that varies when measured."[12] Variables are also empirical units that can be identified through one of the five senses. Accordingly, a variable is an element that has precise meaning in the physical world. Generally, variables are universally understood and easily described. *Weight* is a good example of a variable. When discussing weight with peers or colleagues, universally understood concepts of pounds, ounces, or tons are immediately recognized as valid descriptors of weight. If a variable is incapable of being defined with a generalized descriptor, it may cause problems in communication with leadership peers. Take, for example, a colleague who suggests that her new china cabinet is very "heavy." Based on this description alone, can we accurately describe the weight of the cabinet, or do we need more information? How about a provider who suggests that he just encountered a "large customer" at the pharmacy. "Large" might mean physically obese, tall, or perhaps even muscular. For this reason, variables by themselves are not adequate to communicate concepts in leadership and model building.

The notion of "something that can be measured, and whose measurement can vary or change" is the essence of a variable. An example of a common variable in the health professions is patient body type, which is a variable that can be described by both height and weight. *Height* can be measured, yet varies by person, as does weight. In contrast, a constant is a property that "does not vary";[13] it is unchanging. Variables are essential to leadership theory confirmation through model and hypothesis testing because they are the properties or items that are tested to see whether the theory is confirmed. The importance of variables is that they vary; they change so that empirical testing can be accomplished. If the model is full of constants that do not vary, how could

you test whether the model is true to reality? Moreover, how could such a model help someone to be a better leader if everything stayed the same?

CONSTANTS

Constants are those concepts that do not vary; however, depending on what you are studying, a concept may be either a constant or a variable. An example would be the study of prostate cancer: Would gender be a variable or a constant in this study? Although gender is important, only males get prostate cancer. Given that gender would not vary, it is a constant in this example. High-risk pregnancy would be another example where gender would not vary, because only females would be included in the study. In contrast, in a population-based heart disease study, gender could vary, because each observation could be either male or female; thus gender would be a variable in this situation. The variable—gender in this case—would be a nominal, mutually exclusive, and categorically exhaustive (you can be either male or female, but not both, and you have to be one or the other) variable that could vary. Many times the situation or context dictates whether a concept is a variable or a constant.

OPERATIONALIZATION

Each variable has an operational definition and an operational process for measurement. An operational definition is the exact description of the conceptual property—the variable—under empirical study:

> An operational definition identifies one or more specific observable conditions [or characteristics] or events and then tells the researcher how to measure that event. Typically, there are several operational definition possibilities for variables and values. The operation chosen will often have an immediate impact on the course of the research, especially the findings.[14]

The operational process for measurement is important because it lists the steps in the measurement of the variable as it is operationally defined. Some variables are observed and measured with a tape measure or ruler (such as height); some are categorized (such as shirt size being small, medium, or large); still others use survey measurement (such as conflict management styles). This brings us to the important construct of measurement.

MEASURES

Derived from variables are operationalized measures—that is, operationalized descriptions of variables that must be capable of numerical identification. Operationalizing is the process of quantifying a variable using appropriate, numerical, descriptive terms. Additionally, measures must be universally understood and are classically categorized as continuous (1 to *n*, with *n* equal to infinity), dichotomous or binary (e.g., yes or no; on or off), or categorical (e.g., Caucasian, African American, Latino, multiracial). If measures are incapable of being operationalized through continuous, dichotomous, or categorical identification, the measure may not have enough precise significance to be valid in describing or testing the theoretical model under study.

Another aspect of measurement is numbering taxonomy. Measurements can be categorized into four distinct types (a taxonomy): nominal, ordinal/categorical, interval, and ratio (discussed later in this section). Each type of number has distinct properties associated with it. For example, if you asked a health leader how many subordinates he or she leads, you could get four different answers based on the numbering taxonomy employed; all four answers would be true and correct. If you asked, "Do you have more than 10 subordinates?" you could get a yes or no (nominal) answer. If you asked, "Which group best describes your number of subordinates: 5 or fewer, 6 to 10, 11 to 15, 16 to 20, and so on," you would get a categorical answer. If you asked, "How many subordinates do you lead exactly?" you could get an answer of 17. If you had no subordinates then you would have ratio data (from the taxonomy) because ratio data require an absolute zero. Depending on the number taxonomy used, data can be changed. You can go down the numbering taxonomy, such as from ratio to ordinal/categorical, but you cannot group or change data to go up the taxonomy, as nominal data cannot ever be changed to

interval or ratio data once nominal data are the only data captured. With an answer of 17 subordinates, you could group the data (16 to 20) or categorize the answer into the "yes, more than 10" grouping; however, you cannot manipulate the data from a yes or no answer into a hierarchical group or a pure number.

Why not always use exact numbers? There are two reasons:

- Some variables are not exact, but rather are inherently hierarchically grouped (e.g., place in a race) or categorical (e.g., gender).
- It tends to cost more in resources, time, money, attention, and materials to obtain precision or higher-order data such as interval or ratio taxonomical data.

As already mentioned, the four types of number taxonomy data are nominal, ordinal, interval, and ratio.[15,16] Interval and ratio data are frequently identified as "continuous" data in the literature. Of note, ratio data can be transformed into interval, ordinal, or nominal data; interval data can be transformed into ordinal or nominal data; and ordinal data can be transformed into nominal data. Nominal data, however, cannot be transformed. A researcher can transform data down the taxonomy (ratio down to nominal), but never up the taxonomy. **Table B-1** presents the distinctions of each type of numbering taxonomy.

Variables should be capable of several different methods of operationalization. For example, the variable *age* can be operationalized as a continuous, categorical, or binary variable, depending on how the researcher chooses to define and measure this variable. The following section discusses this process in more detail.

Table B-1 Number Taxonomy Measures

Type	Definition	Scale Transformation
Nominal	Codes are assigned as labels to observations and are mutually exclusive and categorically exhaustive, such as gender (male = 1, female = 2). Also known as categorical or binary variables.	One-to-one, where each observation assigned a label code must be recoded as a group
Ordinal	Numbers coded to observations are in rank or sequential order, such as the result of a race (e.g., first, second, third place).	Monotonic increasing or decreasing as long as order is maintained
Interval	A quantitative score is given to an observation where the interval between scores holds meaning (e.g., observation B is 2 times as much as observation A, observation C is 3¼ less than observation D). Examples include height in meters or temperature on a Celsius scale.	Positive linear
Ratio	Observations are given a quantitative score as in the interval scale number, but an absolute zero is possible (e.g., on the Kelvin temperature scale).	Positive similarities such as multiplication

Operationalizing Measures

To operationalize the variable *age*, we first must associate the variable with a specific unit of analysis (such as an organization, a team, or an individual). Next, we create a brief definition of the variable *age* that supports the unit of analysis under study; for example, we may say that age is defined as the number of years associated with a human individual's life. This statement includes two important features. First, it qualifies age in terms of years. Second, it provides a reference group for age, where a potential range for a life span is universally understood. Given this information, it becomes possible to operationalize age in several different ways: (1) as a continuous variable (interval or ratio data); (2) as a binary (nominal) variable; and (3) as a hierarchical group variable (ordinal), as illustrated in **Table B-2**.

In Table B-2, we arbitrarily established cutoff points for categorical and dichotomous variables that help support the issue under study. The categorical description of age also could have been classified using quarter-century marks or 5-year increments. The selection of a category is up to the executive analyzing the data. Finally, if the executive is interested in partitioning age-eligible Medicare recipients from those not eligible for Medicare, setting a break point at age 65 provides an opportunity to analyze the two different groups.

Measurement is vital to empirical assessment and evaluation, and measurements taken must be both reliable and valid. *Reliability* is the "consistency of an operationalized measure."[17] This concept applies to both the measurement apparatus or method and the person or machine doing the measuring. *Validity* focuses on the notion of measuring what is intended to be measured. An unreliable measure is also invalid, whereas an invalid measure can still be reliable—that is, you can measure the wrong thing correctly with repetitive and consistent results. Within the concept of validity, specific kinds of validity are distinguished:

- *Face validity* refers to whether a measure, on its face, seems to be related to the concept that is presumably being measured.

- *Predictive validity* refers to whether a new measure of something has the same predictive relationship with something else that the old measure had.
- *Convergent validity* refers to whether two different measures of presumably the same thing are consistent with each other—whether they converge to give the same measurement.
- *Criterion validity* is a test of a measure when the measure has several different parts or indicators in it—compound measures. Each part, or criterion, of the measure should have a relationship with all the parts in the measure for the variable to which the first measure is related in a hypothesis.
- *Content validity* tests whether the measure has sufficient content [does it cover or contain enough measurement of the property or characteristic] in it to be acceptable.[18]

Not all variables lend themselves to operationalized measures through all three metrics. For example, the variable *racial category* does not lend itself to a continuous measure. The most appropriate nomenclature for race is a category, where the researcher selects racial categories of interest in the study for analysis.

The process of operationalizing measures is critically important in the business world and in the health industry. A requirement to gather, manage, and measure outcomes from data implies a continuous process. Before data can be collected and analyzed, however, they must be operationalized in a consistent and logical manner. The Balanced Scorecard developed by Kaplan and Norton is an example of a quality-oriented tool that requires executives to select and define not only constructs of interest to measure, but also valid and reliable variables capable of identification through operationalized measures that provide meaningful data for trend analysis.[19]

The last step in operationalizing variables is the construction of a code sheet. Whenever variables are tested in a hypothetical relationship, it is not the variables themselves that are actually tested, but rather the operationalized units of the variables. This step is a necessary precursor to loading data into a statistical software program such as SPSS, SAS, Minitab, or Excel. When we operationalize data for statistical software manipulation, we create code sheets and coding methodology.

A code sheet is a very simple explanation of how operationalized units of a variable will be used in the study. The researcher must keep in mind the assumptions of the test when building a code sheet. For example, parametric and nonparametric tests require different assumptions, which should be incorporated into the code sheet. Although numerous examples of building code sheets are available that

---

Table B-2 Operationalized Variable: Age

Age is defined as the number of years associated with a human individual's life.
Continuous (interval or ratio data): 1 to *n* (e.g., 105)
Hierarchical group or category (ordinal data): 0–10, 11–20, 21–30, 31–40, 41–50, 51–60, 61–70, 71–80, 81–90, 91–100, *n* > 101
Binary (nominal data): Medicare age eligible? Yes or No (Medicare eligibility = 65 years of age or older)

Table B-3 Example Code Sheet for the Variable Education

Label	Description	Operationalized
Education	Highest education degree obtained by member	Taxonomy = Ordinal 1 = High school degree 2 = Associate's degree 3 = Bachelor's degree 4 = Master's degree 5 = JD (law degree) 6 = MD (medical degree) 7 = PhD (doctorate)

demonstrate how data may be operationalized in a study, **Table B-3** provides one proven example of success—in this case, a code sheet is created for the variable *education*.

A MODEL OF HEALTH

Leaders in the health professions will most certainly discuss the construct of *health* on a daily basis. **Figure B-5** presents a conceptual model of health that should look relatively familiar. As we have discussed, health is a concept (i.e., construct) that has numerous meanings to several different brackets of patients. For example, an 82-year-old male of average weight and height may describe being *healthy* in a very different manner than an 18-year-old male of average weight and height. How might a provider standardize these two definitions of health status in a manner that provides meaning across a population of patients? We can do this easily with the modeling of constructs, variables, and measures. Although it may be seamless to a patient, a provider collects variable and measurement information on a patient with each and every encounter.

Let us consider your last visit to your healthcare provider. During this encounter your provider collected variable information such as height, weight, heart rate, blood pressure, and body mass index. Your provider also may have collected blood to evaluate your cholesterol level and blood sugar. All of this variable information is then operationalized and measured in a manner that is consistent within the health profession. Based on the operationalized information gathered from the measurements, your provider can present a universally accepted and well-understood concept of the construct of *health*. For example, the following are two outcomes for measuring health from two patient encounters:

> *Example 1:* A 91-year-old white female presents to the provider. She is 5'2", 250 pounds, has a blood pressure of 220/140, and presents with an above average heart rate (tachycardia). Blood work confirms high blood sugar and high cholesterol.
>
> *Example 2:* A 24-year-old Latino male presents to the provider. He is 5'9", 170 pounds, has a blood pressure of 120/70, and presents with a normal heartbeat. Lab results suggest normal levels of cholesterol and blood sugar.

Based on these two examples, which patient is in better "health"? Furthermore, which patient might require follow-up tests and/or education to achieve a "greater level of health" over a period of time?

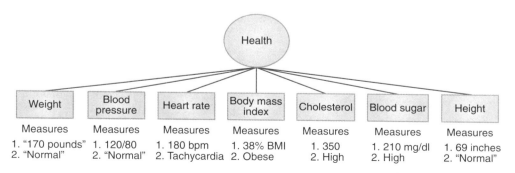

FIGURE B-5 Conceptual model of health using constructs as circles, variables as rectangles, and measures as operationalized units.

Construct, variable, and measurement information is collected by a variety of stakeholders in the health professions all the time.[20,21] Leaders collect similar types of information when evaluating issues such as employee performance and productivity. Such information may be used later in rating an employee for annual merit raises and/or promotion. Similar organization metrics can be collected by leaders to measure organizational productivity, efficiency, effectiveness, and success.

KEY RELATIONSHIPS: LEADERSHIP MODELS TO THEORIES TO ACCEPTED THEORIES

As noted earlier in this chapter, a theory has undergone scientific and practical scrutiny, albeit at various levels of intensity, to determine its value, truth, and validity. In contrast, a model has not yet met a level of academic and practical scrutiny for scientific validation, so its value is yet to be determined. Both theories and models require ecological validity—that is, the ability to represent and present reality well—for scholars and practitioners to study and utilize them. Once a leadership model achieves the designation of a theory, however, how is the theory justified and placed within the greater context of leadership studies and understanding? There is no perfect answer to this question, although the system of evaluation presented here is ecologically valid:

> The word "criteria" is the plural of the term "criterion." A criterion is a standard of judgment such as an examination score of 85% is a grade of "B" or 95% is a grade of "A." Here are five criteria that are generally used when comparing theories, and a new theory satisfying these will then replace a previously accepted theory.

1. The previously accepted theory gives an acceptable explanation of something so the new theory must give the same results;
2. New theory explains something that the previously accepted theory either got wrong or, more commonly, did not apply;
3. The new theory makes a prediction that is later verified;
4. The new theory is elegant, has aesthetic quality, is simple, [is] powerful, and includes universal symmetries that are simple, easy to remember or apply, and/or are expressed as some symmetry of nature,

and/or are powerful enough to be used in many applications; and
5. Provide a deeper insight or link to another branch of knowledge.[22]

DESCRIPTIVE AND PRESCRIPTIVE LEADERSHIP MODELS REVISITED: A CONCEPTUAL MODEL OF A LEADERSHIP THEORY ON MOTIVATION

Leadership theories and models can be descriptive, prescriptive, or both descriptive and prescriptive. Descriptive theories and models illustrate, define, and capture the description of leadership phenomena but do not recommend or prescribe actions, behaviors, or processes to employ. Prescriptive theories and models provide recommendations to the leader practitioner with regard to actions, behaviors, or processes to employ in order to be a successful leader. Some leadership theories and models both describe and prescribe.

As an example, let us explore an application of a leadership theory—in this case, a motivational theory introduced by Edwin Locke—to measure organizational outcomes such as satisfaction and performance and investigate this theory's connection to other motivational theories. As you read about Locke's theory, try to list the constructs, concepts, and variables from this leadership motivational theory.

Goal-setting theory[23] was first introduced by Edwin A. Locke in 1968, when he published the classic article "Toward a Theory of Task Motivation and Incentives" in the journal *Organizational Behavior and Human Performance*. Since the late 1960s, considerable attention has been given to applying goal-setting theory in industry and management situations. Locke, along with other contributors such as Gary Latham, performed laboratory and field experiments; the most widely publicized were field studies conducted in the 1970s in conjunction with the logging industry.[24] During the past few decades, Locke's emphasis has focused on the area of applied goal-setting theory with regard to improved performance in complex business tasks. In 1992, Locke and others studied the relationship between goal-setting and expectancy theory.[25] Studies over the past 35 or more years were performed in an effort to learn more about the potential for improving performance by using goal setting as a motivational technique.

This theory can be disassembled into constructs, concepts, and variables. (Try to list or draw the elements of this theory on your own.) First, Locke's basic assumptions and ideas are important to understand.

Goals are the aim of an action or behavior. Goals can be set for any verifiable or measurable outcome. Locke's basic assumption is that goals are immediate regulators of human action.[26] An individual synthesizes *direction*, *effort*, and *persistence* to accomplish goals. To maximize goal setting, *specific and challenging goals are set to focus action and effort over time to accomplish tasks*. From 1968 to 1980, 90% of studies showed that specific, well-defined, and challenging goals led to greater improved performance than did vague and easy goals.[27-32] Individuals must commit to set goals to produce results; the more difficult (challenging yet reasonable) the goal, the better the individual will perform. Individuals need management support (feedback, reward mechanisms, and required resources [time, training, and material goods]) to maximize performance when applying goal setting.[33] To apply this theory, Locke suggests seven steps[34] to follow to optimize goal setting:

1. Specify objectives or tasks to be done.
2. Specify how performance will be measured.
3. Specify the standard to be reached.
4. Specify the time frame involved.
5. Prioritize goals.
6. Rate goals as to difficulty and importance.
7. Determine the coordination requirements.

Managers must ensure they set goals that do not conflict with each other or conflict with organizational goals. For groups, every group member should have verifiable specific goals, as well as a group goal to counter the tendency toward "social loafing." Smaller groups (three to eight people) are more effective than larger ones. Potential negative issues related to this theory include excessive risk taking, excessive competition, and goal failure, all of which can diminish members' confidence and create unwanted stress. A graphic illustration, like that shown in **Figure B-6**, should assist in understanding this theory.

Can you list the constructs, variables, and process of goal-setting theory? How would you operationalize the variables? How would you measure them if you conducted a study to see how goal setting works in a healthcare organization?

Goal-setting theory is readily integrated with other motivational theories as well. Although goal setting is a principal attribute of many motivational and performance theories, recent research has largely focused on locus of control theory influences and expectancy theory relationships. Locus of control theory suggests that people acquire motivation either through an internal catalyst (internalizers) or via an external catalyst (externalizers). Integration of goal-setting theory with locus of control theory has revealed that internalizers tend to have better performance than externalizers.[35] Both of these theories also relate very well to expectancy theory, in that the goals we set are based on the outcomes we hope to achieve.

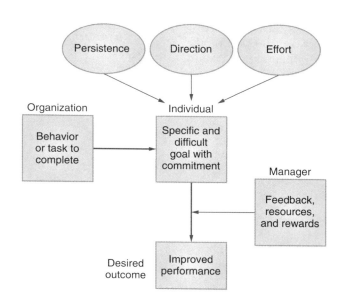

FIGURE B-6 Goal-setting theory.

Another motivational theory, expectancy theory, may be integrated with goal-setting theory in that goal setting is negatively related to valence (setting low goals does not satisfy individuals as well as setting high goals), and instrumentality is positively related to goal setting (achieving difficult goals gives the individual a greater sense of achievement, self-efficacy, and skill improvement than achieving easy goals).[36] To illustrate the connection of goal-setting theory to expectancy theory, the following summary is provided. Can you see how the constructs relate?

Expectancy theory was developed by Victor Vroom in 1964. This theory combines motivation and the process of leadership.[37] With expectancy theory, subordinate behavior and action are seen as the result of the subordinate making conscious choices among alternatives such as a reward or no reward. Constructs of this theory are valence, expectancy, and instrumentality. Valence concerns the affective/emotional orientations that subordinates have regarding rewards based on outcomes; this construct focuses on the extent to which the subordinate has extrinsic motivation (see Herzberg's two-factor theory or hygiene theory; extrinsic motivation refers to money, promotion, time off, or some other external reward) or intrinsic motivation (e.g., satisfaction, self-esteem, self-efficacy). Leaders must understand which type of reward will best motivate the subordinate, given his or her wants and needs. Expectancy is the subordinate's expectations, confidence, knowledge, skills, and abilities to perform a task or action. Leaders should remove barriers and enhance resources appropriately to allow the subordinate to perform to his or her maximum ability. Instrumentality is the perception of the subordinate concerning receiving the reward for the task or action performed based on the resulting outcome. Leaders should fulfill promises to subordinates; that is, leaders should reward subordinates for their performance outcomes.

A formula for this theory would be

Motivation = Valence × Expectancy (Instrumentality)

Expectancy theory is closely tied to social exchange theory and the transactional leadership model. **Figure B-7** illustrates its major precepts.

Which constructs make up goal-setting theory? Clearly, persistence, direction or focus, effort, and performance are constructs. Also, managerial feedback, resources and rewards, and organizational behaviors and tasks are constructs. Concepts from each construct may be identified, such as time on task and attention, and then operationally defined as variables. Because each variable observation changes or varies, the total model is evaluated against performance. Can you operationally define the variables that make up the concepts of the constructs of goal-setting theory? How would you operationally define the variables of this theory? Could you operationally define the variables of goal-setting theory and expectancy theory to merge these theories into a larger model? Can you synthesize goal-setting theory, expectancy theory, and the theory of planned behavior (see **Figure B-8**)? Review the graphics from the three theories and think about where constructs of the theories connect. Do any of the constructs in the three frameworks contradict other constructs? If there is contradiction, can you resolve the tension between constructs? What variables could you operationalize and measure? Would the variables move in one direction or both directions (increase and decrease)? What hypotheses could you develop based on the movement of the variables?

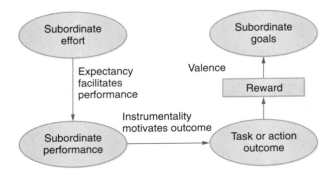

FIGURE B-7 Expectancy theory.

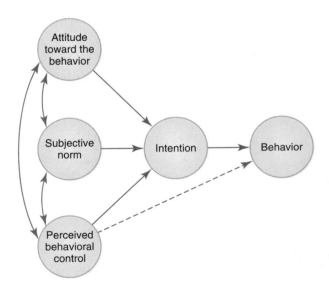

FIGURE B-8 Theory of planned behavior.

Reproduced from Ajzen, I. (1991). The theory of planned behavior. *Organizational Behavior and Human Decision Processes, 50,* 179–211, with permission from Elsevier.

SUMMARY

This chapter presented the underlying fundamentals of theory. A brief overview and definition of theory was presented, followed by a dissection of a theory into its components—constructs, concepts, variables and constants, and measures. Measurement, reliability, validity, and number taxonomy were discussed as well. Visual and graphical tools were used to illustrate how a conceptual model and a theory measure specific outcomes based on leadership principles. Understanding the process of building empirically measurable healthcare and leadership theories and models may be one of the more underrated aspects of leader development in the health system today. The knowledge and ability needed to build conceptual models of leadership and evaluate existing leadership theories and models based on measurement of outcomes of those theories will prove valuable.

DISCUSSION QUESTIONS

1. Why is the study of theory important in the study of leadership in health organizations?
2. What examples can you give in relation to health or leadership to define and distinguish the basic elements and relationships of a theory that can be applied to this field?
3. How would you apply goal-setting theory's constructs and variables in an organizational setting? How would you apply operational variables to your answer? How about expectancy theory?
4. Distinguish conceptual models from theory.
5. How could you design a simple model of leadership principles or applications? Summarize the relationships between the model's theoretical elements and the application of leadership principles.
6. Critique the social sciences' use of theory within the context of leadership as a discipline.

EXERCISES

1. Review the discussion of goal-setting theory and expectancy theory in this chapter, and list the theories, constructs, and variables associated with those theories.
2. Summarize the social sciences hierarchy of a theory or model, and explain how this hierarchy works in terms of hypothesis testing.
3. Using the health industry as a context, modify goal-setting theory by incorporating an additional construct with at least two variables, operationally define the variables, and show how you would measure the variables, including the type of number taxonomy used.
4. Break down, diagram, and label your modified goal-setting model. Write a paragraph explaining how your model differs from the original theory proposed by Locke and Latham.
5. Select two of the following articles or those provided by your instructor. Categorize each construct and variable studied and/or discussed in that article. Next, reorganize the constructs and variables into one model and operationally define each variable and how it is to be measured.
   a. Calhoun, J. G., Dollett, L., Sinioris, M. E., Wainio, J. A., Butler, P. W., Griffith, J. R.,
   & Warden, G. L. (2008). Development of an interprofessional competency model for healthcare leadership. *Journal of Healthcare Management*, *53*(6), 375–389.
   b. Bartling, C. (1996). Leadership for the information age. *Association Management*, *46*(8), 61–66.
   c. Church, A. H., & Waclawski, J. (1998). The relationship between individual personality orientation and executive leadership behavior. *Journal of Occupational and Organizational Psychology*, *71*(part 2), 99–125.
   d. Chambers, H. (1999). The agencies of leadership. *Executive Excellence*, *16*(8), 12.
   e. Dering, N. (1998). Leadership in quality organizations. *Journal of Quality and Participation*, *21*(1), 32–35.
   f. Kent, T., Johnson, J. A., & Graber, D. A. (1996). Leadership in the formation of new health care environments. *Health Care Supervisor*, *15*(2), 27–34.
6. A coworker comes back from visiting a new primary care clinic that was recently built. You ask her how it went, and she replies, "I really liked it.

That is really a *high-quality* new primary care facility." Based on the modeling exercises presented in this chapter, construct a conceptual model of *high quality* for the primary care clinic that presents no less than three variables and two measures for each variable in your word picture. Be sure to use good operationalization techniques. Appraise, conclude, and justify how the variables in your model will vary, and hypothesize what will cause the variables to vary or change.

REFERENCES

1. Bass, B. (1990). *Bass & Stogdill's handbook of leadership: Theory, research and managerial applications* (3rd ed.). New York: Free Press.
2. Stevens, D. (2009). Man on the moon. Retrieved from http://dcstevens1.wordpress.com/2009/10/21/man-on-the-moon/.
3. Smoot, G. (n.d.). Scientific theory or model. Retrieved from http://aether.lbl.gov/www/classes/p10/theory.html.
4. Kerlinger, F. N. (1986). *Foundations of behavioral research* (3rd ed.). New York: Holt, Rinehart, and Winston.
5. Kerlinger, F. N. (1979). *Behavioral research: A conceptual approach*. New York: Holt, Rinehart, and Winston.
6. Jary, D., & Jary, J. (1995). The transformations of Anthony Giddens: The continuing story of structuration theory. *Theory, Culture and Society, 12*(2), 141–160.
7. Jary, D., & Jary, J. (1995). *Dictionary of sociology.* Glasgow/New York: HarperCollins.
8. Smoot, note 3.
9. Coppola, M. N. (2008). Anatomy and physiology of theory. In J. A. Johnson (Ed.), *Health organizations: Theory, behavior, and development* (pp. 9–28). Sudbury, MA: Jones and Bartlett.
10. SLAC, National Accelerator Laboratory, Stanford University. (n.d.). Research. Retrieved from http://www6.slac.stanford.edu/research/.
11. Graham, R. B. (2012). The purpose of pain scales. Retrieved from http://www.intelihealth.com/IH/ihtIH/WSIHW000/29721/32087.html.
12. Botsch, B. (2008). APLS 301 scope and research methods in political science: Concepts, variables, and measurement. Retrieved from http://www.usca.edu/polisci/apls301/concepts.htm.
13. Botsch, note 12.
14. Yee, W. S. L. (n.d.) Inter-observer reliability: Sniffy's behaviours. Retrieved from https://docs.google.com/a/kaplan.edu/document/d/1HJojbHJx408Gk5W7-47sFAjBaXHkzQkREHI0uIfvJGY/preview.
15. Stevens, S. (1951). Mathematics, measurement and psychophysics. In S. Stevens (Ed.), *Handbook of experimental psychology* (pp. 1–49). New York: Wiley.
16. Stevens, S. (1946). On the theory of scales of measurement. *Science, 103*, 677–680.
17. Botsch, note 12.
18. Botsch, note 12.
19. Kaplan, R. S., & Norton, D. P. (1992). The balanced scorecard: Measures that drive performance. *Harvard Business Review, 70*(1), 71–79.
20. Coppola, M. N., Ledlow, G. R., & Fulton, L. (2010, September 7–9). Understanding the language of healthcare. Texas Organization of Rural and Community Health (TORCH) Annual Conference.
21. Coppola, M. N., & Ledlow, G. R. (2012, October). Innovations in teaching health communication. Faculty Development Session, Texas Tech University Health Sciences Center.
22. Smoot, note 3.
23. Locke, E. A. (1968, May). Toward a theory of task motivation and incentives. *Organizational Behavior and Human Performance*, 157–189.
24. Latham, G. P., & Locke, E. A. (1979). Goal-setting: A motivational technique that works. *Organizational Dynamics, 8*(2), 68–80.
25. Mento, A. J., Locke, E. A., & Klein, H. J. (1992). Relationship of goal level to valence and instrumentality. *Journal of Applied Psychology, 77*(4), 395–405.
26. Locke, note 23.
27. Ivancevich, J. M., & Matteson, M. T. (1993). *Organizational behavior and management*. Burr Ridge, IL: Richard D. Irwin.
28. Locke, E. A., Shaw, K. N., Saari, L. M., & Latham, G. P. (1981). Goal setting and task performance: 1969–1980. *Psychological Bulletin, 90*(1), 125–152.
29. Locke, E. A., Gist, M. E., & Taylor, M. S. (1987). Organizational behavior: Group structure, process, and effectiveness. *Journal of Management, 13*(2), 237–257.
30. Locke, E. A., & Chesney, A. A. (1991). Relationships among goal difficulty, business strategies, and

performance on a complex management simulation task. *Academy of Management Journal, 34*(2), 400–424.

31. Locke, E. A. (1986). *Generalizing from laboratory to field settings.* Lexington, MA: Lexington Books.

32. Locke, E. A., & Latham, G. P. (1984). *Goal setting: A motivational technique that works!* Englewood Cliffs, NJ: Prentice Hall.

33. Locke & Latham, note 32.

34. Locke & Latham, note 32.

35. Locke et al., note 28.

36. Mento et al., note 25.

37. 12Manage. (n.d.). Expectancy theory (Vroom). Retrieved from http://www.12manage.com/methods _vroom_expectancy_theory.html.

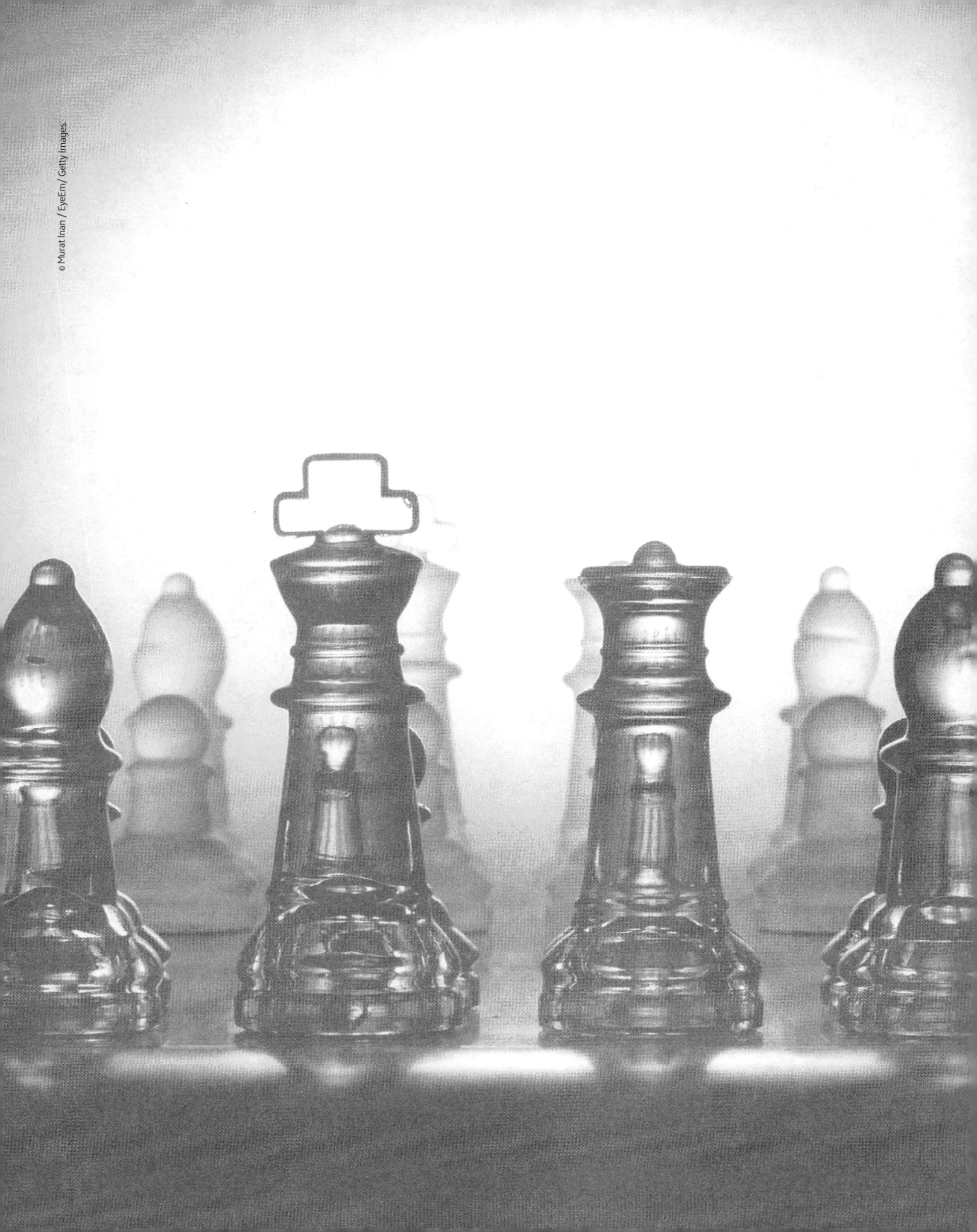
© Murat Inan / EyeEm/ Getty Images.

Appendix C

The Omnibus Leadership Model by Dr. M. Nicholas Coppola

THE OMNIBUS LEADERSHIP MODEL[1]

In 1905, the world-famous Carnegie Museum of Natural History placed the bones of a prized *Apatosaurus* on review. The bones remained on display until 1992, when the fossil was reexamined by a different team of paleontologists. These late-century paleontologists noticed that the dinosaur had been assembled incorrectly and that the wrong head had been placed on the dinosaur almost 90 years earlier.[2] Over the course of the twentieth century, hundreds (perhaps thousands) of scholars and academics had viewed the bones and admired the symmetry and perfection of the fossil—never noticing the 90-year-old error the original paleontologists had made. No one ever questioned whether the fossil has been assembled incorrectly or whether this world-famous museum had made an error. On the contrary, because the museum itself stood as an authoritarian benchmark of quality and distinction, it is quite possible that many other museums, paleontologists, and scholars had used this fossil as a standard on which other scholarly ventures were based. It was a profound error, and one that took nearly three generations of scholars to correct.

Given the weighty nature of this mistake, and the overall humor in placing a wrong head on a skeleton, your authors would like to use this example as a starting point from which to explore the possibility that the study of leadership is likewise suffering from an ancient error in construction. We propose that (in some cases) the study of leadership has become a calculus formula that has become memorized, but never derived. By this we mean that for generations younger scholars have been presented with information that is suggested to be true, but may more likely be a strongly supported opinion.

It has been suggested that there are as many methods to define leadership as there are ways to measure it. From a research perspective, this flexibility is often very beneficial, because the purpose of research is to look at things in increasing levels of complexity, with the ultimate goal of discerning intricate parts of the puzzle. But is it possible that, in the literature of leadership theory, the level of complexities has become so intricate that the larger picture is no longer visible? A review of leadership theory suggests the possibility that the answer to this question is "yes."

Furthermore, is it possible that the study of leadership has suffered from theory creep? The original conception of creep is attributed to former U.S. Secretary of Defense Casper Weinberger, who suggested that *creep* is the absence of a uniform vision, and who noted that this condition results in constant change.[3] The end product of creep results in people solving problems that have no relationship to the original project or process at all. In other words, *the wrong fight is fought.*

The study of leadership theory may have also suffered from theoretical creep. A review of leadership theories in the twentieth century suggests leadership studies have shifted from the broad and wide-ranging trait and "great man" theories to discriminate research efforts that reflect more of an application of unit models of decision making or satisfaction, rather than theory. Supporting this premise, some authors have suggested the problem with organizational theories is that the wrong unit of analysis is applied to inappropriate situations. Furthermore, many authors suggest previous studies may not be looking at leadership issues, but rather at evaluating supervisory and interpersonal characteristics.[4–9]

EARLY PRECEDENTS FOR MISAPPLIED THEORIES

Early anthropological and scientific literature was regularly flawed and full of assumptions and opinions often presumed to be fact until new insights came to light. A whimsical example is the "flat earth theory," which was largely abandoned after the invention of the telescope and the circumnavigation of the globe by early mariners. Other scientific research is less amusing and could produce harmful consequences.

For example, in the early 1900s through the 1930s, the practice of eugenics was accepted in the United States. An estimated 60,000 people were sterilized when researchers of the era suggested persons with disabilities were a menace to society and could not contribute to humanity.[10,11] Thirty-five states enforced eugenics-related laws, and the practice was endorsed by the U.S. Supreme Court in the 1927 *Buck v. Bell* decision, in which Justice Oliver Wendell Holmes declared that "three generations of imbeciles are enough."[12] Later, in the early 1940s, faulty research by the U.S. Army Air Corps supported previous research and literature that suggested African Americans were incapable of flying modern aircraft due to intelligence gaps as compared to their white counterparts.[13]

Situations in which new scientific theories replace older ones are constantly documented in the literature. Paleontologist Jack Horner of the Museum of the Rockies posits that *Tyrannosaurus rex* ("tyrant lizard king") could not have been a predator. Horner traced back the literature behind the naming of *T. rex* by its original discoverer, Henry Osborne, in 1905. Osborne speculated that *T. rex*'s big teeth and head must have been used in a predatory capacity. This assumption became a widely accepted, often cited, and frequently quoted part of paleontology literature for almost a century. Almost 100 years after the discovery, however, new scientific analysis of the skull and teeth suggested that *T. rex* was actually a scavenger.[14]

The organizational literature is likewise peppered with misnomers and reevaluated ideas. Weber's "Protestant work ethic" (PWE) posited that "work gives meaning to life."[15] This theory gained some popular support in early organizational literature, but examination of the literature by later scholars failed to find support for the PWE theory in contemporary literature. As early as 1990, Peter Drucker suggested that society is in need of many new models in leadership and management. "[The] old theories are feeling the weight of increasing complexities,"[16] he said.

In respect to this effort, earlier attempts to develop a uniform framework for effective leadership analysis have translated into significant academic challenges for researchers in this field. Although the term *leadership* is relatively new to the English language, the idea of leadership has existed for thousands of years. Researchers well recognize that certain individuals stand out from others in a group setting and ultimately direct the group to achieve a specific goal. These individuals have, for centuries, been recognized as leaders. Some such leaders may be associated with business or the military, whereas others become prominent politicians or social activists. Whatever the environmental setting may be, one fact is clear: There is little consensus on exactly what leadership is and which processes create an effective leader.[17]

Leadership is one of the most widely debated and broadly defined micro-organization theories within the realm of organizational behavior. As a result, the discussion of leadership and leaders has transcended traditional boundaries and is often incorrectly extended to describe behavior and phenomena associated with managers, supervisors, coaches, educators, celebrities, political representatives, inspirational personnel, sports figures, and subject matter experts. Despite the well-respected body of literature that distinctly separates leadership from other identifiers, the "leadership" label continues to be used to describe a plethora of activity in society.[18] The overuse and misuse of the term *leader* make it difficult to study the concept of leadership and differentiate the concept of "leaders" from managers, supervisors, and popular personality figures.

Because of this misapplication, the terms *leader* and *leadership* have dominated fashionable connotations associated with nonequivalent positions, resulting in a popularly accepted, though largely incorrect, hierarchy. According to this "pecking order," being a leader is better than being just a manager, supervisor, or subject matter expert. Being designated as a leader rather than a manager (or something else) results in an artificial perception of status, which translates into a "feel-good" perception for the individual. Perhaps this notion is in part associated with competition for the best employees and other cultural changes that have occurred within society in the last century. A review of classified ads in *The Washington Post* for senior-level healthcare personnel will turn up few vacancies for "business managers," but it will likely indicate that several positions for "industry leaders" are available.

As a result of these applications, leadership-, management-, and supervisory-related terms have become synonymous within the literature and society. Consequently, leadership constructs are no longer perceived as distinct and mutually exclusive. A review of the literature suggests there is no single construct unique to leadership theory. Researchers working within the leadership theory field are often forced to borrow from the abundance of micro-organizational theories in the discipline to explain phenomena associated with leadership theory.

In response to these propositions, a new model of leadership, originally developed by Coppola at the Army Medical Department Center and School, Academy of Health Sciences, Fort Sam Houston, Texas, is offered here for purposes of discussion, thought, and reflection.[19] This model takes into account constructs and concepts that many traditional models of leadership do not include. These items include higher order, environment, and individual culture composite elements.

Reviewing Leadership as a New Problem

The study of traditional leadership theory does not always study leadership itself, but rather the outcomes of leaders and the antecedent factors that constitute management practices. Several weaknesses are associated with the traditional leadership models that have been previously published. However, all models have potential for improvement. To begin with, few of the models attempt to define leadership theory before building models that explain the phenomena associated with it. For example, Yukl has suggested that there are at least seven (and perhaps many more) different definitions of leadership that can be found within the literature.[20–22] On which of the various definitions of leadership are the models based when they are tested? Without a uniform definition of leadership, and without agreement on measures and variables, outcomes are most certainly interpreted broadly.

The Euclidean management philosophies of the 1970s and 1980s, in which many of these leadership models have their roots, have since been replaced with more interactive, matrix-like, collaborative, and participatory-based models. These models were introduced to accommodate the paradigm shift in employee expectations, generational changes, and societal expectations (such as more women in the workforce) that has occurred in the last two to four decades. As a result, the application and study of leadership models have not kept pace with this paradigm shift in its totality.

Yukl's research exposes a wide variety of ideas on what constitutes leadership. The existing literature on leadership theory also promotes this definitional gap. Researchers have proposed a variety of theories: trait-based theories, transformational theories, contingency theories, and normative theories. The strength of these theoretical approaches lies in the fact that scholars generally accept them as reliable frameworks for evaluating distinct aspects of leadership. In reality, significant weaknesses exist because no one model can successfully explain all past behavior or predict all future behavior in an omnibus fashion. This differs from the study of constructs and measures in other academic fields. For example, scholars in the health field have regarded Donabedian's model of healthcare quality as a panacea for establishing a basis for any discussion of the subject in any health organization. Similarly, Mintzberg's typology for organizational analysis is a staple for deconstructing organizational hierarchical elements into manageable groups for efficiency and performance analysis.[23,24]

Brief Overview of Theory

In the mid-1980s, Samuel Bacharach, building on the earlier works of Popper, Kerlinger, and Duban, developed criteria for evaluating theory that have become the benchmark for modern theoretical assessment in organizational literature.[25–28] According to Bacharach, a theory is a statement of relationships among concepts within a set of boundary assumptions and constructs. In this system of constructs and variables, the constructs are related to one another by propositions and the variables are related to one another by hypotheses. As a result, theory is a linguistic device used to organize a complex empirical world.

Similarly, Kerlinger noted that the essence of hypothesis testing is to test the relationship expressed by the variables in the hypotheses, rather than to test the individual variables themselves. Unfortunately, a majority of the leadership literature is centered on testing unit variables such as task accomplishment and satisfaction rather than more broadly defined leadership constructs. Moreover, as discussed previously, the overwhelming majority of leadership studies focus primarily on the outcomes of management and not leadership. These traditions suggest that modern-day thinkers must redirect their efforts and concentrate on defining and testing leadership as a construct.

The New Model

Albert Einstein once said, "Nearly every great advance in science arises from a crisis in the old theory, through an endeavor to find a way out of the difficulties created; we must examine old ideas, old theories, although they belong to the past, for this is the only way to understand the importance of the new ones and the extent of their validity."[29] As suggested, Ledlow and Coppola defined leadership as the ability to assess, develop, maintain, and change organizational culture and strategic systems to optimally meet the needs and expectations of the external environment by moral means. With this definition in mind, some alternatives and suggestions for studying leadership from a theoretical perspective are offered here.

In response to the problems inherent in traditional leadership theory outlined, we posit a series of propositions using the framework developed by Coppola, Kerlinger, Whetten, and Wittgenstein,[30–33] which stipulates that propositions, or statements of opinion based on related facts, are true when describing relationships. The proposition technique allows relevant prose to coalesce around various arguments offered in the literature that lack empirical support. Following this analysis, semantic differential is used to place ideas of similar meaning into categories. The creation of these categories then allows for the presentation of simple sentences describing concepts. These concepts are then used as valid foundations for continuing the research stream. Although the statements may not always be exact, they are offered as reliable and trustworthy until additional research suggests otherwise or more definitive evidence of disconfirmation is provided. Research historically suggests that empirical evidence most often flows from the advancements of theory, qualitative analysis, and supposition.[34]

The proposed "omnibus leadership model," discussed later here, borrows from previous literature in the field and provides a different aperture for evaluating leaders and leadership theory based on the following propositions:

Proposition 1: Leadership theory has become analogous to a calculus formula that is memorized, but not derived.

In the past, leadership theories and models have followed a pattern similar to that of earlier defunct theories such as the "flat earth" theory and the theory of eugenics—namely, scholars and students memorized the theories and models and passed them on to future generations without ever studying the phenomena firsthand. Likewise, few students have ever done the mathematical calculations to derive the degrees associated with a circle and triangle; rather, they accept the notion that a circle is 360 degrees and the angles within a triangle add up to 180 degrees. We do not dispute these mathematical facts, but do take pause at the widespread acceptance without validation of some of the early leadership literature.

Proposition 2: Early models of leadership theory applied a managerial framework to the study of leadership that failed to correctly differentiate other disciplines from leadership.

Many of the early models of leadership looked at managerial outcomes and not the factors (i.e., constructs) influencing those outcomes for leadership.

Proposition 3: It is necessary to reevaluate leadership models to discern whether incorrect units of analyses or misapplied variables have been extended to the explanation of phenomena associated with leadership theory.

Although we do not suggest that all leader models are inherently incorrect or flawed, we do suggest that—similar to other theoretical disciplines that have acknowledged evolution in their discipline—the study of leadership is more a study of the validation of outcomes attributed to the leader or leadership team than forecasted issues coupled with actions or style selection. This requires prospective and retrospective assessment.

Proposition 4: The tautology of the terms leadership *and* leader *has allowed for the unarrested use and application of the theory in literature.*

The lack of a clear definition of leadership, combined with the lack of a clear understanding of what constitutes the construct of leadership, results in outcomes that do not maximize validity, reliability, and the ability to generalize across situations.

Proposition 5: Leadership theory lacks universally defined constructs and variables.

Dissimilar to the study of quality in health care, where Donabedian's framework has become a benchmark with which to frame results, or the study of evolution, where Darwin's Theory of Evolution dominates the landscape, scholars in the management sciences lack a clear signpost for acuity in the leadership field for study. This lack of grounding decreases consistency. In essence, leadership remains in a perpetual "theory building" cycle.

Proposition 6: Leadership theory lacks a defined conceptual model.

No one conceptual model stands out as a panacea for leadership study. This is dissimilar to the proposition offered by the U.S. Constitution, which clearly states that U.S. citizens have the "right to bear arms."

Proposition 7: Traditional leadership theories do not differentiate between leadership and dictatorship.

Leaders who are self-serving, and who also have an agenda for harm and misery, are often labeled as "leaders" because society is unable to place them into any other designation when considering traditional leadership models. Adolf Hitler and Osama bin Laden are only two examples; they are labeled "leaders" by default. Interestingly, the preponderance of the literature associated with Benito Mussolini describes the Italian ruler as "the Italian dictator" and not as a leader; this is unique in the literature of historical despots.

Why a New Model?

When applying traditional leadership models, Adolf Hitler might be described as an effective leader, or at least as someone who demonstrated leadership skills by successfully rebuilding Germany after World War I. A retrospective application of path–goal leadership theory might also justify this position. Without question, Hitler initially inspired hundreds of thousands of followers to join his fascist movement in both Europe and the United States in the late 1930s. A retrospective application of transformational leadership theory might help explain Hitler's success in this regard. Nevertheless, to refer to Hitler as a leader is insulting to the profession of leadership. Hitler is not thought of as a highly regarded leader in the study of leadership theory today; he is considered, at best, to have been a despot and a dictator. Certainly, a model must be created that allows for the differentiation of leadership and dictatorship.

To test this proposition, 170 commissioned U.S. military officers were asked to participate in a leadership test at Fort Sam Houston, Texas, over the period 2004–2006. The test was designed to test an individual's perception of the definition of *leadership* based on a narrative. This narrative was read aloud to a class of graduate students (who were also Army, Navy, Air Force, or Coast Guard officers) in advance, so the entire class heard the narrative at the same time. After the narrative was read, the officers were asked to turn over a piece of paper that had been placed on their desks and circle the answer choice they thought was most representative of the narrative.

Each class was divided in half so that the narrative was the same. One side of the class had a picture of Adolf Hitler on top of the page; the other side had a picture of Martin Luther King, Jr., on the top of the page. The test was designed to see if the picture of a well-known and accepted leadership figure such as Martin Luther King, Jr., would cause the test takers to support the leadership narrative, whereas the picture of Adolf Hitler would bias the results. The entire one-page test is presented here (including the two pictures used—**Figures C-1** and **C-2**), and the test results appear in **Table C-1**.

The results reveal that military officers were uncomfortable with the option of labeling Adolf Hitler as a leader.

METHODOLOGY

One side of the room received the following narrative, with a picture of Adolf Hitler appearing on the top of the page. The other side of the room received the same narrative, with a picture of Martin Luther King, Jr., appearing at the top of the page. Neither side of the class knew that the other side was looking at a different picture.

FIGURE C-1 Martin Luther King, Jr.

Reproduced courtesy of Prints & Photographs Division, Library of Congress [LC-USZ62-126559]. Photograph by Dick DeMarsico.

FIGURE C-2 Adolf Hitler.

Reproduced courtesy of Prints & Photographs Division, Library of Congress [LC-USZ62-48839].

It had been several years since the world war. With the war now over, people began looking for a national figure to solve social problems and injustices. Clearly, the country was divided and in need of change. Although many people of the nation were united and content with the status quo, he considered his people and nation to be downtrodden. He dreamed of a better place for his people and thought that his country could be greater than what it was. Slowly, over the years, millions listened and followed him. He inspired people like few before him had ever done. He was also successful in inspiring and motivating people, and accomplishing change. This change and his ability to motivate people were immense and dramatic, and can still be felt to this day. Modern scholars still study his methods and wonder how he did it. Years after his death, people still read his books and are moved by the memory of his dream. Select **one answer** that best describes this narrative.

This is an example of:

A. a national public figure.
B. a man with a vision.
C. leadership.
D. effective strategic management.
E. none of the above.

Table C-1 Results of Leadership Quiz Based on Character Perception		
Question Response	Hitler (n = 85)	King (n = 85)
A national public figure	34	9
A man with a vision	16	14
Leadership	9	62
Effective strategic management	14	0
None of the above	12	0

n = 170 military officers over the period 2004–2008.

Only 9 of 85 students (10.5%) felt comfortable with the leader answer when they thought Adolf Hitler's image was associated with the narrative and options. This was not true of the other half of the class, who selected "leader" 73% of the time (n = 62/85 students) when they assumed that Martin Luther King, Jr.'s picture was associated with the narrative and choices.

Clearly, this exploratory test on image perceptions of leadership with trained military officers in graduate school suggests a problem with perceptions associated with the leadership designation of historical figures. To overcome this dilemma, future leadership models must be capable of screening out despots and dictators from traditional leadership frameworks. The omnibus leadership model provides for this adjustment through its higher order, environment, and individual culture composite elements, thereby correcting the problem.

Constructs of the Omnibus Leadership Model

Traditional models of leadership focus on outcomes and trace those outcomes back to specific leadership traits, characteristics, or behaviors, with little emphasis placed on the values associated with intrinsic goal-directed behavior. The "nature versus nurture" debate has long existed within the study of leadership. Are leaders born, or can they be made? The environment certainly plays a role in fostering goal-directed behavior, as do family values, available resources, and education (including both didactic and spiritual education). Nevertheless, these constructs are often viewed as confounding variables rather than as leadership progenitors in traditional leadership models. This is a weakness within traditional leadership study.

Furthermore, traditional leader theories fail to fully integrate the various aspects of confounding variables into one multifaceted model that allows for a wider range and

utility of leadership study. Specifically, constructs such as cultural distinctiveness, higher power influences, and environmental pressures are often disregarded as antecedent constructs for forecasting leader outcomes or explaining past leader behavior. At the same time, these constructs are excellent theoretical examples for forecasting leader outcomes under appropriate conditions.

For example, in the era of the War on Terror, some leaders and followers feel that they are driven to goal-directed behavior through a higher power mandate. Separate from the realm that is considered religion or spirituality in its common understanding, a "higher power" is often classified as a greater belief in a mantra, or distinctive icon, that guides and directs leader behavior and followership in a predictable manner. Rarely, however, does a discussion of how a higher power affects the values and goal-directed behavior of leaders take place. In fact, many leadership scholars completely ignore the construct of a higher power influence when examining leadership. Some suggest it is politically incorrect to consider this factor, whereas others posit that it is too difficult to measure and evaluate it. Regardless, the study of a higher power influence on leadership is a burgeoning field of interest in the scholarly community.[35–37]

As previously discussed, the preponderance of traditional leadership models focus on outcomes, using indicators of satisfaction and productivity as indices of success. In doing so, many established models fail to take into account various aspects of the environment and individual culture. Clearly, culture and the environment have profound effects on the study of leadership theory. As a result, an integrated theoretical model developed by Coppola[38] suggests a solution to this problem. The omnibus leadership model (OLM) borrows from previous literature in the field and provides a different aperture for evaluating leaders and leadership theory. This model offers three spatial dimensional constructs—higher order, individual culture, and environment—as signposts for other variables or constructs. Furthermore, from these spatial dimensions, three other constructs—beneficence, character traits, and resources—may be derived.

Higher Order Construct

Within the health and general management environment, the topic of spirituality in leadership is often considered taboo and, indeed, a career-ending conversation for executives and practitioners. Even so, it is well known that spiritual principles are the basis for many values and enduring beliefs that guide the ethical framework and moral development of health leadership practices in our society. Therefore, spirituality (i.e., higher order) as a construct of discussion and examination in health leadership practice should not be overlooked in future research examining leadership theory.

In 2008, a survey of religion performed by Baylor University[39] found that more than 85% of the U.S. population consider themselves to be "religious." Furthermore, leadership research conducted by other authors suggests that the absence of the study of spirituality and/or a higher power in leadership study has been a distinct flaw in the traditional study of a leader's ability to influence others and to inspire followership. End-of-life decisions and early pregnancy termination are only two of the issues faced by health executives today that have relevance to this construct; these issues have strong spiritual roots that influence and inform decision making. Obviously, the study of a higher power is necessary in health leadership. More importantly, it opens the conversation about spirituality in leadership and brings it to the table for a professional and intellectual discussion.

Higher-order principles guide the construct of *beneficence*, or the practice of "doing good," against the construct of *malevolence*, or the practice of "doing bad." These principles are themselves derived from family values, spiritual teachings, education, "herd mentalities" in the community, and individual interpretation of the aforementioned spatial dimensions, whether they be consistent or inconsistent with practices or norms of behavior. Certainly, higher-order principles guide the development of many leaders, and this construct should not be overlooked in future leadership studies.

Individual Culture Construct

From the individual cultural spatial dimension, the construct of character traits may be derived. Trait theory itself dominated the bulk of traditional leadership methodology over the previous century, and little additional discussion seemed to have been warranted. Nevertheless, it is now clear that cultural distinctiveness acts as an immutable object in the study of leadership theory. Some Asian and Middle Eastern societies clearly favor gender in the practice of leadership hierarchy, whereas other societies are more gender neutral. Age is likewise a factor in many Asian societies and is often used as a proxy suggesting that experience equates with competence. As a result, it would be inappropriate to apply a transformational leadership model to the evaluation of some societies due to the hierarchical gender- and age-based traits associated with those cultures. For example, in traditional Chinese and North Korean cultures, inquisitiveness and outspokenness may be perceived in a negative light, as opposed to the Western perception that these behaviors demonstrate a search for understanding and an extroverted approach.

An individual's birthplace culture, or the culture in which he or she lives, will imprint an endurable mark of distinctiveness on the individual that will follow him or her over the course of the person's lifetime. Although not entirely immutable, the culture in which an individual is raised or lives will dominate and forecast choices in leader decisions for as long as the person is in charge of people, policy, or other decision-making elements.

Environment Construct

The environment in which many leaders operate is critically important to a leader's success, as Fiedler suggested in his model decades ago.[40] The extent to which the literature has addressed the relationship between individuals and the environment is minimal. In fact, the preponderance of leadership theory ignores the environment altogether. Short of trait theory, very few studies attempt to tie traditional leadership theory to the environment in a manner that predicts and forecasts possible outcomes. In reality, by identifying the environment in which a leader will function, individuals can take advantage of factors in the environment to fit the current situation and maximize outcomes. This approach supports the multidimensional and complex idea that leadership processes include an ecologically valid two-way component between the leader and the environment[41] and that followers are embedded in the environmental context.

Leaders cannot execute their vision, inspire followership, and employ legitimate and charismatic attributes unless appropriate resources are available in the environment to assist in the communication of the leader's message. If the environment lacks appropriate resources to assist in the transfer and the communication of the leader's intent, the leader may not have a significant enough followership to lead anything. For this reason, the environmental construct is a necessary precursor to resource availability. Furthermore, leader recognition is not possible without appropriate resources to deliver the leader's message.

Resources[42] have attracted a reasonable amount of attention in traditional leadership study; however, resources are generally viewed in older theories as variables unto themselves and not as constructs for measurement. In the OLM, resources may be accessed through both human followership and logistical means. For example, in the modern study of leadership, vehicles for message delivery have become exponentially available to small groups of individuals who may in the past have been hermetically sealed from the preponderance of the world's culture. The advent of the Internet has allowed small fringe groups of previously marginalized people to gain standing and respect in the greater world community. Through a provocative website whose message inspires followership, a lone marginalized individual may find standing and prominence on the world stage. Clearly, environmental resources have gained prominence as vehicles for leadership followership.

THE OMNIBUS LEADERSHIP MODEL: A SUMMARY

The OLM meets the needs of future leadership researchers by including the spatial dimensions of higher order, individual culture, and environment. **Table C-2** provides a template for this model. **Figure C-3** illustrates the conceptual model of the omnibus leadership theory. The benefit of this theory derives from its ability to capture constructs that assist in explaining why certain leaders are driven to leadership decisions. For example, many leader decisions are based on values learned from childhood, relating to cultural and spiritual teachings that can be acted on in favorable environments. In understanding and applying this model, the foundations on which some leaders base their decisions become clear, as does why some leaders have widespread followership. In fact, followership based on cultural and higher-order issues cannot be overlooked in this modern era of the War on Terror and an increasingly globalized society.

The OLM provides a framework for screening and evaluating real leaders from the despots and the infamous. For example, using this model as a guide, Hitler is clearly screened out of the leadership category due to his evil nature and malevolence. His actions and outcomes resulted in sociopathic murder and do not qualify him as a leader of any sort in modern times. Likewise, support of suicide bombers causes some modern-day figures to be similarly ruled out of leadership consideration because these acts are obviously nonbeneficent.[43–45]

All leaders are guided by some higher-order principles that may present themselves as unconscious drivers for maintaining enduring beliefs and adopting certain values. Rokeach, in the values–beliefs–attitudes model, suggested that values form the bedrock of who we are as people and, consequently, as leaders.[46] However, without an understanding of the higher-order principles and values that guide a leader, it is not possible to fully understand retrospective actions or forecast future behavior in a consistent manner.

MEASURING THE MODEL

Methods for measuring the OLM in the near term may rely on observational and nonexperimental studies. Donabedian proposed a similar observational methodology with

Table C-2 Omnibus Leadership Model			
Spatial Dimension	**Construct**	**Description**	**Variables**
Higher order	Beneficence or malevolence	Altruism or sadism	Actions • Self-serving versus other-serving • Teamwork: glory "me" versus glory "we"
Individual (culture)	Character	Extraversion or introversion Type A or B personality archetypes	Traits, abilities, and skills
Environment	Resources stability Turbidity dynamic	Human followership and logistical availability	Outcomes • Action versus reaction • Flight versus fight

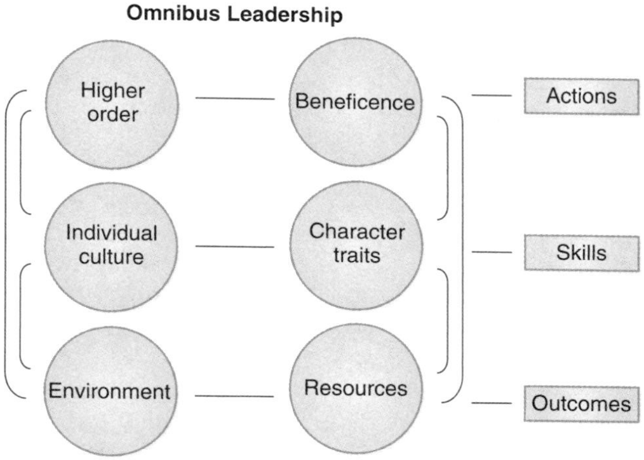

Omnibus Leadership

FIGURE C-3 Conceptual model of the omnibus leadership model.

the now renowned structure–process–outcome quality model in 1966. Donabedian's original article contained few insights into means of empirical measurement other than to qualify review actions as having merit, based on normative and accepted practices in the field. Donabedian suggested that subject matter experts and panels were required to evaluate his new model.[47] Similar methodologies are necessary for evaluation of the OLM. For example, it was not until the passing of the Health Maintenance Organization Act of 1973 that scholars turned to Donabedian's theoretical model to help guide health organizations toward developing quality models. If not for the passage of this act and the requirement for health organizations to make an argument for quality in their organizations, Donabedian's model may have languished in obscurity for years or decades—or perhaps it would never have been used at all.

A similar argument can be made for John Nash's self-named Nash equilibrium (NE) theory, which was first developed in 1950. The NE theory, and later the Nash bargaining solution (NBS), became the basis for game theory. Nash's concepts were largely regarded as theoretical and intangible when first produced. In subsequent years, however, they were used as the basis for U.S. economic policy making and resulted in the awarding of the Nobel Prize to Nash in 1994. Many readers may recall seeing Nash's life portrayed in the movie *A Beautiful Mind*.[48]

Traditional leadership models have typically employed true experimental and nonexperimental methods within their leadership frameworks. This approach would continue to be applicable with the OLM. Subjects and data may continue to be collected and analyzed using traditional practices and procedures. However, the OLM will help guide the researcher toward qualifying specific constructs of leadership for discerning certain phenomena.

In closing, perhaps the Latin phrase *res ipsa loquitur* ("the thing speaks for itself") may suggest additional structure for the OLM. Leadership is action oriented: One knows it when one sees it. As a result, leadership theory may continue to confound research efforts. Perhaps leadership scholars must be satisfied with the appreciation of leadership as an art more than a science after all—at least until better theory testing methods are viable.

REFERENCES

1. Ledlow, G., Coppola, N., & Cwiek, M. (2008). Leadership and transformation. In J. A. Johnson (Ed.), *Organizational theory, behavior and development* (pp. 193–212). Sudbury, MA: Jones and Bartlett.
2. American Museum of Natural History. (n.d.). *Apatosaurus*. Retrieved from http://www.amnh.org /exhibitions/permanent-exhibitions/fossil-halls /hall-of-saurischian-dinosaurs/apatosaurus.
3. Crocker, C. (1995). The lessons of Somalia. *Foreign Affairs, 74*, 2–8.
4. Mowday, R. T., & Sutton, R. I. (1993). Organizational behavior: Linking individuals and groups to organizational contexts. *Annual Review of Psychology, 44*, 195–229.
5. Antoinette, S. P., & Bedeian, A. (1994). Leader–follower exchange quality: The role of personnel

and interpersonal attributes. *Academy of Management Journal, 37,* 990–1001.

6. Norris, W. R., & Vecchio, R. P. (1992). Situation leadership theory: A replication. *Group and Organizational Management, 17,* 331–343.

7. Weick, K. E. (1995). What theory is not, theorizing is. *Administrative Science Quarterly, 40,* 385–390.

8. Roberts, K. H., & Glick, W. (1981). The job characteristics approach to task design: A critical review of the literature. *Journal of Applied Psychology, 66,* 193–217.

9. Lowe, K. B., & Gardner, W. L. (2001). Ten years of *The Leadership Quarterly*: Contributions and challenges for the future. *Leadership Quarterly, 11,* 459–514.

10. Price, C. (2008). Eugenics revisited. *Clearly Caring Magazine, 28*(2), 42–43.

11. Worthington, G. E. (1925). Compulsory sterilization laws. *Journal of Social Hygiene, 11,* 257–271.

12. Parfrey, A. (1990). Eugenics: The orphaned science. In A. Parfrey (Ed.), *Apocalypse culture* (pp. 217–228). Los Angeles, CA: Feral House.

13. Dryden, C. (1997). *A-train: Memoirs of a Tuskegee airman.* Tuscaloosa, AL: University of Alabama Press.

14. McDonald, K. A. (1994, Nov. 16). The iconoclastic fossil hunter. *Chronicle of Higher Education,* A9–A17.

15. Weber, M. (1904–1905/1930). *The Protestant ethic and the spirit of capitalism.* New York: Scribner's.

16. Coppola, M. N. (2004). A propositional perspective of leadership: Is the wrong head on the model? *Journal of International Research in Business Disciplines, Business Research Yearbook, 11,* 620–625.

17. Coppola, M. N., & Lafrance, K. (2005). *The omnibus model* [Unpublished White paper]. San Antonio, TX: U.S. Army Medical Department Center and School, Academy of Health Sciences.

18. Coppola, note 16.

19. Coppola, M. N. (2004). *The omnibus model* [White paper]. San Antonio, TX: U.S. Army Medical Department Center and School, Academy of Health Sciences.

20. Yukl, G. (1998). *Leadership in organizations* (4th ed.). Englewood Cliffs, NJ: Prentice Hall.

21. Yukl, note 20.

22. Yukl, G., & Van Fleet, D. D. (1992). Theory and research on leadership in organizations. In M. D. Dunnette & L. M. Hough (Eds.), *Handbook of industrial and organizational psychology* (Vol. 3, no. 1, pp. 147–197). Palo Alto, CA: Consulting Psychologists Press.

23. Donabedian, A. (1966). Evaluating the quality of medical care. *Millbank Memorial Federation of Quality, 44,* 166–203.

24. Mintzberg, H. (1979). *The structure of organizations.* Upper Saddle River, NJ: Prentice Hall.

25. Bacharach, S. B. (1989). Organizational theories: Some criteria for evaluation. *Academy of Management Review, 14,* 490–495.

26. Kerlinger, F. (1973). *Foundations of behavioral research.* New York: Rinehart and Winston.

27. Popper, K. (1959). *The logic of scientific discovery.* New York: Harper & Row.

28. Dubin, R. (1978). *Theory building* (rev. ed.). New York: Free Press.

29. Einstein, A., & Leopold, I. (1938). *The evolution of physics.* New York: Harper & Row.

30. Coppola, note 16.

31. Whetten, D. A. (1989). What constitutes a theoretical contribution? *Academy of Management Journal, 14,* 490–495.

32. Kerlinger, note 26.

33. Wittgenstein, L. (1972). *On certainty* (G. E. M. Anscombe, Ed.). New York: Harper Torch Books.

34. Coppola, M. N., Pasupathy, R., Posteraro, R., Fulton, L. V., & Aliff, M. M. (2013). Barriers and stakeholder dynamics to health policy reform. *International Journal of Food, Nutrition and Public Health, 6*(1), 67–81.

35. Jordan, S. (2006). *The effects of religious preference and the frequency of spirituality on the retention and attrition rates among soldiers* [Dissertation]. Retrieved from http://www.bookpump.com/dps/pdf-b/1123922b.pdf.

36. Fry, L. W. (2003). Toward a theory of spiritual leadership. *Leadership Quarterly, 14,* 693–727.

37. Russell, R. F., & Stone, A. G. (2002). A review of servant leadership attributes: Developing a practical model. *Leadership and Organizational Development Journal, 23*(3), 145–157.

38. Coppola, note 16.

39. Baylor University, Institute for Studies of Religion. (2008). Baylor religion survey.

40. Blair, G. M. (1997, Feb. 7). Contingency models. Retrieved from http://www.see.ed.ac.uk/~gerard/MENG/ME96/Documents/Styles/conti.html.

41. Coppola & Lafrance, note 17.

42. Goodman, R. M. (1998). Identifying and defining the dimensions of community capacity to provide a basis for measurement. *Health Education and Behavior, 25*(3), 258–278.

43. Wintrobe, R. (2003). *Can suicide bombers be rational?* [White paper]. Ontario, Canada: Department of Economics, University of Western Ontario.

44. Xenophon. (1948). Hiero, or Tyrannicus. Reprinted in L. Strauss, *On tyranny* (pp. 2–11). New York: Political Science Classics.

45. Raskovich, A. (1996). Ye shall have no other gods before me: A legal–economic analysis of the rise of Yahweh. *Journal of Institutional and Theoretical Economics, 152,* 449–471.

46. Rokeach, M. (1968). *Beliefs, attitudes, and values: A theory of organization and change.* San Francisco: Jossey-Bass.

47. Donabedian, note 23.

48. Nasar, S. (2001). *A beautiful mind: The life of mathematical genius and Nobel laureate John Nash.* New York: Touchstone.

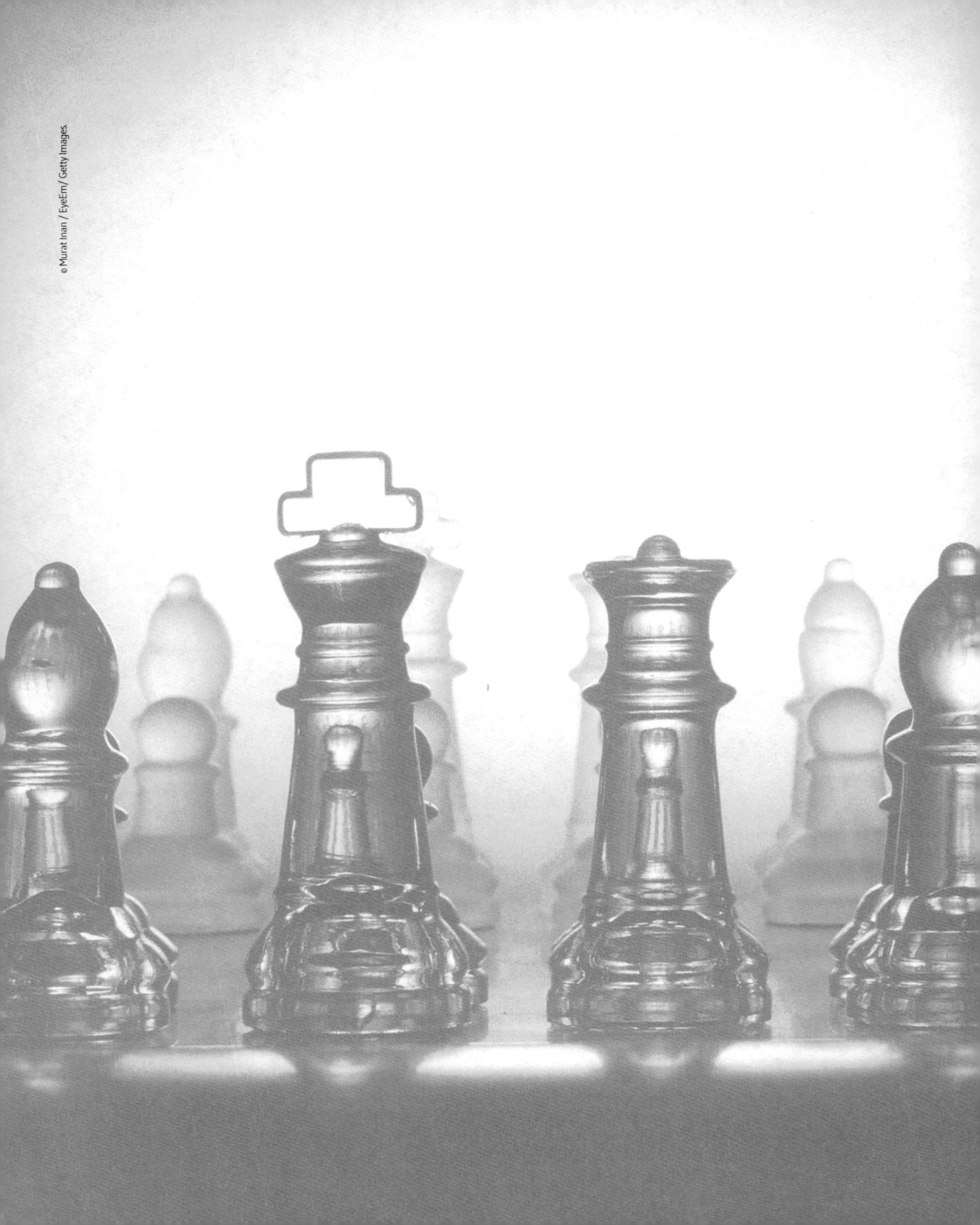

INDEX

Note: Page numbers followed by *f* and *t* denote figures and tables.

360-degree evaluation, 289

A

AACSB. *See* Association to Advance Collegiate Schools of Business
ability, 108, 464
absenteeism, 286
ACA. *See* Affordable Care Act
academy culture, 228
access to health care, 41–42
    employers views on, 316–317
        Parity of Health Care model and, 318
    patients' views on, 314
    providers' views on, 315
accommodating, 125
accountability culture, 451–452
accountable care organization (ACO), 53
ACHE. *See* American College of Healthcare Executives
achievement culture, 227
ACO. *See* accountable care organization
ACS. *See* American College of Surgeons
acting on information, process of, 121
action orientation, 227*t*
action steps, 212–214
active learning techniques, 383
activities of daily living (ADLs), 467
adaptation issues, external, 225
adjourning stage, 169
administrative skills, 16, 68
administrators, as leaders, 309
Adrian, A., 451
adventurer, 31
advocacy, defined, 255
Aetna, 312
affective domain, Bloom's taxonomy of, 110*t*
affiliation, Schutz's theory of, 112–113, 130
Affordable Care Act (ACA), 39, 42, 44, 45, 48, 53, 320, 397–398
African perspective of leadership styles, 332
age, 45, 469, 470, 470*t*
Agency for Healthcare Research and Quality (AHRQ), 299
agency theory, 200
agenda power, 335
aggressiveness, 227*t*

aging workforce, 428
AHA. *See* American Hospital Association
AHRQ. *See* Agency for Healthcare Research and Quality
AIG. *See* American International Group
Ajzen, I., 34
Alexander the Great, 63, 64
alienated individuals, 185
alignment, leadership team, 189–190
Align phase, PAARP model, 183
alliances, 117–120
allied health, 104*t*
All Too Human (Stephanopoulos), 25
AMA. *See* American Medical Association
ambiguity, 121, 122*f*, 129, 145
American Association of Colleges of Nursing, 184
American College of Healthcare Executives (ACHE), 42, 48, 100–101, 107*t*, 251, 252, 319, 423
American College of Surgeons (ACS), 100, 283, 296
American Dental Association, 104
American Hospital Association (AHA), 104, 251, 398, 404
    equity care report, 398–399
American International Group (AIG), 252
American Medical Association (AMA), 104, 277
    Code of Ethics, 250–251
American Medical Center, Code of Corporate Compliance, 262–275
American Nurses Association, 104
American Organization of Nurse Executives (AONE), 101, 107*t*
American Productivity and Quality Center (APQC) research, 234
American Society for Healthcare Human Resources Association (ASHHRA), 50
Anabasis (Xenophon), 64
analytical leader, 190
analytical manager, 190
analytics, 402
Anti-Kickback Statute, Medicare/Medicaid, 266–267
AONE. *See* American Organization of Nurse Executives
Applebaum, W., 456
approved provider, 231
Argyris, C., 69, 86*t*, 197

Argyris's *Personality and Organization theory* (1957), 69, 86*t*
Army Air Corps, 480
army leadership model, 82–84, 83*f*, 88*t*
art, leadership as, 10–11
art leadership model, 187, 200
    analysis and comparison with other model, 201–203, 202*t*, 203*f*
ASHHRA. *See* American Society for Healthcare Human Resources Association
Ashkenas, R., 79–80
Asian perspective of leadership styles, 331–332
Assemble phase, PAARP model, 182
assessments. *See also* personality assessments
    benchmarking, 285–286, 303*t*
    effectiveness. *See* effectiveness
    efficacy, 297–298
    efficiency. *See* efficiency
    emotional intelligence and self-efficacy, 99, 284
    of internal environment, 214–220
    leadership, 24, 31–33
    leadership team, 189–190
    market share/growth, 285
    models, 289–300
    national systems, 286–287
    objectives, 288
    optimization, 294, 303*t*
    performance, 296–297, 303*t*
    planning, 284–285
    quality, 298–300, 303*t*
    satisfaction, absenteeism, and turnover, 286
    situational, 443
    surveys, 288–289
    360-degree evaluation, 289
Association of University Programs in Health Administration (AUPHA), 100, 101–102, 103, 108*t*, 251
Association to Advance Collegiate Schools of Business (AACSB), 103
attention, 195
    decision making, 145
attitudes, 226, 337
AUPHA. *See* Association of University Programs in Health Administration
aural learners, 30
authentic leadership, distinction of, 112
automobile insurance to consumers, 311

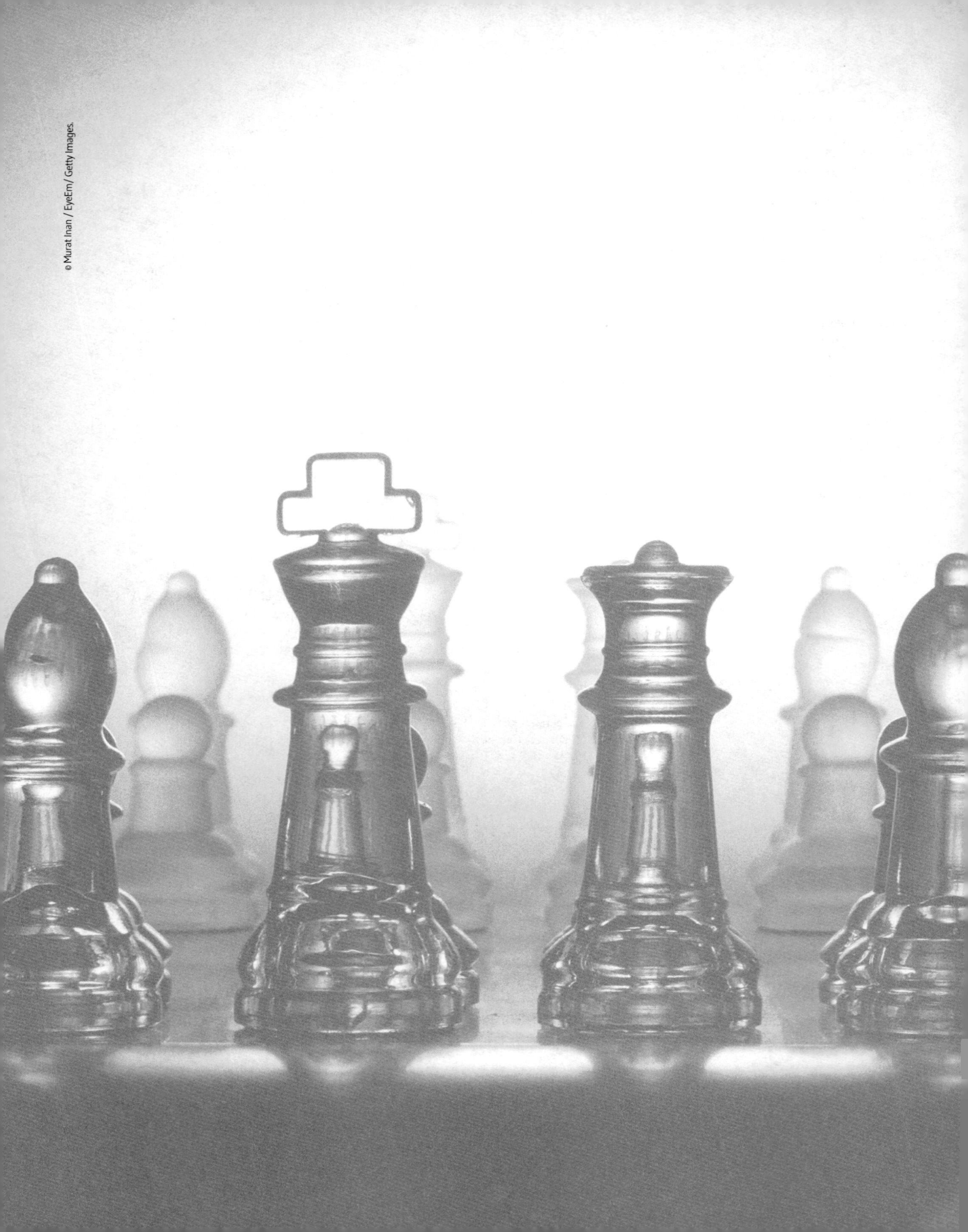